Advance Praise for *Garner's Guidelines for Drafting and Editing Contracts*

"More than a style guide, this book gets at core issues in contract drafting, helping you say what you mean—clearly, directly, and helpfully. Garner's principles strip away the clutter and help the key points shine through. This is essential reading for any lawyer who writes."

—Kent Walker
Chief Legal Officer, Google

"If the definition of genius is taking the complex and making it simple, Garner is the Einstein of legal writing. His plain-English approach to contract drafting is a reminder that too often our profession has it backward—putting archaic jargon and tortured syntax over comprehension and readability. Even the most experienced attorney can learn something from the simple, yet never simplistic, principles of this illuminating new guide."

—Bradley J. Butwin
Chair, O'Melveny & Myers LLP
New York

"Bryan Garner is on a mission: *Garner's Guidelines for Drafting and Editing Contracts* seeks to effect a revolution in transactional drafting. He urges a move away from rote replication of past 'models,' to a considered, practical approach guided by a desire to communicate effectively and avoid costly litigation. Like Garner's previous work, the book is an engaging read, full of helpful examples, and an essential resource for anyone who values clarity of written expression."

—Philip M. Genty
Everett B. Birch Innovative Teaching Clinical Professor
in Professional Responsibility, Columbia Law School
New York

Advance Praise for *Garner's Guidelines for Drafting and Editing Contracts*

"I attended Bryan Garner's daylong course on advanced legal drafting in the spring of 2002. It's no exaggeration to say that that course changed my entire practice. Not a day goes by that I don't apply the principles I learned then. And I've read the course manual to tatters. Now comes *Garner's Guidelines for Drafting and Editing Contracts*. It's the book I've wanted for years. It's the book the legal professional has needed for decades."

—William M. Klimon
Member, Caplin & Drysdale, Chartered
Washington, D.C.

"At last, a book from Garner on writing contracts. From all evidence, drafting is a subject neglected in law schools and a craft never learned by most lawyers. Here, Garner offers the course and instruction the profession sorely needs. He does for the drafter what he did for the advocate in *The Winning Brief*: with a multitude of compelling illustrations, he offers lawyers comprehensive, start-to-finish advice on producing better work product for clients. Every lawyer—including litigators and trial lawyers—can learn a lot from these pages."

—Randall Tietjen
Partner, Robins Kaplan LLP
Minneapolis

"This is the only book on contract drafting you will ever need. A world-class expert in the language of the law himself, Bryan Garner has read everything anyone else has ever written on contract drafting, assembled all the good ideas in one place, and presented them in an organized fashion. Garner provides numerous examples showing how actual contract provisions can be made clearer and more concise and has enriched the book with scores of quotations from leading experts.

"Garner persuasively redirects drafters from the dusty cowpaths seldom encountered outside of contracts on to a fresh, crisp, and direct road easy for lawyer and layperson alike to follow and understand."

—George Davidson
Senior Counsel, Hughes Hubbard & Reed LLP
New York

Advance Praise for *Garner's Guidelines for Drafting and Editing Contracts*

"Bryan Garner, more than anyone else, has taught me that just because you're writing a legal instrument you don't have to talk funny. Here his very first section shows a compelling combination of this lesson with the myriad practical concerns that guide the lawyer toward sound substance as well as clear expression. Know the business. Understand trade practices. Strive for a deal that works for both parties. This is must reading."

—Edward H. Cooper
Thomas M. Cooley Professor of Law Emeritus
The University of Michigan Law School
Ann Arbor

"Bryan Garner knows his stuff. And he shares it in this book. His advice runs the gamut: from plain-English directives to drafting techniques, usage, and formatting, *Garner's Guidelines for Drafting and Editing Contracts* delivers the goods. If you follow his advice, you'll write better contracts, negotiate better deals, and maybe—just maybe—the world will be a better place."

—David Pendarvis
Global General Counsel, ResMed Inc.
San Diego

"Kudos to Bryan Garner for this book. It is thoughtful, practical, witty, and highly accessible. The many 'Not This/But This' comparisons are a treasure. *Garner's Guidelines for Drafting and Editing Contracts* will occupy a central place on my credenza, next to Garner's other excellent guides."

—Henry Morris Jr.
Partner, Arent Fox LLP
Washington, D.C.

"Bryan Garner reminds us once again that good grammar is not simply an aesthetic but a legal virtue that every lawyer should practice—and every client should treasure. Ludwig Wittgenstein famously wrote that 'philosophical problems arise when language goes on holiday.' So too do legal problems."

—Roger Pilon
B. Kenneth Simon Chair in Constitutional Studies
Cato Institute
Washington, D.C.

Advance Praise for *Garner's Guidelines for Drafting and Editing Contracts*

"Drafting contracts is an art that is difficult to master and even more challenging to teach. *Garner's Guidelines for Drafting and Editing Contracts* is the best guide I have seen. The blackletter approach and the before-and-after examples provide a gateway to mastering this exacting skill. It is a must read!"

—Robert C. Berring
Walter Perry Johnson Professor of Law Emeritus
University of California at Berkeley School of Law

"Much as he has so skillfully done for courtroom advocacy, Bryan Garner invokes his formidable expertise in language and writing—dispensed with wit, humor, logic, and helpful illustration—to bring clarity and common sense to contract drafting. As a trial lawyer, I find this call to my transactional peers particularly compelling: Garner's blueprints promise more effective and efficient contract enforcement."

—Luke L. Dauchot
Partner, Kirkland & Ellis LLP
Chicago

"Private contracts can invite sloppy drafting. Unlike statutes, which are public, and legal briefs, which are publicly available, contracts are the exclusive province of parties and their lawyers, who often recycle ancient legal forms. But if a disagreement arises, they must argue before a judge over what they meant—and at least one side ends up losing. Garner explains how to draft a clear, meaningful agreement that will capture the parties' intent, anticipate potential disagreements up front, and avoid the need for after-the-fact interpretation."

—Brian Melendez
Partner, Barnes & Thornburg LLP
Minneapolis

"Multiple coats of paint on a door, as Bryan Garner reminds us in his new book on contract drafting, make the door harder to open. And with this new book, he does what he has done for thousands of brief-writing lawyers—teach them how to peel the unnecessary from their writing, leaving it shorter and simpler, and with the door to understanding much easier to open."

—E. King Poor
Partner, Quarles & Brady LLP
Chicago

Advance Praise for *Garner's Guidelines for Drafting and Editing Contracts*

"As someone who litigates contracts, I have a request: Don't buy this book. Half the cases I've handled in the last 15 years would not have existed had the parties used the lessons that Bryan Garner lays out. When lawyers apply rigorous technique—and stop relying on cluttered forms and half-baked history—contracts work as designed. For transaction lawyers, this book is the best business-development investment you will make this year."

—Paul J. Kiernan
Partner, Holland & Knight LLP
Washington, D.C.

"All successful negotiations end in agreements, which require precision. In this seminal text, Bryan Garner demonstrates how agreements should be written and read. It's an indispensable toolkit for drafting effectively. A practitioner who absorbs the knowledge contained in this book will help clients achieve confidence about their future dealings. The book is essential not just for transactional lawyers—but for *all* lawyers."

—Eric O. English
Managing Partner, Resolution Strategies LLP
Portland, Oregon

"This superb drafting guide should be required reading for transactional lawyers. It is much more than a technical manual on syntax and style—its strategic approach to drafting will make the reader a better *lawyer*, not just a superior *drafter*. Despite the complex and detailed subject matter, Garner's engaging, conversational tone makes the material easy to assimilate. His frequent 'Not this/But this' illustrations highlight the lessons set out in the text. Garner's goal is to help the reader better serve the client while maintaining a good relationship with opposing counsel. Ignore his advice at your own risk!"

—David Simon Sokolow
Distinguished Senior Lecturer
The University of Texas School of Law
Austin

Garner's Guidelines for Drafting and Editing Contracts

Other Books Written or Edited by Bryan A. Garner

Black's Law Dictionary
(Thomson Reuters, 11th ed. 2019)

Garner's Dictionary of Legal Usage
with foreword by Judge Thomas M. Reavley
(Oxford Univ. Press, 3d ed. 2011)

Garner's Modern English Usage
(Oxford Univ. Press, 4th ed. 2016)

Reading Law: The Interpretation of Legal Texts
with Justice Antonin Scalia
(Thomson/West, 2012)

Making Your Case: The Art of Persuading Judges
with Justice Antonin Scalia
(Thomson/West, 2008)

Nino and Me: An Intimate Portrait of Scalia's Last Ten Years
(Threshold Editions, 2019)

The Law of Judicial Precedent
with 12 judicial coauthors, including Justices Neil Gorsuch and Brett Kavanaugh; foreword by Justice Stephen Breyer
(Thomson Reuters, 2016)

Guidelines for Drafting and Editing Legislation
with foreword by Judge Harriet Lansing
(RosePen, 2016)

The Winning Brief: 100 Tips for Persuasive Briefing in Trial and Appellate Courts
(Oxford Univ. Press, 3d ed. 2014)

The Redbook: A Manual on Legal Style
(West, 4th ed. 2018)

Garner on Language and Writing
with foreword by Justice Ruth Bader Ginsburg
(ABA, 2009)

Legal Writing in Plain English
(Univ. of Chicago Press, 2d ed. 2013)

The Elements of Legal Style
with foreword by Charles Alan Wright
(Oxford Univ. Press, 2d ed. 2002)

The Chicago Guide to Grammar, Usage, and Punctuation
(Univ. of Chicago Press, 2016)

The Chicago Manual of Style, Ch. 5, "Grammar and Usage"
(Univ. of Chicago Press, 17th ed. 2017)

HBR Guide to Better Business Writing
(Harvard Business Review, 2013)

Quack This Way: David Foster Wallace and Bryan A. Garner Talk Language and Writing
(RosePen, 2013)

The Winning Oral Argument
(West, 2009)

Ethical Communications for Lawyers
(LawProse, 2009)

Securities Disclosure in Plain English
(CCH, 1999)

The Rules of Golf in Plain English
with Jeffrey Kuhn (Univ. of Chicago Press, 4th ed. 2016)

A New Miscellany-at-Law
by Sir Robert Megarry (Hart, 2005)

Texas, Our Texas: Remembrances of the University
(Eakin Press, 1984)

Basic Law Terms
(West Group, 1999)

Criminal Law Terms
(West Group, 2000)

Family Law Terms
(West Group, 2001)

Business Law Terms
(West Group, 1999)

Garner's Guidelines for Drafting and Editing Contracts

by

Bryan A. Garner

WEST ACADEMIC PUBLISHING

Bryan A. Garner, author and lexicographer, has written more than 20 books on legal language, advocacy, business writing, English grammar, and more, including *Garner's Dictionary of Legal Usage*, *Garner's Modern English Usage*, and two books with the late Justice Antonin Scalia: *Making Your Case: The Art of Persuading Judges* and *Reading Law: The Interpretation of Legal Texts*.

Garner is the editor in chief of *Black's Law Dictionary* and Distinguished Research Professor of Law at Southern Methodist University. He founded LawProse Inc., a Dallas-based training and consulting company, in 1990.

Through LawProse, Garner teaches continuing-legal-education seminars on many subjects, including transactional drafting. He has been engaged to revise major corporate contracts for more than three dozen Fortune 500 companies, including car manufacturers, technology companies, real-estate developers, credit-card companies, insurance companies, telecommunications companies, investment companies, soft-drink manufacturers, banks, homebuilding companies, mortgage companies, and oil-and-gas companies. He has taught contract drafting for the technology-transfer departments at more than a dozen major American universities. During the past 29 years, he has trained tens of thousands of lawyers worldwide in transactional drafting.

His monthly column in the *ABA Journal*, "Bryan Garner on Words," is a perennial favorite among readers. In 2010, in a ceremony at the Library of Congress, he received the Burton Award for Legal-Writing and Reference-Book Author of the Decade.

ISBN: 978-1-64242-669-4

Library of Congress Cataloguing-in-Publication Data
Garner, Bryan A.
Garner's Guidelines for Drafting and Editing Contracts / Bryan A. Garner

Includes bibliographical references and index.
1. Legal composition. 2. English language—usage.
3. English language—style. 4. Law—United States—terminology.
5. Law—United States—contracts. 6. Law—United States—language.
7. Printing, practical—United States—style manuals.

Published by LEG, Inc. d/b/a West Academic
444 Cedar Street, Suite 700
St. Paul, MN 55101
1-877-888-1330

Printed in the United States of America.

To the memory of
Sandra W. Cheng
(1952–2018)

Board of Advisers

Contents

Introduction

Contract drafting is a specialized form of expository prose—although it's not as specialized as many would make it. That is, the subject matter can largely be expressed in normal idiomatic English, as opposed to the archaic jargon so commonly associated with it. When you draft using good style, and you use techniques that maximize readability and comprehension—without sacrificing precision—you're achieving plain English.

How important is plain English? Extremely—if we want clients to understand what they're agreeing to, counterparties to do the same, and lawyers to review their own work competently. But plain English is hard to achieve because of the traditional deviations from it in transactional practice.

Some of these deviations result from the inherent idiosyncrasies of contract drafting. What makes a contract different from ordinary prose is that (1) it deals almost exclusively with future events (whether things will or will not happen or be done in the future), and therefore subtle questions of tense must be considered; (2) it has binding force in allocating rights, duties, and risks, and it therefore requires a great deal of care because it must create a promise or group of promises that the law will enforce (in some way recognize as a duty); (3) it typically contains many lists, which must be presented in a readable way; (4) it is shorn of all emotive words, a fact that creates a barrier between writer and reader, given that it's therefore also shorn of human interest for most readers; and (5) it is predictably going to be read in a hostile way—subjected, essentially, to bad-faith misreadings that it should be able to withstand. No other types of writing apart from legislative and regulatory drafting have these characteristics. Contract drafting really amounts to private legislation.

Too many transactional drafters work from earlier forms without giving them sufficient critical thought. It's all too easy to assume that a document that "worked" before will work again and, as a result, to suppose that any "tinkering" could be exceedingly dangerous. The inclination is to consider forms or precedents to be more or less frozen as stated: any revisions, it is feared, could bring on potential liabilities for the slightest unintended change in meaning. This complacent, perfunctory approach militates against rising above predecessors' mediocrity. Even if a given drafter is willing to make significant revisions, the form itself may reflect a series of iterations from more ancient precedents. The result is similar to layering multiple coats of paint onto a door: eventually, opening and closing it requires serious exertion.

For the experienced, skillful drafter, it's child's play to discover both substantive and stylistic inadequacies in widely used forms—even those published as "models" in formbooks. Child's play. That's one reason so many provisions from formbooks are used throughout this text as negative examples. Legal drafters should approach existing forms with lots of skepticism. Only then will they think critically enough about the documents they're preparing.

But why concentrate so much on style in the first place? Why not confine one's skepticism to matters of substance? The reason, borne out by my decades of experience, is that a focus on style is usually a necessary precursor to improving the content. Substantive deficiencies are typically—not often, but typically—teased out only by improving the style. Only by translating thick slabs of legalese into readable, idiomatic prose can you think more clearly about what's being said and consider its soundness. That's not to say that every stylistic improvement amounts to a substantive upgrade, but that the cumulative effect of such enhancements allows drafters to engage in higher-level thinking. You'll see that for yourself throughout this text.

One major lesson pervading the book is the importance of acquiring, through practice, a *method* or *technique*. It's true in all fields. Just as a competent musician must practice scales and arpeggios, or as a competitive golfer must practice to achieve a reliably repeatable swing, so too must a contract drafter develop a systematic approach to the craft. In the right-hand columns of the "Not This/But This" examples throughout this book, you'll see a great similarity in the *technique* of setting out provisions, no matter what the subject matter. By contrast, in the left-hand columns—which derive from existing forms used throughout the United States—you'll see a bewildering disparity of conventions, sometimes even within a single example.

This deplorable situation exists in almost all law firms and legal departments across the land. Whenever I see a dozen or so contracts from a single law firm, government agency, or corporate department, a mere glance at the documents reveals variable conventions in such easily noticeable things as the numbering of provisions, page layout, and headings. A closer inspection of the documents invariably reveals a much more profound series of preventable flaws—all traceable to the lawyers' lacking any discernible *method* or *technique*. On the whole, they don't have one. Nor did their predecessors. So the documents end up being a mishmash on basic issues such as stating duties, rights, and risks. And it's not just a mishmash of style; it could be a mishmash of substance. Only two things might reveal mangled substance: (1) a close reading probably accompanying a stylistic overhaul, in which substantive flaws will be made evident, or (2) litigation testing the document, an eventuality that's possible only if one party has a high enough economic incentive to sue.

Throughout the book, you'll find that the right-hand columns (the "But This" versions) yield up their meanings much more efficiently than their counterparts. It's predictable. They've been written with an actual reader in mind. They show communicative fervor—the ardent desire to get a point across to the reader with minimal effort on the reader's part. But this desire is just a start. They also show *technique*.

Technique consists of an extensive storehouse of know-how. Just as a competent flutist must know the four fingerings for producing a B-flat, depending on the octave and musical context, and just as a competitive golfer must know the difference between a chip, a pitch, and a flop shot and how to execute each one skillfully, a competent drafter must know not just how to create an exception to a stated rule, but also when to put it before the rule, when to put it after the rule in the same sentence, and when to put it in a totally separate sentence—as well as how best to do each of these things. All are necessary to the competent drafter.

And just as B-flat is only one of 37 notes within the range of a standard C flute, stating exceptions to rules is but one of 52 common syntactic patterns that drafters must master. (Okay, I made up that number, but it's probably close.) The point is that mastery of a craft requires the ability to execute an abundance of particular skills. Only when all those particulars are at one's command can the overall performance possibly be excellent.

❧ ❧ ❧

You might wonder why the book's recommendations are so copiously illustrated with "Not This/But This" examples—and why so many of those examples derive from published formbooks. The answer has many facets. First, it's important to show that the recommendations actually work in practice. Second, it's good to see how they work in a great variety of contracts. Third, it's useful to know the types of contractual provisions that authors and publishers present as "models." Fourth, it's beneficial to the readers of this book to discern the deficiencies in these "models"—and therefore to develop a healthy skepticism for formbooks. And as for all the passages derived from the work product of law firms and legal departments, the pages of this book fairly exemplify the wide variety of drafting practices that exist today. For these private documents, all names have been fictionalized.

In all the "Not This/But This" side-by-side comparisons that follow, you may well spot legal issues or gaps not adequately dealt with in the right-hand columns. Despite the care that has gone into the revisions, it would be shocking if you couldn't, given the many subtle problems embedded in the left-hand columns. The purpose here isn't to guarantee that all legal deficiencies have been addressed in each example but instead to show the great value of concentrating on style, wording, and presentation. All of us can more readily focus on substance once we put it in high relief. But as for warranting that all deficiencies have been remedied in every example, I'll simply rely on the old standby that life is too short to try solving all the world's problems.

On the other hand, this book is intended to help solve one major problem, which is that those on the transactional side of law practice—"office practitioners" or "deal lawyers," as they're often called—have traditionally been underprepared for their work. Law-school training in writing skills has always been litigation-oriented. Even in the course universally called "Contracts," most American law students never actually see a contract. Instead, they read judicial opinions in which contractual disputes have been decided. If medical schools functioned as law schools do, the students would examine nothing but cadavers.

Although law students learn doctrine, they learn next to nothing about the techniques of drafting contracts that will do what they're intended to do: answer the parties' queries about relative rights, duties, and risks without giving either side enough doubt to contest points in court. That's the best standard—not whether a disputed clause is ultimately upheld in court over a legal challenge. Why? Litigation over a contractual term is ordinarily to be considered a disaster: it's costly, time-consuming, and anxiety-ridden. So the best standard to hold oneself to is that of expressing contractual terms so precisely and unambiguously as to quell potential litigation. You want to draft so well that no lawyer would take a case to challenge whether the contractual term really means what it says.

All this takes skill with words, attention to detail, knowledge of law, an understanding of business, an appreciation of human motives, and enlightenment about the ways of the world. The last five aren't in themselves enough: you must have skill with words. That's what this book is mostly about. If you acquire the skill and you know the law, you'll do well. But don't do as so many other lawyers have done: don't assume that your handling of words and sentences is better than it actually is.

You must *always* remember that contract drafting isn't just a process of getting the words right. Not at all. The goal is to get the other side to do what your client wants. In achieving this, you mustn't poison the business relationship with unnecessary acrimony or subject it to a death by a thousand edits. Contract drafting typically takes place in the context of a negotiation. And a perfect written product is only one goal in negotiating—usually a subordinate one.

The main goal is to get the deal done for your client on favorable terms. That's why a good transactional lawyer will avoid a "correct edit" if the counterparty's lawyer's poor word choice or similar sloppiness creates an advantage for the client. The knowing but tight-lipped practitioner understands that an overmeticulous insistence on stylistic perfection can work to one's own disadvantage. The key is knowing the difference, which involves many trade-offs, including value judgments about what is and isn't worth fighting over in the short time available. Are you providing good value for the fees you're charging? Are you avoiding unnecessary discord? If your opposite number (the counterparty's lawyer) is addicted to the redundancy *sell, transfer, assign, and convey*, for instance, should you really insist on the stylistic "purity" advocated by this or any other style manual? Are you going to bill your client for futile time you've spent trying to educate a peer? These are questions worth considering as you work to develop judgment and finesse.

The conventions outlined here assume that you control the draft. The purpose of this book is to show the best techniques for myriad stylistic issues. You shouldn't adopt a hidebound insistence on the conventions. But neither should you pass your career in ignorance of them.

Bryan A. Garner
Boston
December 2018

A. Fundamental Principles

The practicalities of contract drafting

§ 1 Use your skills the best you can in the circumstances.

Before writing a single sentence, you must have complete and accurate knowledge of what the parties are trying to accomplish. Even though you'll be mostly concerned with your client's needs, you must understand that there are at least two sides to the deal: the document you prepare must, in the end, work for both. Yet the parties probably won't have worked through all the points that must be settled. You may well need to help them finish their negotiations—if only by supplying a draft in which those points have been resolved as even-handedly as possible in ways your client will approve.

You should also determine whether you're specifying actions and outcomes or (as may be appropriate for a contract of long duration) merely describing responsibility, authority, and process. Long-duration contracts often depend on creating a structure for making decisions instead of defining the outcomes of those decisions.

You'll be summoning all your knowledge about the nature of the business involved, the trade practices within the field, the likely pitfalls against which your client must be protected, the law applicable to the deal, and the intricacies of unambiguously stating rights, duties, authorizations, conditions, exceptions, representations, warranties, and liabilities. It's a tall order, to say the least.

If it's a company's take-it-or-leave-it contract, such as a consumer contract, then only one side has a say in its content and form. Still, if you're drafting such a document, and you're thoroughly protecting your own side, you should try to be fair and equitable—or at least *seem* so. Your client is going to be bound to do something; otherwise, the contract would

> "Early in my practice I asked the lawyer with whom I was negotiating an agreement the meaning of a provision in his draft. 'I don't know what it means,' he replied, 'but it is always found in this type of agreement.' . . . Ideally, an attorney should research the substance of the transaction and the history of the agreement to understand the role of each provision. While a practitioner cannot always take the time for the research, it is important to take the first step and determine the meaning of the provision. If you don't know what it means, how do you expect it to be meaningful to your client or to a court?" Scott J. Burnham, *The Contract Drafting Guidebook* § 16.1, at 338 (1992).

be illusory. You can't reduce your client's level of risk to zero. And if you try, you and your client will be faulted if the contract is tested in litigation. Under the principle of *contra proferentem*—literally, "against the offerer"—all ambiguities will be resolved against the drafting party (your client). Further, you should remember that a consumer contract is partly a business document. To use the current jargon, it's a "customer-facing" document. What people think about your client is based in part on the documents they're asked to sign. If you think you can outsmart the consumers with sharp provisions, you're probably just exposing your unwitting client to bad PR. In consumer contracts, extremely lopsided, inequitable drafting is bad business.

And in negotiated business-to-business contracts, it's a waste of time and money. (See § 2.)

One advantage of plain-language drafting is that it tends to be fair because it's easily comprehended. You can be fair but firm, protecting your client against all sorts of unfortunate eventualities. But you shouldn't gratuitously make provisions unconscionable.

If the contract is between two sides represented by counsel, then one side usually offers to do the first draft, with the understanding that there will naturally be some back-and-forth between the sides. As a matter of practice, it's good to be the lawyer preparing the first draft: there are dozens of subtle ways in which a first draft benefits the client for whom it's been drafted. For one thing, you'll be thinking through the deal more actively rather than learning and reacting to someone else's ideas. For another thing, to the extent you value good drafting, you'll have the advantage of preparing a document that already looks like one of the right-hand columns in this book. If you leave the first draft to the other side, you'll almost certainly receive a draft resembling one of the left-hand columns. Mediocre to poor drafting is ubiquitous.

Sometimes sophisticated clients will agree at the outset what precedent to use as the basis for a new transaction. If that's so, you will begin with the final draft from the transaction in which the precedent was used, scour it for deal-specific provisions that were unique to the earlier transaction, and update the draft for any new terms agreed to by the parties. This type of drafting is on the passive side, but often it's just the reality of modern law practice.

If you *aren't* able to do the first draft—and there will inevitably be times when you aren't—then you must be realistic about your role. You certainly can't mark up the draft to comply with every injunction in this book. Nor, generally speaking, can you revise it thoroughly to make it stylistically suitable to you and to me. That's just not realistic, and it squanders precious negotiating capital on immaterial points. It would be an insult to opposing counsel (but see the following paragraph), and it would probably waste your own client's money. How you approach the problem depends on the situation—the size of the deal, the players involved, and their working relationships.

If the draft you've received is hopelessly flawed in both content and style, you might float a new draft that cures all the problems—as if you were in fact the initial drafter. This approach requires great diplomacy. You mustn't denigrate the other side's efforts. You must win them over if possible. You're floating a new draft in hopes that it will be accepted as *the* working draft. As a matter of process, you'd be well advised to call your counterpart with a heads-up to preview the rationale for outsized revisions rather than just dropping a wholesale rewrite on the other side without warning.

But if most of the flaws are stylistic, you're probably stuck with the other side's first draft. (Once again, you can see why it's advantageous to have *your* draft be the initial foray.) You must read as skillfully and penetratingly as you can to see that your client gets the deal it wants. You must be practical, winnowing the unimportant items from the important ones. You'll be doing this, of course, having already discussed the client's most vital concerns. You'll be bringing to bear your own knowledge of deals, of business, and of how people behave and misbehave. You'll be thinking about motivations, incentives, and potential risks.

In such a review—when the other side has done a first draft that is stylistically flawed but substantively acceptable as a starting point—you'll be doing your best to separate stylistic comments from substantive ones. Abstain from stylistic comments altogether unless you become convinced

> "Hope for improved drafting lies in every lawyer's talent for visualizing hypothetical situations. By testing each idea in his document with potential variations in circumstance and by evaluating the significance of those variations for the idea his document requires, the lawyer-draftsman can more confidently determine whether the idea must include given events, conditions, or conduct and whether the word which he is inclined to use is likely to express that idea to the user of the document."
> Maurice B. Kirk, *Legal Drafting: Curing Unexpressive Language*, 3 Tex. Tech. L. Rev. 23, 54 (1971).

that what is seemingly a stylistic comment actually affects substance, as when poor phrasing introduces ambiguity.

Yet this is a tricky matter. If the other side's draft has a typo or two, or a mispunctuated provision that you simply can't pass over in good conscience, you may fix it as a matter of course. How long will it take? If you're an accomplished editor, it happens automatically. Just be sure you're not dwelling on matters of style, lest you be written off as a mere proofreader who isn't concerned about the heart of the transaction.

Avoid raising pedantic objections that have no real-world consequences. This, too, is a tricky matter: one person's care is another person's pedantry.

Things can get quite complicated when there are more than two parties or when there are multiple agreements among which consistency must be ensured. It's not pedantry to seek that consistency.

For the most part, this book assumes that *you* control the draft, nobody else. It assumes that you want a style that reinforces good content—a style that reveals the content with minimal effort by readers. The style here presented is an acquired set of techniques that will work again and again in any number of transactional documents. Once you acquire them, you'd no sooner depart from them than a professional golfer would purposely hit bad shots or a professional musician would purposely play out of tune.

§ 2 In your general approach, avoid "extreme drafting" that puts an unreasonable onus on the counterparty—especially if the contract is part of a long-term relationship.

A brilliant Dallas lawyer named J. Cullen Aderhold tells an instructive story. As a young lawyer, he once thought his duty as a negotiator and drafter was to produce the most burdensome contract possible in favor of his client. About 1986, he negotiated a contract for the serial purchase and leaseback of 25 stores, for an aggregate purchase of $100 million. He negotiated an extremely tough contract favoring his client (we'll call the company "Schickel"), which was the buyer. Ecstatic over the results, Schickel closed on the first store quickly and quite profitably. But the seller

> "If a word adds meaning, it belongs. But if it is just there to give the appearance of significance to an otherwise short (which is not the same as inconsequential) text, it should be eliminated." Carl Felsenfeld & Alan Siegel, *Writing Contracts in Plain English* 117 (1981).

soon realized what a lopsided contract he had signed and immediately began looking for ways to break it. Schickel and Aderhold spent the next six months dealing with the seller's repeated attempts to terminate the contract, and Schickel wasn't able to close even the second purchase under the contract.

As Schickel and Aderhold were considering whether to sue to enforce the contract, the seller was acquired by Wal-Mart. But as Wal-Mart's attorneys were reviewing the seller's contracts, they came across the Schickel contract and required the seller to buy out Schickel's rights under that contract as a condition of closing the acquisition. As a result of that happenstance, the seller paid Schickel a fixed sum to terminate the contract, but it was less than Schickel would have made on the second transaction, and considerably less than it would have made had all 25 transactions closed.

This experience illustrates that burdensome contracts damage relationships and that a lawyer who negotiates one disserves the client. Any long-term relationship—whether it's a serial sale-leaseback, a lease, a loan, a license agreement, a franchise agreement, or any other long-lived contract—should be a win-win situation for both parties. In a win-lose contract, the party that perceives itself to be the loser will devote substantial energy to wriggling out of the deal, taking constant potshots at the perceived oppressor. The winner, in turn, will devote unnecessary time and effort and legal fees in attempting to preserve the benefit of the bargain.

The overbearing approach in drafting can likewise be a problem in one-shot contracts such as purchase contracts. How so? The unduly aggressive lawyer drives up costs (especially in the form of legal fees), draws out negotiations unnecessarily, and risks losing the deal altogether. Negotiations often stall or completely halt if one side's lawyer is too difficult.

One common type of overdrafting involves confidentiality clauses, which often obligate the recipient of confidential information to destroy all copies, paper and electronic, on request. Of course, now that virtually all communications and documents are stored in electronic form, any given piece of information will exist not only in current storage but also in backup archival media in any number of copies. The only way for a recipient to delete all copies would be to retrieve every single instance of backup media and then locate, identify, and delete the information in question. That would sometimes involve pulling disks from bomb-proof caverns. And it would sometimes involve gaining the cooperation of cloud-computing providers who don't have explicit procedures for permanent erasures.

In short, such overdrafted clauses simply can't be complied with. Some lawyers therefore refuse to agree to them. Instead, on behalf of their clients, they offer a clause requiring commercially reasonable efforts to remove pertinent data from current storage and to refrain from accessing the data if later retrieved from backup.

A further possible safeguard is to provide that each document of exceptional sensitivity must be flagged in advance so that the recipient must arrange to transfer it by means other than e-mail, to store it securely, and to delete it immediately when it is no longer needed. One experienced lawyer who takes this approach is Fletcher James of Leesburg, Virginia. He reports that after a decade of routinely using such a clause, only twice has a counterparty called for the secure channel.

The lesson here is twofold: don't make others promise things that they can't possibly fulfill, and never allow your client to agree to make unreasonable promises that couldn't reasonably be fulfilled.

§ 3 Know what you want to say.

The first step in drafting is thinking hard about the ends you seek to achieve. Until you've figured out what you want to say, you have no real need for a keyboard or a dictaphone.

When you're asked to prepare a contract, you'll probably need to go through six steps:

1. Learn all you can about the deal. Ask the client (or your supervisor) to explain as fully as possible what the client's purpose is—and what the client's concerns are.
2. Find out what communications have occurred with the other party about the proposed deal. If the parties are sophisticated, they may have a term sheet, which is a preliminary document containing such essentials as the goods or services involved, prices, and deadlines. If not, you may be called on to prepare the initial draft of a term sheet—an exercise that will require a thoroughgoing familiarity with the key business points.
3. Ask about (and negotiate if necessary) your own deadline for circulating a polished first draft. (Never circulate a draft that hasn't been pretty well cleaned up.)
4. Make a concise list of the key aims of the contract. Brainstorm about the practicalities of the deal from your own experience as a legal adviser. Develop notes to supplement the term sheet.

5. See what has been done before: look for relevant forms so that you can mine them for useful ideas. Just remember that it's the *ideas* you're looking for, not verbiage. As we'll see again and again, you should be wary of predecessors' wordings.
6. Consider scheduling a call with the client to ask follow-up questions. Often the client will need to be prodded to consider ancillary terms important to the deal.

You'll need to consider whether the parties have a preexisting relationship. If they do, you need to think about what effect your own involvement will have. Be sure that your impact is positive from your client's perspective.

Just as the artist normally works from preliminary sketches, you may find term sheets and checklists to be extremely helpful. They'll minimize the risk that you'll overlook something important, and they can facilitate a logical structure for the contract. So insist on creating one to set forth the parties, the basic agreement or grant, the applicable territory, the applicable period, the bases for termination, terms relating to confidentiality, governing law, which terms ought to survive the ending of the contract, and so on.

It's normally a good idea to have your client approve the term sheet before going further. Your side's version of the term sheet may then be shared—and negotiated—with the other side. Such a procedure can save time in the long run.

Meanwhile, during the approval process, you'll have worked out many of the lawyerly particulars that will protect your client if the deal goes bad in any of several ways. You're aiming to assimilate the components so that you can make the contract an integrated whole as opposed to a collection of disparate provisions. You'll be selecting appropriate ideas and fitting them together.

At the same time, you'll need to think about not just what to include in the contract but also what to exclude.

Once you have an acceptable draft, you may circulate it to your internal team (such as it is). You might add comment bubbles in the draft with flagged terms or alternative wordings that still need to be discussed

> "The lawyer must have a considerable knowledge of the nature of the business involved in the transaction . . . . Without clarity of comprehension, there can be no clarity of style." Frank E. Cooper, *Writing in Law Practice* 271 (1963).

internally. Incorporating these queries directly into the draft can ensure that the client can consider important questions and that pending issues won't get lost in ongoing communications. Another strategy, if you're not sure about the content of a paragraph, is to add a heading for a term and leave the actual content "TBD" (to be determined). This practice efficiently flags for the client that you're considering a major topic but need further discussion. For example:

> **3. FEES.**
> **3.1 Fees.** Company will provide the Service upon Customer's timely payment of the fees for the Service as described in the Order Form ("Fees"). The Fees are payable on a [monthly/annual] basis (where available) depending upon the Purchase Terms.
> **3.2 Recurring Payment.** [TBD].
> **3.3 Taxes.** Customer shall pay all applicable taxes, levies, duties, or similar government assessments of any nature, including, for example, value-added, sales, use, or withholding taxes, assessable by any jurisdiction whatsoever (collectively, "Taxes") for the use of the Service.

Bryan Garner: Customers will probably be making recurrent payments. During our upcoming call, let's plan on discussing the exact terms that will dictate these payments.

You'll want to incorporate or otherwise take account of your colleagues' comments. Depending on your situation, you may have specialists in regulatory work, environmental law, tax, or real estate with useful points. Once you've dealt with those, you may need to schedule a call with the client to walk through the draft and get reactions to various points. Then you'll update the draft yet again. Once everyone on your team is satisfied, you can send a clean initial draft to the counterparty's counsel.

But again, we're assuming a certain type of situation: a complex transaction in which you're the principal drafter.

The situation could well be different. Sometimes clients have their own basic forms for deals, and you'll be expected to work on the fringes of more or less voluminous documentation. That won't just be a matter of "filling in the blanks," as the cynical joke about transactional lawyers goes. You might be reading hundreds of pages to verify the soundness of a client's forms.

One thing to be aware of here is the undesirability of "joker" provisions that have nothing to do with this particular deal. If some term in the contract is clearly a remnant of an earlier deal with a different configuration, remove it. Joker provisions can haunt your client in all sorts of unpredictable ways. So if a contractual term in a form has no plausible bearing on the current deal, you must cut it.

In a related vein, if you've used a past document as your template, ensure that all references to a former client and its counterparties have been removed.

§ 4 Learn to review a contract knowledgeably and efficiently.

A good first step is to read through the entire contract afresh, even if you worked on an earlier version of it, to make sure all the sections gibe. You'd be surprised how often you can find "busts" in some thoroughly vetted contracts—cross-references to sections that no longer exist, sections that seem to contradict each other, capitalized terms that are never defined, and so on. The probability of finding busts is higher the more complicated a document becomes, particularly if complicated financial terms have been translated (invariably poorly) into prose. By reading the contract from start to finish, rather than focusing on certain sections or isolated pieces, you'll identify the holes.

There's another point here: during the negotiations in the middle and late stages of a complex deal, everybody will be so focused on specific provisions or terms that it will be easy to lose sight of the forest for the trees. Especially if you're the initial drafter, it's best to do the global review and cleanup at the outset to streamline the noncontroversial sections. They'll probably remain untouched after the initial turn.

One deal lawyer I know undertakes this threshold review working backward. He reads each major division of the document in reverse order because the front sections typically receive the most focus. This approach mitigates the risk of fatigue in reviewing the last 20 pages of an 80-page contract. It will also help you discern the treacherous but seemingly benign provisions that some drafters slip in toward the end of a contract.

Early in your reading, focus on precisely how terms have been defined. As tempting as it may be to plunge into editing, you must ensure that you have a fair understanding of the stipulated meanings contained in definitions. Only after grasping their import should you think about making

> "A constant challenge is drafting for the 'reader in bad faith.' In other words, you need to make meaning so clear that a reader who would prefer another meaning cannot support it." Barbara Child, *Drafting Legal Documents* 3 (2d ed. 1992).

substantive edits. Only then will you be able to test the efficacy of provisions by reading them in light of the definitions.

In the later stages of working on a contract, it becomes easy to fixate on points that get contested toward the very end. And it's tempting, once a consensus is reached, to send out a draft "as is" for signatures. But if you have the luxury of time—and a client who will allow you to do so—take a break and get a full night of sleep. Then print the draft and read the hard copy one last time pretending that you've never seen it before. You'll be surprised by the little errors you've overlooked, even if you've spent weeks up to this point improving the draft.

By the way, insist on being utterly honest with yourself about whether you truly understand the provisions. That's especially so with forms. If you can't quite get your mind around a provision, demand that you must clarify until understanding comes. Reject the idea that if you're in doubt, you must leave a provision alone—or even that you should leave it in.

§ 5 Establish efficient protocols for working with counterparties.

Typically, once one party sends an initial draft of a document (or set of documents) to the other, that other side will review and then send back a revised draft with a redline against the initial one. To move negotiations forward efficiently, be careful to always revise the most current draft. Redlining (or "blacklining," as it's often called) is considered important, but fortunately if a revising party overlooks it, computers can now compare two versions of a document and make a redline pretty readily. (That's a luxury we didn't have just a generation ago.) Many practitioners will provide the redlined version together with a clean version of the revised draft. The original drafter will then review the changes and, depending on how far apart the parties are, either revise again and send over a new draft with a new redline or else schedule a call with all the parties to review the changes page by page (or using an issues list drafted by one of the teams). This process is repeated until there are no more redlines. When the parties have a version they agree on, they can sign it after any other conditions to signing have been satisfied.

In multiparty negotiations, or those in which several groups are reviewing a draft contract, it's often wise to avoid track changes and instead use a comment matrix to gather and manage comments.

§ 6 Date your drafts.

Every draft should identify the source or editor and bear a date, and probably even a time. You want to ensure that changes have been physically marked on a draft either by handwriting or by tracking all changes on the computer. Many drafters hand-mark their changes before they're inserted into the document, and they may well put their initials at the head of the first page: "BAG Master [date]." (The *BAG* is for *Bryan A. Garner*: I follow this practice.) So when a new draft is printed, you can proofread the new draft against your edited master to ensure that all edits have been properly made. Today, of course, computers will do the redlining on the latest draft by comparison with an appropriately specified earlier draft. It's crucial that a new draft explicitly identify the earlier draft from which the current draft is showing changes.

Mechanics come into play on the many versions of a document. If you start with a precedent, you might save it to your system and identify it by adding *Original* or *Version 1.* You can easily "version up" to make your initial draft and then run a redline against the original or against any previous version. You'll want to version up every time a draft is sent to anyone for comment, whether internally or to clients, and each version should be labeled and dated (for example, "BAG comments 8/27/18" or "BAG comments based on client feedback 9/1/18"). Likewise, when you receive a revised version marked against a prior version (version 1) that you circulated, you should save in your system that revised version (version 2), and then create another (version 3) in which you make your incremental revisions. When you send a new draft back to the other side, the redline will be version 3 compared to version 2.

Sometimes you'll want to label new drafts for specific provisions that are being negotiated ("BAG comments on insurance payments" or "BAG comments to build in second funding option"). Having everything in the system and methodically labeled this way will be critical to organizing deals effectively. Those involved should be vigilant to make and maintain

> "To send a retyped or reprinted draft without showing what amendments, or further amendments, have been made is disconcerting to the other party, quite apart from obliging him, or an assistant, to spend time making comparisons to discern the changes." L.W. Melville, *The Draftsman's Handbook* § 4.20, at 45 (2d ed. 1991).

these records: revisions can be fast-paced or under the pressure of time, as when parties accelerate the closing date. Ultimately you should be able, with ease, to refer to specific points that took place in negotiations years ago and to see where you started and where you ended up. That could be useful in developing strategies for new deals or reminding clients why a certain provision ended up as it did.

To ensure that a working draft isn't inadvertently considered final or ready for signing, label the document clearly as "DRAFT" (preferably in red ink) both in the title and in the header or footer.

§ 7 Retain the final, signed version with the permanent client file in a separate, conspicuously marked folder.

Preservation needs are situational, but generally a fully signed contract should be maintained in a place that's easy to locate. You'll want to arrange your computer folders logically and thoroughly so that they're easily accessible, and you may wish to keep scans of all operative contracts. Scans are usually best: sometimes small but important changes get made at the last moment, and these may not be reflected in the final native-file draft.

When a major deal closes, the lawyers on all sides typically confirm who will prepare the "closing sets" for the deal (or "closing bibles," as they're sometimes called). Leading up to the closing, all sides confirm their sign-off on the final versions, and these are used to assemble the authoritative closing set. If a counterparty prepares closing sets, it's sound practice to have a junior professional run redlines of every document against the putative final version to ensure accuracy.

These days, most closing sets are electronic, but attorneys who practiced before the digital age often have shelves and shelves of old closing sets. Even if they're stored digitally in a secure cloud, they should be organized by client and by deal, so that whenever a client calls to ask a question—"How did we handle construction delays in Project Piranha?" or "Do you have a copy of the side letter from Project Penguin?"—the answer is just a few clicks away.

§ 8 Adhere most strongly to the conventions recommended in this book when you're the principal or responsible drafter.

It bears repeating: you can't have much influence on other practitioners' drafting style. So don't insist that they use your numbering system (§ 24), your formatting (§§ 35–46), your modal verbs (§ 47—unless there's a really troublesome provision in which *shall* clearly means *may*), or your preferred placement of definitions (§§ 102–103). Don't expect them to share your aversion to romanettes (§ 26), to the generic masculine pronoun (§ 71), to provisos (§ 116), to the omission of the serial comma (§ 129), to *which* as a restrictive relative pronoun (§ 143), or to many other words and phrases, including but not limited to *including but not limited to*.

That's not to say that you shouldn't feel passionate about these matters of technique. You should—precisely because they'll make you more effective. It's just that as ardently as you might adopt these conventions and as important as they might be to you personally, you can't successfully proselytize about them to any practitioners other than junior colleagues. It's a matter of personal pride you'll take in holding yourself to high standards. The "rules" are much more lax in the world at large.

Everything that follows in this book assumes that you have full discretion to adopt the very best practices available to you as a contract drafter.

"[M]any lawyers resist giving up the use of terms of art, asserting this will cause confusion and precipitate needless litigation. This fear is largely without foundation. First, most terms of art are not as precise and fixed in legal meaning as their defenders contend. Consider, for example, the multiple meanings that the courts have given to 'appurtenances,' 'fixtures,' and 'tenantable'—words that real-estate lawyers consider sacrosanct terms of art, but that have proved not to be. Second, some terms of art have a fixed meaning, but one that is so general it is virtually worthless in a drafted document." Thomas R. Haggard & George W. Kuney, *Legal Drafting: Process, Techniques, and Exercises* 263 (2d ed. 2007).

Accuracy

§ 9 Be alert to errors, misstatements, and ambiguities.

Read drafts critically—even hypercritically. Be sure you've actually said what you mean to say. Identify and address instances of substantive error, ambiguity, and curable vagueness. Understand that ambiguity is the cancer of contract drafting. Although vagueness is sometimes purposeful and desirable (e.g., *within a reasonable time*), you should sharpen the wording when you can (e.g., *within 30 days* or *within 24 hours*). If it's possible in the circumstances, a specific time and date will often work better (e.g., *by 5:00 p.m. ET on June 30, 2020*).

When it comes to accuracy, be especially alert to the possibility that some provisions will make no literal sense at all. They're often perpetuated in deal after deal. That they exist at all is something of a marvel; that they're sometimes embedded in frequently used forms is even more so. After all, you'd think that transactional lawyers would adopt a protocol of reading and rereading each contract that goes out the door. Given that critical thinking and close reading are prized habits for lawyers, contradictory or outright nonsensical provisions should be exceedingly rare. Alas, they're not.

Most seasoned lawyers can recall anecdotes of contractual monstrosities. One involves a malpractice claim against a law firm: a mortgage had somehow been prepared in the early 1980s with a crucial line dropped. The resulting sentence made no sense. The firm had prepared dozens if not hundreds of mortgages with the same language missing, resulting in an incomplete sentence devoid of meaning—and the little sense it did seem to make resulted in a disposition that no sane drafter could have wanted. It seems that a typist had mistakenly skipped a line and kept on typing. Nobody caught the error until a problem emerged in the early 2000s.

By that time, the faulty contract had long since become entrenched as the "firm form." A secretarial gaffe from a generation before had become permanently ensconced in the form.

That's one of the pratfalls that forms, or precedents, encourage: a blind reliance on what's "worked" before. Forms often lull drafters into a false sense of security. If it worked last time, it's surely reliable. "Don't touch a word of it," I've heard drafters say. "It's time-tested, and most of the provisions have probably been litigated."

This, too, is lunacy. As David Mellinkoff demonstrated in his classic book *The Language of the Law* (1963), litigated forms typically have glaring problems in them. That's usually why they invite the litigation in the first place. Yet for most of the 20th century, American legal publishers collected and disseminated "litigated forms" as if they were prized: the ambiguities within them had been adjudicated and settled. Yet if, say, the Arizona Supreme Court decides a contractual ambiguity one way, the California Supreme Court may decide it differently, and the New York Court of Appeals even differently from the others. All because nobody simply redrafted the ambiguity to fix the problem. After all, if a redrafted form hasn't been litigated, how could it be recommended over wording that has?

I once attended a lecture by an expert on mechanic's liens. He cited a recent state supreme court's decision in which, in a critical provision, the court held that *shall* meant *may*. (Such holdings are common, given the pervasive sloppiness with which legal drafters use the word *shall*. See § 47.) After noting the decision, he emphatically recommended that all drafters in the state should use *shall* in this provision because they know what it means there: it means *may*. When I asked why drafters shouldn't simply use *may*, he said he had no idea what that might be held to mean. After all, it hadn't been adjudicated.

This mindset leads to all kinds of drafting perversions.

But then there are simple lapses in attentive reading. Lawyers often send me "busts" they encounter. I received an e-mail quoting this provision from a loan document:

> On January 1 of each year during the term of the Loan, Borrower shall furnish and supply Lender each of the Lender's monthly bank statements for the preceding twelve (12) months.

Did you see that? How in the world can the borrower be at liberty to obtain the lender's bank statements in order to give them to the lender? Is the borrower being appointed attorney-in-fact to retrieve those statements from the lender's banker?

Of course, the second instance of *Lender* should be *Borrower*.

Typos of that kind—actually swapping the parties—are most common in contracts that contain correlative designations ending in *-ee* and *-or*: *employer/employee*, *licensor/licensee*, *mortgagor/mortgagee*, etc. Using both in a given legal instrument should be forbidden. It almost guarantees errors of

> "A controversy is normally an exploitation of a systematic set of misunderstandings for war-like purposes." I.A. Richards, *The Philosophy of Rhetoric* 39 (1936).

this kind. Yet many intellectual-property lawyers prepare licensing agreements with *licensor/licensee.*

The problems are threefold: (1) whenever part of such a document is typed anew, clerical errors are likely to occur; (2) the sameness of the party designations leads to cognitive difficulties for all readers—including the drafters themselves—because the only visual difference is the two-character suffix at the end; and (3) clients tend to resent such documents not just for their unreadability, but also for their appearing to be forms that the lawyer took little care in adapting, apart from the preamble.

"I'm paying you this fee for a form you took off your server?" the client is likely to think if not say. A simple search-and-replace maneuver makes the entire document look tailor-made. When you can, you ought to use the parties' actual names. Bad: *Vendor/Vendee.* Better: *Seller/Buyer.* Best: *Williams/Johnson.* And if you use the parties' names, you yourself will read the document with greater comprehension and attentiveness.

Consider an example from an apartment lease. The drafter has adopted the ghastly practice of putting party designations in all caps:

> LESSEE shall not, without the LESSOR's written consent, make any alteration in the Leased Premises and LESSEE will not deface or permit the defacing of any part of the Leased Premises. LESSEE shall not do or suffer anything to be done on the Leased Premises which will increase the rate of fire insurance on the building. LESSEE shall not use any shades, awnings, or window guards, except such as shall be approved by Landlord. LESSEE will not keep or harbor any animal in the Leased Premises without first obtaining the written consent of LESSOR. LESSEE will not permit the accumulation of waste or refuse matter. LESSEE will not assign this Lease or underlet the Leased Premises or any part thereof without the LESSEE's written consent, which consent must not be unreasonably withheld by LESSOR.

The shouted names (in all caps) are distracting, to say the least. They detract from anyone's ability to read the paragraph. Then there's the weird vacillation between *shall* and *will.* Then there's the incorrect use of *shall* (nonmandatory) in the fourth instance. Then there's the switch from *permit* in the first sentence to the archaic *suffer* in the second. Then there's the bizarre switch in midparagraph from "Lessor" to "Landlord." Then there's the obtuse phrase *refuse matter,* in which many ordinary readers would read *refuse* as a verb: the tenant will not refuse matter. But of course the intent is to use *refuse* in its noun sense, with the redundant word *matter.* Wouldn't the plain word *trash* suffice?

But did you notice the clear bust in that passage? The final instance of *lessee* should be *lessor*. This is a silly error—but one that could cost the landlord many a headache.

Granted, you might use surnames in a contract like this one, but if your client is a landlord with many tenants, positional labels may be best. They must be different in form: *Landlord* and *Tenant* would be much preferable to *Lessor* and *Lessee*. You're far less prone to error that way. Here's how that provision might read:

> 3.2 **Prohibited activities.** Tenant must not:
> (A) make any alteration in the Leased Premises without first obtaining the Landlord's written consent;
> (B) use any shades, awnings, or window guards without first obtaining the Landlord's written consent;
> (C) keep or harbor any animal in the Leased Premises without first obtaining the Landlord's written consent;
> (D) assign this Lease or sublet any part of the Leased Premises without first obtaining the Landlord's written consent;
> (E) deface or permit the defacing of any part of the Leased Premises;
> (F) do or permit anything to be done on the Leased Premises that will increase the cost of fire insurance; or
> (G) permit the accumulation of waste or trash.

That's a fairly simple redraft. It adds a helpful heading. It uses vertical listing, which results in tighter wording. It simplifies the language, thereby promoting better compliance by a tenant who now has a better chance of comprehending what's prohibited. And it groups the items more sensibly. Granted, other organizational strategies are possible.

You might have noticed that I completely eliminated the requirement of not unreasonably withholding consent to subletting. If you represent the landlord, you surely don't want that. Why not just allow your client to have full discretion? You don't want to impose unnecessary burdens on the client.

> "'Superstition' would be the best word to describe the law's attitude toward forms. Like a gambler unwilling to wash his lucky shirt lest it lose some of its magic, the average lawyer wouldn't change a comma in a trusted boilerplate form." Adam Freedman, *The Party of the First Part: The Curious World of Legalese* 31 (2007).

In any event, the big point is that we've eliminated the bust: the misidentification of a party. When you adopt sounder practices in contract drafting, you promote critical thinking and prevent error.

	NOT THIS:	BUT THIS:	
The ambiguity here arises from the adverbial phrase *as the arbitrators may direct*: it might modify *apportioned* (surely the intended meaning) or both *apportioned* and *borne* (a bad-faith misreading that arises if the arbitrators are silent about expenses).	Ex. 1 The expense of the arbitration shall be borne by the losing party or apportioned between the parties as the arbitrators may direct. **Purchase Agreement from a major law firm**	The losing party will bear the cost of the arbitration unless the arbitrators apportion the expenses differently.	The most important word in the revision is *unless.*
Bimonthly can mean "every two months" or "twice a month." It's better to be clear by using *twice a month.*	Ex. 2 5.2 The Contractor's Fee will be payable on a bimonthly basis during the course of the Project. **Construction Contract from a major law firm**	**5.2 Payment Schedule.** In accordance with the Payment Schedule in § 4, Franklin will pay Calvin's Construction the Contractor's Fee twice a month during the course of the Project.	It's good practice to check with the client's accounting department to determine and then document its customary practice, such as paying on the 1st and 15th.
Shall indicates that the car is mandatory, but *may* gives the Director discretion to approve or disapprove. Could *is married* be interpreted as *gets married*?	Ex. 3 1. <u>Courtesy Automobile:</u> Coach shall receive a courtesy automobile or a car allowance as may be approved in writing by the Director of Intercollegiate Athletics. Coach shall be eligible for an additional courtesy automobile or car allowance if he is married during the Term. **College-Football Head-Coach Employment Agreement for a major university**	**2.1 Courtesy automobile.** Kirk is entitled to a courtesy automobile or a car allowance. If Kirk is married or gets married during the term of this contract, Kirk will be entitled to a second courtesy automobile or car allowance. The specifics of the car arrangements are subject to approval by the Director of Intercollegiate Athletics.	
What is the earliest date on which one party can terminate under this language? It's not clear whether the notice of intent to terminate can be given before the Initial Term ends.	Ex. 4 (b) <u>Termination Without Cause.</u> Following the expiration of the Initial Term, this Agreement may be terminated by either party, without cause, provided that the terminating party has given proper and unambiguous notice of intent to terminate to the other party at least ninety (90) days in advance of the effective date of termination. **Gas-Station Lease**	**4.2 Termination without cause.** Either party may terminate this Agreement without cause if: (A) the terminating party gives the other party proper and unambiguous notice at least 90 days before the effective date of termination; and (B) the effective date of termination falls after the Initial Term ends.	The rewrite makes it clear that the notice may be given during the Initial Term as long as the effective date of termination falls after the Initial Term ends.

"The use of purely legal words in a document meant for laymen merely creates confusion and mystification. Mystification is not communication, and unless the document communicates its intent and meaning in unmistakable language to the laymen, it utterly fails to accomplish its purpose." Sidney F. Parham Jr., *The Fundamentals of Legal Writing* 42 (1967).

NOT THIS:	BUT THIS:
Ex. 5 *[Misplaced modifier: conjunction* that. *Is the contractor merely* agreeing *before beginning services or* agreeing to furnish *before beginning services?]* Contractor hereby agrees prior to commencement of the services contemplated hereunder that it shall furnish to Client satisfactory evidence of the insurance coverage required hereunder and the certificate shall provide a thirty (30) day written notification provision that notice to Client is required to be sent prior to cancellation of or material change to such insurance. **Independent-Contractor-Services Agreement from 3 Nancy Saint-Paul, Texas Legal Practice Forms 3d *Independent Contractor Agreements* § 50:3, at 712 (2016)**	Before beginning services under this Agreement, Costello must give Empyrean satisfactory evidence of the required insurance coverage. The certificate must require that written notice be sent to Empyrean at least 30 days before canceling or materially changing coverage. *[The rewrite eliminates the conjunction and makes the meaning clearer.]*
Ex. 6 *[The fourth word—the* of*—is a typographical error that makes the provision gibberish. The second* of, *just after the third comma, adds to the nonsensical syntax.]* Notwithstanding the provisions of contained herein, Employee may purchase or otherwise acquire, up to a noncontrolling interest, of any class of securities of any enterprise that may be competitive with Employer and [*name of employer's business*] (but without other participation in the activities of such enterprise) as long as such securities are listed on any national or regional securities exchange or have been registered under Section 12(g) of the Securities Exchange Act of 1934, as amended. **Employment Contract from *Texas Forms Legal & Business* § 11:139, at 338 (2005)**	2.3 **Limits on employee investments.** Despite other provisions of this Agreement, Marcus may purchase or otherwise acquire any class of securities of any enterprise that competes with ICV on 3 conditions: (A) the interest must remain noncontrolling; (B) Marcus cannot otherwise participate in the activities of the competing enterprise; and (C) the securities must be listed on a national or regional securities exchange or have been registered under § 12(g) of the Securities Exchange Act of 1934 (as amended).
Ex. 7 (1) Material Contracts. Except as otherwise set forth in this Agreement, the Company shall not, and shall not permit any of its Subsidiaries to, (i)(A) amend, terminate, cancel, extend, or request any material change in, or agree to any material change in, or (B) waive, release or assign any material right or claim under, any Company Contract or (ii) enter into any material Contract, other than in the ordinary course of business not to exceed $1.0 million per Contract and $5.0 million in the aggregate for all Contracts. *[It's not immediately clear whether the highlighted clause applies to both (i) and (ii) or to only (ii). Only one revision is offered here.]* **Merger Agreement from major entertainment-industry companies**	4.1 **Material Contracts.** Except as otherwise set forth in this Agreement, the Company and its Subsidiaries must not: (A) amend, terminate, cancel, extend, request any material change in, or agree to any material change in any Company Contract; (B) waive, release, or assign any material right or claim under any Company Contract; or (C) enter into any material Contract except in the ordinary course of business up to $1 million per Contract and up to $5 million in the aggregate for all Contracts. *[In this revision, the* other than *clause (changed to* except *here) applies to only (ii) in the original contract.]*

§ 10 Avoid inconsistent usage.

Use a word or phrase consistently to express a single idea. Don't vary your terminology for the sake of "elegant variation." Under the canon of construction known as the presumption of consistent usage,[1] courts presume that a change in wording indicates a change of meaning. So if you use a different word, ensure that it refers to a different thing: some degree of monotony is a necessary evil in legal drafting.

Let's say you represent a company in drafting an employment contract. The template it has used in the past contains several versions of stating permissions:

- The Company may . . .
- The Company may, in its discretion, . . .
- The Company may, in its sole and exclusive discretion, . . .
- The Company has the sole, exclusive, unfettered discretion . . .

A dispute later arises with an employee, Edward Johnson, who objects to the company's actions under a provision stating, "The Company may reassign the employee to another division at any time." The new division is located in a different part of the city and engages in work that Johnson finds less satisfactory given his background and training. He claims that the company should have consulted him and that the reassignment should have been a joint decision. His lawyer argues in court that the operative provision doesn't contain any words used elsewhere in the contract: *may in its discretion . . . sole and exclusive discretion . . . unfettered discretion.* By negative implication the word *may* alone, when contrasted with the other wordings, denotes a kind of discretion that is *joint* (not sole), *nonexclusive*, and *fettered.*

In the end, it doesn't matter which argument—Johnson's or the company's—is upheld. The drafting has embroiled the company in needless

> "If there is anything that characterizes the style of a well-drafted legal document, it is that the drafter always says the same thing the same way and different things differently. Improving style, therefore, amounts to attending consistently to a whole collection of particulars that merit attention throughout any legal document." Barbara Child, *Drafting Legal Documents* 376 (2d ed. 1992).

1 *See* Antonin Scalia & Bryan A. Garner, *Reading Law: The Interpretation of Legal Texts* 170–73 (2012).

litigation. *May* alone would have sufficed until the drafter started embarking on more enthusiastic variations on the theme.

The same difficulties arise with inconsistent wordings relating to duties:

- *shall*
- *agrees that he shall*
- *agrees to*
- *explicitly agrees to*
- *will*
- *promises to*
- *understands that it is his sole responsibility to*

And so on. (See § 47.) Or grounds for acting:

- *for cause*
- *for good cause*
- *for good and sufficient cause*
- *for good cause shown*

Never, seemingly, are these disparate phrasings the result of careful, subtle thought that creates a gradation of standards. If they were, they'd be ludicrously oversubtle. No: they're the stylistic remnants of countless predecessors, each with a different style, coupled with drafters' inertia. Drafters tend to work piecemeal on a contract but never consider overhauling the whole document for consistency of phraseology.

That's a mistake. Don't make it yourself.

NOT THIS:	BUT THIS:
Ex. 1 **17. GOVERNING LAW AND RESOLUTION OF DISPUTES** . . . 17.4 **Mediation.** If the Dispute cannot be settled by direct negotiations within thirty days of initiation of the resolution process, either Party may initiate mediation by giving notice to the other Party. Mediation shall be attended by an individual(s) representing each Party with decision-making authority and the proceeding shall take place in Dallas, Texas. **Master Contractor-Services Contract from a major oil company**	**17. Governing Law and Dispute-Resolution** . . . 17.4 **Mediation.** If the Dispute cannot be settled through direct negotiation within 30 days after the resolution process begins, either Party may initiate mediation by giving notice to the other Party. Each Party must be represented at the mediation by at least 1 person with decision-making authority. The mediation will take place in Dallas, Texas.

Despite some confusion on the subject, *indemnify and hold harmless* is a redundant doublet.

Note the needless variation in wording here.

NOT THIS:	BUT THIS:
Ex. 2 2.5. Performer may not receive any money owed to Contractor, without Contractor's express written permission. 2.6. Performer agrees to indemnify and hold Contractor harmless for any losses of money which Performer receives and Contractor shall not be responsible for any loss, shortage or destruction of the money. . . . 2.9. Performer agrees to hold harmless, indemnify and protect Contractor for any injuries, accidents, problems, disputes or other contingencies that arise as a result of the Performer's performance of this Agreement. **Entertainment-Performance Agreement from 3 Nancy Saint-Paul, Texas Legal Practice Forms 3d *Independent Contractor Agreements* § 50:8 (2016)**	2.5 **Fritz's receipt of money.** Fritz may receive money owed to Pryor only with Pryor's express written permission. If Fritz receives money for Pryor, Pryor is not responsible for any loss, shortage, or destruction of the money. Fritz indemnifies Pryor for the lost, shorted, or destroyed amount. . . . 2.9 **Fritz's further indemnities.** Fritz indemnifies Pryor for injuries, accidents, problems, disputes, or other contingencies resulting from Fritz's performance of this Agreement.
Ex. 3 8. Remedies. Each party agrees that its obligations hereunder are necessary and reasonable in order to protect the other party and the other party's business, and expressly agrees that monetary damages would be inadequate to compensate the other party for any breach of any covenant or agreement set forth herein. Accordingly, each party agrees and acknowledges that any such violation or threatened violation will cause irreparable injury to the other party and that, in addition to any other remedies that may be available, in law, in equity or otherwise, the other party shall be entitled to seek injunctive relief against the breach or threatened breach of this Agreement or the continuation of any such breach, without the necessity of proving actual damages. **Mutual Nondisclosure Agreement from a major consumer-product technology & development company**	8. **Remedies.** Each party's obligations in this Agreement are necessary and reasonable to protect the other party and the other party's business. Because monetary damages would be inadequate to compensate the other party and because a breach or threatened breach will cause irreparable injury to the other party, that party may seek injunctive relief to prevent the breach or threatened breach or the continuation of a breach without need to prove actual damages.[2]

"[I]n legal affairs . . . it is often possible as well as necessary to insist that particular words be used in particular ways." Irving Lee, "They Talk Past Each Other," in *The Ways of Language* 33, 42 (Raymond J. Pflug ed., 1967).

2 As a matter of law, many jurisdictions will not enforce a provision like this one; the court will independently assess whether irreparable harm exists.

NOT THIS:	BUT THIS:
Ex. 4 Section Three. Payment Within [*number of days*] days of the date of this agreement, buyer must pay seller $[*dollar amount of sum*] as an advance on the purchase price of the [*type of mineral*]. This amount must be retained by seller and applied as a credit to buyer's account against any balance that may be due seller at the completion of this contract. Buyer must pay seller the amount provided in this agreement for all [*type of mineral*] shipped under this contract, in the following manner: [*description of shipment*]. For all [*type of mineral*] shipped during any month, payment must be made on or before the [*ordinal number of day*] day of the next succeeding month. The advance payment must be credited to buyer's account on [*date of advance payment*] and applied against any balance due seller at that time on account of [*type of mineral*] previously shipped to buyer. However, if the full quantity of [*type of mineral*] provided in this agreement has not been shipped on or before such date, seller may retain a sufficient amount of the advance payment to cover any shipments then due pending the completion of this sale. **Oil-, Gas-, and Mineral-Rights Agreement from *Texas Forms: Legal & Business* § 3A:343, at 537 (2012)**	**3. Payment.** **3.1 Shipping and payment schedule.** Wilshire will pay Hennings the amount provided in this Agreement for all __________ shipped by Hennings. All __________ shipped in a particular month must be paid for by the 1st day of the next month. **3.2 Advance payment.** Within 15 days after the date of this Agreement, Wilshire will pay Hennings $__________ as an advance on the purchase price. Hennings will apply this payment as a credit to Wilshire's account against any balance that may be due Hennings at the completion of this Agreement. The advance payment will be credited to Wilshire's account on the date the payment is received and applied against any balance then due Hennings for previous shipments. But if the full quantity of __________ provided in this Agreement has not been shipped on or before that date, Hennings may retain enough of the advance payment to cover any shipments then due pending completion of this Agreement.

"Do not use different words in different portions of the contract to describe the same thing. If the contract refers to a 'sedan,' do not refer to it in other portions of the contract by such words as 'automobile,' 'car,' or 'vehicle.'" Frank E. Cooper, *Writing in Law Practice* 278 (1963).

§ 11 Avoid out-of-date or error-ridden forms.

When using forms, be their boss—not their subordinate. Forms are handy. But they're dangerous when they fall into the wrong hands because they readily become cursory fill-in-the-blank exercises. They can stifle thought.

Any seasoned transactional lawyer can recount small horror stories about contracts stipulating to matters that weren't even part of the deal: they were simply remnants from earlier documents. When forms become too great a crutch, that's the inevitable consequence.

So second-guessing existing forms is essential. Second-guess them, both from a legal standpoint and from a plain-English standpoint. Then you'll master them.

Antiquated formbooks are a frequent source of error. Take, for example, a 2005 Texas formbook containing a distribution contract. An antireliance provision in it states: "No representations, promises, guarantees, or warranties were made by us to induce you to execute this Agreement except for what is expressly contained in this Agreement. You agree that no one can guarantee your success in the business."

But under a 2011 Texas Supreme Court decision,[1] any such provision is ineffective unless the antireliance clause includes language specifically disclaiming *reliance*.[2] To be unambiguously effective after 2011, any such clause should say that "there have been no representations and warranties, and you hereby disclaim any reliance on any representations and warranties." As written in the formbook, the clause might be ineffective to deter or overcome a claim of fraudulent inducement.

Sometimes the form is simply wrong or poorly drafted, as you can see in Example 2 below—in which the word *not* has been dropped.

> "An adjudicated form is a form that has attached to it a certificate that there is something terribly wrong with it. If there was not something terribly wrong with it, it never would have been adjudicated. And we publish these form books to the end that the worst mistakes in legal draftsmanship may be preserved and perpetuated."
> Charles A. Beardsley, *Beware of Platitudinous Epistles*, 16 Cal. B.J. 65, 65 (1941).

---

1 *Italian Cowboy Partners, Ltd. v. Prudential Ins. Co. of Am.*, 341 S.W.3d 323 (Tex. 2011) (landlord knowingly misrepresented condition of premises when orally reassuring tenant that building was in perfect condition).

2 *Id.* at 335–36.

One final point about using forms—which might even be contracts you've used before with similar terms. Be sure that no inapplicable remnants remain in your new contract. All references to your former client must be culled, whether actual names, addresses for sending notices, or provisions relating to venue and governing law.

NOT THIS:	BUT THIS:
Ex. 1 (3) The Debtor agrees to deposit and pledge with the Creditor such Security or additional Security as the Creditor may request. The request for such Security may be made by the Creditor by telephone, mail or telegram addressed to the Debtor at the address hereinabove set forth. **General Loan and Collateral Agreement from 1 Lester Nelson, *Digest of Commercial Laws of the World: Forms of Commercial Agreements* § 6-2, at 8 (May 1998)**	(3) **Security deposit.** If the Creditor so requests, the Debtor must deposit and pledge the Security or additional Security with the Creditor. The Creditor may request the Security by telephone, mail, fax, or e-mail addressed to the Debtor.
Ex. 2 D. Within the one (1) year period immediately following the termination of this Agreement, regardless of the reason therefore, Employee shall solicit, induce, aid or suggest to any of the employees, consultants to, or other persons having a substantial contractual relationship with the Company to leave such employ, cease counseling or terminate such contractual relationship with Company. **Restrictive-Covenant Clause of a General Executive-Employment Agreement from 3 Oscar LeRoy Warren, Gloria C. Markuson & Gladys Glickman, *Warren's Forms of Agreements: Business Forms* § 40.4.01, at 40-23 to -24 (Martin D. Fern ed., 1988)**	(D) **Contractual relationships.** For 1 year after termination, the Employee must not encourage, aid, or induce an employee, consultant, or other person with a substantial contractual relationship with the Company to end that relationship.

The telegram reference was surely out of date even in 1998. Telegrams still existed, of course, but were rarely used. E-mail was already on the rise.

This provision erroneously *requires* (not forbids) the employee to induce others to cut their contractual ties with the company. The word *not* is missing. (Also, *therefor* is misspelled *therefore*.)

"Rare is the form that cannot be improved. Most antiquated forms and models, and many modern ones, would benefit from an analysis of both their substance and their style. Many formbooks claim to be 'litigation-tested.' It seems hardly a recommendation for a form that it was the subject of litigation! Having seen the problems caused by the form, the drafter should feel free to improve upon the original." Scott J. Burnham, *The Contract Drafting Guidebook* § 16.2, at 339 (1992).

Clarity and readability

§ 12 Use plain English.

Reject the idea that you're drafting principally for specialists. Granted, it's probably a fiction to think that Grandma Jones (an unsophisticated reader) needs to read and understand your document. It's likewise a fiction to think that people can read and understand the statutes governing their conduct. Indeed, it's probably a fiction to think that even legislators can read and understand most of the statutes they pass.

That's the way of the world. No one but a tax lawyer really understands the Internal Revenue Code. No one but an employee-benefits specialist can read and understand ERISA. No one but a bankruptcy specialist can read and understand the Bankruptcy Code. And no one but a transactional lawyer needs to be able to read and understand your contract. Right?

Wrong. The Internal Revenue Code, ERISA, and the Bankruptcy Code are drafting nightmares. To the true drafting expert, they're abominations.

The point about widening your intended audience is that you'll draft better. It's a fiction, yes, that Grandma Jones should be able to read and understand your document. But it's a useful fiction. It will help you simplify as much as you possibly can. And if you do that, even specialists will be able to grasp your meaning more quickly.

So use the simplest, most straightforward words and sentences you can to express the idea clearly. Whenever language can be simplified without losing meaning, the style needs improving. Your goal is to stay within the bounds of ordinary idiom as much as possible and abstain from jargon. Write natural-sounding sentences, but always with an eye to eradicating imprecision. Whenever your tone becomes stiff and artificial, you're bound to be drafting poorly—and probably imprecisely.

As you'll see throughout this book, using plain English involves much more than word replacements. It involves a whole series of interrelated conventions that enhance a document's clarity—in part by avoiding antiquated practices like these, which can render a contract impenetrable:

> "By exposing the contents of a document, plain language reduces the likelihood of a professional negligence claim against the drafter. Clients who sign a document which is plainly expressed and easily understood will be hard-pressed to convince a court that they did not understand it." Peter Butt & Richard Castle, *Modern Legal Drafting* 89 (2001).

- If you use a single-column format with 9-point type, readers will find it a strain to read your document (see § 38).
- If you use a sans-serif typeface like Arial in the text, you'll double the strain (see § 37).
- If you have a decimal numbering system that involves a third level (1.1.1, 1.1.2, etc.), you'll immediately alienate many readers (see § 24).
- If you insist on lots of definitions for obvious terms—as by saying that *Digitropic Holdings, Inc.* is "hereinafter Digitropic"—you'll weigh down your sentences with galumphing legalisms (see § 93).
- If you run enumerated lists into paragraphs, you'll amass some impenetrable barriers to entry (see § 85).
- If you insist on using the third person no matter what the document, you'll make the text much less engaging (see § 54).
- If you organize from your own point of view and not from the reader's, you'll baffle anyone who really wants to understand (see § 80).
- If you stuff the cover page with unattractively presented minutiae, you'll suggest just how dreadful the rest of the document is likely to be (see §§ 27–28).
- If you use a good deal of unnecessary passive voice, you'll muddle the meaning (see § 66).

These, unfortunately, are all conventions widely used in old-style drafting. And if you start out with any of them, you're drastically hampering yourself.

So begin by liberating yourself from some old habits. Think about the conventions that you've been using and how you might improve on them. And then once you have a good set of conventions, use a consistent format.

NOT THIS:	BUT THIS:
Ex. 1 The developers are desirous that the Invention be utilized to the fullest extent. **License Agreement from a major law firm**	The developers want the Invention to be used to its full potential.

NOT THIS:	BUT THIS:
Ex. 2 7.2 Franchisee does not at any time acquire any rights in the Licensed Marks by virtue of any use thereof. **Franchise-License Agreement**	7.2 **Rights in Licensed Marks.** In using the Licensed Marks, Tomlin does not acquire any intellectual-property rights. It's typically better to use real names—not labels. See § 51.
Ex. 3 It is a condition precedent to the Company's obligation to pay a Loss that the Insured comply with all of the following requirements: . . . . **Insurance Policy from a major insurer**	For us to be responsible for paying a Loss, you must first comply with all the following requirements: . . . .
Ex. 4 (6) Coach shall maintain and enforce conduct (both on and off the field) and disciplinary rules and sanctions, fairly and uniformly for all student-athletes in the Program so as to ensure academic and moral integrity while encouraging excellence. **College-Football Head-Coach Employment Agreement for a major university**	6. **Player conduct.** To encourage excellence and ensure academic and moral integrity, Shaunessey will fairly and uniformly maintain and enforce conduct (both on and off the field), disciplinary rules, and sanctions for all student-athletes in the Program.
Ex. 5 **NOW, THEREFORE,** the parties hereto, in consideration of the mutual covenants and agreements herein contained, promises herein expressed, acknowledged by each of them to be satisfactory and adequate, do hereby agree as follows: **Art-Licensing Agreement from a major law firm**	In consideration of the promises stated in this Agreement, the parties agree as follows: See § 29.
Ex. 6 Now, therefore, in consideration of the above premises and of Indemnitee's continuing to serve the Company directly or, at its request, with another enterprise, and intending to be legally bound hereby, the parties agree as follows: **Indemnification Agreement from a computer-technology company**	In consideration of the promises stated in this Agreement, the parties agree as follows: See § 29.
Ex. 7 (d) Exhibits 4.1D-1 and 4.1D-2 hereto contain, respectively, true and complete copies of the Articles of Incorporation and By-Laws of the Company, and the same have not been amended and are in full force and effect . . . . **Stock-Purchase Acquisition Agreement from Peter Siviglia, *Commercial Agreements: A Lawyer's Guide to Drafting and Negotiating* § 11:4 (2017)**	(D) **Governing documents.** Attached to this Agreement are copies of the Articles of Incorporation (Exhibit 4.1D-1) and the Bylaws (Exhibit 4.1D-2). Both are up to date and in full force . . . .

NOT THIS:	BUT THIS:
Ex. 8 6.4 Survival. Except as otherwise provided, the obligations of Company to make the payments set forth in this Agreement shall survive the expiration or termination of this Agreement only to the extent such obligations had accrued as of the date of such expiration or termination. **Marketing Agreement from a major beverage company**	6.4 **Survival.** Unless this Agreement provides otherwise, when the Agreement expires or terminates, the Company will make all payments that have accrued as of the expiration or termination date.
Ex. 9 A Pricing Agreement shall be in the form of an executed writing (which may be in counterparts), and may be evidenced by an exchange of telegraphic communications or any other rapid transmission device designed to produce a written record of communications transmitted. **Underwriting Agreement from a major grocery chain**	A Pricing Agreement must be in the form of a signed writing (which may be in counterparts) and may be evidenced by an exchange of faxes or e-mailed scans.
Ex. 10 21. Any and all safety equipment, such as traffic control, flagmen, barricades, rigging, fire extinguishers, first aid supplies, etc., as may be necessary or required by any agency having jurisdiction, shall be the sole responsibility of and at the expense of Contractor. . . . All liability shall be the responsibility of the Contractor. Contractor/Sub-contractor shall inaugurate and maintain an accident prevention program and an employee safety-training program. **Agreement for construction of a commercial building**	21. **On-the-Job Safety.** The Contractor must protect everyone around the Work area and will bear full liability for that responsibility. . . . (B) **Programs.** The Contractor and the Subcontractor must jointly create and maintain an accident-prevention program and an employee-safety training program. The building management may request proof of compliance.
Ex. 11 5. **COMPANY PROPERTY.** Upon termination of my employment or at the Company's request before termination, I will deliver to the Company all written and tangible material in my possession, together with all copies thereof, and any other material incorporating or disclosing any Proprietary Information, Inventions, or otherwise relating to the Company's business, and, at Company's request, I will certify in writing that I have fully complied with the foregoing obligation. **Assignment Agreement from a major software-development company**	5. **AllPro's Property.** When my employment ends, or at AllPro's request while I'm still employed, I will give AllPro all written and tangible material in my possession, including all copies and any other material incorporating or disclosing any Proprietary Information or Inventions or otherwise relating to AllPro's business. At AllPro's request, I will certify in writing that I have fully complied with this obligation.

NOT THIS:	BUT THIS:
Ex. 12 It is further agreed that the specifications and drawings form a part of this agreement, and are intended to cooperate, so that any works exhibited in the drawings and not mentioned in the specifications, or vice versa, are to be executed the same as if they were mentioned in the specifications and set forth in the drawings, to the true intent and meaning of said drawings and specifications, without any extra charge whatever. **Building Contract from 2 William Eugene Morse, *Mississippi Legal Forms* 1139 (2d ed. 1977)**	The specifications and drawings are part of this Agreement. To represent the specifications' and drawings' true intent, any works exhibited or mentioned in one but not the other must be executed without extra charge.
Ex. 13 10. Royalty Payment distribution. The Royalty Payment payable to Wasabi Ramen Inc. received by the Company(s) shall be paid over a Charity(ies) to be specially named Wasabi Ramen Charities which must be a Federally approved (#501(c)) tax exempt food related Charity supplying food to the people in need. The Company(s) agree to also make a contribution to the same Charity at the same time licensed Franchise inaugurates its opening of it's stores(s) in a combined amount totaling in accordance with the following schedule: . . . **Franchise-License Agreement**	**10. Royalty Payment Distribution.** Royalties payable to Wasabi Ramen must be paid over to a charity to be named Wasabi Ramen Charities, which must be a federally approved (§ 501(c)) tax-exempt food-related charity supplying food to people in need. The Company will make an additional contribution to the same charity when the licensed Franchise opens its stores in a combined amount in accordance with the following schedule: . . .
Ex. 14 Contractor has investigated the job site for the work and all observable conditions that might affect the progress of the work, and, to the extent that contractor has had access to the Property and buildings located on the Property has satisfied itself as to these conditions. Notwithstanding the foregoing, Owner understands that Contractor may encounter conditions in the Property and buildings located thereon that were not expected and/or that were hidden and that such unforeseen conditions may result in an increase in the cost of the work. **Construction Contract from a major law firm**	**1.3 Jobsite conditions.** (A) **Prior investigation.** To the extent that it has had access to the Property and its buildings, Carlyle Construction has investigated the jobsite and all observable conditions that might affect the work's progress and is satisfied with the conditions. (B) **Unforeseen conditions.** Baxter understands that Carlyle Construction might encounter unexpected or hidden conditions in the Property and its buildings that could increase the costs.

Note that *execute* is used here not in the legal sense but in an architectural sense.

NOT THIS:	BUT THIS:
Ex. 15 5.2 Matters Requiring Investor Director Approval. The Company shall not do any of the following, without Investor Director Consent: . . . (j) Engage any employee or consultant on terms that either his contract cannot be terminated by three months' notice or less or his emoluments and/or commissions or bonuses are or are likely to be at the rate of $200,000 per annum or more or increase the emoluments and/or commissions or bonuses of any employee or consultant to more than $200,000 per annum or vary the terms of employment of any employee earning (or so that after such variation he will, or is likely to earn) more than $200,000 per annum; . . . . **Investment Contract**	**5.2 Matters requiring Investor Director Consent.** The Company will not do any of the following without Investor Director Consent: . . . (J) engage an employee or consultant on terms that: (1) cannot be terminated on 3 months' notice; or (2) entail compensation that is likely to exceed $200,000 a year; (K) change an employee's or consultant's contract to: (1) increase the salary or commissions or bonuses to more than $200,000 a year; (2) vary the employment terms of an employee earning more than $200,000 a year; (3) vary the employment terms so that after the variation the employee will, or is likely to, earn more than $200,000 a year; . . . .

In a 1941 study of contracts cases decided the previous year, Professor Harold Shepherd of Duke University found that 25% of those reaching appellate courts revolved around problems of interpreting the language used: "A good part of the difficulty, we concluded, was traceable directly to incomplete negotiation by the parties and poor draftsmanship either by the parties or their counsel. In many of the cases the courts bluntly said so." Harold Shepard, Book Review, 1 J. Legal Ed. 151, 154 (1948).

> The phrase *yielding and paying* was rather common in the 19th century but now survives only because a few formbooks have antiquated models that use it. Yet another reason to avoid out-of-date formbooks. See § 11.

NOT THIS:	BUT THIS:
Ex. 16 Yielding and paying for the same unto [*name of lessor*] for and during [*his/her*] natural life, then to [*name of beneficiary*] for and during [*his/her*] natural life, if [*he/she*] survives [*his/her*] mother, then upon the death of [*name of beneficiary*] and [*name of beneficiary*]'s heirs, administrators, and assigns, the yearly rental of $[*dollar amount of sum*] for the first 10 years and $[*dollar amount of sum*] per year for the remainder of the term, without any deductions whatever, in quarterly payments of [*number of installments*] installments of $[*dollar amount of sum*] each for the first period and $[*dollar amount of sum*] per quarter for the remainder of the term, in lawful money of the United States, the first payment of which is to be made on [*date of payment*] next, and thereafter on the [*ordinal number of day*] day of [*names of months*], in each and every year of the term. **Rent Provision from Long-Term Lease from 5B Clark A. Nichols, *Nichols Cyclopedia of Legal Forms Annotated* § 118:234 (2011)**	**2. Rent.** **2.1 Annual payments.** For the first 10 years of this lease, the annual rent is $10,000, payable in quarterly installments of $2,500. For the remainder of the term, the annual rent will be $12,000, payable in quarterly installments of $3,000. **2.2 Timing.** Quarterly installments are due on January 1, April 1, July 1, and October 1. The first installment must be paid on the Effective Date on a prorated basis covering the period from that date until the last day of the quarter. **2.3 Recipient of payment.** Jones will pay the rent to Lydia Barlow during her life, and then to Catherine Barlow for her life if she survives Lydia. Upon Catherine's death, tenants will pay the rent to Catherine's heirs, administrators, and assigns.

NOT THIS:	BUT THIS:
Ex. 17 6.1 Purchaser shall not be entitled to assert any claim for indemnification under this section 6.1 unless and until such time as all claims of Purchaser for indemnification hereunder exceed $10,000 ("Seller's Basket") in the aggregate, at which time any and all claims of Purchaser for indemnification in excess of Seller's Basket may be asserted; provided, however, that Seller's Basket shall not be applicable to any damages attributable to (a) noncompliance by Seller with the bulk transfer provisions of the Uniform Commercial Code (or any similar law) in connection with the sale and transfer of the Assets and the Business to Purchaser, (b) the failure of Seller to deliver any of the Assets to Purchaser or to pay or otherwise satisfy any part of the obligations referred to in Clauses (3), (4), and (5) of Section 1.5(b), the obligations referred to in Section 3.7 and any other payment obligations which are presently existing and are not Assumed Obligations, (c) breaches of the representations and warranties contained in Section 2.1(g) or claims under Section 8.1(c), (d) the failure of Seller to comply with Sections 7.1, 7.2 or 7.3, (e) the failure of Seller to perform its obligations under Section 7.14(a), (f) the failure of Seller to make any payment required under Section 1.3, or (g) breach of the representations and warranties in Section 2.1(c) concerning the outstanding principal balance of Bank Debt and the aggregate amount of affiliate receivables. **Asset-Purchase Agreement from a major law firm**	**6.1 Indemnity.** (A) **Fully covered items.** Stanford will fully indemnify Bayworth if Stanford: (1) breaches a representation or warranty contained in § 2.1(g) or 2.1(c); (2) breaches § 8.1(c); (3) fails to comply with the bulk-transfer provisions of the U.C.C. (or any similar law) in selling and transferring the Assets and the Business to Bayworth; (4) fails to deliver any of the Assets to Bayworth or fails to satisfy: (a) any part of the obligations referred to in §§ 1.5(b)(3)–(5) and 3.7; or (b) any other current payment obligations that are not Assumed Obligations; (5) fails to comply with § 7.1, 7.2, 7.3, or 7.14(a); or (6) fails to make a payment required under § 1.3. (B) **Deductible for other items.** If Bayworth seeks indemnities for an item not listed under (A), the claims must together total more than $10,000, and Stanford will indemnify for only the aggregate amount exceeding that threshold.

This is all a single 242-word sentence!

This revision makes explicit what is merely implicit in the original. The breaches have been grouped together. See § 81.

The original provision is surely flawed: there should be a cap for the indemnity. Also, "baskets" of this kind usually apply only to representations and warranties, not to covenants.

"No matter how much time is allowed for the negotiation, there is never time enough to think every issue through in all its possible applications, and never ingenuity enough to anticipate all that does later show up." Harry Shulman, *Reason, Contract, and Law in Labor Relations*, 68 Harv. L. Rev. 999, 1004 (1955).

§ 13 Stick to normal syntax.

Although you must always guard against syntactic ambiguity, your word order should sound natural, not alien. Think about how you would say it if you were a television announcer. The primary appeal of all writing is to the ear—even if what's written is read only in silence.

Consider a common example: *Unless this contract otherwise provides,* . . . . That's not idiomatic English. Would you say *Unless you otherwise say, we'll have a picnic* or *Unless you say otherwise, we'll have a picnic*? The natural, idiomatic word order requires *otherwise* to be at the end of the phrase, not earlier. So you analogize to simpler sentences and arrive at a more sensible wording.

Or let's say you see a provision that reads, *Section 7.1 notwithstanding, all repair costs will be borne by Johnson.* That's a really old-fashioned placement of the adverb *notwithstanding.* In its more usual function, *notwithstanding* appears at the outset of a clause—as an equivalent of *despite.* So the better wording would be *Notwithstanding § 7.1, Johnson will bear all repair costs* or (better yet) *Despite § 7.1, Johnson will bear all repair costs.* See § 149 at p. 430.

Try reading aloud. Listen for awkward syntax. Then bring it into line with normal English usage.

NOT THIS:	BUT THIS:
Ex. 1 Black Fields contains more or less 1000 acres. **Mineral Deed from a major law firm**	Black Fields contains about 1000 acres.
Ex. 2 Each of Assignor and Assignee represents and warrants that it has not been represented by any broker or agent in connection with the execution of this Assignment. **Lease Agreement from Susan A. Halsey et al., *Texas Forms Real Estate* § 2:13, at 204 (2012)**	Each party represents and warrants that it has not been represented by a broker or agent in connection with this Assignment.

"Drafting . . . is first thinking and second composing." Reed Dickerson, *The Fundamentals of Legal Drafting* § 1.2, at 6 (2d ed. 1986).

NOT THIS:	BUT THIS:
Ex. 3 This adverbial qualifier is poorly placed in the sentence. Personnel Service Provider expressly agrees anything herein to the contrary notwithstanding, that it shall indemnify and hold Client Company fully harmless against any damages of any kind whatsoever, including costs and reasonable attorney's fees, Client Company shall incur as a result of injuries to persons or damage to tangible property caused by the negligent acts of, or negligent failure to act by Personnel Service Provider, its employees or agents while on Client Company's premises. **Personnel-Training-Services Agreement from 3 Nancy Saint-Paul, Texas Legal Practice Forms 3d *Independent Contractor Agreements* § 50:9, at 740 (2016)**	Despite anything in this Agreement to the contrary, Personnel Service Provider will indemnify Client Company against any damages (including costs and reasonable attorney fees) that Client Company incurs as a result of: (1) injuries to persons; or (2) damage to tangible property caused by the negligent act or failure to act by Personnel Service Provider or its employees or agents while on Client Company's premises.
Ex. 4 THE TRUSTEE AGREES: 1. Either: (a) That the Entruster, prior to this trust receipt transaction, has had a security interest in the said goods, documents, or instruments, and that such security interest will remain in the Entruster, notwithstanding the delivery of the said goods, documents, or instruments, to the Trustee against this Trust Receipt; or (b) That a security interest has passed or will pass to the Entruster, and will remain in the Entruster as a result of this trust receipt transaction. **Trust Receipt for a Commercial Loan from 15 *Texas Transaction Guide: Legal Forms* § 67A.215[2] (Herbert S. Kendrick & John J. Kendrick Jr. eds., 2017)**	The Trustee stipulates that either: (A) the Entruster had a security interest in the goods, documents, or instruments before the trust-receipt transaction, and that security interest will remain in the Entruster despite the delivery of the goods, documents, or instruments to the Trustee against this Trust Receipt; or (B) a security interest has passed or will pass to the Entruster and will remain with the Entruster based on this trust-receipt transaction.
Ex. 5 VI. Seller agrees that on the Closing Date it will apply so much of the purchase price received by it hereunder as may be necessary and sufficient for the payment of all liabilities of Seller existing on the Closing Date. Seller agrees that Purchaser does not assume, and shall not be obligated to pay, any of the liabilities of Seller under the terms of this Agreement or otherwise. Seller hereby agrees to indemnify and hold Purchaser, its successors and assigns, harmless from and against any and all of Seller's obligations and liabilities, fixed or contingent or otherwise. **Asset-Purchase Agreement from Ludwig Mandel, *The Preparation of Commercial Agreements* 253 (1970)**	6. **Stephens's Liabilities.** On the Closing Date, Stephens will apply a percentage of the purchase price received to pay all of Stephens's liabilities incurred as of that date. Butler does not assume, and is not obligated to pay, any of Stephens's liabilities under this Agreement or otherwise. Stephens indemnifies Butler and Butler's successors and assigns against all of Stephens's liabilities—whether fixed, contingent, or otherwise.

NOT THIS:

Ex. 6

NOW THEREFORE, in consideration of the mutual agreements set forth herein, it is agreed as follows:

First:

At the Closing hereinafter described, Seller will sell to Purchaser and Purchaser will purchase from Seller, Seller's interest in the Partnership, consisting of a [percentage of partnership interest]% interest in the Partnership (the "Interest"), for a total sum of $[dollar amount of purchase price] (the "Purchase Price").

Second:

At the Closing Seller will execute and deliver an assignment of the Interest in the Partnership set forth in paragraph FIRST to Purchaser in the form of Exhibit [designation of exhibit] annexed hereto, and Purchaser will pay the Purchase Price by delivering to Seller certified or bank cashier's checks or, at Seller's option, by wiring funds to accounts designated by Seller, in the amount set forth in paragraph FIRST in full payment of the Purchase Price for the Interest.

Third:

It is a condition precedent to the Closing taking place that (a) the written agreement and consent of the partners of the Partnership (including the family managing partners) to the assignment of the Interest hereunder and to the designation of [name of substitute family managing partner] as substitute family managing partner (for Seller following the Closing) and to the continuation and reconstitution of the partnership; and (b) the written commitment by the Partnership to duly exercise the election allowed under the Internal Revenue Code to increase the basis of the Partnership assets (with reference to the Purchaser) as a result of the transfer of the Interest hereunder; and (c) the written commitment by the Partnership to deliver to Seller financial statements for the year ended [end date of financial statements], shall be obtained (without cost to either party) in the form set forth in Exhibit [designation of exhibit], and delivered to Purchaser and Seller.

Partnership-Interest-Purchase Agreement from 20 Stuart M. Saft, *West's Legal Forms: Commercial Real Estate Transactions* § 7:7, at 286–87 (4th ed. 2012)

BUT THIS:

The parties agree as follows:

1. **Purchase Price.** At the Closing, Sylvan will sell Sylvan's ______% interest in the Partnership to Perlman, and Perlman will purchase it from Sylvan for a sum of $__________.
2. **Deliveries at Closing.** At the Closing, Sylvan will sign and deliver an assignment of Sylvan's interest to Perlman in the form of attached Exhibit A, and Perlman will pay the full purchase price by delivering to Sylvan certified or bank cashier's checks or, at Sylvan's option, by wiring funds to accounts designated by Sylvan.
3. **Closing Conditions.** Before the Closing can take place, the following documents must be obtained (without cost to either party) in the form set forth in Exhibit B and delivered to Perlman and Sylvan:
   (A) the written consent of the partners of the Partnership (including the family managing partners) to the assignment of Sylvan's interest and to the designation of [name of substitute family managing partner] as substitute family managing partner (for Sylvan after Closing) and to the continuation and reconstitution of the Partnership;
   (B) the written commitment by the Partnership to duly exercise the election allowed under the Internal Revenue Code to increase the basis of the Partnership assets (with reference to Perlman) as a result of the transfer of Sylvan's interest; and
   (C) the written commitment by the Partnership to deliver to Sylvan financial statements for the year ended ______.

§ 14 Furnish abundant headings.

Make your principles of organization overt. Use subparts with headings to enhance readability and reinforce meaning. Any subpart that contains at least one full sentence should be introduced by a heading. Good use of headings and white space (see § 46) goes a long way toward making a contract clearer and more readable.

Although this requirement contradicts the prevailing practice in many English-speaking jurisdictions, that contradiction is purposeful: it is one of the most desirable reforms to be made in contract drafting. Headings help readers get their bearings and find the pertinent section when they have questions about the contract's terms. Effective headings help to focus attention that would otherwise drain away from the reader's mind. The many examples in this book illustrate how this requirement should be carried out. Study them. Mimic them.

Headings help not only readers but also drafters, who will necessarily organize their work more logically if they are required to use headings more liberally than has traditionally been done in the past.

> "There is a lengthy research literature showing that well-written and well-placed headings are important. They help the reader to understand what a section of the document is saying and to find information quickly." Janice C. Redish, "How to Draft More Understandable Legal Documents," in *Drafting Documents in Plain Language* 123, 150 (Duncan A. MacDonald chmn., 1979).

NOT THIS:	BUT THIS:
Ex. 1 **Article 12. Breach** Breach of the Agreement. In the event that Licensee fails in a material manner to fulfill any of the terms and conditions of this Agreement, or otherwise breaches this Agreement, Licensor shall have the right, upon written notice to Licensee detailing the claimed breach, to terminate this Agreement, such notice being effective thirty (30) days after having been given and if such breach has not (in the sole discretion of Licensor) been fully cured during such thirty (30) day period; provided, however, that if the breach concerns Licensee's obligation to make payments pursuant to this Agreement, such notice shall be effective ten (10) days after having been given, if such violation has not (in the sole discretion of Licensor) been fully cured by Licensee within said ten (10) day period. This is a confusing heading with two subheadings. **License Agreement from a major law firm**	**12. Breach.** 12.1 **Material breach.** If Lassiter materially fails to fulfill a term of this Agreement or otherwise breaches the Agreement, Mikelson may terminate the Agreement by giving Lassiter written notice detailing the claimed breach. 12.2 **Time for cure and effective termination.** If Lassiter does not fully cure a breach within 30 days after receiving Mikelson's notice under § 12.1, the termination becomes effective 30 days after the date Lassiter received the notice. 12.3 **Breach involving payment; time for cure.** The termination becomes effective 10 days after the date Lassiter receives Mikelson's notice if: (A) the breach concerns Lassiter's duty to make payments under this Agreement; and (B) Lassiter does not fully cure this breach within 10 days after receiving the notice. 12.4 **Cure determined by Mikelson.** Under § 12.2 and § 12.3, Mikelson has sole discretion to determine whether the breach has been "fully cured."

"Good drafting practices can and usually do improve the quality of thought. All good writing tends to do this, but legal drafting does it especially well. First, the emotive element, which often compromises rationality, is at a minimum. Second, legal drafting is the most rigorous writing that I know of. Syntactically, it is not as rigorous as mathematics, but, taken in its full dimensions, it is the most disciplined writing outside, perhaps, poetry." Reed Dickerson, *Teacher's Manual for Materials on Legal Drafting* 21 (1981).

NOT THIS:	BUT THIS:
Ex. 2 (h) During the term of this Agreement, Franchisee shall fully disclose the Improvements to Franchisor, without disclosure of the Improvements to others, and shall obtain Franchisor's written approval prior to using such Improvements. Any such Improvement may be used by Franchisor and all other franchisees without any obligation to Franchisee for royalties or other fees. Franchisee shall assign and does hereby assign to Franchisor, all right, title, and interest in and to the Improvements, including the right to grant sublicenses to any such Improvement. Franchisor, at its discretion, may make application for and own copyrights, patents, trade names, trademarks and service marks relating to any such Improvement and Franchisee shall cooperate with Franchisor in securing such rights. Franchisor may also consider such Improvements as the property and trade secrets of Franchisor. In return, Franchisor shall authorize Franchisee to utilize any Improvement that may be developed by other franchisees and is authorized generally for use by other franchisees. **Franchise-License Agreement**	**12.8 Improvements.** (A) **Disclosure and approval.** Before using an Improvement, Prescott must fully disclose the Improvement to Wilfong and obtain Wilfong's written approval. Prescott must not disclose the Improvement to others. (B) **Assignment.** Prescott assigns to Wilfong all ownership rights to Improvements, including the right to grant sublicenses to the Improvements. Wilfong and all other franchisees may use Improvements without obligation to pay Prescott royalties or other fees. (C) **Intellectual-property rights.** Wilfong may consider an Improvement to be its property and trade secret. Wilfong may apply for and own copyrights, patents, tradenames, trademarks, and servicemarks relating to an Improvement, and Prescott must help Wilfong in securing the rights. (D) **Other franchisee improvements.** Prescott may use any Improvement that is developed by other franchisees and is authorized generally for use by franchisees.

> "Poor organization makes documents hard to understand because there are no connections between one part and the next. Poor organization adds unnecessary length when the same information is repeated in different sections of the document."
> Janice C. Redish, "How to Draft More Understandable Legal Documents," in *Drafting Documents in Plain Language* 123, 133 (Duncan A. MacDonald chmn., 1979).

NOT THIS:	BUT THIS:
Ex. 3 2. **Nature of Agreement.** 2.1 The Company is a provider of online applications that facilitate travel bookings and reservations. Your job responsibilities are as set forth in Exhibit A and may be modified at any time by the Company. These changes may be communicated orally, or in writing. 2.2 This is not a contract for a specific period of time, and is not a promise of continued employment. You are an employee "at-will," which means that the Company can terminate your employment for any reason, with or without "cause," and with or without notice. Your at-will status cannot be changed except by written agreement signed by you and the President of the Company. You, too, can terminate your employment with the Company at any time, with or without cause. 2.3 If you are employed full-time by the Company, you agree to devote your full business time and best efforts to the Company while employed by the Company. You shall not provide products or services similar to those of the Company (either directly or through any other company or entity), except on behalf of the Company. While employed by the Company, you shall not engage in any activity that will have an adverse effect upon your ability to perform the obligations under this Agreement. **Employment Agreement**	2. **Nature of Agreement.** 2.1 **Job responsibilities; modification.** TripPlanner provides online applications that make travel bookings and reservations easier for users. Your job responsibilities are set out in Exhibit A. We may modify those responsibilities at any time and give you oral or written notice of the modifications. 2.2 **Employment is "at will."** This is not a contract for a specific period or a promise of continued employment. You are an at-will employee, which means that TripPlanner can terminate your employment for any reason, with or without cause and with or without notice. Your at-will status cannot be changed except by written agreement signed by you and TripPlanner's president. You, too, can terminate your employment with TripPlanner at any time, with or without cause and with or without notice. 2.3 **Full-time employees; exclusivity.** If you're employed full-time by TripPlanner, you must devote your full business time and best efforts to TripPlanner. You must not provide products or services similar to those offered by TripPlanner (either directly or through another entity), except on TripPlanner's behalf. While employed by TripPlanner, you must not engage in any activity that will hinder your ability to perform your obligations under this Agreement.

Note how the headings give the reader topic signposts, enhancing readability.

"If you're like most lawyers and bureaucrats, you don't know your reader. You do your writing in a vacuum or an air-conditioned ivory tower. This is the way it's always been done, the way you've been taught to do it in college or law school. You try as hard as you can to express your ideas fully and accurately, giving no thought whatever to the poor person who'll have to read and understand what you wrote."
Rudolf Flesch, *How to Write Plain English* 4 (1979).

NOT THIS:	BUT THIS:
Ex. 4 A preliminary guest count must be provided at the time of booking, with a final guest count confirmed seven (7) days prior to the event date. This number will serve as a guaranteed minimum. Tiquewood Catering orders according to your guaranteed guest count and does not produce for overages. No allowance will be made for a decrease in guest count after the guarantee date. Additions to the guest count will be accepted five (5) days prior to the scheduled date of the event and accommodated solely at Tiquewood Catering's discretion, though every reasonable effort will be made to do so. Food and beverage availability may result in product substitutions. Any increase in guest count after the guarantee date will result in a surcharge of 15% plus the original contractual price for each guest added. If your event is a buffet, your final guest count will determine the number of plates supplied for your event. We appreciate your accuracy and honesty in this as it allows us to ensure that your guests will enjoy their experience and that adequate supplies are ordered. Your final guarantee is due before 12 noon seven (7) days prior to your event. This date is July 31st, 2016. Thank you in advance for your timely attention. 25% deposit is due upon booking, this amount $5854.75. Final payment of your balance (based on both this contract and your final guest count) is due on day of your event. If you should cancel the event prior to 60 days of the event you will receive your full deposit, if you should cancel between 30–60 days prior you will receive ½ of your deposit, but if we are able to rebook that day you will be refunded your entire deposit. If you should cancel within 30 days or less you will forfeit your deposit. We accept Visa, MasterCard, Discover, American Express and Corporate or Personal checks. We do not accept cash. When making a payment by check, please make the check payable to: Tiquewood Catering. If the venue allows, we are happy to discuss the possibility of extending the length of your event beyond the end time in your contract. Please note that only an authorized signer or agent is permitted to authorize an event extension. All personnel or staffing fees will be charged at 1.5 times the usual hourly event rate for the extended time. **Catering Contract**	**2.2 Your obligations to us.** (A) **Guest count.** You must give a preliminary guest count when you book your event and give a confirmed guest count before noon 7 days before your event day. Tiquewood Catering will begin planning, ordering, and preparing based on this final guest count. We cannot lower our charge if fewer guests eventually attend. (B) **Deadline for changing guest list.** The number of guests we will accommodate becomes final 5 days before your event. That number will be your final guest count. Up to that day, you may ask to add more guests to your confirmed count. Although we will make every reasonable effort to grant your request, we are not obliged to do so. If we agree to accommodate additional guests, we will add an amount to the final bill: for each additional guest, the original contractual price per guest plus a 15% surcharge. Because the availability of food and beverages is based on your final guest count, some substitutions may be necessary if you add more guests. (C) **Buffet.** If your event is a buffet, we will supply enough food and plates based on your final guest count. (D) **Schedule of deposits and payments.** A 25% deposit is due when you book your event. The remaining balance—based on your final guest count—is due on the day of your event. (E) **Payment methods.** We accept Visa, MasterCard, Discover, American Express, and corporate or personal checks (payable to Tiquewood Catering). We do not accept cash. (F) **Cancellation policy.** If you cancel: (1) 30 or fewer days before your event date, you will forfeit your deposit; (2) 31–60 days before your event date, we will refund half your deposit, and if we can rebook that event date we will refund your full deposit; (3) more than 60 days before your event date, we will refund your full deposit. (G) **Event extensions.** If the venue allows, we are open to discussing extending your event beyond the time stated in your contract. Only a Tiquewood manager can authorize an extension. All our staffing fees will be charged at 1.5 times our usual hourly rate for the extended time.

Note how the lack of a numbering system impairs both readability and citability.

§ 15 Phrase headings to help readers find the information they want.

Much confusion surrounds the use of headings—confusion both philosophical and practical. On the side of philosophy, some drafters have made a false inference from the widespread use of disclaimers about the content of headings—wrongly assuming that headings themselves must be undesirable and therefore shouldn't be used. Others have falsely inferred that there's a canon of construction holding that headings are devoid of meaning. In fact, in the absence of a disclaimer otherwise, the opposite is true. On the side of practice, the use of headings within a single contract is often haphazard and stylistically inconsistent. That's not helpful to the reader.

The most sensible approach to headings can be summed up in five propositions:

- Assign a heading to every provision that consists of at least one grammatically complete sentence. Use headings liberally.
- Ensure that the headings accurately suggest what the provision contains—that's the whole point of this § 15.
- Compile the headings into a table of contents to assess the contract's architectural soundness (see § 79). You'll probably make significant discoveries about how to improve organization. If you're drafting from scratch, start with an outline, which will make it easier to organize and reorganize headings.
- Check to ensure that, to the extent possible, the headings are uniformly pithy.
- Disclaim any substantive effect of headings. They're for readability, preferably not for interpretation.[1]

> "The purpose of writing is to communicate, not to show off. If the reader does not understand, everyone's time will have been wasted and what should have been said will remain effectively unsaid." Mark Adler, *Clarity for Lawyers* 6 (1990).

1 *See* Antonin Scalia & Bryan A. Garner, *Reading Law: The Interpretation of Legal Texts* § 35, at 221–24 (2012) (stating that no heading should ever be allowed to override the plain words of a text, but that the drafter should use them as "useful navigational aids.")

NOT THIS:

Ex. 1

This title doesn't reflect what the provisions are actually about.

The provisions on subcontracting (the last 2 sentences) have no relationship to the heading.

14. ***TITLE AND ENGINEERING DRAWINGS, SPECIFICATIONS***

(a) Any documents, including drawings and specifications produced or acquired by Seller under a Purchase Order will belong to Buyer, subject only to Seller's patent rights, but without any other restrictions on buyer's use, including reproduction, modification, disclosure or distribution of the documents or the information contained therein. To the extent such documents contain original work of authorship created in order to comply with a Purchase Order, the copyrights to such work shall be owned by Buyer in accordance with Section 17. Seller agrees not to label any such documents with a notice asserting that the documents contain confidential or proprietary information of Seller. Any engineering drawing that Seller is required to prepare and furnish to Buyer will conform to the requirements of the local computer aided design standards of the Buyer.

(b) All drawings, know-how, and confidential information supplied to Seller by Buyer and all rights therein will remain the property of Buyer and will be kept confidential by Seller in accordance with Section 16(f). Seller is licensed to use Buyer's drawings, know-how, and confidential information only for the purpose of fulfilling its obligations under a Purchase Order. In addition to the obligations of Section 16(f), Seller will not disclose such drawings to third parties unless this is required for Seller to fulfill its duties under a Purchase Order. Seller will inform Buyer in writing of any third parties to whom Seller subcontracts any of the work required under a Purchase Order specifying in detail the work which has been subcontracted to such third party. Seller will ensure that any third party to whom Seller subcontracts any of the work hereunder is bound by all the terms and conditions relating to such work to which Seller is bound under a Purchase Order.

Global Terms for Production Parts and Nonproduction Goods and Services
General Agreement from a major automobile manufacturer

BUT THIS:

14. **Documents; Intellectual-Property Rights; Confidentiality; Subcontracting.**

14.1 **Documents produced by Burkhalter.**

(A) **Engineering drawings.** Any engineering drawing that Burkhalter prepares and furnishes to Wingo must conform to the requirements of Wingo's local computer-aided design standards.

(B) **Ownership of documents; patent rights.** Subject only to Burkhalter's patent rights, Wingo owns any documents, including drawings and specifications that Burkhalter, produces or acquires under a Purchase Order, and may use them without other restrictions. Wingo is entitled to reproduce, modify, disclose, or distribute the documents or the information they contain.

(C) **Copyright.** To the extent that the documents contain an original work of authorship created to comply with a Purchase Order, Wingo owns the copyrights to the work in accordance with § 17.

(D) **Confidentiality notice.** Burkhalter must not label any such document with a notice asserting that the document contains Burkhalter's confidential or proprietary information.

14.2 **Information produced by Wingo.**

(A) **Burkhalter's license.** Burkhalter is licensed to use Wingo's drawings, know-how, and confidential information only for the purpose of fulfilling its obligations under a Purchase Order.

(B) **Ownership of documents; intellectual-property rights.** Wingo retains ownership of and all rights in drawings, know-how, and confidential information supplied to Burkhalter by Wingo.

(C) **Burkhalter's duty of confidentiality.** In accordance with § 16(f), Burkhalter must keep confidential all drawings, know-how, and confidential information supplied to Burkhalter by Wingo. Burkhalter will not disclose drawings to third parties unless disclosure is required for Burkhalter to fulfill its duties under a Purchase Order.

14.3 **Subcontractors.** If Burkhalter subcontracts any of the work required under a Purchase Order to a third party, Burkhalter must inform Wingo in writing and specify in detail the work that has been subcontracted. Burkhalter must ensure that the subcontractor is bound by all the terms relating to the work to which Burkhalter is bound.

NOT THIS:

Ex. 2

(15) ***JUDICIAL REFERENCE-TRIAL BY JUDGE IN COURT OF COMPETENT JURISDICTION-WAIVER OF TRIAL BY JURY.*** ALL CLAIMS, CAUSES OF ACTION, COUNTER CLAIMS, CROSS-COMPLAINTS, OR DEFENSES BROUGHT BY SELLER, BUYER, OR ANY OTHER THIRD PARTIES OR THEIR SUCCESSORS-IN-INTEREST OR ANY PERSON REPRESENTING BUYER, SELLER OR THEIR SUCCESSORS IN INTEREST (INCLUDING CLASS ACTIONS) ON ANY MATTER WHATSOEVER ARISING OUT OF, OR IN ANY WAY RELATING TO THIS OFFER TO PURCHASE, BUYER'S PURCHASE OF THE RESIDENCE FROM SELLER, BUYER'S OPTIONS, OR THE CONSTRUCTION OF THE RESIDENCE OR THE PROJECT INCLUDING BUT NOT LIMITED TO CLAIMS RELATING TO CONSTRUCTION DEFECT, MISREPRESENTATION OR SELLER'S FAILURE TO DISCLOSE MATERIAL FACTS (HEREIN AFTER COLLECTIVELY "CLAIMS") SHALL BE DETERMINED BY A GENERAL REFERENCE CONDUCTED BY A SINGLE REFEREE APPOINTED PURSUANT TO THE PROVISIONS OF CALIFORNIA CODE OF CIVIL PROCEDURE § 638 ET SEQ. OR ANY SUCCESSOR STATUTES THERETO AND ADMINISTERED BY THE AMERICAN ARBITRATION ASSOCIATION IN ACCORDANCE WITH ITS JUDICIAL REFERENCE PROCEDURES. THE REFERENCE SHALL BE MADE TO A SINGLE REFEREE, WHO SHALL BE A RETIRED JUDGE OF THE SUPERIOR COURT OF THE STATE OF CALIFORNIA. THE REFEREE SHALL TRY ALL ISSUES RELATED TO THE CLAIMS, WHETHER OF FACT OR LAW, AND REPORT A STATEMENT OF DECISIONS. THE REFEREE SHALL HAVE THE POWER TO GRANT ALL LEGAL AND EQUITABLE REMEDIES AND AWARD COMPENSATORY DAMAGES IN THE REPORT OF HIS OR HER STATEMENT OF DECISION, BUT NEITHER THE REFEREE NOR THE COURT IN ENTERING JUDGMENT ON THE REPORT SHALL HAVE THE POWER TO AWARD PUNITIVE DAMAGES. BUYER AND SELLER HEREBY WAIVE THEIR RIGHT TO RECOVER PUNITIVE DAMAGES IN ANY JUDICIAL REFERENCE PROCEEDING BROUGHT TO DECIDE "CLAIMS" AS DEFINED ABOVE. UNLESS THE PARTIES AGREE OTHERWISE: (A) THE PARTIES SHALL BE ENTITLED TO THE SAME DISCOVERY RIGHTS AS THEY WOULD HAVE IN A SUPERIOR COURT ACTION, AND THE REFEREE SHALL OVERSEE DISCOVERY AND MAY ENFORCE ALL DISCOVERY ORDERS IN THE SAME MANNER AS ANY TRIAL COURT JUDGE; (B) THE REFEREE SHALL HAVE THE POWER TO HEAR AND DISPOSE OF MOTIONS IN THE SAME MANNER AS A TRIAL COURT JUDGE; (C) THE REFEREE SHALL APPLY THE RULES OF LAW, INCLUDING RULES OF EVIDENCE, UNLESS EXPRESSLY WAIVED BY ALL PARTIES; (D) THE REFEREE'S STATEMENT OF DECISION SHALL CONTAIN FINDINGS OF FACT AND CONCLUSIONS OF LAW; AND (E) THE REFEREE SHALL HAVE THE AUTHORITY TO RULE ON ALL POST HEARING MOTIONS IN THE SAME MANNER AS A TRIAL JUDGE. BUYER AND SELLER AGREE THAT THEIR AGREEMENT TO SUBMIT ALL "CLAIMS" TO JUDICIAL REFERENCE AND THEIR WAIVER OF THE RIGHT TO PUNITIVE DAMAGES SHALL BE BINDING UPON THEIR RESPECTIVE SUCCESSORS AND ASSIGNEDS AND UPON ALL PERSONS AND ENTITIES ASSERTING RIGHTS OR CLAIMS OR OTHERWISE ACTING ON BEHALF OF SELLER OR BUYER OR THEIR SUCCESSORS AND ASSIGNEDS, INCLUDING ANY HOMEOWNERS' ASSOCIATION. ANY DISPUTE CONCERNING THE VALIDITY OR INTERPRETATION OF THE FOREGOING JUDICIAL REFERENCE PROVISION SHALL BE DECIDED BY A COURT OF COMPETENT JURISDICTION WITHOUT A JURY. IN THE EVENT THE FOREGOING JUDICIAL REFERENCE PROVISION IS HELD INVALID, VOID OR UNENFORCEABLE BY ANY COURT OF COMPETENT JURISDICTION, FOR ANY REASON, OR IF A COURT OTHERWISE FAILS OR REFUSES TO ORDER JUDICIAL REFERENCE OF THE "CLAIMS" (AS DEFINED IN THE PRECEDING PARAGRAPH), BUYER AND SELLER AGREE THAT ALL CLAIMS SHALL BE TRIED BEFORE A JUDGE IN A COURT OF COMPETENT JURISDICTION WITHOUT A JURY. BUYER AND SELLER HEREBY WAIVE THEIR RIGHT TO RECOVER PUNITIVE DAMAGES IN ANY ACTION BROUGHT TO ADJUDICATE CLAIMS. THE JUDGE IN SUCH COURT OF COMPETENT JURISDICTION SHALL HAVE THE POWER TO GRANT ALL LEGAL AND EQUITABLE REMEDIES AND AWARD COMPENSATORY DAMAGES, BUT SHALL NOT HAVE THE POWER TO AWARD PUNITIVE DAMAGES. SELLER AND BUYER EACH HEREBY WAIVE AND COVENANT NOT TO ASSERT THEIR CONSTITUTIONAL RIGHT TO TRIAL BY JURY OF ANY CLAIMS, INCLUDING, BUT NOT LIMITED TO CLAIMS RELATING TO CONSTRUCTION DEFECTS, MISREPRESENTATION OR SELLER'S FAILURE TO DISCLOSE MATERIAL FACTS. SELLER AND BUYER HEREBY COVENANT AND AGREE THAT THEIR MUTUAL WAIVER OF JURY TRIAL AND PUNITIVE DAMAGES SHALL BE BINDING UPON THEIR RESPECTIVE SUCCESSORS AND ASSIGNEDS AND UPON ALL PERSONS AND ENTITIES ASSERTING RIGHTS OR CLAIMS OR OTHERWISE ACTING ON BEHALF OF SELLER OR BUYER OR THEIR SUCCESSORS AND ASSIGNEDS, INCLUDING ANY HOMEOWNERS' ASSOCIATION. EACH PARAGRAPH, PROVISION, SUB-PARAGRAPH, SENTENCE, CLAUSE, PHRASE AND WORD OF THIS PARAGRAPH 15 SHALL BE DEEMED SEVERABLE; AND IN THE EVENT THAT ANY OF THE SAME SHALL FOR ANY REASON BE HELD INVALID BY ANY COURT, SUCH DECISION SHALL NOT AFFECT THE VALIDITY OF THE REMAINING PART OR PORTION OF THIS PARAGRAPH.

Purchase Agreement for Single-Family Home

A California court found this intimidating paragraph to be unconscionable, in part because its heading was misleading and "did not explain the essence of the judicial reference provisions or otherwise convey anything meaningful to the entry-level purchaser."

The first sentence is 139 words, its first subject (*all claims*) separated from its passive-voice predicate (*shall be determined*) by 93 words.

The use of all caps and single-spacing renders the copy very hard to read.

The paragraph is also blatantly repetitious: the waiver language is repeated no fewer than 11 times in various ways.

BUT THIS:

15. **Mandatory Dispute-Resolution Procedures; Waivers of Rights.**

15.1 **Judicial reference of claims.** All claims related to this Agreement must be determined by judicial reference, which means that a court will appoint a single referee under California Code of Civil Procedure § 638 et seq. or its successor. In accordance with the judicial-reference procedures of the American Arbitration Association, the Referee will try all the claims and issue a binding report to be called a "Statement of Decision."

The new headings make it easier for the reader to decipher the content of § 15 and to find a pertinent topic faster.

15.2 **Referee: definition and powers.** The Referee must be a retired judge of the Superior Court of the State of California. The Referee will be vested with the power to grant all legal and equitable remedies and award compensatory damages but cannot award punitive damages. Unless the parties agree otherwise:

(A) the parties are entitled to the same discovery rights as they would have in a Superior Court lawsuit, with the Referee overseeing discovery and enforcing all discovery orders in the same manner as any trial judge;
(B) the Referee may hear and dispose of motions in the same manner as a trial judge;
(C) the Referee must apply the rules of law, including rules of evidence, unless the parties expressly waive them;
(D) the Referee's Statement of Decision must contain findings of fact and conclusions of law; and
(E) the Referee may rule on all posthearing motions in the same manner as a trial judge.

15.3 **Alternative: trial without a jury.** If the judicial-reference provision is held unenforceable for any reason, or if a court fails or refuses to order judicial reference, the claims must be tried before a judge without a jury. The judge may grant all legal and equitable remedies and award compensatory damages but does not have the power to award punitive damages.

15.4 **Waivers of rights to jury and punitive damages.**

(A) **No jury. Any dispute concerning the validity or interpretation of this section must be decided by a judge without a jury. If the claims are adjudicated in a trial instead of a judicial-reference proceeding, the trial must be before a judge without a jury.**
(B) **No right to punitive damages.** Whatever the forum, the parties waive all rights to punitive damages on any claim.

15.5 **Severability.** If a court for any reason holds a provision of this Agreement to be unenforceable, the rest remains fully enforceable.

15.6 **Binding effect of this section.** The duty to submit all claims to judicial reference, the waiver of the right to punitive damages, and the waiver of jury trial are binding on the parties' successors in interest, the parties' assigns, all party representatives, and all other third parties, including any homeowners' association.

> "If a section title cannot be made both succinct and illuminating, it may indicate that the section covers too much territory and should be divided into several sections."
> Reed Dickerson, *The Fundamentals of Legal Drafting* § 8.23, at 190 (2d ed. 1986).

NOT THIS:

Ex. 3

2.5 ***Deliveries.*** Avery Oil will deliver Products at the Marketing Premises on terms and conditions as specified by Avery Oil at its sole discretion from time to time. Franchise Dealer shall take all actions necessary to facilitate the prompt receipt of deliveries, including prompt removal of snow and ice from all fill cap areas. Avery Oil may, but is not obligated to, make single deliveries of Product of less than its standard delivery quantity as specified by Avery Oil from time to time. Franchise Dealer shall take all action necessary to participate in and comply with Avery Oil Product delivery programs and policies in effect from time to time including Avery Oil's Inventory Management System. If Franchise Dealer fails to comply with or participate in Avery Oil's delivery program or policy, without limiting any other remedies available to Avery Oil, Franchise Dealer shall pay to Avery Oil a reasonable charge imposed in accordance with Avery Oil's delivery policy or program to recover administrative or delivery costs resulting from Franchise Dealer's noncompliance with the program or policy. Franchise Dealer shall accept delivery of Product whether or not Franchise Dealer or anyone else representing Franchise Dealer is on the Marketing Premises to receive the delivery. Franchise Dealer shall pay for all Product delivered.

The heading *Deliveries* doesn't warn the reader about the penalty provision. And the dense paragraph doesn't distinguish each party's duties.

2.6 ***Other Terms and Conditions of Sale.*** Franchise Dealer shall use dispensing and storage facilities that are owned by Avery Oil or bear the Avery name or Proprietary Marks only for the storage or sale of the Products. Franchise Dealer shall purchase and resell those Products, grades and specifications, and use those Proprietary Marks, brand names and packaging that are marketed and used by Avery Oil for similar Avery Outlets in Franchise Dealer's area, all as determined by Avery Oil from time to time. Avery Oil may, at its sole option and at any time, add new products or change the grade, specifications, characteristics or delivery package, brand name or other distinctive designation of any Product sold by Avery Oil under this Agreement, and the Products so added or changed are subject to this Agreement. Avery Oil may discontinue the sale of any Product without affecting other rights or obligations of Avery Oil and Franchise Dealer under this Agreement, including Franchise Dealer's obligation to purchase the Contract Volumes for other Products. Avery Oil's license to use Toltec Petroleum's Licensed Trademarks is scheduled to expire February 28, 2018, unless terminated earlier or extended by agreement between the parties. Franchise Dealer understands that Avery Oil's license may terminate in the future, unless extended by agreement of Avery Oil and Toltec Petroleum. If the license terminates, or if Avery Oil determines in good faith that it is appropriate or necessary to discontinue use of the Toltec Petroleum Licensed Trademarks, and convert operations to another brand or trademark, Franchise Dealer and Avery Oil will not be entitled to use Toltec's Marks and Avery Oil will provide a new licensed trademark to Franchise Dealer. Accordingly, nothing in this Agreement grants or shall be construed as granting Franchise Dealer, or any other person, any right, ownership, title or interest therein. Franchise Dealer further acknowledges that all goodwill relating to the licensing rights in the Toltec Marks in the territory covered by this Agreement shall inure to the benefit of Avery Oil. Only Avery Oil has the right to determine what Toltec products will be offered under the System at any time.

Branded Reseller Agreement from a major oil company

The 2.6 heading is unreasonably vague—as are the section's contents—without subsections and subheadings. The omnibus paragraph imposes duties, notes that a license will terminate, and more.

"[The English language] has become, in our day, a level, firm, broad highway, over which all thought and all speech can travel smoothly and safely. Along it the lawyer and the parliamentary agent propel their heavy wagons, clogged with a thousand pieces of curious antiquated machinery—and no wonder, when they charge freightage, not by the weight of the load, combined with the distance, but by the number of impediments which they can manage to offer to the progress of the vehicle." Henry Alford, *The Queen's English* 3–4 (1864).

BUT THIS:

2.5 **Deliveries; duties; penalty fees.** Avery Oil will deliver Products at the Marketing Premises on terms specified from time to time by Avery Oil at its sole discretion. Avery Oil may make single deliveries of Product of less than its standard delivery quantity.

(A) **Lancaster's duties.** Lancaster will:

(1) take all actions necessary to allow the prompt receipt of deliveries, including prompt removal of snow and ice from all fill-cap areas;

(2) accept delivery of Product whether or not Lancaster or anyone else representing Lancaster is on the Marketing Premises at the time of delivery;

(3) take all actions necessary to participate in and comply with Avery Oil Product delivery programs and policies in effect from time to time, including Avery Oil's Inventory Management System; and

(4) pay for all Product delivered.

If a subpart pertains to one party only, try to refer to that party in the heading.

(B) **Failure to comply with delivery program.** If Lancaster fails to comply with or participate in Avery Oil's delivery program or policy, Lancaster will pay Avery Oil a reasonable charge imposed in accordance with Avery Oil's delivery policy or program to recover administrative or delivery costs resulting from Lancaster's noncompliance. This provision does not limit any other remedies available to Avery Oil.

2.6 **Other terms of sale.**

(A) **Dispensing and storage facilities.** Lancaster may use dispensing and storage facilities owned by Avery Oil or bearing the Toltec name or Proprietary Marks only for the storage or sale of the Products.

(B) **Toltec Products available.** Only Avery Oil has the right to determine what Toltec Products will be offered under the System at any time.

(C) **Products and Proprietary Marks.** Lancaster will purchase and resell the Products, grades, and specifications and will use the Proprietary Marks, brand names, and packaging marketed and used by Avery Oil for similar Toltec Outlets in Lancaster's area, all as determined by Avery Oil from time to time. Avery Oil may at any time add new Products or change the grade, specifications, characteristics, or delivery package, brand name, or other distinctive designation of any Product under this Agreement. The Products so added or changed are subject to this Agreement. Avery Oil may discontinue the sale of any Product without affecting other rights or obligations of Avery Oil and Lancaster under this Agreement, including Lancaster's obligation to purchase the Contract Volumes for other Products.

(D) **Termination of Avery Oil's license from Toltec Petroleum.** Avery Oil's license to use Toltec's Trademarks is scheduled to expire September 30, 2025, unless the parties earlier terminate it or extend it. If the license terminates, or if Avery Oil determines in good faith that it is necessary or appropriate to discontinue use of the Toltec's Trademarks and to convert operations to another brand or trademark, Lancaster and Avery Oil will not be entitled to use Toltec's Trademarks, and Avery Oil will provide a new licensed trademark to Lancaster.

(E) **Intellectual property.** Nothing in this Agreement grants or may be construed as granting Lancaster, or any other person, any right, ownership, title, or interest in the intellectual property of Toltec Petroleum.

(F) **Goodwill.** All goodwill relating to the licensing rights in the Toltec's Trademarks in the territory covered by this Agreement inures to the benefit of Avery Oil.

NOT THIS:

Ex. 4

9. **Certain Restrictive Covenants.** Company, Remaining Members and Employee each mutually acknowledge and agree as follows in exchange for the valuable consideration hereinabove described, the receipt and sufficiency of which are acknowledged:

a. Company has obtained and will maintain an advantage over its competitors as a result of name, location and reputation developed at great expense;

b. Company has developed and will preserve the goodwill of Company;

c. Employee's relationship with Company involved the understanding of and access to certain trade secrets and confidential information pertaining to the property, assets, business and operations of Company;

d. All clients/customers subject to the restrictive covenant set forth in subparagraph (g), below, are assets of the Company, regardless of when or by whom acquired;

e. Employee has carefully considered the restrictions contained herein, and Employee specifically agrees that such restrictions are reasonable, necessary and essential to the preservation of the business of Company; and

f. Employee's agreements and covenants under this Paragraph 9, Paragraph 10 and Paragraph 11 are an essential part of the Inducement to Company to enter into this Separation Agreement.

This provision includes an unidentified non-compete clause.

g. In consideration of Company entering into this Separation Agreement, Employee agrees that for a period equal to two (2) years from the date hereof (the "Covenant Period"), Employee shall not directly or indirectly, either individually, or as a principal, partner, member, manager, agent, employee, employer, consultant, shareholder, joint venturer, or investor, or as a director or officer of any corporation, company, partnership or in any other manner or capacity whatsoever;

i. solicit or divert, or attempt to solicit or divert, from Company any business with any client of the Company; or

ii. solicit or divert, or attempt to solicit or divert, from Company any business with any person or entity who was being solicited as a potential client by Company within one (1) year prior to the commencement of this Separation Agreement; or

iii. induce or cause, or attempt to induce or cause, any salesperson, distributor, supplier, vendor, manufacturer, representative, agent or other person transacting business with Company to terminate or modify such relationship or association; or

iv. induce or cause, or attempt to induce or cause, any employee, accountant, member, manager, partner, shareholder, director or officer of Company or any affiliate of Company to leave the employ of Company.

h. In the event Employee violates any of the provisions of this Paragraph 9, or Paragraph 10 or Paragraph 11 during the Covenant Period, the Covenant Period shall be extended for a period of time equal to the period of any such violation.

10. **Confidentiality.** Employee agrees not to disclose or use any confidential or proprietary data of any kind, including, but not limited to, technical or non-technical Information, client lists, client information or any other proprietary information related to the activities of the Company and Employee agrees to return immediately all property of the Company which Employee has in Employee's possession or under Employee's control, except as may be otherwise provided in this Separation Agreement. Employee further agrees that except as otherwise required by legal process, Employee will treat the existence and the terms of this Separation Agreement as well as all Exhibits hereto as confidential and will not disclose any information concerning the terms or existence of this Separation Agreement to anyone other than Employee's legal representatives.

11. **Non-Disparagement.** Each party hereby agrees that it shall refrain from all conduct, verbal or otherwise, that disparages or damages or could disparage or damage the reputation, goodwill, or standing in the community of the other party, or any of its affiliates.

Release and Separation Agreement

BUT THIS:

9. **Restrictive Covenants.**

9.1 **Purposes.** At great expense, the Company has developed and obtained an advantage over its competitors because of its name, location, and reputation, and it has developed goodwill.
(A) The Company wishes to maintain this competitive advantage and preserve its goodwill.
(B) The Employee's relationship with the Company involves understanding and having access to certain trade secrets and confidential information relating to the Company's property, assets, business, and operations. Clients and customers that are subject to § 9.2 are Company assets regardless of when or by whom acquired.
(C) The restrictions in §§ 9.2–9.4 are reasonable, necessary, and essential to preserving the Company's business.
(D) The Employee's agreements and covenants under this § 9 are an essential part of the inducement to the Company to enter into this Separation Agreement.

9.2 **Noncompetition.** For 2 years after the date of this Separation Agreement, the Employee must not directly or indirectly, either individually or as a participant with others in any manner or capacity:
(A) solicit or divert any business with any Company client away from the Company;
(B) solicit or divert from the Company any business with any person or entity that was being solicited as a potential client by the Company within 1 year before the date of this Separation Agreement;
(C) induce or cause any salesperson, distributor, supplier, vendor, manufacturer, representative, agent, or other person transacting business with the Company to terminate or modify their relationship or association;
(D) induce or cause any employee, accountant, member, manager, partner, shareholder, director, or officer of the Company or any of its affiliates to leave the Company's employ; or
(E) attempt to carry out any action prohibited in this section.

9.3 **Confidentiality.** The Employee must not disclose or use any confidential or proprietary data of any kind, including technical or nontechnical information, client lists, client information, or any other proprietary information related to the Company's activities. The Employee agrees to immediately return all Company property that the Employee has in the Employee's possession or under the Employee's control, except as may be otherwise provided in this Separation Agreement. Except as otherwise required by legal process, the Employee will treat the existence of this Separation Agreement as well as all exhibits as confidential and will not disclose any information concerning this Separation Agreement to anyone other than the Employee's legal representatives.

9.4 **Nondisparagement.** Each party must refrain from all conduct, verbal or nonverbal, that disparages or damages or could disparage or damage the other party's reputation or goodwill or that of any of the other party's affiliates.

9.5 **Violation; penalty.** If the Employee violates any provision of this § 9 during the 2-year noncompetition period, that period will be extended for as long as the violation continues.

"Contracts written by lawyers draw upon the law, but most of those contracts are completely unregulated by the law as to form or language. They are not usually required to be clear, or even legible, and too many of them are neither." David Mellinkoff, *Legal Writing: Sense and Nonsense* 77 (1982).

§ 16 Check and, if necessary, improve your average sentence length.

Though sentence length isn't an absolute predictor of readability, it's a very reliable indicator. It's a major factor in most readability formulas.[1] Especially in technical prose, long sentences make for repulsive reading.

So break long compound sentences into two or more sentences. But when doing this, show some linguistic savvy: no choppy, ungainly sentences—just smooth exposition. Aim for an average sentence length of no more than 30 words. (A 20-word maximum is recommended for general expository prose in law.[2]) One way to achieve this goal is to subenumerate: every separately indented subpart counts as a separate sentence, even if it begins with a lowercase letter and ends with a semicolon.

For counting purposes, a "sentence" includes a chunk of text that can be read by itself or by reference to an introductory line shared with other items in a list. The rationale is that when the introductory material is stored separately in memory, each item in the list can be considered by itself. Although it must be taken with what precedes or follows to make up a full sentence in the traditional grammarian's sense, each chunk of text is read independently.

Of course, one of the most notoriously long sentences in traditional contracts is the set of serpentine recitals linked with semicolons and continuing from the first WHEREAS through the end of the NOW, THEREFORE construction. See § 28.

Another horrible sentence-lengthening habit is using *provided that* and *provided, however, that*. Normally, those phrases are best replaced by a capitalized *But* (new sentence). If you're not accustomed to this style, then become accustomed to it right now: it's a technique used eight times in the U.S. Constitution, and it's perfectly proper. See § 116 and § 149 at pp. 435–36.

> "A 240-word sentence, littered with semicolons and words and phrases generally alien to the nonlawyer, is clear in one respect at least: it isn't meant to be read." Carl Felsenfeld & Alan Siegel, *Writing Contracts in Plain English* 23 (1981).

---

1 *See, e.g.*, Rudolf Flesch, *How to Write Plain English: A Book for Lawyers and Consumers* 20–27 (1979); Robert Gunning, *The Technique of Clear Writing* 32–34 (1952).

2 Garner, *Legal Writing in Plain English* § 6, at 27–31 (2d ed. 2013).

<table>
<tr><th>NOT THIS:</th><th>BUT THIS:</th></tr>
<tr><td>Ex. 1
The School District shall pay to the School Bus Inspector for services performed $125 for each completed school bus inspection, for a total not to exceed $6,250.
School-Bus-Inspection Service Agreement from 16A Am. Jur. Legal Forms 2d Schools § 229:194 (Nov. 2017 update)
[Sentence length: 27 words.]</td><td>The School District will pay the School Bus Inspector $125 for each completed school-bus inspection. The total paid must not exceed $6,250.
[Avg. sentence length: 11 words.]</td></tr>
<tr><td>Ex. 2
(a) National hereby engages and retains Parker as a consultant and Parker hereby agrees to perform services for National in the capacity of a consultant in connection with the Business concentrating his efforts primarily to the States of Oklahoma, Kansas and Texas for a term commencing on the date of this Consulting Agreement and ending December 31 of this year.
Consulting Agreement from a major beverage company
[Sentence length: 59 words.]</td><td>(A) Term and territory. National retains Parker as a business consultant from ______________________, 20___ until December 31, 20___. Parker will concentrate his efforts on Oklahoma, Kansas, and Texas.
In the final agreement, the known date and year should be inserted.
[Avg. sentence length: 14 words.]</td></tr>
<tr><td>Ex. 3
17.9 I CERTIFY AND ACKNOWLEDGE THAT I HAVE CAREFULLY READ ALL OF THE PROVISIONS OF THIS AGREEMENT, I UNDERSTAND THIS AGREEMENT AND HAVE BEEN GIVEN THE OPPORTUNITY TO DISCUSS IT WITH INDEPENDENT LEGAL COUNSEL, AND I WILL FULLY AND FAITHFULLY COMPLY WITH ITS PROVISIONS.
It's presumptuous to put a form contract into first person for someone else to sign, though entirely natural to do so for one's own client. See Rudolf Flesch, How to Write Plain English: A Book for Lawyers and Consumers 49–50 (1979).
Assignment Agreement from a major software-development company
[Sentence length: 43 words.]</td><td>17.9 Certification of care. You certify that you:
(A) have carefully read this entire Agreement and understand it;
(B) have had the opportunity to discuss it with your own legal counsel; and
(C) will fully and faithfully comply with it.
Eliminate the all-caps text (see § 42). Also, phrase it in the second person.
[Avg. sentence length: 8 words.]</td></tr>
<tr><td>Ex. 4
(c) The service of beer, wines, and liquors shall be made by the waiters or waitresses, and such sales of beer, wines, and liquors shall be accurately recorded on a separate check from the food check, and such separate checks shall be identified as cocktail bar checks, and payment of such cocktail bar checks shall be made after each serving in a manner prescribed by the owner, and shall not constitute in any manner a part of food income.
Note the poor use of passive voice combined with shall. See § 47.
Food-Management Contract from 5 Christopher J. Miller & Allen D. Choka, Nichols Cyclopedia of Legal Forms Annotated § 99:52 (2017)
[Sentence length: 78 words.]</td><td>(C) Cocktail-bar records. The waiters will serve beer, wine, and liquor. Each sale will be accurately recorded on a cocktail-bar check separate from the food check. Cocktail-bar checks must be paid after each serving in a manner prescribed by the owner; they do not constitute a part of food income.
[Avg. sentence length: 16 words.]</td></tr>
</table>

NOT THIS:	BUT THIS:
Ex. 5 **8.2 Appointment.** In the event that the Company is unable for any reason to secure my signature to any document required to apply for or execute any patent, copyright, mask work or other applications to obtain Proprietary Rights with respect for any Company Invention (including improvements, renewals, extensions, continuations, divisions or continuations in part thereof), I hereby irrevocably designate and appoint the Company and its duly authorized officers and agents as my agents and attorneys-in-fact, which appointment is coupled with an interest, to act for and in my behalf and instead of me, to execute and file any such documents and to do all other lawfully permitted acts to further the purposes stated in Section 8.1, with the same legal force and effect as if executed by me. **Employee-Inventions and Proprietary-Rights Assignment from a major law firm** [Sentence length: 126 words.]	**8.2 Appointment.** Your signature may be needed on documents required to apply for or obtain a patent, copyright, mask work, or something else to obtain Proprietary Rights for a Company Invention (including improvements, renewals, extensions, continuations, divisions, and continuations-in-part). If you are not available to sign a document, you irrevocably designate and appoint the Company and its duly authorized officers and agents as your agents and attorneys-in-fact. They may sign and file a document and do all other lawfully permitted acts for the purposes in § 8.1. On the change from first person to second person, see § 55. [Avg. sentence length: 28 words.]
Ex. 6 Part A-Health and Welfare Plan Section 1-Continuation of Plan . . . Contributions to the Plan will be offset by the expeditious use of such amounts as may at any time be in Special Account A or in one or more special accounts or funds maintained by any insurer, third party administrator or other entity in connection with the Plan and by the use of funds held in trust that are not otherwise needed to pay claims, premiums, or administrative expenses that are payable from funds held in trust; provided, however, that such amounts as may at any time be in that certain special account maintained at the Insurance Company, known as the "Special Account Held in Connection with the Amount for the Close-Out Period," relating to the obligations of the Plan to pay, among other things, benefits incurred but not paid at the time of termination of the Plan in the event such termination should occur, shall be used to pay or provide for Plan benefits as follows: one-third of the balance in such special account as of January 1, 2019, shall be used to pay or provide for benefits that become due and payable during 2019. Do the words *amounts* and *funds* mean the same thing? See § 10. **Imposed Agreement from a major railroad** [Sentence length: 187 words.]	**1. Health and Welfare Plan.** **1.1 Continuation of Plan.** . . . Contributions to the Plan are offset by using the funds in Special Account A or in 1 or more special accounts or funds maintained by an insurer, third-party administrator, or other entity in connection with the Plan. Funds held in trust may also be used if they are not needed to pay claims, premiums, or administrative expenses. But if the Plan terminates, the funds kept at the Insurance Company in the "Special Account Held in Connection with the Amount for the Close-Out Period" must be used to pay or provide for Plan benefits. This includes paying benefits incurred but not paid at the end of the Plan. One-third of the balance in the special account held in connection with the account for the closeout period available on January 1, 2019, must be used to pay or provide benefits that become due during 2019. [Avg. sentence length: 26 words.]

Conciseness

§ 17 Tighten the prose.

Verbosity is a scourge in all writing. Every unnecessary word weighs down a sentence, and the cumulative effect is to burden the reader—especially one who is (to use the psychologists' term) cognitively busy. Tighten wordings as much as is consistent with natural idiom. Under the surplusage canon of construction,[1] courts try to give effect to every word in a contract; they tend to assume that no word is idle or needless.

When wordiness is rampant—the prose clotted with wordy phrases—the best editorial method is simply to rethink the thought. Ask yourself, "What's the real point here?" Then rewrite it, omitting needless details and putting peripheral details in separate sentences. Editors call this process "boiling down."

The revision will doubtless be more concise and readable than the original. What you're doing is avoiding the common sin of burying the crux of the matter in a quagmire of clutter.

Writing experts have long touted the virtues of tightening prose:

- "It is an amiable maxim that words which add nothing to the sense or to the clearness must diminish the force of the expression."[2]
- "Wherever we can make twenty-five words do the work of fifty, we halve the area in which looseness and disorganization can flourish, and by reducing the span of attention required we increase the force of the thought. To make our words count for as much as possible is surely the simplest as well as the hardest secret of style."[3]
- "A sentence should contain no unnecessary words, a paragraph no unnecessary sentences, for the same reason that a drawing should have no unnecessary lines and a machine no unnecessary parts."[4]

---

1 *See* Antonin Scalia & Bryan A. Garner, *Reading Law: The Interpretation of Legal Texts* 174–79 (2012).

2 George Campbell, *Philosophy of Rhetoric* (1776) (as quoted in Alfred Ayres, *The Verbalist* vi (rev. ed. 1911)).

3 Wilson Follett, *Modern American Usage* 14 (1966).

4 William Strunk Jr. & E.B. White, *The Elements of Style* 23 (3d ed. 1979).

- "Once you develop a distaste for surplus words, you will find many word-wasting idioms that can be trimmed from your sentences with no loss of meaning."[5]

So count your savings whenever you edit a phrase down from 12 words to 6, or even 5 down to 1. If *prior to the time when* becomes *before*—as it virtually always can—you're better off. So are your readers.

NOT THIS:	BUT THIS:
Ex. 1 12. Closing Date. Buyer and Seller hereby agree that the Closing Date shall be February 28, 20__. **Purchase Agreement from a major law firm**	**12. Closing Date.** The closing date is February 28, 20__.
Ex. 2 AmeriCon and Provider have entered into an agreement under which AmeriCon is acquiring equipment and other items from Provider. **Purchase Agreement from a major law firm**	AmeriCon has contracted to buy equipment and other items from Wing Software.
Ex. 3 5. Miscellaneous 5.1 Governing Law. This Agreement shall be governed by and construed in accordance with the internal laws of the State of Delaware, without reference to its choice of law rules. **Stockholders Agreement from a major law firm**	**5. Miscellaneous.** **5.1 Governing law.** Delaware law applies to all matters arising under or relating to this Agreement without regard to any choice-of-law rules that might direct the application of another jurisdiction's laws.
Ex. 4 7. **MANAGING SAFE WORK ("MSW") PLAN** 7.1 Contractor shall ensure that its supervisors understand their roles and responsibilities with regard to MSW and translate them into actions and behaviors that are visible. **Master Contractor-Services Agreement from a major energy corporation**	**7. Managing Safe Work ("MSW") Plan.** **7.1 Supervisors' involvement.** The Contractor must ensure that its supervisors understand their roles and responsibilities with MSW and conduct themselves accordingly.
Ex. 5 This Agreement, consisting of Sections 1 through 12, and Appendixes A through C attached hereto (collectively hereinafter referred to as the "Agreement"), is made and entered into as of May 12, 2019. **Purchase Agreement from a major law firm**	This Agreement consists of §§ 1–12 and Appendixes A–C (collectively, the "Agreement"), and is dated May 12, 2019.

See § 49.

See § 34.

5 Richard C. Wydick, *Plain English for Lawyers* 14 (4th ed. 1998).

NOT THIS:	BUT THIS:
Ex. 6 Franchisee shall not use any of the Licensed Marks in any signage, advertising or marketing unless the same shall have been approved in writing by Taxpro prior to such use. In the event of Taxpro modifying or replacing any Licensed Mark, Franchisee shall modify or replace (as Taxpro may direct) any signs or materials to reflect the modified or new Licensed Mark on a timetable designated by Taxpro. **Franchise-License Agreement from a tax-preparation company**	Unless Taxpro so authorizes in writing, you must not use any of the Licensed Marks in signage, advertising, or marketing. If Taxpro modifies or replaces any Licensed Mark, you must—as directed by Taxpro and within Taxpro's designated time—modify or replace any signs or materials to reflect the modified or new Licensed Mark.
Ex. 7 Client understands that any estimates provided by the Firm of the magnitude of the expenses that will be required at certain stages of any litigation asserting a cause of action are not precise, and that the kinds and amounts of expenses required are ultimately a function of many conditions over which the Firm has little or no control, particularly the extent to which the opposition files pretrial motions and engages in its own discovery requests, whether in the nature of interrogatories, depositions, requests for production, or requests for admission, or any other type of discovery allowed by the rules of procedure in the forum in which the dispute is pending. **Fee Agreement from a major law firm**	Early expense numbers are only estimates. Conditions outside our control, especially the opposition's pretrial motions and discovery requests, may raise or lower actual expenses.

"Many legal texts are unnecessarily complex and wholly inappropriate to the needs and abilities of their various audiences. I remember a life assurance policy, still used in India, that begins with a 191-word sentence of pure legalese. A bank overdraft agreement in New Zealand includes a sentence of over 900 words, full of *notwithstandings* and *aforesaids*. Such contracts are unacceptable to me and many customers." Martin Cutts, *Plain English in the Law*, 17 Stat. L. Rev. 50, 50 (1996).

NOT THIS:

Ex. 8

SECTION 7.12—*Post-Merger Arrigo Star Board of Directors.* At the Effective Time, the total number of persons serving on the Board of Directors of Arrigo Star shall be twenty-two (unless otherwise agreed in writing by Tri-Dex and Arrigo Star prior to the Effective Time), half of whom shall be Tri-Dex Directors and half of whom shall be Arrigo Star Directors (as such terms are defined below). No more than six of the twenty-two initial Directors of Arrigo Star shall be employees of Tri-Dex or Arrigo Star; half of the employee directors shall be Tri-Dex Directors and half shall be Arrigo Star Directors (as such terms are defined below). The persons to serve initially on the Board of Directors of Arrigo Star at the Effective Time who are Tri-Dex Directors shall be selected solely by and at the absolute discretion of the Board of Directors of Tri-Dex prior to the Effective Time; and the persons to serve on the Board of Directors of Arrigo Star at the Effective Time who are Arrigo Star Directors shall be selected solely by and at the absolute discretion of the Board of Directors of Arrigo Star prior to the Effective Time. In the event that, prior to the Effective Time, any person so selected to serve on the Board of Directors of Arrigo Star after the Effective Time is unable or unwilling to serve in such position, the Board of Directors which selected such person shall designate another of its members to serve in such person's stead in accordance with the provision of the immediately preceding sentence. From and after the Effective Time and until Manuel R. Diaz ceases to be the Chairman of Arrigo Star, the Board of Directors of Arrigo Star and each Committee of the Board of Directors of Arrigo Star as constituted following each election of Directors shall consist of an equal number of Tri-Dex Directors and Arrigo Star Directors. If, at any time during the period referred to in the immediately preceding sentence, the number of Tri-Dex Directors and Arrigo Star Directors serving, or that would be serving following the next stockholders' meeting at which directors are to be elected, as Directors of Arrigo Star or as members of any Committee of the Board of Directors of Arrigo Star would not be equal, then, subject to the fiduciary duties of the Directors of Arrigo Star, the Board of Directors and the Nominating Committee thereof shall nominate for election at the next stockholders' meeting at which Directors are to be elected such person or persons as may be requested by the remaining Tri-Dex Directors (if the number of Tri-Dex Directors is, or would otherwise become, less than the number of Arrigo Star Directors) or by the remaining Arrigo Star Directors (if the number of Arrigo Star Directors is, or would otherwise become, less than the number of Tri-Dex Directors) to ensure that there shall be an equal number of Tri-Dex Directors and Arrigo Star Directors. The provisions of the preceding sentence shall not apply in respect of any stockholders' meeting which takes place after the date on which Manuel R. Diaz ceases to be Chairman of Arrigo Star, and subsequent to such date, vacancies in the Board of Directors of Arrigo Star shall be filled only by vote of the stockholders. The term "Tri-Dex Director" means (i) any person serving as a Director of Tri-Dex or of a Tri-Dex telephone company on the date hereof who becomes a Director of Arrigo Star at the Effective Time and (ii) any person who becomes a Director of Arrigo Star pursuant to the second preceding sentence and who is designated by the Tri-Dex Directors; and the term "Arrigo Star Director" means (i) any person serving as a Director of Arrigo Star on the date hereof who continues as a Director of Arrigo Star at the Effective Time and (ii) any person who becomes a Director of Arrigo Star pursuant to the second preceding sentence and who is designated by the Arrigo Star Directors.

Merger Agreement

BUT THIS:

7.12 Postmerger Arrigo Star board of directors.

(A) **Board makeup.** After the merger, Arrigo Star's new board of directors will consist of 22 persons—11 Tri-Dex directors and 11 Arrigo Star directors. No more than 6 of the 22 new directors will be employees of Tri-Dex or Arrigo Star (3 from each company). Each company's premerger board has full discretion to select its 11 directors for the postmerger board.

(B) **Replacement directors.** If, before the merger, anyone selected to serve on Arrigo Star's new board of directors is unable or unwilling to serve, the premerger board that selected that person will select a replacement.

(C) **Equal representation.** As long as Manuel R. Diaz is Arrigo Star's chair, Arrigo Star's new board of directors—and each board committee—will consist of an equal number of Tri-Dex directors and Arrigo Star directors. If, during this time, the number of Tri-Dex directors and Arrigo Star directors is about to become unequal, then the new board will nominate for election as director 1 or more persons selected by the remaining Tri-Dex directors or Arrigo Star directors, whichever group is about to become smaller, so that the 2 groups will remain equal in number. Once Manuel R. Diaz is no longer chair, board vacancies will be filled by a vote of the stockholders.

§ 18 Condense phrases into words when possible.

When you can, collapse phrases into single words. For example, never use *person who seeks election to public office through a political campaign* when you can write *political candidate* or just *candidate.*

NOT THIS:	BUT THIS:
Ex. 1 "*Business Day*" means any day other than a Saturday, Sunday or legal holiday in the State of Iowa. **Management-Services Agreement for an assisted-living facility**	"Business Day" means a weekday that is not a legal holiday in Iowa.
Ex. 2 14.1.1 Master Franchisee shall create, develop, prepare, coordinate and implement a Strategic Marketing Plan with respect to each Territory. **International-Franchise Agreement from a major fast-food restaurant**	14.1 **Strategic Marketing Plan.** Mac's Tacos will create, develop, prepare, coordinate, and implement a Strategic Marketing Plan for each Territory.
Ex. 3 22.5 Automatic Termination. Upon the occurrence of a Material Breach specified in Section 22.2.3, this Agreement shall terminate without the need for any Party to take any further action. **Merger Agreement between two major entertainment-industry companies**	22.5 **Automatic termination.** If a Material Breach occurs under § 22.2(C), this Agreement terminates automatically.
Ex. 4 4.8 Medical Supplies. The Provider will be responsible for the costs of prescription or nonprescription drugs or medicines, medical supplies, vitamins, dental work, eye refractions, eyeglasses, or contact lenses that it determines are medically necessary. **Residence-and-Care Agreement executed by a major law firm**	4.8 **Medical supplies.** We will pay the costs of medically necessary prescription or nonprescription drugs, medical supplies, vitamins, dental work, eye refractions, eyeglasses, and contact lenses.
Ex. 5 Purchaser shall have no obligation to make any payment if, at the time such payment would otherwise be due, the Approval Order is stayed, *provided, however*, that Purchaser shall make any such payment within three (3) business days after such stay is lifted but only if, after such stay is lifted, the Approval Order remains in effect. **Purchase-and-Assignment Agreement from a major law firm**	Hoskins need not pay if, at the time payment would otherwise be due, the Approval Order has been stayed. But if the stay is lifted and the Approval Order remains in effect, Hoskins will pay within 3 business days after the stay is lifted.

NOT THIS:	BUT THIS:
Ex. 6 **2. DEVELOPMENT AND DELIVERY** . . . 2.3 **Subcontracting**. Company shall not have the right to subcontract the rights and obligations under this Agreement to any third party without the prior written consent of Developer. In the event of any such subcontracting, Developer shall be solely responsible therefor and shall be liable for all acts or omissions of such subcontractors in the performance of the Development. **License-and-Development Agreement from a computer-technology company**	**2. Development and Delivery.** . . . **2.3 Subcontracting.** Wellstone cannot subcontract its rights and obligations under this Agreement to a third party without Chipco's prior written consent. If subcontracting occurs, Wellstone remains solely responsible and liable for all the subcontractors' acts or omissions in the Development.
Ex. 7 Whereas, the parties hereto agree that the covenants, agreements and restrictions (hereinafter "this covenant") contained herein are necessary to protect the business goodwill, business interests and proprietary rights of [*name of business*] and that the parties hereto have independently discussed, reviewed and had the opportunity of legal counsel to consider this agreement. **Noncompetition Agreement from 3 Nancy Saint-Paul, Texas Legal Practice Forms 3d *Employment Agreements* § 49:9, at 701 (2016)**	The parties have independently discussed, reviewed, and had the opportunity to consult legal counsel about this Agreement and acknowledge that its terms are necessary to protect the business goodwill, business interests, and proprietary rights of [*name of business*].

"Systematic indifference to the way contracts are put together . . . works when the same people repeatedly use the same involved form in the same circumstances, so that no one really bothers to read them to know what they say. These instances do not prove that clear writing is unimportant, but that the labored contract itself—as it turned out—was unnecessary. . . . Clarity counts when the contract counts, especially when there is controversy." David Mellinkoff, *Legal Writing: Sense and Nonsense* 77 (1982).

§ 19 Adopt sensible positions on doublets and triplets of the legal idiom.

Legal drafters are the most redundant of all writers. Part of the reason may be historical: up to about 1700, English drafters were paid by the word. Hence our predecessors had an economic incentive to be verbose.

Although modern drafters, like good stylists, seek to find the right word, they don't force choices on themselves. Instead, they often throw in *all* the choices, seemingly in the hope that one of several will end up being the right word.

This practice is odd, given that most courts say that they must read nothing in a drafted document as being, as they put it, "mere surplusage." Under the surplusage canon, courts are charged to give effect to every word and to regard no words as superfluities. In fact, though, most courts know that in practice lawyers typically follow a different rule—a rule that California has statutorily codified. It is a rule that encourages wordiness: "Superfluity does not vitiate."[1]

The result is that drafters often string out two or more almost-right words. To avoid needless repetitions, try to apply this rule: if one word adequately expresses the meaning of other words, use that word only. That is, if one term names a genus of which the other terms are species, use the genus-word only.

Try to find just the right word—the one that most accurately conveys the meaning. Avoid doublets, triplets, and synonym-strings.[2] Be sure that if you add a near-synonym, you're actually adding meaning.

NOT THIS:	BUT THIS:
Ex. 1 Lewis grants, conveys, transfers, alienates, and assigns exclusively to Ultima all of his right, title, and interest in the Property. **Assignment Agreement from a major law firm**	Lewis assigns his entire interest in the Property to Ultima.
Ex. 2 The Undersigned transfers, assigns, and sets over to MGIPC all of its claims and rights arising out of the aforesaid loss. **Settlement Agreement from a major law firm**	Webber Financial assigns to MGIPC all its claims and rights arising from the loss.

1 Cal. Civ. Code § 3537.

2 *See Garner's Dictionary of Legal Usage* 294–97 (3d ed. 2011).

NOT THIS:	BUT THIS:
Ex. 3 Such right to an injunction shall be cumulative and in addition to, and not in lieu of, any other remedies to which the Employer may show itself to be justly entitled. **Employment Agreement from a major law firm**	Polar Tech has a right to an injunction in addition to its other remedies.
Ex. 4 Tenant must not make alterations, additions, or improvements to the Premises without the prior written consent of Landlord, which consent must not be unreasonably withheld. **Lease Agreement from a major law firm**	Williams will not make a change to the Premises without Stone's prior written consent, which must not be unreasonably withheld.
Ex. 5 Employee hereby represents and warrants to Employer that Employee is not under any impediment, restraint, or disability that would prohibit, hinder, or in any way impair Employee's working ability or relationship with Employer. **Salesperson Agreement from 3 Nancy Saint-Paul, Texas Legal Practice Forms 3d *Employment Agreements* § 49:5, at 679 (2016)**	McNulty represents and warrants that he has no condition that would impair his working ability or relationship with Baltic Sales.
Ex. 6 If Bailee fails, refuses, or indicates its unwillingness to perform any obligation under this agreement, Bailor may, at its option, perform that obligation on behalf of the Bailee and charge to or otherwise recover from Bailee the cost of this performance. **Bailment Agreement from a major law firm**	If Young fails to perform or suggests it won't perform any obligation under this Agreement, Potter may perform that obligation on Young's behalf, and Young must pay for it.
Ex. 7 Owner will indemnify, defend and hold Contractor harmless from all claims, demands, or liability (including reasonable attorneys' fees) arising out of or encountered in connection with this Agreement or the prosecution of work under it. **Construction Contract from a major law firm**	**Indemnity.** Stewart will indemnify and defend All-Star Construction from all liabilities (including reasonable attorneys' fees) arising from or in connection with this Agreement.
Ex. 8 Seller shall cooperate with and assist Buyer in this process, without bearing the costs or expenses incurred or associated therewith, and shall guarantee that Buyer and its representatives and contractors shall have free and unfettered access to the land on which the factory is located so that the work can be performed in a timely and uninterrupted manner. **Grant of Temporary Easement from a major law firm**	Markus must help DeltaCo in this process, at no cost to Markus, and must guarantee that DeltaCo and its representatives and contractors have full access to the land where the factory is located so that the work can be performed timely and without interruption.

On the question of retaining *represents and warrants*, see § 31.

For a full discussion of *indemnify and hold harmless*, as well as variations on the phrase, see § 148 at pp. 392–95.

§ 20 Eliminate zombie nouns.

Drafters often bury would-be verbs in longer derivatives: abstract nouns that give documents a formal, official, legalistic sound. Typically, these "zombie nouns," or nominalizations as they're also called, are found in words having the noun suffixes *-tion*, *-sion*, *-ment*, *-ence*, *-ance*, or *-ity*.

But instead of using a zombie noun such as *repudiation*, try using its kernel verb: *repudiate*. Likewise, *violation* becomes *violate*, *intrusion* becomes *intrude*, *enforcement* becomes *enforce*, *occurrence* becomes *occur*, *acceptance* becomes *accept*, and *conformity* becomes *conform*.

Why bother to carry out these edits? Four reasons:

- You'll often save a couple of words, usually in the form of prepositional phrases that can be eliminated (*made the appointment of Jones* becomes *appointed Jones*).
- You'll avoid weak verbs—*be*-verbs—by replacing them with stronger action verbs (*is in mitigation of* becomes *mitigates*).
- You'll force yourself to say who does what (*Upon the acceptance of the offer* might become *If Smith accepts the offer*). The text then focuses equally on actors and actions instead of referring vaguely to actions.
- As a result of the previous three points, you'll make the writing much less abstract. It will become much easier to read and understand.

In the following list, the zombie noun always introduces at least one unnecessary word—sometimes as many as three:

Instead of:	*Write:*
exhibit resistance	resist
grant a license	license
make a decision	decide
make an assignment	assign
make a payment	pay
make a warranty	warrant
offer a lease	lease
offer a loan	lend

"If you use nominalizations instead of base verbs, surplus words begin to swarm like gnats." Richard C. Wydick, *Plain English for Lawyers* 25 (4th ed. 1998).

offer a rebuttal	rebut
offer testimony	testify
proffer arguments that	argue that
provide an indemnification to	indemnify
provide responses	respond
reach a resolution	resolve
submit an application	apply
take into consideration	consider
undertake the representation of	represent

NOT THIS:	BUT THIS:
Ex. 1 Ballard shall pay for the production of alternative elements which it deems appropriate. **License Agreement**	Ballard will pay to produce alternative elements that it considers appropriate.
Ex. 2 The preparation, filing, and prosecution of all foreign patent applications shall be at the sole expense of the Licensee. **Patent-License Agreement from a major law firm**	PMC Industries will pay the cost of preparing, filing, and prosecuting all foreign patent applications.
Ex. 3 Distributor will make provision for the Customer to receive the Distributor's assistance in basic installation of the Products. **Supplier–Retainer Contract from a major law firm**	Distributor is responsible only for the Products' basic installation.
Ex. 4 (a) ***Mortgage Loan Schedule.*** As of the Cutoff Date, the information contained in the Mortgage Loan Schedule is a true and accurate reflection of the Seller's servicing records with respect to such information in all material respects. **Mortgage-Loan Purchase Agreement between two major financial institutions**	(A) **Mortgage loan schedule.** In all material respects, the Mortgage Loan Schedule accurately reflects Quillco's servicing records as of the Cutoff Date.

For more on the useful distinction between *which* and *that*, see § 143.

The original is vague and highly misleading. The revision is what the drafter actually meant—as revealed after questioning.

"No word or phrase should be used in a legal instrument unless there is a good reason for including it. If none appears, it should be got rid of. Every word should pay its own way. An increase in clarity or readability is adequate payment." Reed Dickerson, *The Fundamentals of Legal Drafting* § 3.7, at 44 (2d ed. 1986).

NOT THIS:	BUT THIS:
Ex. 5 Whereas, the representative of the Union and the KCR has engaged in extensive conferences with the representative of the UTC concerning the subject matter of those notices, and they have reached an Agreement which will be in full satisfaction and disposition of all notices and will resolve all outstanding issues between the parties including the notices referred to above. **Memorandum of Agreement from a railroad company**	The Union and KCR representative has conferred extensively with the UTC representative about the matters covered by the notices. They have reached an Agreement that fully satisfies and disposes of all notices and resolves all outstanding issues between the parties.
Ex. 6 The Player acknowledges that, in the event he is found, in accordance with the terms of the NBA/NBPA Collective Bargaining Agreement, to have engaged in the use, possession or distribution of a "prohibited substance" as defined therein, it will result in the termination of this contract and the Player's immediate dismissal and permanent disqualification from any employment by the Association and any of its teams. **Professional-Basketball-Player Contract**	6.4 **Prohibited-substance policy.** If Howard uses, possesses, or distributes a "prohibited substance" as defined in the NBA/NBPA Collective Bargaining Agreement, this contract will immediately end, and Howard will be immediately dismissed and permanently disqualified from employment by the Association and all its teams.

> "Some lawyers are reluctant to revise cluttered, convoluted language because the courts have 'blessed it' in prior cases. Two problems exist with this logic. First, language that has to be litigated is lacking clarity. Second, the interpretation of each contract depends upon facts and circumstances unique to it, so a ruling in one case is not binding on the next except when the case declares an established usage. Moreover, courts have been known to change their views even when precedent has established usage, so the best practice is to create language that does not require judicial intervention." Lenné Eidson Espenschied, *Contract Drafting: Powerful Prose in Transactional Practice* 59 (3d ed. 2019).

§ 21 Avoid unnecessary detail.

Delete unimportant, extraneous information. If it's only *relatively* unimportant, relegate it to the back of the document.

For many years, old-style drafting made contracts impenetrable to the ordinary reader. It was a needle-in-the-haystack problem: the information a reader might want was buried under so many layers of sludge that it became, in effect, irretrievable. If you include *everything*, you end up imparting *nothing*—because nobody is dogged enough to read it.

Many lawyers fear deletions, even of boilerplate, because they think that deleting something might result in increased potential for liability. The answer to this concern is threefold. First, plain English doesn't mean omitting important information. It only requires you to phrase ideas in words that people can understand in an inviting format. Second, plain-English contracts should reduce potential liability by decreasing the parties' misunderstandings. Third, the lawyers who have learned and who use plain-English principles haven't experienced the kinds of problems that naysayers sometimes warn about.

The following examples show what it means to highlight the important information while subordinating the unimportant. Notice how true the old adage is: less is more. The original versions are loaded with words and information having minimal value for most readers. The revised versions highlight the points most likely to be of immediate concern.

> "Overprecision and overparticularity not only needlessly circumscribe the actions of those who are affected by a legal instrument but make it harder to read, understand, and administer." Reed Dickerson, *The Fundamentals of Legal Drafting* § 3.5, at 41 (2d ed. 1986).

NOT THIS:	BUT THIS:
Ex. 1 In the event said Consumer Price Index shall hereafter be converted to a different standard reference base or otherwise revised, the determination of the percentage increase shall be made with the use of such conversion factor, formula, or table for converting said Index as may be published by the Bureau of Labor Statistics, or if said bureau shall not publish such an Index, then the use of such conversion factor, formula, or table as may be published by Prentice Hall, Inc. or Commerce Clearing House or any nationally recognized publisher of similar statistical information. In the event said Index shall cease to be published, there shall be substituted for said Index such other Cost of Living Index as Licensor and Licensee may agree upon. **Commercial Lease from a major online-search and -advertising company**	If this Consumer Price Index is revised or converted to a different standard-reference base, the percentage increase will be determined by using whatever conversion factor, formula, or table for converting the Index is published by the Bureau of Labor Statistics or its successor.

The last lines deal with absurd contingencies without ever suggesting how to choose between Prentice-Hall, CCH, and other "nationally recognized publishers."

Notice how the last three words deftly, though broadly, replace the absurdly detailed original.

"The attorney's job . . . requires more than transcribing the information the client provides. The attorney needs to think through the structure of this deal with the client, to fill in gaps that the client may not have considered, to find out about particular problems that the contract should address, and to suggest terms necessary to protect the client's interest." Elizabeth Fajans, Mary R. Falk & Helene S. Shapo, *Writing for Law Practice* 479 (2004).

NOT THIS:

Ex. 2

7. **DESCRIPTION OF PET.** Only the following described pet is authorized to be kept in Residents' dwelling unit. **NO substitutions are allowed.** No other pet (including offspring) shall be permitted on the premises by Residents or Residents' guests or occupants, at any time. **NO VISITING PETS.** This prohibition includes birds (except those that are caged), Bull Mastiffs, Bull Terriers, chinchillas, Chow Chows, Doberman Pinschers, ferrets, fish (in tanks 20 gallons or more without adequate insurance naming Serafina Village Leasing as additional insured), German Shepherds, Huskies, iguanas, insects, Malamutes, monkeys, Pit Bulls (aka American Staffordshire Terriers, Staffordshire Bull Terriers, or American Pit Bull Terriers), Pot-Bellied Pigs, rabbits, raccoons, Rhodesian Ridgebacks, rodents of any kind, Rotweillers, skunks, snakes or reptiles of any kind, Tarantulas, and Scorpions or spiders of any kind, weasels. *See SPECIFICALLY PROHIBITED BREEDS.

The provisions are redundant (some dog breeds are named twice) and confusing. Architecturally, the provisions are a mess.

. . .

9. **THE COMBINED WEIGHT OF ANY TWO (2) PETS MAY NOT EXCEED FORTY (40) POUNDS.**
10. **SPECIFICALLY PROHIBITED BREEDS: THE FOLLOWING SPECIFIC BREEDS OF DOGS (OR DOGS MIXED WITH THESE BREEDS) ARE NOT PERMITTED.** Pit Bulls (aka American Staffordshire Terriers, Staffordshire Bull Terriers, or American Pit Bull Terriers), Bull Terriers, Bull Mastiffs, German Shepherds, Huskies, Malamutes, Doberman Pinschers, Rotweillers, Chow Chows, and Rhodesian Ridgebacks. Dogs must be contained in an area so as not to interfere with any maintenance service which has been requested. **No wild animals are permitted** – such as birds (except those that are caged), chinchillas, ferrets, fish (in tanks 20 gallons or more without adequate insurance naming Serafina Village Leasing as additional insured), iguanas, monkeys, pot-bellied pigs, rabbits, raccoons, rodents of any kind, skunks, snakes or reptiles of any kind, tarantulas, scorpions or spiders of any kind, weasels.
11. **SPECIFIC TYPES OF PETS.** The following rules apply to specific types of pets:

    Dogs

    Dogs must be spayed or neutered. Veterinary proof may be required. No puppies (four (4) months or less) are allowed. No adult dog, fully grown, will exceed forty (40) pounds. **In an apartment home, two (2) dogs will be allowed as long as they do not exceed the forty (40) pound weight limit.**

    Cats

    No cat is permitted unless it has been de-clawed and spayed or neutered. Veterinary proof is required. Your cat must be kept in the apartment at all times except when transporting the cat. Under no circumstances are cats allowed on apartment balconies or in common indoor or outdoor areas. Cat litter must be double-bagged in plastic prior to disposal in the garbage. Use of a litter box is required and regular disposal of waste and cleaning is required. You may not dispose of litter in toilets, even if the litter is marked "flushable". Cat litter can cause clogs in the pipes and flooding. Resident shall be responsible for all damage caused by violation of these rules.

    Fish

    Stand must be sturdy. No aquarium with a capacity greater than twenty (20) gallons shall be kept on the Premises or in any apartment. Residents must place aquariums in a safe location in the apartment, on a shelf or table giving the aquarium enough support. Residents shall be responsible for all damage caused by leakage or breakage from any aquarium. Resident shall provide proof of adequate insurance naming Serafina Village Leasing as additionally insured if aquarium is twenty (20) gallons or more.

Pet Agreement for Lease Contract from a residential leasing development

BUT THIS:

7. **Types of Pets Allowed; Rules.** You may keep in your apartment only pets of the following kinds and only under the prescribed rules.
   - 7.1 **Fish.** Fish of all kinds are allowed in tanks of less than 20 gallons. You must place the aquarium in a safe location in the apartment and on a stand, table, or shelf that is a sturdy and adequate support. You are responsible for any damage caused by an aquarium that leaks or breaks. If you seek to have a tank of 20 gallons or more, you must have our written approval after you show proof of adequate insurance against damage naming Serafina Village Leasing as an additional insured.
   - 7.2 **Birds.** Birds of any kind are allowed but must be caged.
   - 7.3 **Cats.**
     - (A) **Veterinary procedures.** Only declawed cats that have been spayed or neutered are allowed. Veterinary proof is required.
     - (B) **Spacial restrictions.** Unless transporting the cat, you must keep it in your apartment at all times. Under no circumstances are cats allowed on apartment balconies or in common indoor or outdoor areas.
     - (C) **Waste.** Your cat must use a litter box. You must regularly clean the litter box and double-bag the used litter and waste in plastic before disposing of them in the garbage. You must not dispose of litter in toilets, even if the litter is marked "flushable," because it can cause clogs in the pipes and flooding.
     - (D) **Liability.** You are responsible for all damage caused by a violation of these rules.
   - 7.4 **Dogs.**
     - (A) **Generally.** A dog must be more than 4 months old, and spayed or neutered. Veterinary proof may be required. A fully grown adult dog cannot weigh more than 40 pounds. Two dogs will be allowed as long as their combined weight is 40 pounds or less.
     - (B) **Prohibited breeds of dog.** You must not keep a dog of the following breeds or one that is mixed with one or more of these breeds: pit bull (aka American Staffordshire terrier, Staffordshire bull terrier, or American pit bull terrier), bull terrier, bullmastiff, German shepherd, husky, malamute, Doberman pinscher, Rottweiler, chow chow, and Rhodesian ridgeback.
8. **Prohibited Animals.** Only the types of pets specified in §§ 7.1–7.4 are allowed. You must not have any others in your apartment at any time. You must not allow any wild animal or other wild creature, domesticated or not, of any kind in your apartment at any time.
9. **Offspring of Pets; Visiting Pets.**
   - 9.1 **Offspring of authorized pets.** You must not have an authorized pet's offspring in your apartment at any time.
   - 9.2 **Visiting pets.** Visiting pets are not allowed in your apartment at any time except for caged birds or fish in tanks of less than 20 gallons.

"Plain language is starting to become part of the psyche .... [T]here is a growing recognition that plain-English legal documents are possible and can be legitimately required. It is an important shift in understanding, displacing the long-held view that legalese was inescapable." Robert Eagleson, *Report from Australia*, 28 Clarity 14, 14 (Aug. 1993).

§ 22 Use general terms for general ideas when the terms are clear.

If you can use general terms to convey the idea with greater clarity, do so. Some degree of vagueness is entirely desirable when you can't possibly foresee every situation that might arise, or when the attempt to enumerate specifics is cumbersome, difficult, or even perilous. In such a circumstance, find a broader expression and use it.

The intent is to forbid everything. But the "including" language may arguably permit some creatures.

	NOT THIS:	BUT THIS:
Ex. 1	**9. Pets.** Tenant shall not keep or harbor in or about the Premises any animals or pets of any kind including, but not limited to, dogs, cats, birds, and marine animals. **Residential Rental Contract**	**9. Pets.** Tenant must not keep or harbor at the Premises any animal or pet of any kind.
Ex. 2	At no time prior to the time of the initial public offering did the underwriters or any officers, directors, employees, or others have knowledge of any facts that would suggest that "Palm View" could not be completed in a timely fashion and in accordance with specifications. **Settlement Agreement**	Before the initial public offering, no one knew or had reason to know that Palm View could not be properly completed on time.
Ex. 3	This release includes, but is not limited to, any claims under any local, state, or federal statute or regulations, or under the common law, including any contract or tort claims such as wrongful discharge, fraud, breach of contract, defamation, tortious interference with business expectancy or contract, intentional or negligent misrepresentation, constructive discharge or infliction of emotional distress. **Settlement Agreement**	This release includes all statutory, regulatory, and common-law claims.

"The notion that there is an inherent antagonism between precision and intelligibility or clarity, that where one is achieved the other must suffer, is palpably false and contrary to the true purpose of language—which is to inform, to edify, to illumine. We write so that another will understand us, and not be left in a fog. If we cannot express our ideas clearly, then we have to question how sure and clear-cut is our understanding of them." Robert Eagleson, *Ensnaring Perceptions on Communication: Underlying Obstacles to Lawyers' Writing Plainly*, 62 Clarity 9, 10 (Nov. 2009).

NOT THIS:	BUT THIS:
Ex. 4 Our consultants agree that all ideas, creations, inventions, discoveries, and improvements, whether or not patentable or copyrightable and whether or not fixed in any mode of expression or reduced to practice, that they have conceived of, alone or jointly with others, or that are suggested by or result from any work performed under our consulting agreements with them, or that relate to our actual or anticipated business, or that result from the use of our facilities, equipment, supplies, or information, belong to us as our sole and exclusive property. **Intellectual-Property Agreement**	Our consultants understand and stipulate that everything they produce in their work for us belongs exclusively to us.
Ex. 5 9. (a) Contractor agrees to and does indemnify and hold harmless Company, its officers, employees and agent from and against any and all loss, cost, expense, claim or liability (including but not limited to attorney's fees) resulting from the injury to or loss of life of any person, including but not limited to officers, employees, agents or guests of Contractor or the officers, employees or agents of Company or the loss of or damage to any property (including but not limited to the property of Contractor or Company) which arises from, is incident to or occurs in connection with the performance or non-performance, whether negligent or otherwise, by Contractor of its obligations under this Agreement or the presence on the property of Company of the officers, employees, agents or guests of Contractor, except for such loss of life or personal injury or property loss or damage which is caused solely by the negligence of Company. The foregoing indemnification shall extend not only to Company but also to any corporation controlled by, controlling or under common control with Company. **Company Dormitory-Restaurant Operation Agreement**	**9. Contractor's Indemnity.** **9.1 Scope of indemnity.** The Contractor indemnifies the Company and its officers, employees, and agents against any loss, cost, expense, claim, or liability (including attorney fees) resulting from anyone's personal injury or loss of life, or the loss of or damage to any property, that arises from, is incident to, or occurs in connection with: (A) the Contractor's performance or nonperformance of its contractual obligations, whether negligent or otherwise; or (B) the presence on the Company's property of the Contractor's officers, employees, agents, or guests. **9.2 Extent of indemnity.** Section 9.1 extends to the Company and also to any corporation controlling, controlled by, or under common control with the Company. **9.3 Company's negligence.** Section 9.1 does not apply if the Company's negligence is the sole cause of loss of life, personal injury, or property loss or damage.

The reader is surely out of breath by the end of this convoluted provision—and probably doesn't remember any specific term.

The reader isn't distracted but instead understands the terms.

NOT THIS:	BUT THIS:
Ex. 6 4.4. *Modification or Dissemination of the Content and Website.* None of Berkman, the Community or its Users shall remove, obscure or alter the Content, or the Website itself, nor shall Berkman, the Community or its Users combine or merge the Content with any other programs or content, except as expressly permitted in the User Agreement. Berkman agrees that Berkman, the Community and its Users will not sub-license, distribute, rent, lease, transfer or otherwise make available the Content to any party outside of the Community, or make the Content accessible to any party by broadcast or transmission, including without limitation by television, cable, satellite, telephone, wireless, closed-circuit or Internet broadcasting, or use the Content for systematic downloading, service bureau redistribution services, printing for fee-for-service purposes and/or making print or electronic copies for transmission to non-subscribers, except as may be expressly permitted in the User Agreement. For the avoidance of doubt, all provisions of this Agreement and the User Agreement relating to the Content shall also govern Content that is edited in accordance with the User Agreement. **Distribution Agreement**	4.4 **Modification or dissemination of the Content and Website.** Except as expressly permitted in the User Agreement, Berkman, the Community, and its Users must not: (A) remove, obscure, or alter the Content or the Website itself; (B) combine or merge the Content with any other programs or content; (C) sublicense, distribute, rent, lease, or transfer the Content or otherwise make it available to any party outside the Community; (D) make the Content accessible to any party by broadcast or transmission of any means; or (E) use the Content for systematic downloading, service-bureau redistribution services, printing for fee-for-service purposes, or making print or electronic copies for transmission to nonsubscribers. 4.5 **Edited Content.** All provisions of this Agreement and the User Agreement relating to the Content also govern Content that is edited in accordance with the User Agreement.

> "I have been plagued all my life by scientists, clergymen, politicians, and even lawyers, who talk like parrots, repeating words and phrases picked up from one another by ear without a moment's thought about their meaning, and accept mere associations of ideas as an easy substitute for logic." George Bernard Shaw, "Preface to *The Miraculous Birth of Language*" (1948), in *George Bernard Shaw on Language* 112, 112–13 (Abraham Tauber ed., 1963).

NOT THIS:

Ex. 7

3. *Release of Claims.* In consideration of the Settlement Payment described in Paragraph 1 of this Agreement, and upon the advice of counsel retained by and on behalf of Yeager, if any, Yeager hereby voluntarily, knowingly and willingly, releases and waives all rights and claims to date of every nature and description, both known and unknown, whether in tort, contract, under statute or regulation or otherwise, including, without limitation, claims regarding any aspect of Yeager's employment or separation from employment with Melchior Inc., or any claims relating to any other event occurring prior to and including the date that Yeager executes this Agreement, against Melchior Inc. and the Melchior Inc. Released Parties, including Hardee. The claims released include, but are not limited to, rights or claims under all federal, state and local constitutional and statutory provisions, ordinances, orders and regulations prohibiting employment discrimination based upon race, color, sex, religion, disability, national origin, military service, marital status, retaliation, employment improprieties and interference with protected activities, including but not limited to: (a) Title VII of the Civil Rights Act of 1964, as amended, 42 U.S.C. § 2000e, *et seq.*; (b) the Civil Rights Act of 1866, 1870 and 1871, 42 U.S.C. § 1981, *et seq.*; (c) the Civil Rights Act of 1991, Pub. L. No. 102-166, 105 Stat. 1071-1100; (d) Constitutions of the United States and the State of Florida; (e) the National Labor Relations Act, as amended, 29 U.S.C. § 151, *et seq.*; (f) the Employee Retirement Income Securities Act of 1974, as amended, 29 U.S.C. § 1001, *et seq.*; (but only as to claims arising thereunder prior to the date hereof); (g) the Americans With Disabilities Act, 42 U.S.C. § 12101, *et seq.*; (h) the Florida Civil Rights Act of 1992, Chapter 760, Florida Statutes; (i) the Family and Medical Leave Act of 1993; (j) the Florida Whistleblower Act, Chapter 448, Florida Statutes; (k) the Age Discrimination in Employment Act of 1967, as amended, 29 U.S.C. § 621, *et seq.*; (l) the Fair Labor Standards Act, 29 U.S.C. § 201, *et seq.*; (m) the Equal Pay Act 29 U.S.C. § 206; (n) the Older Workers Benefit Protection Act, 29 U.S.C. § 621, *et. seq.*; (o) the Uniformed Services Employment and Re-Employment Rights Act, 38 U.S.C. § 4301, *et. seq.*; (p) all other federal, state and local civil rights acts, regulations, orders and executive orders relating to any term, condition or termination of employment and (q) any and all state statutes or judicial decisions relating in any way to any term, condition or termination of employment. The claims released also include, but are not limited to, any and all claims for back pay, front pay, vacation pay or sick pay, bonuses and any other form of compensation or benefits; employment discrimination, wrongful or retaliatory discharge; and any claim in tort, such as, but not limited to, assault, battery, false imprisonment, negligent hiring, negligent retention, defamation, or intentional and/or negligent infliction of emotional distress; promissory estoppel, breach of an express or implied employment contract and for violation of any and all other federal, state or local laws, statutes or ordinances, including specifically any and all common law claims or causes of action of any variety.

Settlement Agreement and Full Release of All Claims

BUT THIS:

3. **Release of Claims.**
   - 3.1 **Advice of counsel.** Yeager has had the opportunity to retain counsel and obtain advice.
   - 3.2 **General release.** In consideration of the Settlement Payment described in § 1 of this Agreement, Yeager voluntarily, knowingly, and willingly releases and waives all rights and claims to date of every nature and description, both known and unknown, relating to all aspects of Yeager's employment or separation from employment with Melchior and all claims relating to any other event occurring before and including the date on which Yeager signs this Agreement against Melchior and the Melchior Released Parties, including Hardee.
   - 3.3 **Claims expressly released.** Yeager expressly releases and waives claims related to employment discrimination, regardless of the basis, and waives all claims under statutes, regulations, orders, executive orders, and judicial decisions relating to all terms of employment.
   - 3.4 **Exception.** Yeager does not release or waive any claim under the Employee Retirement Income Securities Act of 1974, as amended, 29 U.S.C. § 1001 et seq., if the claim arose before the date of this Agreement.

§ 23 Minimize the duplication of ideas.

Eliminate repetitiousness. In old-style drafting, redundant provisions were commonplace. Drafters would say the same thing, more or less, in different places—but often with variable expressions. This habit is dangerous, given that judges are likely to read purposeful changes in sense into variations in wording.[1]

If the identical subject matter is dealt with in two places, and the two passages are irreconcilable, the judicial interpreter is put into an unenviable predicament. (All the while, your client would be suffering through needless litigation.) Some courts hold that the earlier of two irreconcilable passages will control; others hold that the later will control; and still others hold that they're both considered nullities.[2]

NOT THIS:	BUT THIS:
Ex. 1 4. If any work designed or specified by the architect is abandoned or suspended, in whole or in part, the architect is not to be paid for the service rendered on account of it. 5. In the event the project is abandoned or terminated, the architect shall not be entitled to any of the above fees but shall be paid with the rate of one hundred twenty-five dollars ($125.00) per hour for work actually done on the project up until that time of the termination of the work and not to exceed fifty (50) per cent of the basic rate of the architects total fee provided herein. **Contract for architectural services connected to hotel construction**	4. **Developer's Rejection of Architect's Services.** If Architect designs or specifies work for part of the project and Developer abandons or suspends building that part, Developer has rejected the work and Architect will not be paid for the work. 5. **Developer's Termination of Project.** If Developer chooses to terminate the entire project, then instead of the fees on the schedule in § 2, Architect is entitled to payment at the rate of $125 per hour for work done and accepted on the project before termination. The payment cannot exceed 50% of the basic rate of the architect's total fee.

Does the architect get paid or not? These conflicting clauses resulted in litigation.

1 *See* Antonin Scalia & Bryan A. Garner, *Reading Law: The Interpretation of Legal Texts* 170 (2012) ("A word or phrase is presumed to bear the same meaning throughout a text; a material variation in terms suggests a variation in meaning.").

2 *See id.* at 189. *See also, e.g., Guidry v. CSI Blasters/Painters, Inc.*, 724 F.Supp. 435, 437 (W.D. La. 1989) (nullifying mutually repugnant clauses); *Bannin v. Peck*, 52 N.E.2d 599, 599 (N.Y. 1943) (same).

NOT THIS:	BUT THIS:
Ex. 2 1. This agreement is effective as of September 17, 2019. . . . 4. Ennendale is authorized by Oriel National Bank to draw on the account of Manny Riordan up to an aggregate amount of U.S. $63,768.13 available by Ennendale's draft at sight when accompanied by Ennendale's signed statement that the contractor Armin Construction Company has defaulted or failed within ten (10) months to complete the paving improvements required in conjunction with the platting of the Stonybrook Annex, lots 1346–1433. . . . 8. Oriel National Bank hereby engages that Ennendale's draft(s) under and in compliance with the terms of this letter of credit will be duly honored if presented to Oriel National Bank on or before January 1, 2019 together with the document(s) specified herein. **Letter of credit**	1. **Effective Date.** The Effective Date of this Agreement is September 17, 2019. . . . 4. **Authorization for Draws.** Oriel National Bank authorizes Ennendale to draw on the account of Manny Riordan and will honor the drafts at sight if Ennendale presents a signed statement that the contractor Armin Construction Company has defaulted or failed within 10 months of the Effective Date to complete the paving improvements required in conjunction with the platting of the Stonybrook Annex, lots 1346–1433. The aggregate amount of draws is U.S.$63,768.13. . . . 5. **Termination Date.** This Agreement expires 12 months after the Effective Date.

Although draws are permitted for at least 10 months after the effective date, the last provision bars draws after only 3.5 months. No express termination date is stated anywhere.

"Legal thoughts are meant to emerge from the document pure and unsullied, but all too frequently, they are lost to view in an imperfectly designed document that has no internal cohesion. The design is vital to an understanding of the document."
Robert C. Dick, *Legal Drafting* 51 (2d ed. 1985).

Imposing a consistent numbering system

§ 24 Adhere to an exacting system of indented sections and further subsections—preferably the one explained below.

Adopt a numbering system that progresses logically from higher-order to lower-order provisions. The recommended format has major divisions with Arabic numerals; second-level divisions with a single decimal, arranging the numbers that follow the decimal in ascending order from 1 to 999 without regarding them as parts of a mathematical decimal (in sequence: §§ 1.1 . . . 1.99, etc.); third-level divisions signaled by a capital letter in parentheses; fourth-level divisions signaled by an Arabic numeral in parentheses; and fifth-level divisions signaled by lowercase letters in parentheses. Hence:

```
1.  Main Heading.
    1.1 Subheading. -------------------------------------------
        ---------------------------------------------:
        (A) Subheading (if needed). --------------------------
            ---------------------------------------:
            (1) Sub-Subheading (if needed). ------------------
                ----------------------------------------------:
                (a) ------------------------------------------
                    ---------------------------------;
                (b) ------------------------------------------
                    ---------------------------------; or
                (c) ------------------------------------------
                    --------------------------; and
            (2) Sub-Subheading (if needed). ------------------
                ----------------------------------------------.
        (B) Subheading (if needed). --------------------------
            ----------------------------------------------:
            (1) Sub-Subheading (if needed). ------------------
                ---------------------------------------; or
            (2) Sub-Subheading (if needed). ------------------
                ----------------------------------------------.
    1.2 Subheading. -------------------------------------------
        ---------------------------------------------:
        (A) Subheading (if needed). --------------------------
            ---------------------------------------; and
        (B) Subheading (if needed). --------------------------
            ---------------------------------------:
            (1) Sub-Subheading (if needed). ------------------
                ----------------------------------------------:
                (a) ------------------------------------------
                    -------------------------; or
                (b) ------------------------------------------
                    ------------------------------------; and
            (2) Sub-Subheading (if needed). ------------------
                ----------------------------------------------.
```

The recommended form.

This numbering system has many advantages, one being that you'll do better at establishing sets and subsets than you will with other systems. Sections 6.2 and 6.3 must be subsets of 6—whereas if they were merely (b) and (c) you might get sloppy, as experience shows that drafters tend to do. Also, cross-references—to the extent they're needed—become easier, whether you're referring to another provision in the same contract, amending a provision later on, or simply referring to a provision at any time.

Decimal numbering (with only one decimal level) keeps the drafter as well as the readers focused on the main message of each provision. It helps the drafter limit each provision to one main idea.

Although some might say that this type of numbering system is itself legalistic, it really isn't: it appeals to the reader's yearning for sequence and orderliness. And it anchors what otherwise tends to look like floating text.

One last thing: Each subpart should be duly numbered. You should never have multiple subparts (usually in the form of multiple paragraphs) assigned to one number.

A contract's numbering system shouldn't be distracting. Can you imagine discussing this part of the agreement on a conference call with executives, a client, or a sales force? Reading such a long series of numbers aloud wastes time and creates confusion.

NOT THIS:	BUT THIS:
Ex. 1 **14.3 Integration of Equipment Data** . . . **14.3.2 Buyer Furnished Equipment** . . . 14.3.2.5 The BFE Data shall be delivered in digital format (SGML) and/or in Portable Document Format (PDF), as agreed between the Buyer and the Seller. **Purchase Agreement from a major European aeronautic defense and space company**	**14.3 Equipment-data integration.** . . . (B) **Buyer-furnished equipment.** . . . (5) **Delivery format.** The BFE Data must be delivered in digital format (SGML) or in portable document format (PDF), as agreed between the Buyer and the Seller.
Ex. 2 5.2 Promotional Activity. In consideration of the Promotional Funds provided by the Company, Customer agrees to perform the following activities: 5.2.1 Customer and Company will mutually develop and implement an annual program. 5.2.2 Customer will feature and promote Company's frozen carbonated Beverages with appropriate promotional activities. 5.2.3 Customer will conduct mutually agreed promotions and advertising. 5.2.4 [Add additional activities as appropriate] **Marketing Agreement from a major beverage company**	**5.2 Promotional activity.** In exchange for Promotional Funds from the Company, Hubinger will perform appropriate promotional activities, including: (A) mutually developing and implementing an annual program with the Company; (B) featuring and promoting the Company's frozen carbonated beverages; and (C) conducting mutually accepted promotions and advertising.

This simpler numbering system helps people keep up in a busy corporate world. It's readable and keeps any discussion of the contract focused on the content rather than the numbering system.

This format easily allows additional specific activities to be added.

NOT THIS:

Ex. 3

Assignments and Leases. Effective as of the Distribution Date, Fee will (a) assign to the Branded Subsidiary all of Calebra's rights, title, and interest in the Branded Trademarks (as defined herein) and (b) grant to the Branded Subsidiary a nonexclusive royalty-free right to use *Calebra*, *Calebra Foods*, and red, stylized *R* trademarks (collectively, the "Calebra Trademarks") in the United States, its territories and possessions and the Commonwealth of Puerto Rico and military installations on packaging, promotional or advertising materials for a period of one (1) year following the Distribution Date. The "Branded Trademarks" refers to (a) all the Trademarks, other than the Calebra Trademarks and the Yummy Flakes and Scone Devil Trademarks, previously used or currently owned by Calebra Foods or licensed to Calebra Foods or its subsidiaries that are or have been almost always associated with the Branded Business or intended almost always for use therein and (b) certain recipe names used in connection with snack-mix products produced by the Branded Business. The license term relating to the use of the Calebra Trademarks may be extended for a period of no more than one (1) additional year for the purpose of permitting the sale of the materials that remain on hand on the one-year anniversary of the Distribution Date. The Branded Subsidiary will agree that it will (a) make reasonable efforts to conclude the use of such product packaging and promotional and advertising materials by the one-year anniversary of the Distribution Date and (b) not place any orders for such product packaging and advertising or promotional materials at any time after the one-year anniversary of the Distribution Date.

Trademark-License Agreement

Not only is the paragraph run together in violation of § 35, but also the number *one* is doubled up in the "one (1)" fashion, making it look at a glance as if there's another enumeration going on; this violates § 73. Some drafters would change the second (a)–(b) set to (c)–(d). Others would resort to (x)–(y). But then what do you do with the third (a)–(b) set?

"Almost always" introduces a strange standard into the provision. The phrase has been deleted in the revision.

BUT THIS:

7.2 **Assignments and Leases.**

(A) **Calebra's duties.** Effective as of the Distribution Date, Calebra will:

(1) assign to the Branded Subsidiary all of Calebra's right, title, and interest in the Branded Trademarks (see D); and

(2) grant to the Branded Subsidiary a nonexclusive royalty-free right to use *Calebra*, *Calebra Foods*, and red, stylized *R* trademarks—the Calebra Trademarks—in the United States, its territories and possessions, the Commonwealth of Puerto Rico, and military installations on packaging, promotional, or advertising materials for 1 year after the Distribution Date.

(B) **"Branded Trademarks."** The term "Branded Trademarks" means:

(1) all the trademarks, other than the Calebra Trademarks and the Yummy Flakes and Scone Devil Trademarks, that were previously used or are currently owned by Calebra Foods or licensed to Calebra Foods or its subsidiaries and that are or have been associated with the Branded Business or intended for use in that business; and

(2) certain recipe names used for snack-mix products produced by the Branded Business.

(C) **Branded Subsidiary's duties.** The Branded Subsidiary will:

(1) make reasonable efforts to conclude the use of the product-packaging, promotional, and advertising materials by the 1-year anniversary of the Distribution Date; and

(2) place no orders for product-packaging, advertising, or promotional materials anytime after the 1-year anniversary of the Distribution Date.

(D) **Extension of license term.** The license to use the Calebra Trademarks may be extended for no more than 1 additional year after the 1-year anniversary of the Distribution Date to permit the sale of materials still on hand.

The broken-out enumerations and the greater use of headings aren't readily achievable without the numbering system. And once the numbering system is in place, it's possible to improve organization. In this example, the original organization needed to be changed because it plopped a lengthy definition into the middle of the paragraph.

NOT THIS:

Ex. 4

7. **OWNERSHIP**

7.1 Ownership of Proprietary Rights. Subject to Section 7.2 and except for Inventions that I can prove qualify fully under the provisions of California Labor Code section 2870 or other similar law (hereinafter "Section 2870") and that I have set forth in **Exhibit A** (Prior Inventions), I hereby assign and agree to assign in the future (when such Inventions are first reduced to practice or first fixed in a tangible medium, as applicable) to the Company or its designee, my entire right, title, and interest in and to any and all Inventions (and all Proprietary Rights relating to such Inventions) which I may solely or jointly conceive, develop, reduce to practice or otherwise create during my employment with the Company or an affiliate of the Company (a) which relate at the time of creation, conception or reduction to practice to the Company's business or actual or demonstrably anticipated research and development, or (b) which are developed on any amount of the Company's time or with the use of any of the Company's equipment, supplies, facilities or Proprietary Information, or (c) which result from any work I perform for the Company. Inventions assigned to the Company or to a third party as directed by the Company pursuant to Section 7.2 are referred to in this Agreement as **"Company Inventions."**

Employee-Inventions and Proprietary-Rights Assignment Agreement from a major software developer and provider

BUT THIS:

7. **Ownership.**

7.1 **Ownership of proprietary rights.**

(A) **Assignment.** Subject to § 7.2, you assign to the Company and agree to assign to the Company in the future (when an Invention is first reduced to practice or first fixed in a tangible medium, as applicable) all Employee Rights other than those relating to Inventions that you can prove fully qualify under California Labor Code § 2870 or similar law (collectively, "§ 2870") and that you have set forth in Exhibit A (Prior Inventions).

(B) **Definitions for § 7.1.** The following definitions apply in this § 7.1:

(1) "Employee Rights" means all your interests in, and all Proprietary Rights relating to, an Invention that you solely or jointly conceive, develop, reduce to practice, or otherwise create during your employment with the Company, but only if such interests and Proprietary Rights:

(a) relate at the time of creation, conception, or reduction to practice to the Company's business or to actual or demonstrably anticipated research and development;

(b) are developed on the Company's time or with the use of any of the Company's equipment, supplies, facilities, or Proprietary Information; or

(c) result from any work you perform for the Company.

(2) "Company" means the Company or any affiliate of the Company.

(3) "Company Inventions" are inventions assigned to the Company or to a third party as directed by the Company under § 7.2.

"Consistency in numbering is crucial; having chosen a system, the drafter should apply it remorselessly." Peter Butt & Richard Castle, *Modern Legal Drafting* 137 (2001).

NOT THIS:

Ex. 5

(6) For the legal consulting services provided pursuant to paragraph 4, the Company shall pay or provide, as applicable, to Consultant the following: (a) a quarterly retainer of $50,000, payable as of the commencement of the one-year term beginning May 8, 2018 and continuing quarterly thereafter for each quarterly period Consultant is obliged to provide legal consulting services pursuant to paragraph 4, provided that (i) Consultant has provided legal counseling services as reasonably requested in accordance with paragraph 4 for the immediately preceding quarterly period and (ii) with respect to the one-year term beginning May 8, 2019, Consultant has elected to renew the initial 2-year term referenced in paragraph 4 and (iii) with respect to the one-year term beginning May 8, 2020, Consultant has elected to renew the second successive one-year term referenced in paragraph 4; (b) a cellular telephone and fax machine; the cost of maintaining two (2) cellular telephone lines and one (1) fax telephone line; and the cost of a fax machine maintenance agreement; and (c) a Deferred Stock Award (the "Award"), to be awarded as of the effective date of this Agreement, with respect to the 75,000 shares (the "Shares") of the Common Stock of the Company (the "Common Stock"), subject to the following terms and conditions: (i) The Award shall vest and the Shares shall be issued and distributed to Consultant in accordance with the following numbers of shares vesting/distribution dates: 25,000 on May 7, 2019; 25,000 on May 7, 2020; 25,000 on May 7, 2021; provided that (A) with respect to Shares scheduled to vest in 2019, Consultant has provided legal consulting services as reasonably requested in accordance with paragraph 4, (B) with respect to Shares scheduled to vest in 2020, Consultant has elected to renew the initial one-year term referenced in paragraph 4 for the period May 8, 2019 through May 7, 2020 and (C) with respect to Shares scheduled to vest in 2021, Consultant has elected to renew the second successive one-year renewal term referenced in paragraph 4 and has provided legal consulting services as reasonably requested in accordance with paragraph 4 for the period May 8, 2020 through May 7, 2021. (ii) Any unvested portion of the Award shall be forfeited to the Company upon (A) the termination of Consultant's employment with the Company for any reason other than due to Retirement at or after age 65, (B) Consultant's death or Disability prior to the one-year term beginning May 8, 2018 referenced in paragraph 4, or (C) upon Consultant's failure to comply with his obligations under the Agreement or the Agreements described in paragraph 14. In the event of the termination of this Agreement due to Consultant's death or Disability during or after the one-year term beginning May 8, 2018 referenced in paragraph 4, any unvested portion of the Award shall be forfeited on a pro-rata basis upon Consultant's death or Disability as follows: the number of shares to be forfeited shall be the product of 25,000 and a fraction equal to the number of days after Consultant's death or disability remaining in the current one-year term during which Consultant dies or becomes disabled divided by 365. (iii) Consultant will not have the right to receive a certificate for the Shares or vote the Shares or receive dividends on the Shares prior to the date such Shares vest pursuant to the terms of this paragraph 6. However, during the Consulting Term, the Company shall pay to Consultant cash payments in lieu of and equal to dividends otherwise payable with respect to the 75,000 Shares, as such dividends are declared and paid on the Company's Common Stock. The Company's obligations to make payments in lieu of dividends on the 75,000 Shares shall cease once Shares vest pursuant to the terms of this paragraph 6 or in the event the Shares are forfeited. (iv) Until the Shares vest pursuant to the terms of this paragraph 6, such Shares are non-transferable and may not be assigned, pledged or hypothecated and shall not be subject to execution, attachment or similar process. Any attempt to violate these restrictions will result in the immediate forfeiture of the Award and the Shares. (v) Upon the vesting of the Shares pursuant to the terms of this paragraph 6, a Certificate for such Shares will be issued to Consultant by the Transfer Agent. (vi) The terms and provisions of this Award (including, without limitation, the terms and provisions relating to the number and class of Shares subject to this Award) may be adjusted by the Company in the event of any recapitalization, merger, consolidation, reorganization, stock dividend, stock split, split-up or other change in corporate structure affecting the Common Stock. (vii) The Award is made pursuant to the 2011 Performance Incentive Plan (the "Plan") of the Company, to the extent any provision of this Award is inconsistent or in conflict with any term or provision of the Plan, the Plan shall govern. Capitalized terms not otherwise defined herein have the same meaning set forth in the Plan. The Company shall reimburse Consultant for reasonable business expenses incurred in providing services pursuant to this Agreement.

Consulting Agreement with a tobacco company

At first glance, (iii) would seem to have two types of subsets, (b)–(c) and (2)–(1) (the latter in that reversed order). Actually, the romanettes (i)–(iii) all go under (a), and the needless word–numeral pairs "two (2)" and "one (1)" just add to the confusion in this intimidating mass of verbiage.

The first set of romanettes.

Note how odd "two (2)" and "one (1)" are when none of the other numbers are similarly doubled.

Here begins a second set of romanettes. A clear cross-reference to § 6(i) isn't possible.

The numbering system for embedded subparts has shifted here to (A)–(B).

Note how ungainly it is to express mathematical calculations in words alone.

The wording issues in this provision are legion.

This is the last of the second set of romanettes, two of which contained embedded subsets.

BUT THIS:

3. Compensation for Legal-Consulting Services.

3.1 Forms of compensation.

(A) **Cash retainer.** The Company will pay Rhinegold a quarterly retainer of $50,000 when the 1-year term starts on May 8, 2018, and again for each successive quarterly period in which Rhinegold provides legal-consulting services as reasonably requested under § 2. If Rhinegold elects to renew, quarterly payments will continue under the renewal terms described in § 2.

Note how the tiered numbering system, with hanging indents, reinforces meaning.

(B) **Reasonable expenses.** The Company will reimburse Rhinegold for reasonable business expenses incurred in providing services under this Agreement.

(C) **Deferred-stock award.** As of this Agreement's effective date, the Company will award Rhinegold a deferred-stock award of 75,000 shares of the Company's common stock. Until the shares vest under § 3.2, they:

(1) are nontransferable;
(2) cannot be assigned, pledged, or hypothecated; and
(3) are not subject to execution, attachment, or a similar process.

(D) **Cash in lieu of dividends.** For shares that are neither vested nor forfeited, the Company will pay Rhinegold cash equal to the dividends that the Company declares and pays on its common stock.

Consider how much thought must go into devising headings and subheadings like these.

(E) **Communications equipment.** The Company will provide Rhinegold with a cellphone and fax machine, both of which Rhinegold will return to the Company when he no longer provides services under this Agreement. While Rhinegold provides those services, the Company will also pay for 2 cellphone lines, 1 fax line, and a fax-machine maintenance agreement.

3.2 Vesting of deferred stock. When shares vest, the Transfer Agent will issue a Certificate to Rhinegold for them. The shares will vest and the Company will issue and distribute shares according to this schedule and these conditions:

(A) **First vesting:** 25,000 shares on May 7, 2019, if Rhinegold has provided legal-consulting services as reasonably requested during the initial 1-year term;

(B) **Second vesting:** 25,000 shares on May 7, 2020, if Rhinegold has elected to renew for a second 1-year term and has provided legal-consulting services as reasonably requested during the period; and

(C) **Final vesting:** 25,000 shares on May 7, 2021, if Rhinegold has elected to renew for a third 1-year term and has provided legal-consulting services as reasonably requested during the period.

3.3 Forfeiture of unvested shares. Rhinegold will forfeit to the Company any unvested shares if:

(A) he is no longer employed by the Company for a reason other than his retirement at or after age 65;

(B) he fails to meet his obligations under this Agreement or the Agreements described in § 3.7;

According to readability principles, each tabulated subpart counts as a separate "sentence" for purposes of computing average length. See § 16.

(C) he attempts to assign or pledge unvested shares or to subject them to execution, attachment, or a similar process; or

(D) he dies or becomes disabled during or after the 1-year term, beginning May 8, 2018, in which circumstance a pro rata portion of the 25,000 shares applicable to the annual vesting period in which the death or disability occurs will vest and not be forfeited.

3.4 The Company's right to adjust deferred-stock award's terms. The Company may adjust this award (including the terms relating to the number and class of shares subject to this award) if any change occurs in the common stock, including recapitalization, merger, consolidation, reorganization, stock dividend, stock split, and split-up.

3.5 Performance Incentive Plan. The deferred-stock award under § 3.1(C) is made under the Company's 2011 Performance Incentive Plan. If a provision of this award conflicts with a term of the Plan, the Plan governs. Capitalized terms not otherwise defined in this Agreement have the same meanings as in the Plan.

NOT THIS:

Ex. 6

6. Representations and Warranties

6.1. Borrower, Guarantor and Fee Owner respectively represent, warrant and covenant that:

6.1.(a) Borrower is a duly organized and validly existing partnership organized under the laws of the state of Missouri. Guarantor is a duly organized, validly existing corporation organized under the laws of the state of Missouri and is currently in good standing therewith. Fee Owner is a duly organized, validly existing corporation organized under the laws of the State of Missouri and is currently in good standing therewith. Borrower, Guarantor and Fee Owner have the authority and power to own their respective properties, conduct their respective businesses and the same are now being conducted and to consummate the transactions contemplated hereby.

6.1.(b) The general partner of Borrower (hereinafter referred to as the "General Partner") is duly organized and validly existing under the laws of the state of Missouri and is currently in good standing therewith and has the power and authority to conduct its business as the same is now being conducted and to consummate the transactions contemplated hereby.

6.1.(c) Borrower is duly authorized to execute, deliver and perform its obligations under the Loan Documents and all additional agreements, assignments and security arrangements called by thereby, and to incur the Obligations and make the representations, warranties and covenants made therein. This Agreement constitutes, and the other Loan Documents and the additional agreements, assignments and security arrangements called for thereby when issued and delivered hereunder for value received, will constitute the valid and legally binding obligations of Borrower, enforceable in accordance with their respective terms subject, however, to bankruptcy, reorganization and like laws of general application designed for debtors' relief and the principle that specific performance or equitable relief may be subject to the discretion of the tribunal petitioned for such relief.

Purchase Agreement from a major law firm

BUT THIS:

6. **Representations and Warranties.** Knox, Murphy, and FinCo represent and warrant as follows:

(A) Knox is a valid partnership in good standing under Missouri law. Murphy is a valid corporation in good standing under Missouri law. FinCo is a valid corporation in good standing under Missouri law. Knox, Murphy, and FinCo have the authority to own their respective properties, conduct their respective businesses, and complete the transactions in this Agreement.

(B) Knox's general partner, Cox, is duly organized and in good standing under Missouri law and has authority to conduct its current business and to complete the transactions in this Agreement.

(C) Knox is authorized to sign and deliver the Loan Documents and all additional arrangements and to incur and perform the obligations and to make the representations, warranties, and covenants made in them.

(D) This Agreement, the other Loan Documents, and any additional agreements, assignments, and security arrangements, when issued and delivered for value, will constitute Knox's valid and legally binding obligations, subject to bankruptcy, reorganization, and like laws of general application designed for debtors' relief, and to the principle that specific performance or equitable relief may be subject to the discretion of the tribunal petitioned for that relief.

"What is often called 'legal' phraseology is no more than inept writing or the unnecessary use of obscure or entangled phrases." Samuel Goldberg, *Hints on Draftsmanship*, 5 Prac. Law. 39, 40 (1959).

§ 25 Impose consistency in numbering.

Whatever your numbering system, be rigorously consistent. Avoid off-the-wall conventions. In some contracts, for example, an insertion between 5 and 6 becomes 5c or 5m for reasons that will be inscrutable to all but insiders. If the subparts within 5 are 5.1–5.4, then the new insertion could become 5.5. Or if the insertion needs to be between 5.1 and 5.2, either insert and renumber or try 5.1A or (less good) 5.1.5. Or else it could be added to 6—and the main heading for either 5 or 6 could be adjusted to allow for the new matter.

Finally, avoid the phrase "intentionally omitted" after a paragraph number. If something has been omitted, then you should normally renumber the paragraphs so that no gaps are indicated. But this isn't an absolute: if you're negotiating a long, complex contract that has many internal cross-references, you may decide not to fix all the cross-references—especially if the counterparty might force you to reinsert the deleted provisions. So "intentionally omitted" may sometimes prove prudent.

NOT THIS:	BUT THIS:
Ex. 1 3. Employee's Representations and Warranties. 3.1 The Employee represents and warrants that the execution and delivery of this Agreement and the fulfillment of its terms: (i) will not constitute a default under or conflict with any agreement or other instrument to which he is a party or by which he is bound; (ii) do not require the consent of any person or entity. Further, with respect to any past engagement of the Employee with third parties (for purposes hereof, such third parties shall be referred to as "Other Employers"), the Employee represents, warrants and undertakes that: (a) his engagement with the Company is and/or will not be in breach of any of his undertakings toward Other Employers, and (b) he will not disclose to the Company, nor use, in provision of any services to the Company, any proprietary or confidential information belonging to any Other Employer. **Personal Employment Agreement from a nitric-oxide therapeutic company**	**3. Morrison's Representations and Warranties.** **3.1 Entering into the agreement.** Morrison represents and warrants as follows: (A) **Current agreement**. This Agreement does not cause Morrison to: (1) default on or conflict with another agreement that Morrison is a party to or bound by; or (2) obtain consent from another person or entity. (B) **Past employment.** Morrison's engagement with the Company will not: (1) breach Morrison's obligations to a third party arising from past engagements with that third party ("Other Employers"); or (2) involve the use or disclosure of proprietary or confidential information of any Other Employer in Morrison's providing services to the Company.

NOT THIS:	BUT THIS:
Ex. 2 7.6.1 *Service of Notices.* Any notices or other communications given under this Agreement shall be given in writing and may be given by (i) in-person hand delivery; (ii) overnight delivery service; (iii) facsimile transmission to the number or numbers listed below; or (iv) certified mail, with postage prepaid and return receipt requested and shall be deemed properly served upon a party when (x) such notice is received at the address or facsimile number as any party to this Agreement may hereafter designate by written notice served and delivered as described herein; (y) delivery is attempted by one of the methods described herein and is refused; or (z) delivery is attempted by one of the methods described herein and the party to whom such notice has been sent is no longer at the address or facsimile number listed below and has not provided notice of a different address or facsimile number as provided herein. **Purchase & Assignment Agreement from a major law firm**	**7.6 Service of notices.** (A) **Method.** A notice or other communication given under this Agreement must be in writing and given via: (1) in-person hand-delivery; (2) overnight delivery service; (3) fax transmission to the numbers provided in this Agreement; or (4) certified mail, with postage prepaid and return receipt requested. (B) **Proper service.** A notice or communication is properly served on a party when delivery by a method in (A) is attempted and the receiving party: (1) receives it at the address or fax number that the party (a) designated in this Agreement; or (b) later designates by written notice that is delivered by a method specified in (A); (2) refuses it; or (3) is no longer at the address or fax number listed in this Agreement and has not given notice of a different address or fax number.

Note the crazy variation in numbering patterns.

The revision eliminates the romanettes altogether. See § 26.

"Some drafters are concerned that in the process of 'translating' a form into plain language, they will inadvertently change the substantive meaning. Perhaps a horror story circulates to support this concern. 'If it ain't broke,' the opponent might conclude, 'let's not fix it.' I must say I question the premise: if it is not written with clarity, it *is* 'broke.'" Scott J. Burnham, *Drafting and Analyzing Contracts* 288 (3d ed. 2003).

NOT THIS:

Ex. 3

TERMS AND CONDITIONS

1. Owner's Representations and Warranties.

1.01 Sole Proprietor. Owner represents and warrants to Purchaser that Owner is the sole and exclusive proprietor, throughout the world, of that certain original novel written by Owner entitled [*title of work*] (the "Literary Property").

1.02 Facts. Owner represents and warrants to Purchaser that the following statements are true and correct in all respects with respect to the Literary Property:

(i) Owner is the sole author of the Literary Property. As such, Owner represents and warrants that Owner is the sole holder of any and all common law and federally registered copyrights in the Literary Property.

(ii) The Literary Property was first published on [*date of publication*] by [*name of publisher*] under the title [*title of publication*], and was registered for copyright in the name of [*name of author*], under copyright registration number [*registration number*], in the Office of the United States Register of Copyrights, Washington, D.C.

(iii) No motion picture or dramatic version of the Literary Property, or any part of the Literary Property, has been manufactured, produced, presented or authorized; no radio or television development, presentation or program based on the Literary Property, or any part of the Literary Property, has been manufactured, produced, presented, broadcast or authorized; and no written or oral agreements or commitments with respect to the Literary Property or with respect to any right in the Literary Property, have been made or entered into by or on behalf of Owner (except with respect to the publication of the Literary Property as set forth above) prior to this Agreement.

Publishing-Rights Assignment from 1 Lawrence A. Waks & Brad L. Whitlock, *Texas Practice Guide Business Transactions: Entertainment Contracts* § 4:365, at 539 (2017)

BUT THIS:

The Agreement

1. Jenkins's Representations and Warranties. Jenkins represents and warrants to Frobes as follows:

1.1 Authorship. Jenkins is the sole author of the novel entitled [*title of work*]. The term "Literary Property" refers to this novel.

1.2 Ownership. Jenkins is the exclusive worldwide owner of the Literary Property.

1.3 Copyright registration. The Literary Property was registered for copyright in the name of Jenkins, under copyright-registration number [*registration number*], in the Office of the United States Register of Copyrights, Washington, D.C.

1.4 Copyright holder. Jenkins is the sole holder of all copyrights in the Literary Property.

1.5 First publication. The Literary Property was first published on [*date of publication*] by [*name of publisher*] under the title [*title of publication*].

1.6 Derived works. No motion-picture, dramatic, radio, or television version of the Literary Property, or any part of it, has already been manufactured, produced, presented, or authorized.

1.7 No other agreements. Except for the first publication, no written or oral agreement or commitment regarding any right in the Literary Property has been made or entered into by or on behalf of Jenkins before this Agreement.

§ 26 Avoid romanettes except as a last resort.

The term *romanette* is the drafter's word for a lowercase Roman numeral—(i), (ii), (iii), etc.—the type that pervades so much traditional-style drafting. Romanettes typify drafting that does not feature hanging indents (see § 35) but instead consists of margin-to-margin type. If you do try hanging indents with romanettes, their variable width messes up the indents. Hence they're best avoided, or used only as the last (and sixth) level of subenumeration.

What's wrong with roman numerals? The preceding paragraph sets forth two significant drawbacks: (1) they discourage hanging indents, and (2) they promote large blocks of unreadable text. Further, though, they trip up even lawyers, many of whom struggle to write the numerals up to *xx*. It's commonplace to find documents with romanette lists that omit one number in the sequence. (What's missing? one inevitably wonders.) Finally, romanettes signify an underdeveloped numbering system ill-equipped for sophisticated documents. (See § 24.) As a result, you'll often see old-style forms with provisions having subparts with multiple (i)'s, (ii)'s, and (iii)'s. See Example 6 below.

NOT THIS:	BUT THIS:
Ex. 1 6.3. Conduct. Consultant will comply with all applicable [*name of company*] workplace policies including, but limited to: (i) no smoking; (ii) drug-free environment; (iii) dress code; (iv) nonharassment; (v) travel/expense guidelines; (vi) all safety and security policies (including a prohibition against weapons); and (vii) computer security and use policies. **Consulting-Services-Fee Agreement from 3 Nancy Saint-Paul, Texas Legal Practice Forms 3d *Independent Contractor Agreements* § 50:6, at 729 (2016)**	**6.3 Conduct.** Keller will comply with all applicable [*name of company*] workplace policies, including policies on: (A) no smoking; (B) drug-free environment; (C) dress code; (D) nonharassment; (E) travel and expense guidelines; (F) general safety and security (including prohibition of weapons); and (G) computer use and security.

Surely they meant to write: "but *not* limited to."

On the deletion of *but not limited to* (which contained a bad typo in the original), see § 34.

NOT THIS:	BUT THIS:
Ex. 2 3.2 Cooperation. Supplier will cooperate as requested with other Service providers of Griggs to coordinate the provision of Services with the services and systems of such other service providers. Such coordination will include: (i) facilitating with such other relevant service providers the timely resolution of all problems that may arise and impact the Services or the provision thereof, regardless of the actual or suspected root-cause of such problems; (ii) providing information concerning the Services and Provided Resources; and (iii) providing reasonable access to and use of the Provided Resources. **Master Software-License Agreement from a major mobile network**	**3.2 Cooperation.** DonTech will cooperate as requested with Griggs's other service providers to provide Services in coordination with the other service providers' services and systems. The cooperation includes: (A) helping other service providers to timely resolve all problems that may affect the Services, whatever the actual or suspected root cause of the problem might be; (B) providing information about the Services and Provided Resources; and (C) providing reasonable access to and use of the Provided Resources.
Ex. 3 6.1 The completion of the merger shall not occur unless a number of conditions are satisfied: (i) the approval of the merger by the holders of a majority of the Global Tech Shares and OHP Class A common stock, voting as a single class; (ii) the approval of the merger and increase in OHP's issued share capital by the holders of not less than three-fourths of the ordinary shares of OHP entitled to vote at an Extraordinary General Meeting of OHP's shareholders to be held on March 25, 2019; (iii) the nonexistence of an injunction that would be a prohibition of the merger or which would cause a material adverse effect on either OHP or Global Tech; and (iv) the approval of the relevant governmental authorities without the imposition of conditions that would have a material adverse effect on Global Tech, OHP, or Global-OHP. **Merger Agreement**	**6.1 Conditions precedent to the merger.** Global Tech and OHP will not complete the merger unless these conditions are satisfied: (A) the holders of a majority of the Global Tech Shares and OHP Class A common stock must, voting as a single class, approve the merger; (B) at an extraordinary general meeting of OHP's shareholders scheduled for March 25, 2019, the holders of at least three-quarters of OHP's ordinary shares must approve the merger and the increase in OHP's issued share capital; (C) there must not be an injunction that prohibits the merger or that materially harms either OHP or Global Tech; and (D) the relevant government authorities must approve the merger without imposing conditions that would materially harm Global Tech, OHP, or Global-OHP.

"Consistency results from ensuring that each provision corresponds to the total agreement between the parties and meshes with the other provisions in the contract. Address consistency concerns when rewriting and revising." Mary Barnard Ray & Barbara J. Cox, *Beyond the Basics: A Text for Advanced Legal Writing* 91 (2d ed. 2003).

NOT THIS:	BUT THIS:
Ex. 4 Section 10. Verification Period. 10.1 Within five (5) days of the date hereof, Seller shall furnish Purchaser with (i) income and expense statements for the Property for the years 2015, 2016 and 2017, and any similar statements generated by Seller for the current fiscal or calendar year; (ii) any engineering or soil reports relating to the Property in Seller's possession or control; (iii) any environmental audits or reports relating to the Property in Seller's possession or control; (iv) copies of all construction and mechanical warranties in effect with respect to the Property; (v) a copy of the insurance policies described on Exhibit H; and (vi) plans, specifications, engineering data and other related material with respect to the construction, alteration, renovation and rehabilitation to the Hotel in Seller's possession or control. **Purchase Agreement from a major law firm**	**10.1 Verification and documentation.** Within 5 days after the date of this Agreement, Swanson will give Pruitt the following: (A) income and expense statements for the Property covering 2015, 2016, and 2017, and any similar statements generated by Swanson for the current fiscal or calendar year; (B) any engineering or soil reports in Swanson's possession or control relating to the Property; (C) any environmental audits or reports in Swanson's possession or control relating to the Property; (D) copies of all construction and mechanical warranties in effect with respect to the Property; (E) a copy of the insurance policies described in Exhibit H; and (F) plans, specifications, engineering data, and other material in Swanson's possession or control relating to construction, alteration, renovation, and rehabilitation of the Hotel.

> "Highly complex sentences are increasingly difficult to justify as business and professional readers grow more demanding, even when the readers are scientific, engineering, and legal people. In this category fall sentences that contain long series of modifying phrases and clauses piled one on top of the other, like driblets of sand on a sand castle." David W. Ewing, *Writing for Results in Business, Government, and the Professions* 337–38 (1974).

NOT THIS:

Ex. 5

1. RIGHTS GRANTED: Author grants to Publisher during the term of copyright, including renewals and extensions thereof:
(a) The exclusive right in the English language, in the United States of America, the Philippine Republic, and Canada
(i) To print, publish and sell the Work in book form;
(ii) To license publication of the Work (in complete, condensed or abridged versions) by book clubs, including subsidiaries of Publisher;
(iii) To license publication of a reprint edition by another publisher;
(iv) To license publication of the Work (in complete, condensed or abridged versions) or sections therefrom in anthologies and other publications, in mail-order and schoolbook editions, as premiums, and through microfilm and Xerox or other forms of copying;
(v) License periodical publication including magazines, newspapers and digests after book publication to the extent that any such right is relinquished by the first publisher of the same;
(vi) License Electronic Publishing rights, including but not limited to the right to store, record, transmit and retrieve the verbatim text of the Work or parts of the Work by any means, electronic, digital or otherwise, including the right to prepare audio recordings or versions of the text of the Work in connection with display of the text.
(b) Exclusive right to use or license others to use, subject to the approval of Author, the name and likeness of Author, the Work and the title of the Work, in whole or in part, or any adaptation thereof as the basis for trademark or trade name for other products or for any other commercial use in connection with such products.

Professional Book Contract with Commentary from LexisNexis Forms, Form 556-42-1

It's glaring how parts (v) and (vi) are not parallel in structure to parts (i) through (iv).

The adverbial phrase highlighted here is ambiguous: does it modify both *use* and *license others to use*, or just the latter? The revision in the right column resolves the ambiguity in favor of the latter.

BUT THIS:

1. Rights Granted.

1.1 Printing, publishing, and licensing. During the term of copyright, including renewals and extensions, Galliard grants Knoll exclusive English-language rights in the United States, the Philippines, and Canada, to:
(A) print, publish, and sell the Work in book form;
(B) license publication of the Work (in a complete or abridged version) by book clubs, including subsidiaries of Knoll;
(C) license publication of a reprint edition by another publisher;
(D) license publication of the Work (in a complete or abridged version) or sections of the Work in anthologies and other publications, in mail-order and schoolbook editions, as premiums, and through microfilm and Xerox or other forms of copying;
(E) license periodical publication, including magazines, newspapers, and digests, after book publication to the extent that the first publisher relinquishes any right; and
(F) license Electronic Publishing rights, including the right to store, record, send, and retrieve the verbatim text of the Work or parts of it by any electronic, digital, or other means, including audio recordings or displayed text.

1.2 Commercial use of name, likeness, and title. During the term of copyright, including renewals and extensions, Galliard grants Knoll the exclusive right to use or, subject to Galliard's approval, license others to use the name and likeness of Galliard, the Work, and the title of the Work, in whole or part, or any adaptation of it as the basis for trademark or tradename for other products or for any related commercial use.

Sections 1.1 and 1.2 shouldn't be combined: the original limits § 1.1 to the English language, the U.S., Philippines, and Canada, but it does not impose that limit on § 1.2.

NOT THIS:

Ex. 6

ARTICLE VI
COVENANTS OF THE COMPANY

The Company agrees that:

Section 6.01 Conduct of the Company. From the date of this Agreement until the earlier of the Merger Effective Time and the termination of this Agreement, except (x) as prohibited or required by Applicable Law, (y) as set forth in Section 6.01 of the Company Disclosure Schedule, or (z) as otherwise required or expressly contemplated by this Agreement, unless Parent shall otherwise consent in writing (which consent shall not be unreasonably withheld, conditioned or delayed), the Company shall, and shall cause each of its Subsidiaries to, use commercially reasonable efforts to conduct its business in all material respects in the ordinary course of business consistent with past practice and to preserve intact its business organization and relationships with customers, members, suppliers, licensors, licensees and other Third Parties and keep available the services of its present officers and employees; provided that (i) no action by the Company or any of its Subsidiaries to the extent expressly permitted by an exception to any of Section 6.01(a) through Section 6.01(o) will be a breach of this sentence and (ii) if the Company or any of its Subsidiaries seeks the consent of Parent to take any action prohibited by any of Section 6.01(a) through Section 6.01(o), and such consent is withheld by Parent, the failure to take such action will not be deemed to be a breach of this sentence. Without limiting the generality of the foregoing, except (A) as prohibited or required by Applicable Law, (B) as set forth in Section 6.01 of the Company Disclosure Schedule, or (C) as otherwise required or expressly contemplated by this Agreement, without Parent's prior written consent (which consent shall not be unreasonably withheld, conditioned or delayed), the Company shall not, and shall cause each of its Subsidiaries not to:

. . .

(h)(i) make any material loans, advances or capital contributions to, or investments in, any other Person, other than (A) loans, advances, capital contributions or investments (1) by the Company to or in, as applicable, one or more of its wholly owned Subsidiaries or (2) by any Subsidiary of the Company to or in, as applicable, the Company or any wholly owned Subsidiary of the Company, or (B) capital contributions required under the terms of Contracts in effect as of the date hereof, or (ii) incur, assume, guarantee or repurchase or otherwise become liable for any indebtedness for borrowed money, issue or sell any debt securities or any options, warrants or other rights to acquire debt securities or enter into, guarantee or otherwise become liable for any interest rate, swap, currency, commodity or other similar hedging arrangement (in each case, whether, directly or indirectly, on a contingent basis or otherwise), other than (A) additional borrowings under the Credit Agreement (as in effect as of the date hereof) in accordance with the terms thereof and indebtedness under commercial paper arrangements backstopped thereby, provided that (i) the aggregate amount of commercial paper outstanding shall not at any time exceed $750,000,000 and (ii) as of the last day of each fiscal quarter of the Company and as of the Closing Date, the amount of such commercial paper outstanding shall be $0, (B) intercompany indebtedness among the Company and its wholly-owned Subsidiaries or among the Company's wholly-owned Subsidiaries, (C) indebtedness for borrowed money incurred to replace, renew, extend, refinance or refund any existing indebtedness of the Company or any of its Subsidiaries, which indebtedness is (i) on terms that are substantially consistent with those contained in the indebtedness being replaced, renewed, extended, refinanced or refunded (other than the extension of the maturity date thereof) and (ii) not in a principal amount greater than such indebtedness being replaced, renewed, extended, refinanced or refunded or, in the case of any "revolving" credit facility, the aggregate amount that may be incurred under the credit agreement governing such indebtedness being replaced, renewed, extended, refinanced or refunded (as in effect as of the date hereof), (D) guarantees of indebtedness of the Company or its wholly-owned Subsidiaries outstanding on the date hereof or otherwise incurred in compliance with this Section 6.01(h)(ii), (E) in respect of interest rate, swap, currency, commodity or other similar hedging arrangements which (i) are entered into in connection with the restructuring or replacement of up to $500,000,000 in aggregate notional amount of existing hedging arrangements expiring in 2019 into forward contracts, (ii) are entered into in connection with the restructuring or replacement of up to $750,000,000 in aggregate notional amount of existing hedging arrangements expiring in 2020 into forward contracts, or (iii) are entered into in the ordinary course of business consistent with past practice in an aggregate notional amount not to exceed $250,000,000 at any time outstanding, and (F) other indebtedness not to exceed $50,000,000 in the aggregate at any time outstanding pursuant to this subclause (F); . . . .

Agreement and Plan of Merger by major pharmaceutical companies

BUT THIS:

6. Company's Covenants.

6.1 Effective time of covenants. These covenants are effective from the date of this Agreement until the Merger Effective Time or the termination of this Agreement, whichever is earlier.

6.2 Ineffective covenants; breach of covenants.

(A) **Ineffectiveness cure and causes.** If a covenant is ineffective, Parent may consent to it in writing. Consent will not be unreasonably withheld, conditioned, or delayed. A covenant is ineffective if it is contrary to what is prohibited or required by:

(1) applicable law;

(2) § 6.1 of the Company Disclosure Schedule; or

(3) this Agreement.

(B) **No breach.** The Company and its Subsidiaries do not breach this § 6 by:

(1) failing to act as provided by a covenant when the Parent withholds consent to an ineffective covenant; or

(2) acting as expressly permitted by an exception to a covenant.

6.3 Commercially reasonable efforts. The Company will—and will cause each of its Subsidiaries to—use commercially reasonable efforts to conduct its business in all material respects in the ordinary course of business consistently with past practice and to preserve its business organization and relationships with customers, members, suppliers, licensors, licensees, and other Third Parties and keep available the services of its present officers and employees.

6.4 Loans, advances, capital contributions, and investments. The Company and its wholly owned Subsidiaries may make loans, advances, or capital contributions to, or investments in, the Company or any wholly owned Subsidiary, and may make capital contributions required under Contracts in effect as of the date of this Agreement. Otherwise, the Company will not—and will cause each of its Subsidiaries not to—make any material loans, advances, or capital contributions to, or investments in, any other Person.

This is surely overdrafted. The Company can't make any investments?

6.5 Debt. Whether directly or indirectly, on a contingent basis or otherwise, the Company will not—and will cause each of its Subsidiaries not to—incur, assume, guarantee, repurchase, or otherwise become liable for any debt for borrowed money; issue or sell any debt securities, options, warrants, or other rights to acquire debt securities; or enter into, guarantee, or otherwise become liable for any interest rate, swap, currency, commodity, or other similar hedging arrangement. But this covenant against debt does not apply to the following exceptions:

(A) **Credit Agreement.** The Company and its Subsidiaries may borrow under the Credit Agreement in effect as of the date of this Agreement by its terms and according to its commercial-paper arrangements. The aggregate amount of commercial paper outstanding must not exceed $750 million. As of the last day of each fiscal quarter for the Company and as of the Closing Date, the amount of such commercial paper outstanding must be $0.

(B) **Intercompany debt.** The Company and its wholly owned Subsidiaries may incur intercompany debts between the Company and its wholly owned Subsidiaries or among the Company's wholly owned Subsidiaries.

(C) **Existing debt.** The Company and its Subsidiaries may borrow money or otherwise finance debt incurred to replace, renew, extend, or refund any existing debt of the Company or its Subsidiaries, when the new debt:

(1) has terms that are substantially consistent with those for the existing debt (other than the extension of the indebtedness's maturity date); and

(2) is for a principal amount not greater than the existing debt or, in the case of any "revolving" credit facility, not greater than the aggregate amount that may be incurred under the credit agreement governing the existing debt that is in effect as of the date as of the date of this Agreement.

(D) **Guarantees of indebtedness.** The Company or any of its wholly owned Subsidiaries may honor a guarantee of indebtedness that is outstanding on the date of this Agreement or otherwise incurred under an exception to § 6.5.

(E) **Hedging arrangements.** The Company and its wholly owned Subsidiaries may enter into interest-rate, swap, currency, commodity, or other similar hedging arrangements that:

(1) are entered into in the ordinary course of business consistently with past practice in an aggregate notional amount not to exceed $250 million outstanding; or

(2) are in connection with the restructuring or replacement of up to:

(a) $500 million in aggregate amount of existing hedging arrangements expiring in 2019 into forward contracts; and

(b) $750 million in aggregate amount of existing hedging arrangements expiring in 2020 into forward contracts.

(F) **Other debts.** Company and its wholly owned Subsidiaries may create or incur other debt not to exceed $50 million in the aggregate at any time outstanding.

Standard sections and clauses

§ 27 Streamline your preamble and (if you include them) recitals.

Use a simplified form for the preamble, also known as the *commencement*. Normally, you simply want to identify the parties with specificity and to give the effective date (see § 58). If the parties are to be given shorthand names, they should be supplied in parentheses without undue fanfare—that is, no language such as *hereinafter referred to as*.

Although most agreements are for two parties, you'll occasionally need to draft a multiparty agreement. For this type, be sure to name all the parties in the preamble, refer throughout the contract to *all the parties* (never *both parties*), and include a signature block for each party. It's permissible, by the way, to say *between* for three or more parties (just as the Constitution is *between* the several States). *Between* connotes one-on-one reciprocal relations, as opposed to the looser relations connoted by *among*.[1] If you want the contract to bind each party explicitly to each other party, *between* more clearly achieves this effect than *among*. See Example 2 below.

Many drafters like to add quotation marks around the parenthesized parties' names. Doing so makes it clear to all readers that the term is a newly introduced shortened form. It also allows you to search for a defined term electronically by entering, in the search box, the term with quotation marks. But of course the same advantage can be gained by searching for the term with an end-parenthesis.

As for recitals, their purpose is to explain to a neutral interpreter many years in the future just what the parties are trying to accomplish and why. They serve as background for the contract terms, and they're usually stated so briefly and broadly as to be well-suited to that purpose.

When the recitals become unduly detailed, or when the drafter is careless, contradictions may arise between the recitals and the actual terms. An oft-repeated formula with three parts, is often used to solve such a problem: (1) If the operative term and the recitals are both clear but contradictory, the operative term governs. (2) The same result obtains if the operative term is clear but the recital is unclear. (3) But if the operative term is unclear and the recital is clear (and in conflict, seemingly, with the unclear operative term), the recital governs.[2]

---

1 *See Garner's Modern English Usage* 111 (4th ed. 2016).

2 *See* Grover C. Grismore, *Principles of the Law of Contracts* § 107, at 160 (John Edward Murray Jr. ed., rev. ed. 1965).

NOT THIS:	BUT THIS:
Ex. 1 THIS AGREEMENT (the "Agreement") is made and entered into at Seattle, Washington as of this 5th day of April, 2018, by and between Janet D. Halley ("Janet") and Jonathan D. Halley ("Jonathan"). In consideration of the mutual covenants contained herein and other good and valuable consideration, the parties hereto hereby agree as follows: . . . . **Asset-Purchase Agreement from a major law firm**	This Agreement, effective April 10, 2018, is between Janet D. Halley and Jonathan D. Halley, both of Seattle, Washington. The parties agree as follows: . . . .
Ex. 2 This Agreement ("the Agreement") is made among [VENDOR NAME] ("Vendor"), [STUDENT NAME] ("Student"), and [MANAGER NAME] ("Manager") as of the date the student begins working at Vendor's office under the direction of Manager ("Effective Date"). Vendor, Student, and Manager may be referred to individually as "Party" and collectively as "the Parties." **University Bookstore Employment Agreement**	This Agreement, effective September 2, 20__, is between [**Bookstore Name**] (Bookstore), [**Student Name**] (the Student), and [**Manager Name**] (the Manager). The effective date has been scheduled as the Student's first workday. In this Agreement, "Party" means any one of the three; "Parties" means all of them together.

"While the retention of formal preambles is to some extent rooted in tradition, the practical utility of both types of recitals [formal and informal] is reflected in the effect given to them by the courts. They may figure in two ways: (1) as evidence of the intention of the parties, thus operating to explain or even to supplement the operative provisions of the contract; (2) as persuasive or even conclusive evidence of recited facts which have relevance other than as interpretive aids." Note, *The Effect of Recitals in Contracts*, 35 Colum. L. Rev. 565, 567–68 (1935).

<table>
<tr><th>NOT THIS:</th><th>BUT THIS:</th></tr>
<tr><td>Ex. 3
AN AGREEMENT made the 1st day of May, 2018, BETWEEN DESNOES & GEDDES LIMITED, a limited liability company duly incorporated under the laws of Jamaica with registered offices situated at 214 Spanish Town Road, Kingston 11 in the Parish of Saint Andrew (hereinafter referred to as "D&G" which expression for the purposes and intent of this Agreement shall include any subsidiary or affiliate of Desnoes & Geddes Limited) of the ONE PART and the party described in Item 1 of the First Schedule hereto (hereinafter referred to as "the Bottler") of the OTHER PART; . . . .
[Instead of designating "Parts," see § 53.]
Bottling Agreement from 4 Barry Kramer & Allen D. Brufsky, *Trademark Law Practice Forms* § 43:13, at 43-29 to 43-30 (2d ed. 2009)</td><td>This Agreement, effective May 1, 2018, is between Reggae Imports (the Bottler) and Desnoes & Geddes Limited and its subsidiaries or affiliates (D&G). D&G is a limited-liability company incorporated under Jamaican law with registered offices at 214 Spanish Town Road, Kingston 11 in the Parish of Saint Andrew.</td></tr>
<tr><td>Ex. 4
This Agreement is made and entered into this 3rd day of March 2019, by and between Stellich Inc., a corporation ("Company") incorporated in the State of Texas, with its principal business office at 1101 Montgomery Lane, Dallas, Dallas County, Texas, and Mark Bernhardt ("Licensee").
Whereas Company has developed a line of products (the "products").
Whereas Company wishes to market its products in the State of Texas, and Licensee desires to assist Company by contacting prospective users of Company's products to coordinate appointments for representatives of Company.
THEREFORE, for good and valuable consideration, receipt and sufficiency of which is hereby acknowledged, the parties agree as follows:
[It's odd that the form contains no identifying information for the individual.]
License Agreement from 3 *Texas Legal Practice Forms* § 51:2, at 763–64 (2016)</td><td>This Agreement, effective March 3, 2019, is between Stellich Inc., a Texas corporation with its principal place of business at 1101 Montgomery Lane, Dallas, Texas 75225, and Mark Bernhardt, an individual who resides at 7911 Inwood Road, Dallas, Texas 75209. Stellich and Bernhardt enter into this Agreement for Bernhardt to help Stellich market its products in Texas.
In consideration of the promises stated in this Agreement, the parties agree as follows:</td></tr>
</table>

§ 28 Establish the background of the contract (the recitals) as briefly as possible in separate sentences.

If you're to establish the background of the contract in recitals, do so in summary fashion using short declarative sentences—without semicolons and *Whereas*es. What purpose do recitals serve? They should, in general terms, provide useful background information about what the parties seek to accomplish, what assumptions the parties are making, and perhaps the risks associated with the transaction. On the whole, these statements should be succinct synopses, not particularized explanations. After all, they're providing a general background for what led up to the document.

In some contracts, such as buy-sell agreements in which there will be no relationship of any duration between the parties, recitals may be wholly unnecessary. Then again, if there's a real possibility that the contract might be effective for years or even decades, recitals can become extraordinarily important. Although recitals aren't considered "terms" of the contract, a court construing the contract will ordinarily look to the recitals to understand the purposes and motivations that led the parties to enter into it. In short, recitals serve as the equivalent of purpose clauses in legislation.

Because recitals are presumed in contract law not to be contractual terms, some drafters insert a provision (usually as the very first term) incorporating the recitals into the body of the contract. It might say, "The foregoing recitals are hereby incorporated as terms of the agreement," or some similar wording. In doing this, they may have various motives. The first motive may be sheer nervousness about the rule that recitals aren't terms. Here the idea would be simply to ensure that the recitals are in fact part of the contract. Second, they may be trying to upgrade the recitals into representations or even warranties, so that if a recital ends up proving incorrect in some way, that fact might provide grounds for rescission. Why not simply include such things in the representations-and-warranties section? you might ask. The answer typically given is that the drafter believes things can be sneaked into the recitals that would never pass muster

> "If the recitals are clear and the operative part is ambiguous, the recitals govern the construction. If the recitals are ambiguous, and the operative part is clear, the operative part must prevail. If both the recitals and the operative part are clear, but they are inconsistent with each other, the operative part is to be preferred." *In re Moon ex parte Dawes*, [1886] 17 Q.B.D. 275, 286 (Lord Esher, M.R.).

with a counterparty in the reps and warranties. This rationale amounts to a drafting subterfuge that many lawyers engage in and defend, but it may chart a path fraught with peril when judicially scrutinized. Third, they may simply have seen other drafters use such a provision and somehow come to believe that it's advisable for reasons only vaguely contemplated.

The recommendation here is *not* to incorporate recitals as terms of the contract. No explicit promise is made within them (if they're properly done). The law relating to recitals has proceeded as it has for a reason, and there's no good cause to override it.

Traditionally, of course, recitals are introduced by one or (usually) more *Whereas*-clauses, often in tedious succession, each one capitalized (sometimes in all caps for the word *whereas*) even though they're written as one long sentence elongated through the use of semicolons. There's no reason for such serpentine sentences in recitals.

In traditional 19th-century drafting, all the front matter appears in a single sentence having this structure:

> This Agreement, by and between
> ______________________ ("Party of the First Part")
> and ______________________ ("Party of the Second Part"), witnesseth that
>
> Whereas, [assertion]; and
>
> Whereas, [assertion]; and
>
> Whereas, [assertion];
>
> now, therefore, in consideration of the mutual covenants contained herein, and other good and valuable consideration, the receipt and sufficiency of which are hereby acknowledged, the parties agree as follows: . . . .

In fact, in one line of traditional style—a retrograde style, you understand, from the modern viewpoint—every contract consisted of essentially a single sentence because there was no punctuation at all. We've progressed a great deal since then.

Whereas essentially means "given the fact that." The simpler, more straightforward practice is to use a heading such as "Background," "Purposes," or (if you must) "Recitals."

If you're to use recitals, you should generally make them bare-bones recitals. Three to five paragraphs, in bulleted form, should be enough to

> "The more particular the recitals, the more dangerous they are." Barbara Child, *Drafting Legal Documents* 125 (2d ed. 1992).

explain what the parties seek to accomplish, and why. If, for example, an earlier contract is being replaced by a new amended and restated agreement, make sure to refer in the recitals to the earlier agreement and to state clearly that this new contract supersedes the earlier one.

One final point. It's often a good idea to write the background section *after* completing a near-final draft. You must have a comprehensive grasp of all the terms to summarize the contract in clear, logical sentences that all readers can grasp.

NOT THIS:	BUT THIS:
Ex. 1 WHEREAS, Subcontractor wishes to provide Company the said work as set forth herein; and All in the manner and subject to the terms and conditions as hereinafter set forth, NOW, THEREFORE, BE IT KNOWN AND IT IS HEREBY AGREED in consideration of the foregoing premises and mutual covenants herein contained, the parties hereby mutually agree as follows: **Subcontracting Agreement**	In consideration of the promises stated in this Agreement, the Subcontractor and the Company agree as follows: **The Agreement**
Ex. 2 WHEREAS, in recognition of Indemnitee's need for substantial protection against personal liability in order to enhance Indemnitee's continued and effective service to the Company as a director, officer or employee, the Company wishes to provide in this Agreement for the indemnification of and the advancing of expenses to Indemnitee to the fullest extent (whether partial or complete) permitted by law as set forth in this Agreement, and, to the extent insurance is maintained which includes Indemnitee as a covered party, for the coverage of Indemnitee under the Company's directors' and officers' liability insurance policies. **Indemnification Agreement from a technology company**	**Background** Caltex Inc. and Gardiner enter into this Agreement to: • recognize Gardiner's need for substantial protection against personal liability; • enhance Gardiner's continued, effective service to Caltex; and • induce Gardiner to serve as a Caltex director, officer, or employee. **The Agreement** 1. **Indemnification and Expenses.** Caltex will indemnify and advance expenses to Gardiner under this Agreement's terms to the fullest extent allowed by law. 2. **Liability-Insurance Coverage.** To the extent that Caltex maintains insurance that includes Gardiner as a covered party, Caltex will cover Gardiner under its directors' and officers' liability-insurance policies.

This isn't a real recital!

The revision is short and clear and eliminates all the unnecessary legalese.

Note that this is not a grammatical sentence. Incomplete sentences are a common problem with *Whereas*-clauses.

NOT THIS:	BUT THIS:
Ex. 3 **WHEREAS,** Fernley is in the business of providing professional management for Trade Associations and similar groups; and **WHEREAS,** in carrying out such functions, employees of Fernley are placed in positions of trust and confidence with such clientele and develop, with Fernley's encouragement and guidance, close working relationships with members of client associations; and **WHEREAS,** Employee has accepted employment with Fernley as the Director of Operations with responsibilities in the management of the affairs of the Trade Association clients of Fernley; and **WHEREAS,** in such employment Employee will obtain confidential information, as defined hereafter, and develop close personal relationships with the officers and directors of Fernley's Trade Association clients; and **WHEREAS,** as a condition of such employment, Fernley requires that it be assured against the use of confidential information or the employment relationship in a manner contrary to Fernley's interests. **Employment Agreement from a major law firm**	**Background** • Fernley provides professional management for trade associations and similar groups. Fernley employees therefore have positions of trust and confidence with this clientele, and with Fernley's encouragement and guidance, they develop close working relationships with members of these client associations. • Julian Harris has accepted employment with Fernley as director of operations responsible for managing Fernley's trade-association clients' affairs. In this position, Harris will obtain confidential information (as defined below) and develop close personal relationships with the officers and directors of Fernley's trade-association clients. • As a condition of this employment, Fernley requires that Harris must not use confidential information or her employment relationship in any way that adversely affects Fernley's interests.

"The legal mind finds magnetic attraction in redundancy and overkill. It is said that a lawyer never uses one word when two or three will do just as well." *Coca Cola Bottling Co. v. Reeves*, 486 So.2d 374, 383–84 (Miss. 1986) (Robertson, J.).

NOT THIS:	BUT THIS:
Ex. 4 SETTLEMENT AGREEMENT Settlement Agreement dated as of October 30, 2015, by and between E. Clifford, Inc., of 4000 Bridge Street, Short Hills, New Jersey (hereinafter "Clifford"), and Joseph Smith of 200 Mermaid Lane, Short Hills, New Jersey (hereinafter "Smith"). WHEREAS, by a writing dated as of July 15, 2015, Clifford entered into a written contract with Smith to renovate a building on the southeast corner of 19th and Mermaid Lane, Short Hills, New Jersey (hereinafter the "Contract"), in accordance with certain terms, conditions, specifications and drawings referenced in the Contract (hereinafter the "Contract Documents"); WHEREAS, thereafter, Clifford asserted claims against Smith for the performance of extra work and for expenses resulting from delays and disruptions to its work, which claims were submitted to arbitration, pursuant to the Construction Industry Arbitration Rules of the American Arbitration Association, at Case No. 16-110-0005 in Newark, New Jersey (hereinafter referred to as the "arbitration case"); WHEREAS, in the arbitration case, Smith asserted a counterclaim based upon claimed deficiencies in Clifford's performance under the Contract; WHEREAS, neither party admits liability upon the claims of the other; WHEREAS, the arbitration case has not yet been concluded; WHEREAS, the parties now desire to enter into this Settlement Agreement to settle all claims which were or might have been asserted in the arbitration case; NOW, THEREFORE, the parties agree as follows: . . . . **Settlement Agreement from Robert F. Cushman, Michael S. Simon & McNeill Stokes, *Construction Industry Formbook* § 14.10, at 267 (1981 & Supp. 1986)**	**Settlement Agreement** This Settlement Agreement, effective October 30, 2015, is between E. Clifford, Inc., of 4000 Bridge Street, Short Hills, New Jersey, and Joseph Smith, of 200 Mermaid Lane, Short Hills, New Jersey. **Background** • On July 15, 2015, Smith and Clifford entered into a written contract (the "Contract") under which Clifford would renovate a building on the southeast corner of 19th Street and Mermaid Lane in Short Hills, New Jersey. • Clifford has since sued Smith on the Contract. Under the Construction Industry Arbitration Rules of the American Arbitration Association, Clifford's claims went to arbitration as Case No. 16-110-0005 in Newark, New Jersey. At arbitration, Smith counterclaimed. • Although neither party admits liability for the other's claims, the parties now wish to settle all claims that were or might have been asserted. **Terms of Agreement** . . .

NOT THIS:

Ex. 5

RECITALS:

A. WHEREAS, Lender is prepared to make a certain mezzanine loan (the "Loan") to Borrower, pursuant to a Mezzanine Loan Agreement of even date herewith between Borrower and Lender (as the same may be amended, restated, replaced, extended, supplemented or otherwise modified from time to time, the "Loan Agreement"; all capitalized terms used herein but not otherwise defined shall have the respective meanings ascribed to such terms in the Loan Agreement), which Loan shall be evidenced by one or more promissory notes (as the same may be amended, restated, replaced, supplemented or otherwise modified from time to time, collectively, the "Note") and secured by among other things, that certain Pledge and Security Agreement (Mezzanine Loan) of even date herewith, given by Borrower to Lender (as the same may be amended, restated, replaced, supplemented or otherwise modified from time to time, the "Pledge Agreement") encumbering the Collateral (as defined in the Pledge Agreement) described therein.

B. WHEREAS, the Loan is being made in connection with a mortgage loan extended by Goodman Mortgage Company, a New York limited partnership ("Goodman") and Infinity Bank, N.A., a national banking association ("Infinity"; together with Goodman and each of their respective successors and permitted assigns, collectively, "Mortgage Lender") pursuant to the Mortgage Loan Note (as defined in the Loan Agreement), dated of even date herewith, executed by Toys Property Company, LLC, a Delaware limited liability company ("Mortgage Borrower") under which Mortgage Borrower has become indebted, and may from time to time be further indebted, to Mortgage Lender with respect to a loan ("Mortgage Loan") made pursuant to that certain Loan Agreement, of even date herewith between Mortgage Borrower, and Mortgage Lender (as the same may hereafter be amended, restated, extended, replaced, supplemented, or otherwise modified from time to time, the "Mortgage Loan Agreement"), which Mortgage Loan is secured by the Mortgages (as defined in the Mortgage Loan Agreement), encumbering certain real property and the leasehold interests in certain real property (individually and/or collectively, as the context may require, the "Property").

C. WHEREAS, Mortgage Borrower is the owner of the Property.

D. WHEREAS, Borrower is the owner of 100% of the membership interests in Mortgage Borrower.

E. WHEREAS, the Lender is unwilling to make the Loan unless Indemnitor agrees to provide the indemnification, representations, warranties, covenants and other matters described in this Agreement for the benefit of the Indemnified Parties.

F. WHEREAS, Indemnitor is entering into this Agreement to induce the Lender to make the Loan.

Environmental Indemnity Agreement from a major retail toy company

Despite all the definitions in these recitals, it's unclear what the terms "Borrower," "Lender," and "Indemnitor" refer to. Rather than bogging down readers with loads of defined terms, the recitals should simply explain what's happening in plain English. Leave definitions to a definitional section (see §§ 102–103).

BUT THIS:

Facts

- The Lender is prepared to make a mezzanine loan to the Borrower under a Mezzanine Loan Agreement on the effective date of this Agreement. This Loan Agreement will be evidenced by at least one promissory note and the Loan will be secured by, among other things, a Pledge and Security Agreement that the Borrower gives the Lender encumbering the Collateral.
- This Loan is made in connection with a Mortgage Loan extended by Goodman Mortgage Company (Goodman), a New York limited partnership, and Infinity Bank, N.A. (Infinity). Goodman and Infinity are collectively termed the Mortgage Lender. The Mortgage Loan Note was signed and delivered by Toys Property Company, LLC (Toys), a Delaware limited-liability company that has become indebted—and may become further indebted—to the Mortgage Lender under the Mortgage Loan Agreement. The Mortgage Loan is secured by the Mortgages encumbering real property and the leasehold interests in real property. Toys owns the Property and the Borrower owns 100% of the membership interests in Toys.
- The Lender will not make the Loan unless the Indemnitor provides—for the benefit of the Indemnified Parties—the indemnity, representations, warranties, covenants, and other matters described in this Agreement. The Indemnitor therefore enters into this Agreement to induce the Lender to make the Loan.

"The time you spend polishing will depend on the complexity of the contract and the needs and resources of your client. This step requires concentrating on writing rather than substance. For example, read the contract for subjects and verbs too far apart, misspellings, awkward sentence structure, and problems peculiar to your own writing, such as dangling modifiers, overuse of passive voice, or improper use of semicolons. Correct any errors in your grammar, punctuation, usage, and word choice. Your reader will be focused on detail. You must be, too." Mary Barnard Ray & Barbara J. Cox, *Beyond the Basics: A Text for Advanced Legal Writing* 106 (2d ed. 2003).

§ 29 Use a consideration clause that simply betokens a promise for a promise—unless the consideration for covenants is obscure.

Simplify the traditional phrasing by straightforwardly introducing the agreement, which if signed by two parties must necessarily be a bilateral agreement that contains mutual promises. The streamlining is necessary. Consider the phrase *good and valuable consideration*, which has been parroted by lawyers for centuries despite little or no understanding of what the words denote. In fact, only valuable consideration counts for anything in contract law. Good consideration isn't good at all: it's traditionally just the affection one has for another, especially a family member, and affection doesn't give rise to an enforceable contract.[1] Don't worry about how *good* came to be equated with affection: it was the sense given to the word at common law. So the words *good and* are superfluous and always have been—though few lawyers could explain this fact because the full phrase has long been a ritualistic incantation.

Or consider the acknowledgment of receipt and sufficiency. Embedded in most forms is a subject-verb disagreement—a blunder of the most elementary kind. The receipt of consideration is quite a different thing from the sufficiency of the consideration. Hence the phrasing should be *the receipt and sufficiency of which are hereby acknowledged*, not *is*.[2] Yet legions of drafters perpetrate and thereby perpetuate the error.

Why not take the streamlining even further? Why not just say *The parties agree as follows*, or perhaps *The parties therefore agree as follows*? The answer is that in the great majority of instances, such a barebones lead-in will be entirely sufficient. But the recital of consideration—*In consideration of* . . .—contains a useful protection: "if a promise is recited as having been made as consideration, this recital cannot be disputed."[3] The language creates an estoppel to contradict it.[4] Normally, this estoppel doesn't come into play, but the protection may be helpful in anomalous situations. That's why it became more traditional in the first place.

True, a recitation of consideration won't save what purports to be a bilateral contract if one side isn't bound in any way or hasn't promised to do something. But if promises have been made on both sides, the recital confers the slight benefit of estopping the parties to contradict it.

1 *See Garner's Dictionary of Legal Usage* 206–07 (3d ed. 2011) (s.v. "consideration").

2 *See id.* at 755.

3 Grover C. Grismore, *Principles of the Law of Contracts* § 69, at 116–17 (John Edward Murray Jr. ed., rev. ed. 1965).

4 *Id.*

NOT THIS:	BUT THIS:
Ex. 1 NOW THEREFORE, in consideration of the covenants contained in this Agreement, the parties agree as follows: **Sales Agreement**	In consideration of the promises stated in this Agreement, the parties agree as follows:
Ex. 2 **NOW, THEREFORE,** in consideration of the foregoing and the following mutual covenants, and intending legally to be bound, the parties agree as follows: **Employment Agreement from a major law firm**	In consideration of the promises stated in this Agreement, the parties agree as follows:
Ex. 3 NOW, THEREFORE, in consideration of the mutual promises contained herein and for other good and valuable consideration,[5] the receipt and sufficiency of which are hereby acknowledged, Whiteley and Garlow covenant and agree as follows: **Property-Sales Agreement**	In consideration of the promises stated in this Agreement, the parties agree as follows:
Ex. 4 NOW THEREFORE IN CONSIDERATION of the mutual covenants, agreements, representations, and warranties, and in exchange for good and valuable consideration,[6] the receipt and sufficiency of which is hereby acknowledged, the Parties hereby agree as follows: **Confidentiality Agreement from Lynne Ann Frasier, *The Complete Book of Business and Legal Forms* 92 (1998)**	In consideration of the promises stated in this Agreement, the parties agree as follows:

Occasionally, the legal consideration supporting the enforceability of a party's covenants may be obscure. This situation occurs most often when there are multiple parties or when there is a one-sided amendment to an existing agreement. In such a context, recite the precise consideration explicitly. Doing so will help future readers who need to understand why the contract is enforceable.

5 *See Garner's Dictionary of Legal Usage* 206–07 (3d ed. 2011) (s.v. "consideration").

6 Note the (common) subject-verb disagreement that follows the superscript: *the receipt and sufficiency . . . is*. Proper grammar requires *the receipt and sufficiency . . . are*. *See id.* at 755.

§ 30 In the body of the contract, state in precise, readable language the promises, rights, conditions, authorizations, and representations.

Operative clauses must express what each party must do, when the party must do it, what conditions affect the timing or qualities of performance, and (often) the consequences of not performing. A common example is *Contractor is responsible for the safety of persons on or adjacent to the worksite.* Once the contractor signs the agreement, the contractor becomes responsible.

Because the most important aspect of a contract is setting forth the parties' primary obligations, these should appear toward the beginning of the body (see § 80). Ideally, readers of any ilk could quickly discern the gist of what the parties are to do from glancing at the first few clauses after *The parties agree as follows* (see § 29). You might well ask why we care about "readers of any ilk." The answer is that if *they* can readily comprehend, then so can the parties, their employees, their successors, and any arbitrators or judges down the line who must sort out the meaning.

Most of the rest of this book is about how to draft clauses containing clear provisions with utmost skill.

> "Since the purpose of the contract is to state legal rights and duties, it seldom, if ever, involves narration, description, interrogation, or an appeal for action. It contains no pathos, no overtones, no inspiration, no humor, no emotional impact. A style that would be magnificent when probing human nature would be wrong in a contract."
> LeRoy Marceau, *Drafting a Union Contract* § 3.1, at 16 (1965).

§ 31 Understand the distinct purposes of representations and warranties, and express them well.

A representation is a statement of a past or existing fact. A warranty is a guarantee that if a representation later proves to be untrue, the party receiving the guarantee will have an enhanced remedy of some kind, such as immediate rescission of the contract. So the two are distinct. As *Black's Law Dictionary* explains, there are four principal differences: "(1) a warranty is conclusively presumed to be material, while the burden is on the party claiming breach to show that a representation is material; (2) a warranty must be strictly complied with, while substantial truth is the only requirement for a representation; (3) a warranty is an essential part of a contract, while a representation is usu. only a collateral inducement; and (4) an express warranty is usu. written on the face of the contract, while a representation may be written or oral."[1]

Although some have argued that a warranty necessarily subsumes a representation—and it's an arguable point—the universality of coupling representations with warranties, as well as their analytical distinctions, militates in favor of maintaining the dual phrasing: *representations and warranties*. Some will say they don't want a guarantee without a direct statement that something is so. That is, a misrepresentation is typically a kind of lie; a breach of a warranty isn't necessarily a lie at all.

On the whole, it's a mistake to try to bifurcate the representations from the warranties. You'll find it devilishly difficult to parse through the representations and warranties to divvy them up—as hopeless as trying to distinguish *terms* from *conditions*.

> "Overly complicated language leads to multiplicity of interpretation. While we cannot remove the complexity of a particular subject, the difficulty should remain with the content. There is no need for it to spread to the language. On the contrary, the more complex the matter, the greater need for simplicity in language so that readers can concentrate all their energies on the material and not have to dissipate any on unraveling the language." Robert D. Eagleson, *What Plain English Means for Lawyers*, 60 L. Inst. J. 938, 939 (1986).

1 *Black's Law Dictionary* (11th ed. 2019) (under *warranty*). *See Garner's Dictionary of Legal Usage* 775 (3d ed. 2011).

NOT THIS:

Ex. 1

Section 2.10. Depositor's **Representations and Warranties**. The Depositor represents and warrants to the Owner Trustee as of the Closing Date:

(a) Organization and Qualification. The Depositor is duly organized and validly existing as a limited liability company in good standing under the laws of the State of Delaware. The Depositor is qualified as a foreign limited liability company in good standing and has obtained all necessary licenses and approvals in all jurisdictions in which the ownership or lease of its properties or the conduct of its activities requires the qualification, license or approval, unless the failure to obtain the qualifications, licenses or approvals would not reasonably be expected to have a material adverse effect on the Depositor's ability to perform its obligations under this Agreement.

(b) Power, Authority and Enforceability. The Depositor has the power and authority to execute, deliver and perform its obligations under this Agreement. The Depositor has authorized the execution, delivery and performance of this Agreement. This Agreement is the legal, valid and binding obligation of the Depositor enforceable against the Depositor, except as may be limited by insolvency, bankruptcy, reorganization or other similar laws relating to the enforcement of creditors' rights or by general equitable principles.

(c) No Conflicts and No Violation. The completion of the transactions under this Agreement, and the performance of its obligations under this Agreement, will not (i) conflict with, or be a breach or default under, any indenture, mortgage, deed of trust, loan agreement, guarantee or similar document under which the Depositor is a debtor or guarantor, (ii) result in the creation or imposition of any Lien on the Depositor's properties or assets under the terms of any indenture, mortgage, deed of trust, loan agreement, guarantee or similar document (other than the Sale and Servicing Agreement), (iii) violate the Depositor's certificate of formation or limited liability company agreement or (iv) violate a law or, to the Depositor's knowledge, an order, rule or regulation of a federal or State court, regulatory body, administrative agency or other governmental instrumentality having jurisdiction over the Depositor or its properties that applies to the Depositor, which, in each case, would reasonably be expected to have a material adverse effect on the Depositor's ability to perform its obligations under this Agreement.

(d) No Proceedings. To the Depositor's knowledge, there are no proceedings or investigations pending or threatened in writing before a federal or State court, regulatory body, administrative agency or other governmental instrumentality having jurisdiction over the Depositor or its properties (i) asserting the invalidity of this Agreement, (ii) seeking to prevent the completion of the transactions under this Agreement, (iii) seeking a determination or ruling that would reasonably be expected to have a material adverse effect on the Depositor's ability to perform its obligations under, or the validity or enforceability of, this Agreement, or (iv) that would reasonably be expected to (A) affect the treatment of the Notes as indebtedness for U.S. federal income or Applicable Tax State income or franchise tax purposes, (B) be deemed to cause a taxable exchange of the Notes for U.S. federal income tax purposes or (C) cause the Issuer to be treated as an association or publicly traded partnership taxable as a corporation for U.S. federal income tax purposes, in each case, other than proceedings that would not reasonably be expected to have a material adverse effect on the Depositor, the performance by the Depositor of its obligations under, or the validity and enforceability of, the Transaction Documents or the Notes or the tax treatment of the Issuer or the Notes.

Trust Agreement from a major automobile corporation

"[S]implification is not a simple process. Making a document clear is much harder than making it complex." Alan Siegel, "Drafting Simplified Legal Documents: Basic Principles and Their Application," in *Drafting Documents in Plain Language* 175, 177 (Duncan A. MacDonald chmn., 1979).

BUT THIS:

2.10 Depositor's representations and warranties.

(A) **Organization and qualification.** The Depositor represents and warrants that:

(1) it is duly organized and validly existing as a limited-liability company in good standing under Delaware law;

(2) it is qualified as a foreign limited-liability company in good standing; and

(3) it has obtained all necessary licenses and approvals in all jurisdictions in which the ownership or lease of its properties or the conduct of its activities requires the qualification, license, or approval, unless the failure to obtain the qualifications, licenses, or approvals would not reasonably be expected to have a material adverse effect on the Depositor's ability to perform its obligations under this Agreement.

(B) **Power, authority, and enforceability.** The Depositor represents and warrants that:

(1) it has the power and authority to enter into and perform its obligations under this Agreement;

(2) it has authorized the signing, delivery, and performance of this Agreement; and

(3) this Agreement is the legal, valid, and binding obligation of the Depositor, enforceable against the Depositor, except as may be limited by insolvency, bankruptcy, reorganization, or other similar laws relating to the enforcement of creditors' rights or general equitable principles.

(C) **No conflicts and no violation.** The Depositor represents and warrants that the completion of the transactions and the performance of its obligations under this Agreement will not:

(1) conflict with, or be a breach or default under, any indenture, mortgage, deed of trust, loan agreement, guarantee, or similar document under which the Depositor is a debtor or guarantor;

(2) result in the creation or imposition of any Lien on the Depositor's properties or assets under any indenture, mortgage, deed of trust, loan agreement, guarantee, or similar document (other than the Sale and Servicing Agreement);

(3) violate the Depositor's certificate of formation or limited-liability-company agreement;

(4) violate a law that applies to the Depositor and might reasonably be expected to have a material adverse effect on the Depositor's ability to perform its obligations under this Agreement; or

(5) to the Depositor's knowledge as of the effective date of this Agreement, violate an order, rule, or regulation of a federal or state court, regulatory body, administrative agency, or other government instrumentality having jurisdiction over the Depositor or its properties in a way that might reasonably be expected to have a material adverse effect on the Depositor's ability to perform its obligations under this Agreement.

(D) **No proceedings.** The Depositor represents and warrants as follows based on its knowledge as of the effective date of this Agreement:

(1) no proceedings or investigations that do any of the following are pending or threatened before a federal or state court, regulatory body, administrative agency, or other government instrumentality with jurisdiction over the Depositor or its properties:

(a) assert the invalidity of this Agreement;

(b) seek to prevent the completion of the transactions under this Agreement; or

(c) seek a determination or ruling that might reasonably be expected to have a material adverse effect on the Depositor's ability to perform its obligations under this Agreement or on the validity or enforceability of this Agreement;

(2) no proceedings or investigations that might reasonably be expected to do any of the following are pending or threatened before a federal or state court, regulatory body, administrative agency, or other government instrumentality with jurisdiction over the Depositor or its properties:

(a) affect the treatment of the Notes as indebtedness for purposes of the U.S. federal income tax or the Applicable Tax State income tax or franchise-tax;

(b) cause a taxable exchange of the Notes for purposes of the U.S. federal income tax; or

(c) cause the Issuer to be treated for purposes of the U.S. federal income tax as an association or publicly traded partnership taxable as a corporation;

(3) the representations and warranties in § 2.10(D)(2) don't apply to proceedings that could not reasonably be expected to have a material adverse effect on:

(a) the Depositor;

(b) the Depositor's performance of its obligations under Transaction Documents or the Notes;

(c) the validity and enforceability of the Transaction Documents or the Notes; or

(d) the tax treatment of the Issuer or the Notes;

(4) the representations and warranties in § 2.10(D)(2) aren't reasonably expected to:

(a) affect the treatment of the Notes as indebtedness for U.S. federal income- or Applicable Tax State income- or franchise-tax purposes;

(b) be considered to cause a taxable exchange of the Notes for U.S. federal income-tax purposes; or

(c) cause the Issuer to be treated as an association or public traded partnership taxable as a corporation for U.S. federal income-tax purposes.

NOT THIS:

Ex. 2

10. Representations and Warranties of Assignee. Assignee represents and warrants to Assignor that: (i) it has the power and authority to purchase the Loans, the Notes and the other Loan Documents pursuant to the terms of this Agreement; (ii) Assignee has conducted its own due diligence with respect to the acquisition of the Loans, the Notes and the other Loan Documents, including without limitation, (a) the terms, provisions, validity and enforceability of the Loan Documents, (b) the perfection and/or priority of any lien against, security interests in and assignment of any and all of the Collateral therefor, and (c) the value, condition, quality, sufficiency of the description and amount of any such Collateral purportedly covered and affected by the Loan Documents; (iii) except as expressly set forth in this Agreement, Assignee has not relied on any statements of Assignor and is relying solely upon the results of the Assignee's own due diligence, (iv) the person signing this Agreement on behalf of Assignee is duly authorized to do so, (v) Assignee is acquiring the Loans and the Loan Documents for its own account and not with a view to any public sale or distribution thereof and Assignee does not intend to sell, offer for sale or syndicate securities or fractional interests in Assignee in connection with the purchase of the Loans and the Loan Documents, provided however, nothing herein shall be construed or applied to prohibit or otherwise limit Assignee's right to dispose of all or any portion of Assignee's interest in the Loans or the Loan Documents in compliance with all applicable law; (vi) Assignee has such knowledge and experience in financial and business matters so that it is capable of evaluating the merits and risks relating to its purchase of the Loans and the Loan Documents and making an informed purchase and investment decision in connection therewith; (vii) Assignee has made such examination, review and investigation of the facts and circumstances necessary to evaluate the Loans and the Loan Documents as it has deemed necessary or appropriate to form a basis for its evaluation of a purchase of the Loans and the Loan Documents, including but not limited to a review of certain information out of Assignor's credit and collateral files and certain other financial information with respect to the Borrower and Guarantors, and Assignee acknowledges that Assignor has furnished to Assignee, and Assignee has reviewed, such information in confidence and in connection with such investigation, Assignee is assuming all risk with respect to the completeness, accuracy or sufficiency of the Loan Documents. Assignee further acknowledges that in acquiring the Loan Documents, Assignee is assuming the risk of full or partial loss that is inherent with the credit, collateral and collectability risks associated with the quality and character of the Loan Documents; (viii) Assignee has agreed to the Purchase Price on the basis of its own independent investigation and credit evaluation of the Loans and the Loan Documents and Assignee acknowledges that the amount ultimately received by Assignee in respect of the Loans and the Loan Documents may be less than the Purchase Price, and Assignee shall have no recourse to Assignor for any such deficiency; (ix) Assignee has executed and agrees to comply with the terms of Assignor's Confidentiality Agreement (as hereinafter defined) and Assignee is not aware of any circumstances that may lead to a breach thereof; (x) Assignee is a "United States person" within the meaning of Section 7702(a)(30) of the Internal Revenue Code of 1986, as amended; and (xi) Assignee has not engaged any broker or finder or incurred or become obligated to pay any broker's commission or finder's fee in connection with the transactions contemplated by this Agreement.

Agreement Regarding Absolute Assignment of Notes, Liens, and Other Loan Documents, *21st Annual Advanced Real Estate Drafting Course* (State Bar of Texas) Appendix 2, at 11 (2010)

Note the *and/or* in (b)—is due diligence required of either *perfection* or *priority* or both?

As you can see, unpacking the romanettes requires serious thought.

The citation is to the wrong section of the Internal Revenue Code. The error is fixed in the revision on the next page.

"Only as we achieve clarity of expression and ease of comprehension can we genuinely serve the members of our community." Robert Eagleson, *Ensnaring Perceptions on Communication: Underlying Obstacles to Lawyers' Writing Plainly*, 62 Clarity 9, 12 (Nov. 2009).

BUT THIS:

Note that the numbering proceeds directly from 10 to (A), not 10.1, because of the continuous syntax.

10. Representations and Warranties by You. You represent and warrant to us as follows:

(A) you have the power and authority to purchase the Loans, Notes, and other Loan Documents according to this Agreement;

(B) you have conducted your own due diligence for the purchase of the Loans, Notes, and other Loan Documents, including:

(1) the terms and enforceability of the Loan Documents;

(2) the perfection and priority of any lien against, security interest in, and assignment of any Collateral; and

(3) the value, condition, quality, sufficiency of the description, and amount of any Collateral covered or affected by the Loan Documents;

(C) you have not relied on any of our statements except for what is expressly presented in this Agreement, and you rely solely on the results of your own due diligence;

(D) the person signing this Agreement on your behalf is authorized to do so;

(E) you are purchasing the Loans and Loan Documents for your own account and not for a potential public sale or distribution, and you do not intend to sell, offer for sale, or syndicate securities or fractional interests in yourself in connection with the purchase of the Loans and Loan Documents, but this (E) does not deny or limit your right to dispose of all or any part of your interest in the Loans or Loan Documents in compliance with applicable law;

(F) you have enough knowledge of and experience in financial and business matters to be capable of evaluating the merits and risks that might arise from the purchase of the Loans and Loan Documents, and you are capable of making an informed purchase and investment decision;

(G) you have investigated the facts and circumstances that you consider to be necessary and proper to evaluate the Loans and Loan Documents and to form a basis for evaluating a purchase of the Loans and Loan Documents, including reviewing information contained in our credit and collateral files and other financial information about the Borrower and Guarantors;

(H) you have undertaken your review in confidence;

(I) you have agreed to the Purchase Price based on your own independent investigation and credit evaluation of the Loans and Loan Documents;

(J) the amount you ultimately receive from the Loans and Loan Documents may be less than the Purchase Price;

(K) you are assuming all risk relating to the completeness, accuracy, or sufficiency of the Loan Documents;

(L) by acquiring the Loan Documents, you assume the risk of full or partial loss that is inherent in credit, collateral, and collectbility associated with the quality and character of the Loan Documents;

(M) you will have no recourse to us for any deficiency;

(N) you have signed and agreed to comply with our Confidentiality Agreement, and you are not aware of any circumstances that may lead to a breach of it;

(O) you are a "United States person" within the meaning of 26 U.S.C. § 7701(a)(30) of the Internal Revenue Code;

(P) you have not engaged any broker or finder or incurred or become obligated to pay any broker's commission or finder's fee in connection with the transactions of this Agreement;

(Q) the Loans are in default and have been accelerated;

(R) the Mortgaged Property has been posted for foreclosure for a sale scheduled to occur on ____________________, 20__;

(S) Guarantors have filed for Chapter 7 bankruptcy protection;

(T) many mechanic's liens have been filed against the Mortgaged Property; and

(U) you have had the opportunity to inspect the Loan Documents and the Collateral and:

(1) we have made no representation about the accuracy or completeness of the information; and

(2) we sell the Loan Documents, and you purchase them subject to the terms above.

§ 32 Omit the traditional testimonium clause.

If you see an old-fashioned testimonium clause (beginning with *In witness whereof*), delete it. If one party is a business association such as a corporation, all that's necessary is to show that an officer is signing on behalf of the entity. If a warranty of authorization seems desirable, then it should be explicit: "[Signatory] warrants that he [or she] is signing on behalf of the Company and that he [or she] has full authority to bind the Company." Such language is invariably included in the representations and warranties.

NOT THIS:	BUT THIS:
Ex. 1 IN WITNESS WHEREOF, the parties have executed this Agreement as of the date first above written.	Signed: ______________________.
Ex. 2 IN WITNESS WHEREOF, the parties have caused this Agreement to be executed as of the date and place first written above.	Signed: ______________________.
Ex. 3 IN WITNESS WHEREOF, the Corporation has caused this Agreement to be signed by its duly authorized officers, and the Employee has hereunto set his hand and seal on the day and year first above written.	Signed: ______________________.

"Too many of us do not put a sufficient value on our ability to use everyday language and feel that in dealing with our clients we must season our documents with large doses of legal mumbo-jumbo if we are to get the fees that we expect. Unfortunately, this linguistic voodooism more often leads to monumental confusion than to the accomplishment of the intended result." Sidney F. Parham Jr., *The Fundamentals of Legal Writing* 44 (1967).

§ 33 If you must incorporate by reference, do it straightforwardly.

When incorporating exhibits or schedules into the body of a contract, use a simplified, streamlined form.

But think through what you're doing. Incorporating external standards is a common but sometimes treacherous practice. The incorporated standards often use terminology or impose obligations that the drafter doesn't intend. Further, an indiscriminate wholesale incorporation may have other unintended consequences. For example, if a drafter qualifies representations and warranties by referring to specific SEC filings, the effect may be to pick up things such as the "Risk Factors" section, where the sweeping "caveat emptor" statements may undermine the intended effect of more precisely worded representations and warranties.

What's the best simplified, streamlined form? Although you might adopt one of the simpler wordings in the right-hand column below, please consider an "Exhibits Clause" as shown in § 34: "The exhibits attached to this Agreement are an inherent part of it." Then you needn't encumber your references with verbiage relating to incorporation.

NOT THIS:	BUT THIS:
Ex. 1 Gorman shall make the payments in accordance with the payment schedule set forth on Exhibit B attached hereto and made a part hereof as if fully set forth herein. **Settlement Agreement from a major law firm**	Gorman will make payments in accordance with the payment schedule in Exhibit B (attached and incorporated into this Agreement).
Ex. 2 Acceptance of the terms of this Agreement, which incorporates herein by reference the release of claims attached as Addendum A (the "Second Release"), must occur no later than February 28, 2019, twenty-one (21) days following your receipt of this Agreement. **Retirement-Transition Agreement from a global security and aerospace company**	You must accept this Agreement—including the release of claims (the "Second Release") in Addendum A (attached and incorporated into this Agreement)—no later than February 28, 2019, 21 days after you received this Agreement.

"[T]he ordinary contract need not so widely separate lawyer and client. In trying to make the contract clear to clients, the lawyers will also make their contracts clearer to each other." David Mellinkoff, *Legal Writing: Sense and Nonsense* 79 (1982).

§ 34 Adopt default wordings for housekeeping clauses.

Use well-worded standard clauses that don't vary without reason. In practice, lawyers may use dozens of forms containing variant clauses—some inferior to others. The best practice is to have your preferred versions, each with a heading (see § 14). Below are some recommended ones.

8. **Miscellaneous Clauses.**

    8.1 **Entire agreement.** This Agreement represents the entire agreement between the parties. It cannot be changed except by written agreement signed by the parties.

    8.2 **No assignment.** Neither party may assign this Agreement without the other party's prior written consent, which must not be unreasonably withheld. A party's entering into contracts with subcontractors is not considered an assignment.

    8.3 **No waiver.** If either party fails to require the other to perform any term of this Agreement, that failure does not prevent the party from later enforcing that term. If either party waives the other's breach of a term, that waiver is not treated as waiving a later breach of the term.

    8.4 **Successors and representatives.** This Agreement binds and inures to the benefit of the parties and their heirs, personal representatives, successors, and (where permitted) assignees.

    8.5 **Notices.** All notices and other communications required or permitted under this Agreement must be in writing and must be sent or e-mailed to the party at that party's address set forth below or at whatever other address the party specifies in writing.

    8.6 **Severability.** If a court for any reason holds a provision of this Agreement to be unenforceable, the rest remains fully enforceable.

    8.7 **"Including."** Unless the context requires otherwise, the term "including" means "including but not limited to."

    8.8 **Headings.** Headings are for convenience only and do not affect the interpretation of this Agreement.

    8.9 **Exhibits.** The exhibits attached to this Agreement are an inherent part of it.

    8.10 **Governing law.** [California, New York, Texas, etc.] law applies to all matters arising under or relating to this Agreement without regard to any choice-of-law rules that might direct the application of another jurisdiction's laws.

    8.11 **Counterparts.** This Agreement may be signed in counterparts, each one of which is considered an original, but all of which constitute a single instrument.

Two points about these:

First, this is the simplest form of a severability clause. But the provision requires thought. Do you really want an unenforceable provision to be severed no matter what provision it is? A more detailed and explicit severability clause might read this way:

> 8.6 **Severability.** If a court having jurisdiction rules that any provision of this Agreement is invalid or otherwise unenforceable, the parties want the court to interpret this Agreement as follows:
> (A) by modifying the provision to the minimum degree necessary to make it enforceable or, if that modification is not allowed by law, by disregarding the provision;
> (B) by giving effect to the rest of this Agreement;
> (C) by holding the entire Agreement unenforceable if modifying or disregarding the unenforceable provision would destroy an essential purpose of this Agreement.

The substantive point is that "[i]f less than all of an agreement is unenforceable . . . , a court may nevertheless enforce the rest of the agreement in favor of a party who did not engage in serious misconduct if the performance as to which the agreement is unenforceable is not an essential part of the agreed exchange."[1]

Second, the provision about governing law may require research. In some jurisdictions, you may need to say that both the procedural and substantive law of [jurisdiction] applies. Otherwise, statutes of limitations or arbitration rules might not be made applicable.

NOT THIS:	BUT THIS:
Ex. 1 8.04 <u>**Amendments**</u>. No amendment or modification of this agreement shall be deemed effective unless made in writing and signed by the parties to this agreement. **Employment Agreement**	8.4 **Entire agreement.** This Agreement represents the entire agreement between the parties. It cannot be changed except by written agreement signed by the parties.
Ex. 2 8.03 <u>**Prior Agreements**</u>. This agreement contains the entire agreement between Employer and Employee relating to the subject matter hereof, and it supersedes all prior Agreements and understandings with respect to such subject matter. **Employment Agreement**	8.3 **Entire agreement.** This Agreement represents the entire agreement between the parties. It cannot be changed except by written agreement signed by the parties.

1 *See* 2 *Restatement (Second) of the Law of Contracts* § 184, at 30 (1981).

NOT THIS:	BUT THIS:
Ex. 3 **J. CHOICE OF LAW AND CHOICE OF VENUE** The parties agree that this Agreement was executed in [NAME OF COUNTY] County, Texas. Jurisdiction and venue for any action arising as a result of this Agreement shall be in [CITY], [COUNTY NAME] County, Texas and this Agreement shall be construed pursuant to the laws of the State of Texas. **Horse-Boarding Agreement**	(J) **Governing law.** Texas law applies to all matters arising under or relating to this Agreement without regard to any choice-of-law rules that might direct the application of another jurisdiction's laws. (K) **Venue.** Venue for all matters relating to this Agreement is ______ County, Texas.
Ex. 4 37. Texas Law to Govern. The intent of the parties is that Texas law apply to any construction of this agreement and the ownership of the property of the parties. The law of any other state shall apply either to the construction of this agreement or the property of the parties only to the extent absolutely required by law. **Premarital Agreement from 16 John F. Elder, *West's Texas Forms: Family Law* § 2.2, at 51 (4th ed. 2009)**	**37. Governing Law.** Texas law applies to all matters arising under or relating to this Agreement without regard to any choice-of-law rules that might direct the application of another jurisdiction's laws.
Ex. 5 A Party shall not assign or otherwise transfer any of its rights, or delegate or otherwise transfer any of its obligations or performance, under this Agreement, by operation of law or otherwise, to a successor of the assigning Party, by consolidation or merger (whether or not such Party is the surviving corporation); or to a purchaser of all or substantially all of the assigning Party's assets without prior written consent of the other Party. No delegation or other transfer will relieve a Party of any of its obligations or performance under this Agreement. Any purported assignment, delegation or transfer in violation of this Section is void. This Agreement is binding upon and inures to the benefit of the Parties hereto and their respective permitted successors and assigns. **Settlement Agreement**	(D) **No assignment.** Neither party may assign this Agreement, or delegate its performance, without the other party's prior written consent, which must not be unreasonably withheld. (E) **Successors and representatives.** This Agreement binds and inures to the benefit of the parties and their heirs, personal representatives, successors, and (where permitted) assignees.

NOT THIS:	BUT THIS:
Ex. 6 8.05 <u>**No Waiver**</u>. No term or condition of this agreement shall be deemed to have been waived, nor shall there be any estoppel to enforce any provisions of this agreement, except by a statement in writing signed by the party against whom enforcement of the waiver or estoppel is sought. Any written waiver shall not be deemed a continuing waiver unless specifically stated, shall incorporate only as to the specific term or condition waived and shall not constitute a waiver of such term or condition for the future or as to any act other than that specifically waived. The failure of either party to enforce at any time any of the provisions of this agreement shall not be construed as a waiver of such provisions or of the right of such party thereafter to enforce any such provisions. **Employment Agreement**	8.5 **No waiver.** If either party fails to require the other to perform any term of this Agreement, that failure does not prevent the party from later enforcing that term. If either party waives the other's breach of a term, that waiver is not treated as waiving a later breach of the term.
Ex. 7 Section IX. Entire Agreement. a. This written agreement contains the sole and entire agreement between the parties and supersedes any and all other agreements between the parties. The parties acknowledge and agree that neither of them has made any representation with respect to the subject matter of this agreement or any representations inducing the execution and delivery of this agreement, except such representations as are specifically set forth in this agreement, and each of the parties acknowledges that such party has relied on such party's own judgment in entering into the agreement. b. The parties further acknowledge that any statements or representations that may have previously been made by either of them to the other are void and of no effect and that neither of them has relied thereon in connection with such party's dealings with the other. **Contract of Employment from *Texas Forms: Legal & Business* § 11:43, at 101 (2008)**	9. **Entire Agreement.** This Agreement represents the entire agreement between the parties. It cannot be changed except by written agreement signed by the parties.

"The lawyer should not get carried away and include a host of provisions which are neither relevant to the client nor within the ambit of his instructions merely because they look good." Elmer Doonan, *Drafting* § 2.5.1, at 33 (Julie MacFarlane ed., 1995).

NOT THIS:	BUT THIS:
Ex. 8 11. General and Administrative Provisions. This Agreement shall represent the entire agreement by and between the parties, except as otherwise provided in this Agreement and may not be changed except by written agreement signed by Licensor. In the event a dispute or breach occurs regarding this agreement Licensor shall be entitled to its attorney's fees. The failure or delay of Licensor to enforce its rights herein shall not constitute a waiver of its rights under this Agreement, nor shall it be considered a basis for estoppel, either at equity or at law. Licensor may exercise its rights despite the delay or failure to enforce those rights at the time the cause of action, right, or obligation arose. This agreement shall be binding upon and inure to the benefit of the Licensor, its successors and assigns. If any provision of this Agreement is held violative of any applicable law, government rule, or regulation or held to be unenforceable, the invalidity of that specific provision shall not invalidate the remaining provisions of this Agreement. All other provisions and the entirety of this Agreement shall remain in full force and effect. This Agreement shall be subject to and governed by the laws of the State of Texas. Any and all obligations, payments or legal actions shall be in [*name of county*], Texas. Venue for all lawsuits, causes of action, arbitrations, or other disputes shall be [*name of county*], Texas. **Software-License Agreement from 3 Nancy Saint-Paul, Texas Legal Practice Forms 3d *Technology Agreements* § 52:14 (2016)**	**11. General and Administrative Provisions.** 11.1 **Entire agreement.** This Agreement represents the entire agreement between the parties. It cannot be changed except by written agreement signed by the parties. 11.2 **Attorney fees.** If a dispute or breach occurs regarding this Agreement, the Licensor is entitled to attorney fees. 11.3 **No waiver.** If either party fails to require the other to perform any term of this Agreement, that failure does not prevent the party from later enforcing that term. If either party waives the other's breach of a term, that waiver is not treated as waiving a later breach of the term. 11.4 **Successors and assigns.** This Agreement binds and inures to the benefit of the parties and their heirs, personal representatives, successors, and (where permitted) assignees. 11.5 **Severability.** If a court for any reason holds a provision of this Agreement to be unenforceable, the rest remains fully enforceable. 11.6 **Governing law.** Texas law applies to all matters arising under or relating to this Agreement without regard to any choice-of-law rules that might direct the application of another jurisdiction's laws. 11.7 **Venue.** Venue for all lawsuits or other dispute-resolution method is ________ County, Texas.

In many contracts, the Miscellaneous section at the end often appears to have been thrown together at the last minute. You'll do better if you isolate the multiple subjects and provide specific headings.

"Are the performances of the opposing party unambiguously provided for? This is really the nub of the question. Indeed, you would be surprised at the extent to which the question could be rephrased: 'Are there ANY performances by the opposing party which the contract expressly requires?' If the contract has been drafted by or on behalf of the opposing party, the chances are good that this is the relevant question."
David Crump, "The Five Elements of a Contract: Avoiding Ambiguity in Them," 43 Tex. B.J. 370, 371 (1980).

B. Formatting

Understanding the basic decisions

What's the first thing anybody notices about a document? Its overall appearance. And first impressions matter.

But formatting, or "document design," is about much more than first impressions: it's about third and fourth impressions. After all, your reader may spend many hours with your work. If you know how to produce readable pages, you'll minimize readers' headaches and maximize the effortless retrieval of information.

So you must learn something about typography and page layout.[1] Although lawyers formerly didn't have to trouble themselves with these things—because the options were severely limited in the days of typewriters—times have changed. You ignore document design at your peril. Although many colleagues and clients use some form of e-reader, you're wise to assume the primacy of print and to assume that it matters how your document will look if someone prints it.

Few things are more repellent to a reader than a huge block of small type. Readers of contracts (yes, there are some) have to be able to navigate that expanse. Where is the contract term you're looking for? Consider the essence of this chapter if it's typeset this way:

(i) Use a readable typeface; (ii) Create ample white space—and use it meaningfully; (iii) Highlight ideas with attention-getters such as bullets; (iv) Don't use all capitals, and avoid initial capitals; (v) For a long document, make a table of contents; (vi) Never use more than two fonts in a document; (vii) Leave a little more room in your margins than you're required to; (viii) Use initial indents of a quarter of an inch or so; use the tab key or automatic paragraph formatting to keep them consistent; (ix) Use hanging indents that cascade in from the left margin; (x) Use even forward-spacing in your documents: one space between words and one space after punctuation marks (including colons and periods); (xi) Use a hard (nonbreaking) space to avoid breaking lines at inappropriate places; (xii) To ensure that the indentation is consistent throughout the document, use a tab instead of the spacebar for indenting.

or this one?

1. Use a readable typeface.
2. Create ample white space—and use it meaningfully.
3. Highlight ideas with attention-getters such as bullets.
4. Don't use all capitals, and avoid initial capitals.
5. For a long document, make a table of contents.
6. Never use more than two fonts in a document.
7. Leave a little more room in your margins than you're required to.

---

1 *See* Matthew Butterick, *Typography for Lawyers* (2d ed. 2018); Ellen Lupton, *Thinking with Type* (2d ed. 2010); Colin Wheildon, *Type and Layout* (rev. ed. 2005); Robert Bringhurst, *The Elements of Typographic Style* (2002); Philip Brady, *Using Type Right* (1989).

8. Use initial indents of a quarter of an inch or so; use the tab key or automatic paragraph formatting to keep them consistent.
9. Use hanging indents that cascade in from the left margin.
10. Use even forward-spacing in your documents: one space between words and one space after punctuation marks (including colons and periods).
11. Use a hard (nonbreaking) space to avoid breaking lines at inappropriate places.
12. To ensure that the indentation is consistent throughout the document, use a tab instead of the spacebar for indenting.

As for right-margin justification vs. ragged right, there are two schools of thought. Plain-English enthusiasts have traditionally touted a ragged-right margin. But empirical studies show that right-justified text, in the hands of a competent typesetter, is more readable. Neither side of the question is worth a dogmatic stance. You'll notice that the text throughout this book is right-justified.

"[D]esign is recognized as an integral part of any simplification project. The appearance of the finished product should be considered from the start. A document's design is not an afterthought, or a matter of putting ruffles onto an otherwise completed project. The document's appearance fundamentally affects its utility, both as a legal instrument and as a means of communication." Alan Siegel, "Drafting Simplified Legal Documents: Basic Principles and Their Application," in *Drafting Documents in Plain Language* 175, 224 (Duncan A. MacDonald chmn., 1979).

Hanging indents

§ 35 Commit to using hanging indents that cascade from the left margin.

If you're listing items that can't be stated in just a couple of words, break them down into parallel indented provisions. Indenting should progress from the left margin, starting there—not with a first-line indent, as in a letter. The first character of the second line of a subpart should line up precisely with the first character of the subpart's first line. See the examples below.

Although many official printers go margin-to-margin to cut down the number of pages, the result is counterproductive. It makes all the contracts look as if they're "fine print," and readers are inevitably repelled by the monolithic look of the page.

The hanging indent is perhaps the most widely overlooked tool of good drafting. It reveals structure cleanly. Because it's typographically sophisticated, don't assume you'll be able to do it immediately—it takes some setting up. But once you prepare your documents this way, you'll wonder how you ever got by with old-style methods.

NOT THIS:	BUT THIS:
Ex. 1 6. Adjacent Advertising Sign. The Adjacent Sign Master Lease will be in a form reasonably acceptable to Buyer and Seller and will contain provisions providing the following: a. That Seller will be the Master Lessor and Buyer will be the Master Lessee; b. That the term will be for ninety-nine (99) years; c. That Buyer will have the exclusive right in its sole absolute discretion to enter into subleases and assignments with respect to the Adjacent Advertising Sign and will have the right to assign, pledge, or otherwise transfer its interest under the Adjacent Sign Master Lease to third parties without Seller's approval. **Purchase Agreement executed by a major law firm**	6.3 **Adjacent Advertising Sign.** The Adjacent-Sign Master Lease must be in a form reasonably acceptable to the Buyer and the Seller and must provide that: (A) the Seller is the Master Lessor and the Buyer is the Master Lessee; (B) the term is for 99 years; (C) the Buyer may enter into subleases and assignments regarding the Adjacent Advertising Sign without the Seller's approval; and (D) the Buyer may convey its interest under the Adjacent-Sign Master Lease to a third party without the Seller's approval.

"The first job . . . is to draft documents that communicate clearly to your own client." Barbara Child, *Drafting Legal Documents* 2 (2d ed. 1992).

NOT THIS:	BUT THIS:
Ex. 2 (g) <u>Potential Change in Control</u>: shall be deemed to have occurred if (i) the Company enters into an agreement or arrangement, the consummation of which would result in the occurrence of a Change in Control; (ii) any person (including the Company) publicly announces an intention to take or to consider taking actions that, if consummated, would constitute a Change in Control; (iii) any person (other than a trustee or other fiduciary holding securities under an employee benefit plan of the Company acting in such capacity or a corporation owned, directly or indirectly, by the stockholders of the Company in substantially the same proportions as their ownership of stock of the Company), who is or becomes the Beneficial Owner, directly or indirectly, of securities of the Company representing 10% or more of the combined voting power of the Company's then outstanding Voting Securities, increases his beneficial ownership of such securities by 5% or more over the percentage so owned by such person on the date hereof, or (iv) the Board adopts a resolution to the effect that, for purposes of this Agreement, a Potential Change in Control has occurred. **Indemnification Agreement from a computer-technology company**	(G) **Potential change in control.** A Potential Change in Control has occurred if: (1) the Company enters into an agreement or arrangement that would result in a Change in Control; (2) any person (including the Company) publicly announces an intention to take or consider taking actions that would constitute a Change in Control; (3) any person (other than a trustee or other fiduciary holding securities under an employee-benefit plan of the Company acting in that capacity or a corporation owned, directly or indirectly, by the stockholders of the Company in substantially the same proportions as their ownership of Company stock) who is or becomes the Beneficial Owner, directly or indirectly, of Company securities representing 10% or more of the combined voting power of the Company's then-outstanding Voting Securities, increases his or her beneficial ownership of Voting Securities by 5% or more as of the date of this Agreement; or (4) the Board adopts a resolution memorializing that, for purposes of this Agreement, a Potential Change in Control has occurred.

"One of the most hateful acts of the ill-fated Roman tyrant Caligula was inscribing the laws upon pillars so high that the people could not read them. In the opinion of many judges, insurance policies are too long and complex. They might just as well be carved at the top of a Roman pillar." Kenneth S. Wollner, *How to Draft and Interpret Insurance Policies* § 3.3.2, at 51 (1999).

§ 36 Prefer rectilinear indents of the kind illustrated throughout this book.

The left side of a page with hanging indents should show a rectilinear series of cascading provisions—that is, have clean vertical lines for the indented subparts.

The result looks like this:

1.
  1.1
    (A)
      (1)
        (a)

NOT THIS:

Ex. 1

3. Confidentiality. From and after the Closing Date, The Subject Party will, and will cause its Representatives to, keep confidential and not (except, if applicable, in the performance of its duties on behalf of the Covered Parties) directly or indirectly use, disclose, reveal, publish, transfer or provide access to, any and all Covered Party Information without the prior written consent of Tallinn (which may be withheld in its sole discretion). As used in this Agreement, ***"Covered Party Information"*** means all material and information relating to the business, affairs and assets of any Covered Party, including material and information that concerns or relates to such Covered Party's bidding and proposal, technical information, computer hardware or software, administrative, management, operational, data processing, financial, marketing, sales, human resources, business development, planning and/or other business activities, regardless of whether such material and information is maintained in physical, electronic, or other form, that is: (A) gathered, compiled, generated, produced or maintained by such Covered Party through its Representatives, or provided to such Covered Party by its suppliers, service providers or customers; and (B) intended and maintained by such Covered Party or its Representatives, suppliers, service providers or customers to be kept in confidence. The obligations set forth in this Section 3 will not apply to any Covered Party Information where The Subject Party can prove that such material or information: (i) is known or available through other lawful sources not bound by a confidentiality agreement with, or other confidentiality obligation to, any Covered Party; (ii) is or becomes publicly known through no violation of this Agreement or other non-disclosure obligation of The Subject Party or any of its Representatives; (iii) is already in the possession of The Subject Party at the time of disclosure through lawful sources not bound by a confidentiality agreement or other confidentiality obligation as evidenced by The Subject Party's documents and records; (iv) is developed independently by The Subject Party without use of or reference to any Covered Party Information; or (v) is required to be disclosed pursuant to an order of any administrative body or court of competent jurisdiction (provided that (A) the applicable Covered Party is given reasonable prior written notice, (B) The Subject Party cooperates (and causes its Representatives to cooperate) with any reasonable request of any Covered Party to seek to prevent or narrow such disclosure and (C) if after compliance with clauses (A) and (B) such disclosure is still required, The Subject Party and its Representatives only disclose such portion of the Covered Party Information that is expressly required by such order, as it may be subsequently narrowed).

Noncompetition and Nonsolicitation Agreement

BUT THIS:

3. Confidentiality. As of the Closing Date, Kroger will keep Covered Party Information confidential and will not directly or indirectly use, reveal, publish, transfer, or provide access to it without Tallinn's prior written consent, which Tallinn may withhold at its sole discretion. Kroger will also see that its Representatives do the same.

3.1 Exception to obligation. Kroger may disregard confidentiality to the extent necessary to perform its duties on behalf of the Covered Parties.

3.2 Definition of "Covered Party Information."

(A) **Meaning.** "Covered Party Information" means all material and information that, in any form, relates to the business, affairs, or assets of any Covered Party and is:

(1) gathered, compiled, generated, produced, or maintained by the Covered Party through its Representatives or provided to the Covered Party by its suppliers, service providers, or customers; and

(2) intended and maintained by the Covered Party or its Representatives, suppliers, service providers, or customers to be kept in confidence.

(B) **Examples.** "Covered Party Information" includes material and information that concerns the Covered Party's bidding and proposal activities; technical information; computer hardware or software; and administrative, management, operational, data-processing, financial, marketing, sales, human-resources, business-development, planning, and other business activities.

3.3 Obligation not applicable. The obligations in this § 3 do not apply to Covered Party Information if Kroger proves that the material or information:

(A) is known or available through other lawful sources not bound by a confidentiality agreement with, or other confidentiality obligation to, any Covered Party;

(B) is or becomes publicly known without violation by Kroger or any of its Representatives of this § 3 or other nondisclosure obligation;

(C) is already in Kroger's possession at the time of disclosure through lawful sources not bound by a confidentiality agreement or other confidentiality obligation as evidenced by Kroger's documents and records;

(D) is developed independently by Kroger without using or referring to any Covered Party Information; or

(E) must be disclosed under an order of any administrative body or court having jurisdiction, as long as:

(1) the applicable Covered Party is given reasonable prior written notice;

(2) Kroger cooperates (and causes its Representatives to cooperate) with reasonable requests of any Covered Party to seek to prevent or narrow the disclosure; and

(3) Kroger and its Representatives disclose only the part of the Covered Party Information that is expressly required by the final form of the order.

NOT THIS:

Ex. 2

7. Indemnification; Payments; Certain Waivers. Guarantor (i) waives any right or claim of right to cause a marshaling of Borrower's assets or to cause Administrative Agent or any Lender to proceed against any of the security for the Advances or for the obligations guaranteed hereby before proceeding against Guarantor, (ii) agrees that any payments required to be made by Guarantor hereunder shall become due on demand in accordance with the terms of paragraph 2 hereof and without presentment to Borrower, demand for payment or protest, or notice of non-payment or protest, and (iii) except as hereinafter provided, expressly waives and relinquishes all rights and remedies accorded by applicable law to guarantors. Without limiting the generality of the foregoing, Guarantor hereby waives all rights (x) to participate in any claim or remedy Administrative Agent or any Lender may now or hereafter have against Borrower or in any collateral which Administrative Agent or any Lender has or hereafter may acquire for the obligations guaranteed hereby and (y) except as provided below, to contribution, indemnification, set-off, exoneration or reimbursement, whether from Borrower, Guarantor, or any other Person now or hereafter primarily or secondarily liable for any of Borrower's obligations to Administrative Agent and Lenders, and whether arising by contract or operation of law or otherwise by reason of Guarantor's execution, delivery or performance of this Guaranty. Guarantor does not waive and hereby retains all rights of subrogation, contribution, indemnification, set-off or reimbursement against Borrower or any other guarantor that Guarantor may have (the "Undersigned's Rights"); provided, however, that (i) this Guaranty shall neither be contingent upon the existence of the Undersigned's Rights nor subject to any claims or defenses whatsoever which may be asserted in connection with the enforcement or attempted enforcement of the Undersigned's Rights including, without limitation, any claim that the Undersigned's Rights were abrogated by any of Administrative Agent's or any Lender's acts, and (ii) until the Advances shall have been fully and finally paid and satisfied and Lenders shall have no further commitment or other obligation to make Advances or other financial accommodations to Borrower and the Credit Agreement and all other Facility Documents shall have been terminated and shall be of no further force and effect, Guarantor hereby postpones and subordinates (A) the exercise of any and all of the Undersigned's Rights to Administrative Agent and Lenders' rights against Guarantor under this Guaranty or against Borrower under any of the Facility Documents, and (B) any of the Undersigned's Rights to any collateral securing the Advances.

Guaranty of Payment and Performance

Indemnification is mentioned only in a waiver. The payments clause is misplaced here.

Note the second set of romanettes within a single paragraph. See § 26.

"If a document looks terrifying, it does not matter how easy the words are: they will never be read." Alan Siegel, *Language Follows Logic: Practical Lessons in Legal Drafting*, Remarks at Conference of Experts in Clear Legal Drafting, National Center for Administrative Justice (2 June 1978) (as quoted in Reed Dickerson, *Materials on Legal Drafting* 295 (1981)).

BUT THIS:

7. **Payments.** Any payments required to be made by Gerard are due on demand in accordance with § 2 and without presentment to Bernard, demand for payment or protest, or notice of nonpayment or protest.

8. **Certain Waivers.**

8.1 **Waiver of certain rights.** Gerard waives any right or claim of right:

(A) to cause a marshaling of Bernard's assets or to cause Administrative Agent or any Lender to proceed against any of the security for the Advances or for the obligations guaranteed by this Agreement before proceeding against Gerard;

(B) to participate in any claim or remedy that Administrative Agent or any Lender might now or later have against Bernard or in any collateral that Administrative Agent or any Lender has or might later acquire for the obligations guaranteed by this Agreement; and

(C) except as provided in § 8.2, to benefit from contribution, indemnity, setoff, exoneration, or reimbursement, whether from Bernard, Gerard, or any other Person now or later primarily or secondarily liable for any of Bernard's obligations to Administrative Agent and Lenders, and whether arising by contract or operation of law or otherwise, by reason of Gerard's signing, delivery, or performance of this Guaranty;

(D) except as provided in § 8.2, to claim a right or remedy accorded by applicable law to guarantors.

The original section focused on waivers, not payments.

8.2 **Rights not waived.** Gerard retains all rights of subrogation, contribution, indemnity, setoff, and reimbursement against Bernard or any other guarantor that Gerard may have if this Guaranty is neither contingent on the existence of those rights nor subject to any claims or defenses that may be asserted in connection with the enforcement or attempted enforcement of the rights, including any claim that the rights were abrogated by Administrative Agent's or a Lender's acts.

8.3 **Postponement of exercise of Undersigned's Rights.** Gerard will postpone and subordinate the exercise of any of its rights under § 8.2 to Administrative Agent and Lenders' rights against Gerard under this Guaranty or against Bernard under any of the Facility Documents, and any of Gerard's rights to any collateral securing the Advances, until:

(A) the Advances are fully and finally paid and satisfied;

(B) Lenders have no further commitment or other obligation to make Advances or other financial accommodations to Bernard; and

(C) the Credit Agreement and all other Facility Documents have been terminated.

"The legal profession is falling far below its real potentialities, not only in the highly specialized field of legislative drafting but in the general field (which touches every lawyer) of preparing contracts, wills, leases, and conveyances. Basic ability is not hard to find. Basic ability adequately trained is rare." Reed Dickerson, *Legislative Drafting* 4 (1954).

Fonts

§ 37 Prefer a serif font.

In the 1990s, when law offices first began upgrading from the old dot-matrix printers of the 1980s, many lawyers began exuberantly experimenting with all their laser printers' newfound options. The profession—or at least part of it—went through a phase of typographic garishness from which we haven't fully recovered.

One aspect of this unfettered typographic discretion was the widespread adoption of sans-serif typefaces such as Arial. Generally speaking, typographers reserve sans-serif fonts for what is known as *display type*—headlines, for example, or the Helvetica road signs that so effectively draw the eye. (If you haven't seen the documentary movie *Helvetica*, by the way, check it out!)

Sans-serif fonts are good for limited uses in small chunks, such as the running headers in this very book, as well as the boxed *Not This–But This* headings, the contractual attributions at the bottom left-hand sides of the boxes, and the page numbers.

Otherwise, for long spans of words, serif fonts are more conducive to readability. Why? Instead of being uniform straight lines, the serifs—the little protuberances (often called *feet*) coming off the letters of a serif typeface—give each character a distinctive look. Similarly, words themselves have familiar and recognizable shapes. Readers with only a little experience can more easily distinguish letters in the microseconds it takes to discern a word. It's a subliminal effect but a real one.[1]

NOT THIS:	BUT THIS:
Ex. 1 B. This Agreement may be terminated by either party, if there has been a material breach of the terms of this Agreement by the other party and such breach has not been cured within thirty (30) days after receiving written notice of such breach. **Master Development and Distribution Agreement from a major motion-picture studio**	(B) **Termination.** Either party may terminate this Agreement if the other party materially breaches the Agreement and fails to cure the breach within 30 days after receiving written notice of it.

1 *See, e.g.*, A.F. Monk & C. Hulme, "Errors in Proofreading & Evidence for Use of Word Shape in Word Recognition," *in* 11 *Memory and Cognition* 16–23 (1983); A. Pollatsek & K. Rayner, "Eye Movement Control in Reading: The Role of Word Boundaries," *in* 8 *Journal of Experimental Psychology: Human Perception and Performance* 817–33 (1982); M.J. Adams, "Models of Word Recognition," *in* 11 *Cognitive Psychology* 133–76 (1979); P.B. Gough, "One Second of Reading," *in Language by Ear and by Eye* 331–58 (James F. Kavanaugh & Ignatius G. Mattingly eds., 1972).

NOT THIS:

Ex. 2

10 Agreement

a. This written agreement contains the sole and entire agreement between the parties and supersedes any and all other agreements between the parties. The parties acknowledge and agree that neither of them has made any representation with respect to the subject matter of this agreement or any representations inducing the execution and delivery of this agreement, except such representations as are specifically set forth in this agreement, and each of the parties acknowledges that such party has relied on such party's own judgement in entering into the agreement.

b. The parties further acknowledge that any statements or representations that may have previously been made by either of them to the other are void and of no effect and that neither of them has relied thereon in connection with such party's dealings with the other.

Employment Agreement from a major company

BUT THIS:

10. Extent of Agreement.

10.1 Entire agreement. This Agreement represents the entire agreement between the parties. It cannot be changed except by written agreement signed by the parties.

10.2 Prior representations. Every statement or representation previously made by either party to the other is void. Neither party has relied on such a statement or representation when dealing with the other.

"Clarity and readability are more complementary than competitive. Up to a point we can have both. [But a] preoccupation with clarity alone implies that optimum readability is automatic." Reed Dickerson, *The Fundamentals of Legal Drafting* § 8.9, at 175 (2d ed. 1986).

§ 38 Use a font size of 10–14 points.

For the ordinary purposes of a single-column contract, the best default is a 13-point font such as Equity, Garamond, Caslon, or Palatino. If you're using two columns per page, you can reduce the font size to 9 or even 8—but that's only if you're customizing a contract, perhaps because it's for consumers and you're having large numbers professionally printed.

In this book, given the double-column format for most illustrations, the type size is normally 9 points for the side-by-side comparisons. Note that the prose is readable—especially for the special purposes of this book—because the lines in the columns average 45 characters (see § 44).

NOT THIS:

Ex. 1

9.4 Neither party will use the other party's name or trademarks, trade names, service marks, or quote the opinion of any employee of the other party in any advertising, presentations or otherwise without first obtaining the other party's prior written consent.

9.5 The parties are independent contractors and neither party is an employee, agent, servant, representative, partner, or joint venturer of the other or has any authority to assume or create any obligation or liability of any kind on behalf of the other.

Relationship Agreement from a computer-technology company

This copy is set in 7-point type, set solid (with no extra space between lines).

BUT THIS:

9.4 **Prior consent necessary for promotional material.** Neither party may use the other party's name, trademarks, tradenames, or servicemarks, or may quote the opinion of any employee of the other party, in any advertising, presentations, or otherwise without obtaining the other party's prior written consent.

9.5 **Independent-contractor status.** The parties are independent contractors. Neither party is an employee, agent, servant, representative, partner, or joint venturer of the other or has any authority to assume or create any obligation or liability for the other.

This copy is set in 10-point type, with two points of extra space between the lines.

"Good text presentation incorporates the latest techniques to help understanding and avoids things that hinder comprehension. The result is a text that is well organized with type style, layout, page color, line length, and indentations all designed to communicate the message in the clearest possible way." David C. Elliott, *Plain Language: A Global Perspective*, 70 Mich. B.J. 562, 562 (June 1991).

NOT THIS:

Ex. 2

This copy is set in 8-point type with no extra space between the lines.

6. STANDARDS OF MANUFACTURE, QUALITY AND VERIFICATION TESTING

6.1 Prior to any commercialized distribution of each unique implementation of the Licensed Software embedded or otherwise incorporated into Licensee Products, Licensee shall provide Licensor with at least one (1) of each product family of Licensee's implementation for verification testing. In addition, Licensee shall supply Licensor with an evaluation board that provides a socket facility for installation and testing of the Licensed Software embedded or otherwise incorporated into Licensee Products. Licensor shall be entitled to retain in its possession one (1) such copy of the Licensed Software embedded or otherwise incorporated into Licensee Products with corresponding testing materials supplied by Licensee, once certified, for future verification.

Software-License, -Development, and -Distribution Agreement from a digital-technology company

BUT THIS:

This copy is set in 10-point type with two points of extra space between the lines.

6. Standards of Manufacture, Quality, and Verification Testing.

6.1 CNA's responsibilities. Before any commercialized distribution of each unique implementation of the Licensed Software embedded or otherwise incorporated into CNA Products, CNA will provide Revelage with at least 1 of each product family of CNA's implementation for verification testing. In addition, CNA will supply Revelage with an evaluation board that provides a socket facility for installation and testing of the Licensed Software embedded or otherwise incorporated into CNA Products. Revelage may retain 1 copy of the Licensed Software embedded or otherwise incorporated into CNA Products with corresponding testing materials supplied by CNA, once certified, for future verification.

"Nor is it only nonlegal members of the public who are disaffected. Complaints and admissions of personal difficulty in reading all types of legal documents abound from judges and lawyers." Robert D. Eagleson, "Efficiency in Legal Drafting," in *Essays on Legislative Drafting in Honour of J.Q. Ewens CMG, CBE, QC* 13, 14 (1990).

§ 39 Use smart quotes and smart apostrophes.

Straight quotes, which don't jibe well with a serif font, can be caused by all sorts of glitches in computer programs, especially when a document is sent from one computer to another. Fixing them, if the application's default is set to use smart quotes (also called *typographer's quotes*), is usually just a matter of doing a search-and-replace maneuver for all quotation marks (single as well as double). Do the same for apostrophes.

NOT THIS:	BUT THIS:
Ex. 1 As used herein, "Cause" means any of the following: (A) Employee is convicted by a court of competent jurisdiction of, or pleads "no contest" to, a felony or any other crime involving moral turpitude (other than minor traffic violations); . . . . **Employment Agreement from a medicinal-, chemical-, and botanical-products company**	In this Agreement, “Cause” means any of the following: (A) A court convicts Employee of—or Employee pleads “no contest” to—a felony or other crime involving moral turpitude (other than a minor traffic violation); . . . .
Ex. 2 `THIS AGREEMENT entered into as of the 29th day of April, 2016, by and between Rockport Pipeline & Storage Company LLC, a New York limited liability company, hereinafter referred to as "Seller," and Cooperative Energy Company, Inc., a New York corporation, hereinafter referred to as "Customer."` **Natural-Gas-Storage-Services Agreement from a major New York energy company**	This Agreement, effective April 29, 2016, is between Rockport Pipeline & Storage Company LLC (Rockport), a New York limited-liability company, and Cooperative Energy Company, Inc. (Cooperative Energy), a New York corporation. Many drafters would omit the quotation marks altogether and simply put the shorthand names in parentheses. The revision has also changed the ill-advised monospaced Courier font to a proportionally spaced serif face, here Equity Text. See § 37.

> “You can always get curly quotes. Compared to straight quotes, curly quotes are more legible on the page and match the other characters better. Therefore, straight quotes should never, ever appear in your documents.” Matthew Butterick, *Typography for Lawyers* 39 (2010).

Emphasis in text

§ 40 Boldface your headings.

Typographically speaking, most forms are stuck in the typewriter era—when only two means were available for creating visual emphasis: underlining and capitalizing. Boldfacing is largely a post-1980 phenomenon for law-office documents. But so is effective document design generally. In any event, a mere glance at the examples in this section demonstrates how significantly boldfaced headings contribute to readability.

NOT THIS:	BUT THIS:
Ex. 1 10. Successors and Assigns. This Agreement, and all of the terms and provisions hereof, shall be binding upon and shall inure to the benefit of the parties hereto, and their respective legal representatives, heirs, administrators, successors, and assigns. 11. Entire Agreement; Amendments. This Agreement represents the entire agreement between the parties hereto, and no modification or amendment of this Agreement shall be effective unless made by supplemental agreement in writing executed by the parties hereto. 12. Governing Law; Severability. This Agreement shall be governed by and construed in accordance with the laws of the State of Texas, and it is intended to be performed in accordance with, and only to the extent permitted by, all applicable laws, ordinances, rules and regulations of the State of Texas. If any provision of this Agreement, or the application thereto to any person or circumstance, shall, for any reason and to any extent, be invalid or unenforceable, the remainder of this Agreement and the application of such provision to other persons or circumstances shall not be affected thereby, but rather shall be enforced to the greatest extent permitted by law. 13. Notices. All notices or other communications required or permitted to be given pursuant to this Agreement shall be in writing and shall be considered as properly given if mailed from within the United States by first class mail, postage prepaid, and addressed as follows: If to manager: ———. If to owner: ———. **Management Agreement from S. Lee Stevenson Jr. & Dennis H. Taylor, *Texas Legal Practice Forms Contracts* § 2A:74, at 2A-89 (1985)**	**10. Successors and Assigns.** This Agreement binds and inures to the benefit of the parties and their heirs, personal representatives, successors, and (where permitted) assignees. **11. Entire Agreement; Amendments.** This Agreement represents the entire agreement between the parties. It cannot be changed except by written agreement signed by the parties. **12. Governing Law.** Texas law applies to all matters arising under or relating to this Agreement without regard to any choice-of-law rules that might direct the application of another jurisdiction's laws. **13. Severability.** If a court for any reason holds a provision of this Agreement to be unenforceable, the rest remains fully enforceable. **14. Notices.** All notices and other communications required or permitted under this Agreement must be in writing and are considered properly given if mailed from within the United States by first-class mail, postage prepaid, and addressed as follows: (A) If to manager: ____________________. (B) If to owner: ____________________.

NOT THIS:	BUT THIS:
Ex. 2 5. Time of Payment. Within 30 days after delivery. The Seller will not recognize any discount for payment within shorter period. 6. Method of Shipment. In discretion of the Buyer. The Seller will reimburse the Buyer the lesser of truck freight or rail freight from the Seller's plant at [*address of company*] to the Buyer's factory at [*address of factory*]. 7. Risk of Loss and Insurance. Risk of loss on the Buyer from time of delivery to carrier. The Buyer shall provide at its expense insurance thereon insuring the Seller's and the Buyer's interest as they appear, until payment in full to the Seller. 8. Seller to Retain Security Interest Until Paid. The Seller hereby retains a security interest in the goods that are the subject matter of this contract. 9. Time of Delivery. Monday through Friday, during hours of [*range of hours*]. The Seller may ship in lots of not less than [*number of tons*] tons per shipment, but the Buyer shall not be compelled to take more than [*number of tons*] tons in any consecutive period of five business days. 10. Excuse of Delay or Failure to Perform. The Seller shall be excused for any delay or failure to perform due to fire, act of God, or similar catastrophe, strike or labor trouble affecting the Seller or Seller's suppliers or subcontractors, or other cause beyond the Seller's control. 11. Cancellation. The Seller reserves the right to cancel this contract: (1) if the Buyer fails to pay for any shipment when due, or (2) in the event of the Buyer's insolvency or bankruptcy, or (3) if the Seller deems that its prospect of payment is impaired. 12. Controlling Law. This contract shall be interpreted in accordance with the substantive laws of [*name of state*]. **Bulk-Goods Sales Contract from 12A Fred H. Miller, *West's Legal Forms: Commercial Transactions* § 18.10, at 11–12 (4th ed. 2013)**	**5. Time of Payment.** Highlander will pay CGM within 30 days after delivery. There is no discount for early payment. **6. Shipping Method.** CGM will reimburse Highlander for either truck freight or rail freight—whichever is cheaper—from CGM's plant at [*address of company*] to Highlander's factory at [*address of factory*]. The shipping method is at Highlander's discretion. **7. Risk of Loss and Insurance.** Highlander bears the risk of loss from the time CGM delivers the freight to the carrier. Highlander will provide insurance at its own expense for both parties' interests in the shipment until Highlander pays CGM in full. **8. Retained Security Interest.** Until paid in full, CGM retains a security interest in the goods that are the subject matter of this contract. **9. Shipment Size and Delivery Schedule.** CGM will ship in lots of at least ________ tons per shipment. But Highlander is not required to take more than ___ tons in 5 consecutive business days. Shipments may be delivered between 10 a.m. and 5 p.m., Monday through Friday. **10. Excuse for Delay or Failure to Perform.** CGM's delay or failure to perform is excused if it results from: (A) a fire; (B) an act of God or a similar catastrophe; (C) a strike or labor trouble affecting CGM, its suppliers, or its subcontractors; or (D) any other cause beyond CGM's control. **11. Cancellation.** CGM may cancel this contract if: (A) Highlander does not pay for a shipment when due; (B) Highlander becomes insolvent or files bankruptcy; or (C) CGM considers its prospect of payment impaired. **12. Governing Law.** [*Jurisdiction*] law applies to all matters arising under or relating to this Agreement without regard to any choice-of-law rules that might direct the application of another jurisdiction's laws.

May gives the Seller discretion, yet *not less than* indicates a mandatory minimum.

The revision resolves the inconsistency by using *will*.

NOT THIS:	BUT THIS:
Ex. 3 1. Agency. The Artist appoints the Agent to act as his or her exclusive representative: (A) in the following geographical area: ______________ (B) for the markets listed here (specify publishing, advertising, etc.): ______________ The Agent agrees to use his or her best efforts in submitting the Artist's work for the purpose of securing assignments for the Artist. The Agent shall negotiate the terms of any assignment that is offered, but the Artist shall have the right to reject any assignment if he or she finds the terms thereof unacceptable. 2. Promotion. The Artist shall provide the Agent with such samples of work as are from time to time necessary for the purpose of securing assignments. These samples shall remain the property of the Artist and be returned within thirty (30) days of termination of this Agreement. The Agent shall take reasonable efforts to protect the work from loss or damage, but shall be liable for such loss or damage only if caused by the Agent's negligence. Promotional expenses, including but not limited to promotional mailings and paid advertising, shall be paid ______ percent by the Agent and _____ percent by the Artist. The Agent shall bear the expenses of shipping, insurance and similar marketing expenses. 3. Term. This Agreement shall take effect on the _____ day of _____, 20_____, and remain in full force and effect for a term of one year, unless terminated as provided in Paragraph 9. 4. Commissions. The Agent shall be entitled to the following commissions: . . . . **Artist-Agent Agreement from Tad Crawford, *Legal Guide for the Visual Artist* 130 (3d ed. 1989)**	**1. Agency.** **1.1 Scope of representation.** Melville appoints Hubbard to act as exclusive representative for the markets listed here (specify publishing, advertising, etc.): ______________ ______________ ______________ in the following geographical areas: ______________ ______________ ______________ . **1.2 Hubbard's duties.** Hubbard will use best efforts in submitting Melville's work to secure assignments. Hubbard will negotiate any assignment offered. But if Melville considers the terms unacceptable, Melville may reject the assignment. **2. Promotion.** Melville will provide Hubbard work samples when necessary to secure assignments. These samples remain Melville's property and must be returned within 30 days after this Agreement's termination. Hubbard will take reasonable efforts to protect the work from loss or damage but is liable only for loss or damage caused by Hubbard's own negligence. Hubbard will pay ________%, and Melville will pay ________%, of all promotional expenses, which include promotional mailings and paid advertising. Hubbard is responsible for shipping expenses, insurance, and similar marketing expenses. **3. Term.** This Agreement takes effect on ______________ ____, 20_____, for a term of 1 year unless terminated under § 9. **4. Commissions.** Hubbard is entitled to the following commissions: . . . .

§ 41 Never use underlining.

Underlining (or underscoring, as it's sometimes called) is the crude typewriting method for calling attention to text. We also do it in handwriting, since most people can't produce a calligraphic italic. In those contexts, underlining simply means, to the professional typographer, "please set this in italic type."

With the advent of modern word processing, we can now produce boldface and italic type—even boldface italic—with a simple keystroke or mouse click. There's no longer any justification for underlining, which robs the text of interlineated white space, clutters the text, and bumps into descenders such as the lower parts of *g*, *j*, *p*, *q*, and *y*—as well as commas and semicolons. Abstain from underlining.

It's true that many experienced deal lawyers underline (and often boldface as well) all defined terms upon first mention. Nothing that is said here will change their practice, which may concededly be convenient for *them*, as opposed to their readers. Nevertheless, from the viewpoint of general readability and standards of typography, it's a retrograde practice.

NOT THIS:	BUT THIS:
Ex. 1 Except as may be otherwise specifically provided in this Agreement, all notices shall be in writing and shall be deemed to be delivered when deposited in the United States mail, postage prepaid, registered or certified mail, return receipt requested, addressed to the parties at the respective addresses set forth on Exhibit B or at such other addresses as either party may specify by written notice. **Guaranty Agreement from a major law firm**	**16.5 Notices.** All notices and other communications required or permitted under this Agreement must be in writing and must be sent or e-mailed to the party at that party's address set forth below or at whatever other address the party specifies in writing.

"The prose we think of as the traditional lawyers' product gives a feeling of chilly formality. A goal of plain English, on the other hand, is to create a feeling of direct, straightforward communication." Carl Felsenfeld & Alan Siegel, *Writing Contracts in Plain English* 111 (1981).

NOT THIS:	BUT THIS:
Ex. 2 1. Non-Disclosure and Restrictions on Use of Information. (a) Information. For purposes of this Agreement, "Information" shall mean, without limitation, the identity of the Business Opportunity, all intellectual property, strategic information, financial statements or projections, business plans, prototypes, drawings, data, trade secrets, business records, customer lists, supplier agreements, partnership or joint venture agreements, license agreements, marketing plans, employee lists, policies and procedures, information relating to processes, technologies or theory and any or all other information which may be disclosed by the Disclosing Party to the Recipient in accordance with this Agreement. (b) Non-Disclosure of Information. The Recipient acknowledges the competitive value and confidential nature of the Information and the damages that would result to the Disclosing Party if any such information were disclosed, therefore the Information will be kept confidential and shall not be disclosed by the Recipient in any manner whatsoever, in whole or in part, except that: . . . . **Nondisclosure and Noncircumvention Agreement from Jean L. Batman, *Advising the Small Business: Forms and Advice for the Legal Practitioner* 23 (2007)**	**1. Confidential Information.** **1.1 Nondisclosure.** Rogers acknowledges the proprietary nature of the Confidential Information and recognizes the potential damage that could result from its disclosure. Rogers must not disclose Confidential Information in any manner, with the following limited exceptions: . . . . **1.2 Definition.** "Confidential Information" means any information that the Disclosing Party discloses to Rogers under this Agreement. It includes the identity of the Business Opportunity, all intellectual property, strategic information, financial statements or projections, business plans, prototypes, drawings, data, trade secrets, business records, customer lists, supplier agreements, partnership or joint-venture agreements, license agreements, marketing plans, employee lists, policies and procedures, and information relating to processes, technologies, or theory.

§ 42 Forswear all-caps text.

Legal drafters have a long-standing practice of putting important clauses such as disclaimers and limitations of liability into all-caps type. The practice became especially ingrained during the century or so when typewriters were the normal means of preparing legal instruments. Typewriters typically allowed only two methods of emphasizing text: underlining and capping. Drafters with good judgment understood that these admittedly crude methods of emphasizing must be used sparingly.

Over time, legislators and regulators came to enact disclosure obligations requiring certain clauses in legal instruments to be especially prominent. These requirements were often phrased in vague terms such as "in type at least as large and at least as prominent as any other type on the page." For example:

- Haw. Rev. Stat. § 446E-2 (requiring unaccredited degree-granting institutions to make disclosures "in a type size as large or larger than any other text in the catalog, promotional material, or contract for instruction, excluding the name of the unaccredited institution," which must be "presented in a manner reasonably calculated to draw the attention of the reader").
- 12 C.F.R. § 226.17(a)(2) (stating that where the law requires disclosure of the information to the consumer, the terms *finance charge* and *annual percentage rate*, along with their corresponding amount or percentage rate, "shall be more conspicuous than any other disclosure, except the creditor's identity") (the meaning of *conspicuous* had to be determined in litigation: *Smith v. Check-N-Go of Illinois*, 200 F.3d 511, 514–15 (7th Cir. 1999)).
- Tex. Admin. Code § 83.6006 (providing that "disclosures for credit access business transactions must be printed in an easily readable font and type size").
- 15 U.S.C. § 1648 (requiring reverse-mortgage disclosures to be only "in conspicuous type").
- UCC § 2A-214 (Exclusion or Modification of Warranties has been widely adopted. Subsection (2) states: "to exclude or modify the implied warranty of merchantability or any part of it the language must mention 'merchantability,' be in writing, and be conspicuous. . . . [T]o exclude or modify any implied warranty of fitness the exclusion must be by a writing and be conspicuous. Language to exclude all implied warranties of fitness is sufficient if it is in writing, is conspicuous and states, for example, 'There is no warranty that the goods will be fit for a particular purpose.'" UCC 1-201 defines *conspicuous* as "so written, displayed or presented that a reasonable person against which it is to operate ought to have noticed it." But it adds: "Whether a term is 'conspicuous' or not is a decision for the court." At least one court has found that use

of all caps does not render an insurance disclaimer conspicuous. *See Broberg v. Guardian Life Ins.*, 171 Cal. App. 4th 912, 922 (2009)).

But these requirements often proved self-defeating: as the clauses got longer and longer over the years, they became increasingly unreadable, especially when lawyers mistakenly took them to require all caps. It may have been that unscrupulous drafters even maximized the all-caps text just to make the disclosures less and less transparent precisely because parties, especially consumers, couldn't and therefore wouldn't read them. Regardless of motive, though, that was the effect.

When all-caps text became widespread in law offices, boldfacing, italics, and variations in typeface and type size weren't available to most practitioners. Now that these *are* available, the normal typographers' conventions about when to use all-caps text should apply. Here's what the experts say:

- "[Y]ou should never use all caps (unless you have a good reason). For example, all caps is often used to make a piece of type less legible and therefore to de-emphasize it." 1 David Bergsland, *Introduction to Digital Publishing* 282 (2002).
- "Capitalizing an entire word or phrase for emphasis is rarely appropriate in formal prose." *The Chicago Manual of Style* § 7.52, at 433 (17th ed. 2017).
- "Sometimes you will want words and labels to be secondary to other things—lines, shapes, or even other labels—and all caps may be your friend in that instance, since the reader's brain will parse other text more readily, and therefore before parsing the labels in all caps." Julie Steele & Noah Iliinsky, *Designing Data Visualizations: Representing Informational Relationships* 75 (2011).
- "[U]se [caps] judiciously. Caps are suitable for headings shorter than one line (e.g., "TABLE OF AUTHORITIES"), headers, footers, captions, or other labels. Caps work at small point sizes. Caps work well on letterheads and business cards. Always add letterspacing to caps to make them easier to read, and make sure kerning is turned on." Matthew Butterick, *Typography for Lawyers* 87 (2010).
- "All-cap schemes are appropriate and best for title pages of books, main lines in newspaper headings, inscriptions, and small bits that may require special emphasis, but never for continuous reading matter. It is something of an achievement to compose a mass of all caps and have a legible, well-toned page resulting. Careful spacing and more or less editing is required to make such composition pleasing." Andrew R. Andrews, "Some Notes on Type and Typography," in 29 *Printing Art* 33, 39 (Mar. 1917).

- "Full capitals (and small capitals) may be used for displaying text on half-title and title pages, for logos and imprints, and for other types of special presentation and display. . . . Full capitals are usually too prominent to be used for emphasis in open text, but they are sometimes used, as are small capitals, to mimic inscriptions or to reproduce original orthography: 'The earliest Scandinavian coins, inscribed "CNVT REX ÆNOR" ("Cnut, king of Danes"), seem to have been struck . . . no later than 1015.'" *New Hart's Rules: The Oxford Style Guide* § 7.5.2 (2014).

If text is to be upgraded in prominence, the better practice is to change a boldface heading into boldface small-caps text, and then to change regular type into downstyle boldface. The right-hand columns illustrate this technique when appropriate.

NOT THIS:	BUT THIS:
Ex. 1 So long as there is no Event of Default as defined in the LEASE, or event of casualty or condemnation or other event therein specified, as would entitle the landlord under the LEASE to terminate the LEASE or would cause, without any further action of such landlord, the termination of the LEASE or would entitle such landlord to dispossess the TENANT thereunder, the LEASE shall not be terminated, nor shall the TENANT's use, possession, or enjoyment of the LEASED PREMISES be interfered with, nor shall the leasehold estate granted by the LEASE be affected in any other manner, in any summary proceeding or any action or proceeding instituted by OVERLANDLORD under or in connection with the GROUND LEASE. **Ground Lease from *The Sublease and Assignment Deskbook*, Form 7.4, at 375–76 (Brent C. Shaffer ed., 2006)**	If there is no Event of Default as defined in the Lease, or event of casualty or condemnation or other event specified in the Lease, as would entitle the landlord to terminate the Lease or would cause, without further action by the landlord, the termination of the Lease or would entitle the landlord to dispossess the Tenant, then the Lease must not be terminated. Nor must the Tenant's use, possession, or enjoyment of the Leased Premises be interfered with. Nor must the leasehold estate granted by the Lease be affected in any other manner in a proceeding instituted by Overlandlord under or in connection with the Ground Lease.

Notice how this intermittent "shouting" makes little sense if you're trying to read the sentences.

Initial caps are adequate to emphasize defined terms. See § 134. Even though this example is merely illustrating initial-caps vs. all-caps text, the provision is well-nigh unreadable.

"Much that is strange and obscure in legal documents reflects a legal, technological, and cultural milieu that is no longer extant." Howard Darmstadter, *Hereof, Thereof, and Everywhereof* x (2002).

NOT THIS:	BUT THIS:
Ex. 2 I AM AWARE THAT PARACHUTE INSTRUCTION AND JUMPING ARE HAZARDOUS ACTIVITIES, AND I AM VOLUNTARILY PARTICIPATING IN THESE ACTIVITIES WITH KNOWLEDGE OF THE DANGER INVOLVED AND HEREBY AGREE TO ACCEPT ANY AND ALL RISKS OF INJURY OR DEATH. . . . I HAVE CAREFULLY READ THIS AGREEMENT AND FULLY UNDERSTAND ITS CONTENTS. I AM AWARE THAT THIS IS A RELEASE OF LIABILITY AND A CONTRACT BETWEEN MYSELF AND [*NAME OF INSTRUCTION FACILITY*] AND/OR ITS AFFILIATED ORGANIZATIONS AND I HAVE SIGNED IT OF MY OWN FREE WILL. **Parachute-Jumping-Participant Release from 7A *Texas Forms Legal & Business: Contracts, Compromises, Etc.* § 16:70, at 340–41 (2013)**	**3. All Risks Accepted. I am aware that parachute instruction and jumping are hazardous activities. I am voluntarily participating in these activities with knowledge of the danger involved, and I accept all risks of injury or death.** But see § 55. . . . **4. Voluntary Release of Liability. I have carefully read this Agreement and fully understand its contents. I am aware that this is a release of liability and a contract between me and [*name of instruction facility*], and its affiliated organizations, and I have signed it of my own free will.**
Ex. 3 **NOTICE: YOU THE BUYER HAVE OTHER RIGHTS AND REMEDIES UNDER THE TEXAS DECEPTIVE TRADE PRACTICES-CONSUMER PROTECTION ACT WHICH ARE IN ADDITION TO ANY REMEDY WHICH MAY BE AVAILABLE UNDER THIS CONTRACT.** **FOR MORE INFORMATION CONCERNING YOUR RIGHTS, CONTACT THE CONSUMER PROTECTION DIVISION OF THE ATTORNEY GENERAL'S OFFICE, YOUR LOCAL DISTRICT OR COUNTY ATTORNEY OR THE ATTORNEY OF YOUR CHOICE.** **Residential-Service-Company Agreement from 6A *Texas Forms Legal & Business: Contracts, Service and Maintenance* § 11B:30, at 292–93 (2011)**	**Notice: As the buyer, you have other rights and remedies under the Texas Deceptive Trade Practices–Consumer Protection Act in addition to the remedies available under this contract. For more information about your rights, contact the Consumer Protection Division of the Attorney General's Office, your local district or county attorney, or an attorney of your choice.**

NOT THIS:	BUT THIS:
Ex. 4 ADDITIONAL TERMS AND CONDITIONS 1. ACCEPTANCE: This purchase order may be accepted only by either (1) signing and returning the acknowledgment copy prior to the specified delivery date; or (2) delivering the goods or services ordered by the specified delivery date. THIS ORDER IS LIMITED TO THE TERMS AND CONDITIONS SPECIFIED ON THE FACE AND REVERSE OF THIS DOCUMENT AND ANY ATTACHMENTS. BUYER DOES NOT AGREE TO ANY PROPOSED ADDITION, ALTERATION, OR DELETION BY SELLER. THESE TERMS AND CONDITIONS CAN BE VARIED ONLY BY A WRITING SIGNED BY BUYER. ANY FAILURE TO RETURN THE ACKNOWLEDGMENT COPY OF THIS ORDER OR ANY OTHER STATEMENT OR WRITING OF SELLER SHALL NOT ALTER, ADD TO, OR OTHERWISE AFFECT THESE TERMS AND CONDITIONS. **Purchase-Order Form for a Sales Agreement in Robert A. Feldman & Raymond T. Nimmer, *Drafting Effective Contracts: A Practitioner's Guide*, Form 5-2, at 5-197 (2d ed. 2010)**	**5. Additional Terms.** 5.1 **Acceptance.** This purchase order may be accepted only by: (A) signing and returning the acknowledgment copy before the specified delivery date; or (B) delivering the goods or services ordered by the specified delivery date. 5.2 **LIMITATIONS. This order is limited to the terms expressly listed on the face and back of this document and any attachments. Failure to return the acknowledgment copy of this order, or any other statement or writing of Watkins, will not alter, supplement, or otherwise affect these terms.** 5.3 **ALTERATION. This purchase order's terms cannot be altered, supplemented, or waived except by a signed writing by Armstrong.** This revision assumes that there is good legal reason for emphasizing the prominent text.

"Where two or three [parties], or more, are gathered together in contract, they set up a small momentary sovereignty of their own. There is nothing fanciful about this. A contract is a little code for a special occasion. A lease is a little statute for your tenancy of a house you have neither built nor bought. Partnership articles or the charter and by-laws of a corporation are quite an elaborate code of law for those who are concerned. A corporate mortgage is a piece of legislation for a large and shifting population of bondholders, affecting, it is true, only a part of their lives, but affecting that part as completely as experienced and foresighted lawyers working late into the urban night can make it." Charles P. Curtis, *It's Your Law* 42–43 (1954).

NOT THIS:	BUT THIS:
Ex. 5 9. **Limitations of Liability** **9.1 Limitation on Damages**. EXCEPT IN CONNECTION WITH A BREACH OF CONFIDENTIALITY, OR USE OF WOODCREST INC. TECHNOLOGY BEYOND THE SCOPE OF ANY LICENSE GRANTED HEREIN: (I) IN NO EVENT WILL EITHER PARTY BE LIABLE FOR: ANY INDIRECT, MORAL, INCIDENTAL, CONSEQUENTIAL, OR SPECIAL DAMAGES; ANY LOSS OF USE, DATA, OR PROFITS; OR ANY INTERRUPTION OF BUSINESS ARISING OUT OF OR IN CONNECTION WITH THIS AGREEMENT, HOWEVER CAUSED, AND WHETHER OR NOT IT HAS BEEN ADVISED OF THIS POSSIBILITY OF THE DAMAGE; AND (II) THE AGGREGATE LIABILITY OF EITHER PARTY WITH RESPECT TO THIS AGREEMENT WILL NOT EXCEED THE TOTAL AMOUNTS PAID OR PAYABLE BY CUSTOMER PURSUANT TO THIS AGREEMENT FOR THE PRODUCTS AND SERVICES THAT GAVE RISE TO THE LIABILITY WITHIN THE TWELVE (12) MONTHS PRIOR TO THE CLAIM. THE FOREGOING LIMITATIONS AND EXCLUSIONS OF LIABILITY WILL APPLY REGARDLESS OF THE FORM OR SOURCE OF ACTION, AND REGARDLESS OF ANY OBLIGATION STATED UNDER THIS AGREEMENT. THE LIMITATION ON DAMAGES AS SET FORTH IN THE PRIOR SENTENCE WILL APPLY EVEN IN THE EVENT OF A FUNDAMENTAL BREACH OR A BREACH OF THE FUNDAMENTAL TERMS OF THIS AGREEMENT. **Sale and Licensing Agreement from a major software developer and provider**	**9. Limitations of Liability.** **9.1** LIMITATION ON DAMAGES. (A) APPLICABILITY. **The following limitations on and exclusions of liability apply regardless of the form or source of lawsuit and regardless of any obligation stated in this Agreement. They also apply when a Party fundamentally breaches this Agreement.** (B) GENERAL LIMITATIONS. **In no event is either Party liable for any indirect, moral, incidental, consequential, or special damages; any loss of use, data, or profits; or any interruption of business arising from or in connection with this Agreement, however caused, and whether or not the other Party has been told about the possibility of damages.** (C) AGGREGATE LIABILITY. **A Party's aggregate liability is limited under this Agreement to the total amounts paid or payable by Customer within 12 months before the claim for the Products or Services giving rise to the liability.** **9.2 Exceptions.** The limitations in § 9.1 do not apply to a breach of confidentiality or the use of Woodcrest technology beyond the scope of a license granted in this Agreement.

Notice that you're likely to avert your eyes from this type of provision.

Spacing

§ 43 Single-space your documents.

Although it might be tempting for many to say that double-spaced documents are easier to read, that's generally quite false. True, they're easier to hand-edit, if you're working over a draft with standard editorial marks. And they're easier to read if you're reading a speech from a lectern: depending on your eyesight, you might want double-spaced text with a 24-point font. But these are special cases.

If the idea is to read for comprehension—perhaps while flagging passages to negotiate or rewrite—single-spacing is better for four reasons:

1. The document will generally be half as long as it would be otherwise. Length can be costly in all sorts of scenarios, as when a document must be recorded or (as is often true for cities and counties) published.
2. Relatedly, you reach headings twice as often, and therefore you can see organization more readily.
3. What space appears on the page now conveys *meaning*—it's not just regularly interspersed between lines without regard to sense.
4. Readers are accustomed to single-spacing in all their reading of professionally typeset materials: books, magazines, newspapers, etc.

Hence for your polished documents, use single-spacing.

"If it is worth reducing an understanding to writing, it is worth making it adequate."
Samuel Goldberg, *Hints on Draftsmanship*, 5 Prac. Law. 39, 42 (1959).

NOT THIS:

Ex. 1

AGREEMENT

This Agreement is made as of this 11th day of April, 2018, by and among Jacob Reynolds, not personally, but solely in his capacity as receiver of Heloc Company (the "Receiver"); the Creditors Committee (as defined herein), by and through its counsel; Ace, Inc., a Delaware corporation ("Ace"); and Purchaser, Inc., a Delaware corporation ("Purchaser").

RECITALS

A. On May 28, 2017, the State Court entered an order confirming an assignment for the benefit of creditors executed by Heloc Company and appointing the Receiver as receiver of the Heloc Company pursuant to that assignment for the benefit of creditors.

B. Pursuant to that certain Asset Purchase Agreement dated November 1, 2017 (the "APA"), the Heloc Company sold substantially all of its assets to Ace.

"APA" (which suggests the Administrative Procedure Act, or perhaps the American Psychological Association) is a most unfortunate initialism here. It would be better to call it "the Agreement."

C. As of March 1, 2018, Ace was obligated to the Receiver pursuant to that certain Note (the "Note") by and between Ace and the Receiver, which was executed in connection with Ace's purchase of the assets of the Heloc Company, in the total aggregate amount (principal plus accrued and unpaid interest) of $100,000. The Note continues to accrue interest pursuant to its terms.

. . .

Bankruptcy Agreement from a major law firm

BUT THIS:

Agreement

This Agreement, effective April 11, 2018, is between Jacob Reynolds, solely in his capacity as receiver of the Heloc Company; the Creditors Committee (as defined below), by and through its counsel; Ace, Inc., a Delaware corporation; and Bennings, Inc., a Delaware corporation.

Background

- On May 28, 2017, the State Court entered an order confirming an assignment for the benefit of creditors. The assignment, signed by Heloc, appointed Reynolds as its receiver.
- By the Asset-Purchase Agreement dated November 1, 2017 (the Agreement), Heloc sold substantially all its assets to Ace.
- As of March 1, 2018, Ace was obligated to Reynolds under a note between them (the Note), obtained for Ace's purchase of the assets of Heloc, in the aggregate amount (principal plus accrued and unpaid interest) of $100,000. The Note continues to accrue interest by its terms.
- Ace's obligations under the Note are secured by liens on and security interests in all of Ace's assets. These liens and security interests are subordinate only to (a) liens and security interests in the same assets securing obligations owed by Ace to FedEcon Bank (the Bank), and (b) liens and security interests in the same assets securing obligations owed by Ace to GranTrust (Creditor 2).
- As of March 1, 2018, Ace's accounts payable (reported on an accrual basis) totaled about $2 million. More than half that amount represents amounts owed to some of Ace's unsecured trade creditors, some of which were also unsecured creditors of Heloc and are therefore entitled to share in distributions of the Note's proceeds.

For recommendations on stating contract recitals, see § 28.

"Those who draft documents and those who create formbooks rarely consult legal-drafting experts. And legal academia has only just begun to recognize and reward expertise in legal drafting." Wayne Schiess, *Writing for the Legal Audience* 131 (2003).

NOT THIS:

Ex. 2

3. **Separation Payment.** In exchange for agreeing to and complying with the terms of this Agreement (including the general release it contains), Executive will receive from Employer, provided Executive has satisfied the Information Delivery Obligation (as that term is defined herein):

(a) Cash payments equal to the equivalent of Executive's annual base compensation of Four Hundred Thousand Dollars and Zero Cents ($400,000.00) prorated for the period beginning February 1, 2019 and ending on December 31, 2019, less lawful deductions such as, but not limited to, tax withholdings, FICA, and Medicare (the "Severance Payments"). The Severance Payments shall be paid to Executive in equal installments for the period beginning on the Effective Date (as defined in paragraph 25(g) below) and ending on December 31, 2019 in accordance with the Company's usual payroll schedule, less any periods previously paid by the Employer to the Executive after the Separation Date. Payment for the prorated monthly installments of February, March and April, 2019, shall be made on or before May 10, 2019. Thereafter, payments for the remaining monthly installments, will be made in accordance with the Company's usual payroll schedule; and

(b) Cash payment in the amount of $10,000 for paid up-front expenses, less lawful deductions (the "Expense Allocation Payment"). The Expense Allocation Payment shall be paid to Executive in one lump sum on the first payroll date immediately following the execution of this Separation Agreement (as defined in paragraph 24(g) below).

Separation Agreement and General Release

BUT THIS:

3. **Separation Payment.**
   3.1 **General condition.** In exchange for agreeing to and complying with this Separation Agreement, if the Executive has satisfied the Information Delivery Obligation, the Executive will receive from the Employer the cash compensation listed below.
   3.2 **Severance payments.** The severance payments total the Executive's annual base compensation of $400,000 prorated from February 1, 2019, to December 31, 2019, less lawful deductions including tax withholdings, FICA, and Medicare. On or before May 10, 2019, the Employer will pay the Executive the prorated monthly installments for February, March, and April 2019. Employer will pay Executive the remaining severance payments in equal monthly installments in accordance with the Company's usual payroll schedule, beginning on the Effective Date and ending on December 31, 2019, less any periods previously paid by the Employer to the Executive after the Separation Date.
   3.3 **Expense-allocation payment.** An expense-allocation payment of $10,000 will be paid for up-front expenses, less lawful deductions. The Employer will pay the Executive the expense-allocation payment in 1 lump sum on the first payroll date immediately after this Separation Agreement is signed and delivered.

"It may be satisfactory to the lawyer on the winning side of any litigation that his document did not fail his client, but it is better if the document discourages litigation altogether." L.W. Melville, *The Draftsman's Handbook* § 2.01, at 21 (2d ed. 1991).

§ 44 Keep within a range of 45–90 characters per line.

The weakness of the lawyer's much-derided "fine print" is just as much about the length of the lines as it is the size of the type. To squeeze more verbiage into fewer pages, lawyers have traditionally reduced all margins, reduced the type size, and created wall-to-wall characters. By the time a reader reaches the end of a line, it's all but impossible, in the absence of a ruler, to find the beginning of the next. Misusing typography in this way is a sure-fire way of inducing readers *not* to read: the struggle is so great that they'll rebel.

A more creative approach when you're reducing the font size below 11 is to use double-column text. The average number of characters per line will typically be halved. You can often fit all the necessary material into the same number of pages, but in a much more appealing and readable format. The trick involves reducing the number of characters per line.

Remember, though, that the conventional form for negotiated contracts is to use a single-column format with a 13-point (or perhaps 12-point) font.

NOT THIS:

Ex. 1

Lines are about 109 characters wide. That's hard to read.

4. **Taxes.** Prices in the Sales Order do not include taxes. Taxes may be invoiced separately by CalCo, and Customer is responsible for payment of all applicable taxes. Customer must provide a tax exemption claim to CalCo before an invoice is issued. If Customer is required to withhold income taxes from its payment to CalCo, Customer agrees to send to CalCo an official tax receipt within sixty (60) days.

[Average line: 109 characters]

This contract also uses two spaces between sentences instead of one. See § 45.

General Terms from a major software-development company

BUT THIS:

Lines are about 47 characters wide. That's easier to read.

4. **Taxes.** Prices in the Sales Order do not include taxes. Customer is responsible for paying all applicable taxes, which CalCo may invoice separately. Customer must provide a tax-exemption claim to CalCo before an invoice is issued. If Customer is required to withhold income taxes from its payment to CalCo, Customer must send to CalCo an official tax receipt within 60 days.

[Average line: 47 characters]

NOT THIS:

Ex. 2

11. FORCE MAJEURE
Neither party will be liable for any failure to perform acts, other than payment obligations, due to unforeseen circumstances or causes beyond the parties' reasonable control, including, but not limited to, acts of God, war, riot, embargoes, acts of civil or military authorities, acts of terrorism or sabotage, electronic viruses, worms or corrupting microcode, shortage of supply or delay in delivery by vendors, fire, flood, earthquake, accident, strikes, radiation, inability to secure transportation, failure of communications or electrical lines, facilities, fuel, energy, labor or materials.

[Average line: 130 characters]

Terms and Conditions of Sale from a computer-technology company

BUT THIS:

11. Force Majeure.
Neither party will be liable for any failure to perform an act, other than a payment obligation, owing to unforeseen circumstances or causes beyond the party's reasonable control, such as acts of God; war; riot; embargoes; acts of civil or military authorities; acts of terrorism or sabotage; electronic viruses, worms, or corrupting microcode; shortage of supply or delay in delivery by vendors; fire, flood, or earthquake; accident; strikes; radiation; inability to secure transportation; failure of communications or electrical lines; or inaccessibility or inutility of facilities, fuel, energy, labor, or materials.

[Average line: 40 characters]

"A line 50–70 characters long is most comfortable to read. Longer lines may cause fatigue and confusion. Very short lines are also hard to follow, as they require more eye movement and create awkward breaks in the text." Alan Siegel, "Drafting Simplified Legal Documents: Basic Principles and Their Application," in *Drafting Documents in Plain Language* 175, 229 (Duncan A. MacDonald chmn., 1979).

§ 45 Prefer one forward space between sentences, not two.

The settled convention in modern typography is to put one forward space, not two, between sentences (and, some believe, after a colon). When a line of type is short, using two forward spaces after periods can result in an exaggerated and distracting gap, especially if the type is fully justified (to both the left and the right margins). But the single forward space looks more polished regardless of whether the right margin is ragged or justified.

This point is much disputed in law offices, and my own ipse dixit won't suffice for many practitioners. So let me cite authorities with specificity:

- "The typewriter tradition of separating sentences with two word spaces has no place in typesetting. The custom began because the characters of monospaced typefaces used on typewriters were so wide and so open that a single word space—one the same width as a character, including the period—was not wide enough to create a sufficient space between sentences. Proportionally spaced fonts, though, contain word spaces specifically designed to play the sentence-separating role perfectly. Because of this, a double word space at the end of a sentence creates an obvious hole in the line." James Felici, *The Complete Manual of Typography* 80 (2003).
- "Put only one space, not two, following the terminal punctuation of a sentence." Kate R. Turabian, *A Manual for Writers of Research Papers, Theses, and Dissertations* rule A.1.3 (7th ed. 2007).
- "Like most publishers, Chicago advises leaving a single character space, not two spaces, between sentences and after colons used within a sentence, and this recommendation applies to both the manuscript and the published work." *The Chicago Manual of Style* rule 2.9 (17th ed. 2017).
- "I have no idea why so many writers resist the one-space rule. If you're skeptical, pick up any book, newspaper, or magazine and tell me how many spaces there are between sentences." Matthew Butterick, *Typography for Lawyers* 42 (2010).
- "After the *period* at the end of a sentence or abbreviation, the space should be the *normal* one used between the words of the line." Jan Tschichold, *The Form of the Book: Essays on the Morality of Good Design* 95–96 (1991).
- "Some lessons learned in high school are best forgotten. One of them is dotting your i's with hearts and smiley faces. The other is leaving two spaces between sentences. In typesetting, one space only must be left between sentences." Ellen Lupton, *Thinking with Type: A Critical Guide for Designers, Writers, and Students* 166 (2004).

NOT THIS:	BUT THIS:
Ex. 1 2. It is further agreed that Seller may seek authorization from the Commission and/or other appropriate body for such changes to any rates, terms and conditions set forth herein, in Rate Schedule FSS or in the General Terms and Conditions of Seller's FERC Gas Tariff, as may be found necessary to assure Seller just and reasonable rates. Nothing herein contained shall be construed to deny Customer any rights it may have under the Natural Gas Act, as amended, including the right to participate fully in rate proceedings by intervention or otherwise to contest Seller's filing in whole or in part. **Natural-Gas-Storage-Services Agreement from a major New York energy company**	2. **Changes by EPN Gas.** To ensure commercially reasonable rates, EPN Gas may seek authorization from the Commission or other appropriate body to change a rate, term, or condition in this Agreement, the Rate Schedule FSS, or the General Terms and Conditions of EPN Gas's FERC Gas Tariff. Customer is entitled to all rights it may have under the Natural Gas Act, as amended from time to time, including the right to participate in rate proceedings by intervening or otherwise contesting EPN Gas's filing.
Ex. 2 There are no condemnation proceedings pending or, to the best of Seller's knowledge, threatened or contemplated with respect to the Leased Premises. The Company has not received any assessment or other notice with respect to any governmental improvements for which the Leased Premises can be assessed; and no such governmental improvements are threatened, contemplated or pending. The Company has not received any notice of and has no knowledge of any unfulfilled requirements or recommendations of any insurance company, any inspection or rating bureau or any board of underwriters concerning the Leased Premises or any use, operation or occupancy thereof. **Real-Estate Agreement from a major law firm**	No condemnation proceedings are pending or, to the best of the Seller's knowledge, threatened or contemplated that might affect the Leased Premises. The Company has not received any assessment or other notice about any government improvements for which the Leased Premises can be assessed, and no such government improvements are threatened, contemplated, or pending. The Company has not received any notice of and has no knowledge of any unfulfilled requirements or recommendations of any insurance company, any inspection or rating bureau, or any board of underwriters concerning the Leased Premises or its use, operation, or occupancy.

§ 46 Use white space intelligently. Detest density.

Dense writing appears formidable. People tend to put it aside, intending perhaps to get back to it when they might have more time and fortitude. But then they never do. And even if they did, they would put it aside once again because dense writing on technical subjects is deathly dull. But technical writing needn't be that way. In the right hands, it can be engaging.

One essential way to achieve readability is to cultivate both a fear and a loathing of density. Learn to value white space, and leave a good deal of it on every page. Many techniques discussed in this book contribute to meaningful uses of white space:

- headings (§ 14);
- enumerated lists (§ 85);
- cascading left-hand indents (§ 35);
- double columns (§ 44);
- bullets (§ 90); and
- suitable type size (§ 38).

The white space around text is what makes a page look inviting, roomy, and comfortable. The lack of it makes the page look imposing and cramped.

> "Allow your readers to concentrate on substance rather than wading through your vocabulary." Susan L. Brody et al., *Legal Drafting* 116 (1994).

NOT THIS:	BUT THIS:
Ex. 1 6.2 **Termination for Cause.** If either Party materially breaches this Agreement, the non-breaching Party may provide written notice to the breaching Party indicating (i) the nature and basis of the breach, with reference to the applicable provisions of this Agreement; and (ii) the non-breaching Party's intention to terminate all or a portion of the applicable Sales Order(s) related to the breach in accordance with this section. If the breach is not cured within thirty (30) days of the receipt of the written notice, the non-breaching Party can exercise its right to terminate immediately. Either Party may terminate the entire Agreement immediately upon written notice to the breaching Party if the other Party is in breach of the confidentiality provisions of this Agreement. The Company may terminate the Agreement, in whole or in part, upon written notice to Customer if Customer is in breach of the "No Modifications, No Reverse Engineering" Section, or uses Products and Services beyond the scope of the license stated herein. **Terms and Conditions from a computer-software company** [It's quite unclear how the Company might terminate the contract "in part."]	6.2 **Termination for cause.** (A) **Material breach by either party.** If either party materially breaches this Agreement, the nonbreaching party may give the breaching party written notice that states: (1) the nature and basis of the breach, including the applicable provisions; and (2) its intent to terminate under this section all or part of the Sales Order related to the breach. (B) **Time to cure material breach under (A).** If the breaching party does not cure the breach within 30 days after receiving the written notice in (A), the nonbreaching party may immediately terminate this Agreement. (C) **Breach of confidentiality provisions.** If a party breaches this Agreement's confidentiality provisions, the nonbreaching party may terminate this entire Agreement immediately by giving written notice to the breaching party. (D) **Other breaches.** We may immediately terminate this Agreement upon giving you written notice if you: (1) breach the "no modifications, no reverse-engineering" section; or (2) use Products and Services beyond the scope of the license granted in this Agreement.

> "Lawyers sometimes fear that clients will not think they are getting their money's worth unless the agreement contains a sprinkling of legalese. . . . This concern makes no sense. Much of lawyering is communicating in one form or another. Drafting is communicating to the parties, sometimes to third parties, occasionally to a court. If your style is not appropriate to that audience, you are not doing your job." Scott J. Burnham, *Drafting and Analyzing Contracts* 280 (3d ed. 2003).

NOT THIS:	BUT THIS:
Ex. 2 Section Seven. Insurance Contractor will carry and maintain throughout the period of this contract, at contractor's sole cost, compensation and/or employer's liability insurance in an approved company or companies, to cover all classifications of work contemplated under this contract, and also will carry and maintain throughout the period of this contract public liability insurance in an approved company or companies, within the limits of $[*dollar amount of limit per person*] for each person, and $[*dollar amount of limit for accidents*] for each accident. Certificates of insurance coverage shall be furnished company within [*number of days*] days from the date of this agreement. Such insurance shall be adequate to protect both contractor and company from all liability on account of injury or damage done to the persons or property of any and all persons during or in consequence of the performance of the services contracted for in this agreement. The maintenance of such insurance will not in any manner affect contractor's obligation to indemnify company, as provided in Section Eight below, but maintenance of such approved insurance shall be a condition precedent to the payment to contractor of the compensation for the work and services provided for in this contract. **Oil-and-Gas Well-Drilling and -Maintenance Contract from 6A *Texas Forms Legal & Business: Independent Contractors* § 11A:27, at 101 (2011)** [Margin note: This use of *and/or* makes it unclear whether both types are required.]	**7. Insurance.** **7.1 Carried by Contractor.** (A) **Types.** At the Contractor's sole cost, the Contractor must carry throughout the term of this Agreement: (1) compensation and employer's-liability insurance issued by an approved insurer to cover all work classifications contemplated under this Agreement; and (2) public-liability insurance with an approved insurer. (B) **Amounts.** The insurance limits carried in (A) must be at least $_________ for each person and $_________ for each accident. **7.2 Certificates.** Certificates of insurance coverage must be given to the Company within [*number of days*] days after the date of this Agreement. **7.3 Scope of insurance.** This insurance must be adequate to protect both the Contractor and the Company from all liability for injury to a person or property damage resulting from the performance of the services. **7.4 Indemnity.** Maintaining this insurance will not affect the Contractor's obligation to indemnify the Company, as provided in § 8. **7.5 Compensation conditioned on insurance.** The Contractor must maintain this approved insurance as a condition of the Company's payment for its work and services.

NOT THIS:	BUT THIS:
Ex. 3 **V. RELATIONSHIP OF PARTIES** 5.1 Owner and Contractor agree that Contractor is an independent contractor under this Agreement and will in no way be considered to be an agent, partner, joint venturer or employee of Owner and, accordingly, Contractor will not be entitled to any benefits, coverages, or other privileges made available to employees of Owner. Contractor will not undertake to commit Owner to any course of action in relation to third persons, or make any representations to third parties on Owner's behalf, except as requested by Owner. Contractor will not represent that Contractor is an employee or agent of Owner. Owner will not deduct any social security or income taxes from the payments made to Contractor. During the term of Contractor's retention, Contractor will be compensated on a 1099 basis and, accordingly, Contractor will be liable for any and all worker's compensation payments and federal, state, and local employment, sales, use, excise, and other taxes arising out of Contractor's performance of this Agreement and will furnish evidence of compliance or an applicable waiver of requirements to Owner upon request. 5.2 Nothing in this Agreement authorizes Contractor to accept service of any writ, summons or other process or enter any appearance on behalf of Owner in any litigation in the Territory or elsewhere arising out of this Agreement or any order for the Products or otherwise, or in any other manner or subject Owner to the jurisdiction of any court, tribunal or governmental agency. **Commissioned-Sales Agreement from 1 *Stevenson's Texas Legal Practice Forms* § 7:111, at 7-114 to 7-115 (2d ed. 2008)**	**5. Parties' Relationship and Limitations of Authority.** 5.1 **Your independent-contractor status.** You are an independent contractor and not our agent, partner, joint venturer, or employee. 5.2 **Your independent-contractor limitations.** As an independent contractor, you will not: (A) be entitled to any benefit, coverage, or other privilege made available to our employees; (B) unless we ask you to, undertake to commit us to a course of action in relation to a third party or make a representation to a third party on our behalf; (C) assert or represent that you are our employee or agent. 5.3 **Your independent-contractor payments and taxes.** We will not deduct social-security or income taxes from the payments we make to you. You will be compensated on a 1099 basis, and you will be liable for all workers'-compensation payments and all applicable taxes. Upon request, you will give us evidence of compliance or an applicable waiver of requirements. 5.4 **Acceptance of service.** Nothing in this Agreement authorizes you to: (A) accept service of a writ, summons, or other process; (B) enter an appearance on our behalf in any litigation; or (C) subject us in any other manner to the jurisdiction of a court, tribunal, or agency.

"Do not . . . try to keep all sentences within [a prescribed] length. Varying the length avoids monotony and thus promotes readability, so long as the average length stays within bounds. If the average length becomes too long, break up some of the longer sentences." LeRoy Marceau, *Drafting a Union Contract* § 3.9(C), at 23 (1965).

NOT THIS:	BUT THIS:
Ex. 4 2. License To the extent I may have any rights in the Contribution, I hereby grant to Company a perpetual, irrevocable, royalty-free, non-exclusive, sublicensable license to reproduce all or any portion of the Contribution in any media now known or hereafter developed, including electronic media and to perform, display, distribute, transmit, publish, create derivative works of and otherwise use the Contribution and/or such reproductions or modified versions thereof throughout the world, without restriction, including via the Internet, but in each of the foregoing cases solely for non-commercial use. For the avoidance of doubt, the right to perform, display, distribute, transmit, publish, reproduce, create derivative works or use shall also include the right to perform, display, distribute, transmit, publish, reproduce, create derivative works and otherwise use, as set forth in the preceding sentence, and shall also include the right not to perform, display, distribute, transmit, publish, reproduce, create derivative works or use. For the further avoidance of doubt, the preceding license gives Company the right to grant sublicenses to third parties (such as Vimeo, Facebook, iTunes and other websites selected by Company) to perform, display, distribute, transmit, publish, reproduce, create derivative works of and otherwise use the Contribution for non-commercial purposes in any media now known or hereafter developed, including electronic media and via the Internet. **Consent, License, and Release from a major law firm**	1. **Grant of License.** 1.1 **Scope of grant to Reiner.** To the extent that you have any right in the Contribution, you grant to Reiner a perpetual, irrevocable, royalty-free, nonexclusive license to reproduce all or any part of the Contribution in any medium now known or later developed, and to perform, display, distribute, transmit, publish, reproduce, create derivative works of, and otherwise use the Contribution and reproductions or modified versions of it throughout the world. Any use must be for noncommercial purposes. Reiner need not exercise this grant. 1.2 **Sublicenses.** Reiner may grant sublicenses to one or more third parties (such as Vimeo, Facebook, and iTunes) that it selects to perform, display, distribute, transmit, publish, reproduce, create derivative works of, and otherwise use the Contribution for noncommercial purposes in any medium now known or later developed.

The point of this section is white space. But note, incidentally, that the highlighted terms should not be hyphenated. See § 131.

In the list *perform, display, distribute . . .*, note the inconsistent wording (see § 10): the second litany adds *reproduce*.

"Solid pages of text are deadly. They're monotonous, discouraging, and make the reader feel he must concentrate too much." Tyler G. Hicks, *Successful Technical Writing* 151 (1959).

NOT THIS:	BUT THIS:
Ex. 5 2.5 Licensor shall be entitled to sub-license in whole or part the rights of Licensor under the Licensee Licenses to (x) any of its Affiliates or (y) sub-contractors for research and development purposes, in each case from time to time, provided that Licensee's prior written consent (not to be withheld or delayed unreasonably, Licensor acknowledging that it is reasonable for Licensee to withhold consent to sub-licensing to an Affiliate of Licensor, which is itself an Affiliate of a competitor of Licensee) shall be required in respect of any such sub-licensee that is an Affiliate and in which Licensor holds directly or indirectly less than 50% of the voting securities (but for the avoidance of doubt no prior written consent shall be required in respect of any such sub-licensee that is an Affiliate and in which Licensor holds directly or indirectly less than 50% of the voting securities or a sub-contractor for manufacturing or research and development purposes), and provided, further, that any sub-licensee (other than a sub-licensee that is an Affiliate and in which Licensor holds directly or indirectly less than 50% of the voting securities) shall enter in a written sub-license agreement with Licensor and that (i) Licensor shall provide to Licensee a copy of such written sub-license agreement within a maximum period of two (2) weeks from the date of signature of such sub-license agreement, (ii) each such sub-license to an Affiliate of Licensor shall automatically terminate if the sub-licensee ceases to be an Affiliate of Licensor, and (iii) each such sub-license (a) shall contain terms not less onerous than those set forth in this Agreement, including an obligation on the sub-licensee to comply with Licensor's obligations under this Agreement, (b) shall terminate inter alia forthwith upon the expiration or termination of this Agreement for any reason, and (c) shall provide that no sub-licensee shall have any further right to sub-license any rights or to appoint additional sub-licensees. Licensor shall remain primarily responsible and liable to Licensee for the acts or omissions of any of its sub-licensees hereunder, as if the breach had been that of Licensor under this Agreement, and shall take all such actions as may from time to time be necessary in order reasonably to ensure that such sub-licensees comply with their respective obligations under sub-licenses. Promptly upon request by Licensee, Licensor, shall, at its own cost, do all such acts or things reasonably required by Licensee for the purpose of recording a sub-licensee as a registered user or licensee of the Licensee Improvements where it is desirable or necessary to do so. **License Agreement from a major law firm** *The first sentence is 319 words long.*	2.5 **Sublicenses.** Ackerman may from time to time sublicense in whole or part the rights of Ackerman under the Reece Licenses to any of its affiliates or subcontractors on the following terms: (A) **Affiliate ownership.** Whether directly or indirectly, Ackerman may hold no more than 50% of the Affiliate's voting securities. (B) **Reece's consent.** Ackerman must obtain Reece's prior written consent, which will not be withheld or delayed unreasonably, but may be withheld if Ackerman's Affiliate is also an Affiliate of a competitor of Reece. No prior written consent is required if a sublicense is only for manufacturing or for research-and-development purposes. (C) **Sublicense agreements.** If a sublicensee is not an Affiliate in which Ackerman directly or indirectly holds voting securities, Ackerman and the sublicensee must enter into a written sublicense agreement. Ackerman must give Reece a copy of the agreement within 2 weeks after the agreement's signature date. The sublicense must: (1) contain terms at least as rigorous as those set forth in this Agreement, including an obligation that the sublicensee must comply with Ackerman's obligations under this Agreement; (2) not permit the sublicensee to further sublicense any rights or to appoint an additional sublicensee; and (3) terminate automatically if an Affiliate of Ackerman ceases to be an Affiliate, if this Agreement expires, or if this Agreement is terminated for any reason. (D) **Ackerman's responsibility.** Ackerman is primarily responsible and liable to Reece for the acts or omissions of all its sublicensees, as if Ackerman itself breached this Agreement. Ackerman must take all actions that might from time to time be necessary to ensure that sublicensees comply with their obligations under sublicenses. (E) **Recording sublicenses.** If Reece so requests, Ackerman will promptly, at its own cost, do everything reasonably required by Reece to record a sublicensee as a registered user or licensee of the Licensee Improvements. *Note how the cascading hanging indents amount to a smart use of white space.*

C. General Conventions

Obligations and prohibitions generally

§ 47 Adopt a rigorously consistent approach to modal verbs, preferably excluding the word *shall*.

Modal verbs, also known as "helping verbs," convey the mode of action expressed in the main verb, typically to express obligation, necessity, possibility, or intention. The most common ones in English are *will*, *may*, *can*, *should*, and *would*. The least common, in ordinary English, is *shall*. But it's the most common in legal drafting.

Although the widespread use of *shall* within law might be thought of as advantageous, that's hardly true. Because it's not a part of ordinary American English (or Australian English, Irish English, or Scottish English, for that matter), it's a word that most speakers of English grow up not using. At most, it's a part of their recognition vocabulary (as in Shakespeare's *Shall I compare thee to a summer's day?*). In American English, the word exists primarily in two expressions, neither of which is mandatory: *Shall we leave?* and *We shall overcome*.

So most speakers of English grow up without using *shall*, encountering it a few times in literature but never adopting it in their own speech and writing. Meanwhile, those who study English as a second language (ESL) learn an old paradigm that modern English-language grammarians have come to repudiate: *shall* expresses simple futurity in the first person (*I shall*) but command or determination in the second and third persons (*you shall*, *they shall*), while *will* expresses command or determination in the first person (*I will*) but simple futurity in the second and third persons (*you will*, *they will*). Although this formula never described most brands of English[1]—and is devilishly tricky for most people to master (much less understand)—a few people adhere to it tenaciously. According to this

> "To want to retain 'shall' in its obligatory sense when the rest of the world has changed and when there is a suitable alternative is perverse—and doubly so when we acknowledge the inaccurate ways in which lawyers handle 'shall.'" Robert D. Eagleson & Michèle Asprey, *Must We Continue With 'Shall'?*, 63 Austl. L.J. 75, 78 (1989).

1 *See The Chicago Guide to Grammar, Usage, and Punctuation* 96 (2016); *Garner's Modern English Usage* 824–25 (4th ed. 2016).

discredited formula, it's the third-person command that occurs in contracts and statutes: *Provider shall*, *Company shall*, *the district court shall*, *a parolee shall*, etc.

One major problem, however, is that when speakers of English enter the field of law and are barraged by *shalls*, they come to feel as if *shall* is the "drafting verb." They begin to use it indiscriminately in all sorts of sentences, not just those in which the subject of the verb is the duty-bearing agent. I've encountered deal lawyers who say they use *shall* consistently—in every single sentence. But it's not consistency in appearance that matters; it's consistency in meaning.

Here are a few of the variable contexts in which *shall* commonly appears:

- "Employee shall send notice . . . ." (*Shall* imposes a duty on the subject.)
- "Notice shall be sent by Employee . . . ." (*Shall* doesn't impose a duty on the subject, but still it could be read as meaning "is required to." Many courts have held that this type of *shall*, in a given context, means "should.")
- "The Company shall then have a 30-day approval period." (*Shall* means "will"; it's a future-tense verb.)
- "If any notice shall have been mailed to the wrong address . . . ." (*Shall have been* is replaceable with *is*; this is the false future.)
- "Neither party shall disclose the existence or amount of the payment." (*Shall* means "may"; we're negating permission to disclose, not negating a duty to disclose. Those who don't think closely about meanings will simply declare the provision to be "mandatory." Replace *shall* with *has a duty to* or *is required to*, and you'll see that its semantic content cannot be mandatory here.)

> "Did you know that *shall* is the most misused of all words in legal drafting? It may well be conventional wisdom that *shall* imposes an obligation, but well-read drafters know that it is fraught with problems." Wayne Schiess, *Writing for the Legal Audience* 127–28 (2003).

- "The Corporate Secretary shall be reimbursed for all expenses." (*Shall* isn't imposing a duty on the subject of the sentence but instead on an unnamed entity [the Corporation]. The real sense of *shall* is "is entitled to." The better statement would be *The Corporation shall reimburse the Corporate Secretary for all expenses*—assuming *shall* is to be used at all.)
- "All notices shall be printed on 8.5-by-11 inch paper." (This type of nonmaterial requirement will normally be held to mean "should." In other words, *shall* is called a precatory or directory word.)

For existing form contracts, then, the first step is to figure out what all the various *shall*s mean. In a typical law-firm form, *shall* might mean "has a duty to" in perhaps 20% of the instances; "is required to" (with an inanimate object in the subject position) in 30% of the instances; *will* (as a future-tense verb) in 22% of the instances; *is* (in a false-future construction) in 15% of the instances; *may* (usually after a negative word such as *no* or *neither*) in 7% of the instances; and *should* in perhaps 6% of the instances. Figuring out what's what is a considerable challenge for most people, and frankly it's beyond the linguistic ability of many to parse through the senses.

As commonly used, then, *shall* violates the presumption of consistent usage in a great variety of ways. That's the main reason the word invites so much litigation, and why the judicial holdings are so wildly inconsistent in stating what it means.[2] The encyclopedia of litigated terms entitled *Words and Phrases* devotes more than 75 pages to various judicial pronouncements on the variable meanings of *shall. Black's Law Dictionary* records five common senses.[3]

> "Opponents of drafting reform argue that we cannot disturb the sanctity of certain wording found in old documents or contracts because that wording has been steeped in time and we change it at our peril. Although no lawyer can ascribe definitive meanings to the wording, we are expected to observe this warning." Robert C. Dick, *Legal Drafting* 7 (2d ed. 1985).

2 *See Legal Writing in Plain English* 125–26 (2d ed. 2013).
3 *Black's Law Dictionary* 1585 (10th ed. 2014).

But there's another problem. The presumption of consistent usage has a corollary: a change in terminology is presumed to carry with it a change in meaning. And shifting terminology in expressing obligations is commonplace in existing forms. Why? They're typically the product of many drafters over many decades. Nobody has bothered to enforce consistency in wording. So variations like these are pervasive within modern forms:

- "Employee shall . . . ."
- "Employee will . . . ."
- "Employee agrees to . . . ."
- "Employee agrees that she will . . . ."
- "Employee understands that it is her sole responsibility to . . . ."
- "Employee must . . . ."
- "Employee will undertake to . . . ."
- "Employee is responsible for . . . ."
- "Employee agrees to be responsible for . . . ."
- "Employee shall be responsible for . . . ."
- "Employee shall have the duty to . . . ."
- "Employee is required to . . . ."

That's just to get us started. To get a full measure of how profligate lawyers have been with their methods of expressing duties, take out a form contract—either from your law firm or from a published formbook—and start highlighting all the different ways in which requirements are expressed throughout. You're likely to find a dizzying array. (See § 10.)

> "Lawyers write [badly] for three main reasons. The first is inertia. This is the way lawyers have always written. The style is inculcated in law schools, reinforced in legal practice, and mirrored in judicial writing. It is always easier to adopt old styles than to invent new ones. The second is necessity—or, more accurately, perceived necessity. Lawyers write for a potentially hostile audience, in an adversarial ethos. Their documents may be picked over by loophole-seeking opponents. The third reason is insecurity. The pace of modern legal practice reduces the time available to research new ways of expressing old ideas; and when time is short it seems safer to stick to the old rather than risk adopting the new." Peter Butt, *Plain Language and Conveyancing*, Conveyancer & Prop. Law. 256, 258 (July–Aug. 1993).

Here is one typical example that could readily be multiplied hundreds of times over:

NOT THIS:	BUT THIS:
1. Term and Termination. This Agreement shall remain in force for a term of ninety (90) days (the "Term") from the date of this Agreement. This Agreement may be mutually terminated prior to the expiration of the Term, or Lessor may terminate this Agreement upon seven (7) days written notice should Lessee breach any of the provisions of this Agreement, or sooner as set forth in section 5 below. **2. Effective Date.** This Agreement shall become effective only when both parties have signed this document; and the initial payroll has been processed, paid for and received by Lessee. **3. The Employees.** Lessor will lease the employees listed on Exhibit A to Lessee. Lessee's signature shall be affixed to Exhibit A to indicate proper pay status. Lessee will immediately notify Lessor of any change in pay status for any leased employee. No other employees shall become leased to Lessee unless specifically agreed to by Lessor. Lessee agrees to notify Lessor immediately upon the release, termination or cessation of employment of any leased employee. Lessee agrees to cooperate with Lessor in all employment and unemployment matters. Lessor will provide workers' compensation insurance for leased employees when they are performing work in accordance with this Agreement. **4. Cost.** Lessee shall advance to [reimburse] Lessor's payroll account, as appropriate, at least 72 hours prior to a need for disbursement [for] all funds and costs necessary, required and associated with the leased employees. . . . **Agreement to Lease Employees Following Sale of Business from LexisNexis Forms, Form 770-40.4.02, at 1 (2016)**	1. **Term and Termination.** This Agreement will remain in force for 90 days (the "Term") from the date of this Agreement. The parties may mutually end this Agreement before the Term expires. If Hughes breaches a provision of this Agreement, Michaelis may end this Agreement upon 7 days' written notice or sooner as set forth in § 5 below. 2. **Effective Date.** This Agreement is effective only when both parties have signed this document and the initial payroll has been processed, paid for, and received by Hughes. 3. **Leased Employees.** Michaelis will lease to Hughes the employees listed on Exhibit A. Hughes will sign Exhibit A to indicate proper pay status. Hughes will immediately notify Michaelis of any change in pay status for a leased employee. No other employees will be leased to Hughes unless Michaelis agrees. Hughes will notify Michaelis immediately upon a leased employee's release, termination, or cessation of employment. Hughes will cooperate with Michaelis in all employment and unemployment matters. Michaelis will provide workers'-compensation insurance for leased employees when they are performing work under this Agreement. 4. **Cost.** Hughes will advance to Michaelis's payroll account all costs required and associated with the leased employees at least 72 hours before a need for disbursement. . . .

"Lawyers may argue that they use *shall* consistently to impose a duty and that *shall* has a settled meaning in law. Not true and not true." Joseph Kimble, *Lifting the Fog of Legalese* 160 (2006).

So we have two distinct problems that pervade modern contracts: *shall* is used in a great variety of ways, and duties are stated not only with *shall* but also with lots of other words. Confusion is the inevitable result. If you want to avoid thinking about the problems, just take the ostrich-like approach, declare that *shall* is mandatory and *may* permissive, and abstain from any close examination of sentences.

Those who advocate using *shall* in the sense "has a duty to," so that it imposes a duty on the grammatical subject of the sentence, would have contract drafters delete 20–30% of their *shall*s. This approach means full employment for teachers of legal drafting because comparatively few lawyers have the linguistic chops for it. As a whole, lawyers have neither the patience nor the lexical acuity for making all the distinctions necessary for their consistent use of *shall*.[4] Why? Partly because there are just too many instances of the word in a typical contract, and partly because they're not accustomed to this type of linguistic analysis of individual words.

Once again, too, we come back to the point that most native speakers of English aren't even accustomed to using the word. So when they come to be legal drafters, they sprinkle in *shall*s as if they imparted a kind of legal precision. That sense of precision is wholly illusory.

So what are we to do? The simplest, most direct approach is to replace each instance of *shall* with some other, more appropriate term. Given its infamous ambiguity, *shall* is best dropped altogether from modern contract drafting.

But is this approach doable? Sure. Almost every contract I've prepared since 1991 has been without *shall*s. The only (rare) exceptions occurred when a client decided to follow the glossary presented in § 48. That approach requires great care and probably greater skill than the *shall*-less approach. That's so simply because the *shall*-less approach amounts to ordinary English made unambiguous; the *shall*-using approach amounts to unusual English made unambiguous. It's as simple as that.

The multifarious meanings of *shall* can be allocated among *must, will, is, may,* and even *is entitled to.* These substitutions, when carried out, result in the single greatest sentence-level improvement that is possible in modern transactional drafting.

The shift will require many experienced contract drafters to adjust their practices. Many will resist at first because they've grown fond of *shall* and believe (mistakenly, on the whole) that they're using it precisely and consistently. With a little humility and patience, these drafters will

4 *See* Johnson [Lane Greene], *One More Round with* "Shall," The Economist, https://amp.economist.com/Johnson/2011/05/25/one-more-round-with-shall.

almost inevitably come to see the wisdom of eliminating *shall* altogether. It's an issue that affects almost every contractual sentence.

There are two no-*shall* techniques. The first is the default setting for most contracts. Use it when the parties are known to each other.

No-*Shall* Glossary for Negotiated Contracts

will = (expresses a party's promise or a future occurrence)
will not = (expresses a party's negative promise or a future nonoccurrence)
must = (expresses a requirement usually for an inanimate object)
must not = (expresses a negative requirement usually for an inanimate object)
may = has discretion to; is permitted to
is entitled to = has a right to [+ *noun* or *noun phrase*]
can = is legally or physically capable
cannot = is legally or physically incapable

Some will object that this glossary allocates two meanings to *will*. The answer is that *some* degree of polysemy is inherent in all language (even with simple words like *a, an,* and *the*). With this glossary, *will* is in all uses being employed in ordinary, perfectly idiomatic senses. And within a given sentence in drafting that uses the technique properly, the theoretical ambiguity just doesn't occur. Unlike *shall*, the modal verb *will* cannot be used by any sensible speaker of English to mean *is, may, should*, or *is entitled to.* That just doesn't happen.

In English, the usual way to promise you'll do something is to declare that you *will* do it. There's an element of futurity in any such statement. Using *will* in this way (after the introduction stating *The parties agree as follows*) has worked well in thousands if not millions of contracts. And *will*, as a modal verb, hasn't invited anything like the welter of litigation that *shall* has. With this no-*shall* glossary given above, you'll end up with provisions that say, "Company will" (promise to do something in future), "Employee will" (promise to do something in future), "All such sums will

> "[W]hile no legal language, traditional or plain, is likely to be confused with poetry in purpose or content, plain language is less tedious and usually more elegant than legalese." Mark Adler, "The Plain Language Movement," in *The Oxford Handbook of Language and Law* 67, 72 (Peter M. Tiersma & Lawrence M. Solan eds., 2012).

be credited" (future), "No such conduct will be cause for termination" (future), etc. These are ordinary uses of the English language. The glossary covers the most common situations.

It's a different matter with adhesion contracts—that is, nonnegotiable contracts that one party (the powerful one) imposes on another (such as a consumer). In this kind of scenario, in which one party (the little guy) is unknown at the time of the drafting, *will* sounds more like a prediction than the imposition of a duty. The natural default is to use *must* for all requirements and promises for the little guy, and *will* for all promises by the more powerful party. Although *must* sounds bossy when it's used in the ordinary contract between known parties, it doesn't when it's used in adhesion contracts.

No-*Shall* Glossary for Nonnegotiable Contracts

must	=	is required to
must not	=	is required not to
may	=	is permitted to; has discretion to; has a right to; is authorized to [+ *verb*]
is entitled to	=	has a right to [+ *noun* or *noun phrase*]
will	=	(expresses a policy or a future occurrence)
can	=	is legally or physically capable
cannot	=	is legally or physically incapable

Using this glossary, you'll have residential leases that say "We [the landlord] will" and "You [the tenant] must"; car warranties that say "We [the manufacturer] will" and "You [the buyer] must [change the oil on a regular schedule, etc.]"; "We [the lender] will" and "You [the borrower] must . . . ." This style, counterintuitive as it may seem at first glance, reads naturally and is generally unobjectionable to consumers—assuming the rest of the drafting is straightforward and fair (as it ought to be). That is, the rhetoric of *we will/you must* isn't in itself bothersome to most readers. They won't even notice it. In any such contract, by the way, all ambiguities will be resolved against the company and in favor of the consumer.

❧ ❧ ❧

What follows are typical examples of *shall* revised to reflect the guidance of this section.

	NOT THIS:	BUT THIS:
Ex. 1	Each reference to Licensee herein shall be meant to include its Joint Ventures. **License Agreement**	Each reference to City Mart in this Agreement includes its Joint Ventures.
Ex. 2	If the Named Insured shall die, this policy shall cover the Named Insured's spouse. **Insurance Policy from a major underwriter**	If Klein dies, this policy will cover Klein's spouse.
Ex. 3	The premises shall be used by the Tenant for general office purposes and for no other purposes. **Commercial Lease**	Wilcox Resources may use the premises for general office purposes only.
Ex. 4	Employee shall be entitled to reasonable time off for vacations not to exceed five weeks per year. **Employment Agreement**	Marcus Eugene is entitled to reasonable vacation time of no more than 5 weeks a year.
Ex. 5	The Company shall not be liable for, and the Policy shall not apply to, extend to, or cover the following: **Insurance Policy from a major underwriter**	APIC is not liable for, and the Policy does not cover, the following:
Ex. 6	The term of this Agreement shall commence on the date hereof and shall continue for a period of 2 years and 3 months. **License Agreement**	The term of this Agreement begins on October 1, 2018, and continues until December 31, 2020.
Ex. 7	No Confidential Information shall be disclosed by Provider to any third party without the prior written approval of Energico. **Confidentiality Agreement**	CG Medical will not disclose Confidential Information to any third party without Energico's prior written approval.
Ex. 8	It shall be the duty of Agent to use due diligence in finding a purchaser or purchasers for such land and in effecting sale thereof. **General Real-Estate-Agent Contract from 19 Gerry W. Beyer, *West's Texas Forms: Residential Real Estate Transactions* § 2.3, at 18 (4th ed. 2008)**	Stanwick will use due diligence to find one or more purchasers and to sell the land.
Ex. 9	Upon termination of this Agreement for any reason, the Licensor, at its sole discretion shall determine whether any or all sublicenses shall be canceled or assigned to the Licensor. **License Agreement**	If this Agreement terminates for any reason, Nguyen may determine whether any or all sublicenses will be canceled or reassigned to Kim.

Many writers use euphemisms such as *passes away*—a tendency often decried by language commentators. One method to make the provision less harsh is to avoid the verb: *Upon Klein's death . . .*

It's better to use real names—not labels. See § 51.

State the exact date if you have it.

NOT THIS:	BUT THIS:
Ex. 10 Nothing in this article shall create any obligation on the part of the Owner to pay or to see to the payment of any sums to any Subcontractor. **Architect Subcontractor Agreement from 4 Robert W. Stayton, *Stayton Texas Forms Contracts* § 2338, at 591 (1959)**	Nothing in this article requires the Owner to pay or ensure the payment of any amount to a Subcontractor.
Ex. 11 **8. Computer Equipment, Software and Systems** Franchisee at its expense from time to time shall repair, upgrade or replace such equipment and supplies to meet Brean's then-current Technology Standards. **Franchise-License Agreement from an accounting firm**	**8. Computer Equipment, Software, and Systems.** At its sole expense, Franchisee must repair, upgrade, or replace the equipment and supplies to stay current with Brean's Technology Standards as they are updated.
Ex. 12 Allen Inc. shall, during the consulting term, provide Carter and his wife, without charge, with such medical and dental insurance benefits as Allen shall make generally available to its employees. **Consulting Agreement from a major beverage company**	**5. Insurance Benefits.** During the consulting term, Allen will provide Carter and his wife, without charge, the same medical- and dental-insurance benefits that Allen makes available to its employees.
Ex. 13 A. Landlord shall have the right at any time from the date hereof through the end of the term of this lease to substitute, instead of the leased premises, other space (of at least the area of the leased premises) hereinafter referred to as "Substitution Space," in the Building. **Lease Agreement from J. Scott Morris, *Real Estate Tax Planning Forms* 1.115 (1981)**	(A) **Substitution space.** At any time from the date of this lease through the end of its term, the Landlord may substitute other space in the Building of at least the same area for the leased premises.
Ex. 14 **Use of Premises** Lessee shall use the premises for warehousing, industrial, and office uses, or for any other lawful business or purposes with Lessor's written consent which shall not be unreasonably withheld. Lessee agrees to comply with all lawful requirements of the health, police and fire departments and local, state and federal authorities respecting the manner in which it uses the premises. **Lease Agreement from a major law firm**	**7. Use of Premises.** Techno will comply with all local, state, and federal laws respecting the use of the premises. Techno may use the premises for: (A) warehousing, industrial, or office use; or (B) any other lawful purpose with Ault Leasing's written consent, which must not be unreasonably withheld.

"'Shall' sounds a bit like a chorus from Handel's Messiah." Richard Wincor, *Contracts in Plain English* 32 (1976).

NOT THIS:	BUT THIS:
Ex. 15 Any alterations, repairs, construction, reconstruction, additions or improvements to effect Tenant's use of the Premises in compliance with said regulations, ordinances and laws shall be made at Tenant's sole expense, and at Landlord's option, shall be made by Landlord, or by Tenant after Landlord inspects and approves the written contracts of the Tenant's contractors, materialmen and subcontractors, which such contracts shall provide that they cannot be modified in any way without utilizing a written change order approved in writing by both Tenant and by Landlord. **Real-Estate Lease**	(B) **Necessary changes to Premises.** If the Premises must be changed or repaired to facilitate the Tenant's use or to comply with the law, the Tenant will bear the cost. At least 2 weeks before the work begins, the Tenant must submit to the Landlord for inspection and approval all written contracts of the Tenant's contractors, material suppliers, and subcontractors. The contracts must provide that they cannot be modified in any way without a written change order approved in writing by both the Tenant and the Landlord.
Ex. 16 SECTION SIX. POSSIBILITY OF TERMINATION. Nothing contained in this agreement shall constitute, or shall be construed to constitute, a limitation on the right of corporation, or of an affiliated corporation of corporation by whom employee is employed, to terminate employee's employment at any time, with or without cause or notice. It is agreed, however, that if employee shall be employed by corporation and by one or more of its affiliated corporations simultaneously from time to time, or if employee shall be employed by one or more of such corporations simultaneously with the termination of employee's employment by one or more of such corporations, then in either or both of such events no termination of employee's employment within the meaning of Sections Three and Four of this agreement shall be deemed to have occurred. **Stock-Purchase Agreement from 6B Am. Jur. Legal Forms 2d *Corporations* § 74:1364, at 172 (2002)**	**6. Termination.** 6.1 **No limits on termination.** Nothing in this Agreement limits the right of the corporation, or of an affiliated corporation by whom the employee is employed, to terminate the employee at any time, with or without cause or notice. 6.2 **Simultaneous employment.** If the employee is employed simultaneously by the corporation and one or more of its affiliated corporations from time to time, or if the employee is to be employed by one or more of the corporations simultaneously with the termination of the employee's employment by one or more of the other corporations, then in either or both of those events, no termination will occur within the meaning of § 3 or § 4.

"If you mean 'no' member of the class, then if the class appears in the subject, before the copula, say, '*no* member *may* (or *can*)' but do not say, '*no* member *shall.*' 'No' before 'shall' is ambiguous, meaning either that no member has a privilege or that no member has a duty." LeRoy Marceau, *Drafting a Union Contract* § 6.8(B), at 50–51 (1965).

§ 48 If you must use *shall*—either because of institutional pressures or because of personal preference—ensure that it's always replaceable either with "has a duty to" or (less stringently) "is required to."

In the preceding section, we rejected the misleading incantation that *shall* is "always mandatory," and *may* "always permissive." In a typical form that you've inherited, more than 50% of the *shall*s will be something other than mandatory. In varying proportions, they might mean *is* (false future), *will* (true future), *may* (permissive), or even *is entitled to* (entitlement). If you're to use *shall* responsibly—again, my advice is to jettison it altogether—you must have the time and ability to sort through the semantic tangles that it has created in old-school drafting.

So if you want *shall* to be mandatory, you must make it so. If you're determined to stick to *shall*, here's a glossary you can use:

The *Shall*-Using Glossary

shall	=	has a duty to
shall not	=	has a duty not to
must	=	is required to [used for all requirements that are not duties imposed on the subject of the clause]
may	=	has discretion to; is permitted to
may not	=	is not permitted to; is disallowed from
is entitled to	=	has a right to [+ *noun* or *noun phrase*]
will	=	(expresses a future occurrence)
can	=	is legally or physically capable
cannot	=	is legally or physically incapable

What follows are typical uses and misuses of *shall*. The "But This" column reflects adherence to the above glossary. Note, however, that all the other examples throughout this book reflect the guidance of § 47.

NOT THIS:	BUT THIS:
Ex. 1 Note the ambiguity of this sentence: is payment before the 45th day acceptable? All payments under this Agreement are to be paid 45 days from invoice. **Franchise Agreement from a major law firm**	The Dealer shall pay all invoices within 45 days after the invoice date.
Ex. 2 Licensee shall use the name "University of Great State" only to provide truthful and factual information about the licensed cultivars. **License Agreement from a major law firm**	Licensee may use the name "University of Great State" only to provide truthful and factual information about the licensed cultivars.

NOT THIS:	BUT THIS:
Ex. 3 The prevailing party shall be entitled to reasonable attorney fees in addition to costs and necessary disbursements. **Arbitration Agreement from a major law firm**	The prevailing party is entitled to reasonable attorney fees plus costs and necessary disbursements.
Ex. 4 Use of Schedule B services by Tenant shall be paid for by Tenant, which payment shall be made no later than the tenth day succeeding the date of the statement rendered for such services. **Commercial Lease from a major law firm**	Aronson shall pay for its use of Schedule B services no later than 10 days after the date of the statement for those services. **Note also the passive-to-active transformation.**
Ex. 5 The Licensor shall have the right to file, prosecute, or maintain patent applications at its own expense in any country in which the Licensee has not elected to file, prosecute, or maintain patent rights under Article 15. **License Agreement**	Altavista may file, prosecute, or maintain patent applications at its own expense in any country in which Swansen has not elected to file, prosecute, or maintain patent rights under Article 15.
Ex. 6 It is agreed that this Lease shall be an absolutely net lease for the Landlord and that Rent shall be received by the Landlord free of any cost or obligation concerning the Building or the Common Areas, unless specified in this Lease. **Lease Agreement**	This Lease is an absolutely net lease for the Landlord. Unless this Lease specifies otherwise, the Tenant shall pay to the Landlord Rent free of any cost or obligation concerning the Building or the Common Areas.
Ex. 7 Each installment of interest on the Bonds shall be payable as provided in the form thereof set forth in Exhibit A hereto; the Company shall not have any right to extend any interest payment periods for the Bonds as contemplated in Section 301(e) of the Indenture. **Security Interest**	Each installment of interest on the Bonds is payable in the form set forth in Exhibit A. The Company shall not extend any interest-payment periods for the Bonds as contemplated in § 301(e) of the Indenture.
Ex. 8 The Depositary shall not be liable for any governmental taxes, assessments or charges or corporate assessments or charges which may become payable in respect of the Deposited Securities or Receipts, but a ratable part of any and all of the same, whether such tax, assessment or charge becomes payable by reason of any present or future tax, statute, charter provision, by-law, regulation or otherwise, shall be payable by the Holder of this Receipt to the Depositary at any time upon request. **Depositary Receipt**	The Depositary is not liable for any government taxes, assessments, or charges, or corporate assessments or charges, that may become payable for the Deposited Securities or Receipts. But if a ratable part of a government tax, assessment, or charge, or a corporate assessment or charge becomes payable under a present or future tax, statute, charter provision, bylaw, regulation, or otherwise, the Holder of this Receipt shall pay the amount owed to the Depositary upon request.

§ 49 Avoid language of agreement once the terms begin.

After the lead-in to contractual terms (*The parties agree as follows*), the verb *agree* generally shouldn't appear again. Don't say, in the middle of a contract, that *X agrees to* or *It is agreed and understood that.* Everything in the agreement has been agreed and understood. That should be your position. To express the various rights and duties you need to, stick to your glossary for modal verbs.

Some drafters propose using *agrees to* in place of *shall.* This approach has three major drawbacks. First, it's wordy and, because it occurs so frequently, ungainly. Second, because it's ungainly, it's hard to sustain: drafters invariably feel the need to switch to some other wording on second, third, or fourth reference. Third, *agrees to* can be ambiguous when referring to a legal act: if you *agree to indemnify* or *agree to release*, is that a present indemnification or a present release or an agreement to release in the future? Even the performative adverb *hereby* doesn't cure this problem. So *agrees to* predictably, with some verbs, causes ambiguities of immediacy and futurity.

Consider an illustrative case. In 1988, a research fellow at Stanford University "agree[d] to assign" to the University all patent rights resulting from his research there. A short time later, the research fellow also began working with a private company, Cetus, that had developed a Nobel Prize-winning process important to his research. As a condition of employment, Cetus required the research fellow to sign an agreement stating that he would "assign and do[es] hereby assign" patent rights related to his research at Cetus. Some 17 years later, in 2005, Stanford sued Cetus's successor for infringement of a patent resulting from the inventor's research. Faced with two competing assignments of the same invention, the Federal Circuit held that "agree to assign" is a "mere promise to assign rights in the future," while "do hereby assign" is immediately effective.[1] The result: the inventor's agreement with Cetus effectively transferred the same property the inventor had earlier agreed to assign to Stanford, which lost the lawsuit. Stanford appealed to the Supreme Court on other grounds but lost there as well.[2] Whatever the merits of the Federal Circuit's distinction, the episode illustrates one pitfall to be averted by avoiding language of agreement once the terms of a contract begin.

Another pitfall relates to sentences beginning with a condition. Consider this poorly worded sentence from a sales contract: "If Buyer fails

1 *Stanford v. Roche Molecular Sys., Inc.*, 583 F.3d 832 (Fed. Cir. 2009).

2 563 U.S. 776 (2011).

to pay an installment within 30 days of the date such installment is due, Buyer agrees that Seller, at its option, may declare the entire balance then outstanding immediately due and payable." The question raised by this wording is whether the agreement will arise only in the future, upon satisfaction of the condition, or rather occurs upon the signing of the agreement. In essence, the condition has been misplaced. Better syntax would require this instead (assuming we were otherwise to adhere to the poor wording of the provision): "Buyer agrees that, if Buyer fails to pay any installment . . . ." That way, it's a present promise. But the best solution is to eliminate the language of agreement entirely: "If Buyer fails to pay an installment within 30 days after it is due, Seller may declare the entire balance then outstanding immediately due and payable."

The same problem can arise with other constructions. For example: "On the Effective Date, Seller agrees to assign to Buyer the lease of the premises in which the business is located." Once again, is it a present promise or a future one? Granted, it's in the present tense, but that's not determinative because present tense is usual for contracts (see § 64). When the effective date comes, the Seller may contend that it's now time to agree to assign, but that there's been no such agreement yet—only an agreement to agree.

"Come on!" you say. "That's a shyster-style argument!" The argument may frustrate you if you're Buyer's counsel, but it can be made with a straight face. If it's somehow to the Seller's advantage to make the argument, a lawyer can be found to make it. "But the view will ultimately be rejected by a court!" you object. Perhaps so. Yet testing the argument in court is time-consuming and extremely costly for the Buyer, which will probably end up bearing its own litigation costs. The Seller will make the argument only because it has a strong financial incentive to do so. Even if the Buyer's view is ultimately upheld, and the drafter's (perhaps your) true intent is sustained, the drafting has been a failure: it ended up in litigation.

All of which proves the point, once again, that the goal of good drafting is to forestall arguments about meaning. You don't want to give the Seller such an argument, silly as it might seem to us now. It will sound plausible from the pen of a skillful litigator. Using *agree* in the body of a contract can create arguments like this. So avoid it.

What follows are typical instances of language of agreement corrected to reflect the guidance in the blackletter of this section:

NOT THIS:	BUT THIS:
Ex. 1 It is expressly agreed that if Licensee should fail to deliver to Licensor any statement or report, then the Licensor may: . . . **License Agreement from a major law firm**	If AllPro Repair fails to furnish TGK Company with any statement or report, then TGK Company may: . . .
Ex. 2 It is understood that you are not personally responsible for our charges, but rather that they will be billed to you and presented to the insurer. **Physician–Patient Agreement from a hospital**	You are not personally responsible for our charges. We will bill your charges directly to the insurer for payment.
Ex. 3 The parties hereby consent to the exclusive jurisdiction of the courts of the State of Illinois with respect to enforcement of the provisions of this Agreement. **License and Data-Assignment Agreement from a major law firm**	Illinois courts have exclusive jurisdiction over all matters relating to this Agreement.
Ex. 4 It is agreed that no waiver by either party hereto of any breach or default of any of the covenants or agreements herein set forth shall be deemed a waiver as to any subsequent and/or similar breach or default. **Commercial Sublease from a major law firm**	**16.6 No waiver.** If either party fails to require the other to perform any term of this Agreement, that failure does not prevent the party from later enforcing that term. If either party waives the other's breach of a term, that waiver is not treated as waiving a later breach of the term.
Ex. 5 (5) Coach agrees to cooperate in the scheduling of games for the Program and agrees that the authority for and final decisions on such scheduling are with the Men's Athletics Director. **College-Football Head-Coach Employment Agreement from a major university**	(E) **Scheduling.** The Men's Athletics Director has final authority over scheduling the Program's games. Adams will cooperate in that scheduling.
Ex. 6 The Employee agrees that he shall devote all of his professional time, knowledge, and skill to his employment and that he shall perform such duties and occupy such positions and offices as the Board of Directors of the Corporation may from time to time determine. **Employment Agreement from a major law firm**	Cowles will devote all his professional time, knowledge, and skill to his employment and will perform the duties and occupy the positions and offices that Allied Corporation's Board of Directors may determine from time to time.

<table>
<tr><th>NOT THIS:</th><th>BUT THIS:</th></tr>
<tr><td>Ex. 7
Owner agrees to cooperate with Broker, its agents, and cooperating brokers fully with respect to Broker's efforts to sell the Property. Owner agrees to refer to Broker all inquiries received by Owner relating to the purchase or sale of the Property and to conduct all negotiations with prospective buyers of the Property through Broker. Owner further agrees to furnish Broker with such information concerning the Property as Broker may reasonably request.
Residential-Listing Agreement from a major real-estate company</td><td>2.2 Your obligations. As the Property's owner, you must:
(A) cooperate fully with Taylor, with its agents, and with cooperating brokers in Taylor's efforts to sell the Property;
(B) refer to Taylor all inquiries that you receive about the purchase or sale of the Property;
(C) conduct all negotiations with prospective buyers through Taylor; and
(D) furnish Taylor with all information that Taylor may reasonably request about the Property.</td></tr>
<tr><td>Ex. 8
Article II. It is understood and agreed by and between the parties hereto that all the work included in the contract shall be done as approved by the general manager of the owner personally or by duly authorized representative, and that his decision as to the true construction and meaning of the plans and specifications shall be final. It also is understood and agreed by and between the parties hereto that such additional drawings and explanations as may be necessary to detail and illustrate the work to be done are to be furnished by the general manager, and the parties agree to conform to and abide by the same so far as additional drawings or explanations may be consistent with the purpose and intent of the original drawings and specifications referred to in Article I.
Short-Form Contract for Public Project from Jack Kusnet & Owen T. Smith, Modern Construction and Development Forms § 1.79, at 1-132 (1982)</td><td>2. General Manager. Work must be done as approved by the owner's general manager or an authorized representative. The general manager's decision is final on the true construction and meaning of the plans and specifications. The general manager will provide additional drawings and explanations as necessary to detail and illustrate the work to be done. The parties must adhere to the additional drawings and explanations so far as they are consistent with the purpose and intent of the original drawings and specifications referred to in Article 1.

The language beginning so far as seems ill-advised if this form has been prepared by owner's counsel: it gives other parties discretion to reject the GM's additional drawings and explanations.</td></tr>
</table>

"**'It is Understood and Agreed.'** Absurd and sometimes dangerous. There is nothing wrong with 'We agree as follows' or something to that effect once at the beginning of a contract, but repetition of 'It is understood and agreed' adds either nothing or something. If it adds nothing, it ought not to be said. Usually it is the case that it adds nothing, because every clause in the contract is 'understood and agreed' or it would not be written into it. On the other hand, if it adds something, what it adds is a bad thing, namely an implication that other clauses not propped up by this phrase are somehow not understood or agreed on at all." Richard Wincor, *Contracts in Plain English* 29 (1976).

§ 50 Eliminate *may not.*

Change *may not* to *must not* (if it's a duty not to do something) or *cannot* (if it's a legal inability to do something). Idiomatically, *may not* is traditionally a way of denying permission <No, you may not go to that concert>. Sometimes, though, it functions as a near equivalent of *might not* <I may not be able to go>. It's therefore increasingly viewed as a mild expression in all its uses. By contrast, the prohibitory *must not* is unequivocal.

NOT THIS:	BUT THIS:
Ex. 1 The Tenant may not use the premises for any purpose other than general office purposes. **Commercial Lease from a major law firm**	Balfour may use the premises only for general office purposes.
Ex. 2 8.1 This Agreement may not be assigned by either Party without the written consent of the other Party, which consent will not be unreasonably delayed or denied. **Joint-Invention-Administration Agreement from a state technology-trading association**	**8.1 No assignment.** Neither party may assign this Agreement without the other party's prior written consent, which must not be unreasonably withheld.
Ex. 3 E. Entire Agreement. This Agreement contains the entire agreement between the parties and may not be modified or amended except by written instrument signed by both parties. **Joint Marketing Agreement from a telecommunications company**	(E) **Entire agreement.** This Agreement represents the entire agreement between the parties. It cannot be changed except by written agreement signed by the parties.

Party names

§ 51 Prefer real names for the parties.

Let's face it: contracts are generally boring to read. They're stripped of emotion (quite rightly), and for the most part they're devoid of human interest.

One of the few ameliorating devices is to give the participants their names, as opposed to legal-sounding labels. This one step makes the writing more vivid and interesting. It also helps legal drafters review their own work with more alertness. You're less likely to make mistakes. You know the parties—who's who—and so do the parties themselves. Everyone will read with greater comprehension if the principal actors are called by name. For example, you might use the abbreviated term *Ford* to refer to Ford Motor Company.

Admittedly, however, names can sometimes be confusing. For example, there might be multiple parties with similar names, as is common with corporations and their subsidiaries. In that situation, devise a useful alternative. So you might refer to the parent company as *Ford*, the financial subsidiary as *Ford Finance*, and the British subsidiary as *Ford UK*.

Of course, if you're preparing a basic template that includes generic terms, you know that the template will later be used for real clients to negotiate deal terms. When preparing the template you won't have party names, so use positional labels: Company/Employee, College/Student, University/Inventor, even (if you must) Assignor/Assignee. Then use the search-and-replace function to substitute in the actual names as soon as you're drafting for a client.

One qualification, though, about positional labels. If you're sticking to ordinary, idiomatic English (§§ 12–13), you must use articles in the usual way: *the Company*, not *Company* alone; *the Contractor*, not *Contractor*; *the University*, not *University*, etc. Otherwise the prose takes on an alien-sounding tone. Granted, it's a tone that many lawyers are accustomed to, but we must try our best to recapture our sense of normal English.

> "Once the reader is addressed directly and personally, it's natural to unbend and be as straightforward as you'd be in face-to-face conversation." Rudolf Flesch, *How to Write Plain English* 45 (1979).

NOT THIS:	BUT THIS:
Ex. 1 3.3 Housekeeping. You are required to keep your suite in a clean, sanitary and orderly condition and to perform all usual light housekeeping tasks within your Suite. The Provider will provide occasional heavy cleaning services for your Suite as it deems necessary. **Residence-and-Care Agreement from a major law firm**	**3.3 Housekeeping.** You must keep your suite clean, sanitary, and orderly, and perform all usual light-housekeeping tasks. Hill Manor may occasionally provide heavy-cleaning services for your suite.
Ex. 2 3. Conflict of Interest. Associated Counsel shall not accept any employment that shall conflict directly with the interests of the client in the Subject Matter without the prior written consent of the client. In the event that during the pendency of this Agreement, Associated Counsel determines that a conflict of interest exists or has arisen, Associated Counsel shall notify Lead Counsel and the client, and may withdraw from representing any of such clients. **Association Agreement from Vincent Di Lorenzo & Clifford R. Ennico, *Basic Legal Transactions: Attorney-Client Fee Agreements* § 46:34 (2010)**	**3. Conflict of Interest.** Daschle & Dixen will not accept employment that conflicts directly with the client's interests in the Subject Matter without the client's prior written consent. If a conflict arises or is later discovered while this Agreement is in effect, Daschle & Dixen will notify Burton Scarsdale Ludwig and the client. At its own discretion, Daschle & Dixen may then withdraw from representing the client.

"Remember, too, that your reader is the most important person in the universe—or at least your reader thinks so. Don't be afraid to bring the readers into your sentences, and don't be afraid to call them 'you.' The personal form of address will help them understand how the passage relates to them." Richard C. Wydick, *Plain English for Lawyers* 77 (4th ed. 1998).

§ 52 Never use a set of *-or*/*-ee* correlatives.

One of the easiest ways to make a mistake is to differentiate the parties with nothing more than a two-character suffix. You'll be setting yourself up for scrivener's errors. Once a paragraph is loaded with three references to *licensor* and three to *licensee*, somebody at some point will mistype one of the references.

It's permissible to use one of the two correlatives—just not both. You might use (if you must) *McDonald's* and *Franchisee*. You just shouldn't use *Franchisor* and *Franchisee* in the same document.

The only conceivable exceptions are *indemnitor* and *indemnitee*. The argument is that if there are two or more parties, the alternatives are awkward. But it's possible to stick to the rule by writing *indemnifying party* (or even *indemnifier*—a legitimate word) and *indemnitee*.

It's certainly possible to use positional labels in contracts: *Publisher/Author*, *Firm/Client*, *Manufacturer/Transporter*, etc. A contract using such generic names tends to look somewhat like an off-the-server agreement—one not tailor-made. But it does have one signal advantage: *must* tends to work quite well with these generic labels: *Author must deliver the manuscript by December 31* feels much more acceptable than *Liebowitz must deliver* . . . . The positional labels are decidedly less personal.

As we saw in § 51, though, even if you have *Assignor/Assignee* or *Licensor/Licensee* in your templates, replace those designations in your drafts prepared for actual clients. Once you've done that, you'll see the provisions in a new light, with a sharper mind.

NOT THIS:	BUT THIS:
Ex. 1 (a) Independent Contractor Status. The relationship of the parties established by this Agreement is that of vendor and vendee, and all work and duties to be performed by the Salesperson as contemplated by this Agreement shall be performed by it as an independent contractor. **Sales Agreement**	(A) **Independent-contractor status.** The parties' relationship established by this Agreement is that of seller and buyer. Mayfield, as a salesperson, is an independent contractor.

"Even lawyers sometimes get confused over the identity of the *lessor* and the *lessee*, the *mortgagor* and the *mortgagee*, and the *vendor* and the *vendee*." Thomas R. Haggard, *Legal Drafting in a Nutshell* 193 (1996).

NOT THIS:	BUT THIS:
Ex. 2 D. Seller may exercise any and all other rights and remedies even though not contained in this agreement which are now or hereafter become available to a vendor against a vendee who is or becomes in default of this contractual obligations a vendor under a lead sale contract including without limiting the general of the foregoing commencing a quiet title action to establish the validity of Seller's claim to the Premises, bringing an action for unpaid installments or other sums due hereunder, receiving a cancellation of Buyer's interest in this agreement and the Premises pursuing other remedies provided by law and obtaining relief on any other claim arising out of this agreement. Note that *Seller* and *vendor* are both used here. Yes, this is exactly what the contract says: partly gibberish. **Land Installment Contract from a major law firm**	(D) **Standifer's rights and remedies.** If Bilko defaults on a contractual obligation or if another claim arises from this Agreement, Standifer may exercise all rights and pursue all remedies that are then or later become available under this Agreement or by law, including: (1) bringing a quiet-title lawsuit to establish the validity of Standifer's claim to the Premises; (2) suing for unpaid installments or other sums due from Bilko; and (3) canceling Bilko's interest in this Agreement and the Premises.
Ex. 3 2. The option to purchase the property shall commence as of the time of execution of this contract and continue until midnight on [*date of expiration of option*], provided, however, this option may be continued by the Optionee from month to month thereafter for an additional period of [*specify extension period, e.g., 15 consecutive months*] by the payment or tender by the Optionee to the Optionor of the sum of [*specify monthly consideration for extension of option, e.g., $1,000*] per month on or before the first day of each and every month thereafter, provided that proof is furnished to Optionor that Optionee's pursuit in the development of [his or her] project is progressing. **Real Estate Option Contract from Gerry W. Beyer, 13 *West's Texas Forms* § 4.12, at 161 (2001)**	**2. Option Period.** The option to purchase the property begins upon this contract's becoming effective and continues until midnight CT on December 31, 2018. Hollister may continue this option from month to month for an additional 12 months if Hollister: (A) pays Steel City $2,000 per month on or before the first day of each month during the extension period; and (B) provides proof to Steel City that Hollister's development of the project is progressing.

NOT THIS:	BUT THIS:
Ex. 4 (c) Mortgagor will insure the Collateral in the name of the Mortgagee against loss or damage by fire and extend coverage to perils, theft, burglary, pilferage, collision and also, where requested by Mortgagee, against other hazards, with companies, in amounts and under policies (each containing a standard breach of warranty clause) acceptable to Mortgagee, the proceeds to be payable to Mortgagee, and all premiums thereon shall be paid by Mortgagor and the policies assigned and delivered to Mortgagee. Mortgagee shall have the right, but not the obligation, to provide insurance for its interest and charge Mortgagor Mortgagee's cost for such insurance, together with it or its designee's customary charges or fees associated with its insurance. Mortgagor hereby irrevocably appoints Mortgagee as Mortgagor's Attorney-in-Fact to make claim for, receive payment of and execute and endorse all documents, checks or drafts received in payment for any loss or damage under any of said insurance policies and to execute any documents or statements referred to herein. **Security Agreement–Mortgage between a major retail store and a financial-services company** The use of *insure* in the first line is ambiguous. It means to obtain insurance, not to act as insurer.	(C) **Collateral insurance.** Boswell will obtain insurance for the Collateral in Lopez Financial's name against loss or damage by fire, theft, burglary, pilferage, collision and, upon Lopez Financial's written request, other hazards. Boswell will pay the insurance premiums, designate that proceeds are payable to Lopez Financial, and assign and deliver the policies to Lopez Financial. Before Boswell buys a policy, Lopez Financial may exercise approval rights for: (1) the insurer; (2) the policy, which must have a standard breach-of-warranty clause; and (3) the amount of coverage. (D) **Interest insurance.** Lopez Financial may provide insurance for its interest and charge Boswell for the cost of the insurance, together with its own or its designee's customary charges for obtaining that insurance. (E) **Attorney-in-fact for insurance purposes.** Boswell irrevocably appoints Lopez Financial as Boswell's attorney-in-fact to make a claim, receive payments, and sign and endorse all documents, checks, or drafts received in payment for a loss or damage under any such insurance policy, and to sign related documents or statements.

"Lawyers like to distinguish between *bleepors* and *bleepees*. The *bleepor* is the one who bleeps, and the *bleepee* is the one who is bleeped. That's not a wonderful terminological scheme even if you know what bleep you're talking about, as in *grantor/grantee*, *indemnitor/indemnitee*. In cases such as *mortgagor/mortgagee* or *lessor/lessee*, where there's no obvious indication as to who is bleeping whom, the terminological convention has to be committed to memory. Lawyers who work in the area become comfortable with the distinctions, but that's not a good argument for an awkward nomenclature." Howard Darmstadter, *Hereof, Thereof, and Everywhereof* 13 (2002).

NOT THIS:	BUT THIS:
Ex. 5 6. **Insurance.** . . . All premiums on all insurance policies referred to in this section that are required by the Mortgage Loan documents to be paid as of the Cut-off Date have been paid, and such insurance policies name the Mortgagee under the Mortgage Loan and its successors and assigns as a loss payee under a mortgagee endorsement clause or, in the case of the general liability insurance policy, as named or additional insured. Such insurance policies will inure to the benefit of the trustee (or, in the case of a Non-Serviced Mortgage Loan, the applicable Non-Serviced Trustee). Each related Mortgage Loan obligates the related Mortgagor to maintain all such insurance and, at such Mortgagor's failure to do so, authorizes the Mortgagee to maintain such insurance at the Mortgagor's cost and expense and to charge such Mortgagor for related premiums. All such insurance policies (other than commercial liability policies) require at least 10 days' prior written notice to the Mortgagee of termination or cancellation arising because of nonpayment of a premium and at least 30 days' prior written notice to the Mortgagee of termination or cancellation (or such lesser period, not less than 10 days, as may be required by applicable law) arising for any reason other than non-payment of a premium and no such notice has been received by the Mortgage Loan Seller. **Mortgage-Loan Purchase Agreement**	6. **Insurance.** . . . 6.4 **Premiums.** All premiums on insurance policies referred to in this section that the Mortgage Loan documents require to be paid by the Cutoff Date have been paid. 6.5 **Insured and loss payee.** A lender-endorsement clause in the insurance policies names the Lender under the Mortgage Loan and its successors and assigns as loss payees. The general-liability insurance policies name the Lender under the Mortgage Loan and its successors and assigns as named or additional insureds. 6.6 **Beneficiaries.** The insurance policies will inure to the benefit of the trustee (or, in the case of a Nonserviced Mortgage Loan, the applicable Nonserviced Trustee). 6.7 **Insurance maintenance.** Each related Mortgage Loan obligates the related Borrower to maintain the insurance. If the Borrower fails to do so, the related Mortgage Loan authorizes the Lender to maintain the insurance at the Borrower's expense and to charge the Borrower for related premiums. 6.8 **Notice.** (A) **Nonpayment of premium.** If an insurance policy (other than a commercial-liability policy) is at risk of being terminated or canceled for nonpayment of a premium, the Borrower must provide to the Lender at least 10 days' prior written notice. (B) **Other reasons.** If an insurance policy (other than a commercial-liability policy) is at risk of being terminated or canceled for any reason other than nonpayment of a premium and the Mortgage Loan Seller has not received notice, the Borrower must give the Lender at least 30 days' prior written notice. If an applicable law requires a shorter period, the Borrower must give the Lender prior written notice of at least 10 days or the statutory period, whichever is longer.

§ 53 Banish *party of the first part*, etc.

Before the invention of the typewriter in the late 19th century, many contracts were written out in duplicate by scribes—in side-by-side versions on parchment. After the parties signed, the parchment would be halved with a knife or other cutting instrument, usually with angles or notches that would make the pieces match uniquely if laid down together again. One party would take the first half (the party of the first part), and the other party would take the second half (the party of the second part).

Although this terminology had become defunct by the late 1800s, it lingers even today. Yet few lawyers could tell you its origin. It's a prime example of a wordy archaism that needlessly persists.

A noted transactional lawyer recently wrote to say that he'd just reviewed an agreement that defined the party of the first part (doubtless borrowed language) but omitted a party of the second part. Hence no obligations were ever created.

NOT THIS:	BUT THIS:
Ex. 1 3. The First party, at its own cost and expense, shall illuminate the signboard from dusk to midnight; but, if illumination shall not be so provided, for any reason, the First Party shall pay to the Second Party, and the Second Party shall accept, in full settlement thereof, a sum equal to one-third of one day's rent of the signboard for each day in which such illumination shall not be provided. **Advertising Agreement from Saul Gordon, *Gordon's Modern Annotated Forms of Agreement* No. 2-6, at 21 (Stephen Kurzman rev., 1970)**	**3. Night Lighting.** At its expense, Jackson will illuminate the signboard from dusk to midnight. If for any reason Jackson does not provide illumination, it will pay Razorettes a third of a day's rent of the signboard for each day illumination is not provided. Razorettes will accept that payment as full settlement.

"Instead of using those forbidding phrases 'party of the first part' and 'party of the second part,' the contracting parties may be identified just as certainly—and much more understandably—by describing them as 'Seller' and 'Purchaser,' or 'Smith' and 'Jones,' or 'the Company' and 'the Employee.' If this procedure is followed, one can eliminate such old bogeys as 'said,' 'aforesaid,' 'above-named,' 'above-mentioned,' and 'aforementioned.'" Frank E. Cooper, *Writing in Law Practice* 275 (1963).

NOT THIS:	BUT THIS:
Ex. 2 18.01 Sale of the premises to a third party during years 3 through 15 of the lease would be made by the party of the first part (Lessor) directly to the party of the third part with difference between the sale proceeds and the option price (less the rent credit) enuring to the benefit of the parties of the second part (Lessees). In such case, since a prior 21E certificate exists, the funding of a second 21E certificate would be the responsibility of the Tenants. **Lease Agreement from a major law firm**	**18.1 Sale of premises to third party.** If the Owner directly sells the premises to a third party during years 3 through 15 of the lease, the Tenants will be entitled to the difference between the sale proceeds and the option price (less the rent credit). Because a prior 21E certificate exists, the Tenants will be responsible for funding a second 21E certificate.
Ex. 3 NOW, THEREFORE, IT IS MUTUALLY AGREED, AS FOLLOWS: 1. That the Second Party agrees to enter the service of the First Party, and the latter agrees to employ the Second Party, in and about its business, for a term of two (2) years from and after this date, at a salary of twelve hundred dollars ($1,200) a week, payable at the end of each and every week. 2. That, during the term of such employment, the Second Party shall devote all of his time and attention, and give his best effort and skill, exclusively to the business and interests of the First Party, and shall perform such services in and about such business of the First Party as may, from time to time, be assigned to him, and shall, in all respects, do his utmost to further enhance and develop the best interests and welfare of the First Party. **Employment Agreement on Salary Basis from Saul Gordon, *Gordon's Modern Annotated Forms of Agreement* No. 31-14, at 818 (Stephen Kurzman rev., 1970)**	The parties agree as follows: **The Agreement** **1. Employment Relationship.** **1.1 Duration.** We will employ you for 2 years from the date of this Agreement. **1.2 Your duties.** While employed, you must devote all your time and attention and give your best efforts exclusively to our business and interests. You must perform the services that we assign to you and do your utmost to further enhance and develop our best interests and welfare. **1.3 Compensation.** We will pay you $1,200 at the end of each week you work.

Party of the first part (Lessor) = Owner

Party of the second part (Lessee) = Tenant

Party of the third part = third party

"The party of the first part hereinafter known as Jack, and the party of the second part hereinafter known as Jill, ascended or caused to be ascended an elevation of undetermined height and degree of slope, hereinafter referred to as 'hill.'" Don Sandburg, *The Legal Guide to Mother Goose* 7 (1978).

NOT THIS:

Ex. 4

9. It is mutually agreed by the parties to this Contract that if the Party of the Second Part fail or neglect to pay any of the payments required under this contract, within thirty (30) days of their due date, or fails or neglects to perform any of the agreements contained herein, Party of the Second Part shall be deemed in default of this entire contract and the Party of the First Part may at her option:
(1) declare the full balance on the purchase price immediately due and payable and notify Party of the Second Part orally or in writing of same, and the Party of the Second Part shall then have ten (10) days from the receipt of said notice in which to provide Party of the First Part with a written commitment by Party of the Second Part's lending institution that a payoff loan has been approved and upon such approval by the lending institution, Party of the Second Part shall have twenty (20) additional days in which to pay Party of the First Part off in full. If Party of the Second Part does not pay the full balance due within the additional twenty (20) days granted, then the Party of the First Part may file an action against the Party of the Second Part for the balance due under this Contract, including costs and attorney's fees, and for rescission of this contract or for the sale of the property, with the proceeds of said sale to be divided by the court as the respective interests of the parties appear and seller shall be entitled to a personal judgment against Party of the Second Part for any deficiency balance remaining due plus accrued interest, costs and attorney's fees, or
(2) Party of the First Part may waive the default and grant Party of the Second Part a specific additional period of time in which to cure the default by making any payment or performing any agreement required of Party of the First Part. A waiver of one default shall not be a waiver of any other default(s) and Party of the First Part shall retain their options with regard to those other defaults, and should Party of the Second Part fail to cure the default after Party of the First Part have granted additional time to do so, the Party of the First Part may pursue any other remedies provided herein or
(3) Party of the First Part may pursue any legal or equitable remedy available under the laws of the Commonwealth of Kentucky including, but not limited to, an action to enforce the contract and to recover the purchase price, or to rescind the Contract.
It is understood by all parties that the Party of the First Part shall have sole discretion in determining which of the above options to pursue in the event Party of the Second Part is in default. Party of the Second Part agrees to pay Party of the First Part's reasonable attorney's fees and any court costs which Party of the First Part may incur with the exercise of his options in the event of Party of the Second Part's default.

Contract for Sale of Land from a major law firm

BUT THIS:

9. Default and Remedies.

9.1 Carlyle's default. Carlyle will be in default of the entire contract if he fails to make a required payment within 30 days after the due date or fails to perform any other duty under this contract.

9.2 Martel's options for remedies. If Carlyle defaults, Martel may, at her option, pursue the following remedies:

(A) **Acceleration.** Martel may declare the full balance on the purchase price immediately due and notify Carlyle orally or in writing. Carlyle will then have 10 days after receiving notice to give Martel a written commitment from Carlyle's lending institution that it has approved a payoff loan. Upon the institution's approval, Carlyle will have 20 more days to pay Martel in full.

(B) **Lawsuit.** If Carlyle's lending institution approves a payoff loan but Carlyle doesn't pay the full balance due within the 20 days allowed under (A), Martel may file a lawsuit for:

(1) the balance due;

(2) rescission of this contract; or

(3) sale of the property, with the sale proceeds being divided by the court as the respective interests of the parties appear; and, if a deficiency balance still remains due, a personal judgment against Carlyle for that amount plus accrued interest.

(C) **Other remedies.** Martel may pursue any other legal or equitable remedy available under Kentucky law.

9.3 Waiver. Martel may waive the default and grant Carlyle a specific additional period in which to cure the default by payment or other performance. If Carlyle fails to cure the default, Martel may pursue any available remedies. A waiver of one default does not waive any other default; Martel retains all options regarding other defaults.

9.4 Litigation expenses. If Carlyle's default results in a successful outcome for Martel, Carlyle will pay Martel's reasonable attorney fees and any court costs that are incurred.

§ 54 Consider using first- and second-person pronouns (*we* and *you*) in employment contracts, consumer contracts, and the like.

In a consumer contract, as well as in other adhesion contracts, try *you* and *we* instead of legal terms to designate the parties.

Lawyers generally avoid pronouns, and often with good reason: to avoid an ambiguous reference. But in many types of documents—such as consumer documents, letter agreements, and fee agreements—first-person and second-person pronouns help you communicate more quickly and just as unambiguously as you would if you repeated nouns at every turn. Typically, the document becomes far more readable and therefore clearer. And you immediately eliminate all problems associated with sexist language.

First- and second-person pronouns are personal words. They add human interest. With their friendly tone, they pull readers into the document. And in technical writing, that's especially important. Rudolf Flesch, a leading figure in plain-English circles, was one of the first to explain the need for *you*:

> Keep a running conversation with your reader. Use the second-person pronoun whenever you can. Translate everything into *you* language. *This applies to citizens over 65 = if you're over 65, this applies to you. It must be remembered that = you must remember. Many people don't realize = perhaps you don't realize.* Always write directly to *you*, the person you're trying to reach with your written message. Don't write in mental isolation; reach out to your reader.[1]

Likewise, the words *we* and *our*—in reference to your client—make corporations and other legal entities sound as if they have genuine personalities (as they typically do). Businesspeople usually appreciate this down-to-earth approach over the sterile, distancing effect of third-person prose.

But be careful with the word *we*. Drafters sometimes fall into ambiguity in letter agreements especially—when the intention is to use *we* alternatively to denote the drafter's client on the one hand, and the writer and recipient jointly on the other. If you're following the approach outlined here, you must renounce the first-person plural to denote both writer and recipient.

1 Rudolf Flesch, *How to Be Brief: An Index to Simple Writing* 114 (1962).

NOT THIS:	BUT THIS:
Ex. 1 The deductible is the amount that the Insured must pay before the Plan will pay other hospital, surgical, and medical benefits. **Insurance Policy from a major underwriter**	The deductible is the amount that you must pay before we pay other hospital, surgical, and medical costs.
Ex. 2 3.7. Damages for Breach of Contract. In the event of a breach of this Agreement by Employee, Employer may recover from Employee any and all damages that Employer may sustain as a result of the breach of this Agreement. This includes Employer's legal fees. **Salesperson Agreement from 3 Nancy Saint-Paul, Texas Legal Practice Forms 3d *Employment Agreements* § 49:5, at 679 (2016)**	**3.7 Damages for breach of contract.** If you breach this Agreement, we may recover from you any costs that we incur as a result of your breach, including legal fees.
Ex. 3 Client will promptly pay all costs and expenses of litigation monthly. The firm will periodically send to Client, for direct payment by Client, invoices received by the Firm from third parties such as court reporters, expert witnesses, and reproduction centers for services rendered on Client's behalf. Client agrees to pay third-party invoices when due. **Fee Agreement from a major law firm**	You must promptly pay all costs and expenses of litigation each month. We will periodically send you invoices we receive from third parties—such as court reporters, expert witnesses, and copy centers—and you must promptly pay those by their due dates.
Ex. 4 Section VII. Expenses Employer agrees to reimburse employee for all expenses reasonably incurred in performing duties pursuant to this agreement. Such expenses include travel undertaken on behalf of employer, entertainment conducted for purposes of promotion of employer's business, and fees for educational programs relevant to employee's current or future positions with employer. **Employment Contract from *Texas Forms: Legal & Business* § 11:44, at 106 (2008)**	**7. Expenses.** We will reimburse you for all expenses you reasonably incur in performing your duties under this Agreement, including travel you undertake on our behalf, entertainment to promote our business, and educational programs related to your current or future positions with us.

"Using personal pronouns will make your writing job easier. All circumlocutions consume time and energy. The third-person circumlocution can drain both writer and reader." Ernst Jacobi, *Writing at Work: Dos, Don'ts, and How Tos* 59 (1976).

§ 55 Avoid first-person ghostwriting for a counterparty.

Generally, it sounds phony when a form contract puts words into the mouth of a counterparty. Don't say *I* or *we* when you're referring to a signatory on the other side. Make it *you*. The silliness of first-person drafting is that it purports to be in the counterparty's voice, and the words written typically bear little if any relation to how the person might speak or write. Hence there's a kind of insincerity about it. If the document ever gets tested, the adjudicator is more likely than not to conclude that the drafting party has taken advantage or overreached.

NOT THIS:	BUT THIS:
Ex. 1 In consideration of my employment or continued employment by Addison Systems Incorporated or a subsidiary thereof (collectively, the "**Company**") and the compensation now and hereafter paid to me, I acknowledge and agree that: 1. **NO CONFLICT.** During the term of my employment, I will perform for the Company such duties as may be designated by the Company from time to time and will devote my best efforts to the interests of the Company. I represent that I have not entered into, and will not enter into, any agreement, either written or oral, in conflict with this Agreement. 2. **AT WILL EMPLOYMENT.** I understand and agree that nothing in this Agreement shall confer any right with respect to continuation of employment by the Company and that my employment is "at will" and subject to termination by the Company or by me at any time for any reason or no reason and with or without advance notice. **Employee-Inventions and Proprietary-Rights Assignment Agreement from a major multinational computer-software company**	In consideration of your employment or continued employment by Addison Systems Incorporated or its subsidiary ("we," "us," or "our") and of the compensation we pay to you, you agree to the following: 1. **No Conflict.** While employed, you will perform for us as we direct and will devote your best efforts to our interests. You represent and warrant that you have not and will not enter into any agreement, either written or oral, in conflict with this Agreement. 2. **At-Will Employment.** Nothing in this Agreement confers any right to your continued employment by us. Your employment is "at will" and subject to termination by us or by you at any time for any reason, or for no reason at all, with or without prior notice.

Quaere whether this release and waiver would be enforceable against an employee.

"Legalese and traditional style persist for the same reasons as always—habit, inertia, fear of change, the overwhelming influence of poor models, the rote use of forms, and notions of self-interest (prestige and control). Not to mention lack of skill." Joseph Kimble, *Plain English: A Charter for Clear Writing*, 9 Thomas M. Cooley L. Rev. 1, 22 (1992).

NOT THIS:

Ex. 2

Employee Liability Waiver and Indemnification Agreement

An agreement between an employer and an employee releasing and indemnifying the employer from liability for accidents, injuries, or other damages the employee suffers while engaged in and employer-sponsored activity or while using employer-provided equipment or facilities.

Employee Release and Waiver of Liability and Indemnification Agreement

In consideration of being permitted to participate in [SPECIFIED ACTIVITY/ACTIVITIES], I, [EMPLOYEE NAME], hereby release, waive, discharge, and covenant not to sue [EMPLOYER NAME], its parents, subsidiaries or other affiliates, officers, agents, or employees ("**Releasees**") from any and all liability, claims, demands, actions and causes of action of any kind or nature arising out of or related to any loss, damage, or injury, including death, that I or any of my property may sustain resulting from my participation in or in any way connected with my participation in such [activity/activities], regardless of whether such loss is caused by the negligence of the Releasees and regardless of whether such liability arises in tort, contract, strict liability, or otherwise.

I understand that participation in [this activity/these activities] involves an inherent risk of personal injury and even death, and I hereby elect to voluntarily participate in said [activity/activities], knowing that the [activity/activities] may be hazardous to me and my property. I understand that [EMPLOYER NAME] does not require me to participate in [this activity/activities]. I assume full responsibility for any risks of loss, property damage, or personal injury, including death, that I or my property may sustain as a result of being engaged in such [activity/activities], whether caused by the negligence of the Releasees or otherwise, including as a result of negligent rescue operations. I hereby acknowledge that I know of no medical reason why I should not participate in [this activity/these activities].

I hereby acknowledge that [EMPLOYER NAME] has advised me to consult a physician before engaging in such [activity/activities]. In the event of an emergency, I authorize [EMPLOYER NAME] to secure from any licensed hospital, physician, or medical personnel any treatment deemed necessary for my immediate care. I agree that I will be responsible for payment of any and all medical services rendered. I understand that alcohol may be served at [this activity/these activities], and I acknowledge that [EMPLOYER NAME] requires me to act responsibly during and on the way to and from the [activity/activities] with regard to my alcohol consumption.

Employee-Liability-Waiver-and-Indemnification Agreement from an employers' trade association

BUT THIS:

Employee Release and Waiver of Liability and Indemnification Agreement

Background

This release and waiver, effective [date], is by John N. Frankel in favor of his employer, Positano Enterprises, Inc. Throughout, Frankel is referred to by *you* and *your*. Positano is referred to by *we*, *us*, and *our*.

Release and Waiver

1. **Release of Liability.** In participating in [specified activity], you release, waive, and discharge us, our parent corporation, our subsidiaries, and our other affiliates, as well as our officers, agents, or employees from all liabilities, claims, demands, and lawsuits of any kind related to any loss, damage, or injury, including death, that you or your property may sustain from participating in [activity/activities], even if the loss is caused by our negligence and regardless of whether liability arises in tort, contract, strict liability, or otherwise.
2. **Acceptance of Risk.** You understand that participating in [specified activity] involves an inherent risk of personal injury and even death, and you elect to participate voluntarily knowing that [specified activity] may be hazardous to you and your property. You understand that we do not require your participation in [specified activity]. You assume full responsibility for any risks of loss, property damage, or personal injury, including death, that you or your property may sustain, including any negligent rescue operations. You acknowledge that you know of no medical reason why you should not participate.
3. **Medical Services.** You acknowledge that we have advised you to consult a physician before participating in [specified activity]. In an emergency, you authorize us to secure from any licensed hospital, physician, or medical personnel any treatment considered necessary for your immediate care. You agree to pay for all medical services rendered. You understand that alcohol may be served at [specified activity] and acknowledge that we require you to act responsibly during and on the way to and from [specified activity] regarding your alcohol consumption.

"Sometimes, slavishly copied precedents are not merely inappropriate to the particular transaction: they are dangerous or even wrong. 'Botched clauses' find their way into the precedent books; and once there, they are perpetuated." Peter Butt & Richard Castle, *Modern Legal Drafting* 11 (2001).

§ 56 Never put parties' names (or other words) in all-caps text.

Some drafters have adopted the unfortunate habit of putting parties' names, and occasionally other words as well, in all capitals each time they appear. The effect is one of intermittent shouting. The drafters afflicted with this eccentricity know little about readability. Don't be one of them.

For more information on proper capitalization of defined terms, see § 134.

NOT THIS:	BUT THIS:
Ex. 1 11.8 In the event that DAVIS REFINEMENT makes an IMPROVEMENT, and LICENSEE wishes to use such IMPROVEMENT in LICENSEE's IMPLEMENTATION, LICENSEE agrees to qualify the IMPLEMENTATION incorporating the IMPROVEMENT prior to commercialized distribution of the same. Such qualification shall occur through the same process set forth in this Section 11 unless otherwise mutually agreed to by the Parties in writing. **License Agreement from a major digital-technology company**	**11.8 Qualifying Improvements.** If Davis Refinement makes an Improvement and the Licensee wants to use that Improvement in the Licensee's Implementation, the Licensee must first qualify the Implementation that incorporates the Improvement before commercialized distribution of it. Unless Davis and the Licensee agree otherwise in writing, this qualification must occur through the process set forth in this § 11.
Ex. 2 19. TENANT hereby agrees that LANDLORD may at any time enter the PREMISES and at any time perform work therein that LANDLORD is required to perform for SUBTENANT. TENANT further agrees that any entry into the PREMISES by LANDLORD and any work performed in the PREMISES by LANDLORD for SUBTENANT shall not impose liability upon LANDLORD or entitle TENANT to terminate the LEASE, abate the rent, seek compensation from LANDLORD, reduce TENANT's obligations under the LEASE, or increase TENANT's rights under the LEASE. **Consent to Sublease from *The Sublease and Assignment Deskbook* Form 7.6, at 462 (Brent C. Shaffer ed., 2d ed., 2013).**	**19. Entry on Premises for Subtenant Work.** The Landlord may at any time enter the Premises to perform required work for the Subtenant. The Landlord's doing so will not impose liability on the Landlord or entitle the Tenant to terminate the Lease, abate the rent, seek compensation from the Landlord, reduce the Tenant's obligations, or increase the Tenant's rights under the Lease.

NOT THIS:	BUT THIS:
Ex. 3 10. Tenant's Property. Any communications equipment, building, wires, cables, conduits, or pipes installed by TENANT for TENANT's exclusive use shall remain the property of TENANT, and LANDLORD waives any lien rights it may have concerning the communications equipment, building, wires, cables, conduit or pipes. Any device or other equipment erected or installed by LANDLORD for LANDLORD's exclusive use shall remain the property of LANDLORD, and TENANT waives any lien rights it may have concerning LANDLORD's equipment. TENANT shall remove all of its communication equipment at its sole expense, except as provided for herein, on or before the expiration or earlier termination of the lease and shall make any necessary repairs to the property to return it to its prelease condition. **Shared-Communications-Facility Lease from *The Commercial Lease Formbook* Form § 4-1, at 418 (Dennis M. Horn ed., 2004)**	**10. Property Rights.** Any communications equipment, building, wires, cables, conduits, or pipes that Larson installs for its exclusive use remain Larson's property. Willis Management waives any lien rights on them. Property that Willis Management builds or installs for its own exclusive use will remain its own property. Larson waives any lien rights on it. Except as allowed in this Agreement, Larson will remove all its communications equipment at its sole expense when or before the lease expires or terminates and will make any repairs needed to return the property to its prelease condition.

"Clients from all walks may simply wish to know what the effective date of a contract is. Three or more dates can often be found in a contract: the date inserted on the date line at the beginning of the contract and the dates inserted on the date lines following signature lines. Much of the clutter and confusion about these multiple dates can be avoided by simple but incisive language, such as a provision specifying which date is the effective one." R.A. Feldman, *Drafting Effective Contracts: A Practitioner's Guide* § 2-B.9[b], at 83 (Supp. 1992).

Dating the contract

§ 57 Understand the conventions about effective dates, signing dates, and backdating.

Having a definitive date when a contract becomes effective is often a matter of no small significance. One problem occurs when no date is given at all, of course. More commonly, though, a proliferation of dates (as with a single agreement containing a "contract date," an "effective date," and then maybe differing dates of signing) can give rise to all sorts of timing issues. The better drafting practice is to have a single effective date either announced at the outset or stated to occur upon the addition of the final signature. In the latter circumstance, care must be taken to ensure that all signatories include the dates of the signatures—something that doesn't always happen.

For a simple contract, inserting "dated [date]," "dated as of [date]," or "effective [date]" in the preamble is quite common. For example: "This Agreement, dated 31 January 2017, is between . . . ." The date specified is typically the date on which the parties sign and deliver.

Some advisers to this book prefer always to include the effective date in the preamble with no dates next to the signatures. They often use a defined term (i.e., "Effective Date") so that the date itself needs to appear only once—where the term is defined—to avoid discrepancies in the document in case lawyers on either side of the deal fail to catch every instance where a date appears. These drafters also tend to set other important dates based on the Effective Date (for example, "Target Flip Date" might be defined as "the date that is 9 years after the Effective Date"). Exceptions are dates that must be hard-coded into the document, usually for regulatory or financial-statement reasons (e.g., "Sponsor must deliver financial statements for quarters ending March 31, June 30, September 30, and December 31 of each year, beginning for the quarter ending December 31, 2019," or "Sponsor represents and warrants that construction on the project began before December 31, 2019").

Other advisers say that to insist on a uniform rule for dating all contracts would be to impose a foolish consistency. On this view, the "best practice" may depend on the nature of the deal or agreement. There may be good reasons underlying some of the variations that exist. For example, in some commercial transactions, a contract's effective date may be determined by a future act that needs specification, such as "upon approval by the Bankruptcy Court."

On the other hand, sometimes it *is* important to date signatures, and the contract becomes effective on the date when the last signatory signs. This practice is common with home-purchase agreements: we don't want an offer to buy or sell property to exist without including the deal's terms. Normally, such a contract will include a provision saying that the offer represented by this document as signed by the Buyer will terminate if not accepted within 5 days after the date of the Buyer's signing. The acceptance is shown, as specified in the offer, by the Seller's signing and delivering the contract to the Buyer.

Generally, no one in a sophisticated or high-value transaction objects to including the effective date in the preamble, but individuals (usually landowners) or small-business owners sometimes prefer to date their signatures. If the other side really cares, it's probably not worth fighting about. It just requires thorough review of the final document to make sure all dates are correct. That's easy enough, though it might add slightly more expense in lawyer time.

Many large business transactions have multiple agreements and complex closings. Normally it's desirable, for convenience, to date them all the same. In modern practice, signatures are collected on various separate signature pages (often one party to a page) and put together at the office of the lawyer where the deal will close. These are delivered without dates on the signature pages under a formal or informal agreement that the lawyer will "release" the signature pages when all parties agree that the deal can be closed. In this type of situation, the effective date is generally recited in the preamble. Sometimes it's also used as part of the contract's title or on a cover sheet.

But sometimes it's prudent—even necessary—to state more than one date. Contracts can quite legitimately be backdated, for example: under the tax code, say, a partnership agreement for a given tax year can be amended with effect for that year up to the date for filing of the tax return for that year (not including extensions). In such a case, it's good practice to note explicitly both the signing date and the effective date (that is, the earlier date to which the contract is being made effective). Such a contract might say: "This Amendment to the AB Partnership is being signed by A and B this 31 January 2019 but with effect as of 1 January 2018, as provided below." Under current law, you're allowed to make a partnership amendment effective with respect to a year (2018) if you amend before the tax return for that year is due (e.g., March 15, 2019, for the 2018 return).

Two other illustrations of backdating come to mind. First, backdating may occur when a contract is to be effective from the date of the parties' informal agreement (six months, say, before the document's signing). Both parties might date their signatures in this instance to provide unambiguous evidence of what they were doing. Second, in settlement-and-release papers for certain employment cases, an effective date starts the clock for payment of the settlement amount, and a signature date triggers the running of a seven-day time within which the employee may revoke the agreement (the dates often coincide at seven days after signature).

Yet backdating an agreement can create problems if the backdating fabricates the occurrence of an event and harms a third party or violates the law. For example, in a professional-services agreement, federal law provides that an entity engaging a physician must not pay the physician for services rendered unless the physician signs the agreement before treatment or within 90 days after. To avoid running afoul of federal law, the physician must date the signature on the date actually signed; the agreement should not be backdated in an attempt to circumvent the law. Even if the backdating accurately memorializes an event (and neither misleads a third party nor violates the law), the backdating may create unwanted factual and legal issues unless the backdating is explicitly disclosed in the agreement itself to put third parties on notice. Having an "effective date" and a "signed date" may be enough disclosure or notice to avoid these undesirable factual and legal issues. But if the contract is private to the parties and raises no issues of third-party reliance, and backdating doesn't violate the law, then backdating should present no problems.

It's common for contracts with utilities or other semigovernment bodies to get sloppy with dating. Sometimes no date at all appears—just "______, 2019" where a date should be. This can create many problems when one is trying to determine when warranties or statutes of limitation expire or to calculate milestone deadlines that need to be based on contractor deadlines or obligations.

Given the great variety of possible approaches to contract drafting and their underlying justifications, this book can't take an invariable stand on what drafters should do—except to encourage drafters to make considered, unambiguous choices.

NOT THIS:	BUT THIS:
Ex. 1 This could be ambiguous. The date of signing? Another date in the contract that could be considered the "Contract Date"? "*Effective Date*" means the date of this Agreement. **Management-Services Agreement from an assisted-living facility**	"Effective Date" means the date of the last signatory's signing. *or use an exact date*: "Effective Date" means July 1, 2018.

NOT THIS:	BUT THIS:
Ex. 2	
Incontestability: This policy shall be incontestable except for nonpayment of premiums, provided two years shall have elapsed from its date of issue. . . . In witness whereof, the company has caused this policy to be executed this 23d day of August, 2018. **Life-Insurance Policy**	**5.2 Incontestability.** After 2 years from this policy's date of issue, the policy is incontestable except for nonpayment of premiums. The date of issue is the date on which the insured signs the policy. . . . Signed: August 23, 2018.
Ex. 3	
1.1 TERM. This Agreement shall become effective on the Contract Date and shall commence on the Utility Transfer Date immediately following such Effective Date and continue for the term as designated on the "Retail Electric Agreement" and after such date unless terminated pursuant to Paragraph 1.2. **Retail Electric Agreement**	**1.1 Term.** This Agreement is effective on the Contract Date, which is the date on which the last party signs. Your service will begin on the first meter-reading date (as set by the Local Distribution Utility) that falls immediately after the Contract Date and will continue for at least 36 months. Service will continue after that time unless terminated under § 1.2.

The "date of issue" was not defined in the policy, and no other dates were specified. A court determined that the execution date was also the contractual date of issue.

If the Agreement becomes effective on the *Contract Date*, then shouldn't the *Effective Date* be the same as the *Contract Date*? Very confusing!

The revision sticks with *Contract Date* only and states the exact term (36 months) from the Retail Electric Agreement instead of merely cross-referencing to it.

"All legal instruments, including contracts, are communications, and they are addressed not merely to courts. . . . The main audience, of course, consists of the parties to the contract. The problem is to tell them what they need to know about the specifics of the deal without bogging them down in unnecessary detail." Reed Dickerson, "Achieving Clarity in Contracts," in *Drafting Documents in Plain Language* 109, 109 (Duncan A. MacDonald chmn., 1979).

§ 58 Consider putting the effective date in the preamble.

If an effective date is to be given up front, the recommended wording is as follows:

This Agreement, effective [date], is between [names of parties].

This wording allows for an effective date that might differ from the signing date. In fact, the contract may well not include the dates of signing at all. Given that the date appears in the opening sentence, there should be no doubt about the exact date when the contract takes effect.

If you prefer not to say "effective" for some reason, you can modify the preambular language to this:

This Agreement, dated [date], is between [names of parties].

	NOT THIS:	BUT THIS:
Ex. 1	EXECUTED on the date set forth in the acknowledgment below, to be effective on and as of the date first above written. **Mortgage, Rent-Assignment, and Security Agreement from a major financial institution and healthcare clinic**	This Agreement, effective [date], is between [names of parties].
Ex. 2	This Systems Integrator Agreement (the "Agreement") by and between Parker Corporation, a Delaware corporation having its principal place of business at 1036 Hartman Ave., Elkhart, KS 67950, and Steamgears, Inc. ("Integrator"), a Florida corporation having its principal place of business at 17 Main St., Suite J, Fleming Island, FL 32003, is entered into as of the date last written below ("the Effective Date"). **System-Integrator Agreement from a major corporation**	This Systems-Integrator Agreement (the "Agreement"), effective [date], is between Parker Corporation (Parker), a Delaware corporation having its principal place of business at 1036 Hartman Ave., Elkhart, KS 67950, and Steamgears, Inc. (Integrator), a Florida corporation having its principal place of business at 17 Main St., Suite J, Fleming Island, FL 32003.

Even if the contract is signed on a different date, there should be no doubt about the exact date that the contract takes effect if this language is used in the preamble.

The problem with the phrasing "date last written below" is that the Effective Date can be unintentionally changed. If copies are signed and exchanged by electronic means, an Effective Date is created. But if the hard-copy originals are exchanged and signed later, a party could argue that the newly signed document's date supersedes that of the electronic version and creates a new Effective Date.

§ 59 Be careful with dated signatures.

If the signatures are to be dated, you should omit the date in the preamble unless the express purpose is to have an effective date different from that of the last signatory's signing. Don't create confusion by including more dates than necessary. If the contract is to be signed electronically, a date will almost certainly be automatically supplied with each signature—hence you'd want to omit the effective date from the opening sentence. If it's to be signed manually, and you have reason to date the signatures without having a different effective date, you should omit the effective date from the opening sentence.

Dating signatures might be done in two ways. The first is to set forth the person's typed name (and title, if acting on behalf of an entity) followed by the date:

____________________________ Date: _______________
[*Typed name and title just under the line*]

____________________________ Date: _______________
[*Typed name and title just under the line*]

____________________________ Date: _______________
[*Typed name and title just under the line*]

This agreement becomes effective upon the date of the final signing.

The second method is to give one effective date at the end, without dates of specific signatures:

____
[*Typed name and title just under the line*]

____
[*Typed name and title just under the line*]

____
[*Typed name and title just under the line*]

Effective Date: _______________
[*Filled-in date*]

With this second version, the effective date is the only one that's important—not the dates of signing. Given the frequency with which signatories neglect to date their signatures, despite blanks for them, this strategy can be effective (assuming the effective-date blank isn't similarly neglected!).

NOT THIS:

Ex. 1

The agreement's effective date could be clearer.

IN WITNESS WHEREOF, the Parties hereto have caused this Agreement to be executed by their respective authorized representatives effective as of the date last written below.

Selvang Services, LLC	Roemer Hotels, Inc.
By: /s/ Clarissa O'Flynn	By: /s/ Allie C. Berger
Name: Clarissa O'Flynn	Name: Allie C. Berger
Title: President & CEO	Title: President & CEO
Date: June 9, 2017	Date: September 15, 2017

Master Services Agreement

BUT THIS:

This Agreement is effective as of the date of the last signature.

Selvang Services, LLC	**Roemer Hotels, Inc.**
By: /s/ ______	By: /s/ ______
Name: Clarissa O'Flynn	Name: Allie C. Berger
Title: President & CEO	Title: President & CEO
Date: ______	Date: ______

Although the revision is clearer, note the potential complexity of ascertaining the effective date.

or:

______

Clarissa O'Flynn, President & CEO of Selvang Services, LLC

______

Allie C. Berger, President & CEO of Roemer Hotels, Inc.

Ditto.

"In stating a date, be specific. Don't make the reader refer to some other part of the contract to find it. And don't make him compute it by counting a certain number of days from some other date; he will perhaps not know whether to include or exclude the first and last days." LeRoy Marceau, *Drafting a Union Contract* § 5.3(E), at 37 (1965).

NOT THIS:

Ex. 2

[Page 1]

The preamble on page 1 includes one date: the effective date.

THIS TECHNOLOGY COLLABORATION AGREEMENT (the "Agreement") is made and entered into this 11th day of March 2018 ("Effective Date") by and between Logomark, a Delaware corporation ("Logomark") and Technology Pro Company ("Company"), referred to collectively as the "Parties" or each individually as a "Party."

. . .

[Page 11]

IN WITNESS WHEREOF, the Parties have entered into this Agreement as of the Effective Date written above.

Logomark

By: ______________________

Name (print): ______________________

Title: ______________________

Date: ______________________

But the signatures on page 11 also include date lines. The proliferation of dates can cause confusion.

Technology Pro Company

By: ______________________

Name (print): ______________________

Title: ______________________

Date: ______________________

Technology Collaboration Agreement between two multinational technology companies

BUT THIS:

[Page 1]

This is the recommended wording for the preamble.

This Agreement, effective March 11, 2018, is between Logomark, Inc. (Logomark), a Delaware corporation, and Technology Pro Company (Company), a Texas corporation.

. . .

[Page 11]

Logomark

By: ______________________

Name (print): ______________________

Title: ______________________

Dates are omitted in signature blocks to avoid confusion.

Technology Pro Company

By: ______________________

Name (print): ______________________

Title: ______________________

§ 60 Consider an effective-date clause.

Some drafters like to add an effective-date clause that reads:

> **14. Effective Date.** This Agreement is effective on the date when both parties have signed it, as indicated by the last date in the signature blocks below.

Although some might argue that this type of provision is unnecessary, it can harmlessly remove doubt about timing issues relating to effectiveness.

Having conditions on effectiveness leads to complications—often undesirable ones. As you'll see in Examples 1 and 2, readers may find it difficult if not impossible to know precisely when the contract took effect.

Also, as you'll see in Example 4, it's important to be clear both in your mind and in your drafting that there can be a difference between the closing (or consummation) of the transaction and the effectiveness of the agreement itself. In the original Example 4, the two dates are confounded.

NOT THIS:	BUT THIS:
Ex. 1 The period of this contract commences upon its signing by both parties and the Purchaser providing the owner with all required bonds and certificates of insurance. **Sample Timber-Sales Contract from A. Jeff Martin et al., *Lake States Woodlands Bulletin: Marketing Timber* 8 (1996)**	**5. Effective Date.** This contract is effective when (1) both parties have signed the contract; and (2) the Buyer has provided the owner with all required bonds and certificates of insurance.
Ex. 2 ARTICLE VI EFFECTIVENESS Section 6.01 *Effectiveness.* This **Agreement** shall not become effective until the date on which all conditions to effectiveness of the **Settlement Agreement** that are set forth in Article VI thereof are satisfied or waived by the parties thereto (the "***Effective Date***"). **Master Restructuring Agreement between two major corporations**	**6. Effectiveness.** **6.1 Effective date.** This Agreement becomes effective when the parties have either satisfied or waived all the conditions in this § 6 of the Settlement Agreement.
Ex. 3 9. The **"Effective Date"** of this Assignment shall be the later to occur of (a) December 6, 2017, and (b) the date on which the Assignment Consideration shall have been duly paid to Assignor and cleared collection (with such adjustments for the Transfer Apportionments as are required). **Assignment and Assumption of Lease from a major office-supply company**	**9. Effective Date.** The effective date of this Assignment is the later of: (A) December 6, 2017; or (B) the date on which the Assignment Consideration paid to Assignor has cleared collection (with any necessary adjustments for the Transfer Apportionments).

NOT THIS:	BUT THIS:
Ex. 4 The parties hereto contemplate, and agree to make good faith efforts in order to accomplish a closing of the transactions described herein at a time and place agreeable to all of the parties, with the closing date (for all purposes herein referred to as the "Effective Date") being within sixty (60) days after Regis Max Corporation has notified the LLCs in writing that it is prepared to fully perform all of its obligations set forth below or will do so on the Effective Date by executing and delivering such documents as may be necessary, providing evidence of their compliance with their obligations hereunder, or will make such payments as are necessary to comply with their undertakings pursuant to this Agreement. **Franchise-Transfer Agreement from a chain-restaurant group**	3. **Closing Date.** The Parties will make good-faith efforts to close the described transactions at a time and place agreeable to all Parties. The closing date ("Closing Date") will be within 60 days after Regis Max notifies the LLCs in writing that it is prepared to fully perform all its obligations set forth below. On the Closing Date, Regis Max will either sign and deliver all necessary documents that provide evidence of the LLCs' compliance with their obligations under this Agreement, or make the necessary payments to comply with their undertakings under this Agreement.

The effective-date clause is ambiguous. And it confusingly equates the closing date with the effective date.

"From early in a lawyer's training, . . . timidity becomes synonymous with professionalism. So it is not surprising that the basic rule in writing contracts is: 'If a problem can be foreseen, draft for it.'" Carl Felsenfeld & Alan Siegel, *Writing Contracts in Plain English* 56 (1981).

§ 61 Be savvy about other dates mentioned in the contract.

Given that a draft contract often amounts to an offer—the party presenting it to the other side doesn't know whether items will be further negotiated—it can be wise not to give particular dates throughout but instead to base them on either the date of the contract or its effective date. That is, if the draft presented to the other party on May 1 says that the contract is dated May 1, it isn't wise to specify deadlines of May 8 and May 15; it's probably better to specify 7 and 14 days after the contract's effective date. That way, if the contract ends up being negotiated through May 9, there's no need to alter those provisions relating to time. The 7-day and 14-day deadlines take effect on May 9. In brief, it's probably shortsighted—even risky—to send out a draft or a final contract with lots of specific trigger dates as opposed to relative dates calculated from the contract date.

NOT THIS:	BUT THIS:
Ex. 1 This Settlement and Mutual Release ("Agreement") is made and entered into as of the **Effective Date**, defined herein below, by and between SLOVIN APPAREL, a California corporation, MELINDA KWAN, an individual, and DETER THORPE, an individual. . . . (2) KWAN asserts that KWAN has made investment for the sum of $50,000.00 to the Corporation in exchange for her shares. If, upon the objective judgment of Mr. Edward Gruenewald based on the generally acceptable accounting principle, there is credible evidence of an investment by KWAN to the Corporation and no gross negligence or intentional wrongdoing by KWAN in the operation prior to the date of execution of this Agreement, then SLOVIN APPAREL shall make the full refund of the amount that turned out as KWAN's investment, within two (2) business days from the date of completion of the above-mentioned accounting by Mr. Edward Gruenewald, CPA, or the date of execution of this Agreement by the parties, whichever date is later. **Settlement and Mutual Release from a major law firm**	This Settlement and Mutual Release is between Slovin Apparel, a California corporation, Melinda Kwan, an individual, and Deter Thorpe, an individual. The Effective Date is the date on which the last party signs this Agreement. . . . 2. **Kwan's Investment Claim.** Kwan claims that she invested $50,000 in Slovin Apparel in exchange for her shares. Edward Gruenewald, CPA, will perform an accounting to independently determine, based on generally acceptable accounting principles: (A) credible evidence of Kwan's investment; (B) how much Kwan invested; and (C) whether Kwan engaged in gross negligence or intentional wrongdoing in the operation before the Effective Date. 3. **Settlement of Kwan's Claim.** If Gruenewald's accounting finds that Kwan invested and committed no gross negligence or intentional wrongdoing, then Slovin Apparel will fully refund the amount that the accounting identifies as Kwan's investment. The refund must be paid within 2 business days after either the date when the accounting is completed or the Effective Date, whichever is later.

The original uses both *Effective Date* and *date of execution*. The rewrite sticks to *Effective Date* and defines it as the date that the last party signs (since the parties might not all sign on the same day).

The rewrite avoids all caps for the parties' names. See § 56.

Here it makes sense to use relative dates based on the Effective Date, rather than a specific trigger date.

NOT THIS:	BUT THIS:
Ex. 2 This Convertible Promissory Note, dated May 19, 2017, (the "Note"), is by and between **Cornet Vintage Manufacturing, Inc.**, a Minnesota corporation (the "Company"), its successors and assigns, and **Low Prairie Holdings, LLC**, to which the Company is issuing this Note as ("Holder"). This Note is being issued pursuant to exemptions from registration under the Securities Act of 1933 of the United States, as amended. ***1. PRINCIPAL, INTEREST, MATURITY DATE.*** In consideration of complete and total satisfaction of a prior unsecured, undocumented loan to the Company in the same amount and effective the same date as this convertible promissory note and without further recourse for that loan other than the terms of this note, satisfying and superseding all obligations of the prior debt, The Company, its successors and assigns, hereby promises to pay to the Holder, or its successors or assigns, in immediately available funds, the total principal sum of SEVENTY NINE THOUSAND DOLLARS **($79,000.00 U.S.)** under the terms and conditions of this Note. The principal hereof and any unpaid and continuing to accrue interest thereon shall be due and payable to the Holder (unless such payment date is accelerated as provided in Section 8 hereof) not later than six months from the Effective Date, or **November 19, 2017 (the "Maturity Date")**. Payment of all amounts due hereunder shall be made at the address of the Holder provided for in Section 10 hereof. Interest on the unpaid principal balance of this Note shall accrue from the above date first written and shall continue to accrue until all unpaid principal and interest is paid in full. Interest shall be calculated at the simple interest rate of six percent (6%) per annum. **Note-Conversion Notice** What does *above date first written* refer to: May 19, 2017, the undefined Effective Date, or November 19, 2017?	This Convertible Promissory Note, effective May 19, 2017, is between Cornet Vintage Manufacturing, Inc. (Cornet), a Minnesota corporation, its successors and assigns, and Low Prairie Holdings, LLC (Low Prairie), to which Cornet is issuing this Note as holder. This Note is issued under exemptions from registration under the Securities Act of 1933 of the United States, as amended. Now only one date appears above the Interest provision: May 19, 2017. 1. **Loan Description.** Low Prairie previously made an unsecured, undocumented loan to Cornet in the same amount and effective the same date as this Note. Low Prairie has no further recourse for that loan other than the terms of this Note, which satisfies and supersedes all obligations of the prior debt. 1.1 **Principal.** Cornet, its successors, or its assigns will pay Low Prairie, its successors, or its assigns, the principal sum of $79,000 under the terms of this Note. 1.2 **Interest.** Interest is calculated at the simple interest rate of 6% per annum. Interest on the unpaid principal balance of this Note accrues beginning on the effective date and will continue to accrue until all unpaid principal and interest has been paid in full. 1.3 **Maturity.** Unless this Note's payment date is accelerated under § 8, the maturity date is November 19, 2017. This is the latest date on which this Note will become due. 1.4 **Payment.** When due, this Note's principal, remaining accrued interest, and any other amounts due must be paid to Low Prairie at the address stated in § 10.

"Drafting . . . is certainly not a matter of mindless imitation of the past. Drafting is a critical lawyering skill. Like other lawyering skills, drafting can be done well or poorly. Doing it well is something *that can be taught and learned.*" Thomas R. Haggard, *Legal Drafting in a Nutshell* vi (1996).

Grammatical number

§ 62 Prefer the singular over the plural if it's a realistic option.

The simple fact is that the singular always includes the plural: *No person may bring a gun onto these premises* means that it is likewise impermissible to bring two or more guns onto the premises. *An employee may request reassignment* means that all employees who meet the specified qualifications are entitled to request reassignment—not just one employee.

But the opposite often doesn't hold: the plural frequently excludes the singular. *If the employee parks vehicles at the jobsite* . . . arguably doesn't apply to the employee who parks just one. And *No independent contractor may store personal tools at the jobsite* arguably doesn't apply to a single hammer. "Common sense," you may object, "pretty clearly shows what's intended." But the point of good drafting is to forestall arguments that can be readily prevented. The singular-vs.-plural issue is a classic instance.

Even so, the preference for the singular number isn't an absolute rule. Occasionally the plural unambiguously avoids sexist language (e.g., § 71, Example 11) or fits a context in which the plural is the natural choice.

NOT THIS:	BUT THIS:
Ex. 1 12.8.1.1 The policy(ies) shall indicate that it is primary to any other insurance and the insurance company(ies) providing such policy(ies) shall be liable thereunder for the full amount of any loss or claim. **Insurance Agreement from a major law firm**	12.8 **Liability insurance.** The policy must indicate that: (A) it is primary to any other insurance; and (B) the insurance company providing the policy is liable for the full amount of any loss or claim.
Ex. 2 12. <u>Counterparts and Authority</u>. This Agreement may be executed in multiple counterparts, each of which shall be deemed an original and all of which together shall constitute one and the same document. Landlord and Tenant each warrant to the other that the person or persons executing this Agreement on its behalf has or have authority to do so and that such execution has fully obligated and bound such party to all terms and provisions of this Agreement. **Lease Agreement from a major law firm**	12. **Counterparts and Authority.** This Agreement may be signed in counterparts, each one of which is considered an original, but all of which constitute a single instrument. The parties stipulate that each person signing this Agreement on a party's behalf has authority to do so and that the signing fully binds that party to this Agreement.

Note the syntactic awkwardness of alternatives in number.

NOT THIS:	BUT THIS:
Ex. 3 Conducting Business with Partnership The Partners may lend money to; borrow money from; act as a surety, guarantor or endorser for; guarantee or assume specific obligations of; provide collateral for; or transact other business with the Partnership, including entering into any contract with the Partnership. **Limited-Liability-Partnership Agreement from 4 Nancy Saint-Paul, Texas Legal Practice Forms 3d *Partnerships and Limited Liability Partnerships* § 62:45, at 549 (2016)**	**10. Conducting Business with Partnership.** A Partner may transact business with the Partnership, including entering into any contract with the Partnership. A Partner may also: (A) lend money to the Partnership; (B) borrow money from the Partnership; (C) act as a surety, guarantor, or endorser for the Partnership; (D) guarantee or assume specific obligations of the Partnership; or (E) provide collateral for the Partnership.

§ 63 Avoid parenthesized singular/plural alternatives.

Avoid alternative singular/plural forms such as *Borrower(s)* and *Debtor(s)*. Remember that the singular typically includes the plural (see § 62).

	NOT THIS:	BUT THIS:
Ex. 1	Brazoria Mortgage warrants that it has taken all actions necessary . . . to assert and obtain on behalf of the lender a deficiency judgment against the borrower(s) if required by Mortgage Guaranty. **Mortgage Agreement from a major law firm**	Brazoria Mortgage represents and warrants that it has taken all actions necessary . . . to assert and obtain on behalf of the lender a deficiency judgment against the borrower if required by Mortgage Guaranty. *Find out whether there's one borrower or more and draft accordingly.*
Ex. 2	The purpose of this agreement is to set forth the terms and conditions to which all parties will adhere during the term of the policy(ies) shown in the schedule attached hereto. An additional purpose is to provide the means by which any dividend arising from said policy(ies) may be returned to the Insured. **Service Agreement from a major law firm**	This Agreement has two purposes: (1) to set forth the terms that will bind all parties during the term of the policies shown in the attached schedule; and (2) to provide the means by which a dividend on any policy may be returned to the Insured. *Ditto for policies.*
Ex. 3	**12.7 Railroad Insurance Requirements** 12.7.1 Commercial General Liability Insurance. . . . 12.7.1.1 The policy(ies) shall indicate that it is primary to any other insurance except Railroad Protective Liability Insurance and the insurance company(ies) providing such policy(ies) shall be liable thereunder for the full amount of any loss or claim . . . . **Railroad-Station UOM Agreement from a major law firm**	**12.7 Railroad insurance requirements.** (A) **Commercial general-liability insurance.** . . . The policy must indicate that it is primary to any other insurance except Railroad Protective Liability Insurance. The insurance company providing the policy is liable for the full amount of any loss or claim . . . .

"With traditional drafting there is more chance of making or missing a mistake buried in obscure language. If we draft in plain English—especially if starting a document from scratch—we will be thinking more carefully about the meaning of what we write than if we re-use a traditional precedent." Mark Adler, *Clarity for Lawyers* 76 (1990).

NOT THIS:	BUT THIS:
Ex. 4 **12.4 Closing.** The Closing of any purchase or sale pursuant to this Article 12 shall be held at the time and on the date specified by written notice by the **buyer(s)** to the **seller(s)** (the "Buy-Sell Closing Date"), which date shall be within sixty (60) days after the end of the Option Period. Such Closing shall take place at the principal office of the Company. At such Closing, the Members shall, if applicable, each pay one-half of the fees and expenses of the Appraisers and the third valuation expert participating in the determination of the Appraised Value. The specified purchase price shall be paid by the **buyer(s)** in immediately available funds at the Buy-Sell Closing Date, and the **seller(s)** shall execute, seal, and deliver for and on their behalf, all documents that may be necessary or appropriate, in the reasonable opinion of counsel to the **buyer(s)**, to effect such sale free and clear of all liens and encumbrances. **LLC Operating Agreement from a major law firm**	**12.4 Closing.** The Closing will take place at the Company's principal office. (A) **"Buy-Sell Closing Date" defined.** For a purchase or sale under Article 12, the Buyer must give the Seller written notice of the date and time for Closing, which must occur within 60 days after the end of the Option Period. (B) **Payment for appraisal.** At the Closing, the Members will, if applicable, each pay 50% of the fees and expenses of the Appraisers and the third valuation expert involved in determining the Appraised Value. (C) **Purchase price and documents.** The Buyer will pay the specified purchase price in immediately available funds at the Closing. The Seller will sign and deliver all documents that may be necessary or appropriate, in the reasonable opinion of the Buyer's counsel, to effect the sale free and clear of all liens and encumbrances.

"Transactional practice . . . involves understanding the parties' deal and then translating the business terms into a transactional structure that uses contract, commercial, and other business-law principles to govern the parties' relationship. It also involves making an appropriate record along the way as negotiations and documentation continue so that, should the deal break down and litigation ensue, litigation attorneys can present the case in the light most favorable to the client."
Thomas R. Haggard & George W. Kuney, *Legal Drafting: Process, Techniques, and Exercises* 25 (2007).

Tense

§ 64 Prefer the present tense when a provision can be worded naturally in the present.

Use the present tense unless the past or future tense clarifies the idea. Avoid the future perfect tense (*shall have been served*, etc.).

NOT THIS:	BUT THIS:
Ex. 1 4.4 Neither Foundation nor University shall be obligated to spend any funds on this Project other than those provided by Sponsor under this Article 4. **Research Agreement from a major university research foundation**	4.4 **Other expenses.** Rocky Foundation and the University need not spend funds on this Project other than those provided by the Sponsor under this Article 4.
Ex. 2 If any portion or portions of this Agreement shall be, for any reason, invalid or unenforceable, the remaining portion or portions shall nevertheless be valid and enforceable. **Employment Contract from a major law firm**	(E) **Severability.** If a court for any reason holds a provision of this Agreement to be unenforceable, the rest remains fully enforceable.
Ex. 3 The rights of the registered holder of this Warrant shall be subject to the following further terms and conditions: . . . While this Warrant remains outstanding, this Warrant shall be fully exercisable, in whole or in part, as of the date hereof (the "Exercisability Date"). **Warrant to Purchase Units**	The rights of this Warrant's registered holder are subject to the following terms and conditions: . . . . While this Warrant remains outstanding, it is fully exercisable, in whole or in part, as of its effective date.
Ex. 4 Nothing in this Section 4, or any other provision of this Agreement, shall be construed to prohibit Employee from reporting conduct to, providing truthful information to, or participating in any investigation or proceeding brought or conducted by any federal or state government agency or self-regulatory organization. **Nondisclosure and Nonsolicitation Agreement**	(G) **Investigations.** Nothing in this Agreement prohibits the Employee from reporting conduct to, providing truthful information to, or participating in any investigation or proceeding brought or conducted by any federal or state government agency or self-regulatory organization.

See § 34.

NOT THIS:	BUT THIS:
Ex. 5 Licensee agrees to affix to all Pharmaceutical Products for sale to third parties (and not Pharmaceutical Products held for internal use) that utilize the Licensor IP and any promotional and packaging material in connection with such Pharmaceutical Products, such Marks and notices of the Licensor IP, as shall be reasonably requested by Licensor, to the extent practicable and consistent with commercial practice. **Pharma License Agreement**	4.3 **Display of Marks and notices.** To the extent practicable and consistent with commercial practice, Promonx will affix the Marks and notices of Blingding IP that Blingding reasonably requests to all Pharmaceutical Products for sale to third parties (and not Pharmaceutical Products held for internal use) that use the Blingding IP and any promotional and packaging material in connection with the Pharmaceutical Products.

"There may be some truth in the cynical thought that lawyers spend half their time trying to understand what other lawyers wrote; and the other half of their days writing things that other lawyers spend half their time trying to understand." Samuel Goldberg, *Hints on Draftsmanship*, 5 Prac. Law. 39, 42 (1959).

§ 65 For a condition precedent, default to the present-perfect tense.

When you're saying that something is permitted once something else has been done, use the present-perfect—write *has done* or *has been done*—not *is done*.[1]

NOT THIS:	BUT THIS:
Ex. 1 Insurance against this peril does not cover loss resulting from freezing while the building is unoccupied unless the Insured shall have exercised due diligence. **Insurance Policy from a major insurer**	Insurance against this peril covers loss resulting from freezing while the building is unoccupied only if the Insured has exercised due diligence.
Ex. 2 It is specifically understood that the above rates do not apply to any other litigation involving Long's Auto that Counsel may have been or will be retained for. **State-Litigation Chief-Counsel Agreement from a major automotive corporation**	These rates do not apply to any other litigation involving Long's Auto that Counsel has been or will be retained for.
Ex. 3 This Agreement shall become effective and shall bind the parties hereto only after entry of an Order (the "Approval Order") by the State Court approving this Agreement and authorizing the Receiver to enter into same. **Purchase & Assignment Agreement from a major law firm**	This Agreement becomes effective and binds the parties only after a state court has ordered its approval and authorized the Receiver to enter into it.

1 For further guidance on this sequence-of-tenses issue, see *Garner's Modern English Usage* 896 (4th ed. 2016) (s.v. "Tenses").

Voice

§ 66 Prefer active voice over passive voice.

The passive voice—which is pervasive in poorly drafted documents—consists of a *be*-verb (or sometimes *get*) combined with a past participle (usually a word ending in *-ed*). In a passive construction, the subject of the clause doesn't perform the action of the verb:

Passive: If this provision *is breached* by Larman, ... (The provision isn't doing the breaching.)

Passive: If this provision *is breached*, ... (The provision still isn't doing the breaching, but now we're not even told who the breacher might be.)

In an active construction, by contrast, the subject of the clause does perform the action of the verb:

Active: If Larman *breaches* this provision, ... (Larman is doing the breaching.)

What's the problem with using passive voice? First, as with zombie nouns, passive voice usually adds a couple of unnecessary words (see § 20). Second, if it doesn't add those unnecessary words, it fails to say squarely who is to do what (unless a cumbersome *by*-phrase is added). Third, it subverts the normal word order for an English sentence, making it a bit harder for readers to process the information.

The opposite of each of those liabilities can be phrased as a benefit gained from using active voice: it saves words, says directly who is to do what, and meets the reader's expectation of an actor–verb–object order.

What is usually most important in drafting is that the active voice makes the actor and obligations obvious. Sometimes the actor that the drafter contemplates does not appear in a passive-voice construction. This leaves open the possibility that parties will argue about who the contemplated actor is. For several reasons—but especially clarity—the drafter should generally draft in the active voice. When feasible, rephrase a passive-voice verb by putting it in active voice.

> "When the draftsman is concentrating on making it plain to the courts that no possible subterfuge is to be tolerated—when he is telling what may *not* be done—his final product is often so complicated that it is not easy to tell what may and should be done." Frank E. Cooper, *Writing in Law Practice* 311 (1963).

When working with a contract, one of my law students found passive-to-active transformations quite enlightening. In an annotation to his final exam, he wrote:

> When I first read the original contract, I thought I understood it fairly well. But as I began to revise the contract, my understanding became increasingly murky. Two specific alterations brought this murkiness to light: (1) changing the passive voice to active voice, and (2) substituting for the terms "Buyer" and "Seller." When I changed the sentences into the active voice, I discovered that in many places I was uncertain who was doing the action: the buyer, the seller, either one, or both. I was often only able to determine which party a provision applied to by repeatedly reading the original. For those that were truly ambiguous rather than just difficult to figure out, I had to apply logic to determine which party the provision *should* pertain to. Additionally, it became very confusing to keep track of which party a given sentence applied to when the text merely referred to the "Buyer" and "Seller." In one section, I actually got the parties confused halfway through the paragraph. It was only after further simplifying the sentence structure and terminology that this mistake became obvious.

Notice that the blackletter injunction for this section says "prefer," as opposed to "always use." The injunction to avoid passive voice should never be taken as an absolute because you'll need the passive in a small percentage of your sentences. But your overwhelming preference—your rebuttable presumption—should be to use the active voice.

For the circumstances in which you might justifiably use passive voice, see § 68.

NOT THIS:	BUT THIS:
Ex. 1 Therefore, it is hereby agreed between Jones and Smith as follows: **Sales Agreement**	Jones and Smith agree as follows:
Ex. 2 This Agreement may be immediately terminated by the Corporation upon the occurrence of any one or more of the following events: . . . **Contracted-Labor Agreement**	Flint Ltd. may immediately terminate this Agreement upon any of the following events: . . .
Ex. 3 All out-of-pocket expenses, if any, incurred by us in connection with your affairs are billed to you as a separate item on your monthly statement. **Vendor Agreement**	We will bill you for out-of-pocket expenses we incur on your behalf. These items will appear separately on your monthly statement.

NOT THIS:	BUT THIS:
Ex. 4 (c) Disinterested Director. A director of the Company who is not and was not a party to the Proceeding in respect of which indemnification is sought by Indemnitee. **Indemnification Agreement from a computer-technology company**	(C) "Disinterested Director" means a company director who is not and was not a party to the Proceeding for which Indemnitee seeks indemnity.
Ex. 5 Reasonable efforts shall be used by the Licensor to amend any patent application to include claims reasonably requested by the Licensee to protect the products contemplated to be sold under this Agreement. **License Agreement from a major law firm**	Carrollton Products will use reasonable efforts[1] to amend any patent application to include a claim that CGM reasonably requests to protect the products that the parties contemplate selling under this Agreement.
Ex. 6 2.2 Reimbursement. Supplier will be reimbursed for travel, living, and other expenses authorized by Global in the Contract Order at reasonable and actual costs. Travel and living expenses will not be reimbursed unless they are in conformance with Global's travel reimbursement policies. **Master Services Agreement from a telecommunications company**	**2.2 Reimbursement.** Global will reimburse Warren for reasonable and actual costs of travel, living, and other expenses authorized by the Contract Order if they're consistent with Global's travel-reimbursement policies.
Ex. 7 Contractor has the right to stop work if any payment or portion thereof, including payment for any extra work, is not made to Contractor. In the event of such nonpayment, Contractor may stop work and keep the job idle until all payments are received and the time for completion will be delayed during such period. **Construction-Contract Form from a major law firm**	**4.6 Nonpayment.** Caleb's Contracting may stop work if Miller fails to pay all or part of a payment, including payment for extra work. This period of nonpayment will extend the time for completing the Project.
Ex. 8 It is understood and agreed that this Agreement is entered into by the parties on a non precedent non prejudicial basis and with the express agreement that it not be referred to in any other proceeding whether it be arbitral or judicial or other forum, including, but not limited to, Presidential Emergency Boards and factfinding proceedings. **Memorandum of Agreement from a railroad company**	The parties enter this Agreement on a nonprecedential, nonprejudicial basis and agree not to refer to it in any other proceeding whether arbitral, judicial, or otherwise, including Presidential Emergency Boards and fact-finding proceedings.

A hidden passive: *that are contemplated*. It turns out to be a double passive with *to be sold*.

1 Consider making this a best-efforts clause if you're CGM's counsel. See § 148 at pp. 390–92.

NOT THIS:	BUT THIS:
Ex. 9 13. SEVERABILITY. Should any provision of this Agreement be held, by a court of competent jurisdiction, to be invalid or unenforceable, such invalidity or unenforceability shall not render the entire Agreement invalid or unenforceable, and this Agreement and each other provision hereof shall be enforceable and valid to the fullest extent permitted by law. **Executive-Employment Agreement from a major floral company**	**13. Severability.** If a court for any reason holds a provision of this Agreement to be unenforceable, the rest remains fully enforceable.
Ex. 10 In case any Notes shall have been authenticated, but not delivered, by the Trustee then in office, any successor by merger, conversion or consolidation to such authenticating Trustee may adopt such authentication and deliver the Notes so authenticated with the same effect as if such successor Trustee had itself authenticated such Notes. **Senior-Secured-First-Lien-Notes Indenture from a major healthcare company** [Margin note: Again, a hidden passive appears: *have not been delivered.*]	For Notes that a Trustee has authenticated but not delivered, a successor Trustee by merger, conversion, or consolidation may adopt that authentication and deliver those Notes as if the successor Trustee has authenticated them.
Ex. 11 The Parties agree that, should another coaching opportunity be presented to Coach during the Term of this Agreement, Coach must notify the Men's Athletics Director of such opportunity or interest and permission must be given to Coach by the Men's Athletics Director before any discussions can be held by Coach or his representative with the anticipated coaching position principals. Such permission shall not be withheld unreasonably. **College-Football Head-Coach Employment Agreement for a major university** [Margin note: Three passive constructions in one sentence—four altogether.]	**5.2 Other coaching offers.** If Adams learns of another coaching opportunity in which he is interested during the Term of this Agreement, Adams will promptly notify the Men's Athletics Director of the opportunity. Only with the Men's Athletics Director's permission may Adams or his representative participate in discussions with the new-coaching-position principals. The Men's Athletics Director will not unreasonably withhold permission.
Ex. 12 One person designated by the Management Committee shall be appointed Treasurer of the Joint Venture. The Treasurer shall keep for the Joint Venture a separate set of full and current books of account, upon such basis as the Management Committee may determine. Such books of account shall be kept and maintained at the principal office of the Joint Venture, and, along with all other records of the Joint Venture, shall be open for inspection by the parties to the Joint Venture at mutually convenient times. **Joint-Venture Agreement from Robert F. Cushman, Michael S. Simon, and McNeill Stokes, *The Construction Industry Formbook* § 7.15, at 267 (1979)**	The Management Committee will appoint the Treasurer of the Joint Venture to maintain the Joint Venture's accounting records on a basis specified by the Committee. The Treasurer will keep the accounting records at the Joint Venture's principal office. The accounting records and all other records of the Joint Venture must remain open for the parties' inspection at mutually convenient times.

§ 67 When feasible, replace passive voice with an adjective.

Often you can rephrase a passive-voice verb by substituting an adjective. If this technique improves the phrasing, use it.

NOT THIS:	BUT THIS:
Ex. 1 (c) In the event that Grantor fails to provide Grantee with Pre-Securitization Financials on or before the date they are due, and if such failure continues for two (2) business days following notice of same from Grantee, then, in addition to all other rights and remedies of Grantee hereunder, Grantor shall pay to Grantee, at Grantee's option and in its sole discretion, an amount equal to $10,000.00 for each Pre-Securitization Financial that is not delivered. **Mortgage, Rent-Assignment, and Security Agreement from a major law firm**	(C) **Penalty for undelivered Financials.** If Drucker fails to give Brockman the presecuritization Financials on or before the due date and does not provide them within 2 business days after Brockman notifies Drucker of the failure: (1) Drucker will pay Brockman, at Brockman's option and in its sole discretion, $10,000 for each undelivered presecuritization Financial; and (2) Brockman may exercise all other rights and remedies under this Agreement.
Ex. 2 13. Employees shall make a good faith effort to take their vacations within one year of the accrual date. However, a maximum of four (4) weeks of unused vacation may be carried over. Any such vacation time that is carried over shall be paid at the wage rate in effect at the time the vacation was earned. Employees who have unused vacation time that was previously accrued (prior to May 1, 2018) shall have five years to use their accrued unused vacation time. **Collective-Bargaining Agreement from a major law firm**	**13. Accrued Vacation Time.** An Employee may accrue no more than 4 weeks of carried-over vacation time and must make a good-faith effort to use that time within 1 year after the accrual date. Carried-over vacation time is payable at the wage rate in effect when the Employee earned it. An Employee who has accrued unused vacation time before May 1, 2018, has 5 years to use it.

It's better to draft in the singular, so *Employees* was changed to *Employee*. See § 62.

> "Repetition is a poor substitute for careful proofreading." Reed Dickerson, *The Fundamentals of Legal Drafting* § 6.6, at 125 (2d ed. 1986).

NOT THIS:	BUT THIS:
Ex. 3 **Article V Arbitration** (a) As a condition precedent to any right of action hereunder, any dispute arising out of this Agreement shall be submitted to the decision of a board of arbitration composed of two arbitrators and an umpire, meeting at the Company's administrative and executive offices in Florida mutually agreed by the parties to this Agreement. Written notice of intent to enter arbitration will be supplied to the Florida Insurance Department by the party intending to demand arbitration, prior to formal submission to the board of arbitrators. A notice requesting arbitration shall be in writing and given by the claimant to the other party in accordance with Article VII (g) of this Agreement. The notice requesting arbitration shall state in particulars all principal issues to be resolved and shall set a date for the hearing, which date shall be no sooner than 90 days and no later than 120 days from the date that the notice requesting arbitration is mailed. **Administration-and-Management-Services Agreement from a major law firm**	**5. Arbitration.** **5.1 Mandatory arbitration.** Unless the parties agree otherwise, any dispute arising from this Agreement must be submitted to an arbitration board comprising 2 arbitrators and an umpire, meeting at the Company's executive offices in Florida. **5.2 Notices.** (A) **To other party.** Under Article 7(G) of this Agreement, the party requesting arbitration will give written notice to the other party. The notice must describe the principal issues to be resolved and set a date for the hearing at least 90 days and no more than 120 days after the date that the notice is mailed. (B) **To Insurance Department.** The party requesting arbitration must give written notice of that intent to the Florida Insurance Department before formal submission to the arbitration board.
Ex. 4 5.5 *Payments Upon Termination.* (a) *Termination Without Cause or For Good Reason.* If Employer terminates Employee without Cause pursuant to Section 5.1(b) or Employee terminates for Good Reason pursuant to Section 5.2(a)(i), Employer shall pay to Employee in a lump sum in cash on the effective date of such termination, or within 30 days thereafter (i) any portion of Employee's Annual Salary for the remainder of the Term that has not been paid; (ii) any compensation previously deferred by Employee (together with any accrued interest or earnings thereon) that has not yet been paid; and (iii) any accrued but unpaid incentive compensation under Section 4.2(a)(ii) for any period prior to the date of termination; and (iv) all other unpaid, accrued and earned benefits due to Employee including unpaid vacation pay. **Employment Agreement from a major law firm**	**5.5 Payments upon Termination.** (A) **Termination Without Cause or for Good Reason.** If Tallman terminates Miller without Cause under § 5.1(B) or Miller resigns for Good Reason under § 5.2(A)(1), then within 30 days after the termination's effective date, Tallman will pay to Miller in a lump sum in cash: (1) any unpaid part of Miller's Annual Salary for the remainder of the Term; (2) any unpaid compensation that Miller deferred plus any accrued but unpaid interest or earnings on that amount; (3) any accrued but unpaid incentive compensation under § 4.2(A)(2) for any period before the date of termination; and (4) any other unpaid, accrued, and earned benefit owed to Miller, including unpaid vacation pay.

§ 68 Use passive voice in limited circumstances.

Occasionally you'll encounter a sentence that seems better in the passive voice. Don't give in easily: cast it in the active voice anyway. If the result sounds bad, then try another way of expressing the thought. If that still doesn't work, then keep the passive-voice construction. Typically, this situation arises when the actor, once named, gets in the way of the information. In other words, changing from passive to active sometimes results in an unsuitable change of emphasis. For example, you're better off saying *The following information is unaudited* instead of *Our auditors haven't assessed the following information.* The focus is rightly on the information—not on the auditors.

Passive voice is justified primarily in these four circumstances: (1) when naming the actor would unduly narrow the meaning or impede the sentence flow; (2) when, in a contract dealing with such matters as building and safety codes, human actors don't appear much in requirements relating to things; (3) when the passive voice is the most natural, elegant way to achieve gender-neutrality; and (4) when the passive voice keeps the focus appropriately on the recipient of the verb's action. The verb phrase *is entitled to* is justified when it means *has a right to.*

NOT THIS:	BUT THIS:
Ex. 1 The remedies of the seller hereunder may be exercised successively or concurrently. The adoption of one or more remedies does not prevent the seller from exercising any other or further remedy given to it by this contract. **Sales-contract clause from 1 Allen E. Smith & Nancy Saint-Paul, *West's Texas Forms: Creditors' Remedies & Debtors' Rights* § 5.4, at 127 (4th ed. 2009)**	14.1 **Seller's cumulative remedies.** The seller's remedies under this contract may be exercised successively or concurrently. Adopting one remedy does not limit the seller's exercise of another.
Ex. 2 None of the activities permitted by this Agreement may be performed by Franchisee from any location under the name "Winn Premium" or any name other than "Winn" unless authorized by Winn in writing. **Franchise-License Agreement from a tax-preparation company**	4.5 **Use of name.** Unless Winn so authorizes in writing, Franchisee must not perform any activity permitted by this Agreement anywhere under the name "Winn Premium" or any name other than "Winn."

This use of passive voice is permissible because it keeps the focus on the remedies rather than the seller.

Permitted is also passive voice here—it's a shortened form of *"that are permitted."*

The passive voice is justified here because it keeps the focus on Franchisee.

NOT THIS:	BUT THIS:
Ex. 3 If the whole or any substantial part of the condominium is taken or condemned by any public authority for any use or purpose, the term hereof shall end upon, and not before, the date when possession of the part so taken shall be required for such use or purposes, and without apportionment of the condemnation award which shall be paid entirely to Lessor. Current rent shall be apportioned as of the date of such termination. **Condominium-Lease Agreement from *Texas Forms: Legal & Business* § 9:120, at 489 (2015)**	If a public authority takes or condemns all or a substantial part of the condominium for any use or purpose, this lease's term will end upon the public authority's taking possession. Arrowhead is entitled to the entire condemnation award but will apportion the current rent payment as of the termination date.

The passive phrase *is entitled to* has the active sense *has a right to.*

Positives and negatives

§ 69 Prefer positive statements over negative ones.

Who cannot unmisgivingly say that negatives are not lacking in unmistakability when used other than sparingly?

Whenever you can recast a negative statement as a positive one without changing the meaning, do it. You'll save readers from needless mental exertion. Instead of *No more than one proposal may be presented at a time*, write *Only one proposal may be presented at a time.*

NOT THIS:	BUT THIS:
Ex. 1 No assets of Seller not expressly set forth on Schedule A are included in this agreement. **Agreement for the Purchase and Sale of Selected Assets from Robert A. Feldman & Raymond T. Nimmer, *Drafting Effective Contracts: A Practitioner's Guide*, Form 2-1, at 2-51 (2d ed. 2010)**	This Agreement covers only the assets expressly listed on Schedule A.
Ex. 2 Licensee will not use any Mark outside the Territory or on or in association with any product other than the Goods. **Trademark-License Agreement from Peter Siviglia, *Commercial Agreements: A Lawyer's Guide to Drafting and Negotiating* § 10-4 (2017)**	Reynolds may use a Mark only inside the Territory and only in association with products specified as Goods.
Ex. 3 17. Modifications. No amendment or modification of any of the terms and conditions of this Agreement shall be effective unless such modification is expressed in writing and signed by both of the parties hereto. **Marketing Agreement from a major beverage company**	17. **Modification.** To be valid, an amendment or modification of this Agreement must be in writing and signed by both parties.
Ex. 4 B. Conditions Precedent to Funding Under Credit Facilities. Roadster shall not be obligated to provide Vehicle Financing or Capital Loans unless and until the following conditions precedent are met before each credit advance: **Loan and Security Agreement from a major automotive corporation**	2. **Conditions Precedent to Funding Under Credit Facilities.** Roadster will provide Vehicle Financing or Capital Loans only if the following conditions precedent are met before each credit advance:

NOT THIS:	BUT THIS:
Ex. 5 The exercise prices of those options shall be determined by the board of directors and may not be less than the greater of the fair market value or the nominal value of the underlying ordinary shares on the date of the grant. **Stock-Sales Agreement**	The board of directors will determine the exercise prices of the options. But the prices must be at least the fair market value or the nominal value of the underlying ordinary shares on the date of the grant—whichever amount is higher.

"The lawyer who deliberately builds obscurity into a contract is betting that a court will interpret the language to mean what he or she *intends* but is not willing to make clear. This is a gamble at the client's expense, and the consequences can be severe." Lenné Eidson Espenschied, *Contract Drafting: Powerful Prose in Transactional Practice* 59 (3d ed. 2019).

§ 70 Use negative statements when necessary.

Prohibitions are typically negative by their very nature. The preference for positive statements is only that—a preference, not an absolute. Use negatives sensibly when there are no appropriate alternatives.

NOT THIS:	BUT THIS:
Ex. 1 Assignments. Provider acknowledges that Company is relying upon the unique expertise and capability of Provider. Except as set forth specifically below in this Section 9, none of this Agreement, the Work or money due Provider hereunder shall be assigned or transferred in whole or in part by Provider, voluntarily or by operation of law, except with the prior written consent of the Company, and any attempt to do so without such written consent shall be void. **Construction Agreement for solar-to-steam demonstration plant**	(C) **Assignments.** Docking Light & Power is relying on Lanham Construction's unique expertise and capability. Except as specifically set forth in this § 9, Lanham Construction cannot assign or transfer any part of this Agreement, the Work, or the money due to Lanham Construction, voluntarily or by operation of law, unless Docking Light & Power gives written consent. Any assignment without that consent is void.
Ex. 2 2.02 *Corporate Authority of Seller* The execution, delivery, and performance of this agreement by Seller has been duly authorized by all necessary corporate action and is enforceable in accordance with its terms. Such execution, delivery, and performance does not, and the consummation of the transactions contemplated will not (a) result in a material breach of any provision of, or constitute a material default under the articles of incorporation or bylaws of Seller, or agreement or instrument to which Seller is a party or by which it is bound, or (b) require the consent or approval of any other person or governmental agency or authority. **Asset-Sales Agreement from Robert A. Feldman & Raymond T. Nimmer, *Drafting Effective Contracts: A Practitioner's Guide*, Form 2-1, at 2-52 (2d ed. 2010)**	(B) **Corporate authority.** Turner's signing, delivery, and performance of this Agreement have been duly authorized by corporate action, and its terms are enforceable. The signing, delivery, performance, and completion of transactions under this Agreement do not: (1) create a material breach of an agreement or instrument to which Turner is a party or by which it is bound; (2) create a material default under Turner's articles of incorporation or bylaws; or (3) require the consent or approval of another person or government agency or authority.

Note the subject–verb disagreement in the original: a plural subject followed by *has*.

Gender-neutrality

§ 71 Strive to achieve invisible neutrality.

With few exceptions, contracts apply to all people without regard to sex. To preserve credibility and fairness, avoid using the pronouns *he* or *she* and the nouns *man* or *woman* whenever possible and practical. Some useful techniques for gender-neutral writing are:

1. Delete personal pronouns whenever possible. Instead of "a conference between a client and his attorney," write "a conference between a client and the client's attorney" or "an attorney–client conference."
2. Use a gender-neutral noun or pronoun such as *anyone*, *client*, *decedent*, *human*, *one*, *person*, or *someone* instead of *man* or *woman*.
3. Repeat the noun if you can keep repetition to a minimum.
4. Use an article (*a*, *an*, *the*) instead of a possessive pronoun.
5. Use gender-neutral titles (e.g., *police officer*, *firefighter*, *mail carrier*) for gender-specific titles (e.g., *policeman*, *fireman*, *mailman*).
6. Reword the sentence to avoid the need for gender-specific words.
7. Use a plural antecedent (e.g., *contractors* for *contractor*) so you can use a plural pronoun (but see § 62).
8. Use plural constructions (*they*, *them*, *their*) instead of singular ones (*he*, *she*, *his*, *her*) (but again, see § 62).
9. Substitute the phrase *he or she* or the phrase *him or her* when you must use gender-specific pronouns.

Ideally, the question of sexist language or its avoidance will never arise in the reader's mind. True, *he or she* still draws some attention to itself—and if it becomes frequent, it's distracting. But sometimes it will be the best you can do: it cannot and should not be viewed as anathema when it is sparingly used. Rather, it's contrivances such as *s/he* and *(s)he* that are unacceptable to a large proportion of readers, just as the singular *they* still is for many.

> "A patriarchal language, such as English, frequently employs male-biased words and phrases. Modern society demands that new approaches be taken . . . for the drafting of documents." Robert C. Dick, *Legal Drafting* 169 (2d ed. 1985).

NOT THIS:	BUT THIS:
Ex. 1 Except as hereinafter provided, neither party will sell, transfer or encumber all or any portion of her interest in the Apartment or the furniture or furnishings of the Apartment. **Purchase Agreement for Co-owned Investment Property from Peter Siviglia, *Commercial Agreements: A Lawyer's Guide to Drafting and Negotiating* § 9A-2 (2017)**	Unless this Agreement provides otherwise, neither party may sell, assign, or encumber an interest in the Apartment or its furniture or furnishings.
Ex. 2 (b) SUBCONTRACTOR will furnish all barricades, warning signs, lights, flagmen, policemen and any other traffic control items necessary to adequately protect the traveling public in the performance of this SUBCONTRACT. **Subcontract Agreement (2007)**	(B) While performing this work, the Subcontractor will furnish flaggers and police officers as well as all barricades, warning signs, lights, and any other traffic-control items needed to protect the traveling public. When possible, prefer gender-neutral job titles, but eschew contrived ones. Technique #5.
Ex. 3 *ARTICLE IV* *Grievance Procedure* ***Arbitration:*** The arbitrator shall, in any case upon which he/she has the power to rule under the provisions of this Agreement, hold hearings upon the issue, make such investigations, as he/she shall deem necessary to a proper decision and render his/her decision in writing within a reasonable time. Said decisions shall be final and binding upon all parties to this Agreement. **Collective-Bargaining Contract (2005)**	**4. Grievance Procedure.** **4.1 Arbitration.** In a case properly submitted to arbitration, the arbitrator's decisions are final and binding on all parties. The arbitrator's powers and duties are to: (A) hold hearings about the issue; (B) investigate as necessary to reach a proper decision; and (C) render a decision in writing within a reasonable time.
Ex. 4 *ARTICLE III* *NO STRIKES* *Section 1.* A strike is defined as the refusal of an employee, in concerted action with others, to report for duty, or his/her willful absence from his/her position, or his/her stoppage of work, or his/her abstinence in whole or in part from the performance of the duties of employment as established by this Agreement or as established in a collective bargaining Agreement between the City and the Association expiring immediately preceding the alleged strike. **Collective-Bargaining Agreement (2005)**	**3. No Strikes.** **3.1 Definition of *strike*.** A strike is the refusal of employees in concerted action to report for duty, their willful absence from their positions, their stoppage of work, or their abstinence in whole or in part from performing the duties of employment as established by this Agreement or as established in a collective-bargaining agreement between the City and the Association ending immediately before the employees' concerted action. The plural antecedent (*employees*) takes the genderless third-person (*they, them, their*). Techniques #7 and 8.

NOT THIS:	BUT THIS:
Ex. 5 **SECTION 19. UNION STEWARD** G. In the event of layoffs due to lack of work, the Steward shall be the last employee, within his classification (journeyman, working foreman, foreman), to be laid off. In no event shall a Steward be laid off due to lack of work, unless he has not been employed on the project from which he is laid off for at least thirty (30) working days, and provided, further, that he is qualified and competent to perform the work available. **Master Agreement covering drywall, acoustical workers, and lathers in Hawaii (2007)**	**19. Union Steward.** **19.7 Layoffs.** If a layoff occurs because of a lack of work, the Steward must be the last employee within his or her classification (journeyman, working supervisor, supervisor) to be laid off. If the Steward is qualified and competent to perform the work available, the Steward must not be laid off unless he or she has been employed on the project from which he or she has been laid off for fewer than 30 working days.
Ex. 6 **Section 1.** There shall be no limitations as to the amount of work a man shall perform during his working day; it being understood that the workman shall perform a fair and honest day's work. . . . **Section 2.** Conditions . . . (b) Whenever an engineer or apprentice engineer is employed intermittently to operate a machine, he shall do such work during the period when his machine cannot be operated as may be determined by the Lead Engineer. **Agreement Covering Wages and Working Conditions (2007)**	**1. Limits on Workload.** The amount of work an employee may perform during the workday is not subject to limits. It's understood that the employee will perform a fair and honest day's work. . . . **2. Conditions.** . . . (B) **Engineers operating machines.** When an engineer or apprentice engineer is employed to intermittently operate a machine that is inoperable, the Lead Engineer will determine what work the engineer should do until the machine is back in service.
Ex. 7 (b) <u>Acceleration of Distributions on Death.</u> During the first month of the first calendar quarter following the death of a current or former Director, the entire unpaid balance of his Nongrandfathered Account shall automatically be paid in a single lump sum notwithstanding any valid written installment distribution election then in effect. **Directors' Deferred-Compensation Plan from a major fast-food restaurant**	(B) **Accelerating distributions upon death.** During the first month of the first calendar quarter after a current or former Director dies, the entire unpaid balance of the Director's Nongrandfathered Account must be paid automatically in a single lump sum—despite any valid written installment-distribution election then in effect.

The phrase *he or she* and its corresponding objective and possessive forms can be grating when overused, but they are acceptable in moderation. Technique #9.

Note the term *journeyman*, for which many readers would consider *journeyperson* an absurd replacement.

This short subsection employs techniques #1, 2, 3, 4, and 5.

This subsection employs techniques #1, 3, and 4.

NOT THIS:	BUT THIS:
Ex. 8 3.2 Transfers Subject to Right of First Refusal. A Stockholder has the right to Transfer all, but not less than all, of her respective Shares of Common Stock during her lifetime to any prospective third-party transferee (the "Transferee"), subject to the right of first refusal in favor of the non-transferring Stockholder to purchase all, but not less than all, of the Shares offered by the transferring Stockholder. **Stockholders Agreement from a major law firm**	**3.2 Transfers subject to right of first refusal.** While living, a Stockholder may Transfer all—but no less than all—of that Stockholder's Shares of Common Stock. The nontransferring Stockholder has a right of first refusal to purchase all—but no less than all—of the Shares offered by the transferring Stockholder. If the right is not exercised, a prospective third-party transferee may acquire the Shares.
Ex. 9 **Article 6** **No Retention Rights** Nothing in this Agreement shall confer upon the Purchaser any right to continue in Service for any period of specific duration or interfere with or otherwise restrict in any way the rights of the Company (or any Parent or Subsidiary employing or retaining the Purchaser) or of the Purchaser, which rights are hereby expressly reserved by each, to terminate his or her Service at any time and for any reason, with or without cause. **Founder's Stock-Purchase Agreement from a major law firm**	**6. No Retention Rights.** The Buyer has no right to continue in Service for any specific period. The Buyer and the Company (including any Parent or Subsidiary employing or retaining the Buyer) each have the right to end the Buyer's Service at any time and for any reason, with or without cause. The Buyer cannot in any way restrict the Company's right to end the Buyer's Service.
Ex. 10 Once a yardmaster, who has established seniority as such, has been assigned to a Right of Appointment position and has worked thereon for more than 60 full shifts, if s/he is subsequently removed from the Right of Appointment position and another employee is assigned to the Right of Appointment position, the employee who is removed may challenge his removal through the formal grievance procedure. To successfully challenge his removal from the Right of Appointment position s/he must show that the carrier's decision to remove him or her from the position was without just cause. **Memorandum of Agreement from a railroad company**	**8.1 Yardmaster's challenge of removal.** A yardmaster with established seniority may file a grievance challenging removal if the yardmaster: (A) has been assigned to a Right of Appointment position; (B) has worked in that position for more than 60 full shifts; and (C) is later removed and another employee is assigned to the position. **8.2 Standard of proof.** To challenge the removal successfully, the removed yardmaster must show that the carrier's removal decision was without just cause.

NOT THIS:	BUT THIS:
Ex. 11 **Section 5. Lay-offs and Discharges** 5.1 Employers reserve the right to employ and discharge Employees. However, Employees shall not be laid off or fired or otherwise prevented from working without just cause, and notice of such just cause shall be given to the Employee immediately upon his discharge, firing, layoff or if he is otherwise prevented from working, and further, such notice of the aforesaid cause or causes shall be delivered to the Union in writing within forty-eight (48) hours of the time that such Employee shall cease working. **Collective-Bargaining Agreement (2000)** *[Note: The sentence switches from the plural* Employees *to the single* Employee, *which requires a gender-specific pronoun.]*	**5. Layoffs and Discharges.** **5.1 Just cause and notice required.** Employers reserve the right to employ and discharge Employees. Employees must not be laid off or fired or otherwise prevented from working without just cause. Employees must be given notice of the just cause immediately upon being discharged, laid off, or otherwise prevented from working. An Employer must deliver written notice of the cause or causes to the Union within 48 hours after the time when one or more Employees stop working. *[Note: Revising the sentence clarified it and made the personal pronouns unnecessary. Technique #6.]*
Ex. 12 ***SECTION 2. WAGES AND UNION DUES*** . . . (B) Overtime to be paid at the rate of time and one-half (1-1/2). Any man ordered to work on Saturday to be paid at the rate of time and one-half (1-1/2). Time clocks are to be installed in Employers' barns. A man, who during the day, performs any higher paid work shall be paid such higher rate for the entire day. . . . ***SECTION 3. HOURS OF WORK*** . . . A man who finishes his day's work at a barn other than the barn from which he began his day's work will be entitled to transportation and pay back to the starting barn. **New York City Heavy-Construction and Excavating Contract (1999)**	**2. Wages and Union Dues.** . . . **2.2 Overtime pay.** Overtime must be paid at the rate of time and a half (1½). An employee ordered to work on Saturday must be paid at the rate of 1½. Time clocks must be installed in the employers' barns. **2.3 Pay for performing higher-paid work.** An employee who during the day performs any higher-paid work must be paid the higher rate for the entire day. **3. Hours of Work.** . . . **3.4 Workday ending at different barn.** An employee who finishes the day's work at a barn other than the barn at which the day's work began is entitled to transportation back to the starting barn and pay for the time spent in transit.

NOT THIS:	BUT THIS:
Ex. 13 **6.10 Work Rules and Job Conditions.** The following work rules and job conditions shall apply to all jobs and work sites: . . . (n) If the Employer moves a laborer from one jobsite to another jobsite, the Employer shall require the laborer to check in with the other job's Job Steward when he or she arrives at the new site, or, if there is no job steward at the site, the Employer shall immediately report the move to the local union having jurisdiction over the job site. When laborers are moved from one job site to another job site in the course of a day they shall travel from one site to the other site during company time. No laborer will travel from one site to the other site while on his meal break. **Collective-Bargaining Agreement (2007)**	6.10 **Work rules and job conditions.** The following work rules and job conditions apply to all jobs and worksites: . . . (N) **Moving from one jobsite to another.** The employer may move laborers from one jobsite to another, but: (1) a laborer may travel to the new jobsite only on company time; (2) a laborer must not travel to another jobsite while on a meal break; and (3) if the other jobsite has a Job Steward, the Employer must require the laborer to check in with the Job Steward upon arriving at the new jobsite; otherwise, the Employer must immediately report the move to the local union having jurisdiction over the jobsite.

A simple rephrasing can sometimes eliminate the need for gender-based pronouns. Technique #6.

Numbers, percentages, and currency

§ 72 Prefer numerals over written-out numbers.

Written-out numbers are harder to read than numerals simply because they're typographically undifferentiated from other words. Although in general prose it's customary (except with dollar amounts) to spell out one through ten and then to use numerals, in contracts it's desirable to use a numerals-only policy. Some drafters italicize *1* to make it stand out as a numeral when it appears solo; although these *Guidelines* haven't adopted that convention, it's worth considering.

As for large numbers, past one million, the recommended style is to use words in place of sequential zeros (*$5 million*, *$5.3 million*) unless there is a particularity in any of the last five digits (*$5,320,000*, *$4,326,515*).

NOT THIS:	BUT THIS:
Ex. 1 Licensee agrees to pay the Licensor two hundred thousand dollars ($200,000) within seven (7) days after the execution of this agreement. **License Agreement from a major law firm**	Markels will pay Brill $200,000 within 7 days after the signing of this Agreement.
Ex. 2 Notwithstanding any other provision of this Agreement, the Purchase Price shall not exceed Four Billion Dollars ($4,000,000,000). **Mortgage-Loan Purchase Agreement between two major financial institutions**	Despite any other provision in this Agreement, the Purchase Price cannot exceed $4 billion.
Ex. 3 The parties have agreed that for purposes of this Agreement, the current fair market value of the Property is Three Hundred Eighty-Nine Thousand Six Hundred Sixty-Seven and 00/100 Dollars ($389,667.00). **Purchase Contract from a major law firm**	Under this Agreement, the current fair market value of the Property is $389,667.

"I favor writing all numbers in their numerical rather than their alphabetic form unless the typeface we are using produces ambiguity, as used to happen to the first number and twelfth letter on the old typewriters. Printing numbers rather than spelling them helps readers grasp the message more readily." Robert Eagleson, *Writing Numbers*, 30 Clarity 14, 14 (Mar. 1994).

NOT THIS:	BUT THIS:
Ex. 4 4.2 The authorized shares of stock of the corporation shall be divided into two classes of shares of common stock. Class A shall consist of five hundred (500) shares without par value, and Class B shall consist of five hundred (500) shares without par value. **Certificate-of-Incorporation Form from Peter Siviglia, *Commercial Agreements: A Lawyer's Guide to Drafting and Negotiating* § 8:2 (2017)**	**4.2 Authorized shares.** The authorized shares of the corporation's stock will be divided into 2 common-stock classes: Class A and Class B. Each class will consist of 500 shares without par value.
Ex. 5 Principal and interest shall be due and payable in monthly installments of THREE THOUSAND DOLLARS or more, each, payable on the FIRST (1ST) day of each and every calendar month, the first payment being due on AUGUST 1, 2018, and continuing regularly thereafter until JULY 1, 2024, when the entire amount hereof, principal and interest then remaining unpaid, shall be then due and payable; . . . **Real-Estate Lien Note**	Principal and interest is due and payable in monthly installments of at least $3,000, payable on the 1st day of each month, the first payment being due on August 1, 2018, and then continuing regularly until July 1, 2024, when the entire amount of principal and interest then remaining unpaid is due; . . .
Ex. 6 WHEREAS, the Borrower has requested the Lender to (a) make a term loan to the Borrower in the aggregate principal amount of FOUR MILLION AND NO/100 DOLLARS ($4,000,000.00); (b) to make available to the Borrower a revolving line of credit for loans and letters of credit in an amount not to exceed SIX MILLION AND NO/100 DOLLARS ($6,000,000.00); and (c) to make available to Borrower a capital expenditures line of credit for loans in an amount not to exceed ONE MILLION AND NO/100 DOLLARS ($1,000,000.00), which extensions of credit the Borrower will use for Borrower's working capital needs and general business purposes. **Term-Loan Agreement from a major law firm**	Borrelis has asked Capital Bank to extend 3 types of credit for working capital and general business purposes: (A) a term loan in the aggregate principal amount of $4 million; (B) a revolving line of credit for loans and letters of credit not to total more than $6 million; and (C) a capital-expenditures line of credit for loans not to total more than $1 million.

NOT THIS:	BUT THIS:
Ex. 7 In addition to said Payment Schedule, the following Payment terms shall apply: On or before the first (1st) and fifteenth (15th) calendar days of each month, Contractor will submit invoices, bills, and statements to Owner documenting the construction costs, fees and expenses for the Work for the preceding fifteen (15) calendar days. Owner will review such invoices, bills and statement, and other documentary evidence within five (5) days after receipt thereof and deliver to Contractor within said period a written statement either (i) approving the invoices, bill and statements, and other documentary evidence or (ii) reasonably disapproving certain items and explaining its reason for such disapproval. **Construction-Contract Form from a major law firm**	4.4 **Payment Terms.** (A) **Invoice submission.** On or before both the 1st and 15th calendar days of each month, Hill Country Roofing will submit to DuPree invoices, bills, and statements documenting the construction fees and expenses for the Work during the preceding 15 calendar days. (B) **Invoice review.** Within 5 days after receipt, DuPree will review the invoices, bills, statements, and other documentary evidence and deliver a written statement to Hill Country Roofing either: (1) approving the invoices, bills, or statements; or (2) reasonably disapproving certain items and explaining the reasons.

Is there a difference between *costs* and *expenses*? See § 19 *doublets and triplets*.

Note how the rewrite eliminates the romanettes. See § 26.

"Every lawyer is forced to draft something eventually. And when that document—no matter how poor it is in form or substance—does not precipitate an immediate end to the world, the pendulum often swings to the opposite extreme. Unnecessary fear is replaced by dangerous indifference or unwarranted confidence. Drafting is regarded either as an inherent lawyering ability or merely a mechanical function that can be performed by emulating what is contained in form books or the yellowing files of the long-departed founder of the firm." Thomas R. Haggard, *Legal Drafting in a Nutshell* vi (1996).

§ 73 Don't use word-numeral doublets—a hallmark of amateurishness.

The age-old convention of doubling up words and numerals—a holdover from scribal days when it was possible for fraudsters to falsify parchments by altering numerals—is no longer justified in contracts. The doubling encumbers sentences and creates opportunities for discrepancy. Remember: writing a contract isn't the same as writing a check.

NOT THIS:	BUT THIS:
Ex. 1 At Creighton's request, Franchisee shall submit to Creighton a profit and loss statement covering operations, including management, administrative, and general expenses, during the previous twelve (12) month period beginning May 1 of the prior calendar year through April 30 of the current year. **Franchise-License Agreement**	At Creighton's request, the Franchisee must submit to Creighton a profit-and-loss statement covering operations, including management, administrative, and general expenses for the previous 12-month period beginning May 1 of the previous calendar year through April 30 of the current year.
Ex. 2 2.3 Purchase Price. The Purchase Price for the Assets shall be Fourteen Million Two Hundred Forty-Three Thousand (14,243,000) shares of XYLink, Inc. Common Stock ("Common Stock") on the Closing Date. The Common Stock shall be issued to the Seller within fifteen (15) days of the Closing Date. **Asset-Purchase Agreement from a major retail chain**	2.3 **Purchase Price.** The Purchase Price for the Assets is 14,243,000 shares of XYLink Common Stock on the Closing Date. The Common Stock will be issued to the Seller within 15 days after the Closing Date.
Ex. 3 Section 1.1 <u>Sale and Purchase of Shares</u>. On and subject to the terms and conditions of this Agreement, effective as of the Closing Date, Buyer shall purchase from Seller, and Seller shall sell to Buyer, Eleven Million Two Hundred and Twenty Five Thousand (11,250,000) shares of common stock (the "**Shares**") of the Company registered in the name of Seller for the consideration specified in Section 1.2 and upon the terms and conditions set forth in this Agreement. **Stock Sale & Purchase Agreement from a major construction contractor**	1.1 **Sale and purchase of shares.** On the Closing Date, Bonham will purchase from Stein—for the consideration specified in § 1.2—11,225,000 shares of Company common stock registered in Stein's name.

So which is it, 11,225,000 or 11,250,000? This significant drafting error is a risk created by word–numeral doublets.

Also note the redundancy in the first clause and the last clause.

NOT THIS:	BUT THIS:
Ex. 4 Now, therefore, it is mutually agreed, as follows: 1. That the Seller sells to the Buyer, and the Buyer purchases from the Seller, five hundred (500) shares of capital stock of the Corporation, of the par value of one hundred dollars ($100) each, together with all dividends, incomes and issues therefrom, and all rights of preemption, for the sum of seventy-five thousand dollars ($75,000). **Sale-of-Stock Contract from Saul Gordon, revised by Stephen Kurzman, *Gordon's Modern Annotated Forms of Agreement* § 69-8, at 1684 (1970)**	Erwin will sell and Byrne will purchase 500 shares of the Corporation's capital stock with the par value of $100 per share. The purchase price of $75,000 entitles Byrne to the shares, to all dividends, incomes, and issues from them, and to all rights of preemption.
Ex. 5 9. Tenant warrants that all goods and personal property to be placed by Tenant in the room hereby rented by Tenant, shall be Tenant's own property and shall be subject to levy and sale by the Landlord unless so listed by Tenant on the reverse side of all three (3) copies of this agreement. In the event that paragraph 8 of this agreement is placed into full force and effect, Tenant agrees to hold Landlord harmless and indemnify Landlord in the event property is sold which belongs to a party other than Tenant and not so indicated on the reverse side of all three (3) copies. **Mini-Storage Rental Agreement from 15 Gerry W. Beyer, *West's Texas Forms: Real Property* § 16.36, at 275 (2d ed. 2001)**	**9. Stone Crossing's Sale of Property.** Terry represents and warrants that he owns all goods and personal property (collectively "property") in the rented room and that the goods and property are subject to levy and sale by Stone Crossing—except for any property that Terry listed on the reverse side of all 3 copies of this Agreement. If § 8 of this Agreement applies, Terry will indemnify Stone Crossing if Stone Crossing sells property belonging to another party and that property is not listed on the reverse side of all 3 copies.
Ex. 6 10. DISABILITY In the event that Employee shall be permanently disabled for a period of more than three (3) months, Employee shall receive compensation for three (3) months after commencement of disability, as provided in Schedule [C]. Employee's full compensation shall be reinstated upon Employee's return to employment and the discharge of Employee's full duties hereunder. Notwithstanding anything in this Agreement to the contrary, Employer may terminate this Agreement at any time after Employee has been absent from Employee's employment, for whatever cause, for a continuous period of more than three (3) months, and all obligations of Employer hereunder shall cease upon any such termination. **Corporate-Manager Agreement from 3 Nancy Saint-Paul, Texas Legal Practice Forms 3d *Employment Agreements* § 49:7, at 697 (2016)**	**10. Disability.** **10.1 Disability and compensation.** If Ramirez becomes permanently disabled for more than 3 months, Pickwick PC will compensate Ramirez under Schedule C for the 3 months after the disability begins and will reinstate Ramirez's full compensation upon Ramirez's return to employment and discharge of full duties under this Agreement. **10.2 Termination option.** Despite anything in this Agreement to the contrary, Pickwick PC may terminate this Agreement at any time if Ramirez has been continuously absent from employment, for whatever cause, for over 3 months. If that happens, Pickwick PC will have no further obligations under this Agreement.

NOT THIS:	BUT THIS:
Ex. 7 4. Indemnification Process and Appeal. (a) Indemnification Payment. Indemnitee shall be entitled to indemnification of Expenses, and shall receive payment thereof, from the Company in accordance with this Agreement within thirty (30) calendar days after Indemnitee has made written demand on the Company for indemnification (which written demand shall include such documentation and information as is reasonably available to Indemnitee and is reasonably necessary to determine whether and to what extent Indemnitee is entitled to indemnification), unless the Reviewing Party has provided a written determination to the Company that Indemnitee is not entitled to indemnification under applicable law. The Reviewing Party making the determination with respect to Indemnitee's entitlement to indemnification shall notify Indemnitee of such written determination no later than two (2) business days thereafter. **Indemnification Agreement from a computer-technology company**	**4. Indemnity Process and Appeal.** **4.1 Indemnity payment.** Anderson is entitled to indemnity and payment of Expenses by HC Financial within 30 calendar days after giving HC Financial written demand for indemnity along with documentation and information that is reasonably available to Anderson and reasonably necessary for HC Financial to determine whether and to what extent Anderson qualifies for indemnity. The Reviewing Party must notify Anderson of its determination within 2 business days.

NOT THIS:

Ex. 8

Article II

PURCHASE AND ASSIGNMENT OF THE NOTE

. . .

2.2 Payments from Purchaser. In consideration of the Assignment, Purchaser agrees to pay to the Receiver the Purchase Price (as defined in Section 2.2.4 below), pursuant to the following schedule:

2.2.1 Purchaser shall pay ten thousand dollars ($10,000.00) on the third (3rd) business day after entry of the Approval Order (the "Closing Date").

2.2.2 Purchaser shall pay one hundred twenty-five thousand dollars ($25,000.00) upon delivery to Purchaser of executed, written agreements (the "Vendor Commitments"), in form and substance satisfactory to Purchaser, from the following members of the Creditors Committee, to do business with Purchaser on such business terms (which may include, without limitation, credit and payment terms) as Purchaser and each such member shall mutually agree: ABC Corp., DEF Corp., GHI Corp. Notwithstanding anything in this Agreement to the contrary, Purchaser shall be permanently relieved of any obligation to pay the $25,000 installment described in this Section 2.2.2 if the Vendor Commitments described herein are not delivered to Purchaser on or before the first date upon which the payment described in 2.2.3 below becomes due (regardless of whether or not the Approval Order is stayed on that date), provided, however, that such date may be extended by agreement among no fewer than all of the parties to this Agreement.

Agreement in Bankruptcy from a major law firm

This example has a blatant discrepancy between the words and the numbers: $25,000 vs. $125,000.

BUT THIS:

2. Purchase and Assignment of the Note.

. . .

2.2 Payments from Franklin Industries. In consideration of the Assignment, Franklin Industries will pay the Receiver the Purchase Price (as defined in § 2.4), as follows:

(A) $10,000 on the third business day after entry of the Approval Order; and

(B) $25,000 upon delivery of signed commitments from Creditors Committee members ABC Corp., DEF Corp., and GHI Corp. to do business with Franklin Industries on the business terms (which may include credit and payment terms) that Franklin Industries and each member mutually agree on; these commitments must be in form and substance satisfactory to Franklin Industries.

2.3 Exception. Franklin Industries will be permanently relieved of any obligation to pay the $25,000 installment described in § 2.2(B) if the commitments have not been delivered to Franklin Industries on or before the first date on which the payment described in § 2.4 becomes due (whether or not the Approval Order is stayed on that date). This date may be extended by agreement of all the parties to this Agreement.

"One way to foster consistency is to use a style manual—always the same style manual—whenever in doubt." LeRoy Marceau, *Drafting a Union Contract* § 3.2(D), at 17 (1965).

§ 74 Prefer the percent sign (%) and section sign (§) over the words.

We're after efficient communication and error prevention. *Thirty-three percent* is slower, more cumbersome, and more prone to error than *33%*. And *§ 6.4(a)* is quicker and more reliable than *subdivision (a) of section 6.4*.

Although some argue that "§" is alien to the general public and therefore confusing, the general public is likewise probably unfamiliar with the pilcrow—the backward P with two downstrokes to mark a paragraph: ¶. Even so, people generally have no difficulty with the pilcrow and focus instead on the number that follows it. They see that they're reading something with numbered paragraphs—a different kind of writing from what they're accustomed to.

The same goes for "§." It's one character, not four (*sec.*) or seven (*section*). The cumulative benefit in streamlining is tremendous—and readers no longer have to focus on a full two words, "section 474," when the attention should be on a single unit: § 474.

Further, it takes only a few seconds to become accustomed to this abbreviated form. It doesn't tax readers unduly. In fact, it does the opposite: it spares them the trouble of reading empty words.

NOT THIS:	BUT THIS:
Ex. 1 Any such Improvement shall be deemed confidential information of IncomeAce and shall be subject to the limitations set forth in Section 12. **Franchise-License Agreement from a tax-preparation company**	Any Improvement is confidential information of IncomeAce and subject to the limitations in § 12.
Ex. 2 1.3. **Affiliates:** means any corporation, company or other entity in which more than fifty percent (50%) of the voting shares or outstanding capital stock are owned or controlled, directly or indirectly, by a Party. **General Terms from a major software-development company**	**1.3 Affiliate.** *Affiliate* means a corporation, company, or other entity for which a Party owns or controls, directly or indirectly, more than 50% of the voting shares or outstanding capital stock.
Ex. 3 **Section 2.08** <u>**Helping Families Act.**</u> The Purchaser shall deliver the Section 404 Notice required by the Helping Families Act with respect to each Mortgage Loan to each Mortgagor in accordance with applicable law within thirty (30) days after the Closing Date and shall bear all costs associated with providing such notices. **Mortgage-Loan Purchase Agreement between two major financial institutions**	**2.8 Helping Families Act.** As required by the Helping Families Act, JRM will deliver within 30 days after the Closing Date the § 404 Notice to each Borrower for each Mortgage Loan. JRM will pay all costs associated with providing the Notices.

Adding *Section* here just clutters the document.

Ex. 4

NOT THIS:	BUT THIS:
9. Duration and Termination. This Agreement shall become effective as of the date first above written and shall continue until terminated in accordance with the following sentence or until the provision of all Services hereunder has expired as provided in Section 3 hereof. This Agreement may be terminated at any time by (i) the mutual written consent of the parties; (ii) by either Seller or Purchaser, immediately upon notice to the other, in the event that the other commences a case as debtor or has any such case or proceeding commenced against it, or otherwise ceases to function as a going concern; (iii) by Seller, immediately upon notice to Purchaser and the Company, in the event that Purchaser or the Company fails to pay any statement delivered by Seller pursuant to Section 4 hereof within 30 days of the issuance of such statement by Seller (it being understood that nothing in this Section 9 shall modify the payment obligations set forth in Section 4), or (iv) by Seller or Purchaser, immediately upon notice to the other, in the event that the other defaults in the performance of its obligations pursuant hereto in any material respect and such default continues for 30 days following written notice to the other party specifying such default in reasonable detail. Upon the expiration or termination of this Agreement pursuant to this Section 9, the rights and obligations of the parties hereunder shall terminate, except for the rights and obligations of the parties under Section 4, Section 6, Section 7, Section 8 and Section 9 hereof, which shall survive such expiration or termination without limitation. Upon such expiration or termination, Seller shall cease to have any obligation to provide any Services, and each party will promptly deliver to the other all data, programs, software materials, and other properties owned by the other and held by it in connection with the performance of this Agreement. Each party will assist the other at such other party's request and expense in effecting an orderly termination of this Agreement. **Transition-Services Agreement from a major oil company**	9. **Duration and Termination.** This Agreement is effective as of the date stated above and continues until terminated under § 9.1, 9.2, or 9.3, or until the provision of all Services in this Agreement has expired as provided in § 3. 9.1 **Mutual termination.** The parties may mutually consent in writing to terminate this Agreement at any time. 9.2 **Termination by Seller only.** If the Buyer or the Company fails after 30 days to pay a statement delivered by the Seller under § 4 of this Agreement, the Seller may terminate this Agreement immediately by giving notice to the Buyer and the Company. Nothing in this § 9 modifies the payment obligations set forth in § 4. 9.3 **Termination by the Buyer or the Seller.** The Buyer or the Seller may immediately and unilaterally terminate this Agreement by giving notice to the other party if: (A) the other party begins a case as a debtor or if a bankruptcy proceeding is begun against that party, or if that party otherwise stops functioning as a going concern; or (B) the other party materially defaults in performing its obligations under this Agreement and the default continues for 30 days after the defaulting party receives written notice specifying the default in reasonable detail. 9.4 **Parties' rights and obligations.** When this Agreement expires or terminates under this § 9, the parties' rights and obligations will end. But the parties' rights and obligations under §§ 4, 6, 7, 8, and 9 survive expiration or termination without limitation. Upon expiration or termination: (A) the Seller has no obligation to provide any Services; (B) each party must promptly deliver to the other all data, programs, software materials, and other properties owned by the other and held in connection with performing this Agreement; and (C) each party will help the other at the other party's request and expense in effecting an orderly termination of this Agreement. *The drafting here could doubtless be improved: the cross-referencing suggests architectural deficiencies.*

§ 75 Scratch ".00" on round dollar amounts.

Don't use zeros as part of round dollar amounts. Prefer "$50" over "$50.00." Contracts rarely show cents, which take up extra space and can cause printing errors. Only a contract that needs cents displayed should contain the period and the two extra numerals.

	NOT THIS:	BUT THIS:
Ex. 1	The Licensee must pay to the Licensor a license-maintenance fee of $50,000.00 beginning on the first anniversary date of the effective date of this Agreement. **License Agreement from a major law firm**	Irving will pay Findlay a license-maintenance fee of $50,000 on each anniversary date of the effective date of this Agreement or the next business day.
Ex. 2	1. <u>**Payment.**</u> Concurrently with the full execution of this Agreement, Buyer shall pay the sum of Five Hundred Dollars ($500) and No Cents ($.00) by check made payable to Seller and delivered to Seller's attorney. **Settlement Agreement executed by a major law firm**	1. **Payment.** Upon the full signing and delivery of this Agreement, Mitchell will pay $500 by check payable to Ray and delivered to Ray's attorney.
Ex. 3	IN NO EVENT WILL EITHER PARTY'S TOTAL LIABILITY TO THE OTHER PARTY FOR CLAIMS UNDER THIS AGREEMENT EXCEED FIFTEEN MILLION DOLLARS ($15,000,000.00 USD). **Relationship Agreement from a computer-technology company**	**Neither party's total liability to the other party for claims under this Agreement may exceed US$15 million.**

This wording makes it clear that this is an annual renewal fee. The last five words cover unusual circumstances (such as leap day, perhaps).

Avoid using all caps for emphasis. Boldface is more effective and much easier to read. See § 42.

If the agreement deals with cross-border transactions, the normal construction is to write *US$15 million*—never *USD* after the number.

§ 76 Use calculations, diagrams, charts, and other graphics when they help clarify complicated information.

Envision how best to display complex information. Be ingenious. But make sure your graphics are easily understood and can be easily referred to. If necessary, retain a competent compositor to lay out your graphics.

It's often best to include express calculations algebraically and to include worked-out examples. Why? Mathematical wordings are subject to misuse and misunderstandings. For example, *product* denotes multiplication. *Sum* denotes addition. *Difference* denotes subtraction. Yet many lawyers forget these distinctions and misuse terms in verbally expressed calculations.

Tables can be a moderate challenge in contract drafting. But if the drafting staff includes someone with some proficiency in typesetting, tables can be dealt with readily.

Three books by Edward Tufte are invaluable in learning how to incorporate graphic elements effectively:

- *Envisioning Information* (1990).
- *The Visual Display of Quantitative Information* (2001).
- *Beautiful Evidence* (2006).

Make sure that your graphs and diagrams are easily accessible and almost instantly comprehensible. Even old-style documents used graphs and diagrams. The problem was that they often meant very little to anyone other than accountants. "That's fine," say some accountants, "because we know what we're looking for." But it's not fine for anyone else. So test your formulas on a high-school kid who does reasonably well in math. (You're testing your document, remember, not the kid.) If the high-schooler can readily work out the problem with a set of assumed (realistic) numbers, you've done well.

> "The main problem with tables and charts is to remember to use them. It is all too easy to get carried away with the flow of narrative prose and end up describing something that should be displayed in a table or chart. Anything that is measured in numbers and units—e.g., 3 minutes, 10 seconds, 50 horsepower, 70 feet—is easier to tabulate than to describe; anything showing measurable changes is easier to plot on a chart than to describe in words. Tables and charts are easier for both writer and reader. They are to be preferred in all but the simplest case." Ernst Jacobi, *Writing at Work: Dos, Don'ts, and How Tos* 145 (1976).

NOT THIS:	BUT THIS:
Ex. 1 "CPI Increase" means: for each Lease Year after the Commencement Date, the CPI for the CPI Reference Month for that Lease Year divided by the CPI for the CPI Reference Month for the immediately preceding Lease Year minus 1 times 100 with the resulting product in no event being less than 1. **Lease Agreement from a major law firm**	"CPI Increase" means the percentage established by the following calculation: For each Lease Year after the Commencement Date, first divide the CPI for the CPI Reference Month for that Lease Year by the CPI for the CPI Reference Month for the immediately preceding Lease Year. Next, subtract 1 from that result and then multiply by 100. The final number must not be less than 1. For example, if the CPI for January 2019 equals 155 and the CPI for January 2020 equals 162, then the calculation would be: Step 1: 162 ÷ 155 = 1.045 Step 2: 1.045 − 1 = .045 Step 3: .045 × 100 = 4.5%. The CPI Increase would be 4.5%.

"Many attorneys go through provisions requiring numerical calculations much too quickly. This unfortunate tendency is made worse by the fact that many attorneys rarely are required to make calculations more complicated than figuring the tip on a restaurant bill, and consequently many have difficulty understanding the mathematics of some . . . provisions. This is a sad state of affairs, since many of these provisions will have a dramatic effect on the client's financial health." David W. Barron, "Simplifying Lease Calculations," in American Law Institute–American Bar Association, ALI-ABA's *Practice Checklist Manual for Drafting Leases* 73, 74 (Mark T. Carroll ed., 1994).

NOT THIS:	BUT THIS:
Ex. 2 ARTICLE II CONVERSION OF SHARES; EXCHANGE OF CERTIFICATES . . . Section 2.05 *Effect of the Merger on Company Stock Options, Company Restricted Shares and RSUs.* (a) Each outstanding option to acquire shares of Company Common Stock (each, a "*Company Stock Option*"), whether or not then vested or exercisable, that is outstanding immediately prior to the Effective Time shall, as of immediately prior to the Effective Time (and except for (x) Company Stock Options as to which the treatment in the Merger is hereafter separately agreed by Parent and the holder thereof in compliance with Section 5.01 (c), which Company Stock Options shall be treated as so agreed and (y) Company Stock Options which are being exercised pursuant to an Irrevocable Option Election), become fully vested and, subject to the terms of the Company Stock Plans, be converted into the right to receive a payment in cash, payable in U.S. dollars and without interest, equal to the product of (i) the excess, if any, of (x) the Cash Election Price over (y) the exercise price per share of Company Common Stock subject to such Company Stock Option, *multiplied by* (ii) the number of shares of Company Common Stock for which such Company Stock Option shall not theretofore have been exercised. The Surviving Corporation shall pay the holders of Company Stock Options the cash payments described in this Section 2.05(a) on or as soon as reasonably practicable after the date on which the Effective Time occurs, but in any event within two (2) Business Days thereafter. **Technology-Collaboration Agreement from a computer-technology developer** Note the ambiguity: (x) and (y) each have two meanings: stock options with different treatments and two types of stock prices. Also, "the excess . . . of [price] over [price]" is a verbose direction to subtract, yet *over* suggests division.	**2. Conversion of Shares; Exchange of Certificates.** . . . **2.5 Effect of merger on Company Stock Options, company restricted shares, and RSUs.** (A) **Company Stock Options.** An outstanding option to acquire shares of Company Common Stock is a "Company Stock Option." Except for Company Stock Options that are covered by a separate agreement (see § 5.1(C)) or that are being exercised under an Irrevocable Option Election, a Company Stock Option, whether or not then vested or exercisable, that exists immediately before the Effective Time is fully vested. Subject to the Company Stock Plans, it may be converted into the right to receive a cash payment in U.S. dollars and without interest. (B) **Calculation of Company-Stock-Option payment.** The payment amount is the product of the difference between the Cash Election Price and the exercise price per share of Company Common Stock subject to the Company Stock Option (if the difference is greater than zero) multiplied by the number of shares of Company Common Stock for which the Company Stock Option has not been exercised. For example, if the Cash Election Price were \$100 per share, the exercise price \$80 per share, and the Company Common Stock Option of 60 shares exercised for 15 shares, this would be the calculation: Step 1: \$100 share – \$80 share = \$20 per share Step 2: 60 unexercised shares – 15 exercised shares = 45 unexercised shares Step 3: \$20 per share × 45 shares = \$900 payment (C) **Time of payment.** The Surviving Corporation will pay the cash payments described in (B) to the holders of Company Stock Options no later than 2 Business Days after the Effective Time.

Cross-references

§ 77 Eliminate cross-references if you can readily do so through reorganization.

A cross-reference to a faraway provision often—perhaps even typically—signals poor organization. Try repositioning the provisions so that related items stay right together.

A notorious example of cross-referencing gone awry appears in the Internal Revenue Code:

> For purposes of paragraph (3), an organization described in paragraph (2) shall be deemed to include an organization described in section 501(c)(4), (5), or (6) which would be described in paragraph (2) if it were an organization described in section 501(c)(3). [I.R.C. § 509(a).]

Some years ago, this provision won the "Wooliness Award" from the Texas State Bar's Plain-Language Committee. The only way to understand what it's saying is to hold in mind the several other provisions referred to—an achievement that can take even tax lawyers many years of hard work.

Though contracts almost never do anything quite so atrocious, they do often send readers elsewhere to understand something that's supposedly being discussed here and now. Better that you distill whatever it is you're saying here and now. Make it understandable here and now. And in great moderation, tell your readers where they can find further information or original source material if they'll need it.

In sum, avoid sending the reader to other documents to understand a provision in the document you're writing. Make your documents self-contained. If you need to refer to another document, summarize what you're referring to. Do this accurately and concisely and conversationally, without simply regurgitating provisions from those other documents.

> "Cross-references, far from helping readers to understand, poison any attempts to write clearly and simply. The ordinary reader considers cross-references an unmitigated nuisance. His eyes refuse to even see them." Rudolf Flesch, *How to Write Plain English* 81 (1979).

NOT THIS:	BUT THIS:
Ex. 1 *Basic Compensation* 2.01 As compensation for the hours of service actually rendered under this Agreement, the Employee will be paid by the Employer at the rate of $28.00 per hour, to be computed and paid weekly on Friday of each week during the period of employment. *Overtime Compensation* 2.02 The compensation under this Agreement is for a five-day workweek, Monday through Friday, of 40 hours. The Employee will receive overtime compensation at the rate of one and one-half times the amount specified in Paragraph 2.01 for any time worked in excess of 8 hours during a regular workday and for any time worked on Saturday. The Employee will be paid at the rate of two times the amount specified in Paragraph 2.01 for hours worked on Sundays and holidays. **Employment Contract from 10 *Texas Transaction Guide: Legal Forms* § 57.200[2], at 57–117 (Herbert S. Kendrick & John J. Kendrick Jr. eds., 2018)**	**2.1 Basic compensation.** As compensation for work under this Agreement, the Employer will pay the Employee $28 per hour, paid weekly on every Friday during the employment period. **2.2 Overtime compensation.** The Employee's compensation under this Agreement is for a 5-day, 40-hour workweek, Monday through Friday. The Employer will pay the Employee $42 per hour for time worked over 8 hours during a regular workday and for any time worked on Saturday. The Employer will pay the Employee $56 per hour for time worked on Sunday and a holiday. Eliminate the reader's need to look at another section by being specific.
Ex. 2 **Investment Decisions** 1.03. The assets in the Escrow Fund shall be invested at the sole discretion and direction of Purchaser. All assets held under this Escrow Agreement shall be registered in the nominee's name or names that the Escrow Agent selects. . . . ARTICLE 2 DUTIES OF ESCROW AGENT **Investment by Agent** 2.01. The Escrow Agent shall receive and hold the Escrow Fund pursuant to the terms of this Escrow Agreement and shall invest the Escrow Fund as provided in Paragraph 1.03, above. Any interest or other income earned by the assets held in the Escrow Fund shall also be invested in accordance with the procedures set forth in Paragraph 1.03, above, until the Escrow Fund is disbursed as provided below. **Escrow-Fund Agreement from 6 *Texas Transaction Guide: Legal Forms* § 35.202[2], at 35–84 (Herbert S. Kendrick & John J. Kendrick Jr. eds., 2018)** Section 2.01 refers back to 1.03, which is supposed to list terms and procedures for investing. But 1.03 makes only a vague statement about the Purchaser's having sole discretion to invest.	**1.3. Investment decisions.** The Buyer has the sole discretion to invest the assets in the Escrow Fund. All assets held under this Escrow Agreement must be registered in the name of the nominee selected by the Escrow Agent. . . . **2. Duties of the Escrow Agent.** **2.1 Investment by the Escrow Agent.** The Escrow Agent will receive and hold the Escrow Fund and invest it in accordance with § 1.3. Any interest or other income earned by the assets held in the Escrow Fund must also be invested in accordance with § 1.3 until the Escrow Fund is disbursed as provided below.

§ 78 Use the power of your computer to update cross-references automatically, but check cross-references manually before the documents are signed.

Be careful. Having drafts moving back and forth among editors can cause difficulties because many editors don't know how to use dynamic cross-references. Also, if style separators or hidden paragraphs are used, the references may end up distorted. Track changes, too, can wreak havoc with dynamic cross-references. But they're still often preferable because they're less likely to become outdated, and they'll alert you to deleted references.

Cross-referencing to paragraphs within exhibits is challenging because Word (which has become universal) doesn't yet cross-reference effectively across files. So if you're cross-referencing across documents, you'll need to proof carefully in any event. You might be well advised to create a side table of references to guide the proofing. All this is terribly time-consuming, but it's essential for accuracy.

Though it's good to use computing shortcuts, they can't be trusted as foolproof. Everyone knows the fallibility of spell-checkers: they're no substitute for careful proofreading. Nor are cross-references to be trusted without verification. Both user errors and computer glitches must be guarded against—and the only reliable way is doing it manually.

So as a draft nears completion, do a final read-through to ensure that all section references are correct and defined terms consistent. Especially when a draft involves multiple authors and is negotiated through several rounds, small mistakes are likely to creep in unnoticed (extra periods, duplicated words, repeated definitions, etc.). Consider having an associate, a paralegal, or an assistant proofread the contract for spelling, grammar, formatting, and consistency of definitions. If you'll take the time to train a secretary or assistant to proofread contracts, the effort will repay dividends time and again.

D. Structure

Organization

§ 79 Provide a table of contents for any contract of six or more pages.

For any contract of more than a few pages, consider preparing a table of contents. Doing so creates three salient advantages: (1) You'll understand the structure more readily—and so will your readers. (2) You'll think more critically about the necessity or desirability of reorganizing. (3) You'll be better equipped to evaluate the accuracy of your headings. If you doubt these points, just try creating a table of contents for any contract lacking one. You're almost certain to be surprised at the deficiencies you'll find.

NOT THIS:

Ex. 1

TABLE OF CONTENTS

1. BACKGROUND 1
2. DEFINITIONS 1
3. LICENSE GRANT AND TERM 6
4. DUE DILIGENCE 8
5. LICENSE ISSUE ROYALTY; LICENSE MAINTENANCE ROYALTY; MILESTONE ROYALTIES 8
6. EARNED ROYALTIES; MINIMUM ROYALTY PAYMENTS 10
7. SUBLICENSES 13
8. CONFIDENTIALITY AND PUBLICITY 14
9. REPORTS, RECORDS AND INSPECTIONS 15
10. PATENT PROTECTION 16
11. INFRINGEMENT AND LITIGATION 17
12. USE OF UNIVERSITY'S NAME 19
13. TERMINATION 19
14. INDEMNIFICATION; INSURANCE; WARRANTIES 21
15. NOTICES 23
16. INVENTOR AGREEMENTS 24
17. LAWS, FORUM AND REGULATIONS 24
18. MISCELLANEOUS 24

Product-License Agreement from a major university

None of the contract's subsections have subheadings. Two main headings cover the same subject matter (royalties).

"The first point is that drafting is a form of communication. Too many lawyers write as if they were writing a note to remind themselves (and the court) of what the deal was. They forget that drafting is directed to various kinds of audiences and that in each case the nature of the audience or audiences dictates the concepts, structure, and language that should be used." Reed Dickerson, *Teacher's Manual for Materials on Legal Drafting* 20 (1981).

BUT THIS:

Table of Contents

> Creating a table of contents revealed an unlabeled and misplaced clause. ▶

> All royalty-related clauses are now collected under one heading.

> No terms addressed publicity.

> ◀ *Regulations* was redundant.

NOT THIS:

Ex. 2

Table of Contents

1. Instrument Identified 1
2. Parties 1
3. Purpose of Agreement 1
4. Disclosures 1
5. Written Disclosure Attached 2

Separate Property of Prospective Husband.... 2

6. Property Owned or Claimed Before Marriage 2
7. Property Acquired by Gift................ 2
8. Property Acquired by Devise or Descent ... 2
9. Recovery for Personal Injuries 2
10. Income or Property From Separate Property 2
11. Management of Separate Property 3

Separate Property of Prospective Wife 3

12. Property Owned or Claimed Before Marriage 3
13. Property Acquired by Gift................ 3
14. Property Acquired by Devise or Descent 3
15. Recovery for Personal Injuries 3
16. Income or Property From Separate Property 3
17. Management of Separate Property 3

Community Property...................... 4

18. Remainder Shall be Community.......... 4
19. Joint Bank Account 4
20. House 4

Partition and Exchange 4

21. Partition of All Community Property...... 4
22. Meeting to Partition...................... 4

Management of Properties 4

23. Separate Property....................... 4
24. Community Property..................... 5

Record Keeping 5

25. Records to be Kept...................... 5
26. Separate Bank Accounts 5
27. Attorney to be Consulted 5

Wills.................................... 5

28. Agreement to Make Wills............... 5
29. Will of Prospective Husband 5
30. Will of Prospective Wife 5

Spousal Support.......................... 5

31. Support Obligation...................... 5
32. Support During Marriage 6
33. Support Upon Separation or Divorce 6

Divorce Not Intended 6

34. Intent to Remain Married 6
35. Recognition of Possibility of Divorce...... 6

Other Provisions.......................... 6

36. Domicile 6
37. Texas Law to Govern 6
38. Venue................................... 6
39. Amendment 6

Texas Premarital Agreement

BUT THIS:

Table of Contents

1. Background 1
- 1.1 Parties 1
- 1.2 Purpose 1

2. Disclosures 1
- 2.1 General disclosures 1
- 2.2 Written disclosure attached 2

3. Separate Property of Prospective Husband 2
- 3.1 Property owned or claimed before marriage 2
- 3.2 Property acquired by gift............. 2
- 3.3 Property acquired by devise or descent 2
- 3.4 Recovery for personal injuries 2
- 3.5 Income or property from separate property 2
- 3.6 Management of separate property.....3

4. Separate Property of Prospective Wife.....3
- 4.1 Property owned or claimed before marriage 3
- 4.2 Property acquired by gift..............3
- 4.3 Property acquired by devise or descent 3
- 4.4 Recovery for personal injuries 3
- 4.5 Income or property from separate property 3
- 4.6 Management of separate property.....3

5. Community Property 4
- 5.1 Generally 4
- 5.2 Joint bank account 4
- 5.3 House 4

6. Partition and Exchange 4
- 6.1 Partition of all community property 4
- 6.2 Meeting to partition................. 4

7. Management of Properties 4
- 7.1 Management of separate property..... 4
- 7.2 Management of community property 5

8. Recordkeeping..........................5
- 8.1 Records to be kept 5
- 8.2 Separate bank accounts................5
- 8.3 Attorney to be consulted..............5

9. Wills.....................................5
- 9.1 Agreement to make wills..............5
- 9.2 Will of prospective husband 5
- 9.3 Will of prospective wife...............5

10. Spousal Support 5
- 10.1 Support obligation....................5
- 10.2 Support during marriage............ 6
- 10.3 Support upon separation or divorce.... 6

11. Divorce Not Intended.................. 6
- 11.1 Intent to remain married............ 6
- 11.2 Recognition of possibility of divorce ... 6

12. Other Provisions 6
- 12.1 Domicile 6
- 12.2 Texas law to govern 6
- 12.3 Venue 6
- 12.4 Amendment 6

§ 80 Arrange provisions sensibly.

Organize your documents logically and clearly so that finding and referring to provisions in them is relatively easy. Do this by adhering as much as possible to these organizational principles:

- Put rules before exceptions.
- Put more broadly applicable provisions before narrowly applicable ones (except with residual "catchall" provisions).
- Follow the chronological order of contemplated events.
- Couple requirements with deadlines.
- Put remedies or penalties after substantive standards and exceptions.

Remember: plain English is concerned with readers—what they need to know and when they need to know it. Old-style drafting was content to let readers fend for themselves. The cardinal rule is to organize according to the likely reader's need for information and probable expectations about how it would best be formatted.

NOT THIS:	BUT THIS:
Ex. 1 "Permitted Use:" Lessee may continuously use and occupy the premises for the purpose of wind energy conversion to electricity on the premises, including, without limitation: (a) the collection and transmission by lessee of wind generated electric power on the premises; (b) the construction, installation, operation and maintenance by lessee of wind turbines, transmission lines and other related equipment and facilities on the premises (the "Improvements") for their use or operation in conjunction with large wind turbines on the premises (the "Wind Energy Projects"); and (c) access by lessee to and from wind energy projects on the premises and for any purposes incidental thereto. Lessee shall be entitled to use or remove any improvements, if any, now located on the premises solely for the purpose herein intended. *The last sentence fits more logically with the first.* **Wind-Energy Lease from 7A William B. Burford, *West's Texas Forms: Minerals, Oil & Gas* § 19:6, at 290 (4th ed. 2008)**	(A) **Permitted use.** To convert wind energy to electricity, Burgdorf may use or occupy the premises and may use or remove any of Allen's improvements now located on the premises. This includes Burgdorf's right to: (1) collect and transmit wind-generated electric power; (2) construct, install, operate, or maintain the wind turbines, transmission lines, or related equipment or facilities for use with large wind turbines on the premises; and (3) have access to the premises for the wind-energy projects and related purposes. *The revision removes the defined terms. The definitions for* Improvements *and* Wind-Energy Projects *should be in a separate section or subsection.* *Note that 6 zombie nouns were easily changed to verbs in the revision. See § 20.*

NOT THIS:	BUT THIS:
Ex. 2 **ARTICLE 9 - CONFIDENTIALITY** 9.1 The parties agree to consider as strictly confidential and to treat as such all information, regardless of its nature and its support, collected during the execution of this Contract, including the clauses of this Contract (hereinafter "<u>Confidential Information</u>"). 9.2 Notwithstanding the clauses in paragraph 9.1, MONTE VESPER will be authorized, in application of its status as a listed company, to disclose this Confidential Information if this information should be revealed further to a requirement of a regulation in effect, particularly if it relates to the stock exchange or if this information should be revealed further to an injunction by a judicial or administrative authority, with the provision that GANVERS is informed and consulted beforehand regarding the terms of disclosure of this information. 9.3 All information known by the public is deemed non-confidential unless it is compiled in a manner unknown to the public. 9.4 The parties agree to not disclose or allow to be disclosed, directly or indirectly or through a third party, in whole or in part, any Confidential Information of which they are aware, to any third party whatsoever, with the exception of employees and/or subcontractors requiring this information to carry out their obligations. 9.5 The parties agree, in this regard, to take any necessary measures with respect to employees and/or beneficiaries in order that they be subjected to this same obligation of confidentiality. 9.6 The parties agree not to use the Confidential Information in a context other than that of this contract. 9.7 Each party agrees to return upon request all documents or supporting documents, as well as any copies thereof, from the other party which contain Confidential Information that will have been submitted to it in connection with the execution of this Contract. **Joint-Venture Agreement from a major law firm**	**9. Confidentiality.** **9.1 Confidential Information.** The parties must treat as strictly secret all Confidential Information—meaning this Contract and all information, regardless of its nature and support, collected during the performance of this Contract. Information known to the public is not Confidential Information unless it is compiled in a manner unknown to the public. The parties must not disclose or allow to be disclosed to any third party, directly, indirectly, or through a third party, in whole or in part, any Confidential Information that they are aware of except information required for employees or subcontractors to carry out their obligations. The parties must not use the Confidential Information in a way unrelated to this Contract. **9.2 Disclosure.** As long as Ganvers is informed and consulted beforehand about the terms of disclosure of certain Confidential Information, Monte Vesper—in its status as a listed company—is authorized to disclose this Confidential Information if necessary to meet a requirement of a regulation in effect (especially one related to the stock exchange) or a judicial or administrative injunction. **9.3 Employee confidentiality.** The parties must make best efforts to ensure that employees and beneficiaries are subject to this same obligation of confidentiality. **9.4 Confidential Information return policy.** Upon request, each party must return all originals and copies of documents or supporting documents that contain Confidential Information submitted by the other party in connection with this Contract.

Note that this *execution* means "performance," not "signing." See § 149 at pp. 414–15.

In the original, §§ 9.3, 9.4, and 9.6 don't merit being independent subsections: they belong under the general information in § 9.1. Also note the inconsistent use of capitalized *Contract*.

NOT THIS:

Ex. 3

SECTION FOUR.
CATTLE TO CONFORM TO THOSE EXHIBITED

Seller covenants that the cattle when delivered shall conform to the cattle that were exhibited to buy on [*date*], at [*location*], by [*name of sales representative*], the sales representative of seller.

SECTION FIVE.
DISEASE INSPECTION

Seller shall cause the cattle to pass federal, state, and all other necessary inspections for all diseases, brands, and marks at the expense of seller [*specify period of time, such as: before loading at the above time and place*]. No sick, crippled, off-colored cattle, or any other cattle failing to pass the above inspections, are to be counted or loaded at such time and place.

SECTION SIX.
INSPECTION BY BUYER

A. Buyer shall have the right to examine the cattle on their arrival as specified above. Within [*number*] business days after such arrival, [*he/she*] must give notice to seller [*specify, such as: by telegraph or confirmed by mail*], of any claim for damages on account of the condition, quality, or grade of the cattle, and must specify the basis of [*his/her*] claim in detail.

B. Buyer's failure to comply with these provisions shall constitute irrevocable acceptance of the cattle and bind [*him/her*] to pay the contract price for the cattle.

SECTION SEVEN.
BASES FOR REJECTION

For the purposes of determining whether buyer has a reasonable basis for rejecting any of the cattle shipped pursuant to this agreement, there shall be sufficient reason for rejection if the cattle have failed to pass any of the inspections specified in Section Five of this agreement.

SECTION EIGHT.
INSPECTION BY THIRD PARTY IN EVENT OF DISPUTES

In the event of any claim or dispute arising under this agreement, [*name of third party*] shall make an inspection of the cattle and shall furnish each party to this agreement with a copy of [*his*][*her*][*its*] findings of fact. [*If appropriate, add: Such findings shall be binding on seller and buyer in regard to any adjustment under this agreement or in the event of any litigation arising under and pursuant to this agreement.*]

SECTION NINE.
SELLER'S WARRANTIES

A. Seller warrants that the cattle shall be free from any and all liens and encumbrances, and further warrants that [*he*][*she*] will defend title to the cattle and indemnify buyer from and against any and all loss or damage on account of such liens, encumbrances, or other defects in title.

B. Seller further warrants that the cattle shall be in good merchantable condition prior to loading at the above-specified time and place.

SECTION TEN.
PAYMENT OF BALANCE OF PURCHASE PRICE

[*Dollar amount*], the balance of the purchase price after deduction of [*dollar amount*] paid pursuant to the provisions of Section One of this agreement, shall be paid by buyer to seller when the cattle are loaded on the cars as specified above.

SECTION ELEVEN.
WEIGHING

A. The cattle shall be weighed on the day of loading on buyer's cattle cars or other carrier on certified scales prior to loading.

B. The cattle shall be taken off feed and water at daylight on the date of weighing, and kept off feed and water until after they have been weighed.

C. The costs of such weighing shall be borne by [*name*].

SECTION TWELVE.
TRANSFER OF TITLE; INDEMNIFICATION OF BUYER

Title to the cattle that are the subject of this agreement shall remain in seller until after the weighing and loading on buyer's cattle cars or other carrier of the cattle as set forth above. Until the cattle are so loaded, seller will indemnify buyer from and against any and all actions or claims arising out of the terms of this agreement or the shipping of cattle pursuant to this agreement and from and against any and all damages or injuries arising from such matters.

SECTION THIRTEEN.
RISK OF LOSS

The risk of loss from any casualty to the cattle regardless of the cause of such casualty shall be on seller until the cattle have been accepted by buyer as specified in this agreement.

Livestock-Purchase Agreement from 2A Am. Jur. Legal Forms 2d *Animals* § 20:5, at 18–20 (2004)

BUT THIS:

4. **Condition of Cattle.** The cattle must meet the following physical standards:
   4.1 **Cattle as advertised.** When delivered, the cattle must substantially conform to the cattle that our sales representative, [*name*], showed for sale on [*date*] at [*location*].
   4.2 **Disease and other inspections.** At our sole expense, we will put the cattle through all required federal, state, and other inspections for diseases, brands, and marks within [*period of time*] before delivery. We will deliver only cattle that pass these inspections.
   4.3 **Weighing.** Beginning at daylight on the delivery day, we will take the cattle off feed and water. The cattle will be weighed that day at [*our/your*] expense on your carrier's cars or on a certified scale.
5. **Our Warranties.** We warrant that title to the cattle is free of encumbrances and that the cattle will be in good merchantable condition when delivered.

The information has been thoroughly rearranged for logical progression and ease of reading.

6. **Title; Risk of Loss.**
   6.1 **Transfer of title.** We own title to the cattle until after the cattle are weighed and loaded for shipping. At that time, title will transfer to you.
   6.2 **Risk of loss.** We bear the risk of loss regardless of the cause until you accept the cattle.
7. **Your Inspection; Rejection or Acceptance.**
   7.1 **Inspection on arrival.** You may inspect the cattle when they arrive at your destination.
   7.2 **Rejection.** If you reject any cattle, you must notify us within ______ business days after arrival by [*specify means*], stating the specific reasons for your rejection and any claims for damages relating to the cattle's condition. Acceptable reasons for rejecting cattle include:
      (A) failure to pass an inspection required under § 4.2;
      (B) a defect in title, including liens and other encumbrances; and
      (C) defects in the cattle's condition, quality, or grade.
   7.3 **Presumed acceptance.** If you fail to inspect the cattle or to comply with § 7.2, your failure constitutes irrevocable acceptance of the cattle and will bind you to pay the contract price.
8. **Third-Party Inspection.** If we dispute the reason for your rejection, [*name of appointed inspector*] will inspect the cattle and produce written findings of fact, delivering copies to each of us. Those findings will bind each of us in any later litigation relating to this Agreement or an adjustment to it.
9. **Indemnity.**
   9.1 **Generally.** We will indemnify you against all claims arising from this Agreement until the cattle have been loaded.
   9.2 **Title defense.** We will defend title to the cattle and indemnify you against loss or damage because of any encumbrance or other defect in title to the cattle.
   9.3 **Shipping.** We will indemnify you against damages or injuries arising from the cattle's shipping.
10. **Final Payment.** The final payment is the remaining balance of the purchase price, calculated as the agreed price minus the amount already paid under § 1. You must pay this amount when the cattle are loaded for shipment to you.

§ 81 Group related items together.

Things of like kind need to be kept together, not separated. Otherwise, the drafting seems hodgepodge. An added benefit of headings (see § 14) is that they'll help you arrange related ideas sensibly.

NOT THIS:	BUT THIS:
Ex. 1 **7. Training and Other Assistance** Hawley shall furnish Franchisee with information to assist Franchisee in establishing an operating budget, and shall provide Franchisee with initial training in the preparation of tax returns and tax office management, in such manner as Hawley may determine. Franchisee shall complete such training satisfactorily at such times and at such places as Hawley designates. Such training shall be provided by Hawley without charge, but Franchisee shall bear the cost of attending such training, including, without limitation, the cost of travel, room and board, and employee salaries. **Franchise-License Agreement**	**7.1 Training.** (A) **Initial training.** Hawley will provide information to help Wilson Accounting establish an operating budget and will provide Wilson Accounting initial training in tax-return preparation and tax-office management. Wilson Accounting will satisfactorily complete the training at the times and places that Hawley designates. (B) **Cost.** Although Hawley will provide training without charge, Wilson Accounting will bear the costs of attending the training, including travel expenses and employee salaries.
Ex. 2 4.2 Delay of Application for Berkley Products and Services. If a Customer delays activation of its service during the thirty (30) days preceding the scheduled installation, normal charges for local distribution facilities will apply to Customer from the scheduled date of installation. If the delay exists for more than thirty (30) days after the scheduled installation date, Berkley may consider the delay a cancellation of the Application for Service, and Berkley will be relieved of any obligation to provide or initiate service pursuant to the Application of Service. **Master Services Agreement from a telecommunications company**	**4.2 Delay of Application for Service.** (A) **Within 30 days before scheduled installation date.** If Maxis delays activation of its service during the 30 days before the scheduled installation date, Maxis will still owe Berkley the normal charges for local distribution facilities from the scheduled installation date. (B) **More than 30 days after scheduled installation date.** If the delay continues for more than 30 days after the scheduled installation date, Berkley may consider the delay a cancellation, and Berkley will be relieved of any duty to provide service under the Application for Service.

> "The substance of the contract should be built up, provision by provision, with a reason for including every item. 'Because it's been there before' is not reason enough."
> Carl Felsenfeld & Alan Siegel, *Writing Contracts in Plain English* 48 (1981).

NOT THIS:	BUT THIS:
Ex. 3 9. The breach by Lessee of any obligations arising hereunder shall not work a forfeiture or termination of this Lease nor cause a termination or reversion of the estate created hereby nor be grounds for cancellation hereof in whole or in part unless Lessor shall notify Lessee in writing of the facts relied upon in claiming a breach hereof, and Lessee, if in default, shall have sixty (60) days after receipt of such notice in which to commence the compliance with the obligations imposed by virtue of this instrument, and if Lessee shall fail to do so then Lessor shall have grounds for action in a court of law or such remedy to which he may feel entitled. After the discovery of oil, gas or other hydrocarbons in paying quantities on the lands covered by this Lease, or pooled therewith, Lessee shall reasonably develop the acreage retained hereunder, but in discharging this obligation Lessee shall not be required to drill more than one well per eighty (80) acres of area retained hereunder and capable of producing oil in paying quantities, and one well per six hundred forty (640) acres of the area retained hereunder and capable of producing gas or other hydrocarbons in paying quantities, plus a tolerance of ten per-cent in the case of either an oil well or a gas well. **Oil-and-Gas Lease from a major law firm**	**9. Mitchell's Duty to Develop.** **9.1 Generally.** After the discovery of oil, gas, or other hydrocarbons in paying quantities on the lands covered by this Lease or pooled with those lands, Mitchell will reasonably develop the acreage as follows: (A) **Oil.** For each 80 acres plus a 10% tolerance, at least 1 well capable of producing oil in paying quantities. (B) **Gas.** For each 640 acres plus a 10% tolerance, at least 1 well capable of producing gas or other hydrocarbons in paying quantities. **9.2 If Mitchell breaches the lease.** (A) **Lessor to give notice.** If the Lessor believes Mitchell to be in breach, the Lessor must notify Mitchell in writing of the facts underlying the alleged breach. Otherwise, a breach does not: (1) terminate or forfeit this Lease; (2) terminate the mineral estate or cause it to revert; or (3) constitute grounds for canceling this Lease. (B) **Mitchell's obligation upon receiving notice.** Once Mitchell receives notice of a breach, it has 60 days to begin to meet its lease obligations—or else the Lessor may seek remedies as it sees fit.

This original provision is a structural mess.

The first paragraph is set apart and given its own heading instead of being lumped in with the others in the original.

Note that the paragraphs are organized chronologically: duty–breach–notice–Mitchell's obligations upon receiving notice.

"It is true that when a judge reads the words of a contract he may jump to the instant and confident opinion that they have but one reasonable meaning and that he knows what it is. A greater familiarity with dictionaries and the usages of words, a better understanding of the uncertainties of language, and a comparative study of more cases in the field of interpretation, will make one beware of holding such an opinion so recklessly arrived at." Arthur L. Corbin, *Corbin on Contracts* § 535, at 496–97 (1952).

NOT THIS:	BUT THIS:
Ex. 4 5. The Design Professional shall respond in writing to all formal design review comments with regard to the disposition of; or actions taken on such comments. 6. The Design Professional shall include a revision history on the drawings, including the issue dates and descriptions of the revisions. 7. A complete design analysis shall be submitted along with the final documents. The design analysis shall include all calculations, design criteria, applicable standards, etc. needed for equipment and material selection, sizing, detailing, etc. 7.1 The design analysis shall be presented on 8-1/2" x 11" paper except that larger sheets may be used when required for graphs or other special calculation forms. All sheets shall be in reproducible form. The material may be typewritten, hand lettered, handwritten or a combination thereof, provided it is legible. Side margins shall be 1-inch minimum to permit side binding and head-to-head printing. Bottom margins shall be 1-1/4" with page numbers centered 1-inch from the bottom. 7.2 The Design Professional shall provide record document design analysis in reproducible form designated as "FINAL DESIGN ANALYSIS." If a project is abandoned before completion the Design Analysis should be submitted at that point. 8. The Design Professional shall provide record document specifications of furnishings and interior finishes, when applicable. The specifications shall include materials, colors and location. Provide one hard copy and one electronic copy. 9. The Design Professional shall review Operation and Maintenance Manuals and the Constructor's marked-up construction documents reflecting all as-built changes. **Construction Contract ("Design Document Requirements") from a major law firm**	**5. Design Professional Requirements.** 5.1 **Specifics on furnishings and interior.** The Design Professional must provide record-document specifications of furnishings and interior finishes, when applicable. The specifications must include materials, colors, and location. One hard copy and one electronic copy must be provided. 5.2 **Reviewing other documents.** The Design Professional must review Operation and Maintenance Manuals and the Constructor's marked-up construction documents reflecting all as-built changes. 5.3 **Response to comments.** The Design Professional must respond in writing to all formal design-review comments, explaining the disposition of or actions taken on those comments. 5.4 **Information about revisions.** The Design Professional must include a revision history on the drawings, including the issue dates and descriptions of the revisions. 5.5 **Design analysis.** Along with the final documents, the Design Professional must provide a written analysis of the record-document design in reproducible form and specifically designated: "Final Design Analysis." If a project is abandoned before completion, the Design Professional must submit the design analysis upon abandonment. For more requirements for the Final Design Analysis, see § 6. **6. Final Design Analysis.** 6.1 **Requirements.** A complete design analysis must be submitted along with the final documents. The analysis must include all calculations, design criteria, applicable standards, and anything else needed for equipment and material selection, sizing, detailing, etc. 6.2 **Format.** The design analysis must be on 8½"×11" paper, but larger sheets may be used when needed for graphs or other special calculation forms. All sheets must be in reproducible form. The material may be typewritten, hand-lettered, handwritten, or a combination, but must be legible. Side margins must be at least 1" to permit side binding and head-to-head printing. Bottom margins must be 1¼" with page numbers centered 1" from the bottom.

Note how the new § 5 groups all the Design Professional's responsibilities into one place.

Structural divisions

§ 82 Use subparts to maximize readability.

The parts of a contract are preferably sequenced with a one-level decimal followed by an outline form alternating between letters and numerals. The typical contract, managed properly, won't need more than five levels of breakdown. Subitems (as shown below) should rarely if ever be reached. Throughout this book, the "But This" examples follow our recommended format—without any hand-wringing about the terminology. Every citation is preceded simply by the section symbol (§ 6, or § 6.2, or § 6.2(A)(1)(a)(ii), etc.).

§ 6.2(A)(1)(a)(ii)

---

§ 6. [section: major-division heading]
 6.2 [subsection] [If heading is appropriate—otherwise, straight to (A).]
 (A) [paragraph]
 (1) [subparagraph]
 (a) [item]
 (ii) [subitem]

When is a heading appropriate for a subsection? Whenever each of the coordinate subsections contains at least one complete sentence.

NOT THIS:	BUT THIS:
Ex. 1 **5. Initial Deposit** As partial security for Franchisee's faithful performance of this Agreement, Franchisee is depositing with Stokes the amount of $2,500, the receipt of which is acknowledged by Stokes. Such deposit may be held by Stokes without interest to Franchisee; may be commingled with Stokes's other funds; may be applied by Stokes at any time to the payment of any amounts owed to it by Franchisee and to the payment of all costs and expenses, including attorneys fees, incurred by Stokes in enforcing this Agreement and shall be forfeited by Franchisee if Stokes terminates this Agreement pursuant to Sections 13 or 14 hereof. The forfeiture by Franchisee or application by Stokes of the deposit, or any portion thereof, shall not affect any other rights or remedies Stokes may have at law or in equity, constitute liquidated damages or otherwise limit the damages or legal or equitable remedies available to Stokes. **Franchise-License Agreement**	**5. Initial Deposit.** **5.1 Partial security.** As partial security for Wilson's faithful performance of this Agreement, Wilson has deposited $2,500 with Stokes, and Stokes has acknowledged receipt. Stokes may hold this deposit without interest to Wilson, may commingle it with Stokes's other funds, and may apply it at any time to the payment of any amounts that Wilson owes to Stokes or to any costs and expenses, including attorney fees, that Stokes incurs in enforcing this Agreement. If Stokes terminates this Agreement under § 13 or 14, Wilson will forfeit the deposit. **5.2 Preservation of other rights and remedies.** If any part of the deposit is applied or forfeited as described in § 5.1, other rights and remedies remain unaffected. The application or forfeiture does not constitute liquidated damages or otherwise limit Stokes's damages or remedies.

NOT THIS:	BUT THIS:
Ex. 2 § 5.5 **Seller's remedies on default.** On default by buyer, seller has the option of refusing to perform further under this and any other existing contracts between the parties. Seller may elect his or her remedy. Seller may rescind any contracts between the parties and hold buyer liable for all damages and losses occasioned thereby. In the alternative, seller may resell, at public or private sale, undelivered goods covered by this and any other existing contracts between the parties as seller may elect. Seller is not liable to buyer for any profit on such resale but buyer remains liable to seller for the difference between (a) the contract price of the goods and all expenses of storage and resale; and (b) the resale price of the goods. **Uniform Commercial Code Sales Contract from 1 Allen E. Smith & Nancy Saint-Paul, West's Texas Forms: Creditors' Remedies & Debtors' Rights § 5.5, at 127 (4th ed. 2009)**	**5.5 Quillco's remedies upon default.** (A) **Generally.** If Hawley defaults, Quillco may refuse further performance under this or another existing contract between the parties and elect to: (1) rescind any contracts between the parties while holding Hawley liable for all pertinent damages and losses; or (2) resell, at public or private sale, undelivered goods covered by this and any other existing contracts between the parties. (B) **Hawley's liability.** Under § 5.5(A)(2), Quillco is not liable to Hawley for any profit from a resale, but Hawley remains liable to Quillco for the contract price of the goods plus all of Quillco's storage and resale expenses, minus the resale price of the goods.

NOT THIS:

Ex. 3

14.21. Confidentiality and Publicity. Other than as may be required by applicable Law and regulation or by any governmental or regulatory authority, no Party shall disclose to any person (including for the avoidance of doubt, any other Consenting Stakeholder), other than legal, accounting, financial and other advisors to the Company Parties (who are under obligations of confidentiality to the Company Parties with respect to such disclosure, and whose compliance with such obligations the Company Parties shall be responsible for), the name or the principal amount or percentage of the Company Claims/Interests held by any Consenting Stakeholder or any of its respective subsidiaries (including, for the avoidance of doubt, any Company Claims/Interests acquired pursuant to any Transfer); provided, however, that the Company Parties shall be permitted to disclose at any time the aggregate principal amount of, and aggregate percentage of, any class of the Company Claims/Interests held by the Consenting Stakeholders collectively; and, provided, further, that the Company Parties may disclose the names of any Consenting Stakeholder (at the institution level) at a hearing in connection with the Chapter 11 Cases, but not the principal amount or percentage of the Company Claims/Interests held by any such Consenting Stakeholder or any of its respective subsidiaries (including, for the avoidance of doubt, any Company Claims/Interests acquired pursuant to any Transfer). Notwithstanding the foregoing, the Consenting Stakeholders hereby consent to the disclosure of the execution, terms and contents of this Agreement by the Company Parties in the Definitive Documents or as otherwise required by law or regulation; provided, however, that (i) if any of the Company Parties determines that they are required to attach a copy of this Agreement, any Joinder or Transfer Agreement to any Definitive Documents or any other filing or similar document relating to the transactions contemplated hereby, they will redact any reference to or identifying information concerning a specific Consenting Stakeholder and such Consenting Stakeholder's holdings (including before filing any pleading with the Bankruptcy Court) and (ii) if disclosure of additional identifying information of any Consenting Stakeholders is required by applicable Law, advance notice of the intent to disclose, if permitted by applicable Law, shall be given by the disclosing Party to each Consenting Stakeholder (who shall have the right to seek a protective order prior to disclosure). The Company Parties further agree that such information shall be redacted from "closing sets" or other representations of the fully executed Agreement, any Joinder or Transfer Agreement. Notwithstanding the foregoing, the Company Parties will submit to counsel for the Consenting Stakeholders all press releases, public filings, public announcements or other communications with any news media, in each case, to be made by the Company Parties relating to this Agreement or the transactions contemplated hereby and any amendments thereof at least two (2) Business Days (it being understood that such period may be shortened to the extent there are exigent circumstances that require such public communication to be made to comply with applicable Law) in advance of release and will take such counsel's view with respect to such communications into account. Nothing contained herein shall be deemed to waive, amend or modify the terms of any Confidentiality Agreement.

Restructuring Support Agreement

BUT THIS:

14.21 Confidentiality.

(A) **Nondisclosure.** No Party may disclose confidential information to any person except as permitted under § 14.21(C).

(B) **Confidential information.** The name, the principal amount, and percentage of the Company Claims or Interests, including those acquired by Transfer, held by any Consenting Stakeholder or any of its respective subsidiaries qualify as confidential information.

(C) **Permitted disclosure of confidential information.**

(1) A Party may disclose confidential information:

(a) as required by applicable law and regulation or by any governmental or regulatory authority; or

(b) to the Company Parties' legal, accounting, financial, and other adviser if the adviser is under an obligation of confidentiality to the Company Parties for the disclosure and if the Company Parties are responsible for the adviser's compliance with the obligation.

(2) Company Parties may disclose:

(a) at any time, the aggregate principal amount of, and aggregate percentage of, any class of the Company Claims or Interests held by the Consenting Stakeholders collectively; or

(b) at a hearing in connection with the Chapter 11 Cases, the name of a Consenting Stakeholder (at the institution level) but not the principal amount or percentage of the Company Claims or Interests, including those acquired by Transfer, held by the Consenting Stakeholder or any of its respective subsidiaries.

(D) **Disclosure of Consenting Stakeholders' identifying information.** The Company Parties may disclose the performance, terms, and contents of this Agreement in the Definitive Documents or as otherwise required by law or regulation. References or identifying information related to a specific Consenting Stakeholder and that Consenting Stakeholder's holdings must be redacted:

(1) from "closing sets" or other representations of the fully executed Agreement, a Joinder, or a Transfer Agreement;

(2) from a copy of this Agreement, a Joinder, or a Transfer Agreement that must be attached to any Definitive Documents, a similar document, or a filing relating to the transactions contemplated in this Agreement;

(3) after giving prior notice (if permitted by law) to each Consenting Stakeholder that disclosure is required by law and of the intent to disclose, if the Stakeholder obtains a protective order before disclosure.

(E) **Complete agreement.** Nothing in this Agreement waives, amends, or modifies the terms of the Confidentiality Agreement.

14.22 Publicity. When the Company Parties wish to publicize something relating to this Agreement, an amendment to it, or the transactions contemplated in it, the Company Parties must first submit to counsel for the Consenting Stakeholders all press releases, public filings, public announcements, and other communications with any news media at least 2 business days in advance of release. The period may be shortened if exigent circumstances and law require public communication to be made sooner. The Company Parties must submit to counsel's view regarding the public communication.

"A system of arrangement is suspect whenever changing one part means changing many other parts." Reed Dickerson, *The Fundamentals of Legal Drafting* § 5.8, at 99 (2d ed. 1986).

NOT THIS:

Ex. 4

ARTICLE IV
COVENANTS

The Company covenants and agrees during the term of this Agreement and the Master Forward Confirmation with the Sales Agent, the Forward Seller and the Forward Purchaser as follows:

Section 4.01 Registration Statement and Prospectus. (i) To make no amendment or supplement to the Registration Statement or the Prospectus (other than (x) an amendment or supplement relating solely to the issuance or offering of securities other than the Shares and (y) by means of a Current Report on Form 8-K filed with the Commission under the Exchange Act and incorporated or deemed to be incorporated by reference in the Registration Statement or the Prospectus; provided, that the Company will give prior written notice to the Sales Agent of the intention to file such report and describing the subject matter to be included in such report as soon as reasonably practicable prior to the filing of such report) after the date of delivery of a Transaction Notice and prior to the related Settlement Date at any time prior to having afforded the Sales Agent a reasonable opportunity to review and comment thereon; (ii) to prepare, with respect to any Shares to be sold pursuant to this Agreement and the Master Forward Confirmation, a Pricing Supplement with respect to such Shares in a form previously approved by the Sales Agent and to file such Pricing Supplement pursuant to Rule 424(b) under the Securities Act within the time period required thereby and to deliver such number of copies of each Pricing Supplement to each exchange or market on which such sales were effected, in each case unless delivery and filing of such a Pricing Supplement is not required by applicable law or by the rules and regulations of the Commission; (iii) to make no amendment or supplement to the Registration Statement or the Prospectus (other than (x) an amendment or supplement relating solely to the issuance or offering of securities other than the Shares and (y) by means of an Annual Report on Form 10-K, a Quarterly Report on Form 10-Q, a Current Report on Form 8-K or a Registration Statement on Form 8-A or any amendments thereto filed with the Commission under the Exchange Act and incorporated or deemed to be incorporated by reference into the Registration Statement or the Prospectus except to the extent required by Section 4.01(i)) at any time prior to having afforded the Sales Agent and the Forward Seller a reasonable opportunity to review and comment thereon and to advise the Sales Agent and the Forward Seller promptly when any such amendment to the Registration Statement has been filed or has become effective or any such amendment or supplement to the Prospectus has been filed with the Commission; (iv) to file within the time periods required by the Exchange Act all reports and any definitive proxy or information statements required to be filed by the Company with the Commission pursuant to Section 13(a), 13(c), 14 or 15(d) of the Exchange Act for so long as the delivery of a prospectus is required under the Securities Act or under the blue sky or securities laws of any jurisdiction in connection with the offering or sale of the Shares, and during such same period to advise the Sales Agent and the Forward Seller, promptly after the Company receives notice thereof, of the issuance by the Commission of any stop order or of any order preventing or suspending the use of any prospectus relating to the Shares, of the suspension of the qualification of the Shares for offering or sale in any jurisdiction, of the initiation or threatening of any proceeding for any such purpose, of any request by the Commission for the amendment or supplement of the Registration Statement or the Prospectus or for additional information relating thereto, or the receipt of any comments from the Commission with respect to the Registration Statement or the Prospectus; (v) in the event of the issuance of any such stop order or of any such order preventing or suspending the use of any such prospectus or suspending any such qualification during a Selling Period, to use promptly its commercially reasonable efforts to obtain its withdrawal; in the event any such stop order or such other order is issued outside a Selling Period, the Company will promptly advise the Sales Agent and the Forward Seller as to the issuance thereof and as to whether it intends to seek to obtain its withdrawal; and (vi) to pay the required Commission filing fees relating to the Shares within the time required by Rule 456(b)(1)(i) under the Securities Act without regard to the proviso therein and otherwise in accordance with Rules 456(b) and 457(r) under the Securities Act (including, if applicable, by updating the "Calculation of Registration Fee" table in accordance with Rule 456(b)(1)(ii) either in a post-effective amendment to the Registration Statement or on the cover page of the Prospectus Supplement or any Pricing Supplement filed pursuant to Rule 424(b)).

If, immediately prior to the third anniversary of the filing of the Original Registration Statement, any of the Shares remain unsold under the Sales Agency Agreements, the Company will, prior to such third anniversary and subject to this Section 4.01, file, if it has not already done so, a new automatic shelf registration statement or shelf registration statement, as applicable, relating to the Shares, and, if such registration statement is not an automatic shelf registration statement, will use its reasonable best efforts to cause such registration statement to be declared effective as soon as practicable, and will take all other reasonable actions necessary or appropriate to permit the offering and sale of Shares to continue as contemplated in the expired registration statement relating to such Shares and the Sales Agency Agreements.

Note the unnumbered paragraph here. See § 24.

Sales-Agency Financing Agreement

BUT THIS:

4. **Covenants.**
   4.1 **Registration Statement and Prospectus.** During the term of this Agreement and the Master Forward Confirmation with the Sales Agent, the Forward Seller, and the Forward Purchaser, the following apply:
      (A) **Amendment and supplementation.** The Company may amend or supplement the Registration Statement or the Prospectus only after:
         (1) amending or supplementing solely in relation to the issuance or offering of securities other than the Shares;
         (2) providing that an amendment or supplement is incorporated or treated as incorporated by reference into the Registration Statement or the Prospectus;
         (3) delivering a Transaction Notice;
         (4) giving the Sales Agent written notice after the Transaction Notice is delivered that:
            (a) informs the Sales Agent of the Company's intent to file an Annual Report on Form 10-K, a Quarterly Report on Form 10-Q, a Current Report on Form 8-K, or a Registration Statement on Form 8-A, or an amendment to any of these with the Commission under the Exchange Act;
            (b) describes the subject matter of the report; and
            (c) gives the Sales Agent a reasonable opportunity to review and comment on the report before the related Settlement Date; and
         (5) notifying the Sales Agent and the Forward Seller promptly when the Company:
            (a) files with the Commission an amendment to the Registration Statement or such an amendment becomes effective; or
            (b) files with the Commission an amendment or supplement to the Prospectus.
      (B) **Sales of Shares.** For Shares to be sold under this Agreement and the Master Forward Confirmation, the Company will:
         (1) prepare a Pricing Supplement for the Shares in a form previously approved by the Sales Agent;
         (2) file the Pricing Supplement under Rule 424(b) of the Securities Act within the time required by law or rule; and
         (3) deliver the number of copies of the Pricing Supplement to each exchange or market on which sales have been made, if required by law or rule.
      (C) **Reports and other filings.** If the delivery of a prospectus is required under the Securities Act or under the blue-sky or securities laws of any jurisdiction in connection with the offering or sale of the Shares, the Company will timely file definitive proxy or information statements required under §§ 13(a), 13(c), 14, or 15(d) of the Exchange Act.
      (D) **Stop Order.** If a Stop Order preventing or suspending the use of a prospectus or suspending a qualification is issued before or during a Selling Period, the Company will promptly use commercially reasonable efforts to obtain the Stop Order's withdrawal. If a Stop Order preventing or suspending the use of a prospectus or suspending a qualification is issued outside a Selling Period, the Company will promptly notify the Sales Agent and the Forward Seller of the Stop Order and state whether Company intends to try to obtain the Stop Order's withdrawal. "Stop Order" means any order issued by the Commission that:
         (1) prevents or suspends the use of a prospectus relating to the Shares;
         (2) suspends the qualification of the Shares for offering or sale in any jurisdiction;
         (3) begins or threatens a proceeding for purposes of (1) or (2) above;
         (4) asks the Company to amend or supplement the Registration Statement or the Prospectus;
         (5) asks the Company for additional information related to the Registration Statement or the Prospectus; or
         (6) comments on the Registration Statement or the Prospectus.
      (E) **Commission filing fees.** The Company will pay the required Commission filing fees for the Shares within the time required by Rule 456(b)(1)(i) under the Securities Act, without regard to the proviso in that Rule, and in accordance with Rules 456(b) and 457(r) under the Securities Act. If applicable, the Company will update the "Calculation of Registration Fee" table in accordance with Rule 456(b)(1)(ii) either in a post-effective amendment to the Registration Statement or on the cover page of the Prospectus Supplement or any Pricing Supplement filed under Rule 424(b).
      (F) **Unsold Shares.** If any Shares remain unsold under the Sales Agency Agreements immediately before the third anniversary of the filing of the Original Registration Statement, then before the anniversary and subject to this § 4.1, the Company will take the following measures:
         (1) file a new automatic shelf-registration statement or nonautomatic shelf-registration statement, as applicable, relating to the Shares;
         (2) use its reasonable best efforts to cause a nonautomatic shelf-registration statement to be declared effective as soon as practicable;
         (3) take all other reasonable actions necessary or appropriate to permit the offering and sale of Shares to continue as contemplated in the expired registration statement relating to the Shares and the Sales Agency Agreements.

§ 83 Observe the two-part requirement for subdivided provisions.

At any given level, use a subpart only if there is at least one other corresponding subpart. For example, don't use (A) if you don't have a (B), or (1) if you don't have a (2).

NOT THIS:	BUT THIS:
Ex. 1 ARTICLE III - TERM OF AGREEMENT 1. This Agreement shall be effective as of the date first above written and shall remain in effect for a primary term commencing May 1, 2019 and ending March 31, 2024. **Natural-Gas-Storage-Services Agreement from a major New York energy company**	**3. Term of Agreement.** This Agreement, effective May 1, 2019, remains in effect through March 31, 2024.
Ex. 2 6.2 Technology Transfers. (a) Process Technology. (i) The Parties will jointly make available to Flash Forward the process technology developed under the JMDY Agreement, the Product Development Agreement or the Common R&D Agreement and applicable to the manufacturing and testing of NAND Flash Memory Products and R/W ("Process Technology") on a mutually agreed schedule. (ii) Transfers of Process Technology and process integration for new processes developed pursuant to the JMDY Agreement and that appear on the JMDY Roadmap (as defined in the JMDY Agreement), including those processes developed at ACF or any other facility in accordance with the JMDY Agreement, will be jointly reviewed and discussed by the Parties and will be made in a mutually satisfactory manner. All process integration for new process originating from ACF will be led by Tobanna employees, to the extent reasonably possible. Tobanna and QualDisk will cause their respective employees to cooperate in achieving an efficient transition from development module to operating process and volume production. 6.3 Ramp-Up. The Parties shall expand Y5 Facility NAND Flash Memory Product manufacturing capacity through development of Phase I and Phase II of the Y5 Facility as follows: . . . . **Joint-Venture-Manufacturing Agreement between a major computer company and a tech-storage company**	**6.2 Technology transfers; process technology.** (A) **Availability schedule.** On a schedule acceptable to both, the Parties will jointly make available to Flash Forward the process technology that is developed under the JMDY Agreement, the Product Development Agreement, or the Common R&D Agreement, and that is applicable to the manufacturing and testing of NAND Flash Memory Products and R/W ("Process Technology"). (B) **Cooperation and designated roles.** In a manner acceptable to both, the Parties will jointly review, discuss, and make transfers of Process Technology and process integration for new processes that are developed under the JMDY Agreement and appear on the JMDY Road Map (as defined in the JMDY Agreement), including those processes developed at ACF or any other facility under the JMDY Agreement. To the extent reasonably possible, Tobanna employees will lead all process integration for new process originating from ACF. Tobanna and QualDisk employees will cooperate to transition efficiently from the development module to the operating process and volume production. **6.3 Ramp-up.** Through Phase I and Phase II of the Y5 Facility development, the Parties will expand Y5 Facility NAND Flash Memory Product manufacturing capacity as follows: . . . .

There is no reason to label this "1." when there is no "2."

The revision changes Courier to a proportionally spaced font, Equity Text.

Note that it's better to state exact dates, if known, rather than "the date first above written" or the like. For more on dating a contract, see §§ 57–61.

The original has an (a) with no (b) under § 6.2.

The revision provides two subheadings and eliminates the romanettes.

§ 84 Streamline and simplify references to structural divisions.

Generally, include an appropriate reference when needed for clarity—particularly if the other provision is on a different level or is not near the reference. Repeating the rule number—*subject to § 4(h)*—is shorter and clearer than *subject to item (h) of this section.*

But omit the full reference to a provision number when it's not needed for clarity. For example, when referring to a provision on the same level within the same rule, subdivision, or paragraph, you might state: *(a) Except as provided otherwise in (b), a party must . . . .*

But if the references are particularly intricate and you need to refer to the very subpart in which the reference appears (self-reference), or you need to refer to a larger subpart when you're in a subset of it, simply use *this § 17.4* or *this § 17.4(B)(1).* See Example 3.

	NOT THIS:	BUT THIS:
Ex. 1	13.4 **Termination of individual Services:** Either Party may terminate individual Services (in whole or in part, as opposed to the whole Services Agreement) on the same basis as set out above without terminating the Services Agreement, except as specifically prohibited in any specific Service or Commercial Terms. **Service Agreement from a major communications company**	13.4 **Terminating individual Services.** Unless specifically prohibited in a Service or Commercial Term, either Party may terminate individual Services (in whole or in part) on the basis set out in §§ 13.1–13.3 without terminating the whole Services Agreement.
Ex. 2	8.3 Damages. In the event of any termination of this Agreement, Customer shall pay to Company all of the following amounts: 8.3.1 All advances of funding that were not earned as of termination; plus 8.3.2 The unamortized portion of the cost of installation; plus 8.3.3 Interest on all sums due to Company on the foregoing amounts. **Marketing Agreement from a major beverage company**	8.3 **Damages—amounts owed.** Upon termination of this Agreement, Dahlander will pay the Company the following amounts: (A) all funding advances that were not earned as of termination; (B) the unamortized part of the installation cost; and (C) interest on all sums due to the Company on the amounts in (A) and (B).

"The purposes of clarity are served by grouping in sequence all the paragraphs relating to a particular aspect of the agreement, instead of scattering them throughout the contract." Frank E. Cooper, *Writing in Law Practice* 277 (1963).

NOT THIS

Ex. 3

17.4 Restricted Payments. Prior to the earlier of (1) the Guaranty Covenant Termination Date and (2) the date that is six years after the Commencement Date, Lease Guarantor shall not directly or indirectly (i) declare or pay, or cause to be declared or paid, any dividend, distribution, any other direct or indirect payment or transfer (in each case, in cash, stock, other property, a combination thereof or otherwise) with respect to any of Lease Guarantor's capital stock or other equity interests, (ii) purchase or otherwise acquire or retire for value any of Lease Guarantor's capital stock or other equity interests, or (iii) engage in any other transaction with any direct or indirect holder of Lease Guarantor's capital stock or other equity interests which is similar in purpose or effect to those described above (collectively, a "Restricted Payment"), except that Lease Guarantor can execute (1) any of the transactions outlined above if: (a) Lease Guarantor's equity market capitalization after giving pro forma effect to such dividend, distribution, or other transaction is at least $5.5 billion, (b) the amount of such dividend, distribution, or other transaction (together with any and all other such dividends and distributions and other transactions made under this clause (1)(b) but excluding, for the avoidance of doubt, any dividends, distributions or other transactions to be made under clause (1)(c) or (2) below in such fiscal year), does not exceed, in the aggregate, (x) 25% of the net proceeds, up to a cap of $25 million in any fiscal year, from the disposition of assets by Lease Guarantor and its subsidiaries, plus (y) $100 million from other sources in any fiscal year or (c) Lease Guarantor's equity market capitalization after giving pro forma effect to such dividend, distribution, or other transaction is at least $4.5 billion and the aggregate amount of such dividends, distributions or other transactions made under this clause (c) (excluding, for the avoidance of doubt, any dividends, distributions or other transactions made under clause (1)(b) above or clause (2) below in such fiscal year) is less than or equal to $125 million in any fiscal year and is funded solely by asset sale proceeds or (2) any transaction described in clause (ii) above so long as the aggregate amount of all such transactions made under this clause (2) (excluding for the avoidance of doubt, any such transactions made from and after the Commencement Date under clause (1)(b) or (1)(c)above) is less than or equal to $199,500,000.00 (it being understood that from and after such time that the aggregate amount of all such transactions made from and after the Commencement Date under this clause (2) exceeds $199,500,000.00, no further transactions shall be permitted under this clause (2)). Prior to the earlier of (1) the Guaranty Covenant Termination Date and (2) the date that is six years after the Commencement Date, except as provided in clause (1)(a) or (1)(c) in the preceding sentence, any net proceeds from the disposition of assets by Lease Guarantor or its subsidiaries after the Commencement Date in excess of $25 million that are directly or indirectly distributed to, or otherwise received by, Lease Guarantor in any fiscal year shall not be used to fund any Restricted Payment.

Management and Lease Support Agreement

"Another chief defect in the writing of lawyers is the fact that they use circumlocution rather than straight, blunt speech. They prefer to go round a subject with their words rather than straight to it. In their use of language they prefer a steam shovel rather than a spade—and then they neglect to cast away the rubbish." Urban A. Lavery, *The Language of the Law*, 7 A.B.A.J. 277, 281 (1921).

BUT THIS

17.4 **Restricted Payments.** Except as provided in § 17.4(B), before the earlier of the Guaranty Covenant Termination Date or the date that is 6 years after the Commencement Date, Lease Guarantor will not directly or indirectly make a Restricted Payment.

(A) **Definition.** A Restricted Payment means the Lease Guarantor:

(1) declares or pays, or causes to be declared or paid, in cash, stock, or other property, any dividend, distribution, or any other direct or indirect payment or transfer respecting Lease Guarantor's capital stock or other equity interests;

(2) purchases or otherwise acquires or retires for value any of Lease Guarantor's capital stock or other equity interests; or

(3) engages in any other transaction with any direct or indirect holder of Lease Guarantor's capital stock or other equity interests that is similar in purpose or effect to those described above.

(B) **Payments permitted.** Except as provided in this § 17.4(B), a Restricted Payment must not be funded by net proceeds greater than $25 million from any disposition of assets by Lease Guarantor or its subsidiaries after the Commencement Date and directly or indirectly distributed to, or otherwise received by, Lease Guarantor in any fiscal year. Lease Guarantor may make Restricted Payments under any of the following independent circumstances:

(1) after estimating the effect of paying a Restricted Payment on Lease Guarantor's equity-market capitalization, capitalization is at least:

(a) $5.5 billion; or

(b) $4.5 billion if the Restricted Payment is funded solely by asset-sale proceeds and, in the current fiscal year, the aggregate amount paid under only this § 17.4(B)(1)(b) is less than or equal to $125 million.

(2) in the current fiscal year, the aggregate amounts of Restricted Payments under only this § 17.4(B)(2) do not exceed the sum of:

(a) 25% of the net proceeds from the disposition of assets by Lease Guarantor and its subsidiaries, up to a cap of $25 million; plus

(b) $100 million from other sources.

(3) Lease Guarantor's capital stock or other equity interests are acquired or retired for value and the aggregate amount of payments since the Commencement Date for transactions made under only this § 17.4(B)(3) is less than or equal to $199,500,000.

"Anyone who has had to grapple with the instructions on how to assemble a toy or flat pack furniture will need no reminding of the frustration which arises when these are written in a way that assumes the reader is an expert. Sometimes legal documents, especially old documents, are equally open to this criticism. These difficulties can usually be avoided by using simple language." Elmer Doonan, *Drafting* § 1.9, at 12–13 (Julie MacFarlane ed., 1995).

Enumerations

§ 85 Set off enumerated items as distinct subparts.

Avoid dense blocks of text by laying out numbered or lettered lists on separate lines when possible. Subdivide new paragraphs, subparagraphs, and items in the order in which they naturally occur, assigning each a new number or letter according to its position in the hierarchy. Of course, you'll be using rectilinear indents (see §§ 35–36).

More than any other simple technique, this one displays an orderly mind at work. But when you first carry it out, you'll probably lay bare some disordered thoughts. In itself, that's a big step toward editorial progress.

NOT THIS:	BUT THIS:
Ex. 1 5.2. The date of closing for the purchase of Shares pursuant to this paragraph 5.2 shall be held: (i) 7 days following the appointment of a personal representative for the estate of the deceased Shareholder; (ii) 7 days following the payout of the insurance proceeds, if any, on the death of a Shareholder; or (iii) at such other time as is mutually agreed upon by the estate of the deceased Shareholder and the purchaser, and in no event shall the closing occur more than 120 days following the date of death of the deceased Shareholder (the "Deceased Closing Date"). **Family-Shareholders Agreement from a financial-services company**	**5.2 Deceased closing date.** The closing date for purchasing Shares under this § 5.2 must be within 120 days after the Shareholder's death and, unless the Shareholder's estate and the purchaser agree otherwise, will be the earlier of: (A) 7 days after the appointment of a personal representative for the deceased shareholder's estate; or (B) 7 days after the payout of any insurance proceeds after a Shareholder's death.
Ex. 2 Franchisee shall at all times (a) maintain neat and orderly office(s) which contain adequate space for conducting the Franchised Business and which meet the standards set forth in the Manual; (b) maintain a separate bank account for the Franchised Business; (c) pay in a timely manner all operational expenses including, without limitation, payroll, payroll taxes, rent, utilities and telephone charges, and freights, supplies and other amounts due Black; and (d) maintain public liability insurance and errors and omissions insurance in the amounts specified in the Manual. **Franchise-License Agreement from a Fortune 500 company**	**7.2 Covenants.** Frazee will at all times: (A) maintain a neat and orderly office that contains adequate space for conducting the Franchised Business and meets the Manual's standards; (B) maintain a separate bank account for the Franchised Business; (C) pay on time all operational expenses, including payroll, payroll taxes, rent, utilities, telephone charges, and any freights, supplies, and other amounts owed to Black; and (D) maintain public-liability insurance and errors-and-omissions insurance in the amounts specified in the Manual.

NOT THIS:	BUT THIS:
Ex. 3 4.13 Alzheimer's Disease and Dementias. If you develop Alzheimer's disease or any other dementia while this Agreement is in effect, this Agreement will continue in force, provided that The Provider determines that (1) your condition does not result in conduct that is detrimental to the health, safety, or well-being of you or others at the Community or cause an unreasonable and ongoing disturbance at the Community; (2) your care needs are consistent with care routinely furnished by The Provider; (3) your condition can be cared for at the Community efficiently, lawfully and in a manner that protects your and others' health, safety and well-being; and (4) your condition can be cared for by The Provider without imposing an undue burden on The Provider's staff, facilities, or other resources. **Residence and Care Agreement from a major law firm**	**4.13 Alzheimer's disease and other dementias.** If you develop Alzheimer's disease or any other dementia while this Agreement is in effect, this Agreement will continue in effect if we determine that: (A) your condition does not result in conduct that: (1) is detrimental to the health, safety, or well-being of you or others at the Community; or (2) causes an unreasonable and ongoing disturbance at the Community; (B) your care needs are consistent with the type of care we routinely furnish; and (C) your condition can be cared for: (1) at the Community efficiently, lawfully, and in a manner that protects your and others' health, safety, and well-being; and (2) without imposing an undue burden on our staff, facilities, or other resources.

"There are usually three good reasons for enumerating: reference identification, hierarchy, and sequence. You may want to refer to a specific item later in the text or possibly while discussing it with someone over the telephone. In either case it will be helpful to refer to the item by its specific identifier rather than by calling it 'the third item from the top.' . . . A format combining enumeration and indentation is usually best." Ernst Jacobi, *Writing at Work: Dos, Don'ts, and How Tos* 126 (1976).

<table>
<tr><th>NOT THIS:</th><th>BUT THIS:</th></tr>
<tr><td>Ex. 4
Whenever any cash dividend or other cash distribution or distribution other than cash is made, or whenever rights shall be issued with respect to the deposited securities, or whenever for any reason the depositary causes a change in the number of Techtronic shares that are represented by each Techtronic ADS, or whenever the depositary receives notice of any meeting of holders of Techtronic shares or other deposited securities, or whenever reasonably requested by Techtronic, holders of Techtronic shares will fix a record date (which shall be as near as practicable to any corresponding record date set by Techtronic) (a) for the determination of the owners who will be (i) entitled to receive such dividend, distribution or rights, or the net proceeds of the sale thereof, or (ii) entitled to give instructions for the exercise of voting rights at any such meeting, or (b) on or after which each Techtronic ADS will represent the changed number of Techtronic shares, all subject to the provisions of the Deposit Agreement.
Securities-Sales Agreement</td><td>7.4 Record dates.
(A) Triggering events. The holders of Techtronic shares will fix a record date if:
(1) a cash dividend or other cash or noncash distribution is made;
(2) Techtronic issues rights in the deposited securities;
(3) the depositary for any reason causes a change in the number of Techtronic shares that are represented by each Techtronic ADS;
(4) the depositary receives notice of any meeting of holders of Techtronic shares or other deposited securities; or
(5) Techtronic reasonably requests that the holders fix a record date.
(B) Corresponding record date. If Techtronic sets a corresponding record date, the record date set by the holders must be as near as practicable to that date.
(C) Purposes. The record date may serve either or both of the purposes set forth below.
(1) On the record date, it will be determined which owners are entitled to:
(a) receive a dividend, distribution, or right;
(b) receive the net proceeds of a sale of a dividend, distribution, or right; or
(c) give instructions for exercising voting rights at a meeting of holders of Techtronic shares or other deposited securities.
(2) On or after the record date, Techtronic ADS will announce the changed number of Techtronic shares, all subject to the provisions of the Deposit Agreement.</td></tr>
</table>

> "Why write lengthy narrative when you can pull out main points and list them? Itemizing helps you cut down on words and save readers' time. Consider it for major sections." Jerome H. Perlmutter, *A Practical Guide to Effective Writing* 78 (1965).

§ 86 To enhance readability, consider using an appositive to foreshadow an enumeration.

When introducing an enumeration, consider the utility of an appositive such as *the following* to introduce the list. Though not required, this language is sometimes helpful.

NOT THIS:	BUT THIS:
Ex. 1 The Manual may address, among other subjects, the layout, color schemes, equipment, fixtures, furnishings and décor of an office; the policies and procedures which Franchisee must follow in dealing with customers; the manner in which the business and the services which it offers is to be conducted; and training, advertising and marketing programs. **Franchise-License Agreement** Note the grammatical discord here: plural subject but singular verb (cured in the revision).	**10.1 Manual.** The Manual may address, among other things, the following: (A) an office's layout, color scheme, equipment, fixtures, furnishings, and decor; (B) the policies and procedures that the Franchisee must follow in dealing with customers; (C) the manner in which the business and the services that it offers are to be conducted; and (D) training, advertising, and marketing programs.
Ex. 2 The Player's employment during any year covered by this contract shall include attendance at any training camp, playing the games scheduled for the Club's team during any scheduled season of the Association, playing exhibition games scheduled by the Club during and prior to any scheduled season, playing (if invited to participate) in any of the Association's All-Star Games and attending every event (including, but not limited to, the All-Star Game show and/or banquet) conducted in association with such All-Star Games, and playing the playoff games subsequent to any schedule season. **Player Contract for a professional basketball player**	**1.2 Game participation.** During each year covered by this contract, Larson will participate in all the following: (A) training camps; (B) exhibition games before and during the season; (C) scheduled season games; (D) playoff games after the scheduled season; and (E) if invited to participate, the Association's All-Star Games and associated events, including the All-Star Game show and banquet.

"A clear and definite mind is a rarity; an artist in the use of words is as great a rarity." Arthur L. Corbin, *Corbin on Contracts* § 534, at 491–92 (1952).

NOT THIS:	BUT THIS:
Ex. 3 15. TERMINATION: Buyer may terminate all or any portion of this order at any time by giving notice to Seller. In the event of such termination, Buyer's liability shall be the lesser of: (a) a reasonable price for raw materials, components, work in progress, and any finished units on hand; or (b) the contract price per finished unit, after giving effect to any discount Buyer would otherwise be entitled to. In the event of termination of any separate services specifically ordered, liability shall be the lesser of: (a) a reasonable price for the services rendered prior to termination; or (b) the contract price for services. If any hourly or other time-based rate for services is specified in this purchase order, such rate shall be used in determining a reasonable price. Upon receipt of a termination notice, Buyer shall, unless otherwise directed, cease work and follow Seller's directions as to disposal of work in progress and finished goods. THE FOREGOING STATES BUYER'S ENTIRE LIABILITY FOR TERMINATION. This illogically states that the Buyer is making the goods that the Buyer is purchasing. See § 9. **Long-Form Purchase Order from Robert A. Feldman & Raymond T. Nimmer, *Drafting Effective Contracts: A Practitioner's Guide*, Form 5-2, at 5-200 (2d ed. 2010)**	**15.1 Termination.** Calhoun may terminate all or part of this order at any time by giving notice to Stein. Unless directed otherwise, upon receipt of the notice Stein will stop work and follow Calhoun's directions for disposing of work in progress and finished goods. Note that the ability to terminate at any time without notice might well run afoul of the rule against illusory promises: "If the provision is read as giving the promisor the power to terminate at any time at will, without more, the promise will be held to be illusory. . . . Even if a promisor has a power to terminate at will, the promise will not be held to be illusory if its exercise is conditioned on the occurrence of events beyond the promisor's control."[1] **15.2 Liability.** Calhoun's liability for termination is limited as follows: (A) **General termination.** If all or part of this order is terminated, Calhoun's liability will be the lesser of: (1) a reasonable price for raw materials, components, work in progress, and any finished units on hand; (2) the contract price per finished unit, after giving effect to any discount that Calhoun would otherwise be entitled to. (B) **Termination of specific service.** If a specifically ordered separate service is terminated, Calhoun's liability will be the lesser of: (1) a reasonable price for the services rendered before termination; (2) the contract price for the services. (C) **Hourly or time-based rates.** If the purchase order specifies an hourly or other time-based rate for services, that rate must be used to determine a reasonable price.

"A majority of the readers of your draft will be interested in your broadly applicable proposition. Fewer will be interested in the narrowly applicable. Be kind to both groups, but majority first." Robert E. Keeton, *Guidelines for Drafting, Editing, and Interpreting* § 3.2(a) cmt. a., at 34 (2002).

1 E. Allan Farnsworth, *Contracts* § 2.14, at 79–80 (4th ed. 2004).

§ 87 Put enumerated items in parallel form.

When stating more than one requirement—and the requirements can be stated in parallel form—put them in a grammatically matching format. Grammatical parallelism isn't just a tenet of grammar; it makes for instant understanding. By contrast, unparallel phrasing makes for miscues and double takes. Here's the key: when you have a list of items, make sure that each one matches the others grammatically—typically noun–noun–noun or verb–verb–verb. Don't mix and match.

NOT THIS:	BUT THIS:
Ex. 1 5.5 **Carpet Cleaning.** The Seller shall (a) cause all carpeting in the House to be professionally cleaned before the Closing Date; (b) pay the cost of the cleaning before the Closing Date; (c) the cost of such cleaning shall not exceed $500. **House-Purchase Agreement from a realty company**	5.5 **Carpet cleaning.** Before the Closing Date, the Seller will: (a) arrange to have all carpeting in the House professionally cleaned for $500 or less; and (b) pay the cost of the cleaning.
Ex. 2 9. Indemnities and Limitations of Liability . . . B. Supplier will indemnify and hold harmless[1] Gadgets Inc. Indemnified Parties and Customers against Damages arising from claims by third parties resulting from an act or omission of the Supplier, including claims that Products are: (i) defective; (ii) negligently designed, marked, marketed or manufactured; or (iii) fail to comply with any applicable law or industry standard. **Standard Agreement for Products and Services from a major technology company**	**9. Indemnities and Limitations of Liability.** . . . (B) **Indemnity.** Supplier will indemnify Gadgets Inc. Indemnified Parties and Customers against Damages arising from claims by third parties resulting from Supplier's act or omission, including claims that Products: (1) are defective; (2) are negligently designed, marked, marketed, or manufactured; or (3) fail to comply with an applicable law or industry standard.

Note the nonparallel list: (i) is an adjective, (ii) is a string of participles, and (iii) is an active verb and predicate.

List items become three complete predicates for the shared subject *Products.*

"In drafting, a permanent record is made not only of the transaction involved but also of the lawyer's skill in legal drafting." Elmer Doonan, *Drafting* § 1.3, at 5–6 (Julie MacFarlane ed., 1995).

1 For more on the verbose *indemnify and hold harmless* and the fascinating story of its historical development as well as the majority and minority rules around the U.S., see *Garner's Dictionary of Legal Usage* 443–45 (Oxford Univ. Press, 3d ed. 2011).

NOT THIS:	BUT THIS:
Ex. 3 9. **<u>Transfer of User Personal Data out of the EU.</u>** 9.1 Hatch Inc. may transfer User Personal Data to countries outside the European Union only to the extent that: 9.1.1 User Personal Data is transferred to a territory outside the European Union on terms substantially in accordance with the European Union standard contractual clauses for the transfer of Personal Data to processors established in third countries under Directive; or 9.1.2 that the transfer of User Personal Data does not put any member of the Customer Group in breach of its obligations under Applicable Privacy Law. **Data-Protection Terms from a major communications company**	**9. Transfer of User Personal Data out of the European Union.** **9.1** Hatch Inc. may transfer User Personal Data to countries outside the European Union only to the extent that the transfer: (A) is to a territory outside the European Union on terms substantially in accordance with the European Union standard contractual clauses for the transfer of Personal Data to processors established in third countries under Directive; or (B) does not put any member of the Customer Group in breach of its obligations under Applicable Privacy Law.

Notice the "that that" syntax error from 9.1 to 9.1.2.

"One signal that the document may have been prepared without an outline is provisions that do not easily fit within the document because they are in a different drafting style and appear to have arrived in the document on a cut-and-paste basis. On further examination it may be found that these provisions have not been properly cross-referenced or considered in relation to other provisions in the document so that they overlap, repeat, or contradict other provisions." Elmer Doonan, *Drafting* § 2.6.1, at 36 (Julie MacFarland ed., 1995).

§ 88 Observe the principle of economical parallelism.

To eliminate repetition and verbiage in enumerations, place terms shared by each of the enumerated items in the lead-in to the list. In each of the left-hand columns below, notice the repetitious language—the verbiage—that appears but once in the revised versions. By creating parallel vertical lists in which the lead-in language contains what would otherwise be repeated, we've economized words.

NOT THIS:	BUT THIS:
Ex. 1 PRIVACY POLICY AND DISCLOSURES In certain circumstances we may disclose information about you to third parties if we determine, in our sole discretion, such disclosure is necessary (a) to protect Vacation Inc.'s systems, assets, employees, members and customers; (b) to ensure the integrity and operation of Vacation Inc.'s business and systems; or (c) to comply with legitimate and enforceable governmental requests, subpoenas or court orders. **Website Terms, Conditions and Notices from a major travel agency**	4. **Privacy Policy and Disclosures.** We may disclose information about you to third parties if we determine that disclosure is necessary for us to: (A) protect our systems, assets, employees, members, and customers; (B) ensure the integrity and operation of our business and systems; or (C) comply with a legitimate and enforceable government request, subpoena, or court order.
Ex. 2 (b) The Club may terminate this contract upon written notice to the Player if the Player shall do any of the following: (1) at any time, fail, refuse or neglect to conform his personal conduct to standards of good citizenship; or (2) at any time, fail, in the sole opinion of the Club's management, to exhibit sufficient skill or competitive ability to qualify to continue as a member of the Club's team; or (3) at any time, fail, refuse or neglect to render his services hereunder or in any other manner materially breached this contract. **Professional Basketball Player Contract**	(B) **Termination.** Upon written notice to Alejandro, the Club may terminate this contract if Alejandro at any time: (1) fails, refuses, or neglects to conform his personal conduct to standards of good citizenship; (2) fails—in the sole opinion of the Club's management—to exhibit sufficient skill or competitive ability to qualify as a continuing member of the Club's team; (3) fails, refuses, or neglects to perform his services under this contract; or (4) materially breaches this contract in any other way.

> "Sir Frederick Pollock is right when he says that not even the draftsman of an ordinary lease can produce a really good work 'unless he has a share of artistic feeling in the eminent sense, and takes a certain artistic pride in the quality of his workmanship apart from the reward he will get for it.'" Lord Macmillan, *Law and Other Things* 148–49 (1938).

NOT THIS:	BUT THIS:
Ex. 3 **2.1 Use of Proprietary Information.** All Proprietary Information disclosed by Owner to Recipient during the term of this Agreement must be retained in confidence by Recipient. Recipient shall use the Proprietary Information for the purposes authorized by the Agreement and for no other purpose. Recipient shall not disclose the Proprietary Information (a) to any employee, contractor or representative of Recipient unless disclosure to that person is reasonably related to accomplishing the objective of this Agreement; or (b) to any third party. Recipient shall hold the Proprietary Information in the strictest confidence and take all actions necessary to protect it against any unauthorized disclosure, publication, or use. **Nondisclosure & Intellectual-Property-Protection Agreement Form from a major law firm**	**2.1 Using Proprietary Information.** For Proprietary Information that the Owner discloses to the Recipient during the term of this Agreement, the Recipient must: (A) hold it in the strictest confidence; (B) protect it against unauthorized disclosure, publication, or use; (C) use it only for the purposes authorized by this Agreement; (D) not disclose it to any of its employees, contractors, or representatives unless that disclosure reasonably relates to furthering the Agreement's objective. *Although the original was not necessarily unparallel, the revision is much easier to read with* must *foreshadowing the parallel clauses that follow it.*
Ex. 4 **2. Grant of Franchise** Franchisee may provide the services of the Franchised Business at Approved Locations for any person or firm residing within or outside the Franchise Territory, and may advertise or promote the Franchised Business in media originating within the Franchise Territory, the range of which extends outside the Franchise Territory. Franchisee shall not advertise or promote the Franchised Business in media originating outside the Franchise Territory unless authorized by Burdick in writing to do so. Franchisee shall not use the Licensed Marks in any domain name, operate an Internet web site for the Franchised Business, or promote the Franchised Business on any Internet web site, unless authorized by Burdick in writing to do so. Franchisee shall not advertise or promote the Franchised Business by unsolicited e-mail advertising. *Note that the third prohibition (and only the third) omits* advertise. **Franchise-License Agreement from a Fortune 500 company**	**2. Grant of Franchise.** **2.1 Providing services.** Granite may provide the services of the Franchised Business at Approved Locations for a person or firm residing within or outside the Franchise Territory. **2.2 Media advertising.** Except as limited in this paragraph and § 2.3, Granite may advertise or promote the Franchised Business in media originating within the Franchise Territory, even if the media extends outside the Franchise Territory. Unless authorized by Burdick in writing, Granite will not advertise or promote the Franchised Business: (A) in media originating outside the Franchise Territory; (B) on any Internet website; or (C) by unsolicited e-mail. **2.3 Internet presence.** Unless authorized by Burdick in writing, Granite will not operate an Internet website for the Franchised Business or use the Licensed Marks in any domain name.

NOT THIS:	BUT THIS:
Ex. 5 6.1 Independent Contractor. Consultant understands and agrees that Consultant is serving as an independent contractor of [*name of company*], and that Consultant is not an employee of [*name of company*]. Consultant further understands and agrees that [*name of company*] will not withhold any income or other taxes from the Fees paid to Consultant, and that Consultant is responsible for paying Consultant's own income, social security, Medicare, and other applicable taxes. Consultant further understands and agrees that Consultant will not have any right to the benefits under, or rights and privileges to participate in, [*name of company*]'s employee benefit plans (all of which are made available only to [*name of company*] employees). Consultant further agrees that any future reclassification of Consultant from independent contractor to employee status by a taxing authority will not confer upon Consultant eligibility for any retroactive or prospective [*name of company*] benefits. **Consulting-Services Fee Agreement from 3 Nancy Saint-Paul, Texas Legal Practice Forms 3d *Independent Contractor Agreements* § 50:6, at 728–29 (2016)**	**6. Independent Contractor.** **6.1 Status.** You are an independent contractor, not an employee. **6.2 Taxes.** We will not withhold any taxes from your fees. You must pay all applicable taxes, including income, social-security, Medicare, and other taxes. **6.3 No employee benefits.** As an independent contractor, you cannot participate in our employee-benefit plans. If a taxing authority changes your status from independent contractor to employee, you will not be eligible for any retroactive or prospective benefits under our employee-benefit plans.

Note that the final sentence omits the word *understands*.

The repetitive phrase *understands and agrees that* can be eliminated altogether in the rewrite. See §§ 17 and 49.

"It is not sufficient for you to be satisfied that you think you understand what you have written. It is important that the message be gotten across clearly and easily, so that whoever reads it will react with the thought process it was your design to produce."
Bernard H. Goldstein, *Writing to Be Understood*, Prac. Law., Mar. 1969, at 34, 35.

NOT THIS:	BUT THIS:
Ex. 6 1. (a) Except as provided in Paragraphs 1(d) and 3 of this Agreement, all property owned by each of the Parties before the effective date of this Agreement and any property acquired by any Party, regardless of the time of acquisition, shall remain the separately-owned property of that Party. (b) Except as provided in Paragraphs 1(d) and 3 of this Agreement, all property acquired by gift, bequest, devise, or descent, and the rents, issues, and profits thereof, shall be the separately-owned property of the acquiring party. (c) Except as provided in Paragraphs 1(d) and 3 of this Agreement, all earnings, income, salaries, and commissions generated by each of the Parties shall remain the separately-owned property of the Party who generated or acquired the same. (d) In the event that the Parties jointly purchase household furnishings and furniture pursuant to Paragraph 3 of this Agreement, the same shall be the jointly-owned property of the Parties as provided in Paragraph 3, notwithstanding any language to the contrary contained in Paragraphs 1(a) through 1(c) of this Agreement. **Rental-Sharing Agreement from 22 *Texas Transaction Guide: Legal Forms* § 94A.203[2] (Herbert S. Kendrick & John J. Kendrick Jr. eds., 2017)**	1. **Separate Property.** Except as provided in §§ 2 and 3 of this Agreement: (A) property owned by a Party before the effective date of this Agreement and property acquired by a Party, regardless of the time of acquisition, remain that Party's separately owned property; (B) property acquired by gift, bequest, devise, or descent, and the rents, issues, and profits from that property, are the acquiring Party's separately owned property; and (C) all earnings, income, salaries, and commissions generated by each Party remain the separately owned property of the Party who generated or acquired them. 2. **Jointly Purchased Household Items.** If the Parties jointly purchase household furnishings and furniture under § 3, the purchases will be the Parties' jointly owned property despite language to the contrary in § 1 of this Agreement.

Note the incorrect hyphens in *separately owned property* and *jointly owned property*. See § 133.

§ 89 Avoid unnumbered dangling flush text.

Unnumbered dangling sections—that is, flush-left text after an enumeration—are uncitable and therefore undesirable. Such text can't easily be cited because it has no numbered designation. One way to avoid this problem is to always put enumerations at the end of a sentence—not at the beginning or in the middle. Each subpart must be assigned a letter or number.

There is a notorious instance of unnumbered dangling flush text—too long to print here—in the Bankruptcy Code. It is contemptuously known in the field as "the hanging paragraph." To avoid its scandal, avert your eyes from 11 U.S.C. § 1325(a)(9).

<table>
<tr><th>NOT THIS:</th><th>BUT THIS:</th></tr>
<tr><td>Ex. 1

Owner will reimburse Contractor for the following costs of Work:
2.1 The costs for employees working at the site in direct employ of the Contractor in the performance of the work. Owner agrees to pay Contractor for Contractor's crew working at the site according to Contractor's standard labor rates.
Contractor reserves the right to employ additional workers for the Work as reasonably necessary to meet scheduling requirements. Owner reserves the right to pay only for overtime work that it approves, which approval will not be unreasonably withheld.
2.2 Cost of all materials, equipment, machinery and appliances furnished and incorporated in the Work, including costs of transportation and storage thereof.
Construction-Contract Form from a major law firm

Note the unnumbered two-sentence paragraph that floats in the middle of this section.</td><td>2. Costs.
2.1 Reimbursement. Keeland will reimburse Stair for the following:
(A) wages for Stair's site employees at Stair's standard labor rate; and
(B) materials, equipment, machinery, and appliances supplied and used for the Work, including their transportation and storage.
2.2 Additional workers. Stair may employ additional workers for the Work as reasonably necessary to meet scheduling requirements.
2.3 Overtime. Keeland will pay for overtime work if Keeland approves it. Approval must not be unreasonably withheld.</td></tr>
</table>

> "Occasionally, when you try to convert from legalese to plain language, someone will come forward and assert that you made a mistake. You missed something in translation. You inadvertently changed the substance. . . . But the risk is worth it, and writers should not be dissuaded. Otherwise, the legal profession will never start to level the mountain of bad forms and models that we have created. We'll be stuck with the enormous inefficiencies of traditional style and the frustration it causes. Change is hard, but change has to come." Joseph Kimble, *Lifting the Fog of Legalese* 37–38 (2006).

NOT THIS:	BUT THIS:
Ex. 2 18.1 Any controversy arising under or related to this Agreement and any disputed claim by either party against the other under this Agreement — excluding any dispute relating to the copyright validity or infringement arising under this Agreement — shall be settled by arbitration in accordance with the Licensing Agreement Arbitration Rules of the American Arbitration Association. Upon request of either party, arbitration will be by: (a) A third party arbitrator mutually agreed upon in writing by LICENSEE and UNIVERSITY within thirty (30) days of such arbitration request; or (b) An arbitrator named by the American Arbitration Association. Unnumbered dangling flush text. Judgment upon the award rendered by the Arbitrator shall be final and may be entered in any court having competent jurisdiction. **License Agreement from a major law firm**	**18.1 Dispute resolution.** (A) **Arbitration.** A controversy arising from or related to this Agreement—except a dispute about copyright validity or infringement—must be settled by arbitration according to the Licensing Agreement Arbitration Rules of the American Arbitration Association. (B) **Selection.** The arbitrator may be either: (1) a third party approved in writing by the Licensee and the University within 30 days after the arbitration request; or (2) an arbitrator named by the American Arbitration Association. (C) **Finality.** The arbitrator's award is final. A court having jurisdiction may enter judgment on the award.

"[L]egal drafters are blindly overconfident. They believe that because their forms have been around a long time, the forms must be tried and true—a grossly exaggerated notion." Joseph Kimble, *Lifting the Fog of Legalese* 45 (2006).

Ex. 3

NOT THIS:	BUT THIS:
5. TERMINATION This Agreement may be terminated by Employer upon the occurrence of any of the following events: (a) the death of Employee; (b) at Employer's option, Employee's permanent disability. Employer's option shall be exercised in writing, delivered to Employee and shall be effective on delivery; (c) Employee's failure to comply with one of the following specified material terms or conditions: [*Description of material terms and conditions*]; and/or (d) the operation of employer's business in such a manner as to show an aggregate net income of $[*dollar amount of aggregate net income*] for [*number of months*] consecutive months in excess of [*percentage of net sales*]% of net sales for the months. Upon termination for any of the foregoing causes, Employee shall be entitled to receive only the compensation accrued but unpaid as of the date of termination and shall not be entitled to additional compensation except as expressly provided in this Agreement. If Employee dies during the term of the employment, Employer shall pay to the estate of Employee the compensation which would otherwise be payable to Employee up to the end of the month in which Employee's death occurs. **Corporate-Manager Contract from 3 Nancy Saint-Paul, Texas Legal Practice Forms 3d *Employment Agreements* § 49:7 (2016)**	**5. Termination.** **5.1 Employer's option to terminate.** The Employer may terminate this Agreement if: (A) the Employee dies; (B) the Employee becomes permanently disabled, as determined by the Employer (upon the Employer's exercise of this option by delivery to Employee of its written intent to do so); (C) the Employee fails to comply with one of the following specified material terms or conditions: [*description of material terms*]; or (D) the Employer's business has, over [*number of months*] consecutive months, an aggregate net income of $__________, and the aggregate exceeds _____% of net sales for those months. **5.2 Employee's rights upon termination under § 5.1.** Upon termination under § 5.1, the Employee will receive the accrued compensation unpaid as of the termination date but no additional compensation unless this Agreement expressly provides otherwise. If the Employee dies during the term of the employment, the Employer will pay the Employee's estate the compensation that would otherwise be payable to the Employee up to the end of the month in which the Employee dies.

Note the sentence-ending period within (b) despite the need for continuous syntax.

This paragraph beginning with *Upon* amounts to unnumbered dangling text, even if it's not quite "flush." Remember that every paragraph in a contract ought to be assigned a number or letter.

"Boilerplate need not and should not remain frozen while significant improvement is possible. A provision may have to go through many generations of change before it matures into a reliable, up-to-date module of prefabricated law." Reed Dickerson, *Electronic Aids to the Drafting of Legal Instruments*, 1 Rutgers J. Computers & L. 75, 76 (1970).

NOT THIS:

Ex. 4

In the event that by reason of any change in applicable law or regulation or in the interpretation thereof by any governmental authority charged with the administration, application or interpretation thereof, or by reason of any requirement or directive (whether or not having the force of law) of any governmental authority, occurring after the date hereof:

(a) the Bank should, with respect to the Agreement be subject to any tax, levy, impost, charge, fee, duty, deduction, or withholding of any kind whatsoever (other than any change which affects solely the taxation of the total income of the Bank), or

(b) any change should occur in the taxation of the Bank with respect to the principal or interest payable under the Agreement (other than any change which affects solely the taxation of the total income of the Bank), or

(c) any reserve requirements should be imposed on the commitments to lend;

and if any of the above-mentioned measures should result in an increase in the cost to the Bank of making or maintaining its Advances or commitments to lend hereunder or a reduction in the amount of principal or interest received or receivable by the Bank in respect thereof, then upon notification and demand being made by the Bank for such additional cost or reduction, the Borrower shall pay to the Bank, upon demand being made by the Bank, such additional cost or reduction in rate of return; *provided, however, that* the Borrower shall not be responsible for any such cost or reduction that may accrue to the Bank with respect to the period between the occurrence of the event which gave rise to such cost or reduction and the date on which notification is given by the Bank to the Borrower.

Unnumbered dangling flush text.

For more on *provided, however, that*, see § 116.

Loan Application from a major banking institution

BUT THIS:

8.1 Rate adjustments.

(A) **The Borrower's obligations.** The Borrower must, on demand, pay the Bank additional costs or receive reductions in rates of return if both the following conditions are met:

(1) a law or a government directive, either literally or as applied, changes in a way that:

(a) increases the Bank's costs in making or maintaining its Advances or lending commitments; or

(b) reduces the principal or interest receivable by the Bank; and

(2) any of the following occurs:

(a) the Bank becomes—with respect to this Agreement—subject to a tax, levy, impost, charge, fee, duty, deduction, or withholding of any kind (other than a change that affects only the tax on the Bank's total income);

(b) a change occurs in the Bank's taxes with respect to the principal or interest payable under this Agreement (other than a change that affects solely the tax on the Bank's total income); or

(c) a reserve requirement is imposed on the commitments to lend.

(B) **Exceptions to Borrower's obligations.** The Borrower is not responsible for a cost or reduction that accrues to the Bank between the triggering event and the date when the Bank gives the Borrower notice.

§ 90 Use bullets when desirable.

Use bullets to ease the reading of a list, but only if no citation to an individual item is likely. "Dangling" text (see § 89) is unobjectionable after a list of bulleted items because the numbering sequence hasn't been broken. Although you should use bullets sparingly in contracts, they do make individual items stand out more than when those same items are in a long series inside a block of text.

Bullet dots are extraordinarily useful for guiding the reader's eye from one item to the next in a list. But it's not enough simply to decide that you're going to use bullets. You need to use them well. Here are some guidelines:

- End your introduction to the bulleted list with a colon. It serves as a tether for all the items listed.
- Ensure that the size of your bullets is proportional to the size of your type. You don't want overpowering bullets; the best bullets are typically just a bit smaller than a lowercase "o" filled in with ink.
- Adjust your tab settings so that you'll have a small tab between the bullet and the text. Space the tabs so that they look about the way you see them throughout this book—about .15 inch evenly across the line, with a larger space for a paragraph indent.
- Use a hanging indent (see § 35). That is, don't allow the text to wrap under the bullet; instead, leave the bullet hanging out to the left. If you don't already know the word-processing function for this, you'll need to learn it.
- Single-space within bulleted items. Try to keep your bullet-list items fairly short.
- Keep your items grammatically parallel (see § 87).
- Resist the temptation to experiment with computer-generated boxes, arrows, check marks, and other eye-catchers—the bullet is the silver bullet.

<table>
<tr><th>NOT THIS:</th><th>BUT THIS:</th></tr>
<tr><td>Ex. 1
2. PRICING: Pricing is inclusive of all applicable taxes, freight, packaging, insurance, handling and all other charges, whether similar or dissimilar, unless otherwise indicated on the face of this purchase order.
Purchase Order from Robert A. Feldman & Raymond T. Nimmer, Drafting Effective Contracts: A Practitioner's Guide, Form 5-2, at 5-197 (2d ed. 2010)</td><td>2. Pricing. Unless otherwise noted on the purchase order, pricing includes all applicable:
• taxes;
• freight;
• packaging;
• insurance;
• handling; and
• other charges.</td></tr>
<tr><td>Ex. 2
h) Given the new construction status of this property, the following items are required for submission. All FF&E and finishes require approval of CHI.
Color boards and one (1) set of complete Interior Design specifications are to be submitted for review.
Color boards submitted do not need to be framed but should be on a large, foam-core presentation board with all finishes, furniture, and fixtures identified. These boards will be returned.
Submittal requirements include detailed specifications for all guest rooms and public areas: Artwork, Bed Base/Frame, Bed Set, Bedspreads, Carpet, Carpet Pad, Casegoods, Cove Base, Floor Tile, Interior Signage, Lighting, Mirrors.
Subcontract Agreement</td><td>1.8 Items you must submit. Because the property is new construction, you must submit the items listed below. All FF&E and finishes require CHI approval:
(A) Color boards. Color boards do not need to be framed but should be on large, foam-core presentation boards with all finishes, furniture, and fixtures identified (these boards will be returned); and
(B) Interior-Design specifications. One set of complete Interior-Design specifications must detail the specifications for all the following in guest rooms and public areas:
• artwork;
• bed base/frame;
• bed set;
• bedspreads;
• carpet;
• carpet pad;
• case goods;
• cove base;
• floor tile;
• interior signage;
• lighting; and
• mirrors.</td></tr>
</table>

NOT THIS:	BUT THIS:
Ex. 3 **ARTICLE 4 CONTRACT SUM** 4.1 The Buyer shall pay the Seller the total sum of four hundred thousand dollars ($400,000) subject to additions and deductions as provided in the Contract Document. 4.2 Unit price includes the following: a. Bathroom walls will be cultured marble. b. Toilets will not be more than $100 each. c. Kitchen and bathroom floor will be natural marble no more than $5 a square foot. d. Kitchen counter top will be ready-made bullnose, made in China. e. Cabinets will be oak. Kitchen and bathroom cabinets provided only. f. All water faucets will not be more than $100 each. g. Contractor will provide a stove, dishwasher, and central air-conditioning only. h. Stair railing will be oak and steps will be carpeted. i. Wall-to-wall carpets will not exceed $15 a yard. 4.3 The following items are excluded from unit price. If buyer wants any additional items, he/she does so at his/her expense. Any difference will be paid to the Contractor. a. Any chandeliers b. Jacuzzi c. Extra cabinets (laundry, storage, garage, etc.) d. Fans e. Washer/Dryer f. Fridge g. Microwave Oven **Home Sale and Construction Agreement**	**4. Contract Sum.** 4.1 **Total contract price.** The Buyer will pay the Seller $400,000, subject to additions and deductions as provided in the Contract Document. 4.2 **Items included in unit price.** The unit price includes the following items: (A) bathroom walls made of cultured marble; (B) toilets costing at most $100 each; (C) kitchen and bathroom floors made of natural marble and costing at most $5 a square foot; (D) kitchen countertops of ready-made bullnose (made in China); (E) kitchen and bathroom cabinets made of oak; (F) water faucets costing at most $100 each; (G) stove and dishwasher provided by the Contractor; (H) central air-conditioning provided by the Contractor; (I) stairs with oak railing and carpeted steps; and (J) wall-to-wall carpet costing at most $15 a yard. 4.3 **Items not included in price.** If the Buyer wants an item in addition to those listed in § 4.2, the Buyer will bear the added expense and pay it to the Contractor. The following items are specifically excluded from the unit price: • chandeliers; • Jacuzzi; • extra cabinets (laundry, storage, garage, etc.); • fans; • washer/dryer; • refrigerator; and • microwave oven. *The items in § 4.2 are not bulleted because they might be cited individually.* *The items in § 4.3 are unlikely to be cited individually, so they are more appropriate for a bulleted list.*

> "While two revisions may be enough for an opinion, and three or four for a brief, the preparation of a contract may require ten or twelve revisions." Frank E. Cooper, *Writing in Law Practice* 271 (1963).

NOT THIS:

Ex. 4

XII Apprenticeship

SECTION 1. The parties signatory hereto agree to establish a Joint Apprenticeship Committee in accordance with the provisions of the Iron Workers Apprenticeship and Training Standards, as contained in Section 1, Article XIII of the International Constitution. Said Committee shall formulate and operate an Apprenticeship Program in the local area in conformity with said standards.

(a) Apprentices shall be paid no less than the percentage of the journeymen rate as listed below.

Probationary Period shall be the first one thousand hours.

(b) When an Apprentice is found to be accepting more than his/her specified wage rate, he/she shall be subject to Disciplinary Action by the Joint Apprentice Committee.

(c) Apprentices who receive credit for previous experience in the Trade shall be paid, upon entrance, the wage rate of the period to which such credit advances them.

(d) Apprentices who complete last period and who fail to pass the required journeymen examination may elect to serve another six months, for which they shall be paid the regular last period rate.

1st period	1st Year	60%
2nd period	2nd Year	70%
3rd period		75%
4th period	3rd Year	80%
5th period		85%
6th period		90%

Collective-Bargaining Agreement

BUT THIS:

12. Apprenticeship.

12.1 Joint Apprenticeship Committee. The parties will establish a Joint Apprenticeship Committee under the Iron Workers Apprenticeship and Training Standards in art. XIII, § 1, of the International Constitution. This Committee will formulate and operate an Apprenticeship Program in the local area conforming to the standards and subject to these specifications:

(A) **Probation.** The Probationary Period for an Apprentice is the first 1,000 hours of training.

(B) **Base wages.** An Apprentice must be paid no less than the percentage of the journeyman rate as listed below:

- 1st period 1st year 60%
- 2nd period 2nd year 70%
- 3rd period 75%
- 4th period 3rd year 80%
- 5th period 85%
- 6th period 90%

Bullets are clearer here than numbers because the listed items are already in ascending order.

(C) **Previous experience.** An Apprentice who receives credit for previous experience in the Trade must be paid, upon entrance, the wage rate of the period to which the credit advances them.

(D) **No higher rate allowed.** An Apprentice who accepts more than the specified wage rate will be subject to Disciplinary Action by the Joint Apprentice Committee.

(E) **Failure to make journeyman.** An Apprentice who completes the last period and who fails to pass the required journeyman examination may elect to serve another 6 months and will be paid the regular last-period rate.

§ 91 Use lowercase at the outset of subparts that are technically continuations of the sentence.

As long as the syntax of a sentence flows from one subpart into the next, without a sentence-ending period, begin each enumerated item with a lowercase character—not uppercase. Only stand-alone provisions should begin with a capital letter.

<table>
<tr><th>NOT THIS:</th><th>BUT THIS:</th></tr>
<tr><td>Ex. 1
B. Eligibility. To be eligible for severance benefits, an employee:
1. Must have completed at least ten full years of active service with BNML, or any related company, and,
2. Must be unable, by exercise of seniority, to hold a position on the BNML, and,
3. Must permanently sever the employment relationship with BNML, including, but not limited to, any rights to recall.
Memorandum of Agreement from a railroad company</td><td>6.2 Eligibility. To be eligible for severance benefits, an employee must:
(A) have completed at least 10 full years of active service with BNML or a related company;
(B) be unable, by the exercise of seniority, to hold a position with BNML; and
(C) permanently sever the employment relationship with BNML, including any rights to recall.

Note the economy of parallelism. See § 88.</td></tr>
<tr><td>Ex. 2
a. <u>Right of Termination.</u> The Provider may terminate this Agreement at any time after the Cancellation Period for good and sufficient cause, upon giving you ninety (90) days' written notice. Good and sufficient cause shall include, but is not limited to:
(i) Your failure to perform any of your obligations under this Agreement;
(ii) Your or your guests' failure to abide by the Rules and Regulations of the Community;
(iii) Your behavior or physical or mental condition creates a disturbance at the Community or is detrimental to your own health or safety or that of others; and
(iv) Any material omission or misstatement in your Admission Application, Financial Information Form or any other document filed by you or on your behalf with The Provider.
Residence and Care Agreement from a major law firm</td><td>9.4 Termination.
(A) Right of termination. Upon 90 days' written notice, we may terminate this Agreement for good cause at any time after the Cancellation Period.
(B) Examples of good cause. Good cause includes:
(1) your failure to perform an obligation under this Agreement;
(2) your or your guests' failure to abide by the Rules and Regulations of the Community;
(3) your behavior or physical or mental condition creating a disturbance at the Community or being detrimental to your own or another's health or safety; and
(4) your making any material omission or misstatement in a document filed with us, including the Admission Application Form and the Financial Information Form.

Note: it's recommended to define include to mean "including but not limited to" in a definition section. See § 149 at p. 423. See also §§ 34 and 102.</td></tr>
</table>

§ 92 Avoid unhelpful enumeration, or "splintering."

Occasionally, you'll find that the zeal to create vertical lists will result in a less-readable provision because you've splintered the text. When that happens, put the provision right back together.

NOT THIS:	BUT THIS:
Ex. 1 3. **Delivery** **3.1. Shipment Terms.** The System shall be shipped F.O.B. to Contractor's location. **3.2. Delivery Schedule.** Delivery of the System shall be completed no later than three weeks after execution of this agreement. **System Contract from a major beverage company**	3. **Delivery.** Distributor will ship the System F.O.B. to Imbibico's location within 3 weeks after the signing of this Agreement.
Ex. 2 9. **RETURN AUTHORIZATION PROCESS.** Unless otherwise provided in this Agreement, all returns of Deliverables are at Supplier's expense. Exhibit B lists (i) the return authorization process for Deliverables and (ii) the repair and replacement Services and associated fees for "out of warranty" Deliverables. **Master Purchase Agreement for Technical Deliverables and Related Services Instructions from a major telecommunications company**	9. **Return-Authorization Process.** Unless this Agreement provides otherwise, InTech Resources will pay for all returns of Deliverables. Exhibit B lists the return-authorization process for Deliverables and the repair-and-replacement Services and associated fees for out-of-warranty Deliverables.
Ex. 3 2.2 **Conditions Precedent to Exercise.** The Right of Repurchase shall be exercisable only during the 60-day period following the date when the Purchaser's Service terminates for any reason, with or without Cause, including (without limitation) death or Disability. 2.3 [Lapse of Repurchase Right.] 2.4 **Exercise of Repurchase Right.** The Right of Repurchase shall be exercisable only by written notice delivered to the Purchaser prior to the expiration of the 60-day period specified in Subsection 2.2 above. **Stock-Purchase Agreement from a major law firm**	2.2 **Availability of repurchase right.** MKY's right of repurchase is exercisable only by written notice to QuartzCo within 60 days after the date when QuartzCo's service terminates for any reason, with or without cause, including death or disability.

Key terms and their definitions

§ 93 Be a minimalist when it comes to definitions. But if you introduce a defined term, use it consistently.

Keep to a minimum (hereinafter "Minimize") all defined terms, especially those in the form of midsentence parentheticals (hereinafter collectively "Defined Terms"). Most Defined Terms serve as shorthand forms for the person doing the writing (hereinafter the "Writer"). But they're typically roadblocks (hereinafter "Roadblocks" or "Impediments") for the people who do the reading (hereinafter "Readers"), who undoubtedly wish that the Roadblocks were Minimized. If the Writer uses an Impediment such as a Defined Term without first ensuring that clarity and precision (hereinafter collectively "Accurate Readability") have been improved, the Writer is likely to seem to be willfully obscure to naive Readers (hereinafter "Naive Readers") and doltish to more sophisticated Readers (hereinafter "Sophisticated Readers"). The resulting mishmash (hereinafter "Mishmash") will drive all types of Readers, whether Naive Readers or Sophisticated Readers, away from the document (hereinafter the "Repulsive Effect") precisely because the Mishmash and the effects relating thereto, including but not limited to the Repulsive Effect (hereinafter collectively the "Concomitant Effects"), are inconsistent with Accurate Readability.

Write that way if you must. But you needn't. And you shouldn't.

The advice contained in that initial paragraph—if you took the time to figure it out—is quite counterintuitive to most transactional lawyers, who have come to believe that the more you define terms, the better. Drafting experts have long held the opposite view:

- **1972:** "[A] definition . . . often creates more problems than it solves."[1]
- **1979:** "[D]efinitions don't belong in a legal document. If they just echo the dictionary, they are pointless—like section 441(d)

> "The main use of definitions in legal documents is, of course, to achieve clarity and consistency without burdensome repetition. Just as every word in any legal instrument ought to pay its own way, every definition ought to be limited to filling a real need."
> Reed Dickerson, *The Fundamentals of Legal Drafting* § 7.1, at 138 (2d ed. 1986).

1 Lord Reid in *Brutus v. Cozens*, [1972] 3 W.L.R. 521, 525.

of the Internal Revenue Code, which says, 'For purposes of this subtitle, the term "calendar year" means a period of 12 months ending on December 31.' If they *don't* echo the dictionary but sneak in something extra, they're a piece of trickery and should always be replaced by a straightforward explanation in the text of the document."[2]

- **1992:** "In the realm of definitions, it is usually wise to try to be a minimalist, in other words, to try to convey everything you have to say clearly without using definitions at all."[3]

Prune defined terms by (1) resorting to them only when no other device works well, and (2) trying instead to explain your meaning in the immediate context. The primary justification for defining key terms is to create shorthand references for concepts that would otherwise take up abundant words or syllables. For example:

> "Affiliate" means any natural person or firm, corporation, partnership, limited liability company, association, trust, or other entity that, directly or indirectly, controls, is controlled by, or is under common control with the subject entity.

If you decide that you really need a defined term, then use it rigorously—without variation or periphrasis.

One last point. Forget the idea of defining ordinary words such as *and*, *or*, *shall*, and the like. It's worse than pointless: it's invariably counterproductive. A lease sent to me by in-house counsel contained the following definitions of *and/or* (itself to be avoided—see § 149 at pp. 406–08), *and*, and *or*. It's absurd:

> The term "and/or" means that the precedent and subsequent words grammatically appertaining thereunto are connected thereby in the conjunctive sense (whether cumulatively as the whole thereof, or, if more than two, in any combination of more than one thereof) and also as an equal alternative, in the disjunctive sense; and the word "and" (except

> "If you . . . end up with a definition section, it should have in it as few definitions as possible." Barbara Child, *Drafting Legal Documents* 356 (2d ed. 1992).

2 Rudolf Flesch, *How to Write Plain English: A Book for Lawyers and Consumers* 68–69 (1979).

3 Barbara Child, *Drafting Legal Documents* 356 (2d ed. 1992).

> where specifically restricted to the conjunctive or combinatory sense, as for example by use of the phrase "and (but not or)") ordinarily means that the conjunctive sense should be applied thereunto unless by reason of the context, subject matter, or circumstances then and there concerned, substitution of the disjunctive sense would be reasonably necessary to give meaning to the words used therewith; and the word "or" (except where specifically restricted to the disjunctive sense, as for example by use of the phrase "or (but not and)") means the converse (both ordinarily and substitutionally) of the word "and."

That's no joke. Somebody actually thought this verbiage might help a court. In fact, though, the more common the word, the harder it is to define accurately or helpfully. Try defining *an*, *the*, or *to*. You'll soon find yourself mired in difficulty. The ordinary-meaning canon is your friend. It says that words ought to be given their everyday meanings. But if you try to supply those meanings with definitions, you'll soon find yourself hopelessly mired in incomprehensibility and ambiguity.

Ex. 1

NOT THIS:	BUT THIS:
1. The land covered by this agreement (hereinafter referred to as "Communitized Area") is described as follows: . . . 5. The Communitized Area shall be developed and operated as an entity, with the understanding and agreement between the parties hereto that all communitized substances produced therefrom shall be allocated among the leaseholders comprising said area in the proportion that the acreage interest of each leaseholder bears to the entire acreage interest committed to this agreement. All proceeds, 8/8ths, attributed to unleased Indian, Federal, State or fee land included within the CA area are to be placed in an interest bearing escrow or trust account by the designated operator until the land is leased or ownership is established. **North Dakota Oil-and-Gas Pooling Agreement**	1. **Covered Land.** "Communitized Area" means the land covered by this Agreement: . . . 5. **Communitized Area.** 5.1 **Allocation of substances among leaseholders.** The Communitized Area will be developed and operated as an entity, and all communitized substances produced will be allocated among the leaseholders of the Communitized Area in the proportion that the acreage interest of each leaseholder bears to the entire acreage interest committed to this Agreement. 5.2 **Proceeds for unleased land.** The designated operator must place proceeds, 8/8ths, attributed to unleased Indian, federal, state, or fee land included within the Communitized Area in an interest-bearing escrow or trust account until the land is leased or ownership is established.

After using the defined term elsewhere, the drafter inexplicably changed it to *CA area*, which apparently means *communitized area area.*

NOT THIS:

Ex. 2

Landlord shall have the right at any time during the term of this Lease or any renewal or extension of this Lease to require the Tenant to relocate to other space in the Shopping Mall (the "Substitution Premises"). The Substitution Space shall have approximately the same gross leasable area as the Premises. If Landlord desires to exercise such right, it shall give Tenant not less than at least [*number*] days prior written notification that Tenant is to relocate to another space. Within [*number*] days of receipt of Landlord's notification, Tenant shall then give Landlord written notice of Tenant's election to agree to relocate, or to decline to relocate. Should Tenant fail to give Landlord written notice within [*number*] days of receipt of Landlord's notification, then Tenant shall be deemed to have elected to consent to relocation. If Tenant elects to relocate to the Substitution Space, such relocation shall be at the sole cost of Landlord, including all costs and expenses related to improving the space with leasehold improvements equal to those then in the Premises. After such relocation, all terms, covenants, conditions, provisions, and agreements of this Lease shall continue in full force and effect and shall apply to the Substitution Space except that: (a) if the then unexpired balance of the term of this Lease shall be less than one year, the Term shall be extended so that the unexpired balance of the Term shall be one year from the date of the move; and (b) if the Substitution Space contains more square footage than the presently leased Premises, the Monthly Minimum Rent and Tenant's Pro Rata Share shall be increased proportionately (provided that such increase in the Monthly Minimum Rent and Tenant's Pro Rata Share shall not be in excess of [*maximum rent of substitution space as percentage of previous rent*]% of the Monthly Minimum Rent and Tenant's Pro Rata Share immediately preceding such an increase). If Tenant shall retain possession of the Premises or any part of the Premises following the date set for relocation or termination, Tenant shall be liable to Landlord, for each day of such retention, for double the amount of the daily rental for the last period prior to the date of such expiration or termination, plus actual damages incurred by Landlord resulting from delay by Tenant in surrendering the Premises, including but not limited to any claims made against Landlord by any succeeding tenant to the Premises and Landlord's costs in taking any action to evict Tenant from the Premises. If the Tenant declines to relocate and gives Landlord the required written notice, then within [*number*] days of receipt of the Tenant's election to decline, the Landlord may: (a) give the Tenant notice of the Landlord's election to terminate the Lease and require Tenant to vacate the Premises on the [*ordinal number*] day following the date of the Landlord's initial notice requiring the Tenant to relocate; or (b) elect to continue the Lease on the Premises in force in accordance with its terms.

Shopping-Center Lease from 11A Am. Jur. Legal Forms 2d *Leases of Real Property* § 161:153, at 429 (2006)

Note that the defined term is *Substitution Premises*, but the rest of the provision refers instead to *Substitution Space*. It's also used here in lowercase (in contrast to the term as defined), and in one place as merely *the space*. It's also confusing because the original space is defined as merely the *Premises*.

Using *not less than at least* is unnecessary repetition. *At least* is sufficient.

BUT THIS:

7. **Relocation to Different Space in Mall.**
   - 7.1 **Landlord's right to relocate Tenant.** The Landlord may at any time during the Lease's term or during a renewal or extension of this Lease require the Tenant to relocate to a "Substitution Space." "Substitution Space" means another space in the Shopping Mall having a similar gross leasable area as the Premises. If the Landlord requires the Tenant to relocate to Substitution Space, it must give the Tenant at least ________ days' written notice.
   - 7.2 **Tenant's election.** Within ________ days after receiving the Landlord's notice, the Tenant must give the Landlord written notice of the Tenant's election to either agree or decline to relocate. If the Tenant does not respond within this time, the Tenant will be considered to have agreed to relocate.
   - 7.3 **Cost of relocation.** If the Tenant elects to relocate to the Substitution Space, the relocation will be at the Landlord's sole cost, including all expenses related to improving the Substitution Space with leasehold improvements equal to those in the Premises as of the date of relocation.
   - 7.4 **Lease provisions after relocation.** After the Tenant's relocation, all Lease provisions will continue in full force and will apply to the Substitution Space with the following exceptions:
     - (A) if the unexpired balance of the term of this Lease is less than 1 year, the Term will be extended so that the unexpired balance of the Term is 1 year from the date of the relocation; and
     - (B) if the Substitution Space contains more square footage than the Premises, the Monthly Minimum Rent and Tenant's Pro Rata Share will be increased proportionately. But the increase in the Monthly Minimum Rent and Tenant's Pro Rata Share will not be more than ________% of the Monthly Minimum Rent and the Tenant's Pro Rata Share immediately before the increase.
   - 7.5 **If Tenant declines relocation.** If the Tenant declines to relocate and gives the Landlord the required written notice under § 7.2, then within ________ days after receiving the notice, the Landlord may either:
     - (A) notify the Tenant that the Landlord is terminating the Lease and require the Tenant to vacate the Premises on the _____ day after the date of the Landlord's initial notice requiring the Tenant to relocate (in § 7.1); or
     - (B) continue the current Lease on the Premises according to its provisions.
   - 7.6 **Tenant's holding over.** If the Tenant retains possession of the Premises or any part of the Premises after the date set for relocation or termination, the Tenant must pay the Landlord, for each day of the retention, double the amount of the daily rental for the last period before the relocation or termination date plus actual damages that the Landlord incurs as a result of the Tenant's delay in surrendering the Premises, including any claims made against the Landlord by a succeeding tenant to the Premises and the Landlord's costs in taking action to evict the Tenant from the Premises.

"If you are going to be a committed plain legal drafter, you should do what you can to reduce defined terms in your documents. One way to do that is to create and use a defined term only when you will use the term several times. In my reading of transactional documents, I am surprised at how frequently I see a defined term created and then never used. Even if the defined term is actually used once or even twice, you still might consider not creating it." Wayne Schiess, *Preparing Legal Documents Nonlawyers Can Read and Understand* 24 (2008).

NOT THIS:

Ex. 3

(c) Cause. The Company may terminate the Executive's employment hereunder for Cause. The occurrence of any of the following, as reasonably determined by the Company, shall be a reason for Cause, provided that, if the Company determines that the circumstances constituting Cause are curable, then such circumstances shall not constitute Cause unless and until the Executive has been informed by the Company of the existence of Cause and given an opportunity of ten business days to cure, and such Cause remains uncured at the end of such ten-day period: (1) continued failure by the Executive to satisfactorily perform his/her duties; (2) willful misconduct or gross negligence by the Executive in the performance of his/her duties hereunder, including insubordination; (3) the Executive's conviction or entry of a guilty or nolo contendere plea of any felony or any misdemeanor involving moral turpitude; (4) the Executive's commission of any act involving dishonesty that results in material financial, reputational or other harm, monetary or otherwise, to any member of the Group, including but not limited to an act constituting misappropriation or embezzlement of the property of any member of the Group as determined in good faith by the Board; or (5) any material breach by the Executive of this Agreement.

(d) Good Reason. The Executive may terminate his/her employment hereunder for "Good Reason" upon the occurrence, without the written consent of the Executive, of an event constituting a material breach of this Agreement by the Company that has not been fully cured within ten business days after written notice thereof has been given by the Executive to the Company setting forth in sufficient detail the conduct or activities the Executive believes constitute grounds for Good Reason, including but not limited to: the failure by the Company to pay to the Executive any portion of the Executive's current compensation or to pay to the Executive any portion of an installment of deferred compensation under any deferred compensation program of the Company, within twenty business days of the date such compensation is due.

(e) Without Cause by the Company; Without Good Reason by the Executive. The Company may terminate the Executive's employment hereunder at any time without Cause upon 60-day prior written notice to the Executive. The Executive may terminate the Executive's employment voluntarily for any reason or no reason at any time by giving 60-day prior written notice to the Company.

Employment Agreement

"Lawyers, in contrast to other professionals, rarely bother to find the right word. Instead, they often write down a string of almost right words, hoping that one of them will fit. Another way to solve the problem is by definitions. Use a word that's clearly wrong and then define it to fit." Rudolf Flesch, *How to Write Plain English* 59 (1979).

BUT THIS:

(C) **Cause.** The Company may, in its reasonable determination, immediately terminate the Executive's employment for Cause. "Cause" arises if the Executive:

(1) continually fails to perform the duties satisfactorily;

(2) engages in willful misconduct (including insubordination) or gross negligence in performing the duties;

(3) is convicted of, or enters a plea of guilty or nolo contendere to, any felony or any misdemeanor involving moral turpitude;

(4) commits any act involving dishonesty that results in material financial, reputational, or other harm, monetary or otherwise, to any member of the Group, including an act constituting misappropriation or embezzlement of the property of any member of the Group as determined in good faith by the Board; or

(5) materially breaches this Agreement.

(D) **Curing Cause.** If the Company determines that the circumstances constituting Cause are curable, then the Company will inform the Executive of the existence of Cause and give the Executive 10 business days to cure the circumstances.

(E) **Good Reason.** The Executive may terminate the employment for "Good Reason," giving the Company prior written notice setting forth in sufficient detail the conduct or activities that the Executive believes constitute Good Reason and giving the Company 10 business days to fully cure. "Good Reason" arises when the Company materially breaches this Agreement, as by failing to pay the Executive any part of the Executive's current compensation or any part of an installment of deferred compensation under any deferred-compensation program of the Company, within 20 business days after the date when the compensation is due.

(F) **Termination without Cause by the Company; without Good Reason by the Executive.** The Company may terminate the Executive's employment at any time without Cause upon 60 days' written notice to the Executive. The Executive may terminate employment voluntarily without Good Reason at any time by giving 60 days' written notice to the Company.

"Definitions are often useful in clearing up uncertainties. They can also create problems when they are unnecessarily detailed. In general, they have a strange fascination for legal draftsmen. They are so hard to draft, and cause so much trouble when drafted badly, that the draftsman should define to the least extent possible."
Reed Dickerson, *Teacher's Manual for Materials on Legal Drafting* 132 (1981).

§ 94 Employ precise definitional terminology.

Use precise definitional terms: *means* (= denotes), *includes* (= forms a class that has among its members), and *does not include* (= excludes). Avoid especially *shall mean*, *shall have the meaning*, and other variants.

Occasionally you'll need, for the sake of precision, to create a hypernym or "umbrella" term to capture multiple defined terms. Such a term sometimes allows for efficient reference. For example, if *Type 1 products* are those sold in the automobile industry, and *Type 2 products* are sold in the biking industry, then *Cumulative Products* might be the term you'd use for both types collectively. Keep your terminology intuitive. It would be a mistake, for example, to refer to both types collectively as *Type 3 products* because that term would be another type analogous to Type 1 and Type 2. Once again, you must consider things from your readers' standpoint.

NOT THIS:	BUT THIS:
Ex. 1 As used in this Agreement (including within these paragraphs) the following terms shall have these meanings: "NCAA" shall mean the National Collegiate Athletic Association. "Big 12" shall mean the Big 12 Conference. "University Rules" shall mean the Rules and Regulations of the Board of Regents of the John Adams University System, the rules and policies of the John Adams University System, and the rules and policies of John Adams University. **College-Football Head-Coach Employment Agreement for a major university**	**1.1 Definitions.** (A) "Big 12" means the Big 12 Conference. (B) "NCAA" means the National Collegiate Athletic Association. (C) "University Rules" means the rules and regulations of the Board of Regents of the John Adams University System and the rules and policies of both the System and the University itself.
Ex. 2 "*Base Management Fee*" shall have the meaning set forth in Section 3.01. "*Books and Records*" means all books and records of Manager pertaining to the Facility for the period after the Effective Date, including customer referral lists, reports, plans, projections and advertising and marketing materials and financial and accounting books and records. "*Business Day*" shall mean any day other than a Saturday, Sunday or legal holiday in the State of Iowa. "*Code*" shall have the meaning set forth in Section 6.03. **Management-Services Agreement from an assisted-living facility**	(5) "Base Management Fee" is defined in § 3.1. (6) "Books and Records" means all the Manager's books and records on hand as of or created after the Effective Date that relate to the Facility, including customer-referral lists, reports, plans, projections, advertising and marketing materials, and financial and accounting books and records. (7) "Business Day" means any weekday that is not a legal holiday in the state of Iowa. (8) "Code" is defined in § 6.3.

NOT THIS:	BUT THIS:
Ex. 3 4.9 Date of Contract. Whenever the term "date of this Contract", "Contract date" or other similar term is used in this Contract, such date shall mean the date on which this Contract was executed by the last party to execute this Contract. 4.10 Business Day. Whenever the term "Business Day" is used in this Contract, it shall mean Monday through Friday, excluding Bank holidays on which national banking associations are authorized to be closed. If any date provided for in this Contract shall fall on a day which is not a Business Day, the date provided for shall be deemed to refer to the next Business Day. **Real-Estate-Purchase Contract from a major law firm**	**4.9** "Contract Date" means the date on which this Contract was signed by the last party. **4.10** "Business Day" means a weekday except for a bank holiday on which national banking associations are authorized to be closed. If any date in this Contract falls on a day that is not a Business Day, the date will be treated as the next Business Day. It's much preferable to use one term consistently. See § 10. And on the inadvisability of using the date of the last signature, see §§ 57 and 59.
Ex. 4 2.1 Definitions. For purposes of this Agreement, the following terms shall have the following meanings: (a) "Termination For Cause" shall mean termination by the Company of Executive's employment by the Company for reasons of Executive's conviction of a felony involving moral turpitude, persistent dishonesty or fraud, persistent willful breaches of the material terms of this Agreement, or habitual neglect of the duties which she is required to perform hereunder. (b) "Termination Other Than For Cause" shall mean termination by the Company of Executive's employment by the Company (other than a Termination For Cause). (c) "Voluntary Termination" shall mean termination of Executive's employment with the Company by action of Executive (other than termination by reason of Executive's disability or death as described in Sections 2.6 and 2.7). **Executive-Employment Agreement from Jean L. Batman, *Advising the Small Business: Forms and Advice for the Legal Practitioner* 657 (2007)**	**2.1 Termination definitions.** (A) "Termination for cause" means our termination of your employment because of your: (1) conviction of a felony involving moral turpitude; (2) persistent dishonesty or fraud; (3) persistent willful breaches of this Agreement; or (4) habitual neglect of your duties under this Agreement. (B) "Termination other than for cause" means our termination of your employment for a reason not specified in (A). (C) "Voluntary termination" means termination of your employment with us by your own action for reasons other than disability under § 2.6 or death.

"Unless a definition is considered in the context in which it is used, its inadequacies may not become apparent until the document has been executed, and when it is, normally, too late to take action to deal with the problem." Elmer Doonan, *Drafting* § 4.4, at 85 (Julie MacFarland ed., 1995).

§ 95 Avoid tag-on defined terms—those included in parentheses after the term being defined.

Shorthand names are one thing: *Highland Equity Group* becomes *Highland*. They're not really defined terms as those are usually understood in legal drafting. A defined term isn't a shorthand *name*, but rather a shorthand *term* for something being written about. The normal (and preferred) way to define is to write "X means 'so-and-so.'" If you instead say "So-and-so and so-and-so ('X')," the predictable result is that we often won't know how far back in the sentence the *X* is supposed to reach. Consider this example: "The partnership plans to acquire the structure at #8 Country Club Drive in Canyon, Texas (the 'Place of Business')." Is the place of business the building at #8 Country Club Drive? The full lot on which the building lies? All of Canyon, Texas? The entire state of Texas? Disputatious readers want to know.

Not every tag-on defined term will cause problems. But many will. You don't want to acquire any drafting habit that will frequently raise difficulties. This is one of those.

NOT THIS:	BUT THIS:
Ex. 1 Licensee will make reasonable commercial efforts to use the Trademarks for the above identification purposes, and in connection with all publicity, instructional, sales and promotional material for the Licensed Product, Licensee brochures, marketing materials, GUIs, onscreen or websites ("Licensee Materials"). The rights and obligations concerning the use of the Trademarks shall be as follows: . . . . **Network-Service-Provider and Trademark-License Agreement from a digital technology company**	2.1 **Use of Trademarks.** You will make reasonable commercial efforts to use the Trademarks for the above identification purposes and in connection with Licensee Materials, which are all your instructional, sales, and promotional materials for the Licensed Product, together with your publicity, brochures, marketing materials, user interfaces, onscreen displays, and web content. 2.2 **Rights and obligations.** The rights and obligations for the Trademarks' use are as follows: . . . .

The tag-on defined term *Licensee Materials* isn't necessary. The term isn't used anywhere else in the document. Note the substantive improvements in the revision.

"To evaluate a contract properly, there is no substitute for finding out whether or not the intended readers of that contract understand the content and are able to use this information to answer questions and to guide their conduct." Carl Felsenfeld & Alan Siegel, *Writing Contracts in Plain English* 227 (1981).

<table>
<tr><th>NOT THIS:</th><th>BUT THIS:</th></tr>
<tr><td>Ex. 2

3. PROPRIETARY INFORMATION. My employment creates a relationship of confidence and trust between the Company and me with respect to any and all confidential knowledge, data or information:
(a) Applicable or related to the business of the Company or its actual or demonstrably anticipated research or development; or
(b) Received from an affiliate, client, customer or supplier ("Related Third Party") of the Company, which may be made known to me by the Company or by a Related Third Party, or learned by me in such context during the period of my employment, in respect of which the Company is obligated to maintain the confidentiality thereof and use such information only for certain limited purposes.
Employee-Inventions and Proprietary-Rights Assignment Agreement from a multinational computer-software company</td><td>3. Proprietary Information.
3.1 Confidentiality. Your employment creates a relationship of confidence and trust between us and you with respect to all confidential knowledge, data, or information that is:
(A) applicable or related to our business or its actual or demonstrably anticipated research and development; or
(B) received from a Related Third Party and made known to you by us or by a Related Third Party, or learned by you during your employment, with respect to which we are required to maintain the confidentiality of the information and use it only for certain limited purposes.
3.2 Definition of "Related Third Party." A "Related Third Party" is an affiliate, client, customer, or supplier of the Company.</td></tr>
<tr><td>Ex. 3

SECTION THREE: REPRESENTATIONS AND WARRANTIES OF DEBTOR
3.1 Debtor represents and warrants, and so long as any Indebtedness remains unpaid, shall be deemed continuously to represent and warrant that:
a. Debtor is the sole owner of the Collateral and except for the Security Interest granted herein, the Collateral is not subject to any encumbrance including, but not limited to, any mortgage, pledge, lien, charge, security interest, claim, easement, conditional sale or other type of title retention arrangement, hypothecation, privilege, option, subordination to any right or claim of any other person or organization of any type or form or any other type of restriction including, but not limited to, restrictions with respect to title, transfer, use or possession ("Liens"); and
b. No financing statement, security agreement or other instrument covering the Collateral is on file in any public office except any financing statement that may be filed in connection with this Security Agreement.
Security Agreement</td><td>3. Debtor's Representations and Warranties.
3.1 Encumbrances. Now and for as long as any indebtedness remains unpaid, the Debtor represents and warrants the following:
(A) Ownership. The Debtor is the sole owner of the Collateral.
(B) No restrictions on property. Except for the Security Interest granted here, the Collateral is not subject to any encumbrance, to anyone else's right, or to any other restriction.
3.2 Instruments covering the Collateral. Except for a financing statement that may be filed in connection with this Security Agreement, no financing statement, security agreement, or other instrument covering the Collateral is on file in any public office.</td></tr>
</table>

§ 96 If you define a term, use an everyday shorthand name for it. Avoid alien-sounding acronyms and initialisms.

Remember that you're writing English—plain English—not some hybrid language full of terms you make up. And to the extent that you must define terms, choose words that are both descriptive and immediately comprehensible.

In Example 1 below, "GBFSH1" refers to the Grand Boulevard Family Steakhouse #1. A similar initialism denotes each of the numbers up to 5. The result is a mishmash of GBFSH's. Just by using the word *Restaurant* as opposed to *GBFSH*, you've enhanced clarity for the vast majority of readers.

Example 2 has two problems. First, the reader is served a huge bowl of alphabet soup: ten initialisms are introduced in a single sentence. Second, the example's first initialism, *NFL*, is likely to cause a miscue with most readers—at least those who watch TV in the fall. Moral: don't use an acronym or initialism that carries some other popular meaning.

One other thing about Example 2. If you don't have the shorthand acronyms or initialisms, how are you supposed to refer to Westbrook Marketing Corporation or Precision Dialing Services, Inc. a second time? Do you have to use the full name over and over? The answer, of course, is no. Simply say *Westbrook Marketing* and *Precision Dialing*. And do it without the heavy-handedness of saying, in your first mention, "Westbrook Marketing Corporation ('Westbrook Marketing')," etc. Give your reader an ounce of credit for having some candlepower.

NOT THIS:	BUT THIS:
Ex. 1 On December 14, 2017, GBFSH1, GBFSH2, and GBFSH3 distributed all of their cash available for distribution (net of reserves) of $32,000 (or $40 per Interest), $32,000 (or $36 per Interest), and $36,000 (or $36 per Interest), respectively, to their Limited Partners. GBFSH4 and GBFSH5 had no cash available for distribution at July 31, 2018. Limited Partners in GBFSH1, GBFSH2, and GBFSH3 all have invested in the Grand Boulevard Family Steakhouse concept in a substantially earlier phase of that concept than did the Limited Partners in GBFSH4 and GBFSH5. **Restaurant-Chain Interest-Distribution Agreement**	On December 14, 2017, Restaurants #1–3 distributed all their cash available for distribution (net of reserves) to their limited partners. Restaurant #1 distributed $32,000 (or $40 per Interest); Restaurant #2 distributed $32,000 (or $36 per Interest); and Restaurant #3 distributed $36,000 (or $36 per Interest). Restaurants #4 and #5 had no cash available for distribution on July 31, 2018. Limited partners in Restaurants #1–3 all invested in the Grand Boulevard Family Steakhouse concept at a substantially earlier phase of that concept than the limited partners in Restaurants #4 and #5.

NOT THIS:	BUT THIS:
Ex. 2 The Company's wholly owned subsidiaries and affiliated companies include National Foundation Life Insurance Company ("NFL"), National Financial Insurance Company ("NFIC"), American Insurance Company of Illinois ("AICI"), Westbrook National Life Insurance Company ("WNL") and together with NFL, NFIC, and AICI (the "Insurance Subsidiaries"), Foundation Financial Services, Inc. ("FFS"), Westbrook Marketing Corporation ("WMC"), Precision Dialing Services, Inc. ("PDS"), Westbrook Printing Services, Inc. ("WPS"), Westbrook Funding Corporation ("WFC"), LifeStyles Marketing Group, Inc. ("LifeStyles Marketing"), Senior Benefits, LLC ("Senior Benefits"), American Senior Security Plans, LLC ("ASSP") and Health Care-One Insurance Agency, Inc. ("Health Care-One"). **Holding-Company Agreement**	The Company's wholly owned subsidiaries and affiliated companies are: • National Foundation Life Insurance Company; • National Financial Insurance Company; • American Insurance Company of Illinois; • Westbrook National Life Insurance Company; • Foundation Financial Services, Inc.; • Westbrook Marketing Corporation; • Precision Dialing Services, Inc.; • Westbrook Printing Services, Inc.; • Westbrook Funding Corporation; • Westbrook Marketing Group, Inc.; • Senior Benefits, LLC; • American Senior Security Plans, LLC; and • Healthcare-One Insurance Agency, Inc.

> "If we are complex and pompous in our writing, and we are, why are we? There are many reasons, of course—poor training in college, bad thinking habits, slavish imitation of other bad writing, wrong ideas about readers, lack of hard work, a confusion between dignity and pomposity, and a failure to understand that wisdom goes arm-in-arm with simplicity." John O'Hayre, *Gobbledygook Has Gotta Go* 29 (1966).

§ 97 Define terms in the singular, not the plural.

Anyone with a little experience in law has seen the supposedly curative provision: the singular includes the plural, and the plural includes the singular. The problem is that this "cure" solves nothing. The singular almost always includes the plural, but the reverse often isn't so. If a party is prohibited from bringing "personally owned tools" onto a worksite, does that include a single hammer that is personally owned? The problem arises in any variety of contexts more consequential than that one. The alleged breacher of such a provision will inevitably argue plain meaning: *tools* means two or more. And most contracts lack the supposedly curative provision.

The age-old lesson is to draft in the singular. If the prohibition is against bringing a "personally owned tool" onto a worksite, then bringing five essentially amounts to five breaches. You see?

NOT THIS:	BUT THIS:
Ex. 1 "Unique Activities" means production activities of Middleton at the request of either Member to . . . . **Joint-Venture Manufacturing Agreement between a major computer company and a tech-storage company**	"Unique Activity" means a Middleton production activity, requested by either Member, to . . . .
Ex. 2 Supplier/Contractor agrees to submit a Material Safety Data Sheet ("MSDS"), as defined and prescribed in 29 C.F.R. Section 1910.1200, two (2) days before initial delivery or transport to or use on Buyer's property of any hazardous substances. . . . The Material Safety Data Sheets (MSDSs) kept on file by Buyer for any hazardous substances which are present in such work areas will be made available for review by Supplier/Contractor or such employee(s) upon request. **Hazardous Substances and Material Agreement from 3 *Purchaser's Formbook of Contracts and Agreements* § 24:1, at 1 (2017)**	For any hazardous substance, Biologic will submit a Material Safety Data Sheet ("MSDS"), as defined and prescribed in 29 C.F.R. § 1910.1200, 2 days before the substance's initial delivery to, transport to, or use on Frontier's property. . . . An MSDS kept on file by Frontier for a hazardous substance present in a work area must be available upon request for Biologic's or its employee's review.

> "Drafted documents are multifarious. They are read by a variety of diverse audiences for whom there may be a variety of objectives and whose activities may be governed in a variety of ways." Susan L. Brody et al., *Legal Drafting* 6 (1994).

§ 98 Make your definition a literal substitute for the term being defined.

Make sure that the defined term's part of speech matches the part of speech given in the definition. In lexicographic circles, this is known as the principle of "substitutability." The definition must be able (at least notionally) to fit into a sentence in which the defined term appears. That is, a noun must be defined in words that could replace the noun, a verb must be defined as a verb, and so on.

Because *Protection Period* has no phrase that is clearly in apposition to it, there may be some question about what the protection period is.

NOT THIS:	BUT THIS:
Ex. 1 If within 10 days after said Expiration Date (the "Protection Period") Owner executes an earnest money contract for the sale of the Property, Owner must pay Broker. **Real-Estate-Brokerage Contract from a national realty brokerage**	"Protection period" means the period ending at 5:00 p.m. ET on the 10th day after the Expiration Date. If the Owner enters into an earnest-money contract for the sale of the Property during the Protection Period, then the Owner will pay the Broker.
Ex. 2 (d) Notwithstanding anything to the contrary contained herein, each Holder may pledge or transfer (a "Pledge") its Note to any entity (other than the Borrower or any Affiliate of the Borrower) that has extended a credit facility to such Holder or has entered into a repurchase agreement with such Holder. **Co-Lender Agreement from a major bank**	**4.4 Pledging of Note.** Despite anything in this Agreement to the contrary, a Holder may pledge its Note to any entity (other than the Borrower or any Affiliate of the Borrower) that has either extended a credit facility to Holder or entered into a repurchase agreement with Holder.

The definition uses verbs—*pledge* and *transfer*—but the defined term is a noun: *a Pledge*.

Given that the verb *pledge* here bears its ordinary meaning, there is no cause for making it a defined term.

> "The dangers are obvious: if a word is defined in a sense that is different from or contrary to the meaning ascribed to it by the legal community or the community at large, then there is the danger of the drafter inadvertently using the word in its ordinary sense rather than in its defined sense, making nonsense of the inclusion of the extraordinary meaning." Robert C. Dick, *Legal Drafting* 77 (2d ed. 1985).

§ 99 Never use a completely counterintuitive definition.

Ensure that your definitions seem intuitively right—that is, make sure that the term defined reasonably fits the stipulated definition.

NOT THIS:	BUT THIS:
Ex. 1 1.24 "Sale" means the first sale made on an arm's-length basis to an entity other than an Affiliate. A warranty replacement shall not constitute a Sale. **Patent-License Agreement between two major communication-technology companies**	**1.24** "Initial Sale" means the first sale made at arm's length to a non-Affiliate entity. A warranty replacement is not an Initial Sale.
Ex. 2 *"Billing Records and Customer Files"* — all billing records related to the CPD Product for all CPD Customer Contracts active as of the Closing Date sufficient to enable Buyer to bill Dealers pursuant to the CPD Customer Contracts and including, without limitation, an accounts receivable aging report, and all files for customers of the Business with CPD Customer Contracts active as of the Closing Date, including, without limitation, all agreements, correspondence, and support and maintenance records, all in the form maintained by Seller in the ordinary course prior to the Closing, Billing Records and Customers Files include, inter alia, "Contract Files" comprised of the CPD Customer Contract, including any amendments, modifications or extensions thereof, notices of termination and any buy-out figures that may have been provided by Seller to any Dealer with respect to the CPD Customer Contract; and correspondence and other documentation related to the CPD Product from Seller's "Permanent Dealer Files." **Asset-Purchase Agreement**	**8. Definitions.** **8.1** "Billing Records and Customer Files" means all CPD Customer Contracts active as of the Closing Date, including: (A) billing records related to the CPD Product sufficient to enable the Buyer to bill Dealers under the CPD Customer Contracts; (B) an accounts-receivable aging report for each customer; (C) customer files containing all agreements, correspondence, and support and maintenance records, in the form maintained by Seller in the ordinary course of business before the Closing; (D) Contract Files; and (E) correspondence and other documentation related to the CPD Product from the Seller's Permanent Dealer Files. **8.2** "Contract Files" means the CPD Customer Contract, including any amendments, modifications, or extensions, and notices of termination, and any buyout figures that the Seller may have provided to a Dealer about the CPD Customer Contract.

Defining the term this way creates confusion because both *Sale* and *sale* (and also *Sell* and *sell*) are used throughout the contract.

It's better to add the word *initial* to the defined term denoting a first sale.

The comma after *Closing* creates a run-on sentence.

"Socrates to Hermogenes: 'Well, now, let me take an instance; suppose that I call a man a horse or a horse a man. You mean to say that a man will be rightly called a horse by me individually, and rightly called a man by the rest of the world, and a horse again would be rightly called a man by me and a horse by the world—that is your meaning?'" Plato, *The Collected Dialogues of Plato* 423 (Edith Hamilton & Huntington Cairns eds., 1961).

§ 100 Avoid tautologies in defining.

In the definition, don't use the very term being defined. Doing so is amateurish and question-begging.

	NOT THIS:	BUT THIS:
Ex. 1 (Note the tautologous definition: using the word *rights* in defining the word *rights*.)	"Rights" means rights, remedies, powers, and privileges. **Royalty Agreement from a major law firm**	"Rights" includes remedies, powers, and privileges. (Or delete the definition.)
Ex. 2	3.3 Credited Service: The amount of a Participant's Pension shall be based upon the Participant's period of Credited Service. **Pension Plan from an American multinational food, snack, and beverage company**	**3.3** "Credited Service" means the amount of a Participant's Pension that is based on the recipient's length of qualifying service. (Note the original version's problematically tautologous definition: using *Credited Service* in its own definition.)
Ex. 3	"Feedback" means specific suggestions, comments, or feedback (whether orally or in writing) provided by Company to Bellhouse Corp. on how to change or augment its technology. The Parties agree that Feedback shall not include any proprietary code and that Company is not obligated to provide Feedback. **Technology-Collaboration Agreement from a computer-technology developer**	"Feedback" means the Company's specific suggestions or comments (whether oral or written) on how to change or augment Bellhouse Corp.'s technology. Feedback is not mandatory, and it does not include any proprietary code.
Ex. 4 (The exception *unless otherwise indicated*, if it's to be included at all, should be included in the general lead-in for all definitions: "The following words bear the senses indicated unless noted otherwise.")	The term "*Premises*" means, unless otherwise indicated, all premises where the Named Insured, or his or her spouse, maintains a residence and includes private approaches thereto. **Insurance Policy from a national insurance company**	"Premises" means all physical locations where the Named Insured or his or her spouse maintains a residence, and it includes any private approaches to that residence.

§ 101 Don't put substantive provisions within definitions.

By definition, a definition supplies the meaning of a particular word or phrase. It shouldn't contain rules of any kind. So in a definitional section, we should find only stipulated senses—no obligations or rights.

NOT THIS:	BUT THIS:
Ex. 1 For purposes stating the "Vacate Date" hereof, the term "Vacate Date" shall mean the date that Tenant actually vacates the leased premises, removes all of its property therefrom, and lawfully surrenders possession thereof to Landlord (free of all subtenants, occupants, and encumbrances whatsoever) in the condition (and otherwise in the manner) required by the Lease regardless of whether such date is prior to, during, or after the stated term of the Lease, provided, however, that Tenant and Guarantor shall have (as a condition to the occurrence of the Vacate Date) given Landlord written notice not less than [*number of days*] days in advance of the Vacate Day (time being of the essence) specifying with certainty when that date is to be. **"Good Guy" Guaranty of Lease from Tina S. Wu, *Real Estate Leases*, Form 6 (2013)**	**5. Vacating the Premises.** **5.1 Notice required.** Bolieri and City Bank will give Stonegate written notice that states the Vacate Date at least 30 days before vacating the premises. **5.2 Definition.** "Vacate Date" means the date by which Bolieri will remove all its property and surrender possession of the premises to Stonegate—free of all subtenants, occupants, and encumbrances—in the condition and manner required by the Lease. The Vacate Date may be before, during, or after the Lease term.

"Definitions sometimes hide substantive provisions. This practice is undesirable. Substantive provisions should not be in an interpretation clause. It is wrong to write: 'Completion Date means 30 June 1980, on which date the Purchaser shall pay the residue of purchase money.'" J.K. Aitken, *Piesse—The Elements of Drafting* 37 (7th ed. 1987).

§ 102 Collect in one place the definitions for terms that appear throughout the document. Put provision-specific definitions in their place—using the definition section as an index to find these particular definitions.

Some defined terms appear throughout a contract; others are localized. Those of the first type are usefully collected in a definitional section; those of the second type are best defined in the immediate context within which they appear.

With a provision-specific defined term, generally use it first and then promptly define it—as opposed to defining it before using it. That is, readers do best when they see a term used and then explained, as opposed to encountering an acontextual definition of a term followed by its first substantive use.

Once you decide to use provision-specific definitions, you should make them easily findable by including either index references in the definitional section or a separate index of defined terms after the definitional section. Example 3 is the beginning of such an index from a complex merger agreement. Such an index appears after the full definitional section only if that section already borders on being seriously overloaded (not ideal as judged by the standards of § 93).

NOT THIS:	BUT THIS:
Ex. 1 The Player, while "on the road", shall be paid a meal expense allowance as set forth in the Collective Bargaining Agreement currently in effect between the Association and the National Basketball Players Association. No deductions from such meal expense allowance shall be made for meals served on an airplane. During the training camp period, the meal expense allowance shall be paid in weekly installments commencing with the first week of training camp. **Player Contract for a professional basketball player**	**9.1 Meal expenses.** (A) **On the road.** While on the road, McTavish will receive a meal allowance from the Club in accordance with the collective-bargaining agreement in effect between the Association and the National Basketball Players Association. (B) **Definition of "on the road."** A player is considered "on the road" from the time the Club leaves its home city until the Club arrives back at its home city. (C) **Meal served on airplane.** The Club will not deduct from the allowance in (A) the expense for a meal served on an airplane. (D) **Training camp.** During the training-camp period, the Club will pay McTavish the meal allowance in weekly installments beginning the first week of training camp.

If drafting for a U.S. client, use American-style punctuation consistently (comma inside quotation marks).

NOT THIS:	BUT THIS:
Ex. 2 6.5 **Rooftop Rights.** Commencing on the Lease Commencement Date, Tenant shall continue to have the right to use the Rooftop Equipment it installed under the Existing Lease on the terms set forth in Section 6.6 thereof. Subject to, (A) reasonable construction rules and regulations promulgated by Landlord, (B) the Building standards therefor, and (C) the terms and conditions set forth in Article 8 of this Lease and this Section 6.5, Tenant may install, repair, maintain and use, at Tenant's sole cost and expense, but without the payment of any Base Rent or similar fee or charge, communications devices (the number of which shall be determined by Landlord in its sole and absolute discretion) on the roof of the Building for the sending and receiving of signals or broadcasts (provided that there shall be no generation or transmission of commercial signals or broadcasts) servicing the business conducted by Tenant from within the Premises (the satellite dish is the "Rooftop Equipment"). The **Rooftop Equipment** shall be no larger than (or otherwise occupy a space which is larger than) six (6) feet. Tenant shall be solely responsible for any and all costs incurred or arising in connection with the Rooftop Equipment, including but not limited to costs of electricity and insurance related to the Rooftop Equipment. **Lease Agreement from a business park** *Margin note:* Two types of Rooftop Equipment are identified: the satellite dish and unspecified "communications devices."	**6.5 Rooftop Rights.** (A) **Use of equipment.** As soon as the Lease begins, the Tenant may use the Rooftop Equipment. "Rooftop Equipment" means the satellite dish and similar communications devices installed on the roof of the Building under the Existing Lease on the terms set forth in § 6.6 of that lease for the sending and receiving of signals or broadcasts serving the business conducted by the Tenant within the Premises. (B) **Limitations on equipment.** (1) At the Tenant's sole expense, but without the payment of any Base Rent or similar fee or charge, the Tenant may install, repair, maintain, and use Rooftop Equipment, subject to the reasonable construction rules and the Landlord's regulations, the Building standards for the Rooftop Equipment, and the terms set forth in this § 6.5 and § 8. (2) The Landlord has the sole and absolute discretion to determine the quantity of Rooftop Equipment. But the Rooftop Equipment must not be larger than (or otherwise occupy a space larger than) 6 feet. (3) The Tenant must not use the Rooftop Equipment to generate or send commercial signals or broadcasts.

"Lawyers typically charge hundreds of dollars an hour for encoding their plain language in legalese and for translating legalese back into plain language for their clients. Plain language uses fewer lawyer-hours and reduces the waiting time for work to be done." Mark Adler, "The Plain Language Movement," in *The Oxford Handbook of Language and Law* 67, 72 (Peter M. Tiersma & Lawrence M. Solan eds., 2012).

Ex. 3

Index of Defined Terms

§ 103 Prefer putting a long definitional section at the end of the document—unless you have just a few definitions.

If defined terms appear in multiple sections or pervasively within a contract, collect them in an alphabetically arranged glossary (definition or key-terms section), preferably at the end. If the glossary is extensive, it may serve as an index in some respects. That is, provision-specific definitions won't be moved to the glossary. Instead the glossary will list the key terms, in alphabetical order, with a brief note stating that the term is defined in § XX (whatever it might be).

Transactional lawyers are accustomed to putting definitions at the beginning of their contracts—sometimes 2 pages but sometimes as much as 30 pages of intertwined, heavily cross-referenced, often incomprehensible definitions that would make any lexicographer blush. Businesspeople tend to detest this practice, but the lawyers say this in their own defense: how can you read the document if you don't know what the terms mean?

It's not a good defense. No one—not even the lawyer—slogs dutifully through the definitions before reading a document. Not, that is, unless the reader is an expert in the field who knows precisely what to look for in a given definition. And that reader, who isn't the primary audience for contracts anyway, can just as readily flip to the back of the document to consult the definition.

NOT THIS:	BUT THIS:
Ex. 1 6. INVENTIONS; PROPRIETARY RIGHTS. As used in this Agreement, the term **"Inventions"** means any new or useful art, discovery, improvement or invention whether or not patentable, and all know-how, designs, mask works, formulas, processes, data, manufacturing techniques, ideas, concepts, artwork, typefaces, software, written materials or other copyrightable or patentable works, and techniques and all Proprietary Rights therein. The term **"Proprietary Rights"** means all trade secrets, copyrights, trademarks, mask work rights, patents and other intellectual property rights recognized by the laws of any jurisdiction or country. **Employee-Inventions and Proprietary-Rights Assignment Agreement from a major software developer**	**Definitions** **"Invention"** means any new or useful art, discovery, improvement, or innovation whether or not patentable, and all know-how, designs, mask works, formulas, processes, data, manufacturing techniques, ideas, concepts, artwork, typefaces, software, written materials, or other copyrightable or patentable works and techniques, and all related Proprietary Rights. **"Proprietary Rights"** means all trade secrets, copyrights, trademarks, mask-work rights, patents, and other intellectual-property rights recognized by the laws of any jurisdiction or country.

Note, with the first defined term, the preference for the singular over the plural. See § 62. The second defined term is plural because the singular would never appear in this contract.

NOT THIS:

Ex. 2

3 Terms and Exercise of Warrants.

3.1 Warrant Price. Each Warrant shall, when countersigned by the Warrant Agent, entitle the Registered Holder thereof, subject to the provisions of such Warrant and of this Agreement, to purchase from the Company the number of shares of Class A Common Stock stated therein, at the price of $5.75 per half-share (or $11.50 per whole share), subject to the adjustments provided in Section 4 hereof and in the last sentence of this Section 3.1. The term **"Warrant Price"** as used in this Agreement shall mean the price per share at which Class A Common Stock may be purchased at the time a Warrant is exercised. The Company in its sole discretion may lower the Warrant Price at any time prior to the Expiration Date (as defined below) for a period of not less than twenty (20) Business Days, provided, that the Company shall provide at least twenty (20) days prior written notice of such reduction to Registered Holders of the Warrants and, provided further that any such reduction shall be identical among all of the Warrants.

3.2 Duration of Warrants. A Warrant may be exercised only during the period (the ***"Exercise Period"***) commencing on the date that is thirty (30) days after the date hereof and terminating at 5:00 p.m., New York City time on the date that is five (5) years after the date hereof, (the ***"Expiration Date"***); provided, however, that the exercise of any Warrant shall be subject to the satisfaction of any applicable conditions, as set forth in subsection 3.3.2 below, with respect to an effective registration statement. Each Warrant not exercised on or before the Expiration Date shall become void, and all rights thereunder and all rights in respect thereof under this Agreement shall cease at 5:00 p.m. New York City time on the Expiration Date. The Company in its sole discretion may extend the duration of the Warrants by delaying the Expiration Date; provided, that the Company shall provide at least twenty (20) days prior written notice of any such extension to Registered Holders of the Warrants and, provided further that any such extension shall be identical in duration among all the Warrants.

Warrant Agreement from a major acquisition corporation

BUT THIS:

3. Terms and Exercise of Warrants.

3.1 Warrant Price. When a Warrant is countersigned by the Warrant Agent—and subject to the Warrant's own terms—the Registered Holder of the Warrant may buy from the Company the number of shares of Class A Common Stock stated in the Warrant at the price of $5.75 per half-share (or $11.50 per whole share). Before the Expiration Date, the Warrant Price may be adjusted if adjustment is required under § 4. It may also be adjusted if:

(A) the Company, in its sole discretion, lowers the Warrant Price for at least 20 Business Days;

(B) the Company gives Registered Holders of the Warrants at least 20 days' prior written notice of the Warrant Price reduction; and

(C) the reduction is identical among all the Warrants.

3.2 Duration of Warrants. A Warrant may be exercised only during the Exercise Period and is subject to the satisfaction of any applicable conditions regarding an effective registration statement set forth in § 3.4. If a Warrant is not exercised by 5 p.m. ET on the Expiration Date, it is void. But the Company in its sole discretion may extend the duration of the Warrants by delaying the Expiration Date if:

(A) the Company gives the Registered Holders of the Warrants at least 20 days' written notice of the extension; and

(B) the duration of the extension is identical among all the Warrants.

. . .

[Terms used above and appearing in a lengthy glossary at the end.]

"Expiration Date" means the date that is 5 years after the Effective Date of this Agreement.

"Exercise Period" means the time running from the date beginning 30 days after the Effective Date and ending at 5 p.m. ET on the Expiration Date.

"Warrant Price" means the price per share at which Class A Common Stock may be purchased when a Warrant is exercised.

E. Syntax

Kernel sentence parts

§ 104 Keep the subject and the main verb reasonably close together.

Use a syntactic arrangement that enhances clarity, logic, and readability. Subject and verb shouldn't be widely separated. They should be kept together, preferably toward the beginning of the sentence.

But understand that it's clunky to begin with a subject and then to insert a modifying phrase right after. It's the unidiomatic separation that's bothersome. As in Example 2 below, it's often best to begin the sentence with a reasonably short modifying phrase and then have the subject and verb follow immediately after.

NOT THIS:	BUT THIS:
Ex. 1 The depositary, in order to maintain arrangements from time to time to enable persons that are considered United States residents for purposes of applicable law to receive any rebates, tax credits, or other benefits (pursuant to treaty or otherwise) relating to distributions on the TeleMax ADSs to which such persons are entitled, shall use its best efforts that are reasonable in the circumstances. **Tax-Service Franchise Agreement**	The depositary must use best efforts to maintain arrangements that will enable U.S. residents to receive any available rebates, tax credits, and other benefits relating to the TeleMax ADSs.

The subject, *depositary*, is separated from its verb, *shall use*, by 50 words.

Choose either *best efforts* or *reasonable efforts*, but don't combine the two. See § 148 at pp. 390–92.

"The word *precise* is itself as loose as water, and this paradox has helped to keep alive the dogged belief of lawyers in the precision of their language. Though rarely distinguished, two distinct meanings of *precise* are active in the law. *Precise* can be exact, sharp definition; the second is repetition; and though one sense does not exclude the other, the two are not the same." David Mellinkoff, *The Language of the Law* 295 (1963).

NOT THIS:	BUT THIS:
Ex. 2 **Section 11. Compliance With Regulations, Ordinances and Laws.** With respect to the Premises, Tenant shall be solely responsible for complying with all regulations, ordinances and all other laws which are now in force or which may hereafter be enacted by any applicable governmental body or agency now or hereafter having jurisdiction over the Premises, including, without limitation, the Americans with Disabilities Act and the Occupational Safety and Health Act. Tenant, upon receiving notice of any alleged violation of said regulations, ordinances and laws shall promptly forward a copy of such notice to Landlord. **Standardized Commercial Lease from a major law firm**	**11. Compliance with Laws and Regulations.** **11.1 Harrison's responsibility to comply with laws.** Harrison is solely responsible for complying with all regulations, ordinances, and other laws regarding the Premises, including the Americans with Disabilities Act and the Occupational Safety and Health Act. Upon receiving notice of an alleged violation or noncompliance, Harrison must promptly send Kelly Corp. a copy of the notice.
Ex. 3 18.2 Exculpation and Indemnification. (a) The doing of any act or the failure to do any act by any Covered Person, the effect of which may cause or result in loss or damage to the Company, if done or omitted to be done in good faith reliance upon advice of independent legal counsel or accountants employed by or on behalf of the Company, or if done or omitted to be done in good faith and in a manner reasonably believed to be within the scope of the authority granted by this Agreement and in or not opposed to the best interests of the Company, shall not subject any such person to any liability to the Company or the Members; provided, however, that the foregoing shall not relieve any Person of liability hereunder if it shall have been determined by a court of competent jurisdiction that such Person committed an act or omission that constitutes fraud, Gross Negligence or Willful Misconduct. **Operating Agreement from a major law firm**	**18.2 Exculpation and indemnity.** (A) **Exculpation.** Unless a court having jurisdiction finds that a Covered Person's act or omission causing loss or damage to the Company constituted fraud, gross negligence, or willful misconduct, the act or omission will not subject the Covered Person to liability to the Company or Members if it was done in good faith either: (1) in reliance on the advice of independent legal counsel or accountants employed by or acting on behalf of the Company; or (2) in a way that was reasonably believed to be within the scope of the authority granted by this Agreement and not to conflict with the Company's interests.

The subject, *Tenant,* is separated from its verb, *shall forward,* by 13 words. Also, note the missing comma after *laws.*

The first subject, *doing,* is separated from its verb, *shall not subject,* by 97 words. That makes for text that is hard to sort out.

Note the poor use of passive voice combined with *shall.* See §§ 47 and 66.

§ 105 Keep the main verb and its objects pretty close together.

Most English sentences follow what grammarians call the SVO pattern: subject-verb-object. Unduly separating the verb from its object is yet another type of undesirable syntactic bother. Avoid it.

NOT THIS:	BUT THIS:
Ex. 1 29 words separate the verb phrase, *may designate*, from its object, *Observer.* **3.4 Minority Shareholder Observers** (a) The Majority of the Minority Shareholders may designate, for so long as the Minority Shareholders hold, in aggregate, an Effective Interest in Securities of 5% or more but less than 20%, by notice to the Company one Observer. **Shareholders Agreement**	**3.4 Minority Shareholder Observer.** (A) If the Minority Shareholders hold, in aggregate, an Effective Interest in Securities of 5% or more but less than 20%, a Majority of the Minority Shareholders may designate one Observer and give the Company notice of their decision.
Ex. 2 39 words separate the verb, *will make*, from its object, *statement.* (g) The Company will make generally available to its securityholders as soon as practicable, but in any event not later than eighteen (18) months after the effective date of the Registration Statement (as defined in Rule 158(c) of the 1933 Act Regulations), an earning statement of the Company and its subsidiaries (which need not be audited) complying with Section 11(a) of the 1933 Act and the 1933 Act Regulations thereunder (including, at the option of the Company, Rule 158). **Underwriting Agreement**	(G) As soon as practicable, the Company will make available to security-holders an earning statement for both the Company and its subsidiaries. The statement, which need not be audited, must comply with § 11(a) of the 1933 Act and the 1933 Act Regulations (including, at the Company's option, Rule 158) and be available no later than 18 months after the effective date of the Registration Statement (as defined in Rule 158(c) of the 1933 Act Regulations).
Ex. 3 19 words separate the verb, *shall pay*, from its object, *amount.* The alternatives for *whichever is earlier* are near-gibberish. Unless otherwise agreed to in writing by Agent, Resident shall pay, prior to occupying the Premises or on or before the Commencement Date of the Lease Term, whichever is earlier, an amount equal to the Total Deposits, any other fees and charges, the prorated rent if the Lease Term commences on a day other than the first day of the month, and the first full month of total monthly rent if this Lease commences after the 20th day of any month. **Property-Management Agreement**	**15.3 Resident's initial payment.** Unless the Agent agrees in writing otherwise, before occupying the Premises or on the effective date of the Lease, whichever is earlier, the Resident must pay an amount equal to the sum of the Total Deposits and any other fees and charges, plus either: (A) the prorated rent if the Lease Term begins on a day other than the first day of the month; or (B) the first full month of total monthly rent if this Lease begins after the 20th day of any month.

"When a lawyer—like me—has to read virtually an entire document just to figure out what it is trying to do, you know something is wrong." Timothy Perrin, *Better Writing for Lawyers* 197 (1990).

§ 106 Renounce the idea of putting all qualifications into one sentence.

Don't try to stuff all qualifications into one sentence. It's a hopeless endeavor that leads to syntactic monstrosities.

NOT THIS:	BUT THIS:
Ex. 1 Article XI – Reporting Time 11.4 An employee who is scheduled or notified to report and who does report to work, shall be assigned to employee's regular job, but if employee's regular job is not available employee shall be reassigned to another job of equal pay provided that such other job is available and provided further that employee is qualified to perform the work required of employee in the other job. **Labor Contract** *This 65-word sentence contains 3 qualifications.*	**11. Reporting Time.** **11.4 Work assignment.** An employee who reports to work as scheduled or notified must be assigned to the employee's regular job. The employee may be reassigned to another job only if: (A) the regular job is unavailable; (B) the employee is qualified to perform the work required for the other job; and (C) the pay is the same for the regular job and the other job.
Ex. 2 3.3 Nothing contained herein shall constitute a relinquishment or waiver of the Borrower's rights to any independent claim that the Borrower may have against the Agent or any Lender for the Agent's or such Lender's, as the case may be, gross negligence or willful misconduct; provided that no Lender shall be liable for the conduct of the Agent or any other Lender; provided, further, that the Agent shall not be liable for the conduct of any Lender; provided, however that none of the Agent or any Lender shall be liable to the Borrower for any amounts representing indirect, special, consequential or punitive damages (as opposed to direct or actual damages) suffered by the Borrower. **Term-Loan Agreement** *This 113-word sentence contains 3 qualifications.*	**3.3 Murphey's independent claims.** Murphey does not relinquish or waive her rights to independent claims she might have against the Agent or a Lender for gross negligence or willful misconduct. But the following qualifications apply to a claim: (A) **Agent's liability.** The Agent is not liable for the conduct of any Lender. (B) **Lender's liability.** A Lender is not liable for the conduct of the Agent or any other Lender. (C) **Limited damages.** Murphey may recover only direct or actual damages. Neither the Agent nor the Lenders are liable for indirect, special, consequential, or punitive damages.

NOT THIS:	BUT THIS:
Ex. 3 **Casualty** . . . 22.5 Notwithstanding anything to the contrary contained in this Article: (a) Landlord shall not have any obligation whatsoever to repair, reconstruct, or restore the Premises when the damages resulting from any casualty covered by the provisions of this Article 22 occur during the last twelve (12) months of the Term or any extensions thereof, or for which sufficient insurance proceeds to fully cover the repair and restoration are not received by Landlord (provided that Landlord has maintained the insurance required to be maintained by Landlord under this Lease), but if Landlord determines not to repair such damages Landlord shall notify Tenant and if such damages shall render any material portion of the Premises untenantable Tenant shall have the right to terminate this Lease by notice to Landlord within fifteen (15) days after receipt of Landlord's notice; and (b) in the event the holder of any indebtedness secured by a mortgage or deed of trust covering the Premises or Building requires that any insurance proceeds be applied to such indebtedness, then Landlord shall have the right to terminate this Lease by delivering written notice of termination to Tenant within fifteen (15) days after such requirement is made by any such holder, whereupon this Lease shall end on the date of such damage as if the date of such damage were the date originally fixed in this Lease for the expiration of the Term. **Commercial Lease** This 231-word sentence contains many qualifications.	**22. Casualty.** . . . **22.5 No obligation for repairs.** The Landlord need not repair, reconstruct, or restore the Premises if: (A) the Landlord has maintained the insurance required under this Lease; and (B) the damages caused by a casualty covered by this § 22 occur during the last 12 months of the Term or an extension of the Term; or (C) the Landlord does not receive sufficient insurance proceeds to fully cover repairs and restoration. **22.6 Tenant's termination of Lease.** When § 22.5 applies, the Landlord will notify the Tenant of a decision not to repair damage. If any material part of the Premises is unusable because of the damage, then within 15 days after receiving the Landlord's notice, the Tenant may terminate this Lease by giving the Landlord written notice. **22.7 Landlord's termination of Lease.** If the Landlord receives insurance proceeds for the damage and a holder of a debt secured by a mortgage or deed of trust covering the Premises or Building requires the insurance proceeds to be applied to the debt, then the Landlord may terminate this Lease by giving the Tenant written notice of termination within 15 days after the holder notifies the Landlord of the requirement. Under this § 22.7, the Lease terminates on the date that the damage occurred.

"Most lawyers are as ignorant as their clients of the history of the language of the law. They believe that in their language everything is precise, especially if it's peculiar. Generations of lawyers have accepted the easy rationalization passed on to them. . . . [T]he first thing to know about legal writing is that the peculiarity of the language of the law has nothing to do with precision." David Mellinkoff, *Legal Writing: Sense and Nonsense* 2 (1982).

Principle of end weight

§ 107 Understand that in English, the end of a sentence is the greatest position of emphasis.

Remember that in good English, the last position in the sentence, not the first, is the most important. Try to end sentences emphatically—with a word or phrase that should receive stress.

NOT THIS:	BUT THIS:
Ex. 1 18. **Clean Premises—No Tenancies.** Seller will deliver the Premises to Purchaser vacant and broom-clean and free from all tenancies unless otherwise provided in this Agreement. **One-Family-Home Sales Contract from Vincent Di Lorenzo & Clifford R. Ennico, *Basic Legal Transactions: Real Estate Transactions* § 1:32 (2010)**	**18. Condition upon Delivery.** Unless this Agreement provides otherwise, Standridge will deliver the Premises to Macmillan vacant, broom-clean, and free from all tenancies.
Ex. 2 (11) Debtor may not sell, assign or otherwise dispose of or grant any pledge or security interest in the Security, except as provided in this agreement. **General Loan and Collateral Agreement from 1 Lester Nelson, *Digest of Commercial Laws of the World: Forms of Commercial Agreements* § 6-2, at 11 (May 1998)**	(11) **No transfer.** Unless this Agreement provides otherwise, Davis cannot transfer any part of the Security.

> "In the course of writing a contract, research and careful thought may reveal that apparently useless elaboration is actually significant. But it is sheer laziness to include boilerplate phrases just on the off-chance that they might come in handy."
> Carl Felsenfeld & Alan Siegel, *Writing Contracts in Plain English* 124 (1981).

§ 108 Understand that within a sentence containing set-off enumerations, the end of each provision is a position of emphasis.

Just as the end of a sentence is a position of great emphasis, so too is the end of an enumerated item. So avoid putting unemphatic words there.

Note that the systematic use of vertical lists with hanging indents adds *many* more positions of emphasis to the prose. Hence provisions immediately become more readable.

<table>
<tr><th>NOT THIS:</th><th>BUT THIS:</th></tr>
<tr><td>Ex. 1

5. Non-Solicitation. During the Non-Solicitation Period (as hereinafter defined), Graynor Ltd. shall not in any manner solicit or hire any employees or consultants of the Company, or any Company Affiliate, which shall include employees or consultants: (i) with continuing contracts with the Company or a Company Affiliate; (ii) retained, employed or engaged by the Company or a Company Affiliate but without continuing contracts; or (iii) whose contracts expire or otherwise terminate for any reason preceding or following the first day of the Non-Solicitation Period. During the Non-Solicitation Period, Graynor Ltd. will not influence or attempt to influence any customers or suppliers of the Company, or other third parties doing business with the Company, to divert their business to any individual or entity then in competition with the Company. During the Non-Solicitation Period, Graynor Ltd. will not disrupt, damage, impair, or interfere with the business of the Company in any way. Graynor Ltd. further agrees not to make any negative or disparaging statements about the Company, its affiliates, employees or representatives to any third party. For the purposes of this Agreement, the "Non-Solicitation Period" shall mean a period of two (2) years following the termination of this Agreement.
Professional-Services Contract</td><td>5. Prohibited Conduct.
5.1 Solicitation.
(A) Nonsolicitation of employees and consultants. Graynor will not in any manner solicit or hire any employees or consultants of the Company or a Company Affiliate, including employees or consultants:
(1) who have continuing contracts with the Company or a Company Affiliate;
(2) who are without continuing contracts while retained, employed, or engaged by the Company or a Company Affiliate; or
(3) whose contracts expire or otherwise terminate for any reason before or after the first day of the Nonsolicitation Period.
(B) Definition of "Nonsolicitation Period." The 2-year period after the termination of this Agreement is the "Nonsolicitation Period."
5.2 Other prohibited conduct. Graynor will not:
(A) influence or attempt to influence any customers or suppliers of the Company, or other third parties doing business with the Company, to divert their business to any individual or entity then in competition with the Company;
(B) disrupt, damage, impair, or interfere with the Company's business in any way; or
(C) make any negative or disparaging statements to any third party about the Company or its affiliates, employees, or representatives.</td></tr>
</table>

NOT THIS:

Ex. 2

5. Prepayment of the Loan.

(a) The Loan may not be voluntarily prepaid in any amount, within one (1) year after the date hereof. The Loan may be prepaid in whole or in part upon the terms and conditions set forth herein, commencing one (1) year after the date hereof. The Borrowers shall give the Bank, no later than 10:00 a.m., New York City time, at least thirty (30) days' prior written notice of any proposed prepayment of the Loan, specifying the proposed date of payment and the principal amount to be paid. Each partial prepayment shall be accompanied by all accrued interest on the principal repaid to the date of prepayment. Each partial prepayment of the principal amount shall be in an integral multiple of $100,000 and be accompanied by the payment of all charges outstanding and of all accrued interest on the principal repaid to the date of payment. The Borrowers acknowledge that prepayment or acceleration of the Loan shall result in the Bank incurring additional costs, expenses and/or liabilities and that it is extremely difficult and impractical to ascertain the extent of such costs, expenses and/or liabilities. Therefore, all full or partial prepayments of the Loan shall be accompanied by, and the Borrowers hereby promise to pay, on each date the Loan is prepaid or the date all sums payable hereunder become due and payable, by acceleration or otherwise, in addition to all other sums then owing, an amount (the "Prepayment Fee") determined by the Bank pursuant to the following formula:

(i) no prepayment of the Loan is permitted during the first twelve (12) month period after the twelve (12) month period after the date of this Note;

(ii) two percent (2%) of the amount to be prepaid if prepaid during the second twelve (12) month period after the date of this Note;

(iii) one percent (1%) of the amount to be prepaid if prepaid during the third twelve (12) month period after the date of this Note; and

(iv) no Prepayment Fee if prepaid after the third twelve (12) month period after the date of this Note.

(b) Any partial prepayment shall first be applied to accrued interest then due and then to the unpaid principal in reverse order of maturity.

Notwithstanding the foregoing and in the absence of an Event of Default, there shall be no prepayment penalty associated with the application by the Bank of any casualty or condemnation proceeds to the outstanding principal balance of the Loan.

Promissory Note

BUT THIS:

5. **Loan Prepayment.**
   5.1 **Voluntary prepayment.** For 1 year after the date of this Note, the Loan cannot be voluntarily prepaid in any amount. After that time, the Loan may be prepaid in whole or in part on these terms:
   (A) **Advance notice.** The Borrowers must give the Bank, no later than 10 a.m. ET, at least 30 days' written notice of the proposed prepayment of the Loan, specifying the proposed date of payment and the principal amount to be paid.
   (B) **Partial prepayment.** A partial prepayment of the principal amount must be an integral multiple of $100,000. In addition, the Borrowers must pay all charges outstanding and the interest on the principal accrued up to the date of payment.
   (C) **Prepayment fee.** In addition to all other amounts owing when a full or partial prepayment of the Loan is made, an additional amount may be required as a Prepayment Fee. If prepayment is:
   (1) during the second 12-month period after the date of this Note, the Prepayment Fee is 2% of the amount prepaid;
   (2) during the third 12-month period after the date of this Note, the Prepayment Fee is 1% of the amount prepaid; and
   (3) after the third 12-month period after the date of this Note, there is no Prepayment Fee.
   (D) **Application of partial prepayment.** A partial prepayment is first applied to accrued interest due and then to the unpaid principal in reverse order of maturity.
   5.2 **No prepayment penalty.** Despite § 5.1 and in the absence of an Event of Default, the Bank will apply casualty or condemnation proceeds to the outstanding principal balance of the Loan without charging a Prepayment Fee.

The acceleration language has been moved to another section dealing with acceleration of the loan.

"The complaints about legal language are directed at both its style and its unintelligibility, and these are separate objections. It is a mistake to assume, as many do, that style is faulty only when it clouds meaning, for there is a cry of anger in these protests against style itself. 'Said dog did bite aforementioned leg' will offend critics though its meaning is clear." Robert W. Benson, *The End of Legalese: The Game Is Over*, 13 Rev. L. & Soc. Change 519, 522 (1985).

NOT THIS:

Ex. 3

Section 12. Remedies of Indemnitee.

(a) If (i) a determination is made pursuant to Section 10(b) of this Agreement that Indemnitee is not entitled to indemnification under this Agreement, (ii) advance of Expenses is not timely made pursuant to Sections 8 or 9 of this Agreement, (iii) no determination of entitlement to indemnification shall have been made pursuant to Section 10(b) of this Agreement within 60 days after receipt by the Company of the request for indemnification, (iv) payment of indemnification is not made pursuant to Sections 7 or 9 of this Agreement within ten days after receipt by the Company of a written request therefor, or (v) payment of indemnification pursuant to any other section of this Agreement or the charter or Bylaws of the Company is not made within ten days after a determination has been made that Indemnitee is entitled to indemnification, Indemnitee shall be entitled to an adjudication in an appropriate court located in the State of Maryland, or in any other court of competent jurisdiction, or in an arbitration conducted by a single arbitrator pursuant to the Commercial Arbitration Rules of the American Arbitration Association, of Indemnitee's entitlement to indemnification or advance of Expenses. Indemnitee shall commence a proceeding seeking an adjudication or an award in arbitration within 180 days following the date on which Indemnitee first has the right to commence such proceeding pursuant to this Section 12(a); provided, however, that the foregoing clause shall not apply to a proceeding brought by Indemnitee to enforce Indemnitee's rights under Section 7 of this Agreement. Except as set forth herein, the provisions of Maryland law (without regard to its conflicts of laws rules) shall apply to any such arbitration. The Company shall not oppose Indemnitee's right to seek any such adjudication or award in arbitration.

(b) In any judicial proceeding or arbitration commenced pursuant to this Section 12, Indemnitee shall be presumed to be entitled to indemnification or advance of Expenses, as the case may be, under this Agreement and the Company shall have the burden of proving that Indemnitee is not entitled to indemnification or advance of Expenses, as the case may be. If Indemnitee commences a judicial proceeding or arbitration pursuant to this Section 12, Indemnitee shall not be required to reimburse the Company for any advances pursuant to Section 8 of this Agreement until a final determination is made with respect to Indemnitee's entitlement to indemnification (as to which all rights of appeal have been exhausted or lapsed). The Company shall, to the fullest extent not prohibited by law, be precluded from asserting in any judicial proceeding or arbitration commenced pursuant to this Section 12 that the procedures and presumptions of this Agreement are not valid, binding and enforceable and shall stipulate in any such court or before any such arbitrator that the Company is bound by all of the provisions of this Agreement.

(c) If a determination shall have been made pursuant to Section 10(b) of this Agreement that Indemnitee is entitled to indemnification, the Company shall be bound by such determination in any judicial proceeding or arbitration commenced pursuant to this Section 12, absent a misstatement by Indemnitee of a material fact, or an omission of a material fact necessary to make Indemnitee's statement not materially misleading, in connection with the request for indemnification that was not disclosed in connection with the determination.

(d) In the event that Indemnitee is successful in seeking, pursuant to this Section 12, a judicial adjudication of or an award in arbitration to enforce Indemnitee's rights under, or to recover damages for breach of, this Agreement, Indemnitee shall be entitled to recover from the Company, and shall be indemnified by the Company for, any and all Expenses actually and reasonably incurred by Indemnitee in such judicial adjudication or arbitration. If it shall be determined in such judicial adjudication or arbitration that Indemnitee is entitled to receive part but not all of the indemnification or advance of Expenses sought, the Expenses incurred by Indemnitee in connection with such judicial adjudication or arbitration shall be appropriately prorated.

(e) Interest shall be paid by the Company to Indemnitee at the maximum rate allowed to be charged for judgments under the Courts and Judicial Proceedings Article of the Annotated Code of Maryland for amounts which the Company pays or is obligated to pay for the period (i) commencing with either the tenth day after the date on which the Company was requested to advance Expenses in accordance with Sections 8 or 9 of this Agreement or the 60th day after the date on which the Company was requested to make the determination of entitlement to indemnification under Section 10(b) of this Agreement, as applicable, and (ii) ending on the date such payment is made to Indemnitee by the Company.

Indemnity Agreement

BUT THIS:

12. **Remedies of the Indemnitee.**

12.1 **Right to adjudication and arbitration.** The Indemnitee is entitled to litigate the Indemnitee's right to indemnity or advance of Expenses in any court having jurisdiction, or in an arbitration conducted by a single arbitrator under the Commercial Arbitration Rules of the American Arbitration Association, if any of the following occurs:

(A) **Indemnity denied.** It is determined under § 10.2 that the Indemnitee is not entitled to indemnity.

(B) **Unpaid expenses.** Expenses under § 8 or § 9 are not timely advanced.

(C) **Indemnity undermined.** Within 60 days after the Company receives the request for indemnity under § 10.2, no determination of entitlement has been made.

(D) **Indemnity unpaid.** Indemnity has not been paid within 10 days after:

(1) the Company receives the written request for indemnity under § 7 or § 9; or

(2) the Company determines under any other section of this Agreement or the charter or bylaws of the Company that the Indemnitee is entitled to indemnity.

12.2 **Litigation or arbitration.**

(A) **Beginning proceeding.** Within 180 days after the date on which Indemnitee's right to litigation or arbitration for indemnity or advance of Expenses under this § 12 arises, the Indemnitee must sue or seek an award in arbitration. If the Indemnitee sues to enforce the Indemnitee's rights under § 7, the preceding sentence does not apply.

(B) **Absolute right to proceeding.** In a proceeding brought under this § 12, the Company will not oppose the Indemnitee's right to litigate or arbitrate. To the fullest extent allowed by law, the Company will assert that the procedures and presumptions of this Agreement are valid, binding, and enforceable and will stipulate in a court or before an arbitrator that the Company is bound by this Agreement.

(C) **Presumption of entitlement.** The Indemnitee is presumed to be entitled to indemnity or advance of Expenses. The Company has the burden of proving that the Indemnitee is not entitled.

(D) **Indemnity determination binding.** In litigation or arbitration brought under this § 12, if a determination is made under § 10.2 that the Indemnitee is entitled to indemnity, the Company is bound by that determination. But it is not bound if, in connection with the request for indemnity and the determination, the Indemnitee:

(1) misstated a material fact; or

(2) omitted a material fact necessary to make the Indemnitee's statement not materially misleading.

(E) **No reimbursement by the Indemnitee.** The Indemnitee is not required to reimburse the Company for any advances under § 8 until a final determination is made about the Indemnitee's entitlement to indemnity and all rights of appeal have been exhausted or lapsed.

12.3 **The Indemnitee's recovery.**

(A) **Expenses.** If the Indemnitee prevails in a lawsuit or gains an award in arbitration to enforce the Indemnitee's rights under this Agreement, or to recover damages for its breach, the Company will indemnify the Indemnitee for the Indemnitee's Expenses actually and reasonably incurred. If the Indemnitee is found to be entitled to receive only part of the indemnity or advance Expenses sought, the Indemnitee's Expenses actually and reasonably incurred must be appropriately prorated.

(B) **Interest.** The Company must pay the Indemnitee interest at the maximum rate allowed to be charged for judgments under the Courts and Judicial Proceedings Article of the Annotated Code of Maryland for amounts that the Company pays or becomes obligated to pay. The Company will pay interest:

(1) on an award for advance Expenses under § 8 or § 9, beginning on the 10th day after the date on which the Company receives the request for advance Expenses;

(2) on an award for indemnity under § 10.2, beginning on the 60th day after the date on which the Company receives the request for indemnity; and

(3) for any award, ending on the date that the Company pays the interest to the Indemnitee.

12.4 **Governing law for arbitration.** Maryland law applies to all matters arising under or relating to this Agreement without regard to any choice-of-law rules that might direct the application of another jurisdiction's laws.

Conditions—in general

§ 109 Use *if* as the default term for creating conditions.

Use *if* as the general-purpose way to create a condition. Avoid the old-fashioned *should*, which causes a miscue for many readers. Use *when* (not *where*) if the sentence needs an *if* to introduce another unrelated clause or if the condition is something that may occur with regularity.

NOT THIS:	BUT THIS:
Ex. 1 Upon the happening of any event which shall result in the change or cessation of payments to the Wife hereunder, said change or cessation shall be effective as of the next payment date following the event. **Divorce Agreement from Vincent Di Lorenzo & Clifford R. Ennico, *Basic Legal Transactions: Family Transactions* § 43:35 (2010)**	If an event causes the payments to Maribelle to change or cease under this Agreement, the change or cessation will take effect on the next payment date after the event.
Ex. 2 Should default be made in payment of interest when due, or in the event of default other than in the non-payment of interest when due, the whole sum of principal and interest shall become immediately due and payable without notice, at the option of the holder of this note. **Interest-Only Note from Donald E. Rapp Jr., *Guide to Commercial Real Estate Loan Documentation*, Exhibit 7-1, at 120 (1990)**	If interest is not paid when due, or if a default other than nonpayment of interest occurs, the noteholder may require the entire principal and interest to become due immediately without notice.
Ex. 3 Provider's obligation under this warranty shall be to repair any item of Equipment which is repairable or at its option, overhaul, rebuild, or replace any item of Equipment that has been reported by AmeriCon to Provider as containing a defect in materials or workmanship, and has been determined by Provider, in its reasonable judgment, to be defective. **Aircraft-Services Agreement from a major law firm**	32. **Warranty for Material and Workmanship.** If AmeriCon determines that an item of Equipment is defective in material or workmanship, AmeriCon will notify the Provider of that determination. If the Provider reasonably determines that the Equipment is defective, the Provider must, at its option, either repair the Equipment or overhaul, rebuild, or replace it.

"The minute you read something and you can't understand it, you can be sure it was written by a lawyer. Then if you give it to another lawyer and he don't know just what it means, why you can be sure it was drawn up by a lawyer." Will Rogers, "The Lawyers Talking," 28 July 1935, in 6 *Will Rogers' Weekly Archives* 6:243–244 (Steven K. Graggert ed., 1982).

§ 110 Unearth hidden conditions to make them explicit, using the word *if*.

The little word *if* is among the most important ones in the drafter's vocabulary. Often drafters somehow avoid it, usually by using a noun phrase with many prepositional phrases following. When you see awkwardnesses resembling those in the examples below, try *if*.

NOT THIS:	BUT THIS:
Ex. 1 The insurance covering the interest of the loss payee shall become invalid only because of your conversion or secretion of your covered auto. **Automobile-Insurance Policy from a major insurance company**	If you hide or wrongfully take your covered auto, the insurance covering the interest of the loss payee becomes invalid.
Ex. 2 Failure to sign the Release within this time period will result in a forfeiture of the severance benefits described herein. **Healthcare Company Executive-Employment Agreement**	If you fail to sign the Release within this period, you forfeit the severance benefits in this Agreement.
Ex. 3 ALL LOAN CARS ARE NON-SMOKING. To ensure a clean, smoke-free car for service customers, I agree to pay $30.00 detail fee for smoking in this car. **Service Loan-Car Agreement from a luxury-car dealership**	17. **No Smoking in Loan Cars.** We have a no-smoking policy. If you smoke in this car, you must pay a $30 detail fee.
Ex. 4 Tenant's failure to timely deliver the Exercise Notice during the Exercise Period shall be deemed to constitute Tenant's waiver of its option to extend the initial Term hereunder. **Lease Agreement from a major technology institution**	If Lorentax does not timely deliver the Exercise Notice during the Exercise Period, Lorentax waives the option to extend this Lease's initial Term.
Ex. 5 The failure of either party to require the performance of any term of this Agreement or the waiver by either party of any breach under this Agreement shall not prevent a subsequent enforcement of such term and shall not be deemed a waiver of any subsequent breach. **Merchandising-License Agreement from Gregory J. Battersby & Charles W. Grimes, *License Agreements: Forms and Checklists* § 5.13[C], at 5-150.33 (2d ed. 2017)**	If either party fails to require the other to perform any term of this Agreement, that failure does not prevent the party from later enforcing that term. If either party waives the other's breach of a term, that waiver is not treated as waiving a later breach of the term.

NOT THIS:	BUT THIS:
Ex. 6 You are authorized to complete and use this Master Software License Agreement ("MSLA") if you follow these instructions. Failure to comply with Kindall policy may subject the non-complying employee to disciplinary action. **Master Software-License Agreement Instructions from a major telecommunications company**	8. **Using the Master Software-License Agreement.** If you follow these instructions, you are authorized to complete and use this Master Software-License Agreement ("MSLA") . If you do not comply with Kindall policy, you may be subject to disciplinary action.
Ex. 7 Lessor hereby warrants and agrees to defend the title to the property, and agrees that lessee shall have the right at any time to pay or otherwise satisfy any mortgages, taxes or other liens, or interest and other charges on the property, in the event of a default of payment, and be subrogated to the rights of the holder thereof, and to deduct any amount so paid from royalties and other payments due, or which may become due under this lease. **Coal-and-Lignite Lease from 7A William B. Burford, *West's Texas Forms: Minerals, Oil & Gas* § 19:5, at 288 (4th ed. 2008)**	Stanton will defend the title to the property. If Stanton defaults on a payment, Briggs may satisfy any mortgage, tax, lien, interest, or other charge on the property and be subrogated to the holder's rights. Briggs may then deduct the payment amount from royalties and other payments due under this lease. Using *will* is much clearer than the wordy *hereby warrants and agrees to*. See § 49.
Ex. 8 13. EQUIPMENT CHANGES AND FEATURE ENHANCEMENTS 13.1 **Equipment Changes.** Supplier will provide Equipment Upgrades to Delta Communications at no charge during the 5-year warranty period set forth in Section 19. Supplier will provide Equipment Feature Enhancements to DeltaCom, if requested by DeltaCom, and DeltaCom will pay for those Equipment Feature Enhancements consistent with this Section. DeltaCom is not obligated to pay for any Equipment Feature Enhancement supplied to DeltaCom at the initiative of Supplier unless DeltaCom elects to utilize any new feature included therein. **Master Purchase Agreement for Technical Deliverables and Related Services Instructions from a major telecommunications company**	13. **Equipment Changes and Feature Enhancements.** 13.1 **Equipment changes.** During the 5-year warranty period described in § 19, the Supplier will provide Equipment Upgrades to DeltaCom at no charge. If DeltaCom asks, the Supplier will provide Equipment Feature Enhancements at DeltaCom's expense. If the Supplier provides DeltaCom with a Feature Enhancement that DeltaCom has not requested, DeltaCom need not pay for it unless DeltaCom chooses to use it.

§ 111 If a condition is relatively short and seeing it first would help the reader avoid a miscue, put it at the beginning of the sentence.

The lesson is simple: when an *if*-clause is short, start with it. That way, the reader immediately understands the applicability of a stated consequence. This basic syntactic pattern typically reinforces the principle of end weight (see § 107).

NOT THIS:	BUT THIS:
Ex. 1 Contractor shall be entitled to the entirety of the Contractor's Fee based on the GMP rather than on the actual cost to complete in the event that Contractor completes the project for a sum less than the GMP. **Construction Contract from a major law firm**	Even if the Contractor completes the project for a sum less than the GMP, the Contractor's Fee will be based on the GMP, not on the actual completion cost.
Ex. 2 Support Vendor shall provide Customer with one copy of each new Release, without additional charge. **Help-Desk Agreement from 2 Paul C. Quittmeyer et al., *Computer Software Agreements* § 16.2 (3d ed. 2007)**	If a new Release becomes available, the Support Vendor must provide Customer with 1 copy for no additional charge.
Ex. 3 Approval by Horst of a Transfer shall be subject to and conditioned upon execution by the transferee of the then-current form of Black's franchise agreement and payment of any required deposit. **Franchise-License Agreement from a tax-preparation company**	Before Horst will approve a Transfer, the transferee must sign the then-current form of Black's franchise agreement and pay any required deposit.

"Never worry about insulting your reader's intelligence by writing in plain English. Research has shown that experienced readers prefer a straightforward, direct style intended to convey information. Plain English benefits everyone, readers and writers alike. You are far more likely to irritate your readers if you write as though you are a being from another planet, to be approached only with special permission." Margaret C. McLaren, *Effective Writing: Plain English for Accountants* 6 (1992).

§ 112 If a condition is long and the main clause is short, put the main clause first and move directly into the condition.

Here's the corollary to § 111: when the *if*-clause is long or consists of multiple parts, move it to the end.

NOT THIS:	BUT THIS:
Ex. 1 When there is disagreement between an attending physician and the utilization review/case management contractor, the patient and/or attending physician, after all opportunities for appeal have been exhausted within the utilization review/case management contractor's organization, shall be afforded an opportunity to obtain a review (including if necessary, an examination) by an independent specialist physician. **Employment Agreement from a railroad company**	7.1 **Review by independent specialist physician.** The patient or attending physician may obtain a review by an independent specialist physician, including an examination if necessary, if: (A) an attending physician and the use-review or case-management contractor disagree; and (B) all opportunities for appeal have been exhausted within the use-review or case-management contractor's organization.
Ex. 2 If the Player, in the judgment of the Club's physician, is not in good physical condition at the date of his first scheduled game for the Club, or if, at the beginning of or during any season, he fails to remain in good physical condition (unless such condition results directly from an injury sustained by the Player as a direct result of participating in any basketball practice or game played for the Club during such season), so as to render the Player, in the judgment of the Club's physician, unfit to play skilled basketball, the Club shall have the right to suspend such Player until such time as, in the judgment of the Club's physician, the Player is in sufficiently good physical condition to play skilled basketball. **Player Contract for a professional basketball player**	6.1 **Physical condition.** Adamson must be in sufficiently good physical condition to play skilled basketball at the beginning of the season and throughout the season. 6.2 **Cause for suspension.** The Club may suspend Adamson until the Club's physician renders him fit to play skilled basketball if, in the judgment of the Club's physician: (A) Adamson is not in good-enough physical condition to play skilled basketball at the date of the Club's first scheduled game of a season; or (B) Adamson fails to remain in adequate physical condition to play skilled basketball at any time during a season. 6.3 **Exception for injury during Club play.** The Club cannot suspend Adamson if the unfit condition has resulted directly from an injury sustained as a result of participating in any Club basketball practice or game.

For warnings against using *and/or*, see § 149 at p. 406–08.

This one sentence is 127 words long!

The headings break up this long chunk of text.

NOT THIS:	BUT THIS:
Ex. 3 If, after giving effect to any arrangements for the purchase of the Units of a defaulting Underwriter or Underwriters by you and the Company and the Selling Unitholders as provided in subsection 2.9(a), the aggregate number of such Units which remains unpurchased exceeds one-eleventh of the aggregate number of all the Units to be purchased at such Time of Delivery, or if the company and the Selling Unitholders shall not exercise the right described in subsection 2.9(b) to require non-defaulting Underwriters to purchase Units of a defaulting Underwriter or Underwriters, then this Agreement shall thereupon terminate, without liability on the part of any non-defaulting Underwriter or the Company, the Trustee or the Selling Unitholders, except for the expenses to be borne by the Company, the Trustee, the Selling Unitholders and the Underwriters as provided in Section 6 hereof and the indemnity and contribution agreements in Section 8 hereof; but nothing herein shall relieve a defaulting Underwriter from liability for its default. **Underwriting Agreement**	7. **Termination.** (A) **Events causing termination.** This Agreement terminates if: (1) the aggregate number of a defaulting Underwriter's unpurchased units exceeds 1/11 of the aggregate number of units to be purchased at delivery—taking into account arrangements between you, the Company, and the Selling Unitholders under § 2.9(A); or (2) the Company and the Selling Unitholders do not exercise the right under § 2.9(B) to require non-defaulting Underwriters to purchase a defaulting Underwriter's units. (B) **Effect of termination.** A defaulting Underwriter remains liable despite termination of this Agreement. A nondefaulting Underwriter or the Company, the Trustee, or the Selling Unitholders are not liable when termination occurs except for: (1) expenses they must bear under § 6; and (2) indemnity and contribution agreements under § 8.

"A lot of drafting has been influenced by the belief that every qualification and exception relating to a proposition must be held together in the one sentence. This leads to the production of overlong, convoluted sentences—often of 200, 500, or even 800 words in length. The worst I have seen is a sentence with over 1,200 words in a residential mortgage!" Robert Eagleson, *Ensnaring Perceptions on Communication: Underlying Obstacles to Lawyers' Writing Plainly*, 62 Clarity 9, 10 (Nov. 2009).

NOT THIS:

Ex. 4

Upon the occurrence of any of the following events: (a) Borrower's failure to pay any Guaranteed Indebtedness when due or any other default or event of default under any terms of the Loan Documents; or (b) any representation or warranty made by or on behalf of any Guarantor herein or in any writing furnished in connection with or pursuant to this Guaranty shall be incorrect, false or misleading on the date as of which made; or (c) any Guarantor shall default in the punctual and complete performance or observance of any agreement, covenant, term or condition contained herein or in any instrument given to secure Guarantor's obligations hereunder; or (d) any Guarantor shall fail to pay at maturity, or within any applicable period of grace, any obligation for borrowed monies or advances, or fail to observe or perform any term, covenant or agreement contained in any agreement or obligation by which it is bound evidencing or securing borrowed money for such period of time as would accelerate or would permit the holder therefore of any obligation issued thereunder, to accelerate, the maturity thereof or of any such obligation; or (e) a final judgment or judgments in the aggregate for the payment of money in excess of $10,000 shall be rendered against any Guarantor and the same shall remain undischarged for a period of thirty (30) days during which execution shall not effectively be stayed; or (f) any Guarantor or any other person shall claim, or any court shall find or rule, that Lender does not have a valid lien on any security which may have been provided by any Guarantor or such other person for the Guaranteed Indebtedness; or (g) any Guarantor shall make a general assignment for the benefit of creditors or shall petition or apply to any tribunal for the appointment of a custodian, liquidator, trustee or receiver of all or any substantial part of the business, estate or assets of any Guarantor or shall commence any proceeding relating to such Guarantor or its property under any bankruptcy, reorganization, arrangement, insolvency, readjustment of debt, dissolution or liquidation law of any jurisdiction, whether now or hereafter in effect; or (h) any such petition or application shall be filed or any such proceeding shall be commenced against any Guarantor, and such Guarantor by any act or omission shall indicate approval thereof, consent thereto or acquiescence therein, or an order shall be entered appointing any such custodian, liquidator, trustee or receiver of all or any substantial part of the assets of any Guarantor, or granting relief to any Guarantor or approving the petition in any such proceeding, and such order shall remain in effect for more than thirty (30) days; or (i) any Guarantor shall fail generally to pay its debts as they become due, or suffer any writ of attachment or execution or any similar process to be issued or levied against it or any substantial part of its property which is not released, stayed, bonded or vacated within thirty (30) days after its issue or levy; or (j) any Guarantor shall have concealed, removed, or permitted to be concealed or removed, any part of its property, with intent to hinder, delay or defraud its creditors or any of them, or made or suffered a transfer of any of its property which may be fraudulent under any bankruptcy, fraudulent conveyance or similar law; or shall have made any transfer of its property to or for the benefit of a creditor at a time when other creditors similarly situated have not been paid or shall have suffered or permitted, while insolvent, any creditor to obtain a lien upon any of its property through legal proceedings or distraint which is not vacated within thirty (30) days from the date thereof; or (k) as to any Guarantor who is an individual, such Guarantor shall have died and his estate or a substantial part of such estate shall be distributed by the executor or administrator thereof to his heirs or in accordance with such Guarantor's will prior to all the distributees of such estate or part thereof (by an instrument approved in form and substance by Lender) either (i) jointly and severally assuming all of such deceased Guarantor's obligation hereunder or (ii) to secure the payment of the Guaranteed Indebtedness effectively pledging, mortgaging or otherwise creating a first lien (but without any personal liability on such distributee's part) on a portion of the assets of such estate valued by a qualified appraiser approved by Lender at not less than the principal amount of the Guaranteed Indebtedness then outstanding; or (l) as to any Guarantor which is a corporation, partnership or joint venture, the dissolution, liquidation or termination of existence of such Guarantor or the sale, conveyance, lease or other disposition of a substantial part of the assets of such Guarantor; or (m) any adverse material change shall occur in the assets, liabilities, financial condition, business, operations, affairs or circumstances of any Guarantor; then an event of default under this Guaranty shall have occurred and the holder or holders of the Guaranteed Indebtedness may, at its or their option, declare the unpaid balance of the Guaranteed Indebtedness, together with all interest then accrued thereon, to be immediately due and payable, and thereupon the Guaranteed Indebtedness shall immediately be due and payable without presentation, notice of protest, other notice of dishonor, notice of intent to accelerate, or notice of acceleration, all of which are hereby expressly WAIVED by each Guarantor.

Loan Guaranty from a major bank [Word count: 914]

> 914 words! Can you spot the subject and verb?

> Here we have a common drafting problem: Does the *which*-clause (which should be a *that*-clause) refer to proceedings as well as distraints—or might it refer to *lien*? The revision resolves the ambiguity as if it were meant to refer equally to *lien* and *distraint*. A court interpreting the original wording might invoke the rule of the last antecedent.

BUT THIS:

7. Default.

7.1 Conditions of default. Default under this Guaranty occurs upon any of the following events:

(A) if the Stewarts fail to pay any Guaranteed Indebtedness when due or otherwise default;

(B) if a representation or warranty by or on behalf of a Guarantor, or any writing furnished in connection with or under this Guaranty, proves to have been incorrect, false, or misleading when made;

(C) if a Guarantor fails to timely and completely perform or observe any agreement, term, or condition of this or any other instrument to secure the Guarantor's obligations;

(D) if a Guarantor fails to pay at maturity—or within any applicable grace period—an obligation for borrowed moneys or advances, or to observe or perform any term or promise in an agreement or obligation evidencing or securing borrowed money for whatever period, when that failure would either accelerate or permit the holder of any obligation to accelerate the maturity of the obligation;

(E) if a final judgment (or judgments in the aggregate) for more than $10,000 is rendered against a Guarantor, and the sum is undischarged for 30 days during which execution is not effectively stayed;

(F) if a Guarantor or other person claims—or any court finds or rules—that Lender lacks a valid lien on any security that was provided by a Guarantor (or other person) for the Guaranteed Indebtedness;

(G) if a Guarantor makes a general assignment for the benefit of creditors or petitions or applies to a tribunal to appoint a custodian, liquidator, trustee, or receiver of all or a substantial part of the business, estate, or assets of a Guarantor or begins a proceeding relating to the Guarantor or its property under any bankruptcy, reorganization, arrangement, insolvency, readjustment of debt, dissolution, or liquidation law (whether now or later effective) of any jurisdiction;

(H) if a petition or application under (G) is filed or proceeding begun against a Guarantor, and either:

(1) the Guarantor—by act or omission—approves, consents, or acquiesces; or

(2) an order remaining in effect for more than 30 days:

(a) appoints a custodian, liquidator, trustee, or receiver of all or a substantial part of the Guarantor's assets;

(b) grants relief to the Guarantor; or

(c) approves the petition in such a proceeding;

(I) if a Guarantor fails generally to pay its debts as they become due or suffers a writ of attachment or execution or similar process issued or levied against it (or a substantial part of its property)—and the writ or process is not released, stayed, bonded, or vacated within 30 days after its issue or levy;

(J) if a Guarantor conceals, removes, or permits to be concealed or removed any part of its property with intent to hinder, delay, or defraud its creditors; makes or suffers a property transfer that may be fraudulent under any bankruptcy, fraudulent-conveyance, or similar law; or transfers its property to or for the benefit of a creditor when other similarly situated creditors have not been paid, or suffers or permits, while insolvent, any creditor to obtain either of the following if it is not vacated within 30 days from its date:

(1) a lien on any of its property through legal proceedings; or

(2) a distraint;

(K) if an individual Guarantor dies, and the estate or a substantial part of it is distributed by the executor or administrator to the heirs or according to the Guarantor's will *before* all the distributees of the estate (by an instrument that the Lender approved in form and substance) either:

(1) jointly and severally assume all the deceased Guarantor's obligations under this Guaranty; or

(2) in order to secure payment of the Guaranteed Indebtedness, effectively pledge, mortgage, or otherwise create a first lien (but without the distributee's personal liability) on a part of the estate's assets valued (by a Lender-approved, qualified appraiser) at or above the outstanding principal amount of the Guaranteed Indebtedness;

(L) if a corporate, partnership, or joint-venture Guarantor is dissolved, liquidated, or terminated, or its assets (or a substantial part of them) are sold, conveyed, leased, or otherwise disposed of; or

(M) if the assets, liabilities, financial condition, business, operations, affairs, or circumstances of a Guarantor adversely and materially change.

7.2 Effect of default. Upon default, the holder or holders of the Guaranteed Indebtedness may then—at its or their option—declare immediately due and payable the unpaid balance (plus interest) of the Guaranteed Indebtedness. Each Guarantor will be considered as having waived presentation, notice of protest, other notice of dishonor, notice of intent to accelerate, and notice of acceleration.

[Word count: 763; word reduction: 16%]

The rewrite puts the subject and predicate up front with the conditions following, and omits unnecessary wordiness.

With a long series of conditions, as here, it's good practice to preface each one with *if*. That way, a glance at the middle of the list won't produce a miscue.

Notice how the ambiguity highlighted in the original has been corrected here.

Exceptions

§ 113 Use *except* or *unless* as the default wording for an exception.

As with conditions, lawyers have all sorts of ways to state exceptions—many of them stilted, awkward, or downright ambiguous. Learn to like *except* and *unless*.

NOT THIS:	BUT THIS:
Ex. 1 The term of this agreement shall be for a period of 3 years, commencing on May 1, 2018, and terminating on April 30, 2021, subject, however, to prior termination as provided by this agreement. **Contract of Employment from *Texas Forms* § 11:43, at 99 (2008)**	The term of this Agreement is 3 years—beginning on May 1, 2018, and ending on April 30, 2021—unless termination occurs earlier in accordance with this Agreement.
Ex. 2 During the term hereof, Company hereby engages Consultant and Consultant hereby agrees to serve Company, as an independent contractor. Consultant shall be available to work at reasonable times and for reasonable periods of time to perform such consultation as is required by Company. Consultant shall travel on the business of Company whenever reasonably requested to do so provided such travel is not unreasonably burdensome. Consultant shall generally endeavor to improve the business of Company during the term of this Agreement. **Independent-Contractor Agreement from 1 *Tennessee Legal and Business Forms: Employment and Agency Contracts* § 2.22 (Aug. 2016)**	The Company hereby engages Grace Highfill as an independent contractor for the term of this Agreement. She must be available to work at reasonable times and for reasonable periods to perform the consulting work that the Company requests and must be available to travel on Company business as requested unless the travel would be an unreasonable burden on her. She is generally responsible for improving the Company's business for the term of this Agreement.

§ 114 If an exception needs to be understood before the sentence can be easily read, state it briefly at the beginning of the sentence.

The placement of an exception, like the placement of a condition, involves a judgment call. If it can be stated quickly and succinctly, and it properly contextualizes the sentence, put it at the fore.

NOT THIS:	BUT THIS:
Ex. 1 Owner shall pay builder for the construction of the boat, in full compensation, a fixed price of $30,500, which is not subject to adjustment for escalations and which is otherwise subject to adjustment only by mutual agreement in writing between owner and builder. **Agreement for Construction and Sale of Boat from 3B Am. Jur. Legal Forms 2d *Boats and Boating* § 42:9 (Nov. 2017 update)**	Unless the Owner and the Builder agree otherwise in writing, the Owner will pay the Builder $30,500 for the construction of the boat, without any adjustment for escalations.
Ex. 2 Section 6.1 Covenants of the Company. From the date hereof until the Effective Time, except (i) as set forth in the Company Disclosure Schedule, (ii) as required by applicable Law, (iii) as required or contemplated by this Agreement or (iv) as consented to in writing by Parent (which consent shall not be unreasonably withheld, delayed or conditioned), the Company shall, and shall cause each of its Subsidiaries to, (A) conduct its business in the ordinary course, (B) use its reasonable best efforts to preserve intact its business organizations and relationships with third parties and to keep available the services of its present officers and employees, and (C) use its reasonable best efforts to protect the Company Intellectual Property to the end that the Company's and its Subsidiaries' goodwill and ongoing business shall not be impaired in any material respects as of the Closing Date. **Merger Agreement between two major entertainment-industry companies**	**6.1 Covenants of the Company.** Unless the Company Disclosure Schedule, applicable law, or this Agreement requires otherwise, or unless Parent consents in writing (which consent must not be unreasonably withheld, delayed, or conditioned), from the date of this Agreement until the Effective Time, the Company and its Subsidiaries will: (A) conduct business as usual; (B) use best efforts to keep business organizations and relationships with third parties intact and to keep the services of present officers and employees available; and (C) use best efforts to protect the Company Intellectual Property so that the Company's and its Subsidiaries' goodwill and ongoing business are not materially impaired on the Closing Date. [Although this exception is not short, it's best to put it first because the main provision is long with subsections.] [Choose either *best efforts* or *reasonable efforts*, but don't combine the two. See § 148 at pp. 390–92.]

§ 115 If an exception cannot be stated briefly, or if it refers to truly extraordinary circumstances—and hence no miscue is likely—put it at the end. Or start a new sentence with *But*.

As with conditions, complex and lengthy exceptions should typically follow the kernel sentence—not precede it. And forget the wrongheaded notion that all qualifications (including exceptions) should be packed into a single sentence: sometimes the best approach is to state a general rule in one sentence and then to introduce one or more exceptions in a separate sentence beginning with *But*.

NOT THIS:	BUT THIS:
Ex. 1 Unless the loss results from your conversion, secretion, or embezzlement of your covered auto, the insurance covering the interest of the loss payee shall not become invalid because of your fraudulent acts or omissions. **Automobile-Insurance Policy**	The insurance covering the interest of the loss payee does not become invalid if you act fraudulently unless the loss results from your wrongfully taking, hiding, or embezzling your covered auto.
Ex. 2 Cambrian and Contractor agree that the following general provisions shall at all times apply to and control all Work which may be conducted or carried out by Contractor for Cambrian under any Work Order (except to the extent any work is specifically covered under another Cambrian contract (e.g., Well and Lease Service Master Contract - Water Operations or Master Agreement For Onshore Drilling, Completion, and Workover Operations)) until such Work Order is canceled pursuant to Paragraphs 19 or 20 hereof. **Master Service Agreement from a major oil company**	Until a Work Order is canceled under § 19 or § 20, the following general provisions apply to all Work that Lassiter Construction conducts or carries out for Cambrian under that Work Order unless the work is specifically covered under another Cambrian contract, including a well-and-lease service master contract—water operations or a master agreement for onshore drilling, completion, and workover operations.
Ex. 3 Neither party may assign this Agreement without the prior written consent of the other party, except that Publisher may assign its rights and obligations under this Agreement without the prior written consent of Author to any person or entity that acquires all or substantially all of the business or assets of Publisher. **Book-Publishing Contract**	Neither party may assign this Agreement without the prior written consent of the other party. But without the Author's prior written consent, the Publisher may assign its rights and obligations under this Agreement to any person or entity that acquires all or substantially all of the Publisher's business or assets.

Provisos

§ 116 Reword every instance of *provided that.*

Eliminate this phrase and all variations on it. Provisos can mean *if*, *except*, or *also*—and their uncertain syntactic reach is a recurrent cause of ambiguity. Because the phrase *provided that* sometimes creates a condition, sometimes an exception, and sometimes an additional thought, avoid it in all drafting. Instead, use a more specific term such as *if*, *but*, or *and*—or no term at all.

Often thought to create exceptions only, the phrase *provided, however, that* can also create conditions and mere additions. Reword. Often, as in Examples 2, 6, and 7 below, the best solution is to replace the proviso with a sentence-starting *But*. (If you doubt the grammatical correctness of this technique, you have much to learn: see § 147.)

NOT THIS:	BUT THIS:
Ex. 1 Licensee may cancel this Agreement at any time upon 120 days' written notice to Licensor, provided, however, that such cancellation shall not impair any accrued right of Licensor. **License Agreement from a major law firm**	Calhoun may cancel this Agreement at any time upon 120 days' written notice to Burton, but this cancellation must not impair Burton's accrued rights.
Ex. 2 1.03 Undertaking and Assumption As additional consideration, Buyer assumes and will perform all obligations of Seller arising from the terms of the contracts included in the Selected Assets, provided however, that Buyer's obligations are limited to performance that arises on and after the Effective Date. **Asset-Purchase-and-Sales Agreement from Robert A. Feldman & Raymond T. Nimmer, *Drafting Effective Contracts: A Practitioner's Guide*, Form 2-1, at 2-51 (2d ed. 2010)**	**1.3 Undertaking and assumption.** As additional consideration, Jameson assumes and will perform all of Cowler's obligations under the contracts included in the Selected Assets. But Jameson's obligations are limited to performance that arises on or after the Effective Date.
Ex. 3 17. Equipment Lost in the Well. If the equipment or instruments of Contractor are lost in the well, Oxico shall either recover same without cost to Contractor or pay for such equipment or instruments; provided, however, that this provision shall not apply if such loss is caused by the negligence of Contractor or its subcontractors. **Master Service Agreement from a major oil company**	**17. Equipment Lost in the Well.** If Mulligan's equipment or instruments are lost in the well and the loss is not caused by the negligence of Mulligan or its subcontractors, Oxico will either: (A) pay for the lost equipment or instruments; or (B) recover the equipment or instruments without cost to Mulligan.

NOT THIS:	BUT THIS:
Ex. 4 5. *Use and Operation of Equipment.* Lessee agrees that it will use the Equipment in accordance with this Agreement, provided that any such use is in conformity with all applicable laws and Regulations, any insurance policies, and any warranties of the manufacturer and any maintenance agreements with respect to the Equipment. Lessee shall not permit anyone other than its authorized agents or employees to operate the Equipment. **Individual-to-Corporation Equipment Lease from 5B Amelia Legutki et al., *Nichols Cyclopedia of Legal Forms Annotated* § 117:28 (2013)**	5. **Use of Equipment.** Snelling will use the Equipment in accordance with this Agreement and in conformity with all applicable laws and regulations, insurance policies, manufacturer warranties, and Equipment-maintenance agreements. Snelling will not let anyone other than its authorized agents or employees operate the Equipment.
Ex. 5 Crane's grant of license shall include the right of Luddington to use the MSD 2500 software on specific computers located at specific franchised Luddington stations; provided that Luddington may transfer its rights under the license to the Luddington franchisee who operates the franchised station and provided further that if such franchisee relocates from one Luddington station to a different Luddington station, the franchisee may transfer the MSD 2500 software to the new location. **Software Licensing Agreement from a major technology company**	The license includes Luddington's right to use the MSD 2500 software on specific computers located at specific franchised Luddington stations. Luddington may transfer its rights under the license to the Luddington franchisee that operates the franchised station. If a franchisee relocates from one Luddington station to another, the franchisee may transfer the MSD 2500 software to the new location.
Ex. 6 To provide Buyer with the opportunity to conduct such investigations and inspections as it deems appropriate pursuant to this paragraph, Seller hereby grants Buyer the right to have access to Seller's books and records, and the Property; provided, however, that Buyer shall indemnify Seller from and against any and all claims, actions, demands, expenses, or liabilities arising out of any such inspections or investigations by Buyer. **Consent Agreement from a major law firm**	To conduct investigations and inspections that it considers appropriate under this section, Eubanks may have access to Sanchez's books and records as well as the Property. But Eubanks will indemnify Sanchez from all claims, demands, expenses, or other liabilities arising from such an inspection or investigation.

"[The] ability to uncover the correct rule, and to put it into the simplest form, is one of the marks of the great draftsman. The average draftsman writes a rule which does not quite explain the practice, and must therefore be encumbered by numerous exceptions. . . . The great draftsman writes a rule that almost exactly explains the practice, and therefore need be encumbered with few, if any exceptions." LeRoy Marceau, *Drafting a Union Contract* § 2.4, at 12 (1965).

NOT THIS:	BUT THIS:
Ex. 7 3.8 Cooperation. The Parties shall cooperate to execute and deliver such agreements or other documents they may mutually deem appropriate in order to effectuate the grant of Subsidiary Rights to each of the Subsidiaries; provided, however, that each such agreement and other document shall be consistent with this Agreement and agree that, in the case of any ambiguity or inconsistency, the provisions of this Agreement shall govern and control. **International-Franchise Agreement from a major fast-food restaurant**	**3.8 Cooperation.** The Parties will cooperate in preparing agreements and other documents that they agree are necessary to grant Subsidiary Rights to the Subsidiaries. But each agreement or document must: (A) be consistent with this Agreement; and (B) stipulate that this Agreement will govern and control if an ambiguity or inconsistency arises.
Ex. 8 12. BROKERAGE FEE. Seller, Stockholder and Purchaser each represent that no broker (other than ________________ (the "Broker")) has been involved in this transaction and each party agrees to indemnify and hold the others harmless from payment of any brokerage fee, finder's fee, or commission claimed by any party who claims to have been involved because of association with such party; *provided that* Seller shall (pursuant to an agreement between Seller and Broker) pay all fees owed to the Broker in connection with this transaction. **Purchase Agreement from a law firm**	**12. Brokerage Fee.** The Seller, the Stockholder, and the Buyer each represent that no broker other than ________________ (Broker) has been involved with this transaction. Each party indemnifies the others from a brokerage fee, finder's fee, or commission demanded by any person who claims involvement in this transaction by association with that party. Under an agreement between the Seller and the Broker, the Seller will pay all fees owed to the Broker in connection with this transaction.
Ex. 9 To the extent it is not otherwise applied in accordance with this Section, the deposit shall be refunded to Franchisee two years after the expiration, termination, transfer or other disposition of this Agreement, provided that (i) the deposit shall be refunded within 90 days after the effective date of a transfer upon the death of Franchisee and (ii) upon a transfer to a Controlled Entity, the deposit shall be held by Hemmings in accordance with this Section in satisfaction of the obligations of such Controlled Entity under this Section and Franchisee shall have no further interest in the deposit. **Franchise License Agreement from a tax-preparation company**	**5.3 Refund.** To the extent that it is not otherwise applied or forfeited, Hemmings will refund the deposit to the Franchisee 2 years after the expiration, termination, transfer, or other disposition of this Agreement, with 2 qualifications: (A) upon the Franchisee's death, Hemmings will refund the deposit within 90 days after the effective date of a transfer; and (B) upon a transfer to a Controlled Entity, Hemmings will hold the deposit in accordance with this § 5.3 to satisfy the Controlled Entity's obligations, and the Franchisee will have no further interest in the deposit.

NOT THIS:	BUT THIS:
Ex. 10 Subcontracting of work, including unit exchange, will be done only when genuinely unavoidable because (1) managerial skills are not available on the property but this criterion is not intended to permit subcontracting on the ground that there are not available a sufficient number of supervisory personnel possessing the skills normally held by such personnel; or (2) skilled manpower is not available on the property from active or furloughed employees; or (3) essential equipment is not available on the property; or (4) the required time of completion of the work cannot be met with the skills, personnel or equipment available on the property; or (5) such work cannot be performed by the carrier except at a significantly greater cost, provided that the cost advantage enjoyed by the subcontractor is not based on a standard of wages below that of the prevailing wages paid in the area for the type of work being performed and provided further that if work which is being performed by railroad employees in a railroad facility is subcontracted under this criterion, no employees regularly assigned at that facility at the time of the subcontracting will be furloughed as a result of such subcontracting. **Construction Contract for a railroad company**	7.2 **Subcontracting.** The Contractor may enter into a subcontract for the work only when necessary—for example, when: (A) no managers are available on the property; (B) no skilled employees (active or furloughed) are available on the property; (C) essential equipment is not available on the property; (D) the work cannot be completed within the required time given the personnel and equipment available on the property; or (E) the work cannot be performed by the carrier except at a significantly greater cost, and both of the following conditions are met: (1) the cost advantage enjoyed by the subcontractor is not based on a standard of wages below that of the prevailing wages paid in the area for the type of work being performed; and (2) no railroad employees working in a railroad facility will be furloughed as a result of the subcontract.

> "Nothing causes unclear writing more than cloudy thinking. A concept that the author does not clearly understand is not likely to find its way into clear language."
> Carl Felsenfeld & Alan Siegel, *Writing Contracts in Plain English* 110 (1981).

NOT THIS:	BUT THIS:
Ex. 11 **Section 2. Covenants of Company Parties.** . . . (b) Judicial Proceedings. In the event that any Company Party is requested in any judicial or administrative proceeding to disclose any Protected Information of an XC Party, such Company Party will give the XC Party prompt notice of such request so that the XC Party may seek an appropriate protective order. It is further agreed that if in the absence of a protective order the Company Party is nonetheless compelled by order of any Authority having jurisdiction to disclose Protected Information, the Company Party may disclose such Protected Information without liability hereunder; provided, however, that the Company Party gives the XC Party written notice of the information to be disclosed as far in advance of its disclosure as practicable and that the Company Party use its best efforts to obtain assurances that the Protected Information will be accorded confidential treatment; and further provided, that the Company Party will furnish only that portion of the Protected Information which is legally required. **Confidentiality Agreement from a major law firm**	**2. Company Parties' Covenants.** . . . **2.2 Judicial proceedings.** If a Company Party is asked in a judicial or administrative proceeding to disclose an XC Party's Protected Information, the Company Party must give the XC Party prompt notice of the request so that the XC Party may seek an appropriate protective order. If, in the absence of a protective order, the Company Party is nonetheless compelled to disclose Protected Information by order of an authority with jurisdiction, the Company Party may disclose the Protected Information without liability under this Agreement as long as the Company Party: (A) gives the XC Party written notice of the information being disclosed as far in advance of its disclosure as practicable; (B) furnishes only the Protected Information that is legally required; and (C) uses best efforts to obtain assurances that the Protected Information will be given confidential treatment.

"Taking a professional approach involves recognizing the duty we have as lawyers to assist our readers to understand the law as it affects them. It involves being sensitive to the difficulties the reader may be experiencing, recognizing the level of understanding the reader has and supplying whatever additional information the reader might need. But it does not mean patronizing the reader." Michèle M. Asprey, *Plain Language for Lawyers* 53–54 (1991).

NOT THIS:	BUT THIS:
Ex. 12 Creates a condition. Provided that the Issuing Bank or Escrow Agent has received an Inspection Report, the Purchase Price will be released upon the earliest occurrence of one of the following: (i) receipt by the Escrow Agent or the Issuing Bank of a letter from the Buyer, the Buyer's freight forwarder, if any, or the Buyer's shipper certifying that the Weare Mill is loaded on one or more cargo vessels and in transit to Brazil; or (ii) the expiration of a period of one hundred twenty (120) calendar days following the Delivery Date; Creates an exception. provided, however, that any events or circumstances beyond Buyer's reasonable control which prevent the disassembly, packing or shipment of the Used Steel Mill and/or Incomplete Mill, including both events of force majeure and causes imputable to Seller, shall extend the aforementioned period for the same number of days that such event or circumstance persists, Creates a condition subsequent to the exception. and provided further that if such a period should be extended by such events or circumstances more than one hundred eighty (180) calendar days beyond the Delivery Date, either party may rescind this Agreement by written notice to the other, with a copy to the Escrow Agent or the Issuing Bank in accordance with section 11, hereof, whereupon the portion of the Purchase Price being held in the Escrow Account will be released to the Buyer or the letter of credit will be cancelled, as the case may be, and title to and possession of the Weare Mill will revert to Seller without the need for further action. **Shipping-Company Escrow Agreement from a major law firm**	9.2 **Release of escrow.** If the Issuing Bank or the Escrow Agent receives an Inspection Report, the Purchase Price will be released upon the earlier of: (A) the date when the Escrow Agent or the Issuing Bank receives a letter from either the Buyer or the Buyer's freight-forwarder or shipper certifying that the Weare Mill is loaded on one or more cargo vessels and in transit to Brazil; (B) 120 days past the Delivery Date, with the following qualifications: (1) this 120-day period will be extended for as long as any event or circumstance beyond the buyer's reasonable control—including force majeure and causes imputable to the Seller—prevents disassembling, packing, or shipping the Used Steel Mill or Incomplete Mill; (2) if the period is extended for more than 180 days under (1), either party may rescind this Agreement by giving written notice to the other and forwarding a copy to the Escrow Agent or the Issuing Bank, in accordance with § 11; and (3) if either party rescinds under (2), the part of the Purchase Price held in the Escrow Account will be released to the Buyer or the letter of credit will be canceled, and title to and possession of the Weare Mill will automatically revert to the Seller.

Interruptive phrases

§ 117 Avoid subject-verb and verb-object separation.

Try moving an interruptive phrase from midsentence to the beginning or end. Unless there is some special reason for separating the kernel parts of the sentence—subject, verb, and object—don't do it.

NOT THIS:	BUT THIS:
Ex. 1 The parties, upon notice to all parties within 10 days of any change of addresses, shall have the right to change the above addresses for purposes of this section. **Surgical-Equipment-Maintenance-and-Services Agreement from a major hospital**	A party may change its address for purposes of this section by giving notice to all parties within 10 days after the change.
Ex. 2 The Grantor, at any time or times, by a written instrument, signed and delivered to the Trustee during the Grantor's life, may amend or revoke this instrument in whole or in part. **Sample Revocable-Trust Form from a state agency**	Gehring may personally amend or revoke this instrument in whole or in part at any time by delivering signed, written instructions to the Trustee.
Ex. 3 6.04 *Sales Taxes* Any sales tax payable by reason of transfer and conveyance of the Selected Assets under this agreement shall be paid by Buyer. **Asset Sales & Purchase Agreement from Robert A. Feldman & Raymond T. Nimmer, *Drafting Effective Contracts: A Practitioner's Guide*, Form 2-1, at 2-57 (2d ed. 2010)**	**6.4 Sales tax.** Carroll Leasing will pay all sales tax due for the transfer of the Selected Assets under this Agreement.
Ex. 4 Lessee, during the term of this lease, is to have absolute control and use of the motor trucks in the same manner as though he were the absolute owner thereof. **Memorandum Agreement to Lease Trucks from 12A Fred H. Miller, *West's Legal Forms: Commercial Transactions* § 37:20, at 541 (4th ed. 2013)**	During the term of this lease, Kranter may use and control the motor trucks in the same manner as an absolute owner.

§ 118 Split the verb phrase if you must insert an adverbial phrase.

If an adverb or adverbial phrase modifies a verb phrase, the natural placement of the adverbial element is after the first auxiliary verb (such as *may*, *must*, *will*). That is, contrary to popular belief, there's nothing wrong with splitting a verb phrase (as opposed to an infinitive—which generally ought to be left unsplit if possible). This syntactic ordering is not only permissible according to all reputable grammarians[1] but also empirically verifiable. Consider the ratios in frequency of the following phrasings in modern print sources (using big data):

Verb Phrase Split	Verb Phrase Unsplit	Frequency in Print
can hardly be	hardly can be	110:1
could hardly believe	hardly could believe	410:1
may well believe	well may believe	240:1
might soon be	soon might be	31:1
must soon become	soon must become	141:1
shall promptly notify	promptly shall notify	96:1
should never forget	never should forget	35:1
will automatically become	automatically will become	85:1
will gladly give	gladly will give	235:1
will soon go	soon will go	31:1
would rather have	rather would have	83:1

Many adverbially modified verb phrases are unattested in print in an unsplit form. For example, *promptly must notify* and *accurately must reflect* just don't appear with any appreciable frequency. But their split counterparts are exceedingly common.

The point here is that the English language most comfortably fits adverbs after auxiliary verbs, not before them. So don't strain to put them before. Take the simple sentence *I will go to Cleveland*. The verb phrase is *will go*. Now add the adverb *soon*. The two most natural placements are after *will* and after *Cleveland*: *I will soon go to Cleveland* or *I will go to Cleveland soon*. To say *I soon will go to Cleveland* is possible but highly unusual—enough so that it feels unidiomatic. Also unusual, but merely emphatic, is

1 For a litany of grammarians who have written on the subject, see *Garner's Modern English Usage* 25 (4th ed. 2016) (under "adverbs").

Soon I will go to Cleveland. The most frequent form, empirically speaking, is *I will soon go to Cleveland.*

Some readers might ask, Why put the adverb in the middle when you can send it to the end? *I will go to Cleveland soon.* That's perfectly natural. True enough. But add another qualification: *my favorite city.* This type of complementary grammatical element is common in writing of all kinds. Now you have two choices:

I will soon go to Cleveland, my favorite city.

Soon I will go to Cleveland, my favorite city.

But probably not:

I will go to Cleveland, my favorite city, soon.

In this last version, the adverb is separated too much from the verb phrase.

We've now devoted a lot of space to a simple grammatical point. You might think it's overkill. Perhaps so. But then again, maybe not. All sorts of people are confused by the point, and they ill-advisedly avoid splitting verb phrases. They create awkward-sounding sentences. Given that the issue comes up at least once on every page you produce, you might as well know how to handle it. And if your colleagues are laboring under false impressions about how to handle it, you can simply show them this passage. If they nevertheless persist in their false impressions, then they're mumpsimuses. Don't use that word yourself, but that's what they are: people who persist in doing something the wrong way even after learning the right way.

NOT THIS:	BUT THIS:
Ex. 1 This Agreement automatically will renew for additional, successive, one-year terms unless a party provides written notice of non-renewal to the other party at least 180 days before the end of the then current term. **Product-Relationship Agreement**	This Agreement will automatically renew for successive 1-year terms unless a party provides written notice of nonrenewal to the other party at least 180 days before the end of the then-current term.

The adverb *automatically* correctly appears between the two parts of the verb phrase *will renew.*

"Throughout the body of a contract, you will find many points at which empty words and phrases can be excised, to the attainment not only of brevity but of clarity."
Frank E. Cooper, *Writing in Law Practice* 280 (1963).

NOT THIS:	BUT THIS:
Ex. 2 Seller shall furnish true and correct copies of the Articles of Incorporation and all amendments thereto, the Bylaws as amended and currently in force, all stock records, and all corporate minute books and records of the Company for inspection by the Purchaser. Such stock records accurately must reflect all share transactions and the current stock ownership of the Company. **Stock-Purchase Agreement**	The Seller will provide to the Buyer for inspection accurate copies of the Articles of Incorporation and all amendments, the current bylaws as amended, all stock records, and all corporate minute books and records of the Company. These stock records must accurately reflect all share transactions and the Company's current stock ownership. The adverb *accurately* correctly appears between the two parts of the verb phrase *must reflect*.
Ex. 3 10. Agreement Intended to Benefit Both Parties. This Agreement is intended to economically benefit both Tyrol and Supplier. Should either party be suffering a significant adverse economic impact (measured in relation to the overall scope of the transactions covered by this Agreement) as a result of complying with the terms of this Agreement, such adversely affected party may notify the other party at any time. In such event, the parties agree to meet with each other as soon as possible, but not later than thirty (30) days after such notice. After reviewing all relevant information, the parties as soon as possible will use good faith business efforts to work towards an acceptable arrangement to enable both parties to continue to economically benefit from this Agreement. **Strategic-Alliance Agreement from a major appliance-manufacturing company**	**10. Agreement Intended to Benefit Both Parties.** Tyrol and the Supplier intend this Agreement to provide long-term economic benefits to both parties. If a party suffers a significant adverse economic impact (measured in relation to the overall scope of the transactions covered by this Agreement) as a result of complying with the Agreement's terms, that party may notify the other party at any time. The parties must promptly and in good faith meet, review all relevant information, and work toward an acceptable arrangement to enable both parties to continue benefiting from this Agreement. The meeting must take place no later than 30 days after the notice is delivered.

Modifiers

§ 119 Put related words together.

To avoid ambiguity, place a modifier right beside the word or phrase it modifies. That way, you'll avoid the dreaded "misplaced modifier," which is not just a grammarian's peeve but often a genuine source of ambiguity.

NOT THIS:	BUT THIS:
Ex. 1 3.11 Further Identification of Collateral. Borrower will furnish to Bank from time to time statements and schedules further identifying and describing the Collateral and such other reports in connection with the Collateral as Bank may request, all in reasonable detail. **Loan Application from a major lending institution** Must the Bank's request be in reasonable detail?	3.11 **Further identification of Collateral.** Martori will periodically provide to the Bank detailed statements and schedules further identifying and describing the Collateral, and any other detailed reports that the Bank requests in connection with the Collateral. Should we say *reasonably detailed*? Or is the requirement of reasonableness unhelpfully vague?
Ex. 2 2. *REPRESENTATIONS AND WARRANTIES OF SELLER* . . . 2.05 *Litigation* To Seller's knowledge, there are no lawsuits, proceedings, or governmental investigations pending or threatened against Seller that related to the Selected Assets. **Asset-Sales Agreement from Robert A. Feldman & Raymond T. Nimmer, *Drafting Effective Contracts: A Practitioner's Guide*, Form 2-1, at 2-53 (2d ed. 2010)**	2. **Seller's Representations and Warranties.** . . . 2.5 **Litigation.** The Seller does not know of any pending or threatened lawsuits, proceedings, or government investigations against the Seller in relation to the Selected Assets.

"In the majority of instances . . . poor drafting results from a usually unarticulated notion that documents are meant to be interpreted (i.e., by the lawyer or a court) rather than comprehended (i.e., by the parties)." Margaret Emanual, "Drafting as Advocacy: Adaptation of 'Reader Expectation Theory' to Document Drafting," in Barbara Child, *Teacher's Manual to Accompany Drafting Legal Documents: Principles and Practices* 17, 19 (2d ed. 1992).

§ 120 Reword when moving the modifier doesn't make the meaning clear.

If moving a misplaced modifier won't cure a syntactic ambiguity you've detected, rephrase the sentence completely. Sometimes you'll need a little "preventive grammar" to avoid having issues arise: just recast the sentence entirely if that's the best solution.

NOT THIS:	BUT THIS:
Ex. 1 *Is it up to the Author to say what other works are considered suitable? Or the Publisher?* The Author offers the Publisher an option to acquire the publishing rights under the condition of this Agreement of other works by the Author considered suitable for German publication. **Publishing Contract from a major publisher**	If the Publisher considers other works by the Author to be suitable for German publication, the Publisher may acquire the publishing rights to those works on the same terms as in this Agreement.
Ex. 2 "Access laws" means the Americans with Disabilities Act of 1990, the Fair Housing Amendments Act of 1988, all state and local laws and ordinances related to handicapped access and all rules, regulations, and orders issued pursuant thereto including, without limitation, the Americans with Disabilities Act Accessibility Guidelines for Buildings and Facilities, as may heretofore or hereafter may be amended. *Do only amendments to the Guidelines matter? Or amendments to the laws, etc.?* **Master Loan Agreement from a major insurance company**	"Access laws" means the following: the Americans with Disabilities Act of 1990, the Fair Housing Amendments Act of 1988, all state and local laws and ordinances related to handicapped access, and all rules, regulations, and orders issued under these federal, state, and local laws and ordinances.

> "I'm sorry, but most lawyers are not skilled drafters. It doesn't matter how smart or experienced they are or how many legal documents they have drafted. Most—a supermajority, probably—are lacking. And yet, oddly enough, the poor quality of others' drafting is plain for them to see." Joseph Kimble, *Seeing Through Legalese* 3 (2017).

Prepositional phrases

§ 121 Minimize prepositional phrases generally.

Pack-rat drafters like to use these innocent-looking little words to specify what should not need specifying. The result is an overparticularized, arrhythmic sentence in which the idea is hidden amid the clutter.

Freeloading prepositional phrases make reading difficult because they add to the relational components within sentences. And to understand the sentences, readers must sort out these components. They forestall the action if they precede the predicate, and they are anticlimactic if they come after. By testing each one to ensure that it pays its own way in the sentence, you'll make the provision more readable.

	NOT THIS:	BUT THIS:
Ex. 1	For sales of Licensed Products to an Affiliate or Joint Venture from Licensee at a reduced price from that customarily charged to an unrelated third party, the royalties paid to the Licensor shall be based on the Net Sales of Licensed Products of the Affiliate or Joint Venture to the customers of the Affiliate or the Joint Venture. **Licensing Agreement from a major law firm** [13 prepositions]	If Nelson sells licensed products to an affiliate or joint venture at a price below that ordinarily charged to a third party, the Licensor's royalties will be calculated on the Affiliate's or Joint Venture's Net Sales of those products. [5 prepositions]
Ex. 2	Upon the transfer of all or part of a Partnership Interest, the capital account of the transferor that is attributable to the transferred Partnership Interest or portion thereof shall carry over to the transferee Partner in accordance with the provisions of Treas. Reg. § 1.704-1(b)(2)(iv)(*l*). **Partnership Agreement from a major law firm** [8 prepositions]	Upon the transfer of all or part of a Partnership Interest, the transferor's capital account (or applicable portion) attributable to the transferred Partnership Interest will carry over to the transferee Partner under Treas. Reg. § 1.704-1(b)(2)(iv)(*l*). [6 prepositions]
Ex. 3	On the Delivery Date, representatives of Buyer and Seller will make a joint inspection of the Mill to determine that all of the items listed in Schedule "A" are accounted for and in the same condition as indicated. Upon satisfactory completion of the inspection two original dated reports of the inspection and Buyer's acceptance of delivery of the Mill (the "Inspection Report") will be signed by the parties' representatives. **Purchase Agreement from a major law firm** [13 prepositions]	On the Delivery Date, the Buyer's and the Seller's representatives will jointly inspect the Mill to determine that all items listed in Schedule "A" have been accounted for and are in the same condition. After completing the inspection, the parties' representatives will sign 2 original dated inspection reports and the Buyer's acceptance of delivery of the Mill. [7 prepositions]

Note that the revision involves unearthing a hidden condition: see § 110.

§ 122 Minimize *of*-phrases in particular.

Of-phrases tend to encumber a sentence. Do what you can to minimize them while keeping your language normal and idiomatic. Although all prepositional phrases require some caution, *of* requires it to a greater degree. Use a possessive as opposed to an *of*-phrase when you can do so unambiguously and not too awkwardly.

Many contract drafters have been taught a retrograde dogma: that *of*-genitives should always be preferred to normal possessives—*the convenience of the debtor* as opposed to *the debtor's convenience.* The syntactic consequences of this dogma are cumulatively debilitating to the prose, which becomes ever more ponderous and clumsy. The counteracting preference against *of*-phrases is among the most significant reforms contained in these *Guidelines.*

But remember to keep your language natural-sounding: don't take on a misplaced zeal to eliminate every *of* to such a degree that you stack nouns together in strange ways.

By using this tip, you'll be able to make some real headway on editing your drafts on your computer before printing the document out. Simply search for "[space]of[space]" and scrutinize each sentence you find. You'll probably be able to cut half the *of*s at the very least.

NOT THIS:	BUT THIS:
Ex. 1 In the event of default by Buyer under this Agreement, Seller shall have all the rights and remedies of a secured creditor under the Uniform Commercial Code. **Sales Agreement from Robert A. Feldman & Raymond T. Nimmer, *Drafting Effective Contracts: A Practitioner's Guide*, Form 5-6, at 5-209 (2d ed. 2010)**	If Gusthauer defaults, Alia may exercise all secured-creditor rights and remedies available under the Uniform Commercial Code.
Ex. 2 In the event of an alleged breach or violation by any of the Parties of any of the provisions of this paragraph 5, the Noncompetition Period described above shall be tolled until such alleged breach or violation is resolved. **Noncompetition Agreement from a major law firm**	If a party is accused of violating this § 5, the Noncompetition Period will be tolled until the alleged violation is resolved.

"Our oblique language allows us to exclude more timid clients from their proper part in the decision-making. We should be acting as guides to our clients; if we are to do so they must be able to follow us." Mark Adler, *Clarity for Lawyers* 7 (1990).

§ 123 When you can, change a prepositional phrase to an adjective.

When feasible, change prepositional phrases to adjectives—including phrasal adjectives (see § 133).

NOT THIS:	BUT THIS:
Ex. 1 In connection with any repurchase of a Mortgage Loan hereunder by any Seller, the Finance Company or their respective designee, as applicable, and concurrent with the payment of the Repurchase Price, the Purchaser shall be deemed to have represented and warranted that the statements set forth in Section 3.04(e) and in the Notice of Breach are true and correct in all respects as of such date. **Mortgage-Loan Purchase Agreement between two major financial institutions**	In connection with a Mortgage Loan repurchase by a Seller, by the Finance Company, or by designees of the Seller or Finance Company, and concurrently with the Repurchase Price payment, the Buyer represents and warrants that all statements in § 3.4(E) and in the Notice of Breach are accurate as of the repurchase date.
Ex. 2 EACH PARTY ACKNOWLEDGES AND AGREES THAT ANY CONTROVERSY WHICH MAY ARISE UNDER THIS AGREEMENT IS LIKELY TO INVOLVE COMPLICATED AND DIFFICULT ISSUES, AND THEREFORE, IT HEREBY IRREVOCABLY AND UNCONDITIONALLY WAIVES ANY RIGHT IT MAY HAVE TO A TRIAL BY JURY IN RESPECT OF ANY LITIGATION DIRECTLY OR INDIRECTLY ARISING OUT OF OR RELATING TO THIS AGREEMENT OR THE TRANSACTIONS CONTEMPLATED HEREBY. **Transfer-Restriction Agreement between multinational Internet-based technology company and its founder**	**Because any controversy that arises under this Agreement is likely to involve complicated issues, each Party irrevocably and unconditionally waives any right it may have to a jury trial in litigation directly or indirectly relating to this Agreement or transactions under it.**

Note also that *such date* is unclear. Date of the Notice of Breach? The repurchase?

We're guessing that it's the repurchase date.

For the unadvisability of using all-caps text, see § 42. Notice the awkward spacing it can create.

> "Even when your audience is more sophisticated, you should keep your language as simple and direct as possible. No one wants to read legal documents. The stuffier the document sounds, the less likely it is to be read." Susan L. Brody et al., *Legal Drafting* 116 (1994).

§ 124 When you can, change a prepositional phrase to a possessive.

When feasible, change prepositional phrases to possessives. Avoid the *of*-genitive if a possessive is idiomatically available.

NOT THIS:	BUT THIS:
Ex. 1 8. DEFECTIVE PRODUCTS; WARRANTY Supplier warrants the Products in accordance with the provisions of the Contract. **Consignment Agreement from a major consumer-product technology and development company**	**8. Defective Products; Warranty** The Supplier warrants the Products in accordance with the Contract's provisions.
Ex. 2 The obligations owed by Acme to the Receiver pursuant to the Note are secured by liens on and security interests in all of Acme's assets. **Purchase & Assignment Agreement from a major law firm**	Acme's obligations under the Note are secured by liens on and security interests in all its assets.
Ex. 3 3.2 **Cooperation.** Supplier will cooperate as requested with other Service providers of Griggs to coordinate the provision of Services with the services and systems of such other service providers. **Master Software-License Agreement from a major mobile network**	3.2 **Cooperation.** The Supplier will cooperate as requested with Griggs's other service providers to coordinate their services and systems.
Ex. 4 <u>Product Changes</u> Seller at all times reserves the right in its sole discretion without consent of Buyer to incorporate additions or improvements to Products to be delivered hereunder. **General Terms Agreement for Purchase Order from a major consumer-technology company**	4.3 **Product changes.** Tallian may at any time, without Bistick's consent, incorporate additions or improvements to a Product to be delivered under this Agreement.
Ex. 5 Seller and Purchaser and their respective affiliates may each disclose such information (i) to their affiliates for any purpose reasonably incidental to the purposes of this Agreement, (ii) as is required to be disclosed by law, legal process or requirement of any stock exchange, or (iii) which is or becomes within the public domain (otherwise than through the fault of the recipient party). **Transition-Services Agreement from a major oil company**	The Seller, the Buyer, and their affiliates may disclose information: (A) to their affiliates for any purpose reasonably incidental to this Agreement's purposes; (B) as required under a law, legal process, or stock-exchange requirement; or (C) if it has already become public, unless it was the receiving party's fault that it became public.

For more on *all of*, see that entry in § 148 at pp. 385–86.

For more about preferring the singular over the plural, see § 62.

Punctuation

§ 125 Learn and use standard punctuation.

Use standard punctuation in accordance with *The Redbook: A Manual on Legal Style* (4th ed. 2018) and *The Chicago Manual of Style* (17th ed. 2017). Doing so will ensure that you avoid the embarrassment of elementary blunders; it will also save you from multifarious substantive flaws. Only a few common problems are dealt with in the following sections.

§ 126 Place a colon before an indented enumeration.

Use a colon—not a dash or other punctuation mark—as a lead-in to subparts.

NOT THIS:	BUT THIS:
Ex. 1 4. Manner of Payment of the Purchase Price. At the Closing, Purchaser shall pay the Purchase Price by— (a) the wire transfer of immediately available funds to the account designated by Seller in an amount equal to $45,000, (b) the delivery to Seller of a promissory note of Purchaser in the original principal amount of $100,000, and (c) the delivery to Seller of a promissory note of Purchaser in the original principal amount of $150,000. **Stock-Purchase Agreement** [Margin note: An em-dash is a poor lead-in to subparts.]	4. **Payment of Purchase Price.** At Closing, the Buyer must pay the Purchase Price by: (A) wire-transferring $45,000 in immediately available funds to the Seller's designated account; (B) delivering to Seller a promissory note for $100,000; and (C) delivering to Seller a promissory note for $150,000.
Ex. 2 Licensee's quarterly reports to WLY shall include all information required by WLY with regard to the immediately preceding calendar quarter, the quantity of each type of Certified Licensed Product manufactured or sold, whichever occurs first, and, for such Certified Licensed Products, i. the country of manufacture; ii. the country of sale; iii. the product type; iv. the Licensed Market; and v. the Licensee's brand name. **Product-License Agreement from a major digital-technology company** [Margin note: A comma is a poor lead-in to indented enumerations.] [Margin note: Avoid using romanettes. See § 26.]	(A) **Quarterly reports.** The Licensee's quarterly reports to WLY must include: (1) all information required by WLY regarding the immediately preceding calendar quarter; (2) the quantity of each type of Certified Licensed Product manufactured or sold, whichever occurs first; and (3) for Certified Licensed Products, the following information as well: (a) the country of manufacture; (b) the country of sale; (c) the product type; (d) the Licensed Market; and (e) the Licensee's brand name.

§ 127 Put a semicolon at the end of each nonterminal part.

Put a semicolon at the end of each subpart. End each subpart except the last with a semicolon (with the next to last followed by a conjunction—*and* or *or*).

NOT THIS:	BUT THIS:
Ex. 1 2. Contract Information does not include information that is any of the following: (a) Contractor Background Technology. (b) Available generally to the public, as evidenced by printed publication or similar proof, through no act or omission of Contractor Group. (c) Independently made available to Contractor by a third party with a legal right to disclose that information without restriction. **Master Contractor-Services Contract from a major oil company**	2. **Information Not Included.** Contract Information does not include information that: (A) qualifies as Contractor Background Technology; (B) is available to the general public, as shown by printed publication or similar proof not attributable to any act or omission of the Contractor Group; or (C) has been made available to the Contractor independently by a third party that has a legal right to disclose that information without restriction.
Ex. 2 As used herein, "<u>Indebtedness</u>" means, without duplication, (a) the principal amount of any indebtedness of the Company for borrowed money outstanding as of the Closing, including all prepayment premiums or penalties and other fees and amounts with respect to such indebtedness, (b) any unpaid interest owing on any such indebtedness of the Company, (c) obligations of the Company in respect of capitalized leases and obligations for the deferred purchase price of goods or services (other than trade payables and payroll liabilities incurred in the ordinary course of business) as of the Closing Date, (d) obligations in respect of banker's acceptances or letters of credit issued or created for the account of the Company as of the Closing Date, (e) all indebtedness or obligations of the types referred to in the preceding clauses (a) through (d) of any other person, association or organization secured by any lien on any assets of the Company, even though the Company has not assumed or otherwise become liable for the payment thereof, but excluding customer deposits and interest payable thereon in the ordinary course of business, (f) all guarantees of obligations of the type described in clauses (a) through (e) above of any other person, association or organization, and (g) amounts due or owing from the Company under any deferred compensation program. **Stock-Purchase Agreement from a major law firm** *Without duplication* is confusing. What does this mean?	"Indebtedness" collectively means: (A) the principal that the Company owes for borrowed money outstanding as of the Closing, including all prepayment premiums or penalties and other fees and amounts arising from this debt; (B) any unpaid interest owed on this debt; (C) the Company's obligations for capitalized leases and for the deferred purchase price of goods or services (other than trade payables and payroll liabilities incurred in the ordinary course of business) as of the Closing Date; (D) obligations for the banker's acceptances or letters of credit issued or created for the Company's account as of the Closing Date; (E) all debts or obligations of the types in (A) through (D) of any other person, association, or organization secured by a lien on any Company assets, even if the Company has not assumed or otherwise become liable for paying them, but excluding customer deposits and interest payable in the ordinary course of business; (F) all guarantees of obligations of the types in (A) through (E) of any other person, association, or organization; and (G) amounts due from or owed by the Company under any deferred-compensation program. Semicolons are standard at the ends of subparts.

§ 128 Place a comma after an introductory phrase or subordinate clause.

Generally speaking, an introductory phrase such as *generally speaking* ought to be followed by a comma. The principle applies to most adverbial phrases that appear at the outset of sentences.[1]

NOT THIS:	BUT THIS:
Ex. 1 In the event of any dispute as to the contents of the Manual the master copy maintained by Black shall be controlling. **Franchise-License Agreement from a Fortune 500 company**	If a dispute arises about the Manual's contents, the master copy maintained by Black controls.
Ex. 2 As used in this section "control" means at least the degree of control necessary to grant licenses of the scope and content granted in this Agreement. **Collaboration Agreement from a major computer-technology company**	As used in this section, "Control" means the authority to grant licenses of the scope and content described in this Agreement.

"Letters have been misread, and have failed of their purpose, because of their writers' ignorance of punctuation, indifference to its advantages, or rebellion against its discipline. Such errors, in business, sometimes cost money. In the writing and printing of contracts, they may lead to lawsuits. In the drafting of laws or constitutions, they may cause wars and rebellions, or, at the least, time-wasting debates and expensive delays while the courts interpret." Edward N. Teall, *Putting Words to Work* 7 (1940).

1 *See* Garner, *The Elements of Legal Style* 16–17 (2d ed. 2002).

§ 129 Use the serial comma as well as the serial semicolon.

Use the serial comma or the serial semicolon before *and* or *or* in a series. It prevents more ambiguities than people suspect, and it never creates an ambiguity in competent writing.

NOT THIS:	BUT THIS:
Ex. 1 Seller represents that the Premises have been used for the storage, sale and distribution of petroleum products that may have spilled, leaked, seeped or entered onto or under the ground or into ground waters. **Real-Estate-Sale-and-Purchase Agreement from a major oil refinery**	Vongaard represents that the Premises have been used for the storage, sale, and distribution of petroleum products that may have spilled, leaked, or seeped into or under the ground or into groundwaters.
Ex. 2 5.2 **No other warranties:** Unless expressly set out in the Services Agreement all warranties, representations and conditions which are implied by statute or otherwise are expressly excluded to the extent permitted by Applicable Law. **Service Agreement from a major communications company**	**5.2 No other warranties.** Unless expressly set out in the Services Agreement, all warranties, representations, and conditions that are implied by statute (or otherwise) are expressly excluded to the extent permitted by applicable law.
Ex. 3 The Plan was later amended and restated effective September 19, 1996, July 15, 1997, May 17, 2001, December 3, 2003, March 22, 2007 (at which time the Plan was renamed the "Directors' Deferred Compensation Plan"), and January 1, 2008 to comply with the requirements of Section 409A of the Internal Revenue Code of 1986, as amended (the "Code"). **Directors' Deferred-Compensation Plan from a major fast-food restaurant**	To comply with § 409A of the Internal Revenue Code of 1986, as amended (the "Code"), the Plan was later amended and restated effective September 19, 1996; July 15, 1997; May 17, 2001; December 3, 2003; March 22, 2007 (when the Plan was renamed the "Directors' Deferred Compensation Plan"); and January 1, 2008. Semicolons are needed in this series because the items contain commas. See *Garner's Modern English Usage* 754 (4th ed. 2016).

"In a list of three or more, always insert the serial comma. Some writers insist on omitting the last comma, before the *and* or *or*. . . . But they are not drafting legal documents. Never omit the last comma—doing so can cause misinterpretation. *Chickens, ducks, and geese* is clear. *Chickens, ducks and geese* allows someone—a lawyer or judge—to assert that ducks and geese are a distinct category. Or consider *Smith ordered bacon, eggs and cheese.* Did Smith want eggs mixed with cheese? If you write *Smith ordered bacon, eggs, and cheese* the meaning is clear." Mark Painter, *The Legal Writer* 97 (3d ed. 2005).

§ 130 For important interpolations within a sentence, use the double-dash construction.

Prefer em-dashes to parentheses or commas for interpolated ideas that need emphasis. This represents a major shift for many contract drafters who have been taught to avoid all dashes at all costs. The reason for their reluctance is obscure and ill-founded. Far from creating ambiguities, dashes disambiguate many constructions and make the sense much plainer to readers of contractual texts. The bias against dashes is wayward and backward. Used in moderation, em-dashes are an important part of any good writer's arsenal. Without them, commas must take on too many duties. The commas proliferate, and the writing becomes a slog.

NOT THIS:	BUT THIS:
Ex. 1 1.11 "Project IP" means all Intellectual Property developed or conceived specifically in furtherance of the Collaboration whether developed or conceived jointly or independently by the Parties, including improvements. **Collaboration Agreement from a computer-technology company**	(11) "Project IP" means all Intellectual Property—including Improvements—developed or conceived specifically for the Collaboration, whether the Parties developed or conceived it jointly or independently.
Ex. 2 1. Notice to Lessor. If the leased premises or any structures or improvements on them are damaged or destroyed by fire, tornado, or other casualty, regardless of its cause, Lessee must immediately give Lessor written notice of the damage or destruction. **Casualty-Loss Clause for General Lease from 18 *Texas Transaction Guide: Legal Forms* § 81B.214[2] (Herbert S. Kendrick & John J. Kendrick Jr. eds., 2017)**	1. **Notice to Wyatt.** If the leased premises or a structure or improvement on them is damaged or destroyed by fire, tornado, or other casualty—regardless of its cause—Nielsen must immediately notify Wyatt in writing of the damage or destruction.
Ex. 3 "Custodial care" means the provision of room and board or other supportive care in an institute or in the home (with or without routine nursing care; training activities of daily living and other forms of self-care; or supervisory care by a doctor) to a person who is mentally or physically disabled and who . . . . **Insurance Policy from a national underwriting company**	"Custodial care" means the provision of room and board or other supportive care in an institution or in the home—with or without routine nursing care, training activities of daily living, other forms of self-care, or supervisory care by a doctor—to a person who is mentally or physically disabled and who . . . .

NOT THIS:	BUT THIS:
Ex. 4 4. ADDITIONAL COVENANTS AND AGREEMENTS 4.01 Notice of Assignment Immediately after this Agreement is executed, Buyer and Seller shall notify, in a mutually agreeable written form, all customers and other parties as to whom Buyer has assumed obligations under the terms of this agreement of the fact of assignment of their contracts and Buyer's assumption under it. **Assignments Clause from Asset-Sales Agreement Form in Robert A. Feldman & Raymond T. Nimmer, *Drafting Effective Contracts: A Practitioner's Guide*, Form 2-1, at 2-55 (2d ed. 2010)**	**4. Additional Covenants and Agreements.** 4.1 **Notice of assignment.** Immediately after this Agreement is signed, Manuelle and Rodriquez will notify all affected customers and parties—in a mutually agreeable written form—that their contracts have been assigned and that Manuelle has assumed the obligations under this Agreement.

"If we want to tell things to consumers, we'd better learn to speak their language." Rudolf Flesch, *How to Write Plain English* 32 (1979).

§ 131 Don't hyphenate most prefixed terms.

Eliminate hyphens from prefixed words: *nonparty* and *pretrial*, not *non-party* and *pre-trial*. Exceptions include *cross-claim* and words using the prefix *self-* or *quasi-*. Also, use a hyphen if:

- the solid form might lead the reader to mistake the syllables (*anti-inflammatory*, *co-occurrence*, *non-insider*);
- the main word is a proper name (*non-United States citizen*, *pre-Memorial Day*);
- the prefix is part of a noun phrase (*non-high-school athletics*); or
- there might be any confusion in meaning (*pre-judicial career* vs. *prejudicial testimony*; *re-sign* vs. *resign*).

But remember: the general rule is no hyphens with prefixes. To verify whether a particular word takes a prefix—and it probably doesn't—consult the current edition of *Merriam-Webster's Collegiate Dictionary*. Look under the prefix alone (co-, non-, post-, etc.), not the full word: you'll find a very long list of words with that prefix and how they're written in well-edited English. The following words are illustrative.

coauthor
cocounsel
cocreator
codeveloper
codiscoverer
coexecutor
cofounder
coheir
coinsurance
coinvestor
cooperate
coordinate
cosign
cosponsor
cotenant
coventurer
multiagency
multiauthor
multibank
multifaceted
multicampus
multiclient
multidrug
multihospital
multinational
multipart
multiparty
multipurpose
multitalented
multiyear
nonassertion
noncancelable
noncertified
nonconstitutional
noncontractual
noncriminal
nondiscriminatory
nonexempt
nonfiduciary
nonforfeiture
nonfrivolous
nongovernment
noninfringing
noninjury
nonjusticiable
nonlawyer
nonnegligent
nonnegotiable
nonobvious
nonpayment
nonpracticing
nonprivity
nonremunerative
nonresident
nonreversible
nonsignatory
nonstatutory
nonsubstantive
nontransferable
postcertification
postelection
postfiling
postmarital
postmortem
postnuptial
postrelease
prebankruptcy
precertification
predate
predeceased
preelection
preeminent
preemployment
preemption
preexisting
prefiling
premortgage
prepetition
prestatutory
pretax
prewriting
reaccept
reacquire
reactivate
readmission
reallocation
reannexation
reassessment
rebuy
recategorize
recertify
recodify
rededicate
redraft
reelect
reexport
regrant
relend (but *re-lent*)
resecure
reseller
resupply
rezone
semiannual
semiautomatic
semiautonomous
semicommercial
semiconductor
semimonthly
semiofficial
semipermanent
semiretirement

NOT THIS:	BUT THIS:
Ex. 1 Shipment of Product may originate from either Marathal or its authorized sub-contractors or distributors. **Terms and Conditions of Sale from a computer-technology company**	Either Marathal or its authorized subcontractors or distributors may originate the shipment of Product.
Ex. 2 **1.3.** "Intellectual Property Rights" means patents, . . . utility models, copyrights, trade secrets, mask work rights, and any other form of intellectual property right protection afforded by law under the laws of the United States or the laws of any other jurisdiction or bi-lateral or multi-lateral international treaty regime. **Software-License, -Development, and -Distribution Agreement from a major digital-technology company**	**1.3** "Intellectual-Property Rights" means patents, . . . utility models, copyrights, trade secrets, mask-work rights, and any similar rights afforded by law under the laws of the United States or the laws of any other jurisdiction or bilateral or multilateral international-treaty regime.
Ex. 3 3.1 License from Keytech to Company: Subject to the terms and conditions of this Agreement, Keytech grants Company a non-transferable, non-exclusive, worldwide, royalty-free, perpetual, non-sublicensable license. **Collaboration Agreement from a computer-technology company**	**3.1 License from Keytech to Highgate.** Subject to this Agreement, Keytech grants Highgate a nontransferable, nonexclusive, worldwide, royalty-free, perpetual, nonsublicensable license.

Note that these terms *do* need hyphens because they are phrasal adjectives: *intellectual-property rights, mask-work rights,* and *international-treaty regime.* See § 133.

"If you must qualify a statement, be careful not to let your sentence structure get away from you." Ernst Jacobi, *Writing at Work: Dos, Don'ts, and How Tos* 96 (1976).

§ 132 Avoid comma splices and other common punctuation errors.

Contracts ought to follow standard American punctuation (or, in some other parts of the world, standard British punctuation). If you're rusty, brush up with § 1 (some 65 pages) of *The Redbook: A Manual on Legal Style* (current edition).

One elementary rule is that independent clauses (whole sentences) can't be joined by a comma. It's improper to write *Not all losses are covered, the insurance covers only direct out-of-pocket losses.* A period could make them separate sentences. Or a conjunction could follow the comma. A semicolon could replace that comma. The semicolon could be followed by a conjunctive adverb such as *however* followed by a comma. But a comma alone is incorrect: it creates a "comma splice," which involves joining two independent clauses with only the weak punctuation mark of a comma.[1]

	NOT THIS:	BUT THIS:
Ex. 1	2. Additional Exclusions That Apply Only to Coverage L—Coverage L does not apply to: a. "bodily injury" to "you", and if residents of "your" household, "your" relatives and persons in "your" care or in the care of "your" resident relatives. **Insurance Policy**	**2. Additional Exclusions That Apply Only to Coverage L.** Coverage L does not apply to: (A) "bodily injury" to you, and—if residents of your household—your relatives, and persons in your care or in the care of your resident relatives.
Ex. 2	Time is of the essence, therefore, the Purchaser shall cut all timber or forest products described in paragraph 6 and complete all other performance described herein with reasonable diligence so performance is completed no later than ___________. **Sample Timber-Sales Contract from A. Jeff Martin et al., *Lake States Woodlands Bulletin: Marketing Timber* 8 (1996)**	Because time is of the essence, Corrigan must cut all timber and forest products described in § 6 and complete all other duties under this contract with reasonable diligence and no later than September 30, 2019.

Because there's no comma after *relatives*, the phrase *if residents of your household* modifies *persons in . . . care*, so the exclusion doesn't apply to a nonresident person.

Assuming that the policy's exclusion is meant to apply to *persons in . . . care* regardless of residence, a comma is necessary after *relatives* to limit the modifier's reach.

1 *See Garner's Modern English Usage* 802–03 (4th ed. 2016) (s.v. "Run-On Sentences"); Garner, *The Chicago Guide to Grammar, Usage, and Punctuation* 353, 417 (2016); *The Redbook: A Manual on Legal Style* § 1.4(d), at 5 (4th ed. 2018).

NOT THIS:	BUT THIS:
Ex. 3 **Limited Warranty:** Licensor warrants that the Software, as delivered, will perform substantially in accordance with Licensor's then-current user manual in all material respects, however, Licensor does not warrant that the Software will meet Licensee's needs, be error-free, or operate without interruption. **Software License from a major mobile-communications company**	5.2 **Limited warranty.** Telemotion warrants that the Software, as delivered, will perform substantially in accordance with Axis Communication's then-current user manual in all material respects. But Telemotion does not warrant that the Software will meet Axis Communication's needs, be error-free, or operate without interruption.
Ex. 4 11. Point of Contact. The following persons, will, on behalf of the respective parties, be responsible for the management and administration of this Agreement, including the transmittal or receipt of Confidential Information by any means, however, all Confidential Information exchanged hereunder shall be afforded the protection of this Agreement even if not furnished to the points of contact listed below. **Mutual Nondisclosure Agreement from a major consumer-product technology and development company**	11. **Point of Contact.** Acting for the parties, the following persons are responsible for managing and administering this Agreement, including all means of sending or receiving Confidential Information. But Confidential Information exchanged under this Agreement is subject to this Agreement's protection even if not furnished to the persons listed below.

"The general level of education is a good deal higher than it has been in the past, and people feel that they are entitled to understand the contents of a document. They should be able to read a contract or a will and to have a reasonably good idea of whether their intentions are being carried out." Robert C. Dick, *Legal Drafting* 6 (2d ed. 1985).

§ 133 Hyphenate phrasal adjectives.

For clarity and polish, hyphenate phrasal adjectives. That is, if two or more consecutive words make sense only when understood together as an adjective modifying a noun that follows, those words (excluding the noun) should be hyphenated. For example: *license-maintenance fee*; *malpractice-insurance benefits*; *intensive-care accommodations*; *off-premises coverage*; *profit-sharing plan*; *sonic-boom exclusion.*

But three exceptions apply:

(1) when a two-word phrase contains an adverb ending in *-ly* followed by an adjective <closely held corporation> <federally recognized tribe>;

(2) when the phrase consists of a proper noun <several United States citizens>; and

(3) when the phrase has been naturalized from a foreign language <ex officio member> <prima facie case>.

Below is a list of common phrasal adjectives found in legal drafting. To professional copyeditors, inserting the hyphens comes automatically. If the hyphens look strange to you, then you should start paying closer attention to the hyphens you'll invariably find in professionally edited prose.

above-the-line deduction
accrual-basis taxpayer
actual-cash-value insurance
alternative-dispute-resolution clause
annuity-payment date
antitrust-enforcement practices
asset-purchase agreement
attorney-corporate-client privilege
balance-sheet requirement
bankruptcy-law protection
bond-funded loan
breach-of-contract claim
breach-of-duty-of-good-faith-and-fair-dealing claim
breach-of-fiduciary-duty claim
breach-of-warranty claim
business-judgment rule
choice-of-law clause
collateral-estoppel doctrine
collective-bargaining agreement
commercial-arbitration rules
common-law claims
competitive-pay programs
conflict-of-interest grounds
consumer-credit reporting agency
continuing-breach argument
contract-modification rule

No hyphen here because *exclusive* modifies *remedies*.

copyright-infringement claim
cost-allocation agreement
due-diligence review
employee-benefit plans
exclusive employee-grievance remedies
fair-use doctrine
false-advertising claims
fee-basis compensation
fixed-term employment contract
forum-selection clause
fourth-quarter earnings
fraud-in-the-inducement case
fraud-on-the-market claim
fraudulent-concealment claim
geographic-market definition
going-concern value
golden-parachute provisions
good-faith attempt
good-faith-reliance defense
health-benefit plan
incentive-bonus agreement
independent-review process
insurance-coverage case
joint-venture issues
junk-bond rating
lack-of-consideration argument
late-fee provision
lease-renewal option
limitation-of-liability clause
limited-liability company
liquidated-damages clause
loan-loss provisions
market-performance indicator
market-share agreement
merger-and-acquisition activity
opt-out provisions
out-of-pocket expenses
parol-evidence rule
past-due accounts
patent-licensing agreement
pay-in-kind preferred stock
per-share earnings
price-earnings multiple
public-works contract
quality-control requirements
replacement-cost insurance
research-and-development operations
residential-mortgage-backed securities
restraint-of-trade provision
risk-allocation provisions
second-quarter operating profits
settlement-conference statement
severance-pay plan
short-term debt
state-court breach-of-contract case
statutory-interpretation argument
stock-appreciation rights
stock-option agreement
stock-purchase agreement
stock-sale approval procedure
tax-deficiency determination

tax-law changes
terms-of-service agreement
third-party obligor
title-insurance company
trademark-infringement claims
trade-secret analysis
transfer-on-death deed
unconscionable-contract claim
unemployment-insurance benefits
unfair-business-practice claim
void-for-vagueness doctrine
waiting-period requirements
waiver-of-jury-trial provision
wrongful-discharge claims
wrongful-liquidation case
year-to-year lease
zero-coupon bond

NOT THIS:	BUT THIS:
Ex. 1 In the event of Product shortages or an inability to meet Buyer requested requirements for any reason whatsoever, SBP may allocate production among its customers. **Terms and Conditions of Sale from a computer-technology company**	If there are Product shortages or if Buyer-requested requirements can't be met for any reason, SBP may allocate production among its customers.
Ex. 2 The sale of the Mortgage's Premises is an "arm's length" transaction between parties who are unrelated and unaffiliated by family, marriage, or commercial enterprise; . . . . **Affidavit of Short Sale for Loan Owned by the Federal Home Loan Mortgage Corporation from LexisNexis Forms: *Ohio Residential Real Estate*, Form 4354-2.7 (2015)**	(A) Sale of the Mortgage's Premises is an arm's-length transaction between parties who are unrelated and unaffiliated by family, marriage, or commercial enterprise; . . . .
Ex. 3 (a) In addition to any Elected Deferred Benefits, each Director shall receive a stock equivalent benefit, which shall be determined in the manner described in this Section 3.2 ("Stock Equivalent Benefit") and credited to his or her Nongrandfathered Account. **Directors' Deferred-Compensation Plan from a major fast-food restaurant**	In addition to Elected Deferred Benefits, each Director will also receive a stock-equivalent benefit, which will be credited to the Director's Nongrandfathered Account. "Stock-Equivalent Benefit" is defined in § 3.2.

"A subject may be intricate and may require a lot of previous study and knowledge if we are to come to terms with it, but this difficulty in content does not require a matching difficulty in language. Above all, complexity in matter does not call for complicated, convoluted language." Robert D. Eagleson, *What Plain English Means for Lawyers*, 60 L. Inst. J. 938, 939 (1986).

Capitalization

§ 134 Capitalize defined terms to signal that they've been defined.

Over the years, legal drafters have used a variety of techniques to signal that a particular term has been defined: capitalization, italics, boldface type (an awful choice for this purpose), and even marginal notes. By the 1980s, the settled convention was to use initial capitals for defined terms. It's a technique that works quite acceptably as long as definitions aren't overdone. Given the universal acceptance of the technique, together with its being unobjectionable, you should adopt it.

NOT THIS:	BUT THIS:
Ex. 1 5. During the **Term** of this **Lease**, **Lessor**, or its agents, representatives, or contractors, may enter on the **Property**, among other reasons, to make reasonable examinations, surveys, tests and inspections, including any soil tests and borings on the **Property** as it deems necessary. **Lessor** will repair any damages to the **Property** that may be caused as a result of the tests or borings and will reimburse **Lessee** for any damage occasioned by the tests or borings. **Grazing Lease**	5. **Lessor's Entry onto Property.** During the Term of this Lease, Byers and its agents, representatives, or contractors may enter the Property as necessary to make reasonable examinations, surveys, tests, and inspections, including any soil tests and borings. Byers will repair and will reimburse Shaddick for any damage caused to the Property resulting from the tests or borings.

The old-style way of showing defined terms by making them bold renders the text distracting and harder to read.

"The capable preparation of any paper is an art; it requires effort, skill and training. . . . In order to set forth with clarity the idea that he wishes to express, the attorney must find the exact word that will call up in the mind of the reader the thought that he desires to impart. He must use as much care in his search for the right word as the painter uses in the selection of form and color." George Rossman, *Better English for Lawyers as Draftsmen and Advocates*, 48 A.B.A.J. 1048, 1048–49 (1962).

NOT THIS:

Ex. 2

Section 1. Definitions

. . .

1.2 "JHC ALGORITHM" means any JHC audio decoding algorithm or other post processing technique or technology, including the JHC TECHNOLOGY, within the scope of the claims of the JHC PATENTS, or the subject matter of any KNOW-HOW or LICENSED COPYRIGHTED WORKS.

1.3 "JHC PATENTS" means all (a) patents, utility models, design patents and patent applications set forth in Schedule A, and (b) patents, utility models, design patents and patent applications not set forth in Schedule A but which are owned, controlled or licensable by JHC and necessary or used to implement the JHC TECHNOLOGY or JHC ALGORITHM or both.

1.4 "JHC DECODER" means an integrated circuit enabled by FIRMWARE to decode bitstreams encoded by any or all of the JHC TECHNOLOGY as defined in this Agreement.

1.5 "FIRMWARE" means firmware, in binary, executable, or object code form, in the form of a linkable library, that only performs any or all of the JHC TECHNOLOGY or embodies any JHC ALGORITHM and that is required by and works only in conjunction with an IMPLEMENTATION.

The License Agreement uses all caps for every defined term throughout the document, making it extremely difficult to read. See § 42.

. . .

Section 2. License

. . .

2.2 No right is granted to LICENSEE under this Agreement:
  (i) to use a JHC ALGORITHM for any purpose other than in connection with the development of the FIRMWARE and the development of the IMPLEMENTATION and to embed in, or provide in FIRMWARE with, an IMPLEMENTATION; or
  (ii) to use LICENSED COPYRIGHTED WORKS for any purpose other than to develop FIRMWARE; or
  (iii) with respect to JHC PATENTS other than as set forth in this Agreement; or . . . .

License Agreement from a major digital-technology company

BUT THIS:

1. Definitions.

. . .

1.2 "Firmware" means firmware in binary, executable, or object-code form, in the form of a linkable library, that performs any or all of the JHC Technology or embodies any JHC Algorithm and that is required by and works only in conjunction with an Implementation.

1.3 "JHC Algorithm" means any JHC audio-decoding algorithm or other postprocessing technique or technology, including the JHC Technology, within the scope of the claims of the JHC Patents, or the subject matter of any Know-How or Licensed Copyrighted Works.

1.4 "JHC Patents" means all patents, utility models, design patents, and patent applications that are:
  (A) set forth in Schedule A; or
  (B) not set forth in Schedule A but are owned, controlled, or licensable by JHC and necessary in or used to implement the JHC Technology, JHC Algorithm, or both.

1.5 "JHC Decoder" means an integrated circuit enabled by Firmware to decode bitstreams encoded by any or all of the JHC Technology as defined in this Agreement.

. . .

2. License.

. . .

2.2 No right is granted to Licensee to use:
  (A) a JHC Algorithm for any purpose other than for developing the Firmware and the Implementation and to embed in, or provide in Firmware with, an Implementation; or
  (B) Licensed Copyrighted Works for any purpose other than to develop Firmware; or
  (C) JHC Patents other than as set forth in this Agreement; or . . . .

§ 135 Capitalize the word *agreement* when referring to the very contract into which the parties are entering.

Lawyers almost universally capitalize the word *Agreement* when referring to the very contract in which the word appears. Although there are (picayunish) arguments against always referring to *this Agreement* (as opposed to *this agreement*), the practice is both unexceptionable and arguably useful on occasion—to differentiate the present contract from others that might be referred to.

NOT THIS:	BUT THIS:
Ex. 1 SECTION EIGHT. COMPLETION AND DELIVERY On completion of the boat in accordance with all requirements of this agreement, delivery shall be made to, and acceptance shall be made by, owner. Delivery shall be made within 6 months from the date of the signing of this agreement, it being agreed that time is of the essence in the performance of this agreement. The boat shall be delivered free of liens of any kind, in the water, ready to be used, at the builder's plant at [address of plant]. **Agreement for Construction and Sale of Boat from 3B Am. Jur. Legal Forms 2d *Boats and Boating* § 42:9 (Nov. 2017 update)**	8. **Completion and Delivery.** Upon completion of the boat as required by this Agreement, the Builder will deliver the boat and the Owner will accept it. Because time is of the essence, the Builder must deliver the completed boat within 6 months after the date of signing this Agreement. The boat must be free of liens, ready for use in the water, and available at the Builder's plant at [address of plant].
Ex. 2 3.02 Performance of Duties. Employee agrees to serve Employer faithfully and to the best of her ability and to devote her full time attention and efforts to the position described in Section 3.01 during the term of this agreement. Employee hereby confirms that she is under no contractual commitments inconsistent with her obligations as set forth in this agreement, and that during the term of this agreement, she will not render or perform services for any other entity or person that are inconsistent with the provisions of this agreement. **Employment Agreement**	3.2 **Performance of duties.** During the term of this Agreement, Malone will serve Marine Tech to the best of her ability and will devote her full-time attention and efforts to the position described in § 3.1. Malone is under no contractual commitments inconsistent with her duties set forth here, and during the term of this Agreement she will not render or perform for another entity or person services that are inconsistent with Marine Tech's best interests.

> "Lawyers are paid to exercise legal judgment, not merely to 'cut and paste.'" Susan L. Brody et al., *Legal Drafting* 75 (1994).

§ 136 Otherwise, adhere to the capitalization rules for Standard Written English.

In the absence of good reason to do so, lawyers shouldn't depart from the conventions of Standard Written English. For two guides that treat the subject of capitalization quite comprehensively, see *The Chicago Manual of Style* and *The Redbook: A Manual on Legal Style* (chapter 2).

And remember that with enumerations of sentence predicates or qualifiers that constitute continuations of what is technically a single sentence, each subpart begins with a lowercase word unless some other reason exists to make it uppercase (as with a proper noun or defined term). See § 91.

NOT THIS:	BUT THIS:
Ex. 1 In addition to the personal property in this Agreement conveyed, Grantor in this Agreement assigns to Grantee all of Grantor's right, title, and interest in and to the name "McPherson Auto Repair of Grand Junction" and Grantor binds himself, his successors, legal representatives, and assigns, to forever WARRANT and DEFEND the title to this property unto Grantee, his successors, legal representatives, and assigns, against every person whomsoever lawfully claiming, or to claim, the same or any part thereof. **Contract for the Sale of Property**	In addition to the personal property conveyed by this Agreement, McPherson assigns to Winton his entire interest in the name "McPherson Auto Repair of Grand Junction." McPherson binds himself and his successors, legal representatives, and assigns, to forever warrant and defend against all claimants the title to this property in Winton and his successors, legal representatives, and assigns.

Why are these two verbs in all-caps?

"The advantage that drafting in paragraphs affords is in part the opportunity for division and subdivision into short sentences, or parts of sentences, each standing out clearly to the eye because it commences a new line, and in part the freedom of arrangement and the ease with which an exception, or the like, that refers only to one of several particulars can be isolated and its application made clear." J.K. Aitken, *Piesse—The Elements of Drafting* 30–31 (7th ed. 1987).

NOT THIS:	BUT THIS:
Ex. 2 This Legal, Financial, and Emotional Risk Statement is made, acknowledged, and accepted by Adopting Parent, prospective adoptive parent ("Prospective Adoptive Parent"). The Prospective Adoptive Parent hereby acknowledges, understands, and accepts the following legal, financial, and emotional risks associated with the prospective placement for adoption of a child born in _______ to __________ on ____________ (the "child" or "Child"). The Adoptive parent has requested that the birth mother place the Child into their care/possession upon the Child's release from the hospital. The Adoptive parent, by his/her signature below, acknowledges that the following legal, financial, and emotional risks exist regarding the prospective placement: 1. There are certain legal, financial, and emo tional risks associated with the prospective placement of the Child due to the fact that although the birth mother signed a consent to the adoption placing the children with them, the birth father is unknown and has not had his rights terminated. The Adoptive parent represents by signing below that he/she understands the risks associated with accepting the placement of this child into his/her care/home without the legal consent of the birth father of the child. . . . **Legal-, Financial-, and Emotional-Risk Statement from Jennifer Fairfax, *The Adoption Law Handbook: Practice, Resources, and Forms for Family Law Professionals* 333–34 (2011)**	1. **Background.** This Legal-, Financial-, and Emotional-Risk Statement is made by ______________________ ("Adoptive Parent"). The Adoptive Parent understands and accepts the risks explained in § 2 as associated with the prospective placement for adoption of a child born in ______________________ to ______________________ on ________________ (the "Child"). The Adoptive Parent requests that the birth mother place the Child into the Adoptive Parent's possession upon the Child's release from the hospital. 2. **Risks of placement.** Certain legal, financial, and emotional risks are associated with the prospective placement of the Child. Although the birth mother signed a consent to the adoption placing the Child, the birth father is unknown and has not had his rights terminated. The Adoptive Parent understands the risks associated with accepting the placement of this Child into a home without the legal consent of the Child's birth father. (A) **Birth father.** . . . .

Notice the odd and inconsistent capitalization throughout this document. Why do you need a defined term that is both lowercase and capitalized (*child*)? Why would *Prospective Adoptive Parent* first be all initial caps and then switch to just the first word being capitalized (*Adoptive parent*)?

Now it's more than one child? The form uses the word *children* as well as *child*.

It's not clear whether *Adopting Parent* and *Prospective Adoptive Parent* and *Adoptive parent* are the same person. We're assuming that it's one person.

"Recently my broker handed me a multiple-coverage public-liability insurance policy. I noticed that on the outside it said 'Read your policy.' So I did. In fact, I read it ten times. I still couldn't understand the first sentence, which is about 186 words long. So I called up a friend of mine who is counsel for the company in San Francisco. I asked him what it meant. He did not know either. I doubt whether anyone knows what it means. My broker says I am fully protected. I have to take his word for it."
Robert Littler, *Legal Writing in Law Practice*, 31 Cal. B.J. 28, 31 (1956).

F. Words and Phrases

Big words and unnatural idioms

§ 137 Prefer the familiar word to the unfamiliar. Avoid legalese.

Develop the habit of using (not *utilizing*) the simplest word or phrase (not *vocable*) that's suitable to the context. One of the great flaws in legal writing is hyperformality to the point of stuffiness. You can be unstuffy and plainspoken without being undignified and slangy. What you ought to aim for is a straightforward style that doesn't use pretentious words for everyday ideas.

You'll need some legalisms, of course. If you're dealing with debentures, you're not going to help matters by avoiding the word *debentures*. But don't go whole hog with legalese. Sensitize yourself to the fancy but easily simplifiable legalisms that pervade most legal writing. These are the truly off-putting phrases that make ordinary people resent lawyers' writing, which many may think of as being dense to the point of being impenetrable.

This is a serious matter. In a state-bar survey in the late 1980s, California residents were asked what they cared most about in reforming the legal profession. The number-one answer had nothing to do with containing legal fees or providing legal services to the poor. The number-one answer was that legal documents need simplifying. This is an issue that affects ordinary people—all of them.

And although the profession as a whole has been slow in getting the message, the better lawyer-writers understand it well:

- "Attitudes need to change more than rules of composition need to be memorized. Lawyers must be convinced that there is no purpose, or value, in sounding archaic. This is a tall order. It will take an emotional, almost psychological, pitch to teach many attorneys that there

> "There is no evidence that plain language statutes or documents give rise to more litigation than traditionally worded ones. If anything, experience with standard-form legal documents suggests the reverse: that a well-drawn plain language document needs no judicial clarification. In contrast, court lists constantly contain cases where judges are asked to divine meaning from traditionally worded documents." Peter Butt, *Modern Legal Drafting*, 23 Stat. L. Rev. 12, 17 (2002).

is nothing wrong with sounding like a citizen of the second half of the 20th century. You are no less a lawyer for being understandable."[1]

- "I am particularly careful to avoid jargon, and to write simply and clearly. For certain types of writing a high level of technicality is unavoidable; but in general it is the second-rate intellect that cultivates a pretentious vocabulary and a solemn and portentous style."[2]
- "For a hundred years, good lawyers have been writing without all the garbage and in a simple, direct style."[3]
- "The idea is to avoid any word that does not command instant understanding. Your words should be transparent vehicles that let the reader see your ideas without straining to grasp the meaning. . . . Most of the concepts you struggled to master in law school can be grasped by the average 12-year-old. It is the vocabulary training that makes it such a drudgery."[4]

It's hardly an exaggeration to say that once you learn to write without unnecessary legalese, you'll be a better lawyer.

Remember, though, that you must fight not just legalese but also the other symptoms of hyperformality—the unfortunate wish to use heightened words in otherwise ordinary contexts. The most obvious examples are *prior to* and *subsequent to*, which many unskillful writers instinctively choose in place of *before* and *after.* They'd rather *utilize "prior to"* than *use "before."* People stiffen up when writing, when really they need to relax. They certainly shouldn't be lax in their standards, but they should relax in their tone. It's a hallmark of the skillful writer.

Much of the know-how that you must acquire involves straightforward word choice. (Not: *A significant degree of the knowledge base one must needs attain as a fundamental acquirement inheres in the subject of English diction, especially as it relates to the employment of monosyllabic over polysyllabic vocables.*) Don't use formal words for plain ideas. You shouldn't *proceed through the corridor* when you can *walk down the hall.* You shouldn't *imbibe a beverage* when you can *have a drink.* You shouldn't *prepare a midday meal* when you can *make lunch.* And so on. This goes for all writing, and no less for contracts.

What follows in this section is a set of strong preferences in word choice, with an eye especially on transactional practice. The left-hand side is not a series of *nevers* but rather of *almost-nevers.* Cultivate an aversion to them. By

1 Christopher T. Lutz, "Why Can't Lawyers Write?," in *Appellate Practice Manual* 167, 177 (Priscilla A. Schwab ed., 1992).

2 Judge Richard A. Posner, *How I Write*, 4 Scribes J. Legal Writing 45, 49 (1993).

3 Judge Lynn N. Hughes, as quoted in Bryan A. Garner, *Judges on Effective Writing: The Importance of Plain Language*, 73 Mich. B.J. 326, 326 (1994).

4 James W. McElhaney, *Writing to the Ear*, A.B.A.J., Dec. 1995, at 74, 76.

the way, I'm not saying that the suggested replacements will work in every context under the sun, but they're usually reliable. You'll almost instantly know whether the simpler choice will work in a given context.

Plain-Language Word Choices	
Not This:	**But This:**
abate	lessen, reduce, remove
ab initio	from the beginning
above	[omit, or supply specific reference]
above-mentioned	[omit, or supply specific reference]
absent [a thing]	without
accede to	allow, agree to
accord [an opportunity, etc.]	give
accordingly	so, therefore
afford [an opportunity, etc.]	give
aforementioned	[omit, or supply specific reference]
aforesaid	[omit, or supply specific reference]
aggregate	total, sum
agreeance	agreement
albeit	though, although, even though
all and singular	all, every
and/or	and, or, any or all of the following
appertaining	about, relating to, concerning
approximately	about
appurtenant	about, relating to, concerning
are in receipt of	have received
ascertain	find out
assist	help
assistance	help
at present	now

"In setting forth the agreements of the contracting parties, does not the word 'agree' mean just as much as 'mutually agree' or 'it is understood and agreed' or even 'it is expressly understood, covenanted, and agreed'? Many draftsmen prefer to avoid prefacing each paragraph with a statement of agreement." Frank E. Cooper, *Writing in Law Practice* 280 (1963).

Plain-Language Word Choices	
Not This:	**But This:**
attached hereto *or* thereto	attached
at the present time	now
at the time when	when
at this point in time	now
because of the fact that	because
beforementioned	[omit, or supply specific reference]
below	[supply specific reference]
bring an action (against)	sue
by means of	by
by reason of	because
cease	stop, end
ceteris paribus	other things being equal
chattels	goods
commence	start, begin
consequently	so, therefore
covenant and agree	will, agree, promise
covenanted	agreed
currently	now
date first written hereinabove	effective date
day and date	date
deemed to be	treated as, considered to be
desire	want, wish
despite the fact that	although, even if
determine [in the sense "terminate"]	end, finish, terminate
due to the fact that	because, on grounds that
during such time as	while
during the period of	during
each and every	each
emolument	pay, profit, advantage
enclosed please find	here is, here are, enclosed is, enclosed are
endeavor	try
et al.	and others
et seq.	[supply specific range if possible]
expeditiously	quickly, promptly

Plain-Language Word Choices	
Not This:	**But This:**
expend	spend
expiry	expiration
facilitate	help
for and on behalf of	for
foregoing	[omit, or supply specific reference]
for the duration	during
for the purpose of	to, for
forthwith	immediately, promptly, then
furnish	give
gift [as verb]	give
give, devise, and bequeath	give
goods and chattels	goods
henceforth	from now on
hereafter	from now on
herein	in this Agreement, in this § 5.5 [if you're in a subpart of § 5.5 but referring to all of § 5.5]
hereinabove	[supply specific reference]
hereinafter	in this Agreement *or* [omit]
hereinafter defined as	[omit]
hereinafter referred to as	[omit]
hereof	of this [whatever it is]
hereto	[omit]
heretofore	up to now, until now, before the effective date
hereunder	under this Agreement, etc.
hereunto	on this [whatever it is]
herewith	with this [whatever it is], or [omit]
hitherto	until now, up to now, before the effective date
hold in abeyance	wait, postpone
However [+ comma at start of sentence]	But [no comma following]
implement	carry out, fulfill
in an effort to	to
in consequence of	because, as a result

Plain-Language Word Choices	
Not This:	**But This:**
indemnify and hold harmless	indemnify[5]
indemnify and save harmless	indemnify
indemnify, defend, and hold harmless	indemnify and defend
indicate	show, suggest, tell, say
in excess of	more than
initiate	start, begin
initiate legal proceedings (against)	sue
in initio	in the beginning, from the start
in order that	so that
in order to	to
in personam	personal, personally
in regard to	about, regarding, concerning
in respect of	about, for, as for
institute legal proceedings (against)	sue
inter alia	among other things
interlocutory	temporary, pending a final determination
in the alternative	or
in the course of	while, during
in the event that	if
in the majority of instances	usually, normally
in witness whereof the parties have hereunto set their hands	Signed:
irrespective	regardless
irrespective of the fact that	even though
is authorized to	may
is entitled to [+ verb]	may, can
is not entitled to [+ verb]	cannot
is not permitted to	cannot, must not
is permitted to	may
is required to	must
is prohibited from, is prohibited to	must not
it is lawful for	may, can
last will and testament	will
means and includes	means, includes

5 See § 148 at pp. 392–95.

Plain-Language Word Choices	
Not This:	**But This:**
mortgagee	lender, bank
mortgagor	borrower, homeowner
mutatis mutandis	with the necessary changes, with the appropriate changes
mutually agree	agree
nevertheless	even so
not less than	at least
not more than	no more than, at most
notwithstanding	despite
notwithstanding the fact that	even though, even if
Now, therefore, in consideration . . .	The parties agree as follows:
null and void	void
null, void, and of no effect	void
onus	responsibility, burden
otherwise than	except
pari passu	equally, equal
please find enclosed	here is, here are, enclosed is, enclosed are
prior to	before
proceed	go ahead
proscribe	prohibit
provided, however, that	but [preferably starting a new sentence]
provided that	but, if, as long as
purchase	buy
purchaser	buyer
pursuant to	under, in accordance with, as authorized by, as required by
quantum	amount, number
rectify	correct, make good
regardless of the fact that	even though
relative to	about
release, remise, surrender, and forever quitclaim	release
remit	pay, send
remittance	payment
remuneration	compensation, pay, salary, wages

Plain-Language Word Choices	
Not This:	**But This:**
requisite	required, necessary
requisites	requirements
reside	live
residence [in reference to a structure]	house
rest, residue, and remainder	rest, balance, remainder
retain	keep
said [*or* the said]	this, that, these, those, the
same	it, them
save [as preposition]	except
save and except	except
shall [false future]	[present tense]
shall [true future]	will
shall [e.g., *neither party shall*]	may
shall [imperative]	must, will
subsequently	later, then
subsequent to	after
such [as pointing word]	this, that, these, those, the
terms and conditions	terms
testament	will
testamentary disposition	will, willed gift
thence	then, afterward
thenceforth	from then on, after [date]
thereafter	from then on, after [date]
therefor	for it, for them
therein	in it, in them
thereinafter	later in the [whatever it is], later, afterward
thereof	of it, of them
thereon	on it, on them
thereto	to it, to them
therewith	with it, with them
these presents	this Agreement, etc.
the sum of	[omit]
thus	so, therefore
to wit	namely, that is

Plain-Language Word Choices	
Not This:	**But This:**
transmit	send
uberrimae fidei	of the utmost good faith
undermentioned	[omit, or supply specific reference]
undersigned	I, me, this firm, etc.
undertake	agree, promise, do
until such time as	until
unto	to
upon [other than in reference to time]	on
utilization	use
utilize	use
vendee	buyer
vendor	seller
videlicet	namely, that is
viz. [abbreviation of *videlicet*]	namely, that is
where [stipulated situation]	when, if
whereas . . . whereas . . . whereas	[caption: Background or Recitals]
whereby	in which, by which
whereon	on which
wheresoever	wherever
whether or not [unless the sense is "regardless of whether"]	whether
whosoever	whoever, no matter who, anybody, anyone
will and testament	will
with regard to[6]	about, regarding, concerning
with respect to[6]	about, regarding, concerning
with the result that	so that
you are requested to	please
your attention is drawn to	please note

6 Both *with regard to* and *with respect to* are occasionally all but necessary. That is, the proposed substitutions won't always work. Note that if you were to use the phrase *with regard to*, Standard English requires *regard* as opposed to *regards*. *See Garner's Modern English Usage* 779 (4th ed. 2016). Yet *regards* is correct in the phrases *as regards* and *best regards*.

§ 138 Avoid unnatural idioms that typify legalistic writing.

Not just words, but also sentence structures, can strike readers as legalistic. Think of the phrasings that you'd never use except in legal writing:

> *is entitled to effect the transaction pursuant to*
> *the greater of this and that*
> *each of Bob, Jane, and Mary must do so-and-so*
> *anything in this prospectus to the contrary notwithstanding*

The first three of those phrases you can put into ordinary English. The fourth is a phrase you simply shouldn't need in a document.

It's not easy, of course, learning the plain-English equivalents of legalese. For the lawyer, it's like learning a new language. As Jacques Barzun once said, "Plain English is no one's mother tongue. It has to be worked for."[1] But once you get the knack of it, you'll come to detest woolly-minded legalisms.

NOT THIS:	BUT THIS:
Ex. 1 Each of Westworld and the Westworld subsidiaries has duly filed all federal, state, county, and foreign tax returns required to be filed by it. **Corporate-Conveyance Agreement**	Westworld and its subsidiaries have filed all required federal, state, county, and foreign tax returns.
Ex. 2 The Wellco reorganization will be effected largely pursuant to transactions described in the master separation agreement. **Corporate-Reorganization Agreement**	The Wellco reorganization will take place largely through a series of transactions described in the master separation agreement.

1 As quoted in Rudolf Flesch, *The Art of Readable Writing* 1 (1949; reprint 1974).

Pronouns and their antecedents

§ 139 Use pronouns when it's natural to do so and the construction is unambiguous.

How can you make your prose mind-numbing? Simply repeat nouns ad nauseam without ever using a pronoun such as *it* or *them*. That will do the trick.

Mysteriously, many legal writers seem to believe that you shouldn't ever use a pronoun. Perhaps they've seen sentences in which an *it* or a *them* didn't have a clear antecedent, and from that they've mislearned never to use pronouns. That's the wrong lesson because it leads to exceedingly tedious prose. The true lesson is that you must rid your text of miscues and ambiguities while retaining pronouns—well-used, unambiguous pronouns.

Because pronouns can sometimes be ambiguous, be careful. Yet understand that they're also necessary to a natural, more readable style.

NOT THIS:	BUT THIS:
Ex. 1 20. Effective Date. The parties deem this Agreement to be effective immediately as of the latest date on which one of the Parties executes this Agreement. **Settlement Agreement executed by a major law firm**	**20. Effective Date.** This Agreement is effective on the latest date on which one of the Parties signs it.
Ex. 2 The Bradford Financial bylaws permit special meetings of the stockholders of Bradford Financial to be called by the holders of two-thirds of the outstanding Bradford Financial common stock. **Asset-Purchase Agreement**	Bradford Financial's bylaws permit holders of two-thirds of its outstanding common stock to call a special stockholders' meeting.
Ex. 3 Without limiting any of the remedies provided in the Loan Documents, Indemnitor acknowledges and agrees that the provisions of this Agreement are environmental provisions made by Indemnitor relating to the Property (the "Environmental Provisions"). **Environmental Indemnity Agreement from a major retail toy company**	Without limiting any remedies in the Loan Documents, Toy Joy acknowledges that this Agreement contains environmental-specific provisions about the relevant Property.

For more on *deem*, see § 148 at pp. 387–88.

On the inadvisability of this provision, see §§ 57 and 59.

NOT THIS:	BUT THIS:
Ex. 4 Whereas, the shares of First Party in the Company PT. COALUNA MINING shall be exchanged with forty percent (40%) shares held by Second Party in Second Party's Company in FISH ELECTRONICS INT'L BVI COMPANY NUMBER 2859856 . . . . **Agreement to Transfer and Assign Right over Shares**	Locketi's shares in Coaluna Mining will be exchanged for 40% of the shares held by MacGregor in its Company, Fish Electronics Int'l (BVI Company #2859856) . . . .
Ex. 5 As of the date hereof, the income tax returns of Qualtech and the Qualtech subsidiaries have never been examined by the IRS. There are no material disputes pending, or claims asserted for, taxes or assessments upon Qualtech or any of the Qualtech subsidiaries for which Qualtech does not have adequate reserves, nor has Qualtech or any of the Qualtech subsidiaries given any currently effective waivers extending the statutory period of limitation applicable to any federal, state, county, foreign, or local income tax for any period. **Merger Agreement**	As of the date of this prospectus, the IRS has not examined the tax returns of Qualtech or its subsidiaries. Qualtech has enough reserves to cover pending disputes over or claims for taxes and assessments against Qualtech and its subsidiaries. Neither Qualtech nor any of its subsidiaries has given a currently effective waiver extending the statutory limitation period applicable to any federal, state, county, foreign, or local income tax.

For more on avoiding *First Party* and *Second Party*, see § 53.

"Pronouns help you see the world from a reader's perspective—a must for effective writing—much better than a roundabout, nobody-home, untouched-by-human-hands style. If you avoid personal pronouns, you had better have a superbly sensitive nose for sniffing out and avoiding passive voice. Even then, readers will have to pause and translate third-person references to themselves. At best, third-person writing is a poor substitute for talking to readers directly." Thomas A. Murawski, *Writing Readable Regulations* 33 (1999).

§ 140 Ensure that every pronoun has an antecedent.

Ensure that every pronoun is preceded by a proper referent (noun). An adjective or a possessive cannot properly function as a pronoun's antecedent.

NOT THIS:	BUT THIS:
Ex. 1 8. <u>Governing Law/Choice of Venue</u>. The Award and the provisions of this Agreement are governed by, and subject to, the laws of the State of Washington, as provided in the Plan, without regard for its conflict of laws provisions. **Global Restricted-Stock-Unit Agreement from a major coffeehouse chain**	8. **Governing Law.** Washington law applies to all matters arising under or relating to this Agreement without regard to any choice-of-law rules that might direct the application of another jurisdiction's laws.
Ex. 2 Notwithstanding anything contained herein to the contrary, "Contingent Obligations" shall not be deemed to include guarantees of loan commitments or of construction loans to the extent the same have not been drawn. **Credit-and-Guaranty Agreement from a major bank**	Despite anything in this Agreement to the contrary, "Contingent Obligations" do not include guarantees of loan commitments or of construction loans to the extent that the guarantees have not been drawn. *or* Despite anything in this Agreement to the contrary, "Contingent Obligations" do not include guarantees of loan commitments or of construction loans to the extent that the loans have not been drawn.
Ex. 3 The Administrative Agent, without the request of the Borrower may advance any interest, fee, service charge, or other payment to which any Credit Party is entitled from the Loan Parties pursuant hereto or any other Loan Document and may charge the same to the Loan Account as and when the same become due and payable hereunder, after giving effect to any applicable grace periods, notwithstanding that an Overadvance may result thereby, <u>provided</u> that no advances which create an Overadvance shall be made for any Cash Management Services or Bank Products. **Credit Agreement from a major retailer**	Without the Borrower's request, the Administrative Agent may advance any interest, fee, service charge, or other payment to which a Credit Party is entitled from the Loan Parties or any other Loan Document and may charge the interest, fee, service charge, or other payment to the Loan Account when the interest, fee, service charge, or other payment becomes due, after giving effect to any applicable grace periods, even if an Overadvance may result. But no advance that creates an Overadvance may be made for any Cash Management Services or Bank Products.

What does *its* refer to? The Agreement? The Plan? The Award? The State? We just have to guess.

Same as a pronoun often creates ambiguity. Does it refer to guarantees of both commitments and loans? Or only guarantees?

Because of the ambiguity, we can't be sure which version is correct.

What does *same* refer to? It has four antecedents: *interest, fee, service charge,* and *other payment.*

§ 141 Ensure that every pronoun agrees in number and person with its antecedent.

It's a fundamental point of grammar: a singular antecedent takes a singular pronoun of the same person as the antecedent, and a plural antecedent takes a plural pronoun of the same person as the antecedent.[1]

NOT THIS:	BUT THIS:
Ex. 1 The Trustee or Paying Agent, as applicable, will repay to the Company on the Company's written request any funds they hold for payments on the Notes that remain unclaimed for two years after the date upon which that payment has become due. **First Supplemental Indenture from a major coffeehouse chain**	Upon Breve's written request, the Trustee or Paying Agent, as applicable, must repay to Breve any funds it holds for payment on the Notes if the funds have remained unclaimed for 2 years after the payment's due date.
Ex. 2 If the Seller does not, within 45 (forty-five) days of delivery to them of the Draft Completion Statements, deliver written notice to the Purchaser that it disagrees with the Draft Completion Statements or any item thereof (such notice to state the reasons for the disagreement in reasonable detail including a statement of each disputed item and the amount in dispute and the basis for such dispute) (the "**Seller's Disagreement Notice**" and such items being the "**Disputed Items**"), the Draft Completion Statements shall be final and binding on the Parties for all purposes. **Sale-and-Purchase Agreement from a major office-supply chain**	The Draft Completion Statements will be final and binding on the Parties for all purposes if, within 45 days after delivery of the Draft Completion Statements, SupplyMax does not deliver notice to Tristan that it disagrees with a statement or any related item (stating the reasons for the disagreement in reasonable detail, including identifying each disputed item, the amount in dispute, and the basis for the dispute).

"Contracts are the result of what people say, not what they intend to say. In construing a contract, therefore, the question is not what intention or understanding may have existed in the minds of the parties, but what intention is expressed by the language used." 17 C.J.S. *Contracts* § 310 (1999).

1 *See* Garner, *The Chicago Guide to Grammar, Usage, and Punctuation* § 51, at 38–39 (2016).

NOT THIS:	BUT THIS:
Ex. 3 10. Confidentiality. The Parties agree that to the extent this Agreement, including all the terms and conditions hereof and all the information relating to and required for the performance of Services hereunder, is deemed Confidential Information as provided in Section 13.1 of the Operating Agreement, the Parties agree to abide by all the terms and conditions of Section 13.1 of the Operating Agreement, such provisions being hereby incorporated by reference as though fully set forth herein. Consistent with such provisions, the Parties agree to keep confidential such Confidential Information disclosed to it by the other Party hereunder, and that neither it nor any of its employees or agents, nor any of its Affiliates or the employees or agents of such Affiliates, will reproduce, publish or disclose any Confidential Information of the other party to any third party, unless required by law, but then only on the terms and conditions as set forth in the Operating Agreement. **Services Agreement from a major law firm**	**10. Confidentiality.** To the extent that this Agreement, including all the terms and information relating to and required for the performance of Services under this Agreement, constitutes Confidential Information under the Operating Agreement § 13.1, the Parties will follow the Operating Agreement § 13.1, which is incorporated into this Agreement. Consistently with those provisions, each Party will keep confidential the Confidential Information disclosed to it by the other Party under this Agreement, and neither it nor any of its employees or agents, nor its Affiliates or their employees or agents, will reproduce, publish, or disclose any Confidential Information to any third party, unless required by law, and then only in accordance with the Operating Agreement.

The syntax here switches from plural to singular.

"When we draft in plain language we look at more than just the meaning of the words we are using and how they will be perceived by our readers. We also look at the organization of the words in a sentence, the sentences in a document, and the layout of the document itself. All these things can have an effect on whether the document can be understood by its intended readers, at the level of understanding they need to have." Michèle M. Asprey, *Plain Language for Lawyers* 12 (1991).

§ 142 Avoid cataphora—using a pronoun before telling the reader what its referent is.

Ensure that a referent precedes its pronoun, not vice versa. That is, avoid what rhetoricians call *cataphora* or *anticipatory reference.* Use a noun twice rather than having a pronoun precede its referent.

NOT THIS:	BUT THIS:
Ex. 1 11.04 Tax Position. Unless he or it provides prior written notice to the Company, Member will not take a position on his federal income tax return, in any claim for refund, or in any administrative or legal proceedings that is inconsistent with any information return filed by the Company or with the provisions of this Agreement. **Limited-Liability-Company Agreement for units of liability** Note that the pronouns appear before the noun to which they might refer.	11.4 **Tax position.** Without having provided written notice to the Company, Member will not take a position on Member's individual federal income-tax return with regard to a claim for refund, or in any administrative or legal proceeding, if that position is inconsistent with any information return filed by the Company or with this Agreement.
Ex. 2 UNLESS AND UNTIL IT IS EXCHANGED IN WHOLE OR IN PART FOR NOTES IN DEFINITIVE FORM, THIS NOTE MAY NOT BE TRANSFERRED EXCEPT AS A WHOLE BY THE DEPOSITARY TO A NOMINEE OF THE DEPOSITARY OR BY A NOMINEE OF THE DEPOSITARY TO THE DEPOSITARY OR ANOTHER NOMINEE OF THE DEPOSITARY OR BY THE DEPOSITARY OR ANY SUCH NOMINEE TO A SUCCESSOR DEPOSITARY OR A NOMINEE OF SUCH SUCCESSOR DEPOSITARY. **Senior-Secured-First-Lien-Notes Indenture from a major healthcare company** Note that *it* appears before the noun (*note*) to which it refers. Avoid all caps. See § 42.	**53. Restrictions on Transfer. Unless this Note has been exchanged in whole or in part for Notes in definitive form, it cannot be transferred except as a whole by one of the following:** **(A) the depositary to the depositary's nominee;** **(B) the depositary's nominee to either the depositary or another nominee of the depositary; or** **(C) the depositary or the depositary's nominee to either a successor depositary or the successor depositary's nominee.**

"It is tempting to think that creation of a legal document is a ministerial act, the simple writing down of things already decided. It is easy to assume that document drafting is secondary to substantive legal analysis or the planning of tasks more properly at the center of lawyerly attention." Marc Lauritson, *The Literature of Legal Drafting,* Network 2d, Summer 1994, at 8, 8.

Relative pronouns

§ 143 Distinguish between *that* and *which*. Avoid the nonrestrictive *which*.

Use *that*, not *which*, as a restrictive relative pronoun. This injunction is generally (and usefully) followed in American English: it lends grammatical rigor to avoid the word *which* unless it follows a comma, dash, parenthesis, or preposition. True, this convention isn't followed in British English. But it is highly recommended in all English-language contexts.[1]

What are we talking about? A restrictive *that*-clause is one that's necessary to a sentence's essential meaning; a nonrestrictive *which*-clause (which might, for example, appear within parentheses) could be dropped from the sentence with no loss of essential meaning—as with the parenthetical *which*-clause earlier in this sentence. Consider the substantive differences between these sentences:

> Ex.: Briefing that is helpful should be encouraged in all cases. (*Unhelpful briefing shouldn't be encouraged.*)
>
> Ex.: Briefing, which is helpful, should be encouraged in all cases. (*All briefing should be encouraged.*)

Understand how word choice is reinforced by punctuation. A commaless *which* is ambiguous.

NOT THIS:	BUT THIS:
Ex. 1 "Affiliate" of a party means any entity which, directly or indirectly, controls such party or is under common control with such party . . . . **Shareholder-Voting Agreement from a global Internet-media company**	"Affiliate" of a party means an entity that directly or indirectly controls that party or is under common control with that party . . . .
Ex. 2 Each such payment is for royalties which accrued within the Licensee's most recently completed calendar quarter. **Exclusive-License Agreement from an oncology-research company**	Each payment is for royalties that have accrued within the Licensee's most recently completed calendar quarter.

1 For more on this subject, see *Garner's Modern English Usage* 900–02 (4th ed. 2016); *The Chicago Manual of Style* § 5.250, at 354–55; § 6.27, at 327–28 (17th ed. 2017).

NOT THIS:	BUT THIS:
Ex. 3 "Authorized Service Providers" means service providers which may be used by Provider in the maintenance program and which are more particularly described in Appendix A. **Equipment and Software-Services Agreement between a city and a major technology company**	"Authorized Service Providers" means service providers that the Provider may use in the maintenance program and that are listed in Appendix A.
Ex. 4 <u>Mortgage</u>: The mortgage, deed of trust or other instrument, which creates a lien on the related Mortgaged Property securing the related Mortgage Note. **Mortgage-Loan Purchase Agreement between two major financial institutions**	"Mortgage" means the instrument that creates a lien on the Mortgaged Property securing the Mortgage Note.
Ex. 5 Franchisee shall, at its sole expense, equip each Approved Location with computers and computer-related equipment and supplies which meet Tuke's Technology Standards. **Franchise-License Agreement from a Fortune 500 company**	4.2 **Technology.** At its sole expense, Nguyen will equip each Approved Location with computers, computer-related equipment, and supplies, all of which must meet Tuke's Technology Standards.
Ex. 6 1. Definitions. . . . "Site License" shall mean a license for software which allows use on all CPUs located in an Enterprise Site. **Software-License Agreement from a telecommunications company**	**1. Definitions.** . . . (E) "Site License" means a software license that allows use on all CPUs in an Enterprise Site location.
Ex. 7 Each Person listed in Annex A hereto which is not a party to this Agreement prior to the Effective Date (a "**New Lender**") shall become a Lender Party to this Agreement. **Revolving-Credit-and-Guaranty Agreement from a major automotive manufacturer**	Each Person that is listed in Annex A but is not a party to this Agreement before the Effective Date becomes a Lender Party to this Agreement.
Ex. 8 Seller agrees and acknowledges that Purchaser has relied upon information which has been furnished to Purchaser by Seller regarding the Business and the Company, including certain projections and other forecasts. **Stock-Purchase Agreement from a major law firm**	The Seller acknowledges that the Buyer relied on information that the Seller gave the Buyer about the Business and the Company, including projections and forecasts.

The revision eliminates the tautology in the definition. See § 100.

Notice how you can eliminate the preposition *for* in the phrase "license for software" by changing to an adjective: *software license*. See § 123.

On preferring active voice over passive voice, see § 66.

NOT THIS:	BUT THIS:
Ex. 9 6.5 Discontinuance of Printing/Manufacture. Immediately upon notice from Licensor, Licensee shall discontinue the printing and/or manufacture of Licensed Items at any print shop or factory making such Licensed Items which, in the reasonable opinion of Licensor, are of inferior quality or design. **License Agreement from a major law firm**	6.5 **Discontinuance of printing and manufacturing.** Upon notice from Wallace Industries, Quick Print will immediately stop printing and manufacturing Licensed Items at a print shop or factory making Licensed Items that are—based on Wallace Industries' reasonable opinion—inferior in quality or design.

"Nonlawyers almost invariably prefer plain language, often seeing legalese as a device by which lawyers cynically make themselves expensively indispensable." Mark Adler, "The Plain Language Movement," in *The Oxford Handbook of Language and Law* 67, 73 (Peter M. Tiersma & Lawrence M. Solan eds., 2012).

§ 144 Eliminate remote relatives.

Avoid so-called *remote relatives*—the relative pronoun *that*, *which*, or *who* separated from the noun to which it refers. Place the relative pronoun directly after the word it modifies or rework the sentence.[1]

Sometimes you'll find challenging sentences like this one: "The parties understand that they may later discover facts different from what they now believe to be true that if known could have materially affected this Agreement." The relative pronoun *that* is intended to modify *facts*, which appears ten words before. One thought is to change *that* to *which*: some editors think it more readily skips back over intervening words. But it's not a good solution. The real problem is that the words *that are* have been elided from the original sentence after the word *facts*. They need to be restored, and a conjunction added: "The parties understand that they may later discover facts that are different from what they now believe to be true and that, if known, could have materially affected this Agreement."

NOT THIS:	BUT THIS:
Ex. 1 A rate of pay will be established for the new position of Track Maintainer which will be $1,000 per month effective April 23, 2017. **Memorandum Agreement from a railroad company**	A pay rate of $1,000 per month will be established for the new position of Track Maintainer, effective April 23, 2017.
Ex. 2 Any provision of this Policy which is in conflict with the law of the jurisdiction in which the Insured is located is hereby amended to conform to the minimum requirements of that law. **Insurance Policy from a major underwriter**	Any Policy provision that conflicts with the law of the Insured's local jurisdiction is amended by this clause to conform to the minimum requirements of that law.
Ex. 3 To the extent applicable, the sublicenses include all the rights of and obligations due to the Licensor that are contained in this Agreement including payment of royalties and License Issue Fees provided for in Articles 4 and 5 that are contained in this Agreement. **License Agreement from a major law firm**	To the extent applicable, the sublicenses include all of Finklestein's rights contained in this Agreement—as well as all obligations due to Finklestein—including payment of royalties and License Issue Fees provided for in Articles 4 and 5.

The phrase *that are* need not be expressed in the revision. But the phrase could not be suppressed in the "Not this" version without causing a remote relative.

1 For more on remote relatives, see *Garner's Modern English Usage* 784–86 (4th ed. 2016) (s.v. "Remote Relatives").

NOT THIS:	BUT THIS:
Ex. 4 **4. Nondisclosure** 4.1 All information provided by or through Michelson Co. to Contractor or that Contractor reproduces, produces and delivers to Michelson Co. in the course of this Agreement, shall be the sole and exclusive property of Michelson Co. Unless authorized in writing by Michelson Co., any information obtained by Contractor from Michelson Co. in the course of performing this Agreement which is not publicly available, shall be kept confidential and treated as proprietary, shall not be released in whole or in part without the prior written consent of Michelson Co. and shall not be used except to satisfy the purpose of this Agreement. **Third-Party-Logistics-Services Agreement from a major consumer-product technology and development company**	**4. Nondisclosure.** **4.1 Michelson property.** All information provided by or through Michelson to Gregan or that Gregan reproduces, produces, and delivers to Michelson in the course of this Agreement is the exclusive property of Michelson. Any nonpublic information that Gregan obtains from Michelson in the course of performing this Agreement must be kept confidential and treated as proprietary and must not be released in whole or in part without Michelson's written consent, and may be used only to satisfy this Agreement's purpose.

"Substance and style are analytically separable. It is useful to think about each separately at some points during your overall consideration of a good draft. But it is also useful to remember that good substance and good style are complementary." Robert E. Keeton, *Guidelines for Drafting, Editing, and Interpreting* § 5.2(a) cmt. a., at 56 (2002).

Conjunctions

§ 145 Use *and* and *or* advisedly.

When clauses or phrases are joined conjunctively (*and*) or disjunctively (*or*), put the conjunction at the end of the next-to-last item only—not after each item. Polysyndeton (the repetitive use of *and* or *or* at the end of each item) has no place in legal drafting.

NOT THIS:	BUT THIS:
Ex. 1 13.5 **Effect of termination:** On termination of the Services Agreement or an individual Service, the Customer and its Users shall: (i) stop using the relevant Services; and (ii) return, or make available for collection, any equipment owned by Hatch Inc. in accordance with Hatch Inc.'s reasonable instructions; and (iii) pay any applicable Recovery Charge. **Service Agreement from a major communications company**	13.5 **Effect of termination.** Upon ending the Services Agreement or an individual Service, the Customer and its Users must: (A) stop using the relevant Services; (B) return, or make available for collection, the equipment owned by Hatch in accordance with Hatch's reasonable instructions; and (C) pay the applicable Recovery Charge.
Ex. 2 7.6 *Notices.* 7.6.1 *Service of Notices.* Any notices or other communications given under this Agreement shall be given in writing and may be given by: (i) in-person hand delivery; or (ii) overnight delivery service; or (iii) facsimile transmission to the number or numbers listed below; or (iv) certified mail, with postage prepaid and return receipt requested. **Bankruptcy Agreement from a major law firm**	7.6 **Notice.** (A) **Service of notice.** Any notice or other communication given under this Agreement must be in writing and may be given by: (1) in-person hand-delivery; (2) overnight delivery service; (3) fax to the numbers listed below; or (4) certified mail, with postage prepaid and return receipt requested.

> "Nothing is so embarrassing as to have a client ask what certain language in a contract means and, on looking at it, to discover that this was certain language copied from a form that was in no way applicable to your client's particular matter." John E. Tracy, *Hints on Entering the Practice of Law* 54 (1933).

§ 146 Use *but* instead of *and* to introduce a contrasting idea.

The conjunction *but* is known as an *adversative*: it introduces a contrary idea, not merely an additional one.

NOT THIS:	BUT THIS:
Ex. 1 Buyer and Seller hereby agree that, except as expressly provided herein, the provisions of the Prior Agreement shall be, and remain in full force and effect between Buyer and Seller, and that if any provision of this Purchase Agreement conflicts with the Prior Agreement, then the provisions of this Purchase Agreement shall prevail. **Purchase Agreement from a major law firm**	Unless this Agreement provides otherwise, the Prior Agreement remains in full force. But if any provision of this Purchase Agreement conflicts with the Prior Agreement, then this Purchase Agreement prevails.
Ex. 2 This investment agreement (the "Agreement") is made as of the 2nd day of March, 2015, by and between Kurion Investors, Inc., a South Dakota corporation ("Issuer"), and the undersigned investor (the "Investor"), and shall be effective upon execution of the Merger Agreement, provided, however, that the Merger Agreement, as defined below, is executed on or prior to April 30, 2015, and if not so executed, this Agreement shall be void and have no further force and effect. **Investment Agreement from a major bank**	This investment agreement, effective when the Merger Agreement defined below becomes effective, is between Kurion Investors, Inc. (Kurion), a South Dakota corporation, and the undersigned investor (Investor). But if the Merger Agreement does not become effective on or before April 30, 2015, this Agreement is voided.
Ex. 3 (b) *Acceleration of Expiry Date.* If, at any time when an option granted under the Plan remains unexercised, an Offer is made by an offeror, the Board of Directors may in its sole discretion, upon notifying each Participant of full particulars of the Offer, declare all options granted under the Plan, vested, and declare that the expiry date for the exercise of all unexercised options granted under the Plan is accelerated so that all options will either be exercised or will expire prior to the date upon which Common Shares must be tendered pursuant to the Offer, provided such Offer is completed and, if not completed, the respective Expiry Dates of the options shall revert to the original Expiry Date. **Incentive Stock-Option Plan**	(B) **Acceleration of Expiration Date.** If an offeror makes an Offer for an unexercised option granted under the Plan, the Board of Directors may, upon notifying each Participant of the Offer details, declare all options granted under the Plan vested, and accelerate the expiration date for the exercise of all unexercised options granted under the Plan. The accelerated date for exercise or expiration of all outstanding options must be before the date on which Common Shares will be tendered under the Offer. But if the Offer is not completed, the options will not expire and the options' Expiration Dates will revert to the original Expiration Date.

Expiration is the usual term in World English. *Expiry* is a British English variant.

§ 147 Prefer *But* or *Yet* over *However* as a sentence-starter.

Use *But* or *Yet* to start a sentence in preference to *However* or other even more cumbersome contrasting words.[1] Don't place a comma after an initial *But* or *Yet.*

	NOT THIS:	BUT THIS:
Ex. 1	**Is my personal information secure?** We understand that the security of your personal information is important. We provide reasonable administrative, technical, and physical security controls to protect your personal information. However, despite our efforts, no security controls are 100% effective and Woodcrest Inc. cannot ensure or warrant the security of your personal information. **Privacy Policy from a major software developer and provider**	**Is my personal information secure?** We understand that the security of your personal information is important. We provide reasonable administrative, technical, and physical security controls to protect your personal information. Yet no security controls are 100% effective, and Woodcrest Inc. cannot guarantee the security of your personal information.
Ex. 2	(d) Notifications. The formal notifications as required for use variances in § 208-109C(2)(d) above will not normally be required in the case of a request for an area variance. However, if the situation warrants it, the Chairman of the Zoning Board of Appeals may require the applicant to accomplish such notifications. **Town ordinance concerning zoning board of appeals from Patricia E. Salkin, 4 N.Y. Zoning Law & Prac. § 41:2 (Supp. 2018)**	(D) **Notifications.** The formal notifications required in § 208-109C(2)(d) for use variances will not ordinarily be required when requesting an area variance. But if the situation so warrants, the Chairman of the Zoning Board of Appeals may require the applicant to make the notifications.

1 For a collection of myriad authorities defending this age-old practice, see *Garner's Modern English Usage* 133–34 (4th ed. 2016).

Usage

§ 148 Pay special attention to certain wordings.

Many words and phrases deserve your close scrutiny. These can't be forbidden altogether if they have some legitimate uses. *Where*, for example, is the ordinary locative adverb (denoting place), and it would be wrongheaded to say you should abstain from it completely. On the other hand, you ought to refrain from using it in the legalistic sense of establishing a circumstance. That is, don't use *where* in place of *when* or *if*, which are the ordinary English words for establishing a given circumstance. Usually it's *when* for what seems to be an inevitability (*When John reaches the age of 18*) and *if* for something that might or might not happen (*If the parties divorce before John reaches the age of 18*). But to the ordinary speaker of English, *where* is unusual for stipulating a possible eventuality (*Where the parties divorce before John reaches the age of 18*).

Hence the guidance in this section is cautionary, not prohibitive. It's context-sensitive. If *where* is called for in its usual spatial sense (*where its principal office is located*), keep it; but if it appears in the sense of *when* or *if*, replace it.

all of. Delete *of* when possible—as a matter of tightening. It's simply good editorial practice.

NOT THIS:	BUT THIS:
Ex. 1 2.2 Purchasing and Pricing. Customer agrees that it shall purchase all of its Beverage requirements from Company or an authorized Company distributor designated by Company. **Marketing Agreement from a major beverage company**	**2.2 Purchasing and pricing.** Williamson will purchase all its Beverage requirements from Pop Fizz or an authorized distributor that Pop Fizz designates.
Ex. 2 The Company may terminate this Agreement and/or require the Consultant to cease providing any or all of the Services at any time and for any reason upon written notice to the Consultant. **Consulting-Services Agreement from a major food, snack, and beverage corporation**	Upon written notice to you, we may terminate this Agreement or require you to stop any or all Services at any time and for any reason.

For more about *and/or*, see § 149 at pp. 406–08.

NOT THIS:	BUT THIS:
Ex. 3 Notwithstanding any provision set forth in this Section 2.28, the Borrower hereby retains all of its rights and remedies available to it against any Defaulting Lender pursuant to contract, applicable law or otherwise. **Revolving-Credit-and-Guaranty Agreement from a major automotive manufacturer**	Despite any other provision in § 2.28, the Borrower retains all its rights and remedies available against a Defaulting Lender under any contract, applicable law, or otherwise.

any. Try *a*, *an*, *all*, or *other* instead. But *any* is preferable to *if any* (see § 149 at pp. 421–22). And see *such* [noun + *-s*] *as* (§ 149 at pp. 445–46).

NOT THIS:	BUT THIS:
Ex. 1 The Company shall not make any matching contributions to this Plan for any period after the end of the 2019 Plan Year (the Plan Year that ends on December 31, 2019). **Retirement-Plan Agreement from a global industrial innovation company**	The Company will match contributions to this Plan only until the 2019 Plan Year ends on December 31, 2019. *or* The Company will not match contributions to this Plan after the 2019 Plan Year ends on December 31, 2019.
Ex. 2 B. If CLIENT objects to all or any portion of any invoice, CLIENT shall notify CONSULTANT of the same within fifteen (15) days of receipt of the invoice, give reasons for the objection, and pay that portion of the invoice not in dispute. **Consulting-Services Agreement from a major beverage company**	(B) **Invoice disputes.** If Reid objects to all or part of an invoice, Reid must: (1) notify Voigt of the objection within 15 days after receiving the invoice; (2) give reasons for the objection; and (3) pay the undisputed part of the invoice.

For more about positive and negative statements, see §§ 69–70.

For more on this use of *same*, see § 149 at pp. 440–41.

as amended from time to time. This phrasing means that a statute or document referred to means the then-current version, not the version in effect when the contract was signed. Before using the language, think through whether you really mean it. Then express the idea as clearly as you can.

NOT THIS:	BUT THIS:
Ex. 1 All information exchanged or made available shall be governed by the terms of the Non-Disclosure Agreement, dated as of April 27, 2017, by and between Parent and the Company, as amended by the Confidentiality Supplement, dated May 7, 2017 (as it may be further amended from time to time, the "Confidentiality Agreement"). **Merger Agreement between a major Internet-based retailer and a major grocery chain**	All information exchanged or made available is governed by the Nondisclosure Agreement dated April 27, 2017, between Vines and Kern Co., as amended by the Confidentiality Supplement dated May 7, 2017, and as it may be further amended from time to time.

NOT THIS:	BUT THIS:
Ex. 2 This Master Services Agreement (the "MSA") is entered into by and between Comcell ("Comcell" or "Company"), a Delaware L.L.C., and you (the "Customer") for certain web hosting services provided by Comcell (the "Services").... BY USING THE SERVICES, THE CUSTOMER AGREES THAT (1) CUSTOMER HAS ACCEPTED THE MSA IN ITS ENTIRETY, (2) AGREES TO BE BOUND BY THE MSA (AS AMENDED FROM TIME TO TIME AS PROVIDED IN SECTION 9 OF THE TERMS OF SERVICE), (3) IF THE CUSTOMER IS AN INDIVIDUAL, THEN THE INDIVIDUAL REPRESENTS AND WARRANTS THAT HE OR SHE HAS THE LEGAL RIGHT TO ENTER INTO THE MSA AND IF THE CUSTOMER IS AN ENTITY THEN THE INDIVIDUAL WHO AGREES TO THE MSA REPRESENTS AND WARRANTS THAT HE OR SHE HAS THE AUTHORITY TO BIND SUCH ENTITY AND (4) THIS MSA CONSTITUTES A BINDING AND ENFORCEABLE CONTRACTUAL AGREEMENT BETWEEN COMCELL AND CUSTOMER. **Master Services Agreement from a web-hosting company**	This Master Services Agreement (the MSA) is between Comcell, a Delaware LLC, and you, the customer, for certain web-hosting services provided by Comcell. . . . By using the Services, you: (A) accept the MSA in its entirety; (B) are bound by the MSA and any amendments made from time to time under § 9 of the Terms of Service; (C) represent and warrant that if you are: (1) an individual, you have the legal right to enter into the MSA; or (2) an entity, you as the signer have the authority to bind the entity; and (D) promise to honor this MSA as a binding and enforceable contract between Comcell and you.

The rewrite doesn't eliminate the phrase altogether. Instead, it makes it clear that the customer (*you*) is bound by any amendments that may be made under § 9 in the future.

deem. This word should be confined to creating legal fictions: *all cats are deemed to be dogs*; *all squares are deemed to be circles.* Avoid using it to say that some garden-variety thing is that very thing. If it's a matter of shading a sense or declaring a thing of questionable status to have that status, use *treated as* or *considered* or a present-tense verb such as *is* or *does.*

NOT THIS:	BUT THIS:
Ex. 1 No descriptions other than those in this document shall be deemed a warranty by description or otherwise have any legal effect. **Sales Agreement Terms & Conditions from Robert A. Feldman & Raymond T. Nimmer, *Drafting Effective Contracts: A Practitioner's Guide*, Form 5-6, at 5-209 (2d ed. 2010)**	A description outside this Agreement is not a warranty by description and has no legal effect.

NOT THIS:	BUT THIS:
Ex. 2 Nothing herein will be deemed to require Landlord to develop or construct any such additional buildings or to combine the Building with any other buildings. **Lease Agreement from a major technology institution**	Nothing in this Agreement requires Hortoco to develop or construct additional buildings or to combine the Building with any others.
Ex. 3 2. Effectiveness. The transactions contemplated by this Agreement shall be deemed effective as of 12:01 a.m. Central Standard Time on the date of this Distribution Agreement (the "Effective Date"). **Distribution Agreement from 4 *Texas Legal Practice Forms* § 62:33, at 529 (3d ed. 2016)**	2. **Effectiveness.** The transactions contemplated by this Agreement are effective as of 12:01 a.m. CT on the date of this Distribution Agreement.
Ex. 4 No approval or consent by Landlord shall be deemed or construed to be a representation or warranty by Landlord as to the adequacy, sufficiency, fitness or suitability of the construction or compliance thereof with applicable laws or other requirements. **Lease Agreement from a major tech institution**	DemeCorp's approval or consent is not a representation or warranty of the construction's sufficiency, fitness, suitability, or compliance with applicable laws or other requirements.
Ex. 5 Buyer's taking of possession shall not be deemed a waiver of the contract of sale or in any manner affect the rights of either party under it and shall not be deemed an acceptance of the title to the premises, but possession shall be considered as taken conditionally on, and without prejudice to, the full performance of the contract of sale. **Agreement for Preclosing Possession by Property Purchaser from 13 Gerry W. Beyer, *West's Texas Forms: Real Property* § 6.122, at 340 (2d ed. 2001)**	Hardstark's taking possession does not waive the contract of sale, affect either party's contractual rights, or constitute Hardstark's accepting title to the premises. Rather, Hardstark takes possession—without prejudice—on the condition that the sales contract has been fully performed.

each; every. Prefer *a* or *an*—or sometimes *any* or *all.* But *each* sometimes usefully emphasizes that a provision relates to every single instance of a thing specified.

NOT THIS:	BUT THIS:
Ex. 1 5.2.7 Each Master Franchisee Party agrees that it shall not charge any Franchisee a Royalty in excess of the International Franchisee Royalty. **International-Franchise Agreement from a major fast-food restaurant**	(G) A Master Franchisee Party must not charge a Franchisee a Royalty that exceeds the International Franchisee Royalty.

Of course, using the specific party names instead of these clumsy labels would be a better solution.

NOT THIS:	BUT THIS:
Ex. 2 My opinions expressed below are specifically subject to the following limitations, exceptions, qualifications and assumptions: . . . . (a) I have also assumed that each natural person executing any document, instrument, certificate or agreement that I have reviewed in connection with this opinion was legally competent to do so. **Underwriting Agreement from a major food-service distributor**	My opinions expressed below are subject to the following limitations, exceptions, qualifications, and assumptions: . . . . (A) A natural person signing a document, instrument, certificate, or agreement that I have reviewed for this opinion was legally competent to do so.
Ex. 3 "Financing Subsidiary" means each Subsidiary of the Parent Guarantor organized solely for the purpose of providing financing for the members of the Reporting Group and holding no assets other than loans or advances to other members of the Reporting Group, cash and Cash Equivalents and immaterial amounts of other assets. **Bridge Credit Agreement from a major media and entertainment company**	"Financing Subsidiary" means a Subsidiary of Albutex that has been organized solely to provide financing for the members of the Reporting Group and that holds no assets other than loans or advances to other members of the Reporting Group, cash and Cash Equivalents, and immaterial amounts of other assets.
Ex. 4 11. *Developer Update.* Developer shall notify Remington in writing every ninety (90) calendar days following Developer's execution of this Addendum as to: (a) every Unit in the Project contracted to a non-Remington Buyer; (b) the purchase price specified in every Purchase Agreement with every such non-Remington Buyer; (c) every Remington Buyer's Unit re-contracted in the Project; and (d) the re-contracted purchase price for every such Remington Buyer's Unit. **Addendum to Condominium-Unit-Purchase-and-Sale Agreement from a property-management company**	**11. Developer Update.** After executing this Addendum, Developer must notify Remington in writing every 90 calendar days about: (a) any Unit in the Project that is contracted to a non-Remington Buyer; (b) the purchase price specified in the Purchase Agreement with any non-Remington Buyer; (c) any Remington Buyer's Unit that is recontracted in the Project; and (d) the recontracted purchase price for any Remington Buyer's Unit.

"It very often happens that very important decisions turn on one word, and it is as well that draftsmen should remember that." *Dickerson v. St. Aubyn*, [1944] 1 All E.R. 370, 371 (Du Parcq L.J.).

NOT THIS:	BUT THIS:
Ex. 5 (e) General Compliance with Terms and Applicable Regulation. Seller has operated, and has caused its appointees and nominees to operate, each Designated Plan in a manner that is in material compliance with the terms thereof and with all applicable Regulations. With respect to the Business, every employee, former employee, and every dependent of the foregoing entitled to continuation of benefit coverage under any Benefit Plan sponsored by Seller has been accorded all of the rights to which such person is entitled as a matter of Regulation, including any entitlements arising in connection with the transactions contemplated by this Agreement. **Asset-Purchase-and-Sale Agreement from a major law firm**	(E) **General compliance with terms and regulations.** The Seller has operated, and has caused its appointees and nominees to operate, each Designated Plan in a manner that materially complies with the Plan's terms and with all applicable regulations. Regarding the Business, all employees, former employees, and their dependents who are entitled to continuing benefit coverage under any Seller-sponsored Benefit Plan have been accorded all their rights as a matter of regulation, including all entitlements arising from transactions contemplated by this Agreement. The use of *each* is appropriate here to emphasize that there is more than one Plan that Seller has operated.

earlier of [date] [and *or* or] [date]. Contract drafters often debate whether the proper conjunction in this phrase (and similar phrases such as *later of, lesser of,* and *greater of*) is *or* or *and.* The better idiomatic choice is *or.* Yes, *and* has logic on its side because if we say *the earlier of two dates*, then the sense must be plural (conjunctive *and*), not singular (disjunctive *or*). But the wording with *and* sounds as pedantic—and as wrong—as *a number of people was there.*

One solution to the issue is to omit a conjunction altogether. This old technique is called *asyndeton.* For examples, see the "But This" versions in Example 1 of § 85 and Example 3 of § 86.

efforts (best, reasonable, commercially reasonable, good-faith, etc.). It's common to say that a party must use *best efforts* or *commercially reasonable efforts* or *reasonable efforts* to do something. On the one hand, a promise to use *best efforts* to accomplish something is less onerous than an outright promise to accomplish it; on the other hand, a promise to use *best efforts* is stronger than a promise merely to try to do it or to use *reasonable efforts.* Admittedly, there is no judicially recognized continuum of *efforts*-clauses. The caselaw on any such question, especially when you're considering more than one state, is likely to be muddy. So in a sense, caselaw is beside the point: contract lawyers and litigators and businesspeople rely more on ordinary meaning and conventional understanding than on judicial precedents in such matters. What's in people's heads influences their interpretations and their behavior. And in ordinary English, the phrase *best efforts* denotes a higher degree of assiduity than *reasonable efforts* or *commercially reasonable efforts* or *good-faith efforts*.[1] (The latter three are essentially fungible: use your judgment.) So if the other side is required to achieve something, and it's important to your client, you might well require the promisor to use *best efforts* to achieve it; but if your client is the promisor, you might use one of the less-stringent wordings. It's more a matter of common sense and ordinary understanding than judicial precedent.

Sometimes writers ill-advisedly combine reasonableness with best efforts, as by saying that a party must use *best reasonable efforts*, or *such best efforts as are commercially reasonable*, or *commercially reasonable best efforts*. This mixing of standards has at best a muddying effect. The advice here is to adhere to one of two standards: *commercially reasonable efforts* (or, if it's not a commercial relationship, *reasonable efforts*) for the lower standard; and *best efforts* for the somewhat higher standard of diligence.

NOT THIS:	BUT THIS:
Ex. 1 The Company shall use good faith reasonable efforts to obtain or effect such registration or qualification, but is not required to obtain or effect such registration or qualification. **Nonqualified-Stock-Option-Inducement-Award Agreement**	The Company will act in good faith and use reasonable efforts to achieve the registration or qualification, but it is not required to succeed.
Ex. 2 Both Landlord and Tenant shall use commercially reasonable, good faith, efforts and due diligence to cooperate with each other to complete all phases of the Construction Drawings and the permitting process permitting process .... **Lease Agreement**	Both the Landlord and the Tenant will act in good faith and use commercially reasonable efforts and all due diligence to cooperate with each other to complete all phases of the Construction Drawings and the permitting process ....
Ex. 3 The parties recognize the desirability of maintaining a uniform rate of flow of gas to the Gathering Systems, and Shipper agrees to use its best commercially reasonable efforts to regulate its delivery of Shipper's Gas so that gas shall be made available at the CDPs at as uniform a rate of flow as practicable. **Gas-Gathering Agreement**	The parties recognize the desirability of maintaining a uniform rate of gas flow to the Gathering Systems. The Shipper will use best efforts to regulate its delivery of Shipper's Gas so that gas will be made available at the CDPs at as uniform a rate of flow as practicable.

1 *See Garner's Dictionary of Legal Usage* 108 (3d ed. 2011) ("The orthodox view is that a contractual provision requiring best efforts imposes extraordinary duties of assiduity: a very high standard of care, regardless of whether the required efforts might be commercially unreasonable."); E. Allan Farnsworth, *Contracts* § 7.17, at 495 (4th ed. 2004) ("Although the scope of this [best-efforts] duty is no better defined than is the scope of the duty of good faith, it is clear that the duty of best efforts is more onerous than that of good faith."); *see also* 2 *Restatement (Second) of the Law of Contracts* § 220 (1981) ("An agreement is interpreted in accordance with a relevant usage if each party knew or had reason to know of the usage and neither party knew or had reason to know that the meaning attached by the other was inconsistent with the usage.").

NOT THIS:	BUT THIS:
Ex. 4 The Company will use commercially reasonable best efforts to have this Agreement, all exhibits and schedules thereto and hereto, and any other documents or agreements executed in connection with the transactions contemplated hereunder (the "Transaction Documents") approved by the shareholders. **Securities-Purchase Agreement**	The Company will use best efforts to have this Agreement, all its exhibits and schedules, and any other documents or agreements executed in connection with the transactions contemplated by this Agreement approved by the shareholders.

except as; except if. Use *unless* when you can—especially when referring to some future action by the court or by the parties. Sometimes you'll need *except as* in reference to another contract provision (e.g., *except as permitted in § 9, no party may . . .*) in the sense "except to the extent that."

NOT THIS:	BUT THIS:
Ex. 1 5. **Motor Vehicle Safety** . . . 5.6 Contractor shall ensure that motorcycles or all terrain vehicles ("ATV") are not used for performing the Services except if approved in writing by Company. **Master Contractor-Services Agreement from a major energy corporation**	**5. Motor-Vehicle Safety.** . . . **5.6 Motorcycles and ATVs.** You must ensure that motorcycles and all-terrain vehicles will not be used to perform Services unless we approve the use in writing. It's unnecessary to define the commonly used initialism "ATV" here.
Ex. 2 **10.0 EXPENSES** Except as expressly provided for in a Statement of Work, each Party shall be responsible for its own expenses, charges and costs under this Agreement. **Collaboration Agreement from a computer-technology company**	**10. Expenses.** Unless a Statement of Work provides otherwise, each party is responsible for its own expenses, charges, and costs under this Agreement.
Ex. 3 7.2 Refund – No portion of the Escrow shall be refunded except as provided otherwise herein. The Licensor agrees to also provide Licensee with separations for the Catalog and poster at the Licensor's expense. **License Agreement from a major automotive corporation**	**7.2 Refund.** Unless this Agreement provides otherwise, no part of the Escrow is refundable. Littleton must provide—at its own expense—separations for the Catalog and poster to Complete Auto.

greater of [amount] [and *or* or] [amount]. See *earlier of.*

indemnify (and hold harmless, and save harmless, and defend, etc.). It's common to use *indemnify* alone, but it's perhaps more common to add a caboose to it:

indemnify and hold harmless or *indemnify and save harmless.* Do the additional words contribute meaning?

Traditionally, no. Countless English-language dictionaries from 1676 to the present day have defined *indemnify* as meaning "hold harmless," and *hold harmless* as meaning "indemnify." Both phrases mean to compensate for a loss either anticipated or actually sustained. In *Garner's Dictionary of Legal Usage*, I quote from 26 dictionaries from the 17th century to the 20th to demonstrate the interchangeability of the terms.[2] *Indemnify* is a Latin word that came into English through French; *hold harmless* is pure Anglo-Saxon (that is Old English, predating 1100).

Predictably, though, some courts came to attribute a special meaning to *and hold harmless.* Why read it as surplusage? After all, good drafters aren't supposed to include surplus words in their work. Perhaps the earliest such case was decided by the Minnesota Supreme Court in 1870.[3] The court said that *hold harmless* has a more expansive meaning than *indemnify.* In the early 2000s, a few California courts of appeal have declared that *indemnify* is an indemnitee's offensive right to seek indemnification and *hold harmless* is the putative indemnitor's defensive right not to be subjected to an indemnification claim.[4]

But the majority rule has always been that *indemnify and hold harmless* is a unitary phrase that means nothing more than *indemnify* alone.[5] Of course the question

2 Bryan A. Garner, *Garner's Dictionary of Legal Usage* 443–44 (3d ed. 2011).

3 *Weller v. Eames*, 15 Minn. 461, 467 (1870).

4 *San Diego Unified Sch. Dist. v. Cnty. of San Diego*, 87 Cal. Rptr.3d 796, 809–10 (Cal. Ct. App. 2009); *Queen Villas Homeowners Assn. v. TCB Property Mgmt.*, 56 Cal. Rptr. 3d 528, 534 (Cal. Ct. App. 2007).

5 *See, e.g., Black Hills Excavating Servs., Inc. v. Retail Const. Servs., Inc.*, 877 N.W.2d 318, 324 n.5 (S.D. 2016) ("Indemnify . . . derives from *indemnis* (= harmless) combined with *facere* (to make). Thus, *indemnify* has long been held to be perfectly synonymous with *hold harmless* and *save harmless*."); *Estate of Pearson ex rel. Latta v. Interstate Power & Light Co.*, 700 N.W.2d 333, 344 (Iowa 2005) (declaring that "*hold harmless* is synonymous with *indemnify*."); *Loscher v. Hudson*, 182 P.3d 25, 33 (Kan. Ct. App. 2008) (declaring that "a hold harmless provision in a separation agreement is the same as an indemnity agreement"); *Majkowski v. American Imaging Mgmt. Servs., LLC*, 913 A.2d 572, 588 (Del. Ch. 2006) (noting that "it is often almost second nature for the drafter of a contract to include both phrases in referring to a single indemnification right"); *Long v. McAllister-Long*, 221 S.W.3d 1, 10 (Tenn. Ct. App. 2006) (stating that "[t]he term *hold harmless* is synonymous with the word *indemnify*," so "a *hold harmless agreement* is nothing more or less than an *indemnity agreement*."); *Henthorne v. Legacy Healthcare, Inc.*, 764 N.E.2d 751, 757 (Ind. Ct. App. 2002) (noting that "*save harmless* and *hold harmless* are synonymous with *indemnify* and thus signify no separate duties"); *Missouri Pac. R. Co. v. Sonken-Galamaba Corp.*, 274 S.W. 930, 932 (Mo. Ct. App. 1925) (noting precedents establishing that "*to indemnify* is synonymous with *to save harmless*"); *Majkowski v. American Imaging Mgmt. Servs., LLC*, 913 A.2d 572, 588 (Del. Ch. 2006) (noting that "it is often almost second nature for the drafter of a contract to include both phrases in referring to a single indemnification right"); *Brentnal v. Holmes*, 1 Root (Conn.) 291, 292, 1 Am. Dec. 44 (1791) ("What is meant by *indemnifying* and *saving harmless*? The terms are synonymous and mean the same thing.")

never arises until both terms appear alongside each other—something to be avoided because of the very question whether something different is intended.

Then there's the question about *indemnify and defend.* In most jurisdictions, those two terms do denote different things: paying compensation is different from providing a legal defense.[6] But there are no universals in matters of this kind.

Consider an illustrative case. Assume that your client, a municipality ("the City"), has hired Acme Construction to renovate a municipal theater. The contract obliges Acme to "indemnify the City against all liabilities, claims, demands, damages, or costs that arise from Acme's negligence or willful misconduct while performing the work." Unfortunately, one of Acme's employees leaves a hammer on the sidewalk next to the theater, and a pedestrian trips on it, falls forward, suffers grievous injuries, and incurs substantial medical bills.

If the pedestrian sues both Acme and the City, here's what might happen. First, Acme must pay any judgment or settlement against the City. In most jurisdictions, the City needn't pay first itself; in some jurisdictions, however, it might be required to. But wait. Does Acme pay for its defense costs? Does it matter whether the City hires its own attorneys or lets Acme decide which lawyers to use? The answers are jurisdiction-specific. In one state, California, Acme will bear the defense costs, and the City can decide whether to use attorneys of its own choosing or to let Acme choose.[7] An express indemnity imposes a duty to defend. (That's not universal.) And the duty, again in California, arises when there is a mere potential for indemnity, even when coverage is in doubt and ultimately no liability ensues.[8]

So in California, *indemnify* includes *and defend.*[9] But in other jurisdictions, that's not so.[10]

---

6 *See, e.g., King v. Dallas Fire Ins. Co.*, 85 S.W.3d 185, 187 (Tex. 2002) (affirming that the duty to indemnify and the duty to defend are separate and distinct); *Mt. Hawley Ins. Co. v. Casson Duncan Const., Inc.*, 409 P.3d 619, 621 (Colo. Ct. App. 2016) (noting that an insurer's duty to indemnify an insured depends on whether a policy covers the injury, but the duty to defend does not); *Wyman v. Zeltins*, 142 A.D.2d 913 (N.Y. App. Div. 1988) (noting that a statute expressly provided for duty to defend but did not mention duty to indemnify, so indemnification was not owed).

7 *See* Cal. Civ. Code §§ 2778(3), 2778(4).

8 *See Buss v. Superior Court*, 939 P.2d 766, 775–77 (Cal. 1997) (explaining that duty to defend arises from bargain for coverage of certain claims even when claims are only potential but does not arise when claims are not covered and there is no potential for indemnity).

9 *See* Cal. Civ. Code § 2778(3).

10 *See, e.g., Winshal v. Viacom Intl., Inc.*, 76 A.3d 808, 820 (Del. 2013) (stating that express duty to "indemnify" was not the same as "indemnify and defend"); *Wedge Prods. v. Hartford Equity Sales Co.*, 509 N.E.2d 74, 76 (Ohio 1987) (explaining that a duty to defend arises only when a third-party claim falls within an indemnity clause's specified coverage); *Robin v. Wong*, 971 So.2d 386, 388–89 (La. Ct. App. 2007) (finding that phrase *indemnify and save harmless* did not create a duty to defend).

The question whether the indemnified party must first suffer an actual loss before the indemnity becomes due is also interesting. In California, this question depends on whether the indemnity uses the word *liability* (as in our example). The use of that word entitles the indemnified party to recover from the indemnifying party upon becoming liable without having to pay the judgment or settlement itself.[11] But if the indemnity provision provided only for indemnity against some combination of *claims, demands, damages, and costs*, without mentioning *liabilities*, then the indemnified party would first have to pay the judgment or settlement.[12]

later of [date] [and *or* or] [date]. See *earlier of.*

lesser of [amount] [and *or* or] [amount]. See *earlier of.*

limitation. Unless referring to a statute of limitations, use *limit.*

NOT THIS:	BUT THIS:
Ex. 1 XVI. PRICING . . . B. Where charges are "not to exceed" a specified sum, CONSULTANT shall notify CLIENT before each limit is exceeded and shall not continue to provide services beyond such limit unless CLIENT authorizes an increase in the amount of the limitation. **Consulting-Services Agreement from a major beverage company**	**16. Pricing.** . . . **16.2 Limits.** When charges are "not to exceed" a specified sum, Warren must: (A) notify Preston before exceeding the limit; and (B) discontinue services beyond the limit unless Preston authorizes an increase in the limit amount.
Ex. 2 Notwithstanding anything herein to the contrary, the Company is authorized to disclose to any persons the U.S. federal and state income tax treatment and tax structure of the potential transaction and all materials of any kind (including tax opinions and other tax analyses) provided to the Company relating to that treatment and structure, without the Underwriters' imposing any limitation of any kind. **Underwriting Agreement from a Fortune 500 insurance company**	Despite anything in this Agreement to the contrary, Silva may disclose the U.S. federal and state income-tax treatment and tax structure of the potential transaction and all materials of any kind (including tax opinions and other tax analyses) given to the Company relating to that treatment and structure. This may be done without the Underwriters' imposing limits of any kind.

11 *See* Cal. Civ. Code § 2778(1); *CC-California Plaza Assocs. v. Paller & Goldstein*, 59 Cal. Rptr. 382, 388 (Cal. Ct. App. 1996) (finding that contract expressly indemnified against liabilities, so the indemnitee did not have to pay the damages before seeking indemnification). *See also Showers v. Wadsworth*, 22 P. 663, 664 (Cal. 1889) (noting that language expressly stated that indemnity was against liability, so the plaintiff's right to indemnity arose when the liability was incurred rather than after any payment was made).

12 *See* Cal. Civ. Code § 2778(2); *Gribaldo, Jacobs, Jones & Assocs. v. Aggrippina Versichergunges A.*, 476 P.2d 406, 413 (Cal. 1970) (explaining that indemnity against liability protects the indemnitee from experiencing the consequences of his or her liability, but indemnity against claims only ameliorates the consequences after they've been experienced).

notwithstanding anything in this Agreement to the contrary. Use this phrase advisedly and sparingly—ordinarily, only when (1) you didn't draft the document and you can't possibly, given your circumstance, assure yourself that there *are* conflicting provisions; (2) you know of certain provisions that may be interpreted as being in conflict; or (3) you're drafting a provision with a sweeping effect and want to preclude arguments that its effect is less than sweeping.[13] Prefer *Despite* to *Notwithstanding*. Avoid vague relatives—*notwithstanding the foregoing* and the like—because they may not clearly indicate the antecedent.

The three restrictions are meant to be *extremely* restrictive. Often the phrasing signifies that the drafter has lost control of the document. It's been known to happen that a single document will have three overlapping *notwithstanding*-clauses with no indications of precedence. The different permutations can involve massive amounts of money.

NOT THIS:	BUT THIS:
Ex. 1 (C) Notwithstanding anything contained herein to the contrary, in the event that the Corporation shall be unable to secure and the Employee shall also be unable to secure such malpractice insurance coverage, this Agreement may be immediately terminated for cause by written notice to the Employee by the Corporation. **Employment Contract**	(C) **Malpractice insurance.** Despite anything in this Agreement to the contrary, if TRB Exploration and Phillipps are both unable to secure malpractice-insurance coverage, TRB may immediately terminate this Agreement for cause by giving written notice to Phillipps.
Ex. 2 7.2 Notwithstanding anything to the contrary contained in this Agreement, Sellers hereby agree jointly to indemnify and hold harmless each of the Companies and Buyer, its parent, affiliates, officers, directors, employees, agents, successors, and assigns, from and against any and all damages resulting from any governmental or private third-party claim pending as of the closing date or brought under Ecuadorian law within one year of the closing date, with respect to environmental matters. **Asset-Purchase Agreement** [Margin note: This is defensible under exception #3. But it might be tightened somewhat.] [Margin note: Note the ambiguity about Ecuadorian law: must the governmental or third-party claim pending as of the closing date be one under Ecuadorian law?]	**7.2 Indemnity.** Despite anything in this Agreement to the contrary, the Sellers must indemnify each of the Companies and the Buyer, and all their parents, affiliates, officers, directors, employees, agents, successors, and assigns, from all environment-related damages resulting from any government or private third-party claim pending as of the closing date or brought under Ecuadorian law within 1 year after the closing date.

13 *Garner's Dictionary of Legal Usage* 616 (3d ed. 2011).

NOT THIS:	BUT THIS:
Ex. 3 3.6 Optionee and Optionor shall treat and maintain the other party's proprietary business in confidence, using at least the same degree of care as that party uses to protect its own proprietary information of a like nature for a period from the date of disclosure until 5 years after the date of termination of this Agreement. But all proprietary information must be labeled or marked confidential or as otherwise similarly appropriate by the disclosing party, or if the proprietary information is orally disclosed, then it shall be reduced to writing or some other physically tangible form, marked and labeled as set forth above by the disclosing party and delivered to the receiving party within 30 days of the oral disclosure as a record of the disclosure and the confidential nature thereof. Notwithstanding the foregoing, Optionee may disclose proprietary information to its employees, agents, consultants, and contractors, or as is deemed necessary by Optionee for any purpose set forth or relating to this Agreement, provided that any such party is bound by a like duty of confidentiality. **Collaboration Agreement**	**3.6 Confidentiality.** During the term of this Agreement and for 5 years after it terminates, Randolph and LSJ will keep each other's proprietary business in confidence. Each will use at least the same degree of care as it does in protecting its own proprietary information. All proprietary information must be labeled, marked, or appropriately identified as confidential by the disclosing party. If the proprietary information is orally disclosed, then it must be reduced to writing or some other physically tangible form, marked and labeled by the disclosing party, and delivered to the receiving party within 30 days after the oral disclosure as a record of the disclosure and its confidential nature. Even so, Randolph may disclose proprietary information to its employees, agents, consultants, and contractors as it considers necessary for any purpose relating to this Agreement, as long as any such person is bound by a similar duty of confidentiality.

only. Place this word carefully before the correct word.[14]

NOT THIS:	BUT THIS:
Ex. 1 Any such volume may only be taken into account once. **Sales Agreement**	Any such volume may be taken into account only once.
Ex. 2 15. Amendment. Except as otherwise provided by the Plan, the Company may only alter, amend or terminate the Option with your consent. **Stock-Option-Award Agreement from a major payroll-outsourcing company**	**15. Amendment.** Unless the Plan provides otherwise, the Company may alter, amend, or terminate the Option only with your consent.
Ex. 3 (B) Authorization numbers and codes are issued only by Park Ultra to its customers and may not be sold or otherwise distributed without the written consent of Park Ultra. **Master Services Agreement from a telecommunications company**	(B) Only Park Ultra can issue authorization numbers and codes. Jones must not sell or distribute them without Park Ultra's written consent.

14 *See* Garner, *The Redbook: A Manual on Legal Style* § 11.42, at 232 (4th ed. 2018).

NOT THIS:	BUT THIS:
Ex. 4 17.5 This Agreement is the entire understanding of the parties with respect to the subject matter covered. It may only be amended in a writing executed by an authorized representative of each party. **License Agreement from a major automotive corporation**	(A) **Entire agreement.** This Agreement represents the entire agreement between the parties. It can be changed only by written agreement signed by the parties.
Ex. 5 6.7 Shops, Stores and Retail Outlets. Licensee shall only sell and/or distribute Licensed Items to retail shops or stores which carry comparable prestige merchandise, unless Licensee receives Licensor's advance written approval to do otherwise. **Agreement for Licensing Objects of Art from a major law firm**	6.7 **Shops, stores, and retail outlets.** Unless Alvarez receives prior written approval from Boswick, Alvarez may sell or distribute Licensed Items only to retail shops or stores that carry comparable prestige merchandise.
Ex. 6 In signing this Agreement, you agree that, during the Transition Period, you will only use or access documents, materials, information, property, or systems of the Company and its Affiliates to the extent necessary to perform the job duties described in Section 1(c) of this Agreement. **Executive-Employment Agreement from a major healthcare company**	During the Transition Period, you will use or access Company or Affiliates' documents, materials, information, property, or systems only to the extent necessary to perform the job duties in § 1(c) of this Agreement.

on or before. Try *within* or *no later than*, whichever is more accurate (both include the last day). Avoid *by*, which also includes the last day but is arguably ambiguous.

NOT THIS:	BUT THIS:
Ex. 1 On or before five (5) days after the date of this Agreement, Whatley shall pay to Farley the sum of Four Thousand One Hundred Eighty and 94/100 Dollars ($4,180.94). **Auto-Purchase Agreement**	Whatley will pay Farley $4,180.94 within 5 days after the date of this Agreement.
Ex. 2 Any payment that is not made on or before the Due Date shall bear interest at the rate equal to the "prime" rate as published on such Due Date in the Wall Street Journal, Eastern Edition, for the period from and including the date immediately following the Due Date through and including the date of payment. **Limited-Liability-Company Agreement from a major pharmaceutical-distribution company**	To avoid interest, make your payment no later than the Due Date. Interest is the rate equal to the "prime" rate as published on the Due Date in the *Wall Street Journal*, Eastern Edition. Interest is charged from the date immediately after the Due Date through the date of payment.

NOT THIS:	BUT THIS:
Ex. 3 2. Termination Fee. Parent agrees to pay, or cause to be paid, to the Company (or its designee) on or before June 30, 2017 the Parent Termination Fee in the amount of $325,000,000, by wire transfer of immediately available funds to an account designated in writing by the Company. **Termination Agreement from a major pharmaceutical manufacturing, wholesale, and distribution company**	**2. Termination Fee.** Deware agrees to pay Pollard (or its designee), no later than June 30, 2017, the Parent Termination Fee of $325 million by wire transfer of immediately available funds to an account that Pollard designates in writing.
Ex. 4 You further understand and acknowledge that to be effective, any revocation must be in writing and either personally delivered to the Corporation, care of John T. Long, Senior Vice President, Human Resources or sent by certified mail, return receipt requested to Mr. John T. Long at 324 Rockledge Drive, Bethesda, Maryland 20817, by 5:00 p.m., Bethesda, Maryland time, on or before the eighth calendar day after you sign this Agreement. **Retirement-Transition Agreement from a global security and aerospace company**	**31. Revocation Requirements.** Your revocation must be made in writing no later than 5:00 p.m. ET on the 8th calendar day after you sign this Agreement and either: (A) hand-deliver it to the Corporation, care of John T. Long, Senior Vice President, Human Resources; or (B) send it by certified mail, return receipt requested to John T. Long at 324 Rockledge Drive, Bethesda, Maryland 20817.
Ex. 5 Section 2. Exercise. a) Exercise of the purchase rights represented by this Warrant may be made, in whole or in part, at any time or times on or after the Initial Exercise Date and on or before the Termination Date by delivery to the Company (or such other office or agency of the Company as it may designate by notice in writing to the registered Holder at the address of the Holder appearing on the books of the Company) of a duly executed facsimile copy (or e-mail attachment) of the Notice of Exercise in the form annexed hereto. **Common-Stock-Purchase Warrant from a plant biotechnology company**	**2. Exercise of Purchase Rights.** **2.1 Notice.** The purchase rights represented by this Warrant may be exercised if the Notice of Exercise: (A) is delivered to Flores or an office or agency designated by Flores in a writing given to the registered Holder at the Holder's address listed on Flores's books; and (B) is a duly signed fax copy or e-mail attachment that follows the same format as the form attached to this Warrant. **2.2 Timing.** The purchase rights are available no earlier than the Initial Exercise Date and no later than the Termination Date.

"The authors of legal composition do not seek for readers. They expect to be read and are read only by those who must read them for purposes of business."
J.G. Mackay, *Introduction to an Essay on the Art of Legal Composition Commonly Called Drafting*, 3 L.Q. Rev. 326, 334 (1887).

otherwise. For emphasis, this adverb should usually end a clause—e.g., "Unless this court *directs otherwise* . . . ," not "Unless this court *otherwise directs*." But sometimes, for the sake of parallel phrasing, this term should precede the verb—e.g., "Unless otherwise directed by the court or stipulated by the parties . . . ."

Another point with this word is to avoid introducing comma splices with it (see § 132). That is, don't write *The widgets are deliverable on the last day of each month, otherwise special charges will apply.* Because *otherwise*, like *however*, is an adverb and not a conjunction, the clauses on each side of the comma in that example are improperly joined independent clauses. A stronger mark, such as a period or semicolon, is required.

NOT THIS:	BUT THIS:
Ex. 1 10. Transfer of Option. Except as otherwise determined by the Committee, the Option may not be transferred, assigned or pledged (except by will or the laws of descent and distribution, or pursuant to a domestic relations order). **Stock-Option-Award Agreement from a major law firm**	**10. Transfer of Option.** Unless the Committee determines otherwise, the Option must not be assigned or pledged (except by will or the laws of descent and distribution, or under a domestic-relations order).
Ex. 2 8.1 Closing adjustment. The following adjustment shall be made as of the Closing Date with respect to the Unit: (a) real estate taxes and assessments, if any, (including water charges and sewer rates if separately assessed), through the end of the tax period within which the Closing Date occurs, which shall be either a quarter of a year or one-half, however, that Sponsor shall be reimbursed at closing by Purchaser for the cost of any real estate taxes which Sponsor would not otherwise pay but for an unauthorized delay in closing of title by Purchaser; and (b) Common Charges for the month in which title closes, provided, however, that Sponsor shall be reimbursed by Purchaser for the cost of any Common Charges which Sponsor would not otherwise pay but for an unauthorized delay in closing of title by Purchaser. **Purchase Agreement from a major law firm**	**8.1 Closing adjustments.** The following adjustments will be made on the Unit Closing Date: (A) **Taxes and assessments.** The Sponsor will pay any real-estate taxes and assessments (including water charges and sewer rates if separately assessed) through the end of the current tax period (either a quarter or half a year). If the Buyer delays the Closing Date without authorization, the Buyer will reimburse the Sponsor at closing for the cost of any real-estate taxes that the Sponsor would not pay otherwise. (B) **Common charges.** The Sponsor will pay the Common Charges for the month in which title closes. If the Buyer delays the Closing Date without authorization, the Buyer will reimburse the Sponsor for the cost of any Common Charges that the Sponsor would not pay otherwise.

"In view of the deadening cumulative effect of turgid prose, isn't it worthwhile to make even the perfectly clear more readable?" Reed Dickerson, *Materials on Legal Drafting* 283 (1981).

NOT THIS:	BUT THIS:
Ex. 3 §11. ***Assignment or Transfer of Liabilities.*** Claymore may, from time to time, without notice to Guarantor, assign or transfer any or all of the Obligations or any interest therein; and, notwithstanding any such assignment or transfer or any subsequent assignment or transfer thereof, such Obligations shall be and remain Obligations for the purposes of this Guaranty and each and every immediate and successive assignee or transferee of any of the Obligations or of any such interest therein shall, to the extent of the interest of such assignee or transferee in the Obligations, be entitled to the benefits of this Guaranty to the same extent as if such assignee or transferee were the transferor provided, however, that, unless Claymore shall otherwise consent in writing, Claymore shall have an unimpaired right, prior and superior to that of any such assignee or transferee, to enforce this Guaranty, for the benefit of Claymore, as to those of the Obligations which shall not have been assigned or transferred. **Unconditional-Guaranty Agreement from a major law firm**	**11. Assignment or Transfer of Liabilities.** From time to time and without notice to Guarantor, Claymore may assign any or all of the Obligations or an interest in them. For the purposes of this Guaranty, the Obligations will remain Obligations. To the extent of the assignee's interest in the Obligations, every immediate and successive assignee of an Obligation or an interest in an Obligation is entitled to the benefits of this Guaranty to the same extent as if the assignee were the assignor. But unless Claymore consents otherwise in writing, Claymore has an unimpaired right, prior and superior to that of any assignee, to enforce this Guaranty, for the benefit of Claymore, as to those of the Obligations that have not been assigned.

portion. This word connotes a share of something cut away from a whole. If you mean a constituent part of a whole, use *part* instead.

NOT THIS:	BUT THIS:
Ex. 1 You will repay the Company any portion of your Sign-on Bonus in excess of your Earned Sign-on Bonus. **Employment Agreement/Offer from an American multinational food, snack, and beverage company**	You must repay the Company any part of your Sign-on Bonus in excess of your Earned Sign-on Bonus.
Ex. 2 9. VACATIONS. The Executive shall be entitled to no less than four weeks of paid vacation during each full calendar year of the Term (and a pro rata portion thereof for any portion of the Term that is less than a full calendar year). **Executive-Employment Agreement for a major floral company**	**9. Vacations.** The Executive is entitled to at least 4 weeks of paid vacation during each full calendar year of the Term. The weeks will be prorated for any part of the Term that is less than a full calendar year.

upon. Prefer *on.* Thus, *service on a defendant,* not *service upon a defendant.* But use *upon* when introducing a condition or event—e.g., "Upon being served with a request, a party must . . . ."

NOT THIS:	BUT THIS:
Ex. 1 This Imposed Agreement is based upon the provisions of Public Law 102-29 signed by the President on April 18, 1991. **Imposed Agreement from a railroad company**	This Imposed Agreement is based on Public Law 102-29 signed by the President on April 18, 1991.
Ex. 2 Section 2.18 License Agreement and Credit Default Swap Data. . . . (b) The Credit Default Swap Data shall be made available to the Company pursuant to procedures agreed upon by the Company and the Agent. **Credit Agreement from a major food, snack, and beverage corporation**	**2.18 License Agreement and Credit Default Swap Data.** . . . (B) Sein will make the Credit Default Swap Data available to Ocon according to the procedures agreed on by Ocon and United.
Ex. 3 ShipEx shall keep the Indemnified Party properly informed and provide the Indemnified Party the opportunity to review and comment upon any correspondence, negotiations and other communications by ShipEx with third parties. **Merger Protocol between courier-delivery-services companies**	ShipEx will keep the Indemnified Party properly informed and give the Indemnified Party the opportunity to review and comment on any correspondence, negotiations, and other communications that ShipEx has with third parties.

whenever. This word is often replaceable with a simple *if* or *when.* But it contains an important nuance: "each time and from time to time." Used well, it suggests recurrence—e.g.: "HighTec will charge customer a returned-check fee of $15 whenever the customer pays for service with a check or draft that is not accepted by the institution on which it is written."

NOT THIS:	BUT THIS:
Ex. 1 Whenever the context may require, any pronoun shall include the corresponding masculine, feminine and neuter forms. **First Amendment to Amended and Restated Credit Agreement from a major media and entertainment company**	If the context so requires, a pronoun will include the corresponding masculine, feminine, and neuter forms.

NOT THIS:	BUT THIS:
Ex. 2 Whenever the words "include", "includes", or "including" are used in this Merger Protocol, they are deemed to be followed by the words "without limitation". **Merger Protocol between two courier- and parcel-service companies**	When the word "include," "includes," or "including" appears in this Merger Protocol, it is impliedly followed by the words "without limitation."
Ex. 3 Whenever a statement in this letter is qualified by "to the best of my knowledge" or a similar phrase, it is intended to indicate that I and the other attorneys of the Company do not have current actual knowledge of the inaccuracy of such statement. **Underwriting Agreement from a major biopharmaceutical company**	If a statement in this letter is qualified by "to the best of my knowledge" or a similar phrase, it means that I and the other attorneys of Blitzer Inc. do not have current actual knowledge of that statement's inaccuracy.
Ex. 4 Section 2. Purchase and Sale of Securities by the Underwriters. Whenever the Company determines to make an offering of Securities to be governed by these Standard Provisions, the Company will enter into a Terms Agreement providing for the sale of such Securities to, and the purchase and offering thereof by, the Underwriters. **Underwriting Agreement from an American multinational food, snack, and beverage company**	2. **Purchase and Sale of Securities by the Underwriters.** If the Company decides to make a Securities offering governed by these Standard Provisions, it will enter into a Terms Agreement for the sale of the Securities to—and the purchase and offering by—the Underwriters.
Ex. 5 9.9. Obligations of Parent and of the Company. Whenever this Agreement requires a Subsidiary of Parent to take any action, such requirement shall be deemed to include an undertaking on the part of Parent to cause such Subsidiary to take such action. Whenever this Agreement requires a Subsidiary of the Company to take any action, such requirement shall be deemed to include an undertaking on the part of the Company to cause such Subsidiary to take such action and, after the Effective Time, on the part of the Surviving Corporation to cause such Subsidiary to take such action. **Merger Agreement between major Internet-based retailer and major grocery chain**	9.9 **Obligations of Kern and Vines.** If this Agreement requires a Kern Subsidiary to take an action, that requirement includes an undertaking on the part of Kern to cause the Subsidiary to take the action. If this Agreement requires a Vines Subsidiary to take an action, the requirement includes an undertaking on the part of Vines to cause the Subsidiary to take the action and, after the Effective Time, the Surviving Corporation must cause the Subsidiary to take the action.

NOT THIS:	BUT THIS:
Ex. 6 Section 4.4. Notice of Dividends, etc.; Fixing Record Date for Holders of Receipts. Whenever any cash dividend or other cash distribution shall become payable or any distribution other than cash shall be made, or if rights, preferences or privileges shall at any time be offered, with respect to the Stock, or whenever the Depositary shall receive notice of any meeting at which holders of the Stock are entitled to vote or of which holders of the Stock are entitled to notice, or whenever the Depositary and the Corporation shall decide it is appropriate, the Depositary shall in each such instance fix a record date (which shall be the same date as the record date fixed by the Corporation with respect to or otherwise in accordance with the terms of the Stock) for the determination of the Holders of Receipts who shall be entitled to receive such dividend, distribution, rights, preferences or privileges or the net proceeds of the sale thereof, or to give instructions for the exercise of voting rights at any such meeting, or who shall be entitled to notice of such meeting or for any other appropriate reasons. **Deposit Agreement from a major U.S. bank**	4.4 **Fixing record date for Holders of Receipts; notice of dividends, etc.** (A) **Record date.** The Depositary's record date will be the same date as the record date fixed by the Corporation in accordance with the terms of the Stock. (B) **Fixing record date.** The Depositary will fix a record date when any of the following events occur: (1) a cash dividend or other cash distribution becomes payable or a distribution other than cash will be made; (2) rights, preferences, or privileges are offered, with respect to the Stock; (3) the Depositary receives notice of a meeting at which holders of the Stock are entitled to vote or of which holders of the Stock are entitled to notice; or (4) the Depositary and the Corporation decide it is appropriate to fix a record date. (C) **Purpose.** The record date is used: (1) to identify the Holders of Receipts who are entitled to receive a dividend, distribution, rights, preferences, or privileges, or the net proceeds of their sale; (2) to give instructions for the exercise of voting rights at a meeting; (3) to determine who is entitled to notice of a meeting; and (4) to act on other appropriate matters.

where. If this word is replaceable by *when* or *if*—that is, if it introduces a circumstance of situation—it's legal jargon. But if it's used in its ordinary spatial sense, keep it.

NOT THIS:	BUT THIS:
Ex. 1 Where a disbursement has been duly authorized, the Treasurer will disburse the funds accordingly. **Landlord-Tenant Lease**	When a disbursement has been duly authorized, the Treasurer will disburse the funds accordingly.

§ 149 Avoid these "forbidden words and phrases."

Some expressions deserve to be purged from legal drafting in every likely context. They're either wholly unnecessary or likely to cause problems in predictable ways. Traditionally, a list of such forbidden terms is called an "index expurgatorius," but that's not exactly plain English. Here they're just called forbidden words and phrases.

action (in the sense of "lawsuit"). Prefer *lawsuit*—if for no reason other than avoiding the miscue that ordinary readers will have in thinking that *action* might refer merely to an act.

NOT THIS:	BUT THIS:
Ex. 1 Each of the Parties hereby irrevocably and unconditionally (i) agrees not to commence any such action or proceeding except in such courts . . . . **Transfer-Restriction Agreement between a major technology company specializing in Internet-related services and products and its founder**	Each Party irrevocably and unconditionally: (A) agrees to file a lawsuit or court proceeding only in the agreed-upon courts . . . .
Ex. 2 A. Should CLIENT become involved in any action, proceeding, claim or demand relating to SERVICES performed by CONSULTANT, CONSULTANT shall cooperate with, and assist CLIENT in such action. **Consulting-Services Agreement from a major beverage company**	(A) If Selph becomes involved in a claim or lawsuit relating to Johnson's services, Johnson will cooperate with and help Selph with that claim or lawsuit.
Ex. 3 15. Submission to Jurisdiction; Venue; Waiver of Jury Trial. . . . (b) Each party hereto hereby irrevocably waives, to the fullest extent permitted by applicable law, and agrees not to assert, by stay of motion, as a defense, or otherwise, in any legal action or proceeding brought hereunder in any of the above-named courts, that such action or proceeding is brought in an inconvenient forum, or that venue for the action or proceeding is improper. **Underwriting Agreement from a major airline**	**15. Submission to Jurisdiction; Venue; Waiver of Jury Trial.** . . . (B) **Indemnity.** In any lawsuit or proceeding brought under this Agreement in any of the above-named courts, each party irrevocably waives to the fullest extent permitted by law—and must not assert, by stay of motion, as a defense or otherwise—that the lawsuit or proceeding is brought in an inconvenient forum, or that the venue is improper.

The rewrite states the idea in the positive rather than the negative. See § 69.

aforesaid. See *said.*

and/or. If your goal is to appear at least minimally competent as a legal drafter, banish this ambiguous two-faced term. Use *or* or *and*, or *or . . . or both.* If *and/or* joins the last two items of a list consisting of three or more items, try *any or all of the following* as the lead-in to the list. But remember: if *or* is the right word, use *or*; if *and* is the right word, use *and.*

If you were to analyze transactional documents, you'd find that 75% of the *and/ors* should be *or* and that 25% should be *and.* Look at the true meaning of the sentence, and you'll see that *and/or* makes a hash of it.

Often *and/or* means *or*:

> While we are the largest distributor in this market, some of our competitors may have greater total financial, purchasing, and/or [read *or*] sourcing power than we do.

But sometimes it means *and*:

> The Technology Agreement provides that any party who is a sublicensee must obtain written agreement from each of its employees, agents, officers, *and/or* [read *and*] directors that any Technical Information will not be disclosed to third parties.

And sometimes the way to fix the problem is simply to wake up your brain from the slumber that leads to this sort of nonsense:

> "Controlling interest" means the ownership of enough outstanding voting shares in an issuing corporation to enable the acquiring person to exercise (i) one-fifth or more but less than one-third, (ii) one-third or more but less than a majority, *and/or* (iii) a majority of the voting power of the issuing corporation in the election of directors.

Of course, all that's saying is this:

> "Controlling interest" means the ownership of enough outstanding voting shares in an issuing corporation to enable the acquiring person to exercise at least one-fifth of the corporation's voting power in an election of directors.

Maybe you'll find some close calls with *and/or.* But on reflection, you'll see that they're not so close.

> "Anything *and/or* can do, ordinary English can do better." David Mellinkoff, *Legal Writing: Sense and Nonsense* 56 (1982).

NOT THIS:	BUT THIS:
Ex. 1 The Licensor may continue prosecution and/or maintenance of such applications or patents at its sole discretion and expense. **License Agreement**	Modern Electronics may continue prosecuting or maintaining the applications or patents at its sole discretion and expense.
Ex. 2 If he desires, the Employee may request the consultation, advice, and services of other employees and/or the Board of Directors of the Corporation in the treatment of patients. **Employment Agreement**	In treating patients, Johnson may request the consultation, advice, and services of other employees or the Board of Directors. Use of *may* is all that is needed. *If he desires* is superfluous.
Ex. 3 "Cosmetic surgery" means any operative procedure performed primarily to improve physical appearance, to prevent a mental or nervous disorder through change in bodily form, and/or to change or restore form without correcting or materially improving a bodily malfunction. **Health-Insurance Policy from a major underwriter**	"Cosmetic surgery" means any operation performed primarily to improve physical appearance, to prevent a mental or nervous disorder through change in bodily form, or to change or restore form without correcting or materially improving a bodily malfunction.
Ex. 4 The Licensee shall apply for an extension of the term of any patent included within the Licensor's patent rights if appropriate under the Drug Price Competition and Patent Term Restoration Act of 1984 and/or European, Japanese, and other foreign counterparts of this law. **Patent-License Agreement from a major law firm**	Dogwood will apply for a term extension for any patent included within the University's patent rights if appropriate under the Drug Price Competition and Patent Term Restoration Act of 1984 and European, Japanese, and other foreign counterparts to this law.
Ex. 5 1.17 "**Licensed Tools**" means software and/or hardware tools described as Licensed Tools in Exhibit A, including as applicable, but without limitation tools for designing, compiling, synthesizing or otherwise using the Licensed IP Block(s) and/or manufacturing Licensed Products. **License-and-Development Agreement from a computer-technology company**	**1.17** "Licensed Tools" means software or hardware tools listed in Exhibit A, including tools for designing, compiling, synthesizing, or otherwise using a Licensed IP Block or manufacturing Licensed Products.

"If you read books on legal drafting, you will not find a more widely condemned phrase than *and/or*." Wayne Schiess, *Writing for the Legal Audience* 125 (2003).

NOT THIS:	BUT THIS:
Ex. 6 8. REIMBURSEMENT OF EXPENSES. During the Term, the Company shall pay or reimburse the Executive for all reasonable travel (at first class level), entertainment and other business expenses actually incurred or paid by the Executive in the performance of his duties hereunder upon presentation of expense statements and/or such other supporting information as the Company may reasonably require of the Executive. **Executive-Employment Agreement from a major floral company**	(H) **Reimbursement of expenses.** During the Term, Kulkenhof will pay or reimburse Stoessel for all reasonable travel (at first-class level), entertainment, and other business expense if Stoessel: (1) actually incurs or pays for the expense in performing his duties under this Agreement; and (2) provides expense statements or other supporting information that Kulkenhof reasonably requires.
Ex. 7 I further understand that serious accidents occasionally occur during competitive tennis events and tournaments, and that participants in tennis events occasionally sustain mortal or serious personal injuries, and/or property damage, as a consequence thereof. Knowing the risks of tennis tournaments, nevertheless, I hereby agree to assume those risks and to release and to hold harmless all of the persons or entities mentioned above who (through negligence or carelessness) might otherwise be liable to me (or to my heirs or assigns) for damages. **Tennis-Tournament-Participant Release Form in *Texas Forms: Legal & Business* § 16:74 (2013)**	You understand that serious accidents can occur during competitive tennis events and that as a participant, you might sustain property damage or serious, even mortal personal injury as a result of competing. Knowing this, you assume those risks and release and indemnify all persons or entities mentioned above that—through negligence or carelessness—might otherwise be liable for damages to you, your heirs, or your assigns.

any and all. Use *all* alone.

NOT THIS:	BUT THIS:
Ex. 1 The Company (A) is in compliance, in all material respects, with any and all applicable foreign, federal, state and local laws, rules, regulations, treaties, statutes and codes promulgated by any and all Governmental Authorities. **Common-Stock Underwriting Agreement**	The Company is in compliance with all applicable foreign, federal, state, and local laws, rules, regulations, treaties, statutes and codes promulgated by all Government Authorities.
Ex. 2 The Bank represents and warrants that the Authorized Agent has agreed to act as such agent for service of process and agrees to take any and all action, including the filing of any and all documents and instruments, which may be necessary to continue such appointment in full force and effect as aforesaid. **Medium-Term-Notes Distribution Agreement**	The Authorized Agent has agreed to act as the Bank's agent for service of process and will take all action—including filing all documents and instruments—that might be necessary to continue the Authorized Agent's appointment in full force.

approximately. Use *about* <about 250 cars> or even *some* <some 250 cars>. Only in the sciences is *approximately* a favored word <approximately 3,200 gene sequences>.

	NOT THIS:	BUT THIS:
Ex. 1	The replacement costs will be approximately $9,600. **Purchase Agreement**	The replacement costs will be about $9,600.
Ex. 2	Any amounts due in 2013 related to your separation from service with the Corporation will be subject to a six-month delay until approximately November 1, 2013. **Retirement-Transition Agreement from a global aerospace and defense company**	Any amounts due in 2013 related to your separation from service with the Corporation will be subject to a 6-month delay from this Agreement's effective date.
Ex. 3	The Premises consist of the following space located in the Building: (1) the entire 11th Floor, containing approximately 14,097 rentable square feet (sometimes referred to in this Lease as the "**11th Floor Premises**"); and (2) the entire 12th Floor, containing approximately 14,365 rentable square feet (sometimes referred to in this Lease as the "**12th Floor Premises**"). **Commercial Lease from a major law firm**	The Premises consist of: (A) the entire 11th floor, with about 14,097 rentable square feet (11th-Floor Space); and (B) the entire 12th-floor, with about 14,365 rentable square feet (12th-Floor Space).
Ex. 4	As of September 30, 2016, after giving effect to this offering and the application of the proceeds thereof, we had approximately $4,600 million of senior debt outstanding and approximately $91 million of issued and undrawn letters of credit, and our subsidiaries had approximately $9,605 million of indebtedness and other liabilities outstanding, including medical claims liability, accounts payable and accrued expenses, unearned revenue and other long term liabilities (excluding intercompany liabilities). **Underwriting Agreement from a major healthcare company**	As of September 30, 2016, after giving effect to this offering and the application of the proceeds, we had about $4.6 billion of senior debt outstanding and about $91 million of issued and undrawn letters of credit. Our subsidiaries had about $9.6 billion of indebtedness and other liabilities outstanding, including medical-claim liability, accounts payable and accrued expenses, unearned revenue, and other long-term liabilities (excluding intercompany liabilities).

Why use *approximately* when you can state a date certain?

Note the change from *million* to *billion* in the revised version.

"Plain language exposes errors. Legalese hides inconsistencies and ambiguities. Errors are harder to find in dense and convoluted prose. In this way, plain language helps both lawyers and clients." Peter Butt, *Plain Language and Conveyancing*, Conveyancer & Prop. Law. 256, 265 (July–Aug. 1993).

by and between. Though this is a common expression in contracts, use either *by* or *between.*

NOT THIS:	BUT THIS:
Ex. 1 This is an Agreement by and between Grand Forths Inc. and William Shipley. **Master Development-and-Distribution Agreement from a major motion-picture studio**	This is an Agreement between Grand Forths Inc. and William Shipley.
Ex. 2 THIS AGREEMENT AND PLAN OF MERGER (this "Agreement") is made and entered into as of December 20, 2016 by and between SpinwheelCo LLC, a Delaware limited liability company to be converted to a Delaware corporation following the date hereof ("SpinwheelCo"), R&D Holdings, Inc., a Delaware corporation ("R&D"), and Platforms Inc., a Delaware corporation ("Platforms"). **Merger Agreement from a distributor of healthcare systems, medical supplies, and pharmaceutical products**	This Agreement and Plan of Merger, effective December 20, 2016, is between SpinwheelCo LLC, a Delaware limited-liability company; R&D Holdings Inc., a Delaware corporation; and Platforms Inc., a Delaware corporation. After December 20, 2016, SpinwheelCo will be converted to a Delaware corporation.

commence. Instead of this stilted, hyperformal word, try *begin.* Instead of *commencing* a lawsuit, simply *file* one. See Example 4.

NOT THIS:	BUT THIS:
Ex. 1 The term of this agreement shall commence on May 19, 2017, and shall expire at 12:01 a.m. on August 19, 2019. **Stock-Sale Agreement from a major financial institution**	This Agreement begins on May 19, 2017, and ends at 12:01 a.m. on August 19, 2019.
Ex. 2 "Contract Year" means, except for the first Contract Year, each twelve-month period corresponding to the calendar year. Thus, the first Contract Year shall commence September 1, 2021 and expire December 31, 2021; the second Contract Year shall commence January 1, 2022 and expire December 31, 2022 and so forth. **Master Services Agreement from a major healthcare company**	"Contract Year" generally means each calendar year beginning January 1 and ending December 31. But the first Contract Year begins September 1, 2021, and ends December 31, 2021. The second Contract Year begins January 1, 2022, and ends December 31, 2022, and so forth.

NOT THIS:	BUT THIS:
Ex. 3 The initial term of this Agreement shall commence as of the Effective Date and shall continue for an initial term of twelve (12) consecutive calendar months from the Effective Date of the Agreement, unless sooner terminated as provided in this Agreement. **Distributor Agreement from a major mobile-communications company**	1. **Term.** The term of this Agreement begins on the Effective Date and continues for an initial term of 12 consecutive calendar months from the Effective Date, unless it is terminated sooner under this Agreement.
Ex. 4 (c) Parent shall not make, nor permit of its Affiliates to make, any claim or demand, or commence any Action asserting any claim or demand, including any claim of contribution or indemnification, against the other party, or any related Released Party, with respect to any liability released pursuant to Section 6.01(a). **Limited-Liability-Company Agreement from a major healthcare-products distributor**	(C) **No new claim, demand, or lawsuit.** Steele and its Affiliates will not file a lawsuit or otherwise assert a claim or demand (including a claim of contribution or indemnity) against the other party or a related Released Party about any liability released under § 6.1(A).

We've also reduced the instances of *any* from 6 to 1. See § 148 at p. 386.

commencing _____ and until and including _____. Instead, write *begin(ning)* _____ *and through* _____.

NOT THIS:	BUT THIS:
Ex. 1 Commencing July 1, 2015, and until and including June 30, 2016, Employee shall be paid a salary of $75,000. **CFO Employment Agreement for a major radio and television broadcaster**	Beginning July 1, 2015, and through June 30, 2016, Jacobs will receive a salary of $75,000.
Ex. 2 "Due Period": With respect to any Distribution Date and any Mortgage Loan or Companion Loan (including the Republic Plaza Mortgage Loan Components) the period commencing on the day immediately succeeding the Due Date for such Mortgage Loan or Companion Loan occurring in the month preceding the month in which such Distribution Date occurs and ending on and including the Due Date for such Mortgage Loan or Companion Loan occurring in the month in which such Distribution Date occurs. **Pooling and Servicing Agreement from a multinational banking-and-financial-services holding company**	"Due Period"—with respect to a Distribution Date, Mortgage Loan, or Companion Loan (including the Republic Plaza Mortgage Loan Components)—begins on the day after the Due Date of the previous month's Mortgage or Companion Loan and ends on the Due Date for the Mortgage Loan or Companion Loan occurring in the month when the Distribution Date occurs.

covenants and agrees. If the notion of agreement is important in a given statement—and it usually isn't—then use *agree* alone. Otherwise, simply use the appropriate word of authority: *will*, *may*, *cannot*, etc.

NOT THIS:	BUT THIS:
Ex. 1 (3) Each Settling State further covenants and agrees that it shall not after the occurrence of State Specific Finality sue or seek to establish civil liability against any Released Party based, in whole or in part, upon any of the Released Claims, and further agrees that such covenant and agreement shall be a complete defense to any such civil action or proceeding. **Master Settlement Agreement between 40 states and a major tobacco manufacturer**	(3) After State-Specific Finality occurs, a Settling State must not sue or seek to hold any Released Party civilly liable based, in whole or in part, on a Released Claim. This provision is a complete defense to such a lawsuit or other proceeding.
Ex. 2 The Employee expressly covenants and agrees that for a period of three years immediately following the expiration or termination of the Employee's employment with the Corporation for any reason whatsoever, the Employee will not, at any time, engage in the practice of general urology within a radius of four miles from any office of the Corporation where medical services were rendered by the Employee on behalf of the Corporation. **Employee Noncompetition Agreement from a major law firm**	If Paulsen's employment with SP Inc. ends for any reason, Paulsen will not engage in the practice of general urology for 3 years within 4 miles of any SP Inc. office where Paulsen rendered medical services on its behalf.

except that. Use *but*, preferably at the start of a new sentence. See § 147.

NOT THIS:	BUT THIS:
Ex. 1 Such signs shall be furnished by Killingsworth without charge except that Franklin will be responsible for freight, installation, any personal property taxes and maintenance charges pertaining to the standard signs. **Franchise-License Agreement from a Fortune 500 company**	Killingsworth will furnish the signs at no charge, but Franklin is responsible for freight, installation, and any personal-property taxes and maintenance charges pertaining to them.

> "If a drafter's client has to struggle to make sense of the document being written, how can he or she make sure that the document says what it is supposed to say?" Christopher Balmford, *Adding Value by Writing Clearly*, 111 S. African L.J. 514, 528 (1994).

NOT THIS:	BUT THIS:
Ex. 2 3. Compensation and Benefits. . . . (d) Life Insurance. Executive will be entitled to term life insurance coverage for the benefit of Executive, his family or estate as he may direct provided under the terms of the group policy offered to all employees, except that Employer will pay Executive's portion of the cost thereof. **Employment Agreement from a banking corporation**	**3. Compensation and Benefits.** . . . (D) **Life insurance.** Salters is entitled to term-life insurance—for the benefit of himself, his family, or his estate as he directs—as provided under the group policy offered to all employees. Calaska will pay Salters's part of the cost.
Ex. 3 b *Limitation on Termination for Good Cause.* Nothing in this Section shall diminish The Provider's ability to terminate this Agreement for good and sufficient cause, except that The Provider shall not have good cause for termination under this Section if: (1) you (or your representative) file or lodge a formal or informal complaint with the Department of Social Services, or any other State, county, or city agency; or (2) you participate in an organization, affiliation or association of residents or engage in other similar lawful activity. **Residence-and-Care Agreement from a major law firm**	(B) **Limits on termination for good cause.** This section does not diminish our ability to terminate this Agreement for good cause. But we do not have good cause for termination if: (1) you or your representative files a formal or informal complaint with the Department of Social Services or another state, county, or city agency; or (2) you participate in an organization of residents or engage in other similar lawful activity.

except when. Use *unless.*

NOT THIS:	BUT THIS:
Ex. 1 Whether made pursuant to this clause or by mutual agreement, price adjustments shall not be binding upon CLIENT, except when confirmed in writing by CLIENT. **Consulting-Services Agreement from a major beverage company**	Price adjustments made under this clause or by mutual agreement are not binding on Nguyen unless Nguyen confirms them in writing.
Ex. 2 Presence at a meeting by a Member shall constitute a waiver of any deficiency of notice, except when a Member attends the meeting for the express purpose of objecting, at the beginning of the meeting, to the transaction of any business because the meeting is not called or convened in accordance with this Agreement. **Limited-Liability-Company Agreement from a distributor of healthcare systems, medical supplies, and pharmaceutical products**	A Member's presence at a meeting waives any deficiency of notice unless the Member attends the meeting for the express purpose of objecting to the transaction of business because the meeting is not called or convened in accordance with this Agreement. The Member's objection must be raised at the outset of the meeting.

except with [+ *noun* or *noun phrase*]. Use *unless* instead.

NOT THIS:	BUT THIS:
Ex. 1 All material Taxes with respect to the Purchased Assets have been duly and timely paid except with respect to matters contested in good faith by appropriate proceedings and for which adequate reserves have been provided in accordance with GAAP. **Asset-Purchase Agreement from a major pharmaceutical manufacturing, wholesale, and distribution company**	Material Taxes on the Purchased Assets have been duly and timely paid unless contested in good faith by appropriate proceedings for which adequate reserves have been provided in accordance with GAAP.
Ex. 2 D. The Ceding Company shall not make any changes after the Effective Date in the provisions and conditions of any Policy except with the Reinsurer's prior written consent, including, but not limited to any changes to comply with any applicable law, rule or regulation. **Reinsurance Agreement from a major life-insurance company**	(D) **No changes.** After the Effective Date, York cannot change any terms in a Policy—including changes to comply with an applicable law, rule, or regulation—unless JPT gives prior written consent.
Ex. 3 Section 9.04. Exclusive Remedies. Except with respect to the matters covered by ARTICLE II, and other than with respect to any equitable remedies contemplated by Section 10.13, Seller and Buyer acknowledge and agree that, following the Closing, the indemnification provisions of Section 9.01 and Section 9.02 shall be the sole and exclusive remedies of any Seller Indemnified Party and any Buyer Indemnified Party, respectively, for any losses. **Asset-Purchase Agreement from a major drugstore chain**	9.4 **Exclusive remedies.** Unless covered in § 2 or by an equitable remedy in § 10.13, after the Closing, the indemnity provisions in §§ 9.1 and 9.2 are the only remedies available to a third party that either Pillars or Brenning indemnifies against losses.

execute; execution. In traditional contract terminology, to *execute* a contract is to perform the obligations contained within it.[1] But in modern usage, lawyers refer to the parties' *executing* a contract in the sense of doing what is necessary to make it effective—usually just signing it. Sometimes they mean both signing and delivery, but often it's merely the signing. If anything, this usage has now become predominant, and the traditional usage relating to performance has become old-fashioned.

Although you might not think the dual meanings would ever actually cause a problem, they do from time to time. Not long ago two companies had a preliminary agreement in which one, in order to have an option, was required first to "execute an acquisition agreement" by a given date. When the date came, the execution

1 *See Garner's Dictionary of Legal Usage* 340 (3d ed. 2011) (s.v. "execute").

agreement had been signed but not performed. The option-giving party claimed default; the option-obtaining party claimed full compliance because the acquisition agreement had been signed a day earlier. In the end, the litigation settled after more than a year of skirmishing.

If you mean *sign*, write *sign*; if you mean *sign and deliver*, write that; if you mean *perform*, write that. But avoid *execute* if one of those wordings will suffice. Concededly, though, *execute* in the modern sense can seem more apt when one or both parties are corporations, which can't really be said to *sign* contracts.

The same point holds true for the noun *execution*. Prefer *signing of the Agreement*.

NOT THIS:	BUT THIS:
Ex. 1 Upon your execution, return and non-revocation of the Second Release no earlier than April 30, 2020, you will be eligible to receive the Benefits set forth in Paragraph 2(c). **Retirement-Transition Agreement from a global security and aerospace company**	You will be eligible to receive the Benefits in § 2(C) if you sign, return, and don't revoke the Second Release before April 30, 2020.
Ex. 2 This Agreement shall supersede and replace any prior indemnification agreements entered into by and between LNW Mortgage and Indemnitee and any such prior agreements shall be terminated upon execution of this Agreement. **Indemnification Agreement from a national mortgage-lending corporation**	This Agreement supersedes any existing indemnity agreements between LNW and Pyatt, and those agreements will end upon the signing and delivery of this Agreement.
Ex. 3 (e) Promptly after the execution of this Agreement and also at the Closing Time, the Underwriters shall have received from Knoll's LLP a letter or letters, dated as of the respective dates of delivery thereof, in form and substance reasonably satisfactory to the Representatives. **Underwriting Agreement from a major airline**	(E) Promptly after the signing of this Agreement and also at the Closing Time, Knoll's LLP will send to the Underwriters a letter with the date of delivery in a form and substance reasonably satisfactory to the Representatives.

"When they move beyond excuses and denial statements, writers most frequently express the resistance to change as a defense of either their professionalism, or of a necessary evil employed in the best interests of their client." Philip Knight & Plain Language Institute, *A Plain Language Report: So People Can Understand* 39 (1993).

facsimile. See *telecopy*.

following. When used as an equivalent of *after* to begin a sentence or clause, *following* often results in a misplaced modifier. It can also cause a miscue because readers may think for a moment that it's functioning as a participle. If you mean "after," write *after*.

NOT THIS:	BUT THIS:
Ex. 1 Following the Effective Date, the Borrower shall deliver to the Agent annual renewals of each flood insurance policy or annual renewals of each force-placed flood insurance policy, as applicable. **Revolving-Credit-and-Guaranty Agreement from a major automotive manufacturer**	After the Effective Date, the Borrower must give the Agent annual renewals of each flood-insurance policy or force-placed flood-insurance policy, as applicable.
Ex. 2 9. No Right to Give Public Interviews. For a period of five years following the Retirement Date, without the prior written consent of the Company, Executive shall not . . . . **Executive-Retirement Agreement and General Release of All Claims from a major automotive dealer**	(9) **No right to give public interviews.** Unless Amal gives prior written consent, Charmander will not, for 5 years after the Retirement Date, ...
Ex. 3 6. Termination By Executive. (a) If termination does not follow a Change in Control of Employer or Bank, Executive shall receive the following separation payments: (i) a lump sum payment, payable within thirty (30) days following his termination, equal to six (6) times his then monthly Base Salary amount, and (ii) six (6) monthly installment payments. **Employment Agreement from a banking corporation**	**6. Termination by Executive.** (A) Unless termination follows a Change in Control of Employer or Bank, Stinson will receive the following separation payments: (1) a lump-sum payment, payable within 30 days after his termination, equal to 6 times his then-monthly Base Salary amount; and (2) 6 monthly installment payments.
Ex. 4 (b) Non-Solicitation. Subject to the provisions of Section 4 (e), you agree that, during the Consultancy Period and for a period of twelve (12) months following the end of the Consultancy Period, you will not, without the prior written consent of the Company, through its Chief Human Resources Officer, either directly or indirectly engage in any act that diverts, or is intended to divert, employees from the Company. **Separation Agreement from a major beverage manufacturer**	(B) **Nonsolicitation.** Subject to § 4(E) and unless you receive written consent of Sugarfull's Chief Human Resources Officer, during the Consultancy Period and for 12 months after, you will not engage directly or indirectly in an act that diverts or is intended to divert employees from Sugarfull.

NOT THIS:	BUT THIS:
Ex. 5 (MM) "Warranty Period" means the following: . . . (2) For a particular Product, the longer of either of the following: (a) Eighteen months following the date that the Product is actually delivered. If delivery occurs on more than one day, then eighteen months following the date when delivery is completed. (b) Twelve months following the date on which the Product is installed and placed into first operational use and (if applicable) after completion of all testing. **Master Contractor-Services Contract from a major oil company** *Note the two senses of following in this passage.*	**10.6** "Warranty Period" means the following: . . . (B) For a particular Product, the longer of either: (1) 18 months after the date that the Product is actually delivered or, if delivery occurs on more than 1 day, then 18 months after the date when delivery is completed; or (2) 12 months after the date on which the Product is installed and placed into first operational use and (if applicable) after completion of all testing.

forthwith. This is a fuzzy word with no hint of precision. Use *promptly* (with very little delay) or *immediately* (with no delay) instead. Better yet, state a specific period or deadline.

NOT THIS:	BUT THIS:
Ex. 1 The Company will forthwith prepare and cause to be filed with the Commission an amendment or supplement to the Registration Statement or the Prospectus. **Underwriting Agreement from a major food, snack, and beverage company**	The Company will promptly prepare an amendment or supplement to the Registration Statement or the Prospectus and file it with the Commission.
Ex. 2 If and to the extent such Lender shall not have so made such amount available to the Administrative Agent, such Lender and the Borrower severally agree to pay to the Administrative Agent, forthwith on demand, such corresponding amount (to the extent not previously paid by the other). **Credit Agreement from a major pharmacy chain**	If the Lender does not make the stated amount available to the Administrative Agent, the Lender and the Borrower will be severally liable to pay the Administrative Agent, promptly on demand, the corresponding amount (to the extent not previously paid by the other).

"We should treat precision and clarity as equally important. At the same time, we should look at the underlying substance, along with the language, to see if they can be simplified. More often than not, these three goals are complementary." Joseph Kimble, *Plain English: A Charter for Clear Writing*, 9 Thomas M. Cooley L. Rev. 1, 17–18 (1992).

NOT THIS:	BUT THIS:
Ex. 3 If the Premises are or become infested with vermin as a result of the use of the Premises by Tenant, its agents, servants, employees, contractors, visitors or licensees, Tenant shall forthwith, at Tenant's expense, cause the Premises to be exterminated from time to time to the satisfaction of Landlord and shall employ such licensed exterminators as shall be approved in writing in advance by Landlord. **Lease Agreement from a major law firm**	If the Premises are or become infested with vermin because of its use by the Tenant or Tenant's agents, servants, employees, contractors, visitors, or licensees, the Tenant must immediately hire a licensed exterminator to treat the Premises to the Landlord's satisfaction. The Tenant must pay the cost of extermination. The Landlord is entitled to approve one or more licensed exterminators beforehand.
Ex. 4 On the date of each Loan, the Agent shall be authorized (but not obligated) to advance, for the account of each of the Lenders, the amount of the Loan to be made by it in accordance with its Revolving Credit Commitment Percentage hereunder. Should the Agent do so, each of the Lenders agrees forthwith to reimburse the Agent in immediately available funds for the amount so advanced on its behalf by the Agent, together with interest at the Federal Funds Effective Rate if not so reimbursed on the date due from and including such date but not including the date of reimbursement. **Revolving-Credit-and-Guaranty Agreement from a major automotive manufacturer**	On the date of each Loan, the Agent may advance each Lender's account the amount of the Loan according to its Revolving Credit Commitment Percentage. Upon the advance, each Lender will promptly reimburse the Agent with immediately available funds for the amount advanced on the Lender's behalf. If the Lender does not reimburse by the due date, the Lender will also pay interest at the Federal Funds Effective Rate from and including the advancement date but not including the reimbursement date. *Note how* may *easily takes the place of "shall be authorized (but not obligated) to."*

good and valuable consideration. Use *valuable consideration* instead. The words *good and* are notoriously unnecessary: legally, they contribute nothing because only valuable consideration counts toward making a contract enforceable.[2] *Good consideration* is considered, in the eyes of the law, to be familial affection and the like: it's no good.[3]

NOT THIS:	BUT THIS:
Ex. 1 NOW, THEREFORE, in consideration of the foregoing and the mutual promises, covenants and agreements of the parties hereto, and for other good and valuable consideration the receipt and sufficiency of which are hereby acknowledged, the parties hereto agree as follows: **Limited-Liability-Company Agreement from a distributor of healthcare systems, medical supplies, and pharmaceutical products**	In consideration of their mutual promises, and for valuable consideration, the parties agree as follows:

2 *See Garner's Dictionary of Legal Usage* 206–07 (3d ed. 2011).

3 *Id.*

NOT THIS:	BUT THIS:
Ex. 2 NOW, THEREFORE, in consideration of the foregoing and the mutual promises, agreements and covenants set forth herein, and for other good and valuable consideration the receipt and adequacy of which the Parties acknowledge, the Parties hereby agree as follows: **Transfer-Restriction Agreement between a global Internet-services company and its founder**	In consideration of their mutual promises in this Agreement, and for other valuable consideration, the Parties agree as follows:

herein, hereof, hereto, hereunder, therein, thereof, thereto, and the like. *Here-* and *there-* words are antiquated and often vague. (*Herein* where? This section, this page, this document?) They're usually thrown in to give contracts a musty legal smell. Use everyday words instead, especially demonstrative pronouns such as *this*, *that*, *these*, and *those*. Say *this Agreement* or *this section* instead of *herein*.

Note, however, that *hereby* is a special case: it's a performative adverb that can usefully signify that a given legal act is taking place here and now—that the sentence in which it appears is the very doing of the action described.[4]

NOT THIS:	BUT THIS:
Ex. 1 Notices. All notices required hereunder shall be in writing. **Construction-License-and-Indemnity Agreement from Richard J. Rabbitt & Charles M. Sink, *PreConstruction Agreements in Forms & Substance: Specialized Agreements for the Construction Project* 215 (Carina Y. Ohara, John I. Spangler III & Michael D. Tarullo eds., 2007)**	**Required notices.** All notices must be in writing.

"I don't object to legal terminology where it's necessary to express a legal concept that has no compact equivalent in nonlegal speech. That can't be said of *hereof*, *thereof*, and their ilk. One of the unfortunate effects of their use is that they can be substituted for legal reasoning. I vividly remember that, when I was a kid lawyer, liberally sprinkling *hereof*s and *thereof*s on a document was enough to convince me that I was indeed a hotshot drafter." Howard Darmstadter, *Hereof, Thereof, and Everywhereof* 6 (2002).

4 *See* Richard C. Wydick, *True Confessions of Diddle-Diddle Dumb-Head*, 11 Scribes J. Legal Writing 57, 68–74 (2007).

NOT THIS:	BUT THIS:
Ex. 2 This Agreement shall be binding upon the parties hereto and their respective heirs, successors, and assigns. **Master Development-and-Distribution Agreement from a major motion-picture studio**	(C) **Successors and representatives.** This Agreement binds and inures to the benefit of the parties and their heirs, personal representatives, successors, and (where permitted) assignees.
Ex. 3 The Employee understands that this is a restrictive covenant and fully agrees to the reasonability thereof. **Executive-Confidentiality and Restrictive-Covenant Agreement from a major candy company**	Caldwell understands that this is a restrictive covenant and stipulates to its reasonableness.
Ex. 4 The Placement Shares, when issued, will conform to the description thereof set forth in or incorporated into the Prospectus. **Stock-Sales Agreement from a pharmaceutical company**	When issued, the Placement Shares must conform to their description in the Prospectus.
Ex. 5 Except as expressly set forth herein, Johnson and Jones hereby release each other from all claims. **Settlement Agreement from a major law firm**	Unless this Agreement states otherwise, Johnson and Jones hereby release each other from all claims.
Ex. 6 If the Employee fails to use the full vacation privileges hereunder, the Employee shall not be entitled to additional compensation for such additional time worked. **Employment Agreement from a major law firm**	If Yung fails to use full vacation privileges under this Agreement, Yung is not entitled to additional compensation for the additional time worked.
Ex. 7 The Contractor hereby acknowledges that it has read and agrees to be bound by the conditions of the Company's confidentiality and proprietary information agreement attached hereto as Schedule A, which forms an integral part hereof. **Independent-Contractor Agreement from a major law firm**	Jenkins is bound by the Company's agreement on confidentiality and proprietary information, which is attached as Schedule A and fully incorporated into this Agreement.

"'Hereinbeforementioned' is as unreadable as it is silly. Let's stop writing like we were using quill pens, slumped over a Dickensian desk." Mark P. Painter, *The Legal Writer* 87 (2002).

NOT THIS:	BUT THIS:
Ex. 8 Between the participating carriers listed in Exhibit A attached hereto and hereby made a part hereof, and represented by the National Carriers' Conference Committee, and the employees shown thereon and represented by the Brotherhood of Maintenance of Way Employees. **Introduction to Railroad's Imposed Agreement**	1. **Parties to Agreement.** This Agreement is between the participating carriers listed in Exhibit A and represented by the National Carriers' Conference Committee, and the employees listed in Exhibit A and represented by Brotherhood of Maintenance of Way Employees.

if any. Instead of following the noun with this phrase, try placing *any* before the noun.

NOT THIS:	BUT THIS:
Ex. 1 For the purpose of this Merger Protocol, the Closing Date will be the last day, after extension(s), if any, of the Acceptance Period. **Merger Protocol between courier-delivery-services companies**	Under this Merger Protocol, the Closing Date will be the last day of the Acceptance Period after any extensions.
Ex. 2 If a Participant dies after distribution of his or her Account has begun, the remaining balance of his or her Account (if any) shall be paid to the Participant's Beneficiary in accordance with the method of payment chosen by the Participant. **Retirement-Plan Agreement from a global industrial-innovation company**	If a Participant dies after distribution of the Account has begun, any remaining balance of the Account will be paid to the Participant's Beneficiary using the Participant's chosen payment method.
Ex. 3 5. Brinson shall submit to Albrecht royalty reports within thirty (30) days after the end of each calendar quarter hereafter in which it shall set forth (i) the number of troy ounces of Licensed Products sold and/or used by Brinson during the previous calendar quarter; (ii) the amount (if any) of any alloy which is the subject of a credit actually given by Brinson to customers for returned goods as to which royalties had been previously paid and as to which a credit is being taken by Brinson and (iii) the amount of royalties due. **Patent-Licensing Agreement from 25 Allen Brufsky & Barry Kramer, *West's Legal Forms: Intellectual Property, Patents* § 13.2, at 397 (3d ed. 2004)** *Note the redundancy of the amount (if any) of any alloy.*	5. **Royalty Reports.** Brinson will submit a royalty report to Albrecht within 30 days after the end of each calendar quarter. The report must state: (A) the number of troy ounces of Licensed Products sold or used by Brinson during the previous calendar quarter; (B) the amount of any alloy that is the subject of a credit given by Brinson to customers for returned goods for which royalties had been previously paid and for which a credit is being taken by Brinson; and (C) the amount of royalties due.

NOT THIS:	BUT THIS:
Ex. 4 Any Award granted will be evidenced by a letter or other document delivered in writing by the Company to Grantee (each an "Award Letter"), which Award Letter will contain the terms of each Award including, but not limited to, the date of grant of the Award, the number of shares of Class A Common Shares, no par value, of the Company (the "Class A Common Shares") subject to the Award, the exercise price, if any, (the "Exercise Price"), the expiration date of the Award, if any (the "Expiration Date"), the vesting schedule, if any, and any other restrictions. **Stock-Incentive-Plan-Award Agreement from a major athletic retailer**	For each Award granted, the Company will give Grantee a letter or document verifying the Award (an "Award Letter"). Each Award Letter will list the Award's applicable terms, which may include any of the following: • the Award's grant date; • the number of the Company's Class A Common Shares, no par value ("Class A Common Shares"), subject to the Award; • the exercise price; • the Award's expiration date ("Expiration Date"); • the vesting schedule; and • any other restriction.

in case. Try *if* instead.

NOT THIS:	BUT THIS:
Ex. 1 (g) *Lost Certificates.* In the case of any Certificate that has been lost, stolen or destroyed . . . . **Agreement and Plan of Merger between two manufacturing companies**	(G) **Lost Certificates.** If a Certificate is lost, stolen, or destroyed, ...
Ex. 2 In case the other party fails or refuses to appoint a second arbitrator within the time provided, the first arbitrator appointed will be the sole arbitrator. **Service-and-Maintenance Agreement from *Texas Forms: Legal & Business* § 11B:26, at 270 (2011)**	If the other party fails or refuses to appoint a second arbitrator within the time provided, the first arbitrator appointed will be the sole arbitrator.
Ex. 3 This Merger Protocol terminates immediately by notice in writing given by the Terminating Party to the other Party in case of the other Party having breached the terms of this Merger Protocol. **Merger Protocol between courier-delivery-services companies**	If one party breaches this Merger Protocol, the other party may immediately terminate the Agreement upon delivering written notice of the termination to the breaching party.
Ex. 4 In case the provisions of this Agreement shall be held to be invalid, illegal, or unenforceable in any respect, such invalidity, illegality, or unenforceability shall not affect any other provisions hereof. **Common-Stock-Purchase-Warrant Agreement between a technology company and a venture-capital firm**	**Severability.** If a court for any reason holds a provision of this Agreement to be unenforceable, the rest remains fully enforceable. See § 34.

including but not limited to; including without limitation; including without limiting the generality of the foregoing; etc. The recommended course is to put the following definition in a definitions section: "*Including* means 'including but not limited to.'"

This cautious phrase avoids three canons of construction that can defeat the drafter's intent: the negative-implication canon (saying one thing but not something else suggests that the something else was purposely omitted),[5] the associated-words canon (words of a feather flock together),[6] and the *ejusdem generis* rule (general words that follow specific ones in a list are limited in kind by the specific ones).[7] It is therefore a useful habitual phrase when pairing general words with specific ones.

Ensure that the general words preceding the phrase constitute a genus, and that the specific words following the phrase constitute species. If that is not so, then edit out the phrase *including but not limited to.*

NOT THIS:	BUT THIS:
Ex. 1 All tangible and intangible information, materials and intellectual property, including, without limitation, ideas, concepts, designs, products, methods . . . . **Consulting-Services Agreement from a major food, snack, and beverage corporation**	All tangible and intangible information, materials, and intellectual property, including ideas, concepts, designs, products, methods . . . .
Ex. 2 19. <u>**Confidentiality.**</u> Each of the Parties promises that it shall maintain in confidence and shall not disclose the contents of this Agreement, including, but not limited to, the consideration received or paid by either of the Parties. **Settlement Agreement executed by a major law firm**	**19. Confidentiality.** Neither party may disclose the contents of this Agreement, including the consideration received or paid by either Party.
Ex. 3 Without limiting the generality of the foregoing, you agree not to file any lawsuit seeking monetary damages for yourself and asserting any claims that are lawfully released in this Second Release of Claims. **Retirement-Transition Agreement from a global aerospace, defense, security, and advanced-technologies company**	You must not file a lawsuit that seeks monetary damages for yourself or asserts any claims lawfully released by this Second Release of Claims.

5 *See* Antonin Scalia & Bryan A. Garner, *Reading Law: The Interpretation of Legal Texts* § 10, at 107 (2012).

6 *Id.* § 31, at 195.

7 *Id.* § 32, at 199.

in the event of [+ *zombie noun*[8]]. Try changing to *if* and using the zombie noun's verb form. But sometimes the phrase *in the event of* is all but unavoidable.

NOT THIS:	BUT THIS:
Ex. 1 In the event of any conflict among the provisions of the Plan and this Award Agreement, the provisions of the Plan will be controlling and determinative. **Stock-Option-Award Agreement from a major payroll-outsourcing company**	If the Plan conflicts with this Award Agreement, the Plan controls.
Ex. 2 In the event of any conveyance or transfer of title to the Building, then from and after the date of such conveyance or transfer, the transferor shall be relieved of all liability with respect to obligations of the Landlord hereunder to be performed after the date of such conveyance or transfer. **Lease Agreement from a major tech institution**	If the Building title is transferred, the transferor is not liable for Kishco's lease obligations incurred after the transfer.
Ex. 3 (h) Exclusivity. Unless otherwise determined by the Company in its sole discretion, in the event of a termination of the Executive's employment with the Company for any reason (or no reason) or at any time other than as expressly contemplated by Section 2 hereof, the Executive shall not be entitled to receive any severance payments and/or benefits or other further compensation from the Company hereunder whatsoever, except for the Accrued Compensation and any other rights or benefits to which the Executive is otherwise entitled pursuant to the requirements of applicable law. **Employment Agreement from a major clothing retailer**	(H) **Compensation after termination.** If Cohen's employment with Anderson's Clothing ends for any reason or at any time other than as provided in § 2 of this Agreement, Cohen is not entitled to receive a severance payment or benefit or further compensation from Anderson's Clothing. But Cohen will receive the Accrued Compensation and any other rights or benefits Cohen is otherwise entitled to under law.

in the event that. Use *if.* The phrase *in the event that* is always replaceable.

NOT THIS:	BUT THIS:
Ex. 1 17. Severability. In the event that any provision of this Agreement should be held to be void, voidable or unenforceable, the remaining portions hereof shall remain in full force and effect. **Settlement Agreement executed by major law firm**	17. **Severability.** If a court for any reason holds a provision of this Agreement to be unenforceable, the rest remains fully enforceable.

8 *See* § 20.

NOT THIS:	BUT THIS:
Ex. 2 In the event that Executive's employment is terminated by reason of Executive's Disability or upon the death of Executive, the Company shall be under no further obligation to Executive (or his estate), except to pay the Accrued Benefits. **Employment Agreement from a major deep-discount retailer**	If Hartman's employment ends because of his disability or death, BuyLow has no further obligation to Hartman or his estate except to pay his Accrued Benefits.
Ex. 3 In the event that any patent or claim thereof included within the Licensor's patent rights is held invalid in a final decision by a court of competent jurisdiction and last resort from which no appeal has been or can be taken, all obligation to pay royalties based on the patent or claim ceases as of the date of the final decision. **Assignment of Patent Rights by university technology-transfer department**	If a patent or patent claim within the Licensor's patent rights is held invalid in a final decision by a court and no appeal is sought or available, any obligation to pay royalties based on that patent or claim ends on the date of that decision.
Ex. 4 (l) Specific Enforcement. The Parties acknowledge and agree that irreparable damage would occur in the event that any of the provisions of this Agreement were not performed in accordance with their specific terms or were otherwise breached, and that monetary damages, even if available, would not be an adequate remedy therefor. **Termination Agreement from a major pharmaceutical manufacturing, wholesale, and distribution company**	12. **Specific Enforcement.** If this Agreement is not performed in accordance with its specific terms or is otherwise breached, irreparable damage would occur and monetary damages, even if available, would not be adequate.[9]
Ex. 5 It is understood and agreed that, in the event that you are required to give testimony, the Company is the holder of attorney client privilege and work product protections, that the Company does not intend to waive, expressly or impliedly, said privileges and protections, and that you agree to vigorously protect and resist disclosure of Confidential Information, as herein defined, including but not limited to attorney client privileged, work product protected information, at all times. **Separation Agreement from a major beverage manufacturer**	Koolaah has attorney–client privilege and work-product protections and does not intend to waive these privileges and protections either expressly or impliedly. If you are required to give testimony, you must at all times vigorously protect and resist disclosing Confidential Information, including attorney–client-privileged or work-product-protected information.

This language of agreement is unnecessary. The revision removes it. See § 49.

9 As a matter of law, many jurisdictions will not enforce a provision like this one; the court will independently assess whether irreparable harm exists.

know all men by these presents. This phrase—which is a bombastic way of saying "Heads up!"—continues to drift along in legal drafting like so much deadwood in a stream. Delete as surplusage.

NOT THIS:	BUT THIS:
Ex. 1 KNOW ALL MEN BY THESE PRESENTS that for good and valuable consideration and upon receipt of the amount paid by Federal Guaranty Deposit Corporation ("FGDC"), the undersigned releases FGDC from any further liability arising from any loss due to the default by the borrower under a loan described as follows: **Commercial Loan**	For valuable consideration—and upon receipt of the amount paid by FGDC—the undersigned releases FGDC from any further liability arising from a loss due to the borrower's default on a loan described as follows:
Ex. 2 KNOW ALL MEN BY THESE PRESENTS, that each person whose signature appears below constitutes and appoints Joseph F. Cottinger and Daniel Szekarez, and each of them, with full power to act without the other, such person's true and lawful attorneys-in-fact and agents, with full power of substitution and resubstitution, for him and in his name, place and stead, in any and all capacities, to sign this Registration Statement, and any and all amendments thereto (including post-effective amendments), and to file the same, with exhibits and schedules thereto, and other documents in connection therewith, with the Securities and Exchange Commission. **Power of Attorney for a major life-science company's equity-incentive plan**	Each person whose signature appears below appoints Joseph F. Cottinger and Daniel Szekarez as his or her attorneys in fact and agents, each with full power to act without the other, to sign this Registration Statement and any amendments to it, and to file it and any related documents with the Securities and Exchange Commission.

liens and encumbrances. Because every lien is an encumbrance, this illogical phrase is similar to *cars and vehicles* or *pens and writing instruments.* The more logical phrasing acknowledges that a lien is a species of encumbrance. Make it *liens and other encumbrances.*

NOT THIS:	BUT THIS:
Ex. 1 Seller shall pass to Purchaser upon Delivery good and marketable title to the Aircraft clear of all liens and encumbrances other than any liens created by Purchaser which by their express terms become effective upon passage of title to Purchaser. **Contract for Sale of Aircraft**	Upon Delivery, Seller will pass to Buyer good and marketable title to the Aircraft clear of all liens and other encumbrances other than any liens created by Buyer that by their express terms become effective upon passage of title to Buyer.

NOT THIS:	BUT THIS:
Ex. 2 “Permitted Liens” means liens imposed by Applicable Law that were incurred in the Ordinary Course of Business . . . including carriers’, warehousemen’s and mechanics’ liens, statutory landlords’ liens and other similar liens and encumbrances arising in the Ordinary Course of Business. **Senior-Secured-Loan Agreement**	“Permitted Liens” means liens imposed by Applicable Law that were incurred in the Ordinary Course of Business . . . including carriers’, warehousemen’s, and mechanics’ liens, statutory landlords’ liens, and similar liens and other encumbrances arising in the Ordinary Course of Business.

made and entered into. Avoid this doublet by rephrasing.

NOT THIS:	BUT THIS:
Ex. 1 THIS AGREEMENT (the “Agreement”) is made and entered into this 15th day of May, 2017, by and between Katrina Brim and Drew Hetzler. **Premarital Agreement**	This Agreement, effective May 15, 2017, is between Katrina Brim and Drew Hetzler.
Ex. 2 THIS TAX SHARING AGREEMENT (the “Agreement”) is made and entered into as of October 31, 2016 (the “Effective Date”) by and among Kerley Inc., formerly known as Kerley Department Stores, Inc. (“Kerley”) as Common Parent and those Members whose names appear on Schedule A hereto. **Tax-Sharing Agreement from a major department-store chain**	This Tax-Sharing Agreement, effective October 31, 2016, is between Kerley Inc., formerly known as Kerley Department Stores Inc. (Kerley), as Common Parent and those Members whose names appear on Schedule A attached to this Agreement.
Ex. 3 THIS WORK LETTER AGREEMENT (“**Agreement**”) is made and entered into by and between MOMENTUS, LLC, a California limited liability company (“**Landlord**”), and KELLER CLEANING CORPORATION, a California corporation (“Tenant”), and shall be deemed a part of the lease between Landlord and Tenant to which this Agreement is attached (the “**Lease**”). **Lease Agreement from a major law firm**	This Work-Letter Agreement, effective [date], is between Momentus LLC, a California limited-liability company, and Keller Cleaning Corporation, a California corporation. It is attached to and made part of the Lease between Momentus and Keller Cleaning.

> “[If] you have fallen under the spell of ‘legalese,’ . . . words take on a certain institutional stiffness. When words such as *whereby*, *thereby*, *heretofore*, and *wherein* creep into your vocabulary, put down your pen, take a few deep breaths, and read your work aloud. Your ear will soon tell you just how awkward and antiquated these phrases are.” Gary Blake & Robert W. Bly, *The Elements of Technical Writing* 73 (1993).

not later than. Use *no later than* or *within.* "*Within* 10 days after entry of judgment" is usually better than "*no later than* 10 days after entry of judgment." But the latter may be needed if you want to allow the act to be done before the entry of judgment as well as in the following 10 days.

NOT THIS:	BUT THIS:
Ex. 1 Such determination of entitlement to indemnification shall be made not later than 30 calendar days after receipt by FMC of a written request for indemnification. **Indemnification Agreement from a national mortgage-lending corporation**	The indemnity entitlement will be determined within 30 calendar days after FMC receives a written request for indemnity.
Ex. 2 On the Closing Date, the Company shall repay the Garza Promissory Note Principal Amount in full satisfaction thereof in immediately available funds by wire transfer to an account of Garza with a bank in New York City or London designated by Garza, by notice to the Company, which notice shall be delivered not later than two Business Days prior to the Closing Date. **Agreement of Contribution and Sale from a distributor of healthcare systems, medical supplies, and pharmaceutical products**	On the Closing Date, Elrod Ltd. will repay the Garza Promissory Note Principal Amount in full by wire transfer of immediately available funds to a Garza account with a bank in New York City or London. Garza will designate the account by notice to Elrod Ltd. The notice must be delivered no later than 2 Business Days before the Closing Date.
Ex. 3 (3) If any Product does not satisfy a warranty given in Section 4.4(A), Company may give notice to Contractor of this failure. Provided this notice is given to Contractor not later than thirty days after expiration of the Warranty Period, then at Company's option, Contractor shall replace or repair the non-conforming Product to Company's reasonable satisfaction or refund the full price of the non-conforming Product. **Master Contractor-Services Contract from a major oil company**	(C) **Satisfaction of warranty.** If a Product does not satisfy a warranty given in § 4.4(A), the Company may notify the Contractor of this failure. If the Company gives notice to the Contractor within 30 days after the Warranty Period ends, then at the Company's option, the Contractor will replace or repair the nonconforming Product to the Company's reasonable satisfaction or refund the full price of the nonconforming Product.

not less than; no fewer than. The first phrase best refers to amounts or to mass nouns, the second to number of things. Try using *at least.*

NOT THIS:	BUT THIS:
Ex. 1 Such notices shall be mailed or delivered, as applicable, not less than 20 nor more than 90 days prior to the date fixed for the meeting. **Indenture from a major financial institution**	The notices must be mailed or delivered, as applicable, at least 20 days—but no more than 90 days—before the fixed meeting date.

NOT THIS:	BUT THIS:
Ex. 2 (d) Termination of Employment by the Executive. During the Term, the Executive may terminate employment with the Company with or without Good Reason (as defined below) by delivering to the Company, not less than thirty (30) days prior to the Termination Date, a written notice of termination; provided, that, if such termination of employment is by the Executive with Good Reason, such notice shall state in reasonable detail the facts and circumstances that constitute Good Reason. **Employment Agreement from a major clothing retailer**	(D) **Allastair's termination of employment.** During the Term, Allastair may terminate employment with HL Clothiers with or without Good Reason by giving HL Clothiers written notice of termination at least 30 days before the Termination Date. If Allastair has Good Reason to terminate employment, the written notice must state in reasonable detail the facts and circumstances that constitute Good Reason.

not more than. Try *at most*, *up to*, or *no more than*.

NOT THIS:	BUT THIS:
Ex. 1 The record date if one is selected shall be not more than fifteen days prior to the date of commencement of solicitation of such action. **Indenture from a major financial institution**	If a record date is selected, it must be at most 15 days before the date that solicitation begins.
Ex. 2 Advances by the Depositary shall be made not more than once a month, after the Depositary's receipt of a written request therefor from the Board of Managers, addressed to the Depositary. **Landlord–Tenant Lease for space in a NYC high-rise under construction**	The Depositary may make Advances no more than once a month, after receiving the Board of Managers' written request addressed to the Depositary for an Advance.
Ex. 3 ***Section 2.01.*** *Loans.* (a) *Commitments.* On not more than two Business Days during the Commitment Period, subject to the terms and conditions hereof, each Lender agrees to make Loans to the Borrower in an aggregate principal amount not to exceed the amount of such Lender's Commitment. **Amended and Restated Term-Loan Agreement from a major online social-media and social-networking service**	**2.1 Loans.** (A) On up to 2 Business Days during the Commitment Period, subject to this Agreement, each Lender agrees to make Loans to the Borrower in an aggregate principal amount not to exceed the amount of that Lender's Commitment.

NOT THIS:	BUT THIS:
Ex. 4 The Company shall deliver a census summary (which shall comply with Section 6.14(a) of the Company Disclosure Schedules) (the "Census Summary") on or prior to the date of this Agreement, which Census Summary shall be as of a date not more than ten (10) days prior to the date of this Agreement. **Asset-Purchase Agreement from a major pharmaceutical manufacturing, wholesale, and distribution company**	The Company will deliver a census summary (complying with § 6.14(a) of the Company Disclosure Schedules) within 10 days before the date of this Agreement.
Ex. 5 Notwithstanding the foregoing, the Company and the Guarantors may suspend the offering and sale under a Market Making Registration Statement for a period or periods the Company reasonably determines to be advisable for valid business reasons, but in any event no such period shall be in excess of 45 days and not more than two (2) times during any calendar year during which such Market Making Registration Statement is required to be effective and usable hereunder. **Registration-Rights Agreement from a major food-processing company**	Despite anything in this Agreement to the contrary, Lockmiller and the Guarantors may suspend the offering and sale under a Market-Making Registration Statement for a period that Lockmiller reasonably determines to be advisable for valid business reasons. But no period may exceed 45 days, and at most 2 such periods may be called during a calendar year in which the Market-Making Registration Statement is required to be in effect.

notwithstanding. A literalist drafter or judicial interpreter might ask, "What doesn't withstand what else? Are the limitations of § 3.5 'not withstanding' (i.e., subordinated to) the present section, or is the present section 'not withstanding' (subordinated to) § 3.5?" Try *despite.*

NOT THIS:	BUT THIS:
Ex. 1 The Depositary or the Corporation may, however, act upon any facsimile transmission received by it from the other, notwithstanding that such facsimile transmission shall not subsequently be confirmed by letter or as aforesaid. **Deposit Agreement between two major financial-services corporations**	The Depositary or the Corporation may act on a fax it has received from the other, despite not having confirmation by letter or otherwise.
Ex. 2 Notwithstanding, the non-performance of any obligations of Depositor to deliver Deposit Material under the License Agreement or this Agreement, IPJ Information is entitled to be paid all Service Fees that accrue during the Term of this Agreement. **Three-Party Intellectual-Property Escrow Agreement between three major corporations**	Despite Depositor's noncompliance with a Deposit Material delivery obligation under the License Agreement or this Agreement, IPJ Information is entitled to payment for all Service Fees that accrue during this Agreement's Term.

NOT THIS:	BUT THIS:
Ex. 3 In addition, and notwithstanding the provision of Section 4.2 of this Agreement, if the date of termination is on or before the fifth (5th) anniversary date of the Effective Date, Employer shall pay to Employee within thirty (30) days of termination, a lump sum cash amount equal to Nine Hundred Fifty Thousand Dollars ($950,000) less all Annual Bonus amounts previously paid to Employee pursuant to Section 4.2 (a) (i) hereof and such lump sum payment shall be in lieu of any other Annual Bonus payments due to Employee for the Bonus Period (or any portion thereof). **Employment Agreement from a major law firm**	(B) **Additional payment.** Despite § 4.2 of this Agreement, if the date of termination is on or before the 5th anniversary of the Effective Date, then within 30 days after termination, Miles Software will pay Schwarz an additional lump sum of $950,000 after deducting from that amount all Annual Bonus amounts previously paid to Schwarz under § 4.2(A)(1). This lump-sum payment is in lieu of any other Annual Bonus payments owed to Schwarz for all or any part of the Bonus Period.

notwithstanding the fact that. This verbose, needlessly legalistic introduction can be shortened. Use *even if* or *even though.* Instead of *notwithstanding* alone, try *despite.*

NOT THIS:	BUT THIS:
Ex. 1 Division of the profits and losses shall be on an accrual basis notwithstanding the fact that taxes may be filed on a cash basis. **Joint-Venture Agreement**	Division of profits and losses are on an accrual basis even though taxes may be filed on a cash basis.
Ex. 2 To the extent permitted by applicable law, the aforesaid right of setoff may be exercised by such Lender, notwithstanding the fact that such right of setoff shall not have been exercised by such Lender prior to the making, filing or issuance of, service upon such Lender of, or notice to such Lender of, any petition, assignment for the benefit of creditors, appointment or application for the appointment of a receiver, or issuance of execution, subpoena, order or warrant. **Credit Agreement from a major pharmacy chain**	To the extent permitted by law, the Lender may exercise the right of setoff even if the Lender has not exercised that right before in connection with any type of legal process or proceeding.

on and after. This phrasing conveys the explicit nuance that the given date is included. If it shouldn't be, use *after* or *from*—or some simpler formulation.

NOT THIS:	BUT THIS:
Ex. 1 On and after the date of this Agreement, Johansen shall cooperate with Alexander and execute any documents necessary for Alexander to obtain title insurance and mortgage financing or refinancing relating to the Property. **Residential-Purchase Agreement from a major law firm**	From the date of this Agreement, Johansen will cooperate with Alexander and sign all documents necessary for Alexander to obtain title insurance and mortgage financing or refinancing on the Property.
Ex. 2 SECTION 6. Effect on Loan Documents. The Borrower and the other Loan Parties acknowledge and agree that, on and after the Effective Date, this Amendment and all the other Loan Documents to be executed and delivered by a Loan Party in connection herewith shall constitute a Loan Document for all purposes. **Amendment to Credit Agreement from a major theater-entertainment company**	6. **Effect on Loan Documents.** Burnwood and other Loan Parties agree that from the Effective Date, this Amendment and all the other Loan Documents signed and delivered by a Loan Party in connection with this Agreement are Loan Documents for all purposes.

partially. Unless referring to a quality or a degree of measure, use *partly*. Although few readers will seriously read *partially* as an antonym of *impartially*, the term is simplifiable to *partly*.

NOT THIS:	BUT THIS:
Ex. 1 The defeasance described herein, together with all prior and simultaneous defeasances of Mortgage Loans, brings the total of all fully and partially defeased Mortgage Loans to $____________________, which is _______% of the aggregate Certificate Balance of the Certificates as of the date of the Current Report. **Pooling-and-Servicing Agreement from a multinational banking and financial-services holding company**	The defeasance described in this Agreement, together with all previous and simultaneous defeasances of Mortgage Loans, brings the total of all fully and partly defeased Mortgage Loans to $____________________, which is ______% of the aggregate Certificate Balance of the Certificates as of the date of the Current Report.

NOT THIS:	BUT THIS:
Ex. 2 15.3 *Allocation of Expenses.* In the event a claim is based partially on an indemnified claim described in Section 15.1 and/or Section 15.2, above, and partially on a non-indemnified claim, or is based partially on a claim described in Section 15.1, above, and partially on a claim described in Section 15.2, above, any payments and reasonable attorney fees incurred in connection with such claims are to be apportioned between the Parties in accordance with the degree of cause attributable to each Party. **International-Distribution Agreement from a major law firm**	**15.3 Allocation of expenses.** If a claim is based partly on an indemnified claim described in § 15.1 or § 15.2 or both, and partly on a nonindemnified claim, or based partly on a claim described in § 15.1 and partly on a claim described in § 15.2, any payments and reasonable attorney fees incurred in connection with the claims are apportioned between the Parties in accordance with the degree of cause attributable to each Party.
Ex. 3 Because the primary purpose of our engagement was not to establish or confirm factual matters or financial or accounting matters and because of the wholly or partially non-legal character of many of the statements contained in the Registration Statement, the Prospectus, the Preliminary Prospectus Supplement and the Issuer Free Writing Prospectus, we are not passing upon and do not assume any responsibility for the accuracy, completeness or fairness of the statements contained in the Registration Statement, the Prospectus, the Preliminary Prospectus Supplement or the Issuer Free Writing Prospectus. **Underwriting Agreement from a major food-service distributor**	Because the primary purpose of our engagement was not to establish or confirm factual, financial, or accounting matters and because of the wholly or partly nonlegal character of many statements in the Registration Statement, the Prospectus, the Preliminary Prospectus Supplement, and the Issuer Free Writing Prospectus, we are not passing on—and do not assume any responsibility for—the accuracy, completeness, or fairness of the statements in those documents.
Ex. 4 Seller agrees that prior to the Closing, Seller will not sell or convey any of the 13 model homes, 18 partially completed homes as more specifically described and identified in Schedule 2.1(d)(ii)(A) (the "**Partially Completed Homes**"), any owned design and sales center, or any of the approximately 473 developed, undeveloped, partially developed or undevelopable lots that are part of the Real Property described in Section 2.1(a) hereof, so that all model homes, Partially Completed Homes and lots will be conveyed to Purchaser at Closing. Likewise, Seller agrees that no part of the amenity center or common areas included within the Real Property that have not been deeded previously to an HOA will be transferred or conveyed prior to Closing so that same will be conveyed to Purchaser at Closing. **Asset-Purchase Agreement from a major home-builder**	Before the Closing, Elm Ranch will not sell or convey any of the 13 model homes, the 18 partly completed homes as more specifically described in Schedule 2.1(D)(2)(a) (entitled "Partly Completed Homes"), any owned design-and-sales center, or any of some 473 developed, undeveloped, partly developed, or undevelopable lots that are part of the Real Property described in § 2.1(A). At Closing, Elm Ranch will convey to Callia Homes all these model homes, Partly Completed Homes, and lots, and the part of the amenity center or common areas included within the Real Property that has not been previously deeded to an HOA.

prior to. This legalism should be used only if you routinely use *posterior to* for *after.* (You don't.) Use *before.* Especially avoid *prior to the time when.*

NOT THIS:	BUT THIS:
Ex. 1 These costs include patent-prosecution costs for these inventions incurred by the Licensor prior to the signing of this Agreement. **Patent-Licensing Agreement from a university's office of technology transfer**	These costs include patent-prosecution costs for these inventions incurred by Marcus before the signing of this Agreement.
Ex. 2 3.1 Application Requirements. Prior to and conditioned upon the initial establishment of service, Alpha may require a customer to sign an Application for Service form and to establish credit as provided in these Master Terms and Conditions. **Master Services Agreement from a telecommunications company**	3.1 **Application requirements.** Before establishing service for a customer, Data Experts may require the customer to sign an Application for Service and to establish credit under the Master Terms and Conditions.
Ex. 3 a. Funeral Plans. The Provider encourages you to make funeral arrangements prior to residency. If you have made arrangements regarding funeral plans prior to moving into your Suite, The Provider requires that you furnish it with such information, to be kept as part of your records. **Residence-and-Care Agreement from a major law firm**	(A) **Funeral plans.** We encourage you to make funeral arrangements before moving in. If you have made those arrangements before move-in, you must give us the information to add to your records.
Ex. 4 2.1 Reasonable Efforts. The Parties agree to use their reasonable efforts to complete the Collaboration project as set forth in the applicable Statement of Work, attached hereto as Exhibit A. If a Party takes exception to any element of a proposed Statement of Work, such exception(s) must be mutually resolved by Jarvis and Company prior to the further commencement of any work specified therein. Neither Party shall be obligated to commence work detailed in the Statement of Work prior to both Parties indicating their acceptance of the Statement of Work by sending written confirmation to the other Party. **Collaboration Agreement from a Fortune 500 company in the computer industry**	2.1 **Reasonable efforts.** The Parties will use reasonable efforts to complete the Collaboration project as set forth in the Statement of Work attached as Exhibit A. If a Party objects to any element of a proposed Statement of Work, the Parties must mutually resolve the exception before the specified work begins. Neither Party is obligated to begin the work detailed in the Statement of Work before both Parties accept the Statement of Work by exchanging written confirmation.

provided that; provided, however, that. Reword using more specific language. See § 116.

NOT THIS:	BUT THIS:
Ex. 1 5. Company shall have final authority over the scheduling of the Aircraft, provided, however, that Company will give Executive's requests first priority over other utilization of the aircraft. **Aircraft Time-Sharing Agreement from a major heavy-equipment manufacturing company**	5. **Scheduling.** Viramontes has final authority over the scheduling of the Aircraft. But Viramontes will give Mungor's requests priority over other requests.
Ex. 2 (e) Each Party shall bear its own attorneys' fees and costs incurred in connection with the resolution of any Dispute in accordance with this Article VI; provided that the Parties shall share the fees and expenses of both the mediators and Arbitration Panel equally. **Master Separation Agreement from a major insurance provider**	(E) **Attorney fees.** Each Party will bear its own attorney fees and costs incurred in resolving a Dispute in accordance with § 6 of this Agreement. But the Parties will share the fees and expenses of the mediators and Arbitration Panel equally.
Ex. 3 Following transfer, the Options shall continue to be subject to the same terms and conditions as were applicable to the Options immediately before transfer (including terms and conditions based on the employment status of the Optionee); provided that where appropriate, all references in this Agreement to "Optionee" shall be deemed to refer to the transferee. **Nonstatutory-Stock-Option-Award Agreement from a major financial holding company**	After transfer, the Options are subject to the same terms as applied to the Options immediately before transfer, including terms based on the Option-holder's employment status. Where appropriate, all references in this Agreement to "Option-holder" refer to the transferee.
Ex. 4 SECTION 2.20 Increase in Commitments. (a) The Borrower may, from time to time by written notice to the Administrative Agent (which shall promptly deliver a copy to each of the Lenders), request that the Commitments be increased by an amount not less than $10,000,000 for any such increase; provided that after giving effect to all such increases the total Commitments shall not exceed $2,500,000,000 minus any amount by which the Commitments shall have been reduced pursuant to Section 2.09. **Credit Agreement from a major food-service distributor**	**2.20 Increase in Commitments.** (A) **Notice; limit.** Thompson may request that the Commitments be increased by at least $10 million by written notice to Moore (who will promptly deliver a copy to each Lender). But after giving effect to all increases, the Commitments must not exceed $2.5 billion minus any amount by which the Commitments have been reduced under § 2.9.

NOT THIS:	BUT THIS:
Ex. 5 Parent shall be authorized to consent to a compromise or settlement of such arbitration in full; provided, however, that, unless such compromise or settlement provides for no relief other than the payment of monetary damages by Parent or its Affiliates in an amount not to exceed the amount set forth on Section 6.25 of the Company Disclosure Schedules and makes no admission, Parent shall give the Company advance notice of any proposed compromise or settlement and in no event shall Parent compromise or settle such arbitration without the prior written consent of the Company. **Asset-Purchase Agreement from a major drugstore chain**	Hildebrand may consent to a settlement of an arbitration in full with prior notice to and the written consent of Gauze Co. But no notice or consent is required if the settlement involves no admission and provides no relief other than the payment of damages by Hildebrand or its Affiliates in an amount up to that specified in § 6.25 of the Company Disclosure Schedules.

provisions of. Avoid *the provisions of*—invariably a filler phrase. Ditto with *the terms of.*

NOT THIS:	BUT THIS:
Ex. 1 Section 2.27. *Payment of Obligations.* Subject to the provisions of Section 7.01, upon the maturity (whether by acceleration or otherwise) of any of the Obligations of the Loan Parties under this Agreement or any of the other Loan Documents, the Lenders shall be entitled to immediate payment of such Obligations. **Revolving-Credit-and-Guaranty Agreement from a major automotive manufacturer**	2.27. **Payment of Obligations.** Subject to § 7.1, Lenders are entitled to immediate payment of an Obligation of the Loan Parties—under this Agreement or any other Loan Document—when that Obligation matures (by acceleration or otherwise).
Ex. 2 The Purchaser acknowledges that its failure to comply with the provisions of this paragraph may affect the Purchaser's rights in any such Pending Proceeding, including a dismissal with prejudice or the running of any statute of limitations if any such Pending Proceeding is dismissed. **Mortgage-Loan Purchase Agreement between two major financial institutions**	Polston's failure to comply with this section may affect Polston's rights in a Pending Proceeding, which—if dismissed—may include dismissal with prejudice or the running of a statute of limitations.

"Good architecture directs attention to the nature and relative position of each element in the hierarchy of the client's ideas." Reed Dickerson, *The Fundamentals of Legal Drafting* § 2.3.2, at 16 (2d ed. 1986).

NOT THIS:	BUT THIS:
Ex. 3 (o) The statements set forth in the Pricing Prospectus and Prospectus under the captions "Description of Debt Securities" and "Description of the Notes", insofar as they purport to constitute a summary of the terms of the Securities, and under the captions "Plan of Distribution" and "Underwriting", insofar as they purport to describe the provisions of the laws and documents referred to therein, are accurate, complete and fair in all material respects. **Underwriting Agreement from a Fortune 500 insurance company**	(O) **Representation of accuracy.** The following statements in the Pricing Prospectus and Prospectus are accurate, complete, and fair in all material aspects: (1) statements under the captions "Description of Debt Securities" and "Description of the Notes," to the extent that they summarize the Securities; and (2) statements under the captions "Plan of Distribution" and "Underwriting," to the extent that they describe the law and documents referred to.

pursuant to. This phrase has four meanings in law: (1) in accordance with, under; (2) as required by; (3) as authorized by; and (4) in carrying out.[10] Use *under* or *in accordance with*. Write *under § 3*, not *pursuant to § 3*, or *in accordance with 26 U.S.C. § 1333*, not *pursuant to 26 U.S.C. § 1333*.

NOT THIS:	BUT THIS:
Ex. 1 You may not otherwise disclose the trade secret, except pursuant to court order. **Executive-Employment Agreement from a healthcare company**	You must not otherwise disclose the trade secret except as required by court order.
Ex. 2 The term of the Employee's employment pursuant to this Agreement shall be deemed to have commenced on the Effective Date. **Employment Agreement**	Redman's term of employment under this Agreement begins on the Effective Date.
Ex. 3 Owen shall bear the cost of any discount granted pursuant to any discount program promoted by Allcom in which Owen participates. **Franchise-License Agreement from a Fortune 500 company**	Owen will pay the cost of any discount given under a discount program that Allcom promotes and Owen participates in.
Ex. 4 The Company will reimburse you for your authorized and documented expenses within thirty (30) days of receiving such statement pursuant to its regular business practice. **Executive-Employment Agreement from a healthcare company**	In accordance with its regular business practice, the Company will reimburse you for authorized and documented expenses within 30 days after receiving your statement.

10 *See Garner's Dictionary of Legal Usage* 737–38 (3d ed. 2011).

NOT THIS:	BUT THIS:
Ex. 5 1.2 "Company's Intellectual Property" means any and all: (a) Pre-existing IP of Company; (b) Non-Project IP of Company; and (c) Project IP owned by Company pursuant to the terms of the Agreement. **Collaboration Agreement from a computer-technology company**	**1.2** "Company's Intellectual Property" includes: (A) Preexisting IP of the Company; (B) Nonproject IP of the Company; and (C) Project IP owned by the Company under the Agreement.
Ex. 6 **Section 2.12 Shareholders Agreement Will Terminate at the Effective Time.** AEPP and Oncolix agree and acknowledge that the Shareholders Agreement will terminate and become null and void pursuant to its terms as of the Effective Time. **Merger Agreement between two major oil companies**	**2.12 Shareholders' Agreement termination.** Upon the Effective Time, the Shareholders' Agreement will terminate and become void by its terms.

said, *adj.* Use *the*, *this*, or *that*. Like its siblings, *the said* and *the aforesaid*, *said* used as an article imparts no greater specificity than the definite article *the*—and reeks of legalese.

NOT THIS:	BUT THIS:
Ex. 1 Bergeron, individually, is the sole owner of the Lithotrypter machine; neither the Corporation nor Kranz has an interest in said machine. **Asset-Purchase Agreement**	Bergeron is individually the sole owner of the Lithotrypter machine; neither the Corporation nor Kranz has an interest in the machine.
Ex. 2 The maintenance fee is not due on any anniversary date of the effective date of this Agreement if on said date the Licensee is commercially selling Licensed Products and paying earned royalties to the Licensor. **License Agreement from a major law firm**	The maintenance fee is not due on any anniversary date of the effective date of this Agreement if Goldstein is then commercially selling Licensed Products and paying earned royalties to the University.
Ex. 3 Property insured hereunder while contained inside a building on the premises of the described dwelling, is insured against loss due to change of temperature as the direct result of physical damage to the said dwelling, or equipment therein, caused by a peril insured against. **Insurance Policy**	While contained inside a building on the premises of the described dwelling, property insured under this policy is insured against loss caused by a peril insured against and attributable to a change in temperature as the direct result of physical damage to the dwelling or equipment inside it.

"*The* is one of the most concise and informative words in the language, and much undervalued by lawyers." Mark Adler, *Clarity for Lawyers* 59 (1990).

NOT THIS:	BUT THIS:
Ex. 4 (C) Avery's consultative services shall include identifying customers for the business, visiting customers and potential customers, advising Kade with respect to the needs and the nature of equipment and the quantity of equipment which said customers may require, advising Kade of competitive activities, and similar and related matters. **Consulting Agreement from a major beverage company**	(C) **Consulting services.** Avery's consulting services include: (1) identifying customers for the business; (2) visiting customers and potential customers; (3) advising Kade about the nature and quantity of equipment that the customers may require; and (4) advising Kade of competitive activities and related matters.
Ex. 5 b) New Warrants. This Warrant may be divided or combined with other Warrants upon presentation hereof at the aforesaid office of the Company, together with a written notice specifying the names and denominations in which new Warrants are to be issued, signed by the Holder or its agent or attorney. **Common-Stock-Purchase Warrant from a plant biotechnology company**	(B) **New Warrants.** This Warrant may be divided or combined with other Warrants by presenting it at the Company's office, together with a written notice signed by the Holder or its agent or attorney and stating the names and denominations in which new Warrants are to be issued.
Ex. 6 10. In the event of any disagreement between the Publisher and the Author regarding the interpretation of any of the terms of this Agreement, such dispute shall be referred for hearing and determination to three arbitrators, one to be appointed by the Publisher, one to be appointed by the Author, and the third to be appointed by the two aforesaid arbitrators. The decision of any two of said three arbitrators shall be final and binding upon the parties. **Publishing Contract from a book-publishing company**	**10. Binding Arbitration.** If the Publisher and the Author disagree about the interpretation of a term in this Agreement, they will refer their dispute to 3 arbitrators for a hearing and determination. The Publisher and the Author will each appoint 1 arbitrator. The 2 appointed arbitrators will appoint a third arbitrator. A decision made by 2 of the arbitrators is final and binding on the parties.

"'**Aforesaid.**' A revolting word that has little to recommend it. 'Aforesaid' and its companion, 'The said' whatever you please, accomplish nothing that cannot be dealt with by more exact reference." Richard Wincor, *Contracts in Plain English* 30 (1976).

NOT THIS:	BUT THIS:
Ex. 7 8.2 Neither Foundation nor University makes any warranty that the technology covered by any claim of any patent(s) resulting from Project will not infringe any third party patent and neither Foundation nor University makes any covenant either to defend any infringement charge by a third party or to institute action against infringers of said technology. Neither Foundation nor University makes any warranty of validity of any patent rights, or any other warranty, express or implied related in any way to said technology. **Research Agreement from a major university research foundation**	8.2 **No warranties.** Rocky Foundation and the University do not warrant the validity of any patent rights or any other warranty, express or implied, related to the technology. The Foundation and the University do not warrant that the technology covered by any patent claim resulting from the Project will not infringe any third-party patent. The Foundation and the University will not: (A) defend any infringement charge by a third party; or (B) sue infringers of the technology.

same, *pron.* Use the relevant noun or *it*, *they*, or *them*. When used as a pronoun, *same* imparts faux precision that can actually mask an ambiguity. It lacks the advantage of telling readers whether the antecedent is singular or plural. For an interesting story about how this use of *same* caused a constitutional crisis, see Antonin Scalia & Bryan A. Garner, *Reading Law: The Interpretation of Legal Texts* 144 (2012).

NOT THIS:	BUT THIS:
Ex. 1 No amendment or modification of this Agreement shall be valid unless the same is in writing and signed by the Employee and the Corporation. **Employment Agreement from a major law firm**	No amendment of this Agreement is valid unless it is in writing and signed by Steig and Mactronics.
Ex. 2 5. The undersigned state and agree that each has read and understands that this is a Release in accordance with its terms and each intends to be legally bound by same. **Release from a major automotive corporation**	5. **Binding Nature of Release.** Each party has read this Release, understands that it is a Release in accordance with its terms, and intends to be legally bound by it.

"'**Same.**' Here we have a word that turns up in all sorts of odd places like an unwelcome guest. 'The same XYZ Company' ranks no better than 'the said Company,' and 'XYZ Company will furnish same' ranks even lower. Same what? Business people frequently misuse this word under the impression that it sounds legal." Richard Wincor, *Contracts in Plain English* 31 (1976).

NOT THIS:	BUT THIS:
Ex. 3 13. Effect of Waiver. The failure of the Company at any time to require performance of any provision of this Agreement will in no manner affect the right to enforce the same. **Executive-Retirement Agreement and General Release of All Claims from a major automotive dealer**	13. **Effect of Waiver.** Even if Truance at any time fails to require performance of a provision of this Agreement, that will not affect Truance's right to enforce the provision later.
Ex. 4 4.1 Determination of Effective Date. This Agreement shall become effective and shall bind the parties hereto only after entry of an Order (the "Approval Order") by the State Court approving this Agreement and authorizing the Receiver to enter into the same. **Assignment Agreement (Bankruptcy) from a major law firm**	4.1 **Determination of effective date.** This Agreement will become effective and bind the parties if the state court approves it and enters an Order authorizing the Receiver to enter into it.

so [*verb* + *-ed*] **as to.** This phrase results in cumbersome sentences and unclear verbs. Use [*verb* + *-ed*] *to.*

NOT THIS:	BUT THIS:
Ex. 1 *ARTICLE EIGHT - FIRE AND OTHER CASUALTY INSURANCE* All of the insurance under this Article EIGHT shall be so issued as to cover the several interests of Landlord and Landlord's mortgagee(s). **Master Indenture of Lease**	8. **Fire and Other Casualty Insurance.** All insurance issued must cover the several interests of Landlord and Landlord's mortgagee.
Ex. 2 C. The manner of determining the due allowance from the contract price to be made where the loss is partial or the goods have so deteriorated as to no longer conform to the contract shall be as follows: [*Specification of procedure for determining allowance*]. **Sales Agreement from *Uniform Commercial Code Legal Forms* § 2:901**	(C) **Partial loss.** When only part of the goods are lost or too deteriorated to conform to the contract, the allowance from the contract price is calculated as: [*specification of procedure for determining allowance*].

"Not one . . . in a hundred of those who study for . . . the Bar thinks it incumbent upon him to learn how to write, read, and speak, although he will labor sedulously, with the help of the best masters, to obtain other needful knowledge." Edward W. Cox, *The Arts of Writing, Reading, and Speaking: Letters to a Law Student* 7 (1909).

NOT THIS:	BUT THIS:
Ex. 3 4. All lines, wires, cables and other facilities of the Company's system shall be so located as to cause minimum interference with the safe and proper use of the streets, and with the rights and reasonable convenience of property owners who adjoin any of said streets. All such lines, wires, cables and other facilities shall be maintained so as not to endanger the traveling public, shall be safely erected at a sufficient height so as to permit the passage of all vehicles traveling said roads, and shall be securely affixed and attached to any necessary poles, which poles shall be so located and placed so as not to obstruct traffic or present any safety hazard in and along said roads. **Agreement to Erect and Maintain a Cable-Television Service Line**	4. **Location of equipment.** The Company's lines, wires, cables, and other facilities must be located to cause no more interference than necessary with the safe and proper use of the streets and with the rights and reasonable convenience of adjoining-property owners. They must be safely erected at a height sufficient to permit the passage of all vehicles on the streets and be securely fastened to any necessary poles. The poles must not obstruct traffic or create a safety hazard. The lines, wires, cables, and other facilities must be maintained to ensure the safety of the traveling public.
Ex. 4 D. Lessee may contest the validity or amount of any tax in whole or in part, or endeavor to obtain a reduction of the assessed valuation for the purposes of reducing the Taxes, by an appropriate proceeding commenced and diligently conducted in good faith; provided, however, if the contest of valuation relates solely to the land, Lessee shall notify Lessor prior to commencing any lawsuit. Nothing herein contained, however, shall be so construed as to allow a challenged tax to remain unpaid for such length of time as shall create a lien on the Lessee Site or permit the Lessee Site or any part thereof to be sold by a governmental authority or other person for the non-payment of the same; and, if at any time it shall become necessary or proper so to do, Lessee shall pay the challenged tax, or so much thereof as may be required to prevent the sale or forfeiture of the Lessee Site, or any part thereof. **Ground-Lease Agreement**	(D) **Contest of taxes.** The Lessee may contest the validity or amount of any tax in whole or in part, or try to get the assessed value reduced for purposes of reducing the Taxes, by an appropriate proceeding begun and conducted diligently in good faith. But if the contest about the assessed value relates solely to the land, the Lessee must notify the Owner before filing a lawsuit. (E) **No tax liens.** This Agreement does not allow a challenged tax to remain unpaid if the Lessee's failure to pay would create a lien on the Lessee Site or permit all or part of the Lessee Site to be sold by a government authority or other person for the nonpayment of the tax. The Lessee must pay the challenged tax or as much of it as necessary to prevent the sale or forfeiture of part or all of the Lessee Site.

subsequent to. The phrase is a legal pomposity. Use *after* instead.

NOT THIS:	BUT THIS:
Ex. 1 The lump-sum payments provided for in this Article are payable to each employee who has retired or died subsequent to the beginning of the applicable base period. **Employment Contract**	The lump-sum payments provided for in this section are payable to each employee who has retired or died after the beginning of the applicable base period.

NOT THIS:	BUT THIS:
Ex. 2 Section 8 – Eligibility for Receipt of Lump Sum Payments The lump sum cost-of-living payments provided for in this Article will be payable to each employee subject to this Agreement who has an employment relationship as of the dates such payments are made or has retired or died subsequent to the beginning of the applicable base period used to determine the amount of such payments. **Employment Agreement from a railroad company**	8. **Eligibility to Receive Lump-Sum Payments.** Lump-sum cost-of-living payments will be payable under this section to each employee who is employed on the date payments are made or has retired or died after the beginning of the applicable base period used to determine the payment amount.
Ex. 3 (b) If termination occurs within one (1) year after a Change in Control of Employer or Bank, then as severance pay and in lieu of any further compensation for periods subsequent to the effective date of such termination, Executive shall receive, within thirty (30) days following such termination, an amount in cash equal to 2.99 times his "annualized includable compensation for the base period" (as defined in Section 280G(d)(1) of the Internal Revenue Code of 1986, as amended (the "Code")). **Employment Agreement from a banking corporation**	(B) **Timing and compensation.** If termination occurs within 1 year after a Change in Control of Employer or Bank, Macpherson will receive—within 30 days after his termination—cash equal to 2.99 times his annualized includable compensation for the base period (as defined in § 280G(d)(1) of the Internal Revenue Code of 1986, as amended) as severance pay and in lieu of further compensation for periods after his termination date.

"Unfortunately, many lawyers have tended not only to downgrade important aspects of drafting but to think of themselves as individually accomplished in this respect. It is hard to sell people new clothes if they consider themselves already well accoutered." Reed Dickerson, *The Fundamentals of Legal Drafting* § 1.1, at 2 (2d ed. 1986).

such, *adj.* Use *the*, *this*, or *that*—unless *such* is used in the literate nonlawyer's sense "of that general type" (e.g., *such auctions* means "auctions of that kind").

There is more balderdash afoot about the supposed preciseness of *such* and *said* than about any other drafting convention apart from definitions. Neither *such* nor *said* adds precision, as legal scholars and commentators have long noted.[11] The danger is that these words, when used as demonstrative adjectives (for example, *such property*, *said Company*), make drafters think they're being precise when they really aren't. And the terms are pure legalese: you can always improve on them with ordinary words that are every bit as precise.

NOT THIS:	BUT THIS:
Ex. 1 The invalidity of a provision hereof or thereof in a particular jurisdiction shall not invalidate or render unenforceable such provision in any other jurisdiction. **Extension Agreement from a major aerospace and defense company**	The invalidity of a provision in this Agreement in a given jurisdiction does not render it invalid or unenforceable in any other jurisdiction.
Ex. 2 On the basis of such reviews, the Company has reasonably concluded that such associated costs and liabilities would not have, singularly or in the aggregate, a Material Adverse Effect. **Underwriting Agreement from an investment-banking firm**	Based on these reviews, the Company has reasonably concluded that the associated costs and liabilities would not have, singularly or in the aggregate, a Material Adverse Effect.
Ex. 3 (iv) The definition of "Security Documents" set forth in Section 1.01 of the Credit Agreement is hereby amended by adding the text ", the First Refinancing Amendment Reaffirmation Agreement" after the text "the Mortgages" appearing in such definition. **Refinancing-and-Incremental-Facility Amendment from a major computer-technology company**	(D) **Definitional amendment.** The definition of "Security Documents" in § 1.1 of the Credit Agreement is amended by adding the text ", the First Refinancing Amendment Agreement" after the text "the Mortgages" appearing in the definition.

11 *See, e.g.*, Peter M. Tiersma, *Legal Language* 91 (1999) ("The legal profession's long retention of *said*, *aforesaid*, *same*, and *such* cannot be justified as adding precision or clarity to the text."); David Mellinkoff, *The Language of the Law* 319 (1963) ("Though some lay critics tell us that, worthless elsewhere, *said* is 'traditional' and 'permissible' in the law, it is either unnecessary or dangerous, and should be dropped."). *See also Garner's Modern English Usage* 873 (4th ed. 2016) ("[C]ontrary to what some think, *such* isn't any more precise than *the*, *that*, or *those*.").

NOT THIS:	BUT THIS:
Ex. 4 (iii) Taxes. On the applicable Closing Date, all stock transfer or other taxes (other than income taxes) that are required to be paid in connection with the sale and transfer by such Selling Stockholder of the Shares will be fully paid or provided for by such Selling Stockholder and all laws imposing such taxes will be fully complied with. **Underwriting Agreement from a designer and manufacturer of compact construction equipment**	(3) **Taxes.** On the applicable Closing Date, the Selling Stockholder will: (a) fully pay or provide for all stock-transfer or other taxes (other than income taxes) required in connection with this sale and transfer; and (b) comply with all laws imposing those taxes.
Ex. 5 8. Should the Player suffer an injury as provided in the preceding paragraph, he will submit himself to a medical examination and treatment by a physician designated by the Club. Such examination when made at the request of the Club shall be at its expense, unless made necessary by some act or conduct of the Player contrary to the terms of this contract. **Player Contract for a professional basketball player**	**8. Medical Examinations.** If Calducci suffers an injury under § 7, he must see a Club-designated physician for a medical examination and treatment. If the Club requests the examination, the Club will pay for it unless it is necessary because of conduct by Calducci that is contrary to this Agreement.

such [*noun* + *-s*] **as.** Use *any* [*noun*] (*that*) or *a* [*noun*] (*that*).

NOT THIS:	BUT THIS:
Ex. 1 The terminating shareholder shall execute and deliver to the Corporation such instruments as are necessary and proper to transfer full and complete title. **Stockholders Agreement from a major healthcare-facility developer**	The terminating shareholder must sign and deliver to the Corporation any instrument that is necessary to transfer full and complete title.
Ex. 2 The Depositary will transmit to the Record Holders of Receipts at the Corporation's expense, including applicable fees, such other documents as may be requested by the Corporation. **Deposit Agreement between two major financial-services corporations**	At the Corporation's expense (including applicable fees), the Depositary will send to the Record Holders of Receipts all other documents that the Corporation requests.

> "A liberal sprinkling of the word 'such' through a document does indeed give it a lawyer-like flavor. It is, however, a flavor to be avoided." Carl Felsenfeld & Alan Siegel, *Writing Contracts in Plain English* 145 (1981).

NOT THIS:	BUT THIS:
Ex. 3 d) The Representatives shall have received from Mitchell Campbell LLP, counsel for the Underwriters, such opinion or opinions, dated the Closing Date, with respect to the issuance and sale of the Securities, this Agreement, the Indenture, the Registration Statement, the Disclosure Package, the Prospectus and other related matters as the Representatives may reasonably require, and the Company shall have furnished to such counsel such documents as they request for the purpose of enabling them to pass upon such matters. **Underwriting Agreement from a major food-processing and commodities-trading corporation**	(D) **Legal opinions.** Mitchell Campbell LLP, counsel for the Underwriters, will give the Representatives an opinion or opinions (dated on the Closing Date) about (1) the issuance and sale of the Securities, (2) this Agreement, (3) the Indenture, (4) the Registration Statement, (5) the Disclosure Package, (6) the Prospectus, and (7) other related matters that the Representatives may reasonably require. Scott will give Mitchell Campbell LLP any documents that it requests for the purpose of passing on the matters.

telecopy and facsimile. Both nouns mean the same thing. Try *fax*. But note that scanned PDFs are now the norm, not faxes. Almost any provision referring to faxes should probably also refer to e-mails and scans.

NOT THIS:	BUT THIS:
Ex. 1 Facsimiles of signatures shall constitute acceptable, binding signatures for purposes of this Agreement. **Settlement Agreement between the Department of Justice and a major financial institution**	For purposes of this Agreement, faxed and scanned signatures are acceptable and binding. Note that scanning ought to be acceptable as well.
Ex. 2 Facsimile or photocopied signatures shall be considered as valid signatures as of the date affixed, although the original signature pages shall thereafter be appended. **Settlement Agreement between a state government and major tobacco manufacturers**	Faxed, photocopied, and scanned signatures are valid as of the date affixed, as long as the original signature pages are appended later.
Ex. 3 Notices. All notices or other communications to any party to this Agreement shall be in writing (including, but not limited to, facsimile, telex, telecopy or similar writing) and shall be given at the addresses specified in Exhibit P. **Master Settlement Agreement between 40 states and a major tobacco manufacturer**	**Notices.** A notice or formal communication to a party to this Agreement must be in writing (including by fax or scan) and given at the addresses in Exhibit P.

NOT THIS:	BUT THIS:
Ex. 4 Section 9.2 Notices. All notices and other communications hereunder shall be in writing and shall be deemed to have been duly given or made by a party hereto only upon receipt by the receiving party at the following addresses (if mailed) or the following telecopy numbers (if delivered by facsimile), or at such other address or telecopy number for a party as shall be specified by like notice: . . . . **Merger Agreement from a major entertainment-industry company**	9.2 **Notices.** Notices and communications under this Agreement must be in writing and sent to the appropriate address, fax number, or e-mail address below. They are considered duly given or made by a party only upon the other party's receipt. A party must notify the other party of any address, fax-number, or e-mail changes.

term. Be careful about using this word in more than one sense—to mean both "a period of time" and "a contractual provision." See *provisions of.*

terms of. See *provisions of.*

therefor. This word means "for it," "for them," or "for that." A nonlawyer might misread the word as *therefore* ("consequently"; "for that reason"). Avoid altogether—often merely by deleting it.

NOT THIS:	BUT THIS:
Ex. 1 Procedural details relating to the issue and delivery of Securities, the solicitation of offers to purchase Securities and the payment in each case therefor shall be as set forth in the Administrative Procedure attached hereto as Annex II as it may be amended from time to time by written agreement between the Agents and the Company. **Distribution Agreement from a global innovation company**	Procedural details about the issue and delivery of Securities, the solicitation of offers to purchase Securities, and the payment in each case are set forth in the Administrative Procedure attached to this Agreement as Annex II. The Administrative Procedure may be amended by a written agreement between the Agents and Montoya LLC.
Ex. 2 (b) Cancellation of Dissenting Shares. Each Dissenting Share shall, as a result of the Merger and without any action on the part of the holder of such Dissenting Share, cease to be outstanding, be cancelled without payment of any consideration therefor and shall cease to exist, subject to any rights the holder thereof may have pursuant to Section 4.2(g) and the Texas Business Organizations Code. **Merger Agreement between a major Internet-based retailer and a major grocery chain**	(B) **Cancellation of Dissenting Shares.** Each Dissenting Share will, as a result of the Merger and without action by the holder of the Dissenting Share, cease to be outstanding, be canceled without payment of any consideration, and cease to exist, subject to any rights the holder may have under § 4.2(G) and the Texas Business Organizations Code.

NOT THIS:	BUT THIS:
Ex. 3 2. Rights of Company and Affiliates. This Award Agreement does not affect the right of the Company or any Affiliate to take any corporate action whatsoever, including without limitation its right to recapitalize, reorganize or make other changes in its capital structure or business, merge or consolidate, issue bonds, notes, shares of Common Stock or other securities, including preferred stock, or options therefore, dissolve or liquidate, or sell or transfer any part of its assets or business. Note that *therefor* is also spelled incorrectly. **Stock-Option-Award Agreement from a major payroll-outsourcing company**	**2. Rights of Company and Affiliates.** This Award Agreement does not affect the right of the Company or an Affiliate to take corporate action, including its right to recapitalize, reorganize, or make other changes in its capital structure or business; to merge or consolidate; to issue bonds, notes, shares of Common Stock or other securities, including preferred stock or options; or to dissolve, liquidate, sell, or transfer any part of its assets or business.
Ex. 4 We understand and agree that the above escrow services and closing statement do not include any representation of, or express or implied warranty regarding, the assets of the business sold and that the Escrow Agent and Attorney preparing the closing documents assume no responsibility for the condition of title, sufficiency of instruments conveying title, consideration paid therefor, payment of utilities, receipt or delivery of possession of the business and its assets, future performance of the parties to the purchase and sale, transfer of any insurance policies, leases, or other executory agreements, or any other matters related to the purchase and sale of the above described business, and that all costs, if any, that are not included in this closing statement are designated as out-of-escrow expenses and become the express responsibility of the parties to this Agreement. **Sale-and-Purchase-of-Business Agreement from 1 S. Lee Stevenson Jr., *Texas Legal Practice Forms* § 5:90, at 5-147 (2d ed. 1992)**	The escrow services and closing statement do not include an express or implied warranty about the assets of the business sold. Any costs not included in this closing statement are out-of-escrow expenses and become the parties' responsibility. The Escrow Agent and Attorney preparing the closing documents assume no responsibility for: • the condition of title; • the sufficiency of instruments conveying title; • the consideration paid; • the payment of utilities; • the receipt or delivery of the business and its assets; • the future performance of the parties to the purchase and sale; • the transfer of any insurance policies, leases, other executory agreements; or • other matters related to the purchase and sale of the business.

therein; thereof; thereto. See *herein.*

there is; there are. Generally avoid. Use only if you must refer explicitly to the *existence* of something and no other phrasing will work.[12] There are two things wrong—no, two things are wrong—with *there is* and *there are* in legal drafting. First, these sentence-openers obscure the subject and predicate. Second, they allow the

12 *See* Garner, *The Elements of Legal Style* 143 (2d ed. 2002).

writer to avoid saying precisely who has the duty to do what. As a result, the sentence becomes less clear.

NOT THIS:	BUT THIS:
Ex. 1 There is no fact known to the Seller that has specific application to the Shares . . . . **Stock-Purchase Agreement from a luxury-goods and textiles company**	The Seller knows of no fact that has specific application to the Shares . . . .
Ex. 2 Because of the difficulty of ascertaining damages, there shall be payable to the Landlord the sum of $5,000.00 liquidated damages for each such breach. **Commercial Lease from a property-management company**	Because of the difficulty of ascertaining exact damages, Newsome will pay Finsser $5,000 in liquidated damages for each breach.
Ex. 3 There are no significant arbitration decisions, settlement agreements, injunctions, consent decrees, or conciliation agreements which affect the operation of the Business other than those specifically listed in Appendix 2.01(k) to Sellers' Disclosure Letter. **Asset-Purchase Agreement**	No significant arbitration decisions, settlement agreements, injunctions, consent decrees, or conciliation agreements—other than those listed in Appendix 2.1(K) to Sellers' Disclosure Letter—affect the Business's operation.
Ex. 4 In the event that there is a transfer of a substantial portion of the stock or assets of the Customer that is not in the ordinary course of business, Customer shall cause the acquiring party to ratify this Agreement and assume all of the obligations of Customer hereunder. **Marketing Agreement from a major beverage company**	If Marshall transfers a substantial part of its stock or assets outside the ordinary course of business, the acquiring party must ratify this Agreement and assume all obligations under it.
Ex. 5 Except for Subsidiary Corporation, a Colorado corporation ("*Subsidiary*"), there is no corporation, partnership, joint venture, business trust or other legal entity in which Seller Corp., either directly or indirectly through one or more intermediaries, owns or holds beneficial or record ownership of at least a majority of the outstanding voting shares. **Stock-Purchase Agreement**	Except for Telemix Corporation, a Colorado corporation, Landler Technologies neither owns nor holds beneficial or record ownership of a majority of the outstanding voting shares of any corporation, partnership, joint venture, business trust, or other legal entity—either directly or indirectly through one or more intermediaries.

"One of the virtues of intensive, systematic, and specialized across-the-board checks is that even where they are applied to what appear to be only stylistic aspects of the instrument they often expose substantive discrepancies." Reed Dickerson, *The Fundamentals of Legal Drafting* § 4.9, at 65 (2d ed. 1986).

to wit. Delete altogether or prefer the plain-English *namely* to this archaic phrase.

NOT THIS:	BUT THIS:
Ex. 1 The Buyer hereby agrees to purchase, and pay to the Seller, as consideration for the conveyance to him of the above-described real property, the sum of Fifteen Thousand Dollars and Zero Cents ($15,000.00) in the manner following to-wit: cash at closing. **Real-Estate-Sale Contract**	Maryvale will purchase the real property described above and pay Holland $15,000 in cash at closing.
Ex. 2 If not otherwise specified herein, then the following plumbing fixtures and materials are to be furnished and installed, to wit: . . . . **Standard Form of Plumbing Bid and Contract**	If not specified otherwise, Stockard's Plumbing Outfitters will furnish and install the following plumbing fixtures and materials: . . . .

transmit. A pompous word. Use *send.*

NOT THIS:	BUT THIS:
Ex. 1 10. Notices. All notices and other communications transmitted hereunder shall be in writing and effective only upon receipt. **Underwriting Agreement from a major airline**	**10. Notices.** A notice or other communication sent under this Agreement must be in writing. It is effective on receipt.
Ex. 2 (e) Conformity with EDGAR Filing. The Prospectus delivered to the Agent for use in connection with the sale of the Placement Shares pursuant to this Agreement will be identical to the versions of the Prospectus created to be transmitted to the Commission for filing via EDGAR, except to the extent permitted by Regulation S-T. **Pharmaceutical Company Stock-Sales Agreement**	(E) **Conformity with EDGAR filing.** The Prospectus delivered to the Agent for use with the sale of the Placement Shares under this Agreement must be identical to the Prospectus sent to the Commission for filing via EDGAR, except to the extent permitted by Regulation S-T.

For more on *pursuant to,* see § 149, pp. 437–38.

> "Few things sound as lawyerly as the phrase *to wit*, and beyond sounding lawyerly, it fulfills absolutely no function." Peter M. Tiersma, *Legal Language* 91 (1999).

NOT THIS:	BUT THIS:
Ex. 3 Any notice or other communication is deemed to have been given, if sent by fax or by e-mail, on the date of transmission, if transmitted before 3.00 p.m. (local time at the place of destination) on any Business Day and in any other case on the Business Day, following the date of transmission. **Merger Protocol between courier-delivery-services companies**	A faxed or e-mailed notice or other formal communication is considered given on the date sent if sent before 3.00 p.m. (in the destination's local time) on any Business Day, and in any other case on the next Business Day after the date sent.

utilize. Try the verb *use* instead. And instead of *utilization*, try the noun *use*.

NOT THIS:	BUT THIS:
Ex. 1 4.1 All arbitration proceedings under this Agreement shall be heard by a panel of three arbitrators unless the parties mutually agree to utilize a single arbitrator. **Consulting-Services Agreement from a major beverage company**	**4.1 Number of arbitrators.** Unless the parties agree to use 1 arbitrator, a panel of 3 arbitrators will hear an arbitration proceeding under this Agreement.
Ex. 2 2. <u>Work Order.</u> This contract does not obligate Alpango to request or utilize the Services of Contractor nor does it obligate Contractor to accept a Work Order issued by Alpango. **Master Service Agreement from a major oil company**	2. **Work Order.** Under this contract, Alpango need not request or use Mellinger's services, and Mellinger is not obligated to accept a Work Order issued by Alpango.
Ex. 3 **17.4 Export.** I agree not to export, directly or indirectly, any U.S. technical data acquired from the Company or any products utilizing such data, to countries outside the United States, except in compliance with applicable export laws or regulations. **Assignment Agreement from a major software-development company**	7.4 **Export.** You must not export, directly or indirectly, any U.S. technical data acquired from Digitronics, or any products using this data, to countries outside the United States unless you comply with applicable export laws and regulations.
Ex. 4 16.5 <u>Restrictions of Foreign Carriers.</u> Foreign administrations may impose certain limitations, prohibitions or restrictions that may limit the ability of customers to utilize Pixel Plus products or services. The customer must conform to any limitations, prohibitions, or restrictions imposed by the foreign administration. **Master Services Agreement from a telecommunications company**	**16.5 Foreign-carrier restrictions.** Foreign administrations may impose certain limitations, prohibitions, or restrictions that could affect the customer's ability to use Pixel Plus products or services. The customer must conform to these limitations, prohibitions, or restrictions.

Note that *mutually* is superfluous. *Agree* is sufficient.

On the use of second-person instead of first-person, see § 55.

whereas. In the sense "given the fact that," *whereas* is the archetypal legalism and should be avoided. Instead, use a simple heading above all the recitals. Use straightforward, complete sentences to introduce each recital.

NOT THIS:	BUT THIS:
Ex. 1 Whereas, Licensor has developed an HD audio encoder and decoder and certain related software and documentation, defined as the Licensed Software below. Whereas, Licensee has developed Licensee Products (as defined below). Whereas, Licensee desires to license the Licensed Software, to conduct internal interoperability testing and to distribute the Licensed Licensed Software as a component of the Licensee Products. Whereas, Licensor is willing to license the Licensed Software to Licensee for such use under the terms and conditions of this Agreement. **Software-License, -Development, and -Distribution Agreement from a major digital-technology company**	**Background** • Pilon has developed an HD audio encoder and decoder and certain related software and documentation. • Refrangix has developed a line of products in which the software could be useful. • Refrangix would like to license Pilon's encoder and decoder to conduct internal interoperability testing, and to distribute the software as a component of its products. • Pilon will license the software to Refrangix on the terms set forth in this Agreement.
Ex. 2 WHEREAS: 1. XCo and YCo have each requested the other to make available confidential information concerning the other and their respective business for the purpose of evaluating a joint venture or other business relationship between them in the field of medical training and/or medical equipment (the "**Transaction**"). 2. The Parties agree to exchange such confidential information subject to the provisions of this Agreement. **Confidentiality Agreement from a major law firm**	**Background** • XCo and YCo are considering a joint-venture or other business relationship between them in the field of medical training, medical equipment, or both. • XCo and YCo have each asked the other to make available confidential information about each other and each other's business to evaluate the joint-venture or other business relationship. • XCo and YCo have agreed to exchange this confidential information under this Agreement.

Licensed Licensed Software appears to be an obvious typo.

On the use of bullets, see § 90.

"Nearly every book on legal drafting has declared that *whereas* clauses are obsolete. If you're still using the word, look it up in a drafting text." Wayne Schiess, *Writing for the Legal Audience* 125 (2003).

NOT THIS:	BUT THIS:
Ex. 3 ESCROW AGREEMENT AGREEMENT made this [*ordinal number of day*] day of [*name of month*], [*designation of year*], between [*name of seller*], a [*state of incorporation*] limited partnership (the "Seller"), [*name of purchaser*], a [*state of incorporation*] corporation, (the "Purchaser") and [*name of escrow agent*] (the "Escrow Agent"). WITNESSETH: WHEREAS, the Seller is the owner of certain property located described on Exhibit [*designation of exhibit*] attached hereto (referred to as the "Premises" and the "Property"); and WHEREAS, Seller has contracted to sell and Purchaser has contracted to purchase the Premises pursuant to a certain Agreement for Purchase and Sale (the "Contract") and, WHEREAS, the Contract requires the payment of a $[*dollar amount of deposit*] deposit; and WHEREAS, the parties have agreed to place $[*dollar amount in escrow*] in escrow with the Escrow Agent as additional security for Purchaser's performance. NOW, THEREFORE, for good and valuable consideration, the receipt of which is hereby acknowledged, the parties hereto agree as follows: . . . **Escrow Agreement from 21 Stuart M. Saft, *West's Legal Forms: Commercial Real Estate Transactions* § 16:6, at 282 (4th ed. 2012)**	**Escrow Agreement** **Effective Date:** March 26, 2019 **Parties:** Seller: McAlester Properties, Inc. Buyer: Shoumaker & Brewer (S&B) Escrow Agent: Prudential Land Inc. **Background for Escrow Agreement:** McAlester owns and wishes to sell the property described in the attached Exhibit A. S&B wishes to purchase that property according to the Agreement for Purchase and Sale ("Contract"). The deposit required by the Contract is $10,000. To secure S&B's payment, McAlester and S&B agree to place $5,000 in escrow with Prudential. [The original doesn't make it clear who is paying the escrow amount.] **The parties agree as follows:** **The Agreement** . . .

"The draftsman should not shrink from a useful format merely because it is untraditional." Reed Dickerson, *Materials on Legal Drafting* 298 (1981).

witnesseth. This archaism is a traditional but worthless flourish. *Witnesseth* is not a command, as often assumed: it's a Middle-English third-person verb now written "witnesses."[13] It's a remnant of the phrasing *This Agreement, by and between X and Y, witnesseth that, whereas* . . . Gradually the surrounding language got truncated. There's absolutely no reason to retain *witnesseth.* It's best deleted in modern contracts.

NOT THIS:	BUT THIS:
Ex. 1 **AMENDED AND RESTATED EMPLOYMENT AGREEMENT** THIS AMENDED AND RESTATED EMPLOYMENT AGREEMENT ("***Agreement***") is entered into by and between MEDIA MASTERS INC. ("***Media Masters***" or the "***Company***"), and CURTIS MAHONEY ("***Executive***"). Media Masters and Executive may hereinafter be referred to jointly as the "***Parties.***" **WITNESSETH:** **WHEREAS,** Executive and the Company previously entered into an employment agreement, as amended from time to time, dated September 12, 2017 (the "***Original Effective Date***"); and **WHEREAS,** the Parties desire to amend and restate the employment agreement on the terms and conditions set forth herein. **NOW, THEREFORE,** in consideration of the mutual covenants contained herein, the Parties agree upon the following terms of employment of Executive by the Company: **Amended and Restated Employment Agreement between major movie retailer and company executive**	**Amended and Restated Employment Agreement** This Amended and Restated Employment Agreement is between Media Masters Inc., and Curtis Mahoney. **Background** • Mahoney and Media Masters previously entered into an employment agreement dated September 12, 2017 (the "Original Effective Date"). That agreement has been amended at different times since the Original Effective Date. • Mahoney and Media Masters want to amend and restate the employment agreement. **The Agreement** The parties agree as follows: . . . .

13 *See Garner's Dictionary of Legal Usage* 950 (3d ed. 2011).

NOT THIS:	BUT THIS:
Ex. 2 1. WITNESSETH: That the said Contractor, having been awarded the contract for Little Zoo Choo Choo Track Project Elkhart, Oklahoma In accordance with the proposal therefore, which is bound herewith and for and in consideration of the premises and of the covenants and agreements and of the payments herein specified to be made and performed by the Owner. The Contractor hereby covenants and agrees with the Owner to undertake and execute all of the said work in good, substantial and workmanlike manner, and to furnish all the materials and all tools and labor necessary to properly perform and complete the work ready for use in strict accordance with the plans and specifications, and any revisions thereto in effect at the same time of signing this contract and to accept as full compensation the amount of One Million One Hundred Fourteen Thousand Eight Hundred and Eighty-Four Dollars in same as the attached price quote. **Contract for work on a railroad track**	**The Agreement** 1. **Contractor.** Lehigh Construction, Inc. has been awarded the contract for the Little Zoo Choo-Choo Track Project in Elkhart, Oklahoma. 2. **Financing.** Lehigh's proposal for the Project is attached to this Agreement. Charles Burke, as the owner of Little Zoo, will make the payments specified in the proposal. 3. **Contractor's Performance.** Lehigh will perform the specified work in a good, substantial, and workmanlike manner. It will furnish all the materials, tools, and labor necessary to properly perform and complete the work in strict accordance with the plans and specifications and any revisions to them in effect when this Agreement is signed. 4. **Contractor's Payment.** Burke will pay Lehigh $1,114,884 for the work, as stated in the attached price quote.

§ 150 Know where to find answers to usage questions not covered here.

For matters not covered in these guidelines, please refer to the works listed in the Select Bibliography. On matters of word usage, see especially the current versions of *The Redbook: A Manual on Legal Style*; *Garner's Dictionary of Legal Usage*; *Garner's Modern English Usage*; and *The Chicago Manual of Style*.

On matters of capitalization, compounding, hyphenation, and other mechanical matters, contracts should follow the modern style used by mainstream works of nonfiction. Stay within the bounds of refined English usage of the day—avoiding gratuitous capitalization and other frequent quirks of contractual prose.

> "Lawyers have two common failings. One is that they do not write well, and the other is that they think they do." Carl Felsenfeld, *The Plain English Movement in the United States*, 6 Can. Bus. L.J. 408, 413 (1981–82).

Conclusion

Effective contract drafting isn't easy. It requires hard work—just as all other good writing does. In the end, though, if you acquire this skill and hone it, not only will you be writing much better than most transactional lawyers do, but you'll also be thinking better.

Plain English, the major component of effectiveness in this field, is a matter of good mental hygiene. It's an acquired skill—a habit, really—that is more in demand than ever. Many contracts are now required to be in plain English: franchise agreements and, in many states, consumer contracts and insurance policies.

The legal profession is changing. The way people communicate with each other is changing. As the world becomes increasingly complex, and as information about our world becomes increasingly complex, people yearn for straightforward simplicity. Simple words. Direct sentences. Intelligibility.

Don't ever oversimplify. Just say things as simply and straightforwardly as you can.

APPENDIX A

Statements of Work

Understand the main goals of a statement of work.

(A) **Definition.** A statement of work (SOW[1]) is a contractual document—usually contained in an attachment and incorporated by reference into a broader master agreement (sometimes called a "frame agreement")—defining precisely what one party, such as a supplier or service provider, will do for the other to further a particular project. It typically covers such items as the nature of and standards for deliverables, quality assurance, inspection, and acceptance. An SOW is crucial to making a contract workable, and a good one will save managers time and companies money.

SOWs can run the gamut from simple one-page sets of requirements for building a website to exceedingly long and detailed specifications for building a spacecraft. In what follows, the assumption is that the SOW is a stand-alone attachment to a contract, as opposed to a provision or set of provisions within a contract.

(B) **Objectives.** An SOW must clearly and concisely explain the work to be accomplished. Its broad goal is to provide enough concrete detail to convey what must be done by whom and when, without so much detail as to plunge the reader into the technical weeds. It should outline with reasonable specificity the work to be done, the expected product or result, the employees who are to be involved in the project, the various parties' responsibilities, and so forth. It should be in plain English: a nontechnician (e.g., a contract manager or a judge) should be able to understand what's essential to a successful contractual performance. It should also be accurate: grammatical, consistent, and correct in all cross-references, both internally to the SOW and externally to the master agreement.

(C) **Subordination to agreement.** Nothing in the SOW should change—or purport to change—the master agreement's terms. The SOW must remain subordinate to the master agreement: it just sets forth what must be done and when. The contract itself should contain language making the SOW binding on the burdened party and enforceable by the benefited party. Of course, if there's a seeming discrepancy between the master agreement and the SOW, anyone interpreting the two should, if

1 The term generally used is the initialism *SOW*, normally pronounced /ess-oh-**dəb**-əl-yoo/. The term is sometimes (much less commonly) pronounced as an acronym (/soh/, not /sow/).

possible, try to read them harmoniously. Ideally, the contract and the SOW should expressly refer to each other.

Like a contract, an SOW should provide that it can be changed only by amendment or by a written change order. Any amendment or change order should refer explicitly to the clause being changed.

Think about the specific goals of your SOW.

(A) **The basic elements: who, what, when, where.** Begin by identifying the parties. Refer at the outset to the master agreement to which the SOW is attached. Specify the SOW's effective date. Then describe the ultimate goal of the work to be performed: the expected end result by a specified date. Specify the responsibilities of each party: the language must clearly allocate responsibility for each task to one party or the other. Arrange the SOW to progress from a big-picture description to narrower specifics. For example, a tech company might want a contractor develop a component with certain features. State that, and then break it down into the following project-specific elements:

- A recitation of the parties involved (mirroring the parties to the contract).
- The names of organizational representatives, so that lines of responsibility are clear.
- A high-level description of the project.
- A brief chronological list of the work to be performed.
- The timing (milestones) for completion for each task, whether by relative times (e.g., within 60 days of some event) or hard deadlines (e.g., 5:00 p.m. EDT on May 1 of a specific year).
- Explicit identification of any tasks that are interdependent, and how they are interdependent.
- The cost of each task, broken down as appropriate—payments being earned according to milestones reached (consider making a table for milestones).
- Specific limitations or exceptions.
- The criteria for the acceptance of each deliverable—preferably objective criteria subject to verification.
- A change-order procedure that allows flexibility for changes that become necessary.
- An escalation path for any technical problems encountered.
- Project-level breach provisions aligning with overarching breach provisions within the master agreement.

You may want to consider additional terms for on-site visits while the work is ongoing. Other possibilities might involve additional expenses for travel, additional training requirements, and visa requirements for foreigners.

(B) **Things to exclude.** Avoid including legal provisions such as warranties and limitations of liability: these should be in the master agreement itself, not the SOW, which shouldn't contain any hidden legal provisions.

(C) **Consistency with master contract.** Review the SOW carefully for how it aligns with the master agreement—and any other attachments to that agreement. Ensure that nothing in the SOW conflicts in any way with the master agreement. Don't attempt to override the master agreement in the SOW; instead, that would require an amendment to the master agreement.

Avoid the common pitfalls in SOWs.

(A) **Failing to set forth clear goals.** Sometimes a service provider will have a "form SOW" that describes in vague language various actions it plans to take but never really says, from the counterparty's viewpoint, what the ultimate objective is. That's a poor approach. If the goal, for example, is editorial software that uses artificial intelligence to translate suboptimal documents into plain-English equivalents without substantive change, then say so with some specificity.

(B) **Failing to apportion responsibilities clearly.** Don't make parties jointly responsible for deliverables. There must be a clear delineation of who is to deliver what by when.

Not this: The block must not contain more than . . .
But this: Customer will ensure that the block does not contain more than . . .

Not this: Vendor's contract is required to . . .
But this: Vendor will require that its contractor . . .

Not this: The logic library will be designed with the architectural features to allow it to be interoperable with Acme 10nm 12DG library.
But this: Vendor will design the logic library with architectural features allowing it to be interoperable with Acme 10nm 12DG library.

Not this: The patent block must meet the following requirements: . . .
But this: Vendor will ensure that the patent block meets the following requirements: . . .
Not this: The schedule will set forth . . .
But this: The parties will agree to a schedule setting forth . . .

Keep in mind that because you're so intimately involved in the project, some points may seem obvious to you that may not be so clear to an outsider. The allocation of responsibility must be explicit and fully understandable to a stranger to the deal. For the same reasons, avoid language that merely expresses wishes or desires. Don't use *should*, *would like to*, *wants*, or *wishes*: these so-called *precatory words* create uncertainty about whether an action is required.

Not this: The flowchart should be able to show the relevant criteria for generating design collaterals.
But this: Customer will ensure that the flowchart shows the relevant criteria for generating design collaterals.

Not this: The qualification schedule should feed into the overall project schedule.
But this: The parties will create a qualification schedule comporting with the overall project schedule.

(C) **Rehashing topics already covered in the master agreement.** If you start repeating things that are covered in the master agreement, you're performing not only an unnecessary task but a dangerous one: you're creating the very real possibility of introducing inconsistencies. You're also complicating the process of amendment. Plus, you're not recognizing the limited purposes of an SOW as opposed to the broader legal purposes of the master agreement. In any event, all substantive questions such as ownership, as well as assurances and guarantees, belong in the master agreement, not in the SOW.

An SOW shouldn't address who owns or is entitled to use the outcome of the work performed—or, for that matter, any of the parties' other legal rights. But the question of ownership is sometimes muddied in an SOW using the word *owns* in the colloquial sense of "is responsible for" or "has responsibility for developing." Don't say *Acme owns the design block* if you mean *Acme is responsible for developing the design block.*

(D) **Failing to distinguish hard vs. soft deadlines.** Some deadlines are more important than others. You can use the terms *hard deadline* and *soft deadline* to distinguish them. Consider the difference between "Acme will deliver the block by December 4, 2018" and "Acme will target early December for delivery of the block." You may want to give yourself some flexibility. For example, a company and its contractor may prefer to complete a project before the end of the third quarter of the year even though for legal purposes, the project need only be completed before year's end. The parties could say: "Contractor must use commercially reasonable efforts to complete the project before September 30, 2018, and in any event must complete the project on or before December 31, 2018." Alternatively, if the parties want to give the soft deadline more "teeth," the same sentence could be restyled to offer an incentive for achieving the earlier deadline (or to impose a disincentive for failing to do so): "Contractor must complete the project no later than December 31, 2018. If Contractor completes the project before September 30, 2018, the overall contract price will be raised by 10%."

(E) **Lacking specificity.** If you want to buy an oak tree and you ask to buy a "tree," it's hard to complain when the seller delivers a pine. Similarly, if you want a 2,500-square-foot house with three bedrooms and two and a half bathrooms, you surely wouldn't sign a contract with a builder to erect a "reasonably sized house, with adequate plumbing." You'd be much more specific, whether buying goods or services. If service is an important aspect of the deal, specify the timing of various levels of services. Some will be more important than others. The point is to avoid vagueness when you know the specifics of what you require. Specificity, as opposed to generality, will make both parties happier because it fosters genuine understanding and performance standards. Contractors want to know what they're expected to do, and customers want to know what they're paying for.

(F) **Failing to have adequate drafting safeguards.** Writing unmistakably, in an SOW or elsewhere, is a challenge. Many SOWs fail for too much generality, vagueness, or downright ambiguity. You must take enough time to be clear about what's expected, and then have a second or third set of eyes review important parts. Listen sympathetically (and gratefully) to constructive comments. Whatever you do, don't insulate yourself from criticism and think that something that you've drafted solo, without others' critical review, is likely to succeed. If you're a contract manager at a company, don't wait until the last minute to review your SOW with in-house counsel; discuss your questions in advance.

Study models of exemplary SOWs, as well as explanatory literature.

(A) **Finding exemplars.** Because SOWs can be so varied in length and content, it's a good idea—if you work with them routinely—to build your own collection for the types of contracts you're working with. Although this may take some time, you shouldn't overlook it. Critically study the SOWs you encounter and constantly upgrade your selection of the most admirable ones relevant to your work: explicit, well worded, to the point, and streamlined.

(B) **Further guidance.** For more on on drafting effective SOWs, recommended books are:

- Peter S. Cole & Michael G. Martin, *How to Write a Statement of Work* (6th ed. 2012).
- Michael G. Martin, *The Government Manager's Guide to the Statement of Work* (2014).
- Stanley E. Portny et al., *Project Management: Planning, Scheduling, and Controlling Costs* (2008).
- James Taylor, *Project Scheduling and Cost Control* (2008).
- Glenn J. Voelz, *Contractors in the Government Workplace* (2010) (appendix D).

APPENDIX B

A Model Contract Using These Guidelines

This contract has been edited to reflect the principles embodied in this book. The better the contract to begin with, the easier it is to edit effectively. Because this contract is architecturally sound, editing it was a comparatively straightforward exercise. Even so, constant practice is the only means of maintaining the skill to achieve satisfactory editorial results.

FINDERSEN AUTHORIZED MASTER RESELLER AGREEMENT

Table of Contents

The page numbers in this table of contents are as if for the actual document. Hence they don't match the page numbers of this book.

FINDERSEN AUTHORIZED MASTER RESELLER AGREEMENT

Parties

In this Agreement, the terms "you," "your," and "yours" refer to

____

____

____

a (cross out two) Corporation / Partnership / Sole Proprietorship of the State of ____________________,
having its principal place of business at ____
____,

and the terms "we," "us," "our," and "ours" refer to Findersen, Inc., a Delaware corporation having its principal place of business at 1301 E. Cherokee Road, Canyon, Texas 79015.

Background

- For many years, we have sold certain outer-space products and services through a direct-sales force that we developed and support at great expense.
- We intend to continue direct distribution of these outer-space products and services to customers that, in our judgment based on business or technological reasons, should be served by us.
- We also want to expand our distribution system to include resellers who will solicit other customers and develop other markets for two-way intercom products, wireless integrated systems, site equipment, and aftermarket and accessory products as well as mobile data and dispatch console systems as more fully defined in this Agreement.
- Resellers and dealers need to have a well-defined role in our distribution system so that they can work efficiently and cooperatively with us to expand our product distribution and to provide the highest level of customer satisfaction.

With these goals in mind, the parties agree as follows.

The Agreement

1. **Term.**

   1.1 **Initial term and renewal.** The initial term of this Agreement begins on the Agreement Date and continues through the next December 31. The Agreement will then renew automatically for successive 1-year terms unless:

   (A) one of the parties sends written notice of nonrenewal to the other party at least 30 days before the current term's expiration date; or

   (B) it is otherwise terminated under this Agreement.

1.2 **No obligation to renew.** Nothing in this Agreement creates any express or implied obligation on either party to renew or extend this Agreement or any right to continue this Agreement on the same terms contained in this Agreement. You understand that we will review our distribution strategy and the terms of this Agreement at our discretion.

2. **Products and Prices.**

2.1 **Selected products only.** You will buy and we will sell, under the terms, conditions, limitations, and prices set forth in this Agreement, only those selected Findersen-manufactured and non-Findersen-manufactured outer-space products listed in Attachment A entitled "Products." Those products comprise 7 distinct categories: Scopial, Two-Way Intercom, PQ Professional Series Intercom, Rocketship Shuttling Solutions, Site Equipment, Select System, and Aftermarket and Accessories. Each category contains the specific products that you are authorized to sell. This product listing is also included in your Dealer Price Book for each product category. Price books are posted on Findersen On-Line ("FOL"), our business-to-business e-commerce website. Only those product categories designated with a check mark on Attachment A are a part of your Dealer Price Book.

2.2 **Unique provisions.** This Agreement contains provisions that apply to the reseller relationship between you and us for the purchase and sale of the products. Separate, unique provisions governing purchase and sale of certain products are contained in Attachments B to G.

2.3 **Referrals.** As further consideration for our entering into this Agreement, you agree to promptly refer all inquiries and leads regarding our other products and services not listed in your Dealer Price Book to one of our offices as we may designate.

2.4 **Dealer Price Book.** We will publish your Dealer Price Book from time to time to keep you informed about products and services available, current prices of those products and services, available discounts, delivery schedules, and other terms of sale and doing business with us. The entire contents of your Dealer Price Book are subject to change or withdrawal at any time at our sole discretion upon 30 days' written notice. When we send you written notice of any change or withdrawal, any earlier inconsistent content will be automatically superseded as of the effective date stated in the notice. We may withdraw or change your Dealer Price Book and the design or specifications for the products at any time, in any way, without any liability or obligations to you or your customers.

2.5 **No obligation regarding other products.** You specifically acknowledge the existence of our other products, product lines, and services, and that this Agreement is limited solely to the products listed in your Dealer Price Book. You also specifically acknowledge that we distribute various products and services by other contractual relationships, and that nothing contained in this Agreement creates any express or implied obligation on our part to establish any other contractual relationship with you.

3. **Your Customers and Location.**

3.1 **Retail sales to end-use customers only.** Except as specifically provided in the Additional Terms and Conditions for Aftermarket and Accessory Products contained in Attachment G, you will limit your distribution of the products bought under this Agreement to direct sales to your customers at retail for end use as limited by the terms of this Agreement and as limited by terms contained in § 18.2, "Sales to Government Entities in the United States."

3.2 **Your location.** You will sell our products only from your above-specified location or from another location that we expressly authorize in Attachment I. You must not appoint any sales agent or representative (other than your employees) to perform any part of this Agreement. At our sole discretion upon a duly signed and delivered amendment to this Agreement, we may allow you to appoint one or more specified agents to sell our products.

4. **Pass-Through Provisions.**

Some provisions in this Agreement are, by their sense and context, intended for the end-user customer who buys one or more of the products from you. For each of these provisions—identified in §§ 8, 9, 10, and 13—you will notify your customers, both before and as part of each transaction, of the specific requirements, rights, duties, and limitations contained in the Warranty and Warranty Disclaimer; Software License and Software Warranty; Warranty Disclaimer; Patents, Copyrights, and Trademarks; and FCC and Other Government Matters provisions; and any other provisions that we may from time to time notify you are required.

5. **Orders, Acceptance, Credit Approval.**

5.1 **Purchase and means of placing orders.** A purchase-and-sale occurs only when we accept an order submitted by you. You may submit an order by fax, by e-mail, orally, or through FOL.

5.2 **Acceptance.** Acceptance of an individual order occurs only when we send you our invoice. You may object to it in writing within 10 days after receiving it; if you do not, you acknowledge that it is accurate and final.

5.3 **Terms of acceptance.** Acceptance will be only on the terms of this Agreement, the listed Attachments, and your Dealer Price Book. The only effect of any terms in your purchase order or elsewhere will be to request the time and place of delivery (only to your location or to one or more other locations expressly authorized by Attachment I) and to specify the number of products to be delivered. Those terms will not change these terms in any way.

5.4 **Credit approval.** One of the conditions of acceptance is that you obtain and maintain credit approval from us. You will provide financial information and statements that we request to obtain and maintain your credit approval.

6. **Canceling Orders.**

You may cancel an individual order by giving us notice of the cancellation. We must receive the notice at least 6 days before the order's scheduled shipping date. We will not cancel an individual order if we receive the notice within 5 days before the order's scheduled shipping date. You will pay a 20% restocking charge as liquidated damages—not as a penalty—for any cancellation.

7. **Shipping, Delivery, Payment, Title, and Security.**

7.1 **Charges shown in Dealer Price Book.** Payment, shipping, and handling charges are set forth in your Dealer Price Book. They are subject to change upon 30 days' written notice to you.

7.2 **Invoices.** Each delivery will be invoiced separately without regard to other deliveries. Payment for each invoice will be according to our payment terms set forth in your Dealer Price Book. Payment terms of Net 90 are also available if you are a qualifying dealer as set forth in your Dealer Price Book, with the exception of the Parts and Accessory Price Book.

7.3 **Shipping and delivery dates.** Shipping or delivery dates are our best estimates only. We reserve the right to make deliveries in installments, and this Agreement is severable for those installments. Delivery delay or default of any installment will not relieve you of your obligation to accept and pay for the remaining deliveries. **In no event will we be liable for increased costs, loss of profits or goodwill, or any other incidental or consequential damages caused by late delivery or nondelivery of products.**

7.4 **Title and risk of loss.** Title to products sold and risk of loss will pass to you at the shipping point. You grant us a security interest in and lien on all your existing or after-acquired inventory of the products and all your accounts, chattel paper, instruments, contract rights, general intangibles, and accounts receivable, and the proceeds of those now existing or later arising from your sale or other disposition of the products. You will cooperate in whatever manner is necessary to help us perfect and record that security interest and lien by completing the UCC-1 form attached to this Agreement as Attachment J (or any similar form that may apply) and any other security as we may from time to time request. All security interests and liens will become part of this Agreement.

8. **Warranty and Warranty Disclaimer.**

8.1 **Generally.** We warrant the products contained in your Dealer Price Book under a commercial or limited warranty that is shipped with each product order, except for those orders containing products purchased from the Aftermarket and Accessory Price Book. The warranty for these products is found in the Parts and Accessory Price Book, a hard copy of which will be sent to you and which is also available on FOL. Other than what is stated in the warranties for these products, we make no representation or warranty of any kind. We extend each product warranty not to you but to the original buyer of the products from you. Any such warranty is not assignable or transferable from the original buyer to any later buyer. You will provide the original buyer with the appropriate product warranty and, if applicable, a software license and software warranty (see ¶ 9) before the sale of the products. You must not issue any warranties, guarantees, or licenses that purport to obligate us to any person or entity other than the applicable warranties or license specified here and that we furnish. We may change those warranties from time to time on 30 days' written notice to you. **We do not extend any warranty to you, and all warranties express or implied are specifically excluded, including the implied warranties of merchantability and fitness for a particular purpose.**

8.2 **Your remedy for defects.** If any of our products furnished under this Agreement is initially defective—that is, defective at the time of delivery to you—your sole remedy will be to return it to us for replacement or repair at our sole discretion. All returns must be undamaged in the original container and packing with all accessories and instructions included. You have no right to reject all or any part of any shipment of our products furnished under this Agreement because any or all of our products in the shipment may be initially defective.

9. **Software License and Software Warranty; Warranty Disclaimer.**

A separate Findersen Software License and Software Warranty may apply to certain products and individual items of software. When we advise you that a Findersen Software License and Software Warranty applies to products containing Findersen Software that are purchased from us for resale or relicensing, we will require you and your customers to sign an applicable Findersen Software License before delivering the products and Findersen Software. **We do not extend any software warranty to you, and all warranties express or implied are specifically excluded, including the implied warranties of merchantability and fitness for a particular purpose.**

10. **Patents, Copyrights, and Trademarks.**

10.1 **Indemnity.** If you or your customer becomes a defendant in a suit based on a claim that any Findersen-manufactured product furnished under this Agreement directly infringes a U.S. patent or copyright, you must notify us promptly in writing of the suit. If we receive prompt notice and, at our request, are given control of the suit and all requested help for defense, we will defend the suit at our expense and pay any costs or damages finally awarded. If the use or sale of an allegedly infringing product furnished under this Agreement is enjoined as a result of such a suit, we will, at our option and at no expense to you, either obtain for you or your customer the right to use or sell the product or else substitute an equivalent product that is reasonably acceptable to you or your customer. At our option, we will either extend this indemnity to that product or else accept return of the allegedly infringing product and reimburse you its purchase price less a reasonable charge for reasonable wear and tear. This indemnity does not extend to any suit based on any infringement or alleged infringement of any patent or copyright resulting from the combination of any product furnished under this Agreement with other elements, nor does it extend to any product of your own or your customer's design.

10.2 **Copyrights and mask works.** Laws in the United States and other countries preserve for us certain exclusive rights in the Findersen Software, mask works, and other works of authorship furnished under this Agreement, including the exclusive right to prepare works derived from them, to reproduce them in copies, and to distribute copies of them. These Findersen Software, mask works, and other works of authorship may be used in and redistributed only with the products associated with them. No other use is permitted, including reproduction, modification, or disassembly of Findersen Software, mask works, or other works of authorship, or exercise of exclusive rights in them.

10.3 **Reverse-engineering.** The Findersen Software and products furnished under this Agreement contain valuable trade secrets belonging to us. You must not translate, reverse-engineer, decompile, disassemble, or make any other unauthorized use of the Findersen Software and products. Since unauthorized use of protected Findersen Software and products would greatly diminish the value of those trade secrets and cause us irreparable harm, you acknowledge that we will be entitled—in addition to any other remedies we may have—to equitable relief to protect those trade secrets, including temporary and permanent injunctive relief without proof of damage.

10.4 **Trademark and proprietary marks.** The products shipped under the terms of this Agreement will carry our trademark and proprietary marks or any other logo or proprietary marks that we may expressly agree to in writing before they are used. For certain products that you are authorized to sell, we have designated specific trademarks ("Dealer Trademarks") that you may use. The specific Dealer Trademarks are set forth in the Additional Terms and Conditions for Scopial Products, Two-Way/PQ Professional Series Intercom Products, and Aftermarket and Accessory Products contained in Attachments B, C, and G.

(A) **Validity of marks.** You acknowledge the validity of the trademark "Findersen" and the Dealer Trademarks as well as all other proprietary marks that are affixed to the products. Those trademarks and proprietary marks are and will remain our property.

(B) **No infringement.** You must not do anything to infringe on, harm, or contest the validity of those trademarks or any of our other proprietary marks.

(C) **Use with promotions.** You may use the Dealer Trademarks to promote and sell the products, and you may state that the products are manufactured by us. Unless we specifically provide otherwise, any promotion will be at your sole cost and expense.

(D) **Prohibited use.** You must not use the trademark "Findersen" or the Dealer Trademarks as part of the name under which you conduct business.

(E) **No grant of rights in marks.** Permission to display the word "Findersen," the Dealer Trademarks, or any other proprietary word or symbol owned by us or our affiliates is given only as stated above. Nothing in this Agreement grants you any right, title, or interest in the word "Findersen" (either alone or in association with other words, names, or symbols), in the corporate name of Findersen or any part of that word or name, or in any other trademark or trade name adopted by us or our affiliates.

(F) **Our right to approve use.** To help us protect our trademarks, tradenames, corporate slogans, goodwill, and product designations, you agree not to use any of those marks, names, slogans, or designations in any advertising copy, promotional material, signs, or other written or printed material except in a form that we specifically approve in writing.

(G) **Mandatory discontinuance of use.** If you use any of those marks in a sign, advertisement, or any other material as set forth in (F), you will immediately discontinue their use or display upon termination or expiration of this Agreement.

10.5 **License disclaimer.** Except for the right to use the Findersen Software and products for the purposes provided in this Agreement—or rights that may arise by operation of law—and unless expressly provided, nothing in this Agreement grants you or your customers, either directly or by implication, estoppel, or otherwise, any license or right under any patent, copyright, trademark, or trade secret of ours or of any third party.

11. **Taxes and Insurance.**

11.1 **Taxes and fees.** You must pay all license fees; all sales, use, service-use, occupation, retailer's-occupation, service-occupation, personal-property, and excise taxes; and any other fees, assessments, or taxes that may be assessed or levied by any national, state, or local government or any department or subdivision of any government when the tax or fee is owed as a result of performing under the Agreement or charged against any product you order.

11.2 **Insurance coverage.** At all times during any term of this Agreement, you will obtain and maintain in effect the insurance coverage specified below, at your own expense. You will get policies only with companies satisfactory to us and having an AM Best rating of "A-VIII" or better. You or your insurance agent will furnish us certificates of insurance evidencing the coverages, and each policy will provide us at least 30 days' written notice of any material change to or cancellation of the policy. Unless we expressly agree otherwise in writing, no deductible or self-insured retention may exceed $50,000. A deductible or self-insured retention is your sole responsibility and does not apply to or limit your liability to us. This provision does not limit or expand the scope, application, or limits of coverage; rather, it sets forth your minimum insurance requirements. You may obtain insurance with greater limits or broader coverage as you consider appropriate. At a minimum, though, you will maintain the following types and amounts of coverage:

(A) **Workers' compensation:** statutory coverage required by the state in which the services are performed; the coverage will contain a waiver of subrogation for us;

(B) **Employers' liability with occupational disease:** $1 million per person, aggregate; the policy will contain a waiver of subrogation for us;

(C) **Commercial general-liability insurance:** including personal-injury extension, products and completed-operations coverage, independent-contractor endorsement, and broad-form contractual liability, $1 million combined single limit; the policy will name or list us as an additional insured; and

(D) **Business-automobile liability insurance:** including all owned, leased, hired, loaned, or borrowed vehicles, $1 million combined single limit.

11.3 **Prices exclusive of tax.** Except for any amount of federal, state, or local taxes stated in your Dealer Price Book or otherwise set forth in this Agreement, the prices agreed to exclude any amount for federal, state, or local excise, sales, use, property, retailers'-occupation, or similar taxes. If any such excluded taxes apply to any transaction related to this Agreement, or if we are required to pay or bear the burden of any such tax, the prices set forth in this Agreement will be increased by the amount of those taxes and any interest or penalty incurred. You will pay us the full amount of any such increase no later than 10 days after receiving an invoice for the taxes, or you may provide us a valid resale-exemption certificate as required by state tax authorities to establish your tax-exempt status as a reseller under this Agreement.

12. Excusable Delays.

We are not liable for any delay or failure to perform due to any cause beyond our reasonable control. Those causes include strikes; acts of God; your own acts; transportation interruptions; inability to obtain necessary labor, materials, or facilities; a supplier's default; and our volume of orders at any time rendering deliveries impractical in the ordinary course of business. The delivery schedule will be considered extended by a period equal to the time lost because of an excusable delay. If we are unable to wholly or partly perform because of any cause beyond our reasonable control, we may terminate any order without liability to you or your customers.

13. FCC and Other Government Matters.

The end user of a product is solely responsible for obtaining any licenses or other authorizations required by the Federal Communications Commission or any other federal, state, or local government agency. The end user is solely responsible for complying with applicable FCC rules and regulations and the applicable rules and regulations of any other federal, state, or local government agency. In FCC or other government matters, neither we nor any of our employees is an agent of yours or of the end user. We may, however, help prepare an FCC license application at no charge to the end user. We will establish your obligations regarding any FCC or other government-licensing help required for end users.

14. Compliance with Law.

You must at all times conduct your efforts under the Agreement in strict accordance with all applicable federal, state, and local laws, rules, and regulations, and with the highest commercial standards. You must promptly comply with any notices received from us regarding remedial efforts that we, in our sole discretion, consider necessary to satisfy any law, rule, or regulation, including laws, rules, and regulations regarding warranties, consumer protection, and product safety for our products and services.

15. Nonexclusive Dealer.

You are a nonexclusive dealer. In our sole and unrestricted discretion, without any liability or obligation to you, we may appoint additional dealers or finders for—or make direct or indirect sales or distributions of—any Findersen product or service, similar or dissimilar to those that you sell, or any non-Findersen product or service in your defined area of primary marketing responsibility and elsewhere, anytime, and to anyone.

16. Dealer Product Servicer.

After signing this Agreement, you may be considered for the opportunity to become a Dealer Product Servicer ("DPS"). To be approved as a DPS, you must meet our criteria. Upon our written notification that you have been approved as a DPS, you must sign and deliver the DPS agreement, a copy of which is attached for reference as Attachment H.

17. Confidentiality.

During the term of this Agreement and for 3 years after it terminates or expires, you will maintain in strict confidence all information disclosed to you by us or others, including the contents of your Dealer Price Book and any revisions to it, all price and marketing information, customer lists, drawings, technical information and data, and other information of any nature relating to all our products and services and to their sale or distribution. All information we disclose under this Agreement and information you obtain in connection with this Agreement will be used solely to further the distribution of our products and services.

18. Area and Sales of Products.

18.1 **Distribution.** You will use your best efforts to promote, sell, and service the products in your area as described in the Additional Terms and Conditions for Scopial Products, Two-Way/PQ Professional Series Intercom Products, Rocketship Shuttling Solutions Products, Site Equipment, and Select System Products contained in Attachments B through F.

18.2 **Sales to Government Entities in the United States.** A "Government Entity" is any department, agency, or instrumentality of the U.S. government, or of any state, county, municipal, or local government in the United States, including the District of Columbia and U.S. territories. If you elect to sell products to a Government Entity in the U.S., you do so at your own option and risk. You cannot obligate us as subcontractor or otherwise to any Government Entity. If you transact such sales, you are solely and exclusively responsible for complying with all laws, regulations, and provisions governing sales to any Government Entity. We make no representations, certifications, or warranties whatsoever other than those expressly stated in this Agreement, and in particular we make none with respect to the ability of our products, services, or prices to satisfy any laws, regulations, or provisions governing or relating to sales to any Government Entity, including place of product origin, manufacture, or assembly (e.g., under the Buy American Act or Trade Agreements Act); contracting with small, minority, or diversity suppliers; payment of prevailing wages; or price guarantees and commitments. **Except as specifically provided in the Additional Terms and Conditions for Aftermarket and Accessory products contained in Attachment G, sale of a product by you to any third party who is reselling the product to a Government Entity (e.g., a prime contractor to the U.S. government) is strictly prohibited by terms referred to in this § 18.**

18.3 **Sales outside the United States.** Except as specifically set forth in the Additional Terms and Conditions for Scopial Products contained in Attachment B and the Additional Terms and Conditions for Aftermarket and Accessory Products contained in Attachment G, any direct or indirect distribution, transshipment, or sale of products by you outside the United States is prohibited.

19. Sales Performance.

19.1 **Permitted and prohibited advertising.** You will keep your sales and service personnel properly informed about all our advertising and marketing programs and policies, and will pursue those programs and policies in a way that reflects our high standards, valuable goodwill, and business reputation. To help you promote sales of our products, we may furnish whatever promotional literature and other advertising aids that we consider necessary.

19.2 **Performance standards.** We may, at our sole discretion, set reasonable sales objectives for you for each contract term, and we may consider those objectives, among other factors, in evaluating your sales performance. You will achieve the performance standards set forth in the Findersen Dealer Scorecard found on FOL. No later than 60 days before the end of any term—including the initial term—we will give you performance standards for the next term. If we do not provide new performance standards within that 60-day period, the previous year's standards will apply on a prorated basis until we provide you with new performance standards. Despite any revision of performance standards, the rest of this Agreement will remain in full effect. You acknowledge that this § 19.2 is essential, fair, and reasonable, and that your failure to meet a performance standard will be grounds for us to terminate this Agreement.

19.3 **Marketing reports.** Except as set forth in the Additional Terms and Conditions for Select System products contained in Attachment F, by the first Wednesday of each month that this Agreement is in effect, you will provide us PURPORT21 Reports containing any marketing information that we request, in any form that we designate. You will report customer names, addresses, and phone numbers, the number of units of each product that you sold during the preceding month, and dollar volume of sales by county, customer Standard Industrial Code, or other categories or industry groupings that we request. You will also send us a PURPORT21 Report containing the number of accessories and aftermarket products sold, as well as sales of any other Findersen products that you are authorized to offer. You will provide PURPORT21 Reports to us when requested; failure to do so may result in your becoming ineligible to participate in our Premier Purchase and other marketing programs. If you fail to provide us with any marketing report called for by this Agreement and do not cure that failure within 15 days after receiving notice from us, then, in addition to our other rights and remedies under this Agreement, at law or in equity, we may withhold any further processing of any of your orders until each requested report is provided to us as required by the Agreement.

19.4 **Forecast.** During the term of this Agreement, you will provide us, in a form to be provided by us, a monthly usage forecast to help us maintain an orderly production flow to meet your delivery requirements. If you fail to provide this information, we may consider your failure to be good cause for any excusable delivery delay on our part.

19.5 **Inspection of your facilities.** We may inspect your facilities and operations that relate to your performance under this Agreement during normal business hours and without prior written notice.

20. Ethical Practices.

We have historically depended on product quality and superiority, combined with outstanding support capability, to market our products throughout the world. We believe that we can continue to grow and to prosper without succumbing to legally questionable or unethical demands or practices. You must conduct your business in an ethical manner.

21. Outer-Space Services Exclusion.

Your purchase of products under this Agreement does not include outer-space services such as TMR, community repeater, or other services. You or the end user must enter into separate agreements with the service provider to obtain those services. **We disclaim liability for range, coverage, availability, or operation of any outer-space systems and services.**

22. Party Relationship.

22.1 **No business entity.** This Agreement does not create an agency, joint venture, or partnership between you and us. Neither party may impose or create any obligation or responsibility, express or implied, or make any promise, representation, or warranty on behalf of the other party, other than as expressly provided in this Agreement. Nothing in this Agreement may be construed to make you, your employees, or your agents employees of ours, and you are not entitled to participate in any of our employee-benefit programs. We are not liable to pay wages, to pay for any form of employee insurance, or to assume any other obligation as an employer. We are not responsible to any government agencies for workers'-compensation insurance or any other type of employee insurance, withholding taxes, or social-security taxes for you, your employees, or your agents.

22.2 **No franchise.** The relationship created by this Agreement does not constitute—and is not intended by the parties to constitute—our granting of a franchise to you. No federal, state, or local franchise law is intended by the parties to apply to the parties' relationship, nor will such a law be considered or construed to apply to the formation, operation, administration, termination, or expiration of this Agreement. You expressly confirm that you have not paid and will not pay any franchise fee to us in connection with this Agreement, and that none of the terms, conditions, or amounts provided for in this Agreement can be characterized as constituting a franchise fee.

23. Termination.

23.1 **By either party.** Either party may terminate this Agreement at any time, without cause and for the party's convenience, upon 30 days' written notice to the other party.

23.2 **By us.** We may terminate this Agreement at any time upon the occurrence of any of the following events:

> Although repeating *if* adds a few words to the provision, it avoids making the provision sound like a litany of accusations.

(A) if you fail to meet the sales-performance standards set forth in this Agreement;

(B) if a change in your control, management, or ownership is in our sole opinion, unacceptable to us;

(C) if you cease to function as a going concern, declare bankruptcy, have a receiver appointed for you, or otherwise take advantage of any insolvency law;

(D) if you fail to cure any breach of this Agreement within 15 days after receiving our written notice;

(E) if you misrepresent or omit a material fact in any communication to anyone in connection with this Agreement, about its terms, conditions, or amounts, the performance of this Agreement or any of our products or services referred to by this Agreement;

(F) if you engage in any act or fail to act related to the subject matter of this Agreement when that act or failure to act is illegal or contributes to an unfair or deceptive trade practice violating any applicable federal, state, or local law, or that in the opinion of our counsel constitutes an illegal, unfair, or deceptive act or practice;

(G) if you use a sales agent or representative to perform any obligation of yours under this Agreement without authorization;

(H) if we receive customer complaints that, in our sole opinion, indicate that you are not achieving our standards of total customer satisfaction; or

(I) if you fail to conduct your business in an ethical manner as required by § 20, "Ethical Practices."

24. Effects of Termination or Expiration of Agreement.

24.1 No Damages. **If this Agreement is terminated or expires, or if we cancel any of your orders for products that remain undelivered on the effective date of any termination or expiration of this Agreement, you will not have any claims against us for any damages, including any claim for loss of profits or prospective profits, that are in any way related to the sale or purchase of products or services under this Agreement.**

24.2 **Amounts owed.** All sums owed by either party to the other will become due and payable immediately upon termination of this Agreement.

24.3 **Return of our property held by you.** Within 5 working days after termination or expiration of this Agreement, you will deliver, to any address that we specify, all our property, including all our equipment, customer data, software items, catalogues, drawings, designs, engineering photographs, samples, literature, sales aids, and confidential business information and trade secrets in your possession. You will also return to us any copies you possess of any such materials.

24.4 **No obligation to fill orders.** Upon termination or expiration of this Agreement, we will be relieved of any obligation to make any further shipments under its terms. If this Agreement is terminated, we may cancel any or all of your outstanding accepted but unshipped orders for products. We will have no obligation or liability to you, your prospective customers, or any other party in connection with any such cancellations.

24.5 **Continued acceptance of orders.** If we accept any order for products from you after this Agreement has expired or been terminated, our acceptance cannot be construed as a renewal or extension of this Agreement, or as a waiver of its termination or expiration.

24.6 **Partial survival of Agreement.** This Agreement contains certain terms, provisions, representations, and warranties that by their sense and context are intended to survive this Agreement. Those terms, provisions, representations, and warranties will survive the completion of performances and termination or expiration of this Agreement, including the making of any payments due under this Agreement.

25. Products Remaining in Your Possession.

25.1 **Initial inventory.** Upon termination or expiration of this Agreement, you will notify us in writing of your current inventory of products that you purchased from us.

25.2 **First option to repurchase; joint inventory.** We will have the option—but no obligation—to repurchase all or any part of your remaining inventory. We will have 14 days after the day we receive your inventory to exercise that option. If we exercise the option, both you and we will take a joint inventory of those products that are still in your control. The last products that you purchase will be the first that we repurchase. The repurchase price for each product inventory will be either the net price you paid to us for the inventory or else the price being offered to other dealers at the time of repurchase for the same products, whichever is lower.

25.3 **Sale to third parties: our right of first refusal.** Upon the termination or expiration of this Agreement, we will have a right of first refusal to repurchase any products you bought from us. Before you may sell those products in your control to any third party, you will first offer us in writing the opportunity to repurchase the products for your net purchase price or the price being offered by the third party, whichever is lower. We will have 10 days after receiving your offer to accept or reject it.

25.4 **Delivery.** If we exercise our option to repurchase all or any part of your inventory of products, you will sell it to us as of the date of termination or expiration of this Agreement and deliver it immediately to any place or places that we designate, free and clear of any liens or encumbrances, undamaged, and in its original and unopened packaging. We will bear all delivery costs and expenses unless we terminated this Agreement because you breached it; in that event, you will bear all delivery costs and expenses.

25.5 **Payment.** We will pay you for the repurchased inventory within 30 days after receiving delivery of the products. If you have a debt due and owing to us as of the date our payment for the repurchased products is due to you, we have the right to reduce our payment for the repurchased products by the amount of your debt to us.

25.6 **Your remaining inventory.** If we do not repurchase your entire inventory of products, you may sell any remaining inventory in the normal course of business. Any such sale will remain subject to the terms, conditions, and restrictions of this Agreement.

26. Per-Unit Administrative-Processing Charge.

26.1 **Limitation on product distribution.** You must limit your distribution of the products purchased under this Agreement to your own direct retail sales as specified in § 3.1.

26.2 **Damages from your breach.** You acknowledge that we will incur serious damages if your sale of any product unit fails to comply with the limitation on product distribution. You also acknowledge that the monetary value of those damages is uncertain and difficult to estimate because it includes the costs of recordkeeping, administrative, and operational tasks that we must perform each time the Agreement is breached.

26.3 **Stipulated charge.** In addition to our other rights and remedies under this Agreement, at law or in equity, we have the right to bill you for a per-unit administrative-processing charge for each product unit sold in breach of your limitation on product distribution, as compensation—and not as a penalty—for our expenses caused by your breach. The amount charged will be based on our estimate of the difference between our suggested list price and the dealer purchase price listed in the then-current Dealer Price Book for each product unit in each noncomplying sale, except for Aftermarket and Accessory products. To help us identify each product unit that is subject to the charge, you will give us your full cooperation and access to all your books, contracts, and records related in any way to your sale of product units, and furnish us any other information about your affairs that we consider necessary to make the identification.

26.4 **Payment.** We will invoice you for each per-unit administrative-processing charge. Payment will be due when you receive the invoice. If you fail to pay the invoice within 30 days after the due date, then in addition to our other rights and remedies under this Agreement, at law or in equity, we may withhold any further processing of your product orders until you make the payment.

27. No Waiver.

If either party fails to require the other to perform any term of this Agreement, that failure does not prevent the party from later enforcing that term. If either party waives the other's breach of a term, that waiver is not treated as waiving a later breach of the term.

28. Findersen-Authorized Two-Way Intercom Dealer Agreement Terminated.

Findersen-Authorized Two-Way Intercom Dealer agreements include Professional Series, CTR, LS TMR, Scopial Reseller, and Select System Dealer agreements (collectively, "Dealer Agreements") between you and us for the sale of Findersen-branded products. In consideration of our entering into this Agreement, you will terminate any existing Dealer Agreements and any related software-license agreements upon the signing of this Agreement. Your termination must be in accordance with all the terms of any such Dealer Agreements and software-license agreements. You acknowledge that this Agreement and any software-license agreement entered into in connection with this Agreement supersede any prior Dealer Agreements and that the products available under the prior Dealer Agreements will be available under this Agreement. Your purchases of the products will be governed by this Agreement and its Attachments.

29. Limitations.

29.1 LIMITATION OF LIABILITY. **Except for personal injury and except as provided for in § 10.1, "Patents, Copyrights, and Trademarks: Indemnity," our total liability in any matter arising from or related to this Agreement is limited to the price of the particular product sold under this Agreement with respect to which losses or damages**

are claimed. Your sole remedy is to ask that we either refund the purchase price or else repair or replace the product that is not as warranted, at our option. In no event will we be liable for incidental, special, or consequential damages, including frustration of economic or business expectations; loss of profits; loss of data; cost of capital; cost of substitute products, facilities, or services; downtime cost; or any claim against you by any other party.

29.2 **INSURANCE. You understand that we are not an insurer, that you must obtain all insurance required by this Agreement, and that we do not represent or warrant that any product of ours will avert or prevent occurrences, or their consequences, that are monitored, detected, or controlled with use of the products.**

29.3 **TIME TO SUE. Except for money due on an open account, no lawsuit for any breach of this Agreement may be filed more than 2 years after the claim accrues. When a shorter limitation period is provided by applicable law for a particular claim, no lawsuit may be filed after that period ends.**

29.4 **NO REPRESENTATIONS. Any information, advice, approval, instruction, or cost projection issued by our sales personnel or other representatives will be considered an expression of personal opinion only and will not affect either party's rights and obligations under this Agreement unless it is made a formal amendment to this Agreement as provided in § 30.2(B), "Modification of Agreement: Mutually."**

30. General.

30.1 **Incorporations.** All Attachments, your Dealer Price Book, and any deletions, additions, and revisions to either the Attachments or your Dealer Price Book are incorporated into this Agreement.

30.2 **Modification of Agreement.** Additions, deletions, amendments, and other changes are collectively called "modifications." This Agreement can be modified in 2 ways.

(A) **By us.** We may unilaterally modify your Dealer Price Book or Attachments upon 30 days' written notice to you. If you do not terminate this Agreement within that notice period, your inaction will be considered consent to the modification, and this Agreement will be considered amended accordingly.

(B) **Mutually.** Any other modification to this Agreement must be in writing, contain an explicit statement that it constitutes an amendment to this Agreement, and be signed by you and by one of our authorized officers.

30.3 **Entire agreement.** This Agreement represents the entire agreement between the parties. It cannot be changed except by written agreement signed by the parties.

30.4 **Successors and representatives.** This Agreement binds and inures to the benefit of the parties and their heirs, personal representatives, successors, and (where permitted) assignees.

30.5 **Severability.** If a court for any reason holds a provision of this Agreement unenforceable, the rest remains fully enforceable.

30.6 **Headings.** Headings are for convenience only and do not affect the interpretation of this Agreement.

30.7 **Governing law.** Texas law applies to all matters arising under or relating to this Agreement without regard to any choice-of-law rules that might direct the application of another jurisdiction's laws.

30.8 **Dispute resolution.**

(A) **Nonbinding alternative dispute resolution.** Both parties must try to settle any claim or controversy arising from this Agreement through consultation and negotiation in good faith and in a spirit of mutual cooperation. If those attempts at resolution fail, then either party may demand nonbinding mediation to resolve the dispute. Within 30 days after the party's demand for mediation is received by the other party, both parties will choose a mutually acceptable mediator. Neither party may unreasonably withhold consent to the selection of a mediator. Both parties will share the costs of the mediation equally. By agreement, the parties may postpone mediation until the parties have completed some specified but limited discovery about the dispute. The parties may also agree to replace mediation with some other form of nonbinding alternative dispute resolution.

(B) **Litigation.** If the parties cannot resolve a dispute within 2 months after the initial demand for nonbinding mediation, then either party may submit the dispute to a court located in Cook County, Texas, for resolution. Both parties consent to the court's personal and subject-matter jurisdiction. No alternative-dispute-resolution procedures will be construed under the doctrine of laches, waiver, or estoppel to adversely affect the rights of either party. Nothing will prevent either party from resorting to the judicial proceedings mentioned in this ¶ if good-faith efforts to resolve the dispute using alternative-dispute-resolution procedures have been unsuccessful, or if interim relief from the court is necessary to prevent serious and irreparable injury to one of the parties or to a third party.

30.9 **Attestation.** If you are a corporation, the Attestation should be completed and the corporate seal affixed; a witness is not necessary. If you are an individual or a partnership, the Attestation need not be completed, but a witness should sign it.

30.10 **Notices.** All notices and other communications required or permitted under this Agreement must be in writing and must be sent or e-mailed to the party at that party's address set forth below or at whatever other address the party specifies in writing.

30.11 **Acceptance.** This Agreement is an offer from you to be appointed by us as a dealer in our products as set forth in this Agreement. This Agreement will not become a binding contract between you and us until after the Agreement Date—that is, the date on which we accept this Agreement. Upon acceptance, we will send you a fully signed copy of this Agreement signed by one of our corporate officers who is authorized to make dealer appointments in your geographic area. No act or omission regarding this Agreement or its performance by anyone, including you or us, that occurs before the Agreement Date can be characterized by anyone to constitute acceptance of this Agreement by us or to in any way create a claim in anyone related to the subject matter of this Agreement.

31. Attachments.

The following Attachments are a part of this Agreement:

A. Products

B. Additional Terms and Conditions for Scopial Products

C. Additional Terms and Conditions for Two-Way/PQ Professional Series Intercom Products

D. Additional Terms and Conditions for Rocketship Shuttling Solutions Products

E. Additional Terms and Conditions for Site Equipment

F. Additional Terms and Conditions for Select System Products

G. Additional Terms and Conditions for Aftermarket and Accessory Products

H. Dealer Product Service Agreement

I. Additional Sales Location

J. Uniform Commercial Code UCC-1

The parties consider this Agreement to be signed by their duly authorized representatives on the Agreement Date.

FINDERSEN, INC.

By: ______________________________
(Authorized Signature)

Print Name: ______________________________

Title: Division General Manager

Print Findersen Address for Notices:

____

____

____

DEALER

By: ______________________________
(Authorized Signature)

Print Name: ______________________________

Print Title: ______________________________

Witness or Attest: ______________________________

Print Dealer Address for Notices:

____

____

____

APPENDIX C

A Typical Contract Needing an Overhaul, with Annotations

In Appendixes C–E, the comment boxes are merely illustrative—hardly exhaustive. If every edit necessary were accompanied by a comment box, all the text would be obscured. Hence not every problem is highlighted, but only a few illuminating ones.

With each of the three contracts that follow in Appendixes C–E, the even-numbered pages show the original, and the odd-numbered pages a revision that carries out the techniques discussed and demonstrated throughout the book.

NOT THIS:

Nondisclosure and Confidentiality Agreement

This Nondisclosure and Confidentiality Agreement (the "Agreement"), effective as of ____________________, 20__, is between Johnsonius Enterprises, Inc. (the "Company"), a California corporation, and ________________________________, whose address is ________________________________ (the "Recipient"). It is intended to protect confidential information in the Company's possession from being disclosed by the Recipient.

Background

The Company and the Recipient are considering entering into a business relationship for their mutual benefit. In consideration of the possibility of this relationship, the Company will disclose certain proprietary information about its business so that the two parties may assess whether such a relationship would be to their mutual benefit. To induce the Company to disclose sufficient information, the Recipient undertakes the nondisclosure duties outlined below.

Terms and Conditions

1. Limitations.

1.1 Unprotected Information. The Recipient has no obligation to protect information that:

(A) was known or available to the Recipient before this Agreement without breach of a duty of confidentiality by the Recipient or a third party;

(B) is or becomes available to the public, other than by breach of this Agreement; or

(C) becomes known to the Recipient by a third party without restrictions as to disclosure.

1.2 Disclosure Required by Law. The Recipient may disclose Confidential Information to the extent required by law. But the Recipient must give the Company prompt written notice of the required disclosure and make a reasonable effort to avoid disclosure by seeking a protective order.

2. Nature of Relationship. The Recipient has no obligation to disclose any Confidential Information. This Agreement grants no rights of ownership, licenses, or any other intellectual-property rights. This Agreement does not create any agency, partnership, joint venture, or any other business relationship.

3. Duty Not to Disclose Confidential Information.

3.1 The Meaning of "Confidential Information." As used in this Agreement, Confidential Information means all proprietary information related to the Company, including:

BUT THIS:

Nondisclosure and Confidentiality Agreement

This Nondisclosure and Confidentiality Agreement (this "Agreement"), effective ____________________, 20__, is between Johnsonius Enterprises, Inc. (the "Company"), a California corporation, and ______________________________________, whose address is ______________________________________ (the "Recipient"). It is intended to protect confidential information in the Company's possession from being disclosed by the Recipient.

Background

The Company and the Recipient are considering entering into a business relationship for their mutual benefit. In consideration of the possibility of this relationship, the Company will disclose certain proprietary information about its business so that the two parties may assess whether the relationship would be to their mutual benefit. To induce the Company to disclose sufficient information, the Recipient undertakes the nondisclosure duties outlined below.

The Agreement

1. Duty Not to Disclose Confidential Information.

1.1 **Recipient's duty.** The Recipient must use best efforts in taking precautions to safeguard the Confidential Information, including all precautions that the Company may, in its sole discretion, request. The Recipient may use Confidential Information only for the purposes contemplated by this Agreement. Before the Recipient discloses Confidential Information to any employee, the employee must first sign a nondisclosure agreement identical to the one in Schedule A.

1.2 **The meaning of "Confidential Information."** As used in this Agreement, "Confidential Information" means all proprietary information related to the Company, including:

(A) trade secrets and other intellectual property;

(B) financial information and pricing;

(C) technical information, including research, development, procedures, algorithms, data, designs, and know-how;

(D) business information, including operations, planning, marketing interests, and products;

(E) information collected or developed by the Company regarding its customers; and

(F) any agreement between the Company and the Recipient and the discussions, negotiations, and proposals related to that agreement.

NOT THIS:

(A) trade secrets and other intellectual property;

(B) financial information and pricing;

(C) technical information, including research, development, procedures, algorithms, data, designs, and know-how;

(D) business information, including operations, planning, marketing interests, and products;

(E) information collected or developed by the Company regarding its customers; and

(F) the terms of any agreement between the Company and the Recipient and the discussions, negotiations, and proposals related to that agreement.

3.2 Standard of Care. The Recipient must protect the Confidential Information from both unauthorized use and unauthorized disclosure by exercising the same degree of care that the Recipient uses with respect to information of its own of a similar nature, except that the Recipient must at least use reasonable care.

This is the main provision! It appears much too far into the contract.

3.3 Recipient's Duty. The Recipient must use its best efforts in taking precautions to safeguard the Confidential Information, including all precautions that the Company may, in its sole discretion, request. The Recipient may use Confidential Information only for the purposes contemplated by this Agreement. Before the Recipient discloses Confidential Information to any employee, the employee must first sign a nondisclosure agreement identical to the one in Schedule A.

3.4 Protection Period. The Recipient must protect the Confidential Information for two years from the last date that the Recipient received Confidential Information.

4. Representatives. The parties' representatives for disclosing or receiving information are:

Company: Jeffrey A. Gurlich
Recipient: ______________________________

5. Publicity. The Recipient must not, without the Company's prior written consent, make any news release, public announcement, denial, or confirmation of this Agreement or its subject matter.

6. Right to Enjoin Disclosure. The Recipient's unauthorized disclosure or use of Confidential Information may result in irreparable harm. The Company may therefore seek a temporary restraining order and other injunctive relief to protect its Confidential Information. The Recipient will not raise the defense of an adequate remedy at law. This provision does not alter any other remedies available to either party.

BUT THIS:

1.3 **Standard of care.** The Recipient must protect the Confidential Information from both unauthorized use and unauthorized disclosure by exercising the same degree of care that the Recipient uses regarding similar information of its own. But the Recipient must at least use reasonable care.

1.4 **Protection period.** The Recipient must protect the Confidential Information for 2 years from the last date that the Recipient received Confidential Information.

2. **Representatives.** The parties' representatives for disclosing or receiving information are:

   Company: Jeffrey A. Gurlich

   Recipient: ______________________________

3. **Limitations.**

   3.1 **Unprotected information.** The Recipient has no obligation to protect information that:

   (A) was known or available to the Recipient before this Agreement without breach of a duty of confidentiality by the Recipient or a third party;

   (B) is or becomes available to the public, other than by breach of this Agreement; or

   (C) becomes known to the Recipient by a third party without restrictions on disclosure.

   3.2 **Disclosure required by law.** The Recipient may disclose Confidential Information to the extent required by law. But the Recipient must give the Company prompt written notice of the required disclosure and make a reasonable effort to avoid disclosure by seeking a protective order.

4. **Nature of Relationship.** The Recipient has no obligation to disclose any Confidential Information. This Agreement grants no rights of ownership, licenses, or any other intellectual-property rights. This Agreement does not create any agency, partnership, joint venture, or other business relationship.

5. **Publicity.** The Recipient must not, without the Company's written consent, make any news release, public announcement, denial, or confirmation of this Agreement or its subject matter.

6. **Right to Enjoin Disclosure.** The Recipient's unauthorized disclosure or use of Confidential Information may result in irreparable harm. The Company may therefore seek a temporary restraining order and other injunctive relief to protect its Confidential Information. The Recipient will not raise the defense of an adequate remedy at law. This provision does not alter any other remedies available to either party.

APPENDIX D

A Second Typical Contract Needing an Overhaul, with Annotations

NOT THIS:

This generic heading is unhelpful.

Agreement

THIS AGREEMENT is made and effective as of the 25th day of March 2018 (the "Effective Date") by and between Muensch Fabrics and Fibers Co., a Delaware corporation ("Muensch"), and Bertelon Inc., a New York corporation ("Buyer").

WITNESSETH:

WHEREAS, Buyer wishes to purchase from Muensch certain primary and secondary carpet-backings for manufacture into carpets, and Muensch wishes to sell such backings to Buyer, upon the terms and conditions hereinafter specified:

NOW, THEREFORE, in consideration of the mutual covenants contained herein and other good and valuable consideration, the receipt and sufficiency of which are hereby acknowledged, Muensch and Buyer (jointly "the Parties," and individually a "Party") agree as follows:

The lack of headings in this list make it hard to identify provisions.

1. The products ("Product") to be sold by Muensch and purchased by Buyer hereunder are certain primary and secondary carpet-backings in the styles identified in the attached Exhibit A, and conforming to the Product specifications set forth in the attached Exhibit B.

2. (a) The term of this Agreement shall commence as of the date hereof and shall remain in effect until December 31, 2023, unless and until earlier terminated as set forth in this Section 2. A contract year of this Agreement shall run from January 1 until the following December 31; contract quarters hereunder shall be three (3) month periods commencing January 1, April 1, July 1, and October 1.

(b) Buyer may terminate this Agreement at any time upon ninety (90) days prior written notice to Muensch.

(c) Muensch may terminate this Agreement upon ninety (90) days prior written notice to Buyer in the event that Buyer fails to purchase and receive at least thirty percent (30%) of Buyer's requirements for primary carpet backing, and at least fifty percent (50%) of Buyer's requirements for secondary carpet backing, in any contract quarter of this Agreement.

3. The quantity of Product to be sold and purchased each contract year under this Agreement shall be thirty percent (30%) of Buyer's total requirements for primary carpet backing, and fifty percent (50%) of Buyer's total requirements for secondary carpet backing; provided that Muensch's maximum obligation to supply Product, in all styles of primary and secondary backing in the aggregate, shall not exceed two-thousand pounds (2,000 lbs.) in any contract year hereunder.

BUT THIS:

Carpet-Backing Sales Agreement

This Agreement, effective 25 March 2018, is between Muensch Fabrics and Fibers Co., a Delaware corporation, and Bertelon Inc., a New York corporation. Bertelon wishes to purchase from Muensch certain primary and secondary carpet-backings for manufacture into carpets, and Muensch wishes to sell these backings to Bertelon, on the terms here specified. The parties therefore agree as follows.

The Agreement

1. **Products.** The products ("Product") to be sold are primary and secondary carpet-backings in the styles identified in the attached Exhibit A, and conforming to the Product specifications set forth in the attached Exhibit B.

2. **Duration.**

   2.1 **Basic term.** This Agreement begins on 25 March 2018 and ends 31 December 2023 unless terminated earlier under § 2.2 or § 2.3. A contract year of this Agreement runs from January 1 until the next December 31. Contract quarters are 3-month periods beginning January 1, April 1, July 1, and October 1.

   2.2 **Termination by Bertelon.** Bertelon may terminate this Agreement at any time upon 90 days' written notice to Muensch.

   2.3 **Termination by Muensch.** Muensch may terminate this Agreement upon 90 days' written notice to Bertelon if Bertelon fails to purchase and receive at least 30% of Bertelon's requirements for primary carpet-backing, and at least 50% of Bertelon's requirements for secondary carpet-backing, in any contract quarter of this Agreement.

3. **Quantity.**

   3.1 **In general.** The quantity of Product to be sold and purchased each contract year under this Agreement will be 30% of Bertelon's total requirements for primary carpet-backing and 50% of Bertelon's total requirements for secondary carpet-backing. But Muensch's maximum obligation to supply Product, in all styles of primary and secondary backing in the aggregate, cannot exceed 2,000 pounds in any contract year.

   3.2 **Maximum delivery.** Unless Muensch agrees otherwise, Muensch is not obligated to deliver in any calendar month a total amount of Product

NOT THIS:

Unless otherwise agreed to by Muensch, Muensch shall not be obligated to deliver in any calendar month a total amount of Product (in pounds) in excess of one and one-half (1-1/2) times the average of the monthly purchases of Product by Buyer for the preceding ninety (90) day period. Muensch nevertheless agrees to exercise its best efforts to accommodate Buyer's needs for amounts of Product over the maximum monthly obligation called for by the preceding sentence.

Except as otherwise expressly provided in Exhibit C, the minimum quantity of any other Product shall be one-thousand yards (1,000 yds.) per style.

4. Buyer shall request shipments of Product by submitting firm, written orders to Muensch at least two (2) days prior to the requested Product delivery date. Muensch shall use its best efforts to confirm or reject Buyer's orders within twenty-four (24) hours after receipt. Muensch shall use all reasonable efforts to comply with Buyer's stated delivery requirements but does not guarantee such compliance.

All deliveries of Backing shall be made by truck F.O.B. to locations designated by Buyer. Measurements of deliveries shall be performed at Muensch's manufacturing facilities by Muensch.

Title to and risk of loss of Product sold hereunder shall pass to Buyer when delivered to the F.O.B. point identified in paragraph 4 above.

5. The initial price for each style of Product hereunder, in dollars per yard, is set forth in the attached Exhibit C; said initial prices are firm for all orders submitted by Buyer on or before one year of the effective date of this Agreement.

At any time after 25 March 2019, Muensch may increase the price for any style of Product upon at least thirty (30) days prior written notice to Buyer; provided, however, that no Product price shall be increased by more than six percent (6%) in each contract year hereof.

There is no second exception: shouldn't have a (1) without a (2).

The limitation on price increases set forth in paragraph 5 above shall not: (1) apply to price increases which Muensch can show directly pass through increases in manufacturing costs (as historically calculated by Muensch) or raw materials costs (calculated at actual cost).

If Buyer receives a bona fide offer to buy synthetic primary or secondary carpet backing from a non-affiliated domestic supplier, and such offer is: (i) for synthetic carpet backing of similar quality to a Product sold hereunder; (ii) for a quantity of synthetic carpet backing which is similar to Buyer's expected total purchases (consistent with Buyer's prior purchasing patterns) of such similar Product during the period covered by the offer; and (iii) at a price lower than the price then in effect hereunder for such similar Product, then Buyer may request Muensch, in writing, to meet such offer. Buyer's written request shall advise Muensch of the terms of such offer, including the lower price. Within ten (10) days after Muensch receives Buyer's written request, Muensch shall either meet such offer or allow Buyer to purchase the synthetic carpet backing offered and deduct the quantity so purchased from Buyer's remaining purchase obligation hereunder.

BUT THIS:

(in pounds) in excess of 1½ times the average of the monthly purchases of Product by Bertelon for the preceding 90-day period. Muensch will nevertheless exercise its best efforts to accommodate Bertelon's needs for amounts of Product over the maximum monthly obligation called for by the preceding sentence.

3.3 **Minimum delivery.** Except as expressly provided otherwise in Exhibit C, the minimum quantity of any Product will be 1,000 yards per style.

4. **Delivery, Title, and Risk of Loss.**

4.1 **Shipment orders.** Bertelon will request shipments of Product by submitting firm, written orders to Muensch at least 2 days before the requested Product delivery date. Muensch will use best efforts to confirm or reject Bertelon's orders within 24 hours after receipt. Muensch will use all reasonable efforts to comply with Bertelon's stated delivery requirements but cannot guarantee compliance.

4.2 **F.O.B. terms.** All Product deliveries will be made by truck F.O.B. to locations designated by Bertelon. Muensch will measure the Products at its manufacturing facilities. Title to and risk of loss of Product sold under this Agreement pass to Bertelon when delivered to the F.O.B. point.

5. **Price.**

5.1 **Initial price.** The initial price for each style of Product, in dollars per yard, is set forth in the attached Exhibit C. This initial price is firm for all orders submitted by Bertelon on or before 25 March 2019.

5.2 **Increases through contract period.** At any time after 25 March 2019, Muensch may increase the price for any style of Product upon at least 30 days' written notice to Bertelon. But no Product price may be increased by more than 6% in each contract year, unless Muensch can directly show that the increases result from passed-on increases in manufacturing costs (as historically calculated by Muensch) or raw-material costs (calculated at actual cost).

5.3 **Third-party price strategy.** If Bertelon receives a bona fide offer to buy synthetic primary or secondary carpet-backing from a nonaffiliated domestic supplier, then Bertelon may request in writing that Muensch meet the offer. To take advantage of this term, Bertelon must advise Muensch in writing of the offer, together with the price. Muensch may either meet the offer or allow Bertelon to purchase the synthetic carpet-backing offered and deduct the quantity so purchased from Bertelon's

NOT THIS:

6. Payment shall be made by Buyer not later than thirty (30) days from the date of Muensch's invoice.

Any tax or other governmental charge upon the sale or shipment of Product hereunder now imposed by Federal, State, or Local authorities, or hereinafter effective within the life of this Agreement, shall be added to the price set forth herein and shall be paid by Buyer. Should Buyer claim exemption from any such tax or charge, Buyer will furnish appropriate, fully executed exemption certificates in accordance with the law and regulations of the relevant tax-levying authority in effect at the time of the sale.

If Muensch reasonably determines that Buyer's financial condition has deteriorated and Buyer's credit has become impaired, then Muensch shall have the right to unilaterally change the provisions of this Section 6 and its credit arrangements with Buyer.

7. Muensch warrants title to Product sold hereunder and that Product will conform to the product specifications set forth in the attached Exhibit B. MUENSCH MAKES NO WARRANTY OF MERCHANTABILITY OR FITNESS FOR A PARTICULAR PURPOSE WITH RESPECT TO PRODUCT, AND ALL OTHER WARRANTIES, EXPRESS OR IMPLIED, EXCEPT FOR THOSE EXPRESSLY STATED ABOVE, ARE EXCLUDED. Muensch's liability under this Agreement shall be limited to replacement of Product in respect of which a claim is made or, at Muensch's option, refund of an amount not to exceed the purchase price thereof. Claims hereunder must be made within twenty-eight (28) days after delivery of said Product to Buyer (or, in the case of non-delivery, within fifteen (15) days after the date scheduled for delivery) and Muensch must be given a reasonable opportunity to investigate the claim. IN NO EVENT SHALL EITHER PARTY BE LIABLE FOR ANY INCIDENTAL, SPECIAL, OR CONSEQUENTIAL DAMAGES.

8. Neither Party shall be liable to the other for failure or delay in performing its obligations hereunder to the extent that such failure or delay is due to war, fire, flood, strike, labor trouble, breakdown of equipment or machinery, failure of manufacturing processes, shortages of raw materials, accident, riot, act of court of competent jurisdiction, act or request of governmental authority, reasons relating to health and/or safety of employees or the general public and/or to environmental protection, act of God, or other contingencies beyond the reasonable control of the affected Party. The quantity of Product whose delivery or acceptance is excused pursuant hereto shall be deducted without liability from the quantity otherwise subject to delivery or acceptance, provided that in no event shall Buyer be relieved of the obligation to pay in full for Product previously delivered hereunder. The causes of failure or delay shall be remedied by the affected Party to the extent reasonably possible without undue delay, and performance shall be resumed at the earliest practical time after cessation of such failure or delay; provided, however, that neither Party shall be required to settle a labor dispute against its own best judgment. In the event of Force Majeure affecting Muensch's production of any product, Muensch shall have the right to allocate

BUT THIS:

remaining purchase obligation under this Agreement. This term applies only to a third-party offer that is:

(A) for synthetic carpet-backing of similar quality to a Product sold under this Agreement;

(B) for a quantity of synthetic carpet-backing that is similar to Bertelon's expected total purchases (consistent with Bertelon's prior purchasing patterns) of similar Product during the period covered by the offer; and

(C) at a price lower than the price then in effect under this Agreement for similar Product.

6. **Payment.**

6.1 **Due dates.** Bertelon must pay within 30 days after the date of Muensch's invoice.

6.2 **Taxes.** Any tax or other government charge on the sale or shipment of Product under this Agreement now imposed by federal, state, or local authorities, or later effective within the life of this Agreement, will be added to the price set forth here and will be paid by Bertelon. If Bertelon claims exemption from any such tax or charge, Bertelon will furnish an appropriate, valid exemption certificate in accordance with the law and regulations of the relevant tax-levying authority in effect at the time of the sale.

6.3 **Impaired credit.** If Muensch reasonably determines that Bertelon's financial condition has deteriorated and Bertelon's credit has become impaired, then Muensch may unilaterally change this § 6 and its credit arrangements with Bertelon.

7. **Warranty; Limitation of Liability.** Muensch warrants both title to Product sold and conformity with the Product specifications set forth in the attached Exhibit B. **Muensch makes no warranty of merchantability or fitness for a particular purpose with respect to the Product. All other warranties, express or implied, except for those expressly stated above, are excluded.** Muensch's liability under this Agreement is limited to replacement of Product for which a claim is made or, at Muensch's option, refund of an amount not to exceed the purchase price. A claim must be made within 28 days after delivery of the Product to Bertelon (or, in the case of nondelivery, within 15 days after the date scheduled for delivery), and Muensch must be given a reasonable opportunity to investigate the claim. **In no event is either party liable for any incidental, special, or consequential damages.**

NOT THIS:

its available production in a fair and reasonable manner among its customers and Muensch's own requirements. If any of the events specified in this paragraph shall have occurred, the Party affected shall notify the other Party promptly of the occurrence of such event and potential duration of the interruption.

9. No assignment of this Agreement may be made by either Party without the prior written consent of the other Party, such consent not to be withheld unreasonably, and any assignment without such consent shall be null and void; provided, however, that Muensch may assign this Agreement, without the consent of Buyer, to any affiliate, subsidiary, parent or indirect parent company of Muensch.

10. Waiver by either Party of any breach, or failure to enforce any of the terms and conditions of the Agreement at any time, shall not in any way affect, limit or waive the right of that Party thereafter to enforce the Agreement and compel strict compliance with every term and condition thereof.

11. This Agreement shall be governed by and interpreted under the law of the State of Georgia, excluding any choice of law rules which may direct the application of the laws of any other jurisdiction.

12. All notices and other communications required or contemplated under this Agreement shall be deemed sufficient if given by prepaid registered mail, return receipt requested, or telex, and addressed to Muensch as follows:

Muensch Fabrics and Fibers Company
Attention: Marketing Vice President – Carpet Backing

and to Buyer as follows:

____
____
____
Attention: ________________________

13. This Agreement constitutes the entire agreement and understanding between the Parties and supersedes and terminates any previous oral or written agreement between the Parties with respect to the sale and purchase of Product. There are no oral promises, representations, or warranties. No alteration, modification, or amendment of this Agreement or any Exhibit hereto, or any specification comprising any Exhibit hereto, shall be effective unless in writing and signed by both Parties. No modification or amendment of this Agreement shall be effected by the exchange of purchase orders, sales acknowledgments, shipping invoices and the like having terms inconsistent or additional to those herein.

BUT THIS:

8. **Force Majeure.** Neither party will be liable to the other for failure or delay in performing its obligations under this Agreement to the extent that failure or delay is due to a contingency beyond the affected party's reasonable control, including war, fire, flood, strike, labor trouble, breakdown of equipment or machinery, failure of manufacturing processes, shortages of raw materials, accident, riot, act of court having jurisdiction, act or request of government authority, reasons relating to health or safety of employees or the general public or to environmental protection, or act of God. The quantity of Product whose delivery or acceptance is excused under this term will be deducted without liability from the quantity otherwise subject to delivery or acceptance. But in no event will Bertelon be relieved of the obligation to pay in full for Product previously delivered. The causes of failure or delay must be remedied by the affected party to the extent reasonably possible without undue delay, and performance must be resumed at the earliest practical time after cessation of the failure or delay. But neither party will be required to settle a labor dispute against its own best judgment. If force majeure affects Muensch's production of any Product, Muensch may allocate its available production in a fair and reasonable manner among its customers and by Muensch's own requirements. If any event specified in this § 8 occurs, the affected party must promptly notify the other party of the event and potential duration of the interruption.

9. **No Assignment.** Neither party may assign this Agreement without the other party's written consent, which must not be unreasonably withheld. But Muensch may assign this Agreement, without Bertelon's consent, to any affiliate, subsidiary, parent, or indirect parent company of Muensch.

10. **No Waiver.** If either party fails to require the other to perform any term of this Agreement, that failure does not prevent the party from later enforcing that term. If either party waives the other's breach of a term, that waiver is not treated as waiving a later breach of the term.

11. **Governing Law.** Georgia law applies to all matters arising under or relating to this Agreement without regard to any choice-of-law rules that might direct the application of another jurisdiction's laws.

NOT THIS:

14. This Agreement shall not be binding upon either Party until signed an authorized representative of both Parties.

IN WITNESS WHEREOF, the Parties have caused this Agreement to be du executed as of the day and year first hereinabove written.

Muensch Fabrics and Fibers Company

By ______________________________

Title ______________________________

Date ______________________________

______________________________ ("Buyer")

By ______________________________

Title ______________________________

Date ______________________________

BUT THIS:

12. **Notices.** All notices and other communications required or permitted under this Agreement must be in writing and are sufficient if given by prepaid registered mail, return receipt requested, and addressed

to Muensch as follows:	and to Bertelon as follows:
Muensch Fabrics and Fibers Co.	Bertelon, Inc.
3317 Plainview Drive	2200 Commander Avenue
Suite 6	
Ithaca, New York 14882	Bangor, Maine 04401
Attention:	Attention:
Marketing Vice President, Carpet-Backing	Vice President, Manufacturing

13. **Entire Agreement.** This Agreement represents the entire agreement between the parties. It cannot be changed except by written agreement signed by the parties.

14. **Effective Date.** This Agreement does not bind either party until signed by an authorized representative of both parties. When duly signed by both parties, this Agreement has the effective date of 25 March 2018.

MUENSCH FABRICS AND FIBERS CO.

By ______________________________

Title ______________________________

Date ______________________________

BERTELON, INC.

By ______________________________

Title ______________________________

Date ______________________________

APPENDIX E

A Third Typical Contract Needing an Overhaul, with Annotations

NOT THIS:

AGREEMENT

This Acme Agreement (the "Agreement") is entered as of ________, 20__ by and between ______________________ ("Vendor"), a _________ corporation with its principal place of business at ___________, and Acme, Inc. ("Acme"), a _________ corporation with its principal place of business at 100 Main Street, Boston, Massachusetts 02110 (sometimes collectively the "Parties" and individually a "Party").

WHEREAS, Vendor is engaged in the manufacture of the Products (as hereafter defined);

Whereas-recitals are antiquated.

WHEREAS, Acme wishes to purchase from Vendor certain Products to distribute to Acme's end-user customers with, or integrally incorporated into, Acme's ___________ promises and covenants set forth below, the Parties agree as follows:

The only necessary definition is here. In the revision it is § 5.1.

1. Definitions.

a. "Confidential Information" shall mean, collectively, all know-how, trade secrets, plans, designs, processes, formulas, manufacturing techniques, discoveries, inventions and ideas, product specifications, drawings, photographs, machinery, equipment, devices, tools and apparatus, sales and marketing data and plans, pricing and cost information, customer and supplier information and any other technical or business information, which either Party has heretofore disclosed or revealed, or may hereafter disclose or reveal in connection with the activities contemplated by this Agreement, including all documentation or manifestations of the same, whether in hard copy or in computer data bases, discs, tapes or other computer-related forms, and all such disclosures made verbally, through observation of processes or assets or otherwise. However, Confidential Information shall not include information which: (i) was already known to the receiving Party prior to disclosure hereunder; (ii) was publicly available at the time of such disclosure or subsequently becomes so without violation of the obligations hereunder; (iii) is rightfully received from third parties not under obligations of confidentiality; (iv) is independently acquired or developed by an employee of a Party not having access to Confidential Information of the disclosing Party; or (v) is approved in writing by the disclosing party for release without restriction.

Shall mean is poor phrasing for definitions.

Romanettes in midparagraph signal poor drafting style. See § 26.

b. "Products" shall mean the products set forth on Attachment A hereto together with the documentation provided therewith by Vendor expressly for distribution to end users. Any update or enhancement of a Product that is made generally available by Vendor that is substantially similar thereto and that is marked under the same product number and nomenclature shall be added to Attachment A as a new Product.

c. "Product Materials" shall have the meaning provided in Section 4(c) hereof.

d. "Territory" shall mean the territory set forth on Attachment B hereto.

The spacing is awkward and unsightly.

2. Grant of Rights. Subject to all of the terms and conditions of this Agreement, Vendor hereby grants Acme the non-exclusive right to distribute the Products (as hereafter defined)

BUT THIS:

PURCHASE-AND-SUPPLY AGREEMENT

Background

Melroy International Inc. ("Melroy") is a Delaware corporation with its principal place of business at Austin, Texas.

Acme, Inc. (Acme) is a Massachusetts corporation with its principal place of business at 100 Main Street, Boston, Massachusetts 02110. Melroy manufactures products that Acme wishes to purchase and distribute to Acme's customers within a certain territory, either as separate products or as incorporated into Acme's products. This Agreement grants Acme a nonexclusive license to do so and memorializes each party's rights, promises, and obligations. The products ("Products") are listed in Attachment A to this Agreement, and the territory ("Territory") is specified in Attachment B.

1. **Acme's Requirements.**

Melroy will supply Acme with its required quantities of Products. Acme will provide Melroy with quarterly nonbinding good-faith forecasts of its anticipated requirements and shipping dates for the 3-month period covered by each forecast (or, if shorter, the remaining term of this Agreement). Acme will order at least the number of Products specified in Attachment A within the period specified in the forecast.

Duties are expressed by *will.*

2. **Delivery and Payment.**

Melroy will deliver the Products F.O.B. to Melroy's warehouse or place of production. Title to and risk of loss or damage to the Products pass to Acme at the point of delivery. Acme will pay the suggested end-user prices as shown on Melroy published U.S. price list less the Acme discounts (both set forth in Attachment C). Acme will pay all charges, including transportation costs, insurance premiums, and all taxes (except Melroy's U.S. income taxes), duties, and other government assessments incurred in the transaction. Payment must be made in U.S. dollars in the United States within 30 days after Melroy's invoice.

3. **Melroy's Duties.**

3.1 **Establishing and maintaining escrow for Product Materials.** Promptly after executing this Agreement, and in furtherance of Melroy's obligation under this section, Melroy will place in escrow with a third party mutually acceptable to the parties the Product Materials as they exist on the date of this Agreement. Melroy will promptly update the escrow with any new or modified Product Materials as they become available and notify Acme when it does so. Acme will pay all escrow fees. If a third party licenses any Product Materials to Melroy, the rights and licenses and Melroy's obligation to provide or escrow Product Materials are subject to the terms and restrictions of Melroy's agreement with that third party and Acme's payment of any amounts that would not otherwise be due on account of this Agreement.

NOT THIS:

for use with, or integrally incorporated into, Acme's ____________ products to Acme's customers within the Territory (as hereafter defined).

3. Sale and Purchase: Payment and Supply Terms.

a. Subject to all of the terms and conditions of this Agreement, Vendor agrees to sell to Acme such quantities of Products as Acme orders from Vendor. Acme shall provide Vendor with quarterly nonbinding good-faith forecasts of its anticipated requirements and shipping dates for the three (3) month period following each forecast (or, if shorter, the remaining term of the Agreement). Acme agrees that it will order at least the number of Products specified in Attachment A within the time periods specified therein.

Indents are too big. Use hanging indents. See § 35.

b. Vendor shall deliver the Products F.O.B. Vendor's warehouse or place of production. Title to the Products and risk of loss or damage thereto pass to Acme at the point of delivery. Prices payable by Acme for Products ordered by and shipped to Acme are the suggested end-user prices (in U.S. dollars) set forth on Vendor's published U.S. list prices (which are included in Attachment C), less the Acme discounts set forth on Attachment C. Acme will pay all charges, including without limitation transportation charges and insurance premiums and shall be responsible for all taxes (except Vendor's U.S. income taxes), duties and other governmental assessments in connection with the subject matter of this Agreement. Payment shall be made in U.S. dollars in the United States within 30 days of Vendor's invoice.

4. Vendor Obligations.

a. *Vendor Covenants*. During the term of this Agreement:

1. Vendor will provide Acme, at Vendor's expense, with ____ units of any applicable printed marketing materials for the Products. Additional units shall be provided at direct cost therefor.

2. Vendor will inform Acme within a reasonable time of any changes in the Products and delivery schedules.

Inconsistent numbering system is confusing. See § 24.

3. Subject to the other terms and conditions of this Agreement, Vendor shall promptly fill (by full or partial shipment) Acme's orders for Products.

4. Vendor agrees to provide _____ training program[s] for Acme personnel. Such program[s] shall be given at Acme's main office on a schedule reasonably acceptable to Vendor but commencing no later than ____________ days after Acme's written request. Acme shall bear all Vendor's direct costs in connection with such program[s] including, without limitation, travel, room and board.

b. *Technical Support and Maintenance*. Vendor will provide Acme with technical support and maintenance services and such other reasonable assistance as Acme shall from time to time request.

c. *Assurance of Supply*. Vendor acknowledges and agrees that it is critical to Acme that it have at all times a reliable and continuous supply of Products. Accordingly, should Acme:

(1) institute proceedings to be adjudicated as bankrupt or insolvent or become the subject of a creditor's petition for liquidation or reorganization; or

BUT THIS:

Consistent use of descriptive headings at this level really helps the reader.

3.2 **Filling orders.** Because Acme must maintain a reliable and continuous supply of Products, Melroy will promptly fill Acme's orders for Products by full or partial shipments.

3.3 **Technical support and maintenance.** Melroy will provide Acme with technical support and maintenance services and other reasonable help as Acme may request.

3.4 **Training programs.** Melroy will provide 3 training programs for Acme's personnel. The programs must be given at Acme's main office on a schedule reasonably acceptable to Melroy, but the first program must be held no later than 30 days after Acme's written request. Acme will bear all of Melroy's direct costs in connection with the programs, including travel, room, and board.

3.5 **Marketing materials.** During the term of this Agreement, Melroy will provide Acme, at Melroy's expense, 2 units of any applicable printed marketing materials for the Products. Additional units will be provided at direct cost.

3.6 **Notice of changes.** Melroy will inform Acme within a reasonable time of any changes in the Products and delivery schedules.

3.7 **Inability to supply Products**

(A) Melroy will take the "Escrow Measures" specified in (B) if Melroy:

(1) institutes proceedings to be adjudicated as bankrupt or insolvent or becomes the subject of a creditor's petition for liquidation or reorganization;

Alignment of and spacing between provisions is neat and regular.

(2) becomes insolvent, admits that it cannot pay its debts as they mature, or formally or informally effects a plan or enters into any other arrangement with creditors relating to its inability to meet its debts as they mature; or

(3) becomes unwilling or unable for any reason to supply Acme with its requirements under Attachment A within the period covered.

(B) If a condition specified in (A) is satisfied, then Melroy will take the following "Escrow Measures" by placing in escrow copies of all Product designs and specifications; manufacturing protocols; supplier information; maintenance, training, and support manuals and materials; and all other materials (including materials constituting Melroy's confidential and proprietary information) that Melroy used to manufacture, maintain, or support the Products (collectively, the "Product Materials").

4. **Acme's Duties.**

Unless otherwise provided in this Agreement, Acme will:

(A) not disassemble, decompile, or otherwise reverse-engineer any Products;

(B) use best efforts to successfully market, distribute, and support the Products, whether separate or incorporated into or bundled with Acme Products, including providing installation, training, and other support within the Territory, and to comply with good business practices and all laws and regulations relevant to this Agreement or its subject matter;

NOT THIS:

(2) become insolvent, admit its inability to pay its debts as they mature, or formally or informally effect a plan or enter into any other arrangement with creditors relating to Vendor's inability to meet its debts as they mature; or

(3) be unwilling or unable for any reason to supply Acme with at least the number of Product(s) specified in Attachment A within the time periods specified therein; then, in any such case, Acme shall be entitled to receive from Vendor a copy of all Product designs and specifications, manufacturing protocols, supplier information, maintenance, training and support manuals and materials and all other materials (including, without limitation, materials constituting Confidential Information of Vendor) used by Vendor in the manufacturing, maintenance or support of the Products (the "Product Materials"). In support of the foregoing and promptly after execution of this Agreement, Vendor will place in escrow with a third party mutually acceptable to Acme and Vendor the Product Materials as they exist at the date of this Agreement. Vendor will update the escrow with any new or modified Product Materials promptly as they become available and will notify Acme when it does so. All escrow fees will be borne by Acme. With respect to any Product Materials licensed to Vendor from a third party, the foregoing right and licenses and Vendor's obligation to provide or escrow Product Materials are subject to the terms and restrictions of Vendor's agreement with such third party and the payment by Acme of any amounts that would not otherwise be due on account of this Agreement.

After the semicolon at the end of the second line, this is all dangling text. It applies to all three conditions spelled out above it, but the text itself can't be cited individually. See § 89.

Redundant verbs can cause problems, not prevent them.

5. Acme Covenants and Representations. Except as otherwise provided herein, Acme represents, warrants, and agrees:

a. not to disassemble, decompile or otherwise reverse engineer the Product(s).

b. to use its best efforts to successfully market, distribute, and support (including installation, training, and other support) the Products (or Acme Products which integrally incorporate or are bundled with the Products) within the Territory and to comply with good business practices and all laws and regulations relevant to this Agreement or the subject matter hereof. In its distribution efforts, Acme will use the then-current names used by Vendor for the Products (but will not represent or imply that it is Vendor or is a part of Vendor).

c. to keep Vendor informed as to any problems encountered with Product(s) and any resolutions arrived at for those problems, and to communicate promptly to Vendor any and all modifications, design changes or improvements of the Products suggested by any customer, employee or agent.

d. to comply with the U.S. Foreign Corrupt Practices Act and all applicable export laws, restrictions, and regulations of any United States or foreign agency or authority and not to export or reexport, or authorize the export or reexport of any product, technology or information it obtains or learns pursuant to this Agreement (or any direct product thereof) in violation of any such laws, restrictions or regulation.

6. Confidentiality. Unless otherwise agreed to in writing, each Party shall during the term and for __________ years thereafter, hold in confidence and not use Confidential Information received from the other Party except for the purposes of this Agreement. Each Party shall protect the Confidential Information of the other Party and any jointly developed Confidential Information with the same degree of care as such Party uses to protect its own Confidential Information.

BUT THIS:

(C) use Melroy's then-current names for the Products (but not to represent or imply that Acme is Melroy or is any part of Melroy);

(D) keep Melroy informed about any problem encountered with any Product and any resolution;

(E) inform Melroy promptly of any modification, design change, or improvement to the Products suggested by any customer, employee, or agent; and

(F) comply with the U.S. Foreign Corrupt Practices Act and all applicable export laws, restrictions, and regulations of any United States or foreign agency or authority, and not export or reexport, or authorize the export or reexport of, any Product, direct Product, technology, or information it obtains or learns under this Agreement in violation of those laws, restrictions, or regulations.

5. **Confidentiality.**

5.1 **Confidential information.** Confidential information is technical or business information that either party has disclosed or may disclose in connection with this Agreement, including all know-how, trade secrets, designs, processes, formulas, manufacturing techniques, discoveries, inventions and ideas, product specifications, drawings, photographs, machinery, equipment, devices, tools and apparatus, sales and marketing data and plans, pricing and cost information, customer and supplier information, and documentation and manifestations of them in any form, including hard copy or electronic, and by any means, including oral, written, or observed.

5.2 **Nonconfidential information.** Information is not confidential if the disclosing party approves it for release without restriction or if it:

(A) was already known to the receiving party;

(B) was publicly available when disclosed or is later made available without violating this Agreement;

(C) is rightfully obtained by the receiving party from a third party who does not have an obligation of confidentiality to the other party; or

(D) is developed or acquired by the receiving party independently of the disclosing party's confidential information.

5.3 **Terms and protection.** Unless otherwise agreed to in writing, each party during the term of this Agreement and for 2 years after it terminates will hold in confidence and not use any confidential or proprietary information received from the other party except for the purposes of this Agreement. Each party will protect the confidential and proprietary information of the other party and any such information they jointly develop with the same degree of care that each party uses to protect its own confidential and proprietary information. Except as otherwise provided in this Agreement, the receiving party will upon request return to the disclosing party all the disclosing party's confidential and proprietary information, including all copies. If the materials have been destroyed, the receiving party will give the disclosing party written certification that the information has been destroyed.

NOT THIS:

Two unrelated subjects forced into same section.

Except as otherwise provided in this Agreement, the receiving Party shall return to the disclosing Party all of the latter's Confidential Information upon request, including all copies thereof, or in lieu of such return, issue a written certification that such have been destroyed.

7.1 Warranty; Indemnity.

Vendor warrants to Acme that all Products purchased by Acme hereunder will conform in all respects to the specifications set forth on Attachment D and will be free from defects in workmanship and materials for a period of ________ from the date of delivery thereof. Acme will handle and be responsible for all warranty returns from its customers. Products obtained from Vendor that do not comply with the foregoing warranty and are returned (by Acme only) to Vendor will be repaired or replaced at Vendor's option, provided Acme bears the cost of freight and insurance to the point of repair. Vendor will bear the cost of freight and insurance for return of goods to Acme. If Vendor cannot, or determines that it is not practical to, repair or replace the returned Product, the price therefor paid by Acme will be refunded or credited toward future purchases, at Acme's option. EXCEPT AS SPECIFICALLY PROVIDED IN THIS AGREEMENT, VENDOR MAKES NO OTHER WARRANTIES EXPRESS OR IMPLIED, INCLUDING, WITHOUT LIMITATION, WARRANTIES OF MERCHANTABILITY OR FITNESS FOR A PARTICULAR PURPOSE.

All-caps text is unnecessary and hard to read. See § 42.

b. Vendor shall hold Acme and its officers, directors, agents and employees harmless from liability resulting from infringement by the Product of any United States or foreign patent issued as of the date of delivery of the applicable Product, or any United States or foreign copyright or trademark, provided Vendor is promptly notified of any and all threats, claims and proceedings related thereto and given reasonable assistance and the opportunity to assume control over the defense thereof and negotiations for a settlement or compromise. The foregoing obligation of Vendor does not apply with respect to Product or portions of components thereof (i) that are not supplied by Vendor, (ii) where Acme's use of the Product is incident to an infringement not resulting primarily from the Product or (iii) where Acme's use is not in accordance with this Agreement and all applicable licenses and documentation.

8. Limited Liability. EXCEPT AS OTHERWISE SET FORTH IN THIS AGREEMENT, VENDOR WILL NOT BE LIABLE WITH RESPECT TO ANY SUBJECT MATTER OF THIS AGREEMENT UNDER ANY CONTRACT, NEGLIGENCE, STRICT LIABILITY OR OTHER LEGAL OR EQUITABLE THEORY (I) FOR ANY AMOUNTS IN EXCESS, IN THE AGGREGATE, OF THE SUMS PAID TO VENDOR HEREUNDER OR (II) FOR ANY INCIDENTAL OR CONSEQUENTIAL DAMAGES OR (III) FOR COST OF PROCUREMENT OF SUBSTITUTE GOODS, TECHNOLOGY OR SERVICES. THIS SECTION DOES NOT LIMIT LIABILITY FOR BODILY INJURY OF A PERSON.

9. Relationship of Parties. This Agreement creates no relationship in the nature of joint venture, partnership, limited partnership or agency between the Parties, and the Parties hereby acknowledge that no other facts or relations exist that would create any such relationship between them. Neither Party has the right or authority to assume or to create any obligation or responsibility on

BUT THIS:

6. **Warranty.**

Melroy warrants to Acme that all Products purchased by Acme under this Agreement will conform in all respects to the specifications in Attachment D and will be free from defects in workmanship and materials for 12 months from the date of the Products' delivery. Acme will handle and be responsible for all warranty returns from its customers. Products obtained from Melroy that do not comply with this warranty and are returned by Acme to Melroy will be repaired or replaced at Melroy's option. Acme will bear the cost of freight and insurance to the point of repair, and Melroy will bear the cost of freight and insurance for the return of Products to Acme. If Melroy cannot repair or replace the returned Products, or determines that it is not practical to do so, the price that Acme paid for them will be refunded or credited toward future purchases, at Acme's option. **Except as specifically provided in this Agreement, Melroy makes no other warranties express or implied, including warranties of merchantability or fitness for a particular purpose.**

Boldface type is far easier to read than all-caps type. See § 42.

7. **Indemnity.**

Melroy will hold Acme and its officers, directors, agents, and employees harmless from liability resulting from infringement by any of Melroy's Products of any U.S. or foreign patent issued as of the date of delivery of the applicable Products, or any U.S. or foreign copyright or trademark, if Acme informs Melroy promptly of any threats, claims, and proceedings related to the matter and is given reasonable help and the opportunity to assume control over the defense and negotiations for a settlement or compromise. This Melroy obligation does not apply to Products or portions of Product components that Melroy did not supply. Nor does this Melroy obligation apply if Acme's use of the Product:

(A) is incident to an infringement not resulting primarily from the Products; or
(B) is not in accordance with this Agreement or an applicable license or regulation.

Notice that the *and* in the original version has been changed to *or*, the more logical conjunction here.

8. **Limited Liability.**

8.1 Subject matter. Except as otherwise provided in this Agreement, Melroy is not liable with respect to any subject matter of this Agreement under any contract, negligence, strict liability, or other legal or equitable theory:

(A) for any amounts greater than the total sums paid to Melroy under this Agreement;

(B) for any incidental or consequential damages; or

(C) for the cost of procuring substitute goods, technology, or services.

8.2 Bodily injury. This section does not limit liability for bodily injury of a person.

9. **Relationship of Parties.**

This Agreement creates no joint-venture, partnership, limited-partnership, or agency relationship between the parties. No other facts or relations exist that would create any such relationship between them. Neither party has the right or authority to assume or create any obligation

NOT THIS:

behalf of the other Party except as may, from time to time, be provided in written instruments signed by both Parties.

10. Assignment. This Agreement and the rights hereunder are not transferable or assignable (and any attempted assignment will be void) without the prior written consent of the Parties hereto, except for rights to payment and except to a person or entity who acquires all or substantially all of the assets or business of a Party, whether by sale, merger or otherwise.

11. Term and Termination. Unless terminated earlier as provided herein, this Agreement shall have a term extending from the date of this Agreement to ______________, 20___.

a. This Agreement may be terminated by a Party for cause immediately upon the occurrence of any of the following events:

Terrible formatting with indents much too wide.

1. If the other Party ceases to do business, or otherwise terminates its business operations; or

2. If the other Party shall fail to promptly secure or renew any license, registration, permit, authorization or approval necessary for the conduct of its business in the manner contemplated by this Agreement in any significant country or area of the Territory, or if any such license, registration, permit, authorization or approval is revoked or suspended and not reinstated within ________ days; or

3. If the other Party materially breaches any material provision of this Agreement and fails to fully substantially cure such breach within 30 days (10 days in the case of a failure to pay and immediately in the case of a breach of Section 6) of written notice describing the breach; or

4. If the other Party shall seek protection under any bankruptcy, receivership, trust deed, creditors' arrangement, composition or comparable proceedings or if any such proceeding is instituted against the other (and not dismissed within 120 days). Also, consider whether this is an appropriate basis for termination if there is no breach.

b. Vendor may terminate this Agreement upon 30 days' prior written notice to Acme at any time after Acme has failed during any period to distribute to end-users in arm's-length transactions at least the quantities of Products set forth in Attachment ___ for such period that are not returned.

12. General.

a. *Amendment and Waiver*. Except as otherwise expressly provided herein, any provision of this Agreement may be amended and the observance of any provision of this Agreement may be waived (either generally or in any particular instance and either retroactively or prospectively) only with the written consent of the parties. However, it is the intention of the parties that this Agreement be controlling over additional or different terms of any purchase order, confirmation, invoice, or similar document, even if accepted in writing by both parties and that waivers and amendments shall be effective only if made by nonpreprinted agreements clearly understood by both parties to be an amendment or waiver.

b. *Governing Law*. This Agreement shall be governed by and construed under the laws of the Commonwealth of Massachusetts and the United States without regard to

BUT THIS:

or responsibility on behalf of the other party except as may, from time to time, be provided in written instruments signed by both parties.

10. Term.

This Agreement becomes effective on the date both parties sign it and terminates on December 31, 2014.

11. Termination for Cause.

11.1 By either party. A party may immediately terminate this Agreement for cause if:

(A) the other party ceases to do business or otherwise terminates its business operations;

(B) the other party seeks protection under any bankruptcy, receivership, trust deed, creditors' arrangement, composition, or comparable proceedings, or any such proceeding is instituted against the other and not dismissed within 120 days;

(C) the other party fails to promptly secure or renew any license, registration, permit, authorization, or approval necessary to conduct its business in the manner contemplated by this Agreement in any significant country or area of the Territory, or any such license, registration, permit, authorization, or approval is revoked or suspended and not reinstated within 14 days; or

(D) the other party breaches any material provision of this Agreement and, after receiving written notice of the breach, fails to substantially cure it within 30 days (10 days in the case of a failure to pay and immediately in the case of a breach of § 5).

11.2 By Melroy. Melroy may terminate this Agreement upon 30 days' written notice to Acme at any time if Acme fails during any period to distribute to end-users in arm's-length transactions at least the quantities of Products set forth in Attachment C. Returned Products are not considered undistributed.

12. Amendment and Waiver.

Except as otherwise expressly provided, any provision of this Agreement may be amended and the observance of any provision of this Agreement may be waived (either generally or in any particular instance and either retroactively or prospectively) only with the parties' written consent. This Agreement controls over additional or different terms in any purchase order, confirmation, invoice, or similar document, even if accepted in writing by both parties. Any waiver or amendment is effective only if made by a nonpreprinted agreement that both parties clearly understand to be an amendment or waiver.

13. Arbitration.

Any dispute between the parties arising in connection with this Agreement will, if possible, be settled amicably through direct discussions between the parties. If no agreement is reached, the dispute will be exclusively and finally settled by binding arbitration by 3 arbitrators—1 chosen by Melroy, 1 chosen by Acme, and a third chosen by the 2 arbitrators—in accordance with the rules of the American Arbitration Association. Both parties will cooperate with and abide

NOT THIS:

conflicts of laws provisions thereof and without regard to the United Nations Convention on Contracts for the International Sale of Goods.

c. *Arbitration.* Any disputes between the Parties arising in connection with this Agreement shall, if possible, be settled in an amicable way through direct discussions between the parties. If, however, no agreement is reached, such disputes shall be exclusively and finally settled by binding arbitration between three arbitrators, one chosen by Vendor, one chosen by Acme and a third chosen by the two arbitrators, in accordance with the rules of the American Arbitration Association. Under arbitration, both parties shall cooperate with and agree to abide by the decision of the arbitration proceeding. Arbitration shall take place in the Commonwealth of Massachusetts. English shall be the language used during all proceedings. The cost of the arbitration proceeding shall be borne according to the decision of the arbitrators. Subsequent to the arbitration decision, both parties retain the right to apply to a court of competent jurisdiction for a temporary or preliminary injunction to enforce the confidentiality and limited use obligation contained in this Agreement. In the event that any legal proceeding between the parties, including but not limited to arbitration, is commenced to enforce any of the provisions of this Agreement, each party shall be responsible for its own legal costs and attorneys' fees incurred by it in connection with the prosecution or defense of such action.

d. *Headings.* Headings and captions are for convenience only and are not to be used in the interpretation of this Agreement.

e. *Notices.* Notices under this Agreement shall be sufficient only if in writing and personally delivered by a major commercial rapid delivery courier service, or mailed by certified or registered mail, return receipt requested, to a party at its addresses first set forth herein or as amended by notice pursuant to this subsection.

f. *Entire Agreement.* This Agreement supersedes all proposals, oral or written, all negotiations, conversations, or discussions between or among parties relating to the subject matter of this Agreement and all past dealing or industry custom.

g. *Severability.* If any provision of this Agreement is held to be illegal or unenforceable, that provision shall be limited or eliminated to the minimum extent necessary so that this Agreement shall otherwise remain in full force and effect and enforceable.

BUT THIS:

by the arbitrators' decision. Arbitration will take place in the Commonwealth of Massachusetts. English will be the language used during all proceedings. The arbitration cost will be borne according to the arbitrators' decision. After the arbitration decision, both parties retain the right to apply to a court having jurisdiction for a temporary or preliminary injunction to enforce this Agreement's confidentiality and limited-use obligations. If any legal proceeding between the parties, including arbitration, is begun to enforce this Agreement, each party is responsible for its own legal costs and attorney fees incurred in connection with the lawsuit's prosecution or defense.

14. Miscellaneous Terms.

14.1 **Entire agreement.** This Agreement represents the entire agreement between the parties. It cannot be changed except by written agreement signed by the parties.

14.2 **No assignment.** Neither party may assign this Agreement without the other party's written consent, which must not be unreasonably withheld. A party's entering into contracts with subcontractors is not considered an assignment.

14.3 **Successors and representatives.** This Agreement binds and inures to the benefit of the parties and their heirs, personal representatives, successors, and (where permitted) assignees.

14.4 **Notices.** All notices and other communications required or permitted under this Agreement must be in writing and must be sent or e-mailed to the party at that party's address set forth below or at whatever other address the party specifies in writing.

14.5 **Severability.** If a court for any reason holds a provision of this Agreement to be unenforceable, the rest remains fully enforceable.

14.6 **"Including."** Unless the context requires otherwise, the term "including" means "including but not limited to."

14.7 **Headings.** Headings are for convenience only and do not affect the interpretation of this Agreement.

14.8 **Governing law.** Massachusetts and United States law apply to all matters arising under or relating to this Agreement without regard to any choice-of-law rules that might direct the application of another jurisdiction's laws. The parties expressly exclude the United Nations Convention on Contracts for the International Sale of Goods.

14.9 **Counterparts.** This Agreement may be signed in counterparts, each one of which is considered an original, but all of which constitute a single instrument.

NOT THIS:

ACME, INC.

By: ______________________________
(Authorized Signature)

Print Name: ______________________________

Title: ____________________

Print ACME Address for Notices:

____

____

____

VENDOR

By: ______________________________
(Authorized Signature)

Print Name: ______________________________

Print Title: ______________________________

Witness or Attest: ______________________________

Print Vendor Address for Notices:

____

____

____

EFFECTIVE DATE: ______________

BUT THIS:

ACME, INC.

By: ______________________________
(Authorized Signature)

Print Name: ______________________________

Title: ____________________

Print ACME Address for Notices:

____

____

____

MELROY

By: ______________________________
(Authorized Signature)

Print Name: ______________________________

Print Title: ______________________________

Witness or Attest: ______________________________

Print Melroy Address for Notices:

____

____

____

EFFECTIVE DATE: ____________

Select Bibliography

Books

Aarts, Bas. *Oxford Modern English Grammar*. Oxford: Oxford Univ. Press, 2011.

Adams, Kenneth A. *A Manual of Style for Contract Drafting*. 4th ed. Chicago: American Bar Ass'n, 2018.

Adler, Mark. *Clarity for Lawyers: The Use of Plain English in Legal Writing*. London: Law Soc'y, 1990. 2d ed. *Clarity for Lawyers: Effective Legal Writing*. London: Law Soc'y, 2007.

Asprey, Michèle M. *Plain Language for Lawyers*. Annandale, Aus.: Federation Press, 1991. 4th ed. Leichhart, Aus.: Federation Press, 2010.

Beccaria, Cesare. *An Essay on Crimes and Punishments*. Anon. trans. Rev. ed. Edinburgh: Alexander Donaldson, 1778.

Bentham, Jeremy. *The Works of Jeremy Bentham*. 11 vols. John Bowring, ed. Edinburgh: William Tait, 1843.

Burnham, Scott J. *Drafting and Analyzing Contracts*. 3d ed. Newark: LexisNexis, 2003.

Butt, Peter; and Richard Castle. *Modern Legal Drafting: A Guide to Using Clearer Language*. Cambridge: Cambridge Univ. Press, 2001. 2d ed. 2006.

Child, Barbara. *Drafting Legal Documents: Principles and Practices*. 2d ed. St. Paul: West, 1992.

Coode, George. *On Legislative Expression; or, the Language of Written Law*. 2d ed. London: Thomas Turpin, 1852.

Cook, Robert N. *Legal Drafting*. Rev. ed. Brooklyn: Foundation Press, 1951.

Cutts, Martin. *The Plain English Guide*. Oxford: Oxford Univ. Press, 1995.

Darmstadter, Howard H. *Hereof, Thereof, and Everywhereof: A Contrarian Guide to Legal Drafting*. Chicago: Am. Bar Ass'n, 2002.

Dick, Robert C. *Legal Drafting*. 2d ed. Toronto: Carswell, 1985.

Dickerson, Reed. *The Fundamentals of Legal Drafting*. 2d ed. Boston: Little, Brown & Co., 1986.

Dickerson, Reed. *Materials on Legal Drafting*. St. Paul: West, 1981.

Doonan, Elmer. *Drafting*. Julie MacFarland, ed. London: Cavendish, 1995.

Eagleson, Robert D. *Writing in Plain English*. Canberra: Australian Gov't Pub. Serv., 1990.

Editorial and Design Stylebook. Plain Language Report. Vancouver: Plain Language Inst., 1993.

Espenschied, Lenné Eidson. *Contract Drafting: Powerful Prose in Transactional Practice*. 3d ed. Chicago: American Bar Ass'n, 2019.

Evans, B. Ifor. *The Use of English: Being a Primer of Direct English*. London: Staples Press, 1949.

Fajans, Elizabeth; Mary R. Falk; and Helene S. Shapo. *Writing for Law Practice*. N.Y.: Foundation Press, 2004.

Flesch, Rudolf. *How to Write Plain English: A Book for Lawyers and Consumers*. N.Y.: Harper & Row, 1979.

Freedman, Adam. *The Party of the First Part: The Curious World of Legalese*. N.Y.: Henry Holt & Co., 2007.

Garner, Bryan A. *Garner's Dictionary of Legal Usage*. 3d ed. N.Y. & Oxford: Oxford Univ. Press, 2011.

Garner, Bryan A. *Garner's Modern English Usage*. 4th ed. N.Y. & Oxford: Oxford Univ. Press, 2016.

Garner, Bryan A. *Guidelines for Drafting and Editing Court Rules*. Wash., D.C.: Administrative Office of the U.S. Courts, 1996. [Available in downloadable PDF at www.lawprose.org.]

Garner, Bryan A. *Legal Writing in Plain English*. 2d ed. Chicago: Univ. of Chicago Press, 2013.

Garner, Bryan A. *The Redbook: A Manual on Legal Style*. 4th ed. St. Paul: West Academic Publishing, 2018.

Gunning, Robert. *The Technique of Clear Writing*. N.Y.: McGraw-Hill, 1952.

Haggard, Thomas R. *Legal Drafting in a Nutshell*. St. Paul: West, 1996.

Haggard, Thomas R.; and George W. Kuney. *Legal Drafting: Process, Techniques, and Exercises*. 2d ed. St. Paul: West, 2007.

Kimble, Joseph. *Lifting the Fog of Legalese*. Durham, N.C.: Carolina Academic Press, 2006.

Kimble, Joseph. *Seeing Through Legalese*. Durham, N.C.: Carolina Academic Press, 2017.

Kimble, Joseph. *Writing for Dollars, Writing to Please: The Case for Plain Language in Business, Government, and Law*. Durham, N.C.: Carolina Academic Press, 2012.

MacDonald, Duncan A. (chmn.). *Drafting Documents in Plain Language*. N.Y.: Practising Law Institute, 1979.

Martineau, Robert J.; and Michael B. Salerno. *Legal, Legislative, and Rule Drafting in Plain English*. St. Paul: Thomson/West, 2005.

Mellinkoff, David. *The Language of the Law*. Boston: Little, Brown & Co., 1963.

Mellinkoff, David. *Legal Writing: Sense and Nonsense*. St. Paul: West Pub. Co., 1982.

O'Hayre, John. *Gobbledygook Has Gotta Go*. Washington, D.C.: U.S. Gov't Printing Office, 1966.

Perrin, Timothy. *Better Writing for Lawyers.* Toronto: Law Society of Upper Canada, 1990.

Piesse, E.L. *The Elements of Legal Drafting.* J.K. Aitken & Peter Butt, eds. 10th ed. Sydney: Lawbook Co., 2004.

Plain English Manual. Canberra: Office of Parliamentary Counsel, 1993.

Plain Language Action & Information Network. *Federal Plain Language Guidelines.* May 2011.

Ray, Mary Barnard; and Barbara J. Cox. *Beyond the Basics: A Text for Advanced Legal Writing.* 2d ed. St. Paul: Thomson/West, 2003.

Scalia, Antonin; and Bryan A. Garner. *Reading Law: The Interpretation of Legal Texts.* St. Paul: Thomson Reuters, 2012.

Solan, Lawrence; and Peter M. Tiersma (eds.). *The Oxford Handbook of Language and Law.* Oxford: Oxford Univ. Press, 2012.

Tiersma, Peter M. *Legal Language.* Chicago: Univ. Chicago Press, 1999.

Wincor, Richard. *Contracts in Plain English.* N.Y.: McGraw-Hill, 1976.

Wydick, Richard C. *Plain English for Lawyers.* 5th ed. Durham, N.C.: Carolina Academic Press, 2005.

Articles

Crump, David. *The Five Elements of a Contract: Avoiding Ambiguity in Them.* 43 Tex. B.J. 370 (1980).

Dickerson, Reed. *Clear Legal Drafting: What's Holding Us Back?* 11 ALI-ABA CLE Rev. 3 (1980).

Eagleson, Robert D. *What Is Plain English?* Address at the Singapore Acad. of Law, 27 January 1996.

Eagleson, Robert D.; and Michèle Asprey. *Must We Continue With "Shall"?* 63 Austl. L.J. 75 (1989).

Elliott, David C. *Plain Language: A Global Perspective.* 70 Mich. B.J. 562 (1991).

Kerr, Edward. *Plain Language: Is It Legal?* 52 Law Soc'y J. 52 (1991).

Kimble, Joseph. *Answering the Critics of Plain Language.* 5 Scribes J. Legal Writing 1 (1996–1997).

Kimble, Joseph. *Plain English: A Charter for Clear Writing.* 9 Thomas M. Cooley L. Rev. 1 (1992).

Kirk, Maurice B. *Legal Drafting: Curing Unexpressive Language.* 3 Tex. Tech. L. Rev. 23 (1971).

Llewellyn, Karl. *On the Good, the True, the Beautiful in Law.* 9 U. Chi. L. Rev. 224 (1942).

Mackay, J.G. *Introduction to an Essay on the Art of Legal Composition Commonly Called Drafting.* 3 L.Q. Rev. 326 (1887).

Williams, Glanville. *Language and the Law* (pts. 1–5). 61 L.Q. Rev. 71, 179, 293, 384 (1945), 62 L.Q. Rev. 387 (1946).

General Index

C

E

G

H

I

M

N

Q

R

T

U